THE GREEN GUIDE

Fr. Isler/MICHELIN

French Alps

Travel Publications

Hannay House, 39 Clarendon Road
Watford, Herts WD17 1JA, UK
☎ 01923 205 240 - Fax 01923 205 241
www.ViaMichelin.com
TheGreenGuide-uk@uk.michelin.com

Manufacture française des pneumatiques Michelin
Société en commandite par actions au capital de 304 000 000 EUR
Place des Carmes-Déchaux – 63 Clermont-Ferrand (France)
R.C.S. Clermont-Fd B 855 200 507

No part of this publication may be reproduced in any form
without the prior permission of the publisher

© Michelin et Cie, Propriétaires-éditeurs, 2001
Dépôt légal janvier 2001 – ISBN 2-06-000088-2 – ISSN 0763-1383
Printed in France 12-02/2.3

Typesetting: Euronumérique à Ligugé
Printing and binding: Aubin à Ligugé

Cover design: Carré Noir, Paris 17ᵉ arr.

THE GREEN GUIDE
Spirit of Discovery

Leisure time spent with The Green Guide is also a time for refreshing your spirit, enjoying yourself, and taking advantage of our selection of fine restaurants, hotels and other places for relaxing: immerse yourself in the local culture, discover new horizons, experience the local lifestyle. The Green Guide opens the door for you.

Each year our writers go touring: visiting the sights, devising the driving tours, identifying the highlights, selecting the most attractive hotels and restaurants, checking the routes for the maps and plans.

Each title is compiled with great care, giving you the benefit of regular revisions and Michelin's first-hand knowledge. The Green Guide responds to changing circumstances and takes account of its readers' suggestions; all comments are welcome.

Share with us our enthusiasm for travel, which has led us to discover over 60 destinations in France and other countries. Like us, let yourself be guided by the desire to explore, which is the best motive for travel: the spirit of discovery.

Contents

Wrought-iron campanile

Field of lavender, Albion Plateau

Frescoes in the chapel at Bessans

Winter wonderland

5

Maps

Motorists who plan ahead will always have the appropriate maps to hand. Michelin products are complementary: for each of the sites listed in The Green Guide, map references are indicated which help you find your location on our range of maps. The image below shows the local maps to use for each geographical area covered in this guide.

The **regional maps** at a scale of 1:200 000 nos 232, 237 and 238 are good maps to choose for travelling in a wide area, as they cover the main roads and secondary roads. Both include useful indications for finding tourist attractions. At a quick glance, you can locate and identify the main sights. In addition to identifying the types of road ways, the maps show castles, churches and other religious edifices, scenic viewpoints, megalithic monuments, swimming beaches on lakes and rivers, swimming pools, golf courses, racetracks, airfields, and more.

And remember to travel with the latest edition of the **map of France no 989**, which gives an overall view of the Alpine region and the main access roads which connect it to the rest of France (1:1 000 000 scale). **Atlas** formats are also available, spiral bound, paperback, hardback and the new, convenient Mini France (all including the Paris region, 50 town plans and an index of place names).

Michelin is pleased to offer a route-planning service on the Internet: www.ViaMichelin.com Choose the shortest route, a scenic route, a route without tolls, or the Michelin recommended route to your destination; you can also access information about hotels and restaurants from The Red Guide, and tourists sites from The Green Guide. Bon voyage!

There are a number of useful maps and plans in the guide, listed here:

Thematic maps

Town plans

Local maps for touring

Key

Selected monuments and sights

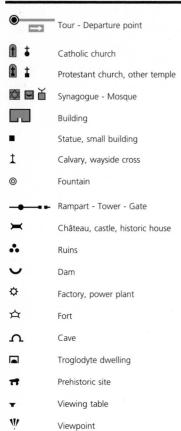

Tour - Departure point

Catholic church

Protestant church, other temple

Synagogue - Mosque

Building

Statue, small building

Calvary, wayside cross

Fountain

Rampart - Tower - Gate

Château, castle, historic house

Ruins

Dam

Factory, power plant

Fort

Cave

Troglodyte dwelling

Prehistoric site

Viewing table

Viewpoint

Other place of interest

Sports and recreation

Racecourse

Skating rink

Outdoor, indoor swimming pool

Multiplex Cinema

Marina, sailing centre

Trail refuge hut

Cable cars, gondolas

Funicular, rack railway

Tourist train

Recreation area, park

Theme, amusement park

Wildlife park, zoo

Gardens, park, arboretum

Bird sanctuary, aviary

Walking tour, footpath

Of special interest to children

Abbreviations

A	Agricultural office (Chambre d'agriculture)
C	Chamber of Commerce (Chambre de commerce)
H	Town hall (Hôtel de ville)
J	Law courts (Palais de justice)
M	Museum (Musée)
P	Local authority offices (Préfecture, sous-préfecture)
POL.	Police station (Police)
👮	Police station (Gendarmerie)
T	Theatre (Théâtre)
U	University (Université)

	Sight	Seaside resort	Winter sports resort	Spa
Highly recommended	★★★	⚲⚲⚲	✻✻✻	♯♯♯
Recommended	★★	⚲⚲	✻✻	♯♯
Interesting	★	⚲	✻	♯

Additional symbols

🛈	Tourist information
▬▬▬ ▭▭	Motorway or other primary route
❶ ❶	Junction: complete, limited
⊏⊐ ▭▭	Pedestrian street
⊺ ⊏ ⊏ ⊏ ⊺	Unsuitable for traffic, street subject to restrictions
▭▭▭ ▭ ▭	Steps - Footpath
🚂 🚉	Train station - Auto-train station
🚌 🚌 S.N.C.F.	Coach (bus) station
▬▪▬▪▬	Tram
⦿	Metro, underground
🄿ᴿ	Park-and-Ride
♿	Access for the disabled
✉	Post office
☏	Telephone
✉	Covered market
⦁×⦁	Barracks
△	Drawbridge
⊔	Quarry
✕	Mine
Ⓑ Ⓕ	Car ferry (river or lake)
⛴	Ferry service: cars and passengers
⛵	Foot passengers only
③	Access route number common to Michelin maps and town plans
Bert (R.)...	Main shopping street
AZ B	Map co-ordinates
▶▶	Visit if time permits

Hotels and restaurants

20 rooms: Number of rooms: price for one person/
€ 38.57/57.17 double room

half-board or Price per person, based
full board: on double occupancy
€ 42.62

⇌ € 6.85 Price of breakfast; when not given, it is included in the price of the room (i.e., for bed-and-breakfast)

120 sites: Number of camp sites and cost
€ 12.18 for 2 people with a car

€ 12.18 *lunch-* Restaurant: fixed-price menus
€ 16.74/38.05 served at lunch only – mini/maxi price fixed menu (lunch and dinner) or à la carte

rest. Lodging where meals are served
€ 16.74/38.05 mini/maxi price fixed menu or à la carte

meal € 15.22 "Family style" meal

reserv Reservation recommended

🚫 No credit cards accepted

🄿 Reserved parking for hotel patrons

The prices correspond to the higher rates of the tourist season

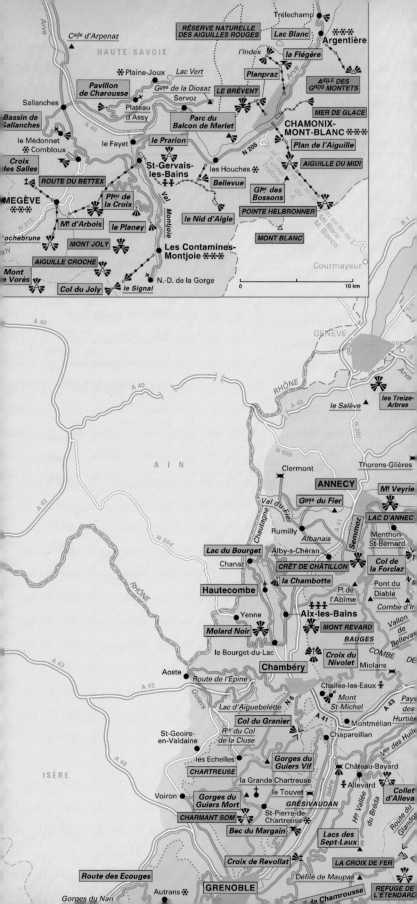

Cade d'Arpenaz

Trélechamp

RÉSERVE NATURELLE
DES AIGUILLES ROUGES

Lac Blanc

Argentière ✻✻✻

HAUTE-SAVOIE

l'Index

la Flégère

❋ Plaine-Joux

Lac Vert

Planpraz

AIGLE DES
GROS MONTETS

Pavillon
de Charousse

Gges de la Diosaz
Servoz

LE BRÉVENT

Plateau
d'Assy

Parc du
Balcon de Merlet

MER DE GLACE

CHAMONIX-
MONT-BLANC ✻✻✻

Sallanches

le Fayet

le Prarion

Plan de l'Aiguille

le Médonnet
❋ Combloux

St-Gervais-
les-Bains

les Houches ✻

AIGUILLE DU MIDI

Croix
des Salles

ROUTE DU BETTEX

Plau de
la Croix

Bellevue

Glier des
Bossons

Bassin de
Sallanches

MEGÈVE
✻✻✻

ochebrune

Mt d'Arbois

le Planey

le Nid d'Aigle

POINTE HELBRONNER

MONT JOLY

Val Montjoie

MONT BLANC

AIGUILLE CROCHE

Les Contamines-
Montjoie ✻✻✻

Courmayeur

Mont
e Vorès

Col du Joly

le Signal

N.-D. de la Gorge

0   10 km

GENÈVE

RHÔNE

les Treize-
Arbres

le Salève

AIN

Clermont

Thorens-Glières

ANNECY

Mt Veyrie

Gges du Fier

Val du Fier

LAC D'ANNEC

Rumilly

Albanais

Menthon-
St-Bernard

Chautagne

Semmoz

Col de
la Forclaz

Lac du Bourget

Alby-s-Chéran

CRÊT DE CHÂTILLON

Chanaz

la Chambotte

Pont du
Diable

Combe d'Ir

Hautecombe

Pt de
l'Abîme

Vallon
de Bellevª

Yenne

Aix-les-Bains

COMBE

Molard Noir

MONT REVARD

le Bourget-du-Lac

BAUGES

Croix du
Nivolet

Miolans

Chambéry

Challes-les-Eaux ✝

Pays
des
Hurtièr

Aoste

Route de l'Épine

Mont
St-Michel

Lac d'Aiguebelette

Montmélian

Chaparaillan

St-Geoire-
en-Valdaine

Col du Granier

Rte du Col
de la Cluse

Château-Bayard

Collet
d'Alleva

les Echelles

Gorges du
Guiers Vif

✝ Allevard

CHARTREUSE

la Grande Chartreuse

le Touvet

Hte Vallée
du Bréda

Route
du Gland

Voiron

Gorges du
Guiers Mort

GRÉSIVAUDAN

St-Pierre-de-
Chartreuse

Lacs des
Sept-Laux

ISÈRE

CHARMANT SOM

Bec du Margain

Croix de Revollat

LA CROIX DE FER

Route des Ecouges

GRENOBLE

Défilé de Maupas

REFUGE DE
L'ÉTENDARD

Gorges du Nan

Autrans ❋

de Chamrousse

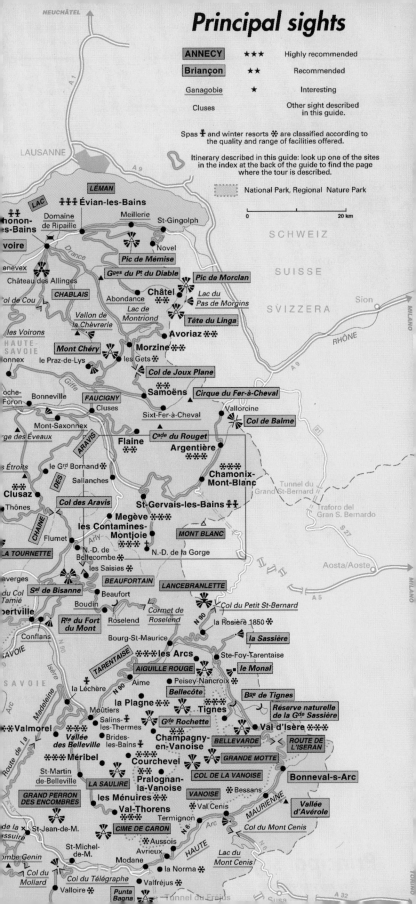

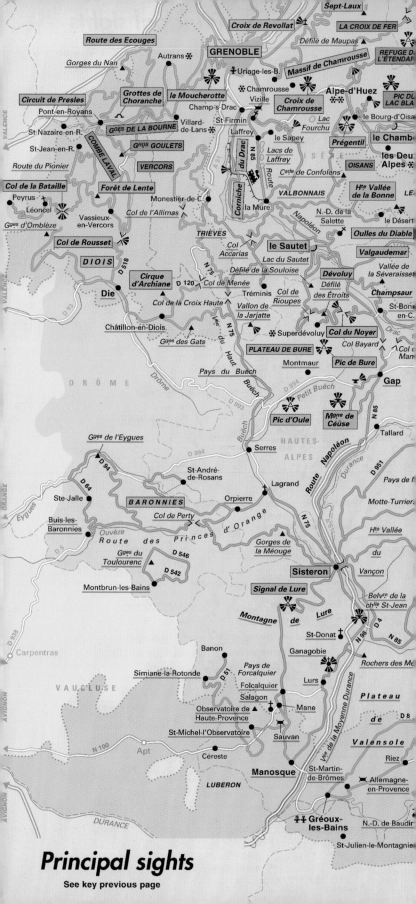

Principal sights

See key previous page

Driving tours

For descriptions of these tours,
turn to the Practical information section following

- ⛪ Religious building
- 🏰 Château, castle or historic house
- 🚂 Tourist train
- ▲ Outstanding natural site
- 🏰 Fortifications
- ❀ Garden, park
- 🏺 Arts and crafts
- ✴ Historic site
- **F** Fresco
- ◑ Sports and recreation area
- ↯ Panorama
- ⛴ Boat trips
- ★ Outstanding man-made site
- 🏯 Old town
- 🏘 Picturesque village
- Ⓒ Regional specialities
- ⌒ Cave
- **M** Museum, art gallery

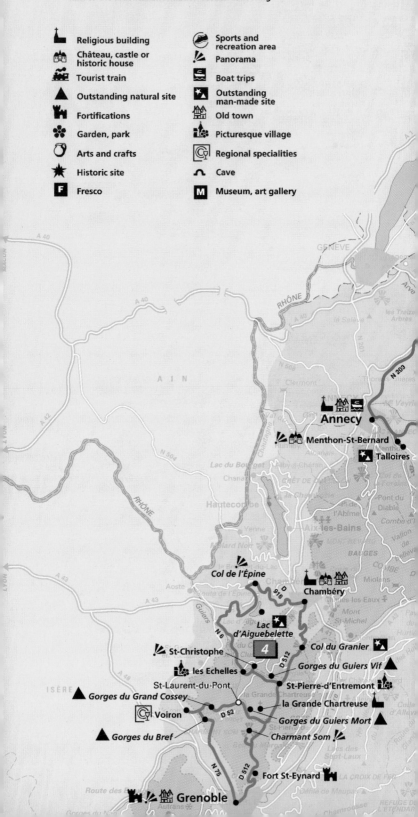

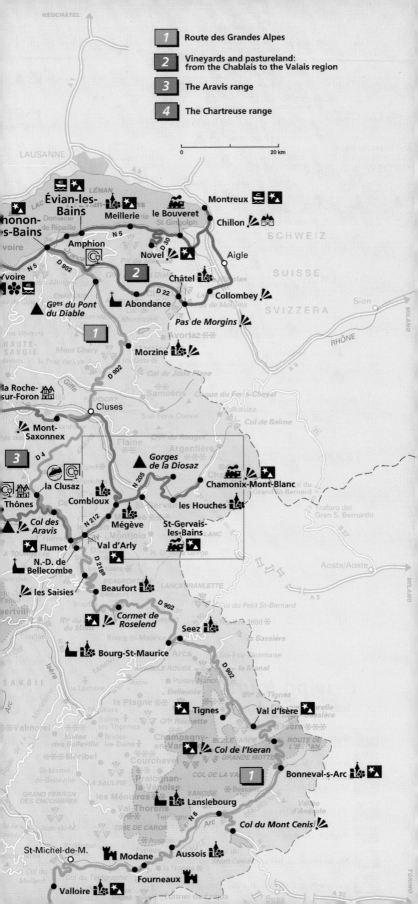

Driving tours
See key previous page

1 Route des Grandes Alpes

5 Vercors, the green fortress

6 Drac and Romanche, corniches and gorges

7 Durance and Ubaye

8 Route Napoléon

9 Haute Provence between Verdon and Durance

10 Vineyards and trees of the Diois region

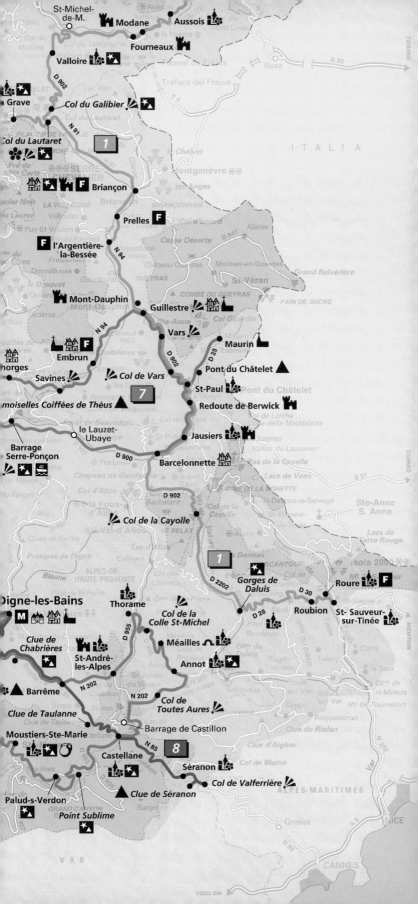

Into the peaks above the Col du Noyer

B. Kaufmann /MICHELIN

Practical information

Planning your trip

Useful addresses

INTERNET

www.ambafrance-us.org
The French Embassy in the USA has a website providing basic information (geography, demographics, history), a news digest and business-related information. It offers special pages for children, and pages devoted to culture, language study and travel, and you can reach other selected French sites (regions, cities, ministries) with a hypertext link.

www.franceguide.com
The French Government Tourist Office / Maison de la France site is packed with practical information and tips for those travelling to France. The home page has a number of links to more specific guidance, for American or Canadian travellers for example, or to the FGTO's London pages.

www.FranceKeys.com
This site has plenty of practical information for visiting France. It covers all the regions, with links to tourist offices and related sites. Very useful for planning the details of your tour in France!

www.fr-holidaystore.co.uk
The French Travel Centre in London has gone on-line with this service, providing information on all of the regions of France, including updated special travel offers and details on available accommodation.

www.visiteurope.com
The European Travel Commission provides useful information on travelling to and around 27 European countries, and includes links to some commercial booking services (ie vehicle hire), rail schedules, weather reports and more.

FRENCH TOURIST OFFICES

For information, brochures, maps and assistance in planning a trip to France travellers should apply to the official French Tourist Office or Maison de la France in their own country:

Australia – New Zealand

Sydney – Level 22, 25 Bligh Street,
NSW 2000 Sydney
☎ (02) 9231 5244 – Fax: (02) 9221 8682.

Canada

Montreal – 1981 Avenue McGill College, Suite 490,
Montreal PQ H3A 2W9
☎ (514) 876 9881 – Fax: (514) 845 4868.

Eire

Dublin – 10 Suffolk Street, Dublin 2
☎ 15 60 235 235

South Africa

P.O. Box 41022, 2024 Craighall,
☎ 00 27 11 880 80 62, Fax 00 27 11 770 16 66.

United Kingdom

London – 178 Piccadilly, London WIV OAL
☎ (0891) 244 123 – Fax: (0171) 493 6594.

United States

East Coast – New York – 444 Madison Avenue,
16th Floor, NY 10022-6903,
☎ (212) 838-7800 – Fax: (212) 838-7855.

Mid West – Chicago – 676 North Michigan Avenue,
Suite 3360, Chicago, IL 60611-2819.
☎ (312) 751-7800 – Fax: (312) 337-6339.

West Coast – Los Angeles – 9454 Wilshire Boulevard,
Suite 715, Los Angeles, CA 90212-2967.
☎ (310) 271-6665 – Fax: (310) 276-2835.
Information can also be requested from **France on Call**,
☎ (202) 659-7779.

LOCAL TOURIST OFFICES

Visitors may also contact local Tourist offices for more precise information, to receive brochures and maps. The addresses and telephone numbers of Tourist offices in the larger towns are listed after the symbol 🖪 in the *Admission times and charges* section at the end of the guide. Below, the addresses are given for local Tourist offices of the *départements* covered in this guide. The index lists the *département* after each town. Address inquiries to the **Comité Départemental du Tourisme (CDT)**:

Rhône-Alpes – Comité Régional de Tourisme, 104 route de Paris, 69260 Charbonnières-les-Bains, ☎ 04 72 59 21 59.

Provence-Alpes-Côte d'Azur – Comité Régional du Tourisme, Espace Colbert, 14 rue Ste-Barbe, 13001 Marseille, ☎ 04 91 39 38 00.

Côte-d'Azur – Comité Régional du Tourisme, 55 promenade des Anglais, BP 1602, 06011 Nice Cedex 1, ☎ 04 93 37 78 78.

Alpes-de-Haute-Provence – Comité départemental du tourisme et des loisirs, 19 rue du Docteur-Honnorat, BP 170, 04005 Digne-les-Bains Cedex, ☎ 04 92 31 57 29.

Drôme – Comité départemental du tourisme, 31 avenue du Président-Herriot. Valence ☎ 04 75 82 19 26. www.vallee-drome.com

Hautes-Alpes – Comité départemental du tourisme, 8bis rue Capitaine-de-Bresson, 05000 Gap, ☎ 04 92 53 62 00.

Haute-Savoie – Agence touristique départemental Haute-Savoie Mont-Blanc, 56 rue Sommeiller, BP 348, 74012 Annecy, ☎ 04 50 51 32 31. www.cdt-hautesavoie.fr

Isère – Comité départemental du tourisme, Maison du tourisme, 14 rue de la République, BP 227, 38019 Grenoble, ☎ 04 76 54 34 36. www.isere-tourisme.com

Savoie – Agence touristique départementale de la Savoie, 24 bd de la Colonne, 73000 Chambéry, ☎ 04 79 85 12 45. www.savoie-tourisme.com

Var – Comité départemental du tourisme, 5 avenue Vauban, BP 5147, 83000 Toulon, ☎ 04 94 09 00 69.

Tourist offices – Further information can be obtained from the tourist offices or *syndicats d'initiative*, as they are called in smaller towns. The addresses and telephone numbers are listed after the symbol 🖪 in the Admission times and charges.

Heritage trails – All over France, since 1975, *routes historiques* have been designated by the Caisse Nationale des Monuments Historiques et des Sites. See the section on Themed Itineraries for the heritage trails in the French Alps.

EMBASSIES AND CONSULATES IN FRANCE

Australia	Embassy	4 rue Jean-Rey, 75015 Paris ☎ 01 40 59 33 00 – Fax: 01 40 59 33 10.
Canada	Embassy	35 avenue Montaigne, 75008 Paris ☎ 01 44 43 29 00 – Fax: 01 44 43 29 99.
Eire	Embassy	4 rue Rude, 75016 Paris ☎ 01 44 17 67 00 – Fax: 01 44 17 67 60.
New Zealand	Embassy	7 ter rue Léonard-de-Vinci, 75016 Paris ☎ 01 45 01 43 43 – Fax: 01 45 01 43 44.
South Africa	Embassy	59 quai d'Orsay, 75007 Paris ☎ 01 53 59 23 23 – Fax: 01 53 59 23 33
UK	Embassy	35 rue du Faubourg St-Honoré, 75008 Paris ☎ 01 44 51 31 00 – Fax: 01 47 53 99 70.
	Consulate	18bis rue d'Anjou, 75008 Paris ☎ 01 44 51 31 00 – Fax 01 44 51 31 27.
	Consulate – Marseille	24 rue du Prado, 13006 Marseille ☎ 04 91 15 72 10 – Fax 04 91 37 47 06
USA	Embassy	2 avenue Gabriel, 75008 Paris ☎ 01 43 12 22 22 – Fax: 01 42 66 97 83.
	Consulate	2 rue St-Florentin, 75001 Paris ☎ 01 42 96 14 88.
	Consulate – Marseille	Place Varian Fry 13006 Marseille ☎ 04 91 54 92 00 – Fax 04 91 55 09 47.

Travellers with special needs

The sights described in this guide which are easily accessible to people of reduced mobility are indicated in the *Admission times and charges* by the symbol ♿ .
Useful information on transportation, holidaymaking and sports associations for the disabled is available from the *Comité National Français de Liaison pour la Réadaptation des Handicapés* (CNRH), 236bis rue de Tolbiac, 75013 Paris.

Next stop Haute-Provence; Gap in the colours of the south

Call their international information number ☎ 01 53 80 66 44, or write to request a catalogue of publications. Web-surfers can find information for slow walkers, mature travellers and others with special needs at www.access-able.com and www.handitel.org. For information on museum access for the disabled contact La Direction, *Les Musées de France, Service Accueil des Publics Spécifiques*, 6 rue des Pyramides, 75041 Paris Cedex 1, ☎ 01 40 15 35 88.

The Red Guide France and the **Michelin Camping Caravaning France** indicate hotels and campsites with facilities suitable for physically handicapped people.

Formalities

Documents

Passport – Nationals of countries within the European Union entering France need only a national identity card (or in the case of the British, a passport). Nationals of other countries must be in possession of a valid national passport. In case of loss or theft report to the embassy or consulate and the local police.

Visa – No **entry visa** is required for Canadian, US or Australian citizens travelling as tourists and staying less than 90 days, except for students planning to study in France. If you think you may need a visa, apply to your local French Consulate.

US citizens should obtain the booklet *Safe Trip Abroad* (US$1), which provides useful information on visa requirements, customs regulations, medical care etc for international travellers. Published by the Government Printing Office, it can be ordered by phone – ☎ (202) 512-1800 – or consulted on-line (www. access.gpo.gov). General passport information is available by phone toll-free from the Federal Information Center (item 5 on the automated menu), ☎ 800-688-9889. US passport application forms can be downloaded from http://travel.state.gov

Customs

Apply to the Customs Office (UK) for a leaflet on customs regulations and the full range of "duty free" allowances; available from HM Customs and Excise, Dorset House, Stamford Street, London SE1 9PS, ☎ 0171 928 3344. The US Customs Service offers a publication *Know Before You Go* for US citizens: for the office nearest you, consult the phone book, Federal Government, US Treasury (www.customs.ustreas.gov).

There are no customs formalities for holidaymakers bringing their caravans into France for a stay of less than six months. No customs document is necessary for pleasure boats and outboard motors for a stay of less than six months but the registration certificate should be kept on board.

Americans can bring home, tax-free, up to US$400 worth of goods; Canadians up to CND$300; Australians up to AUS$400 and New Zealanders up to NZ$700. Persons living in a Member State of the European Union are not restricted in regard to purchasing goods for private use, but the recommended allowances for alcoholic beverages and tobacco are as follows:

Spirits (whisky, gin, vodka etc)	10l	Cigarettes	800
Fortified wines (vermouth, port etc)	20l	Cigarillos	400
Wine (not more than 60 sparkling)	90l	Cigars	200
Beer	110l	Smoking tobacco	1kg

Health

First aid, medical advice and chemists' night service rota are available from chemists/drugstores (pharmacie) identified by the green cross sign.

It is advisable to take out comprehensive insurance coverage as the recipient of medical treatment in French hospitals or clinics must pay the bill. Nationals of non-EU countries should check with their insurance companies about policy limitations. Reimbursement can then be negotiated with the insurance company according to the policy held.

All prescription drugs should be clearly labelled; it is recommended that you carry a copy of the prescription.

British and Irish citizens should apply to the Department of Health and Social Security for Form E 111, which entitles the holder to urgent treatment for accident or unexpected illness in EU countries. A refund of part of the costs of treatment can be obtained on application in person or by post to the local Social Security Offices (Caisse Primaire d'Assurance Maladie). **Americans** concerned about travel and health can contact the International Association for Medical Assistance to Travelers, which can also provide details of English-speaking doctors in different parts of France: ☏ (716) 754-4883.

The American Hospital of Paris is open 24hr for emergencies as well as consultations, with English-speaking staff, at 63 boulevard Victor-Hugo, 92200 Neuilly sur Seine, ☏ 01 46 41 25 25. Accredited by major insurance companies.

The British Hospital is just outside Paris in Levallois-Perret, 3 rue Barbès, ☏ 01 46 39 22 22.

Seasons

Climate

Sports and leisure in the French Alps changes with the seasons. The region's resorts are at their liveliest in winter, when snowy villages and landscapes, and the frequently brilliant blue skies of the south, offer the best-known images of alpine holidays. In the summer, the south generally remains drier than the lush north, but is also considerably hotter, except in the higher hills. Climbers and walkers flock to the whole area in search of striking panoramas and clean mountain air and the water sports centres around Geneva, Le Bourget and Annecy come into their own. Be aware, however, that heat haze may obscure some of the best views in the height of summer.

For any outdoor activity on sea or land, it is useful to have reliable weather forecasts. For general weather reports, dial 08 36 68 02 followed by the two-digit number of the département;

　　　　Alpes de Haute Provence ☏ 04
　　　　Alpes Maritimes ☏ 06
　　　　Drôme ☏ 26
　　　　Haute-de-Savoie ☏ 74
　　　　Hautes-Alpes ☏ 05
　　　　Isère ☏ 38
　　　　Savoie ☏ 73
　　　　Var ☏ 83
　　　　Vaucluse ☏ 06

The Minitel service **36 15 METEO**, **36 15 CIEL** and **36 17 METPLUS** gives weather forecasts for the next 10 days. See also the chapter on Safety on the mountains.

What to pack

As little as possible! Cleaning and laundry services are available everywhere. Most personal items can be replaced at reasonable cost. Try to pack everything into one suitcase and a tote bag. Porter help may be in short supply, and new purchases will add to the original weight. Take an extra tote bag for packing new purchases, shopping at the open-air market, carrying a picnic, etc. Be sure luggage is clearly labelled and old travel tags removed. Do not pack medication in checked luggage, but keep it with you.

Public holidays

Museums and other monuments may be closed or may vary their hours of admission on the following public holidays:

1 January	New Year's Day *(Jour de l'An)*
Easter	Easter Day and Easter Monday *(Pâques)*
1 May	May Day
8 May	VE Day
Thurs 40 days after Easter	Ascension Day *(Ascension)*
7th Sun-Mon after Easter	Whit Sunday and Monday *(Pentecôte)*
14 July	France's National Day (Bastille Day)
15 August	Assumption *(Assomption)*
1 November	All Saints' Day *(Toussaint)*
11 November	Armistice Day
25 December	Christmas Day *(Noël)*

National museums and art galleries are closed on Tuesdays; municipal museums are generally closed on Mondays. In addition to the usual school holidays at Christmas and in the spring and summer, there are long mid-term breaks (10 days to a fortnight) in February and early November.

Time

France is 1hr ahead of Greenwich Mean Time (GMT).

When it is **noon in France**, it is

3am	in Los Angeles
6am	in New York
11am	in Dublin
11am	in London
7pm	in Perth
9pm	in Sydney
11pm	in Auckland

In France "am" and "pm" are not used but the 24-hour clock is widely applied.

Budget

Currency

There are no restrictions on the amount of currency visitors can take into France. However visitors carrying a lot of cash are advised to complete a currency declaration form on arrival, because there are restrictions on currency export.

NOTES AND COINS

The European currency unit, the **euro**, went into circulation on 1 January 2002 and the euro has been the only accepted currency since 17 February 2002. The exchange period for francs, when notes and coins could be converted in any bank, expired in June 2002; they are now only accepted by the Banque de France (3 years for coins and 10 years for notes).

BANKS

Banks are open from 9am to noon and 2pm to 4pm and branches are closed either on Monday or Saturday. Banks close early on the day before a bank holiday. A passport is necessary as identification when cashing travellers' cheques in banks. Commission charges vary, and hotels usually charge more than banks for cashing cheques. One of the most economical ways to use your money in France is by using **ATM machines** to get cash directly from your bank account or to use your credit cards to get cash advances. Be sure to remember your PIN number, you will need it to use cash dispensers and to pay with your card in most shops, restaurants, etc. Code pads are numeric; use a tele-phone pad to translate a letter code into numbers. PIN numbers have 4 digits in France; inquire with the issuing company or bank if the code you usually use is longer. Visa is the most widely accepted credit card, followed by MasterCard; other cards, credit and debit (Diners Club, Plus, Cirrus, etc) are also accepted in some cash machines. American Express is more often accepted in premium establishments. Most places post signs indi-cating the cards they accept; if you don't see such a sign, and want to pay with a card, ask before ordering or making a selection. Cards are widely accepted in shops, hyper-markets, hotels and restaurants, at tollbooths and in petrol stations. If your card is lost or stolen, call one of the following 24-hour hotlines:

American Express	☎ 01 47 77 72 00	**Visa**	☎ 08 36 69 08 80
Mastercard/Eurocard	☎ 01 45 67 84 84	**Diners Club**	☎ 01 49 06 17 50

You must report any loss or theft of credit cards or travellers' cheques to the local police who will issue you with a certificate (useful proof to show the issuing company).

TIPPING

Since a service charge is automatically included in the price of meals and accommoda-tion in France, any additional tip *(pourboire)* is up to the visitor, generally small change, and generally not more than 5%. Taxi drivers and hairdressers are usually tipped 10-15%. As a rule, prices for hotels and restaurants as well as for other goods and serv-ices are significantly less expensive in the French regions than in Paris. Here are a few indicative euro prices, based on surveys conducted by French authorities. Exchange rates change regularly, so you will have to check before you leave for an exact calcula-tion. At press time, the exchange rate for 1€ was: USD 1.01; GBP 0.64; CAD 1.56; AUD 1.83.

Hotel rooms (based on double occupancy) in a city	Euro
1 star (French Tourist board standards)	27.44 – 53.36
2 star	53.36 – 76.22
3 star	76.23 – 121.97
4 star	137.21 – 228.69
4 star (luxury)	228.69 – 381.15

Food and entertainment	Euro
Movie ticket	7.62
River cruise	6.1 – 9.91
Dinner cruise	68.61 – 76.23
In a café:	
Espresso coffee	1.83
Café au lait	3.35
Soda	3.35
Beer	3.25
Mineral water	3.05
Ice cream	4.88
Ham sandwich	3.20
Baguette	0.69
Soda (1 litre in a shop)	2.13
Restaurant meal (3 courses, no wine)	25
Big Mac menu meal	5.34
French daily newspaper	1
Foreign newspaper	1.52 - 2.29
Compact disc	12.00 – 21.00
Telephone card – 50 units	7.47
Telephone card – 120 units	14.86
Cigarettes (pack of 20)	2.44 – 3.50

Public transportation	Euro
Bus, street car, metro	1.25 – 1.31
Book of ten tickets	8.80 – 9.24
Taxi (5km + tip)	9.91 – 10.40
TGV ticket Paris-Lyon 2nd class (one way)	52.10

Restaurants usually charge for meals in two ways: a *menu*, that is a fixed price menu with 2 or 3 courses and sometimes a small pitcher of wine (*pichet de vin* or *vin en carafe*), all for a stated price, or *à la carte*, the more expensive way, with each course ordered separately.

Cafés have very different prices, depending on where they are located. The price of a drink or a coffee is cheaper if you stand at the counter *(comptoir)* than if you sit down *(salle)* and sometimes it is even more expensive if you sit outdoors *(ter-race)*.

Shopping

Most of the larger shops are open Mondays to Saturdays from 9am to 6.30 or 7.30pm. Smaller, individual shops may close during the lunch hour. Food shops – grocers, wine merchants and bakeries – are generally open from 7am to 6.30 or 7.30pm; some open on Sunday mornings. Many food shops close between noon and 2pm and on Mondays. Bakery and pastry shops sometimes close on Wednesdays. Hypermarkets usually stay open non-stop until 9pm or later.

There is a Value Added Tax in France (TVA) of 19.6% on almost every purchase (books and some foods are subject to a lower rate). However, non-European visitors who spend more than 182.94€ in any one participating store can apply for a refund of the VAT. Usually, you fill out a form at the store, showing your passport. Upon leaving the country, you submit all forms to customs for approval (they may want to see the goods, so if possible don't pack them in checked luggage). The refund is usually paid directly into your bank or credit card account, or it can be sent by mail. Big department stores that cater to tourists provide special services to help you; be sure to mention that you plan to seek a refund before you pay for goods (no refund is possible for tax on services). If you are visiting two or more countries within the European Union, you submit the forms only on departure from the last EU country. The refund is worth while for those visitors who would like to buy fashions, furniture or other fairly expensive items, but remember, the minimum amount must be spent in a single shop (though not necessarily on the same day).

People travelling to the USA cannot import plant products or fresh food, including fruit, cheeses and nuts. It is acceptable to carry tinned products or preserves.

Discounts

Significant discounts are available for senior citizens, students, young people under 25, teachers, and groups for public transport, museums and monuments and for some leisure activities such as movies (at certain times of day). Bring student or senior cards with you, and bring along some extra passport-size photos for discount travel cards.
The **International Student Travel Conference** (www.istc.org), global administrator of the International Student and Teacher Identity Cards, is an association of student travel organizations around the world. ISTC members collectively negotiate benefits with airlines, governments, and providers of other goods and services for the student and teacher community, both in their own country and around the world. The non-profit association sells international ID cards for students, young people under 25 and teachers (who may get discounts on museum entrance charges, for example). The ISTC is also active in a network of international education and work exchange programmes. The corporate headquarters address is Herengracht 479, 1017 BS Amsterdam, The Netherlands ☎ 31 20 421 28 00; Fax 31 20 421 28 10.
See the section below on travelling by rail in France for other discounts on public transport.

Tourist Pass: 100 sights for 42€

This pass gives unrestricted access to more than 100 historic buildings managed by the *Centre des Monuments Nationaux*. It is valid for one year throughout France as of the date of purchase and is for sale at the entrance to major historic buildings, monuments and museums. With the pass, you can save time by skipping the wait at the ticket window. For a list of all the monuments, plus details on their history, information on travel, and other entertaining features to help you plan your trip, visit the lively website: www.monuments-france.fr

---

Transport

Getting there and getting around

BY AIR

The various national and other independent airlines operate services to Paris (Roissy-Charles-de-Gaulle and Orly airports). Major companies offering regularly scheduled flights from the UK and the US to one of the key gateway airports (Geneva, Lyon-Satolas and Chambéry) include Air France, American Airlines, Delta and British Airways. Discount flights from London to Grenoble are offered by buzz. There are daily flights from Paris to Grenoble (1hr), Chambéry/Aix-les-Bains (1hr 10min) and Annecy (1hr 15min).
There are also package tour flights with a rail or coach link-up, as well as Fly-Drive schemes. Information, brochures and timetables are available from the airlines or travel agents.

BY SEA (from the UK or Ireland)

There are numerous **cross-Channel** passenger and car ferry services from the United Kingdom and Ireland, as well as the rail Shuttle through the Channel Tunnel (**Le Shuttle-Eurotunnel**, ☎ 0990 353-535). To choose the most suitable route between your port of arrival and your destination use the Michelin Tourist and Motoring Atlas France, Michelin map 911 (which gives travel times and mileages) or Michelin maps from the 1:200 000 series (with the yellow cover). For details apply to travel agencies or to:

P & O Stena Line Ferries	Channel House, Channel View Road, Dover CT17 9JT, ☎ 0990 980 980 or 01304 863 000 (Switchboard), www.p-and-o.com
Hoverspeed	International Hoverport, Marine Parade, Dover, Kent CT17 9TG, ☎ 0990 240 241, Fax 01304 240088, www.hoverspeed.co.uk
Brittany Ferries	Millbay Docks; Plymouth, Devon, PL1 3EW, ☎ 0990 360 360, www.brittany-ferries.com
Portsmouth Commercial Port (and ferry information)	George Byng Way, Portsmouth, Hampshire PO2 8SP, ☎ 01705 297391, Fax 01705 861165
Irish Ferries	50 West Norland Street, Dublin 2, ☎ (353) 16 610 511, www.irishferries.com
Seafrance	Eastern Docks, Dover, Kent, CT16 1JA, ☎ 01304 212696, Fax 01304 240033, www.seafrance.fr

BY RAIL

British Rail and **French Railways** (SNCF) operate a 3hr service via the Channel Tunnel on Eurostar between **London** (Waterloo International Station) and **Paris** (Gare du Nord). Since June 2001, the operation of high-speed TGV trains from **Paris** has greatly reduced the journey time to Albertville (4hr 15min), Annecy (4hr), Chambéry (3hr 30min), Grenoble (3hr) and Thonon-les-Bains (4hr 30min). You can also start your journey in Lille (add 1hr). On Friday evenings during the ski season, a special overnight ski train connects Paris Gare du Nord and the stations of Bourg St-Maurice, Aime la Plagne, Moûtiers, Albertville and Chambéry; prices and timetables for this weekly service can be found on the Rail Europe website, www.raileurope.co.uk.

Eurailpass, **Flexipass**, **Eurailpass Youth**, **EurailDrive Pass** and **Saverpass** are travel passes which may be purchased by residents of countries outside the European Union. In the US, contact your travel agent or **Rail Europe** 2100 Central Ave. Boulder, CO 80301 ☎ 1-800-4-EURAIL or **Europrail International** ☎ 1 888 667 9731. If you are a European resident, you can buy an individual country pass if you are not a resident of the country where you plan to use it. In the UK, contact Europrail at 179 Piccadilly, London W1V OBA ☎ 0990 848 848. Information on schedules can be obtained on websites for these agencies and the **SNCF**, respectively: www.raileurop.com.us, www.eurail.on.ca, www.sncf.fr. At the SNCF site (available in English), you can book ahead, pay with a credit card, and receive your ticket in the mail at home.

There are numerous **discounts** available when you purchase your tickets in France, from 25-50% below the regular rate. These include discounts for using senior cards and youth cards (the photocards must be purchased – 46€ and 44€, respectively), and lower rates for 2-9 people travelling together (no card required, advance purchase necessary). There are a limited number of discount seats available during peak travel times, and the best discounts are available for travel during off-peak periods.

Remember to validate *(composter)* French railway tickets using the orange automatic date-stamping machines at the platform entrance. Failure to do so may result in a fine. The French railway company SNCF operates a **telephone information, reservation and prepayment service in English** from 7am to 10pm (French time). In France call ☎ 08 36 35 35 39 (when calling from outside France, drop the initial 0).

BY COACH

The Alps can also be reached by coach via Paris. **Eurolines** operates ski season services to Chamonix, Grenoble, Annecy, Chambéry and Lyon. For further information, check www.eurolines.com or contact:

London: 52 Grosvenor Gardens, Victoria, London SW1 OAU ☎ 0171 730 8235.
Paris: 28 Avenue du Général-de-Gaulle, 93541 Bagnolet ☎ 01 49 72 51 51.

Motoring in France

The area covered in this guide is easily reached by main motorways and national routes. **Michelin map 911** indicates the main itineraries as well as alternate routes for avoiding heavy traffic during busy holiday periods, and gives estimated travel times. **Michelin map 914** is a detailed atlas of French motorways, indicating tolls, rest areas and services along the route; it includes a table for calculating distances and times. The latest Michelin route-planning service is available on Internet, **www.ViaMichelin.co.uk**. Travellers can work out a precise route using such options as shortest route, scenic route, route avoiding toll roads or the Michelin-recommended route. The site also provides tourist information (hotels, restaurants and attractions).

The roads are very busy during the holiday period, particularly at weekends in July and August, and to avoid traffic congestion it is advisable to follow the recommended secondary routes (signposted as *Bison Futé – itinéraires bis*). The motorway network includes rest areas *(aires)* and petrol stations, usually with restaurant and shopping complexes attached, about every 40km/25mi, so that long-distance drivers have no excuse not to stop for a rest every now and then.

Documents

Travellers from other European Union countries and North America can drive in France with a valid national or home-state **driving licence**. An **international driving licence** is useful because the information on it appears in nine languages (keep in mind that traffic officers are empowered to fine motorists). A permit is available (US$10) from the National Automobile Club, 1151 East Hillsdale Blvd., Foster City, CA 94404 ☎ 650-294-7000 or nationalautoclub.com; or contact your local branch of the American Automobile Association. For the vehicle, it is necessary to have the registration papers (logbook) and a nationality plate of the approved size.

Certain motoring organisations (AAA, AA, RAC) offer accident **insurance** and breakdown service schemes for members. Check with your current insurance company in regard to cover while abroad. If you plan to hire a car using your credit card, check with the company, which may provide liability insurance automatically (and thus save you having to pay the cost for optimum coverage).

Highway code

The minimum driving age is 18. Traffic drives on the right. All passengers must wear **seat belts**. Children under the age of 10 must ride in the back seat. Headlights must be switched on in poor visibility and at night; use sidelights only when the vehicle is stationary.

In the case of a **breakdown**, a red warning triangle or hazard warning lights are obligatory. In the absence of stop signs at intersections, cars must **yield to the right**. Traffic on main roads outside built-up areas (priority indicated by a yellow diamond sign) and on roundabouts has right of way. Vehicles must stop when the lights turn red at road junctions and may filter to the right only when indicated by an amber arrow.

The regulations on **drinking and driving** (limited to 0.50g/l) and **speeding** are strictly enforced – usually by an on-the-spot fine and/or confiscation of the vehicle.

Speed limits – Although liable to modification, these are as follows:
– toll motorways *(autoroutes)* 130kph/80mph (110kph/68mph when raining);
– dual carriageways and motorways without tolls 110kph/68mph (100kph/62mph when raining);
– other roads 90kph/56mph (80kph/50mph when raining) and in towns 50kph/31mph;
– outside lane on motorways during daylight, on level ground and with good visibility
– minimum speed limit of 80kph/50mph.

Remember that on steep, single lane roads in the Alps, as elsewhere in France, the driver heading downhill is expected to pull over or reverse to allow oncoming vehicles to pass.

Parking Regulations – In town there are zones where parking is either restricted or subject to a fee; tickets should be obtained from the ticket machines (*horodateurs* – small change necessary) and displayed inside the windscreen on the driver's side; failure to display may result in a fine, or towing and impoundment. Other parking areas in town may require you to take a ticket when passing through a barrier. To exit, you must pay the parking fee (usually there is a machine located by the exit – *sortie*) and insert

the paid-up card in another machine which will lift the exit gate. Where a blue parking zone is marked by a blue line on the road and a ▣ sign with a white square in the corner, a cardboard disc *(disque de stationnement)* gives 1hr 30min parking, or 2hr 30 min over lunchtime. Discs are available in supermarkets or petrol stations and occasionally given away free.

Tolls – In France, most motorway sections are subject to a toll *(péage)*. You can pay in cash or with a credit card (Visa, Mastercard).

Car rental

There are car rental agencies at airports, railway stations and in all large towns throughout France. Most European cars have manual transmission; automatic cars are available in larger cities only if an advance reservation is made. Drivers must be over 21; between ages 21-25, drivers are required to pay an extra daily fee; some companies allow drivers under 23 only if the reservation has been made through a travel agent. It is relatively expensive to hire a car in France; Americans in particular will notice the difference and should make arrangements before leaving, take advantage of fly-drive offers, or seek advice from a travel agent, specifying requirements.

Central Reservation in France:

Avis: 08 02 05 05 05.
Online booking at www.Avis.fr

SIXT-Eurorent: 0143 33 27 47

Europcar: 08 25 35 23 52

National-CITER: 01 44 38 61 61 (Paris); 08 00 20 21 21 (outside Paris). Online booking at www.citer.fr

Budget France: 08 00 10 00 01

Baron's Limousine: 01 45 30 21 21 (chauffeur-driven)

Hertz France: 01 39 38 38 38

Worldwide Motorhome Rentals offers fully equipped campervans for rent. You can view them on the company's web pages (mhrww.com) or call (US toll-free) US ☏ 888-519-8969; outside the US ☏ 530-389-8316 or Fax 530-389-8316.

Overseas Motorhome Tours Inc. organises escorted tours and individual rental of recreational vehicles: in the US ☏ 800-322-2127; outside the US ☏ 1-310-543-2590; Internet www.omtinc.com

Petrol (US: gas) – French service stations dispense: *sans plomb 98* (super unleaded 98), *sans plomb 95* (super unleaded 95), *diesel/gazole* (diesel) and *GPL* (LPG). Petrol is considerably more expensive in France than in the USA. Prices are listed on signboards on the motorways; it is usually cheaper to fill up after leaving the motorway; check the large hypermarkets on the outskirts of town.

Where to stay, Where to eat

Finding a hotel

THE GREEN GUIDE is pleased to offer a new feature: lists of selected hotels and restaurants for this region. Turn to the sections bordered in blue for descriptions and prices of typical places to stay and eat with local flair. The key on page 9 explains the symbols and abbreviations used in these sections. Use the **map of Places to stay** below to identify recommended places for overnight stops. For an even greater selection, use **The Red Guide France**, with its famously reliable star-rating system and hundreds of establishments all over France.

For further assistance, **Loisirs Accueil** is a booking service that has offices in some French *départements* – contact the tourist offices listed above for further information.
A guide to good-value, family-run hotels, **Logis et Auberges de France**, is available from the French Tourist Office, as are lists of other kinds of accommodation such as hotel-châteaux, bed-and-breakfasts etc.
Relais et châteaux provides information on booking in luxury hotels with character: 15 rue Galvani, 75017 Paris, ☏ 01 45 72 90 00.

Economy Chain Hotels – If you need a place to stop en route, these can be useful, as they are inexpensive (30-45€ for a double room) and generally located near the main road. While breakfast is available, there may not be a restaurant; rooms are small and simple, with a television and bathroom. Central reservation numbers:
– **Akena** ☏ 01 69 84 85 17
– **B&B** ☏ 0 803 00 29 29 (in France); 33 02 98 33 75 00 (when calling from outside France)
– **Mister Bed** ☏ 01 46 14 38 00
– **Villages Hôtel** ☏ 03 80 60 92 70
The hotels listed below are slightly more expensive (from 45€), and offer a few more amenities and services. Central reservation numbers:
– **Campanile, Climat de France, Kyriad** ☏ 01 64 62 46 46
Many chains have online reservations: www.etaphotel; www.ibishotel.com

Renting a cottage, bed and breakfast

The **Maison des Gîtes de France** is an information service on self-catering accommodation in the French Alps (and the rest of France). *Gîtes* are usually cottages or apartments decorated in the local style where visitors can make themselves at home, or bed and breakfast accommodation *(chambres d'hôtes)* which consists of a room and breakfast at a reasonable price.
Contact the Gîtes de France office in Paris: 59 rue St-Lazare, 75439 Paris Cedex 09, ☏ 01 49 70 75 75, or their representative in the UK, **Brittany Ferries** *(address above)*. On the internet, go to www.gites-de-france.fr and click on the flag for the English language version. This site is informative and also has an on-line ordering service so that you can have a catalogue sent to your home in just a couple of days. Two alternatives are Bed and Breakfast France, 94-96 Bell St, Henley-on-Thames, Oxon RG9 1XS, ☏ 01491 578 803; Fax. 01491 410 806; www.bedbreak.com, bookings@bedbreak.demon.co.uk or the guide "Gites d'Etape, Refuges" by A. and S. Mouraret – Rando Editions, B.P. 24, 65421 Ibos, produced with ramblers, mountaineers, skiers, bikers and kayakers in mind. The English language website www.gites-refuges.com allows users search by department or along a given route.

Places to stay: Northern Alps

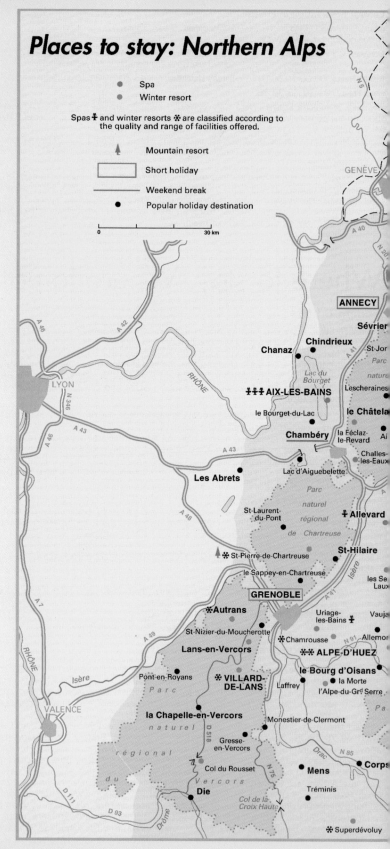

● Spa
● Winter resort

Spas ‡ and winter resorts �֍ are classified according to the quality and range of facilities offered.

▲ Mountain resort

▭ Short holiday

— Weekend break

● Popular holiday destination

0 — — — 30 km

GENÈVE

ANNECY

Sévrier

Chindrieux

St-Jor
Parc

Chanaz

naturel

Lac du
Bourget

Lescheraines

‡‡‡ AIX-LES-BAINS

le Châtela

le Bourget-du-Lac

la Féclaz-
le-Revard

Ai

Chambéry

Challes-
les-Eaux

LYON

A 43

Lac d'Aiguebelette

Les Abrets

Parc

naturel

St-Laurent-
du-Pont

régional

‡ Allevard

de Chartreuse

▲ �֍ St-Pierre-de-Chartreuse

St-Hilaire

le Sappey-en-Chartreuse

GRENOBLE

les Se
Lau

✖ Autrans

Uriage-
les-Bains ‡

Vauja

St-Nizier-du-Moucherotte

✖ Chamrousse

Allemo

Lans-en-Vercors

✖✖ ALPE-D'HUEZ

le Bourg d'Oisans

Pont-en-Royans

✖ VILLARD-
DE-LANS

Laffrey

la Morte

Parc

l'Alpe-du-Grd Serre

VALENCE

Isère

la Chapelle-en-Vercors

Monestier-de-Clermont

Pa

naturel

régional

Gresse-
en-Vercors

Corps

Col du Rousset

Mens

du Vercors

Die

Col de la
Croix Haute

Tréminis

✖ Superdévoluy

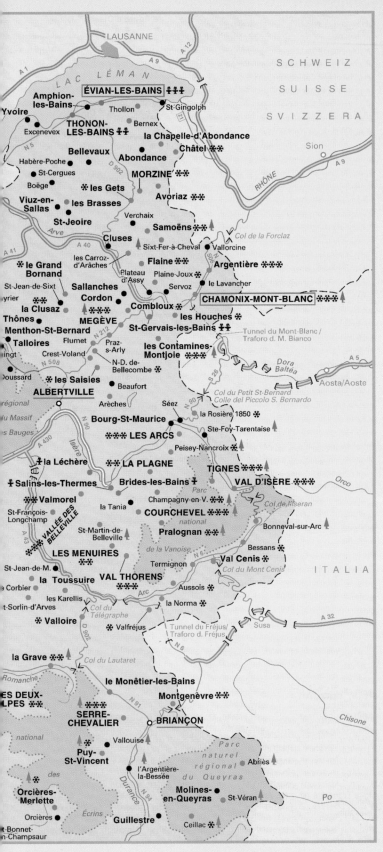

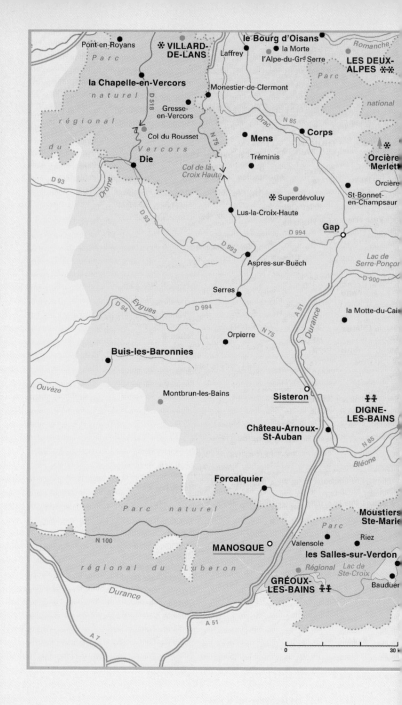

Hostels, camping

To obtain an International Youth Hostel Federation card (there is no age requirement, and there is a "senior card" available too), you should contact the IYHF in your own country for information and membership application (US ☎ 202 783 6161; UK ☎ 1727 855215; Canada ☎ 613-273 7884; Australia ☎ 61-2-9565-1669). There is a new booking service on the internet (iyhf.org), which you may use to reserve rooms as far as 6 months in advance.

There are two main youth hostel associations *(auberges de jeunesse)* in France, the **Ligue Française pour les Auberges de la Jeunesse** (67, rue Vergniaud 73013 Paris, ☎ 01 44 16 78 78) and the **Fédération Unie des Auberges de Jeunesse** (27 rue Pajol, 75018 Paris, ☎ 01 44 89 87 27, Fax 01 44 89 87 10). The Federation has an informative website providing online booking through the International Booking Network: www.fuaj.org

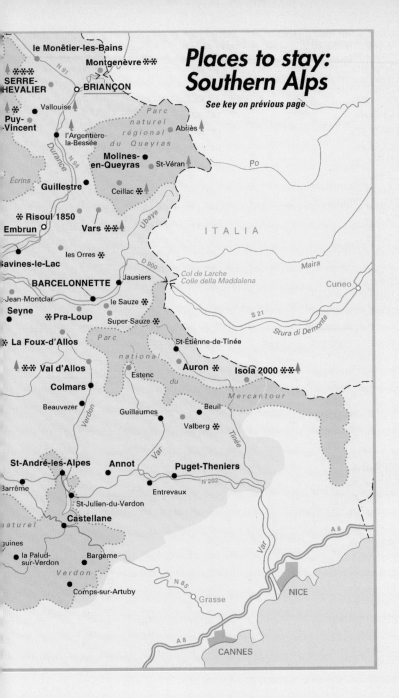

Places to stay:
Southern Alps

See key on prévious page

le Monêtier-les-Bains
Montgenèvre **

SERRE-
CHEVALIER ***
○ BRIANÇON

Vallouise
Puy-
Vincent *

l'Argentière-
la-Bessée

Parc naturel régional du Queyras

Abriès

Molines-
en-Queyras
St-Véran

Guillestre
Ceillac *

Écrins

* Risoul 1850
Embrun ○
Vars **

les Orres *

Savines-le-Lac

BARCELONNETTE
Jausiers

ITALIA

Col de Larche
Colle della Maddalena

Maira

Cuneo

S 21

Stura di Demonte

Jean-Montclar
le Sauze *
Seyne
* Pra-Loup
Super-Sauze *

* La Foux-d'Allos

Parc
national

St-Étienne-de-Tinée

Auron *
Isola 2000 **

Val d'Allos **

Estenc

du

Mercantour

Colmars

Beauvezer

Guillaumes

Beuil

Valberg *

Verdon

St-André-les-Alpes
Annot
Puget-Theniers

Barrême

Entrevaux

N 202

St-Julien-du-Verdon

Castellane

A 8

naturel

guines

la Palud-
sur-Verdon

Bargème

Verdon

Var

Comps-sur-Artuby

N 85

Grasse

NICE

A 8

CANNES

Po

Ubaye

Durance

 Écrins

There are numerous officially graded **camping sites** with varying standards of facilities throughout the French Alps. The **Michelin Camping Caravaning France** guide lists a selection of campsites. The region is popular with campers in the summer months, particularly the areas around the Lac d'Aiguebelette and the Lac d'Annecy, so it is wise to reserve in advance.

Finding a restaurant

Turn to the pages bordered in blue for descriptions and prices of selected places to eat in the different locations covered in this guide. The key on page 9 explains the symbols and abbreviations used in these sections. Use **The Red Guide France**, with its famously reliable star-rating system and hundreds of establishments all over France, for an even greater choice. If you would like to experience a meal in a highly rated restaurant from The Red Guide, be sure to book ahead! In the countryside, restaurants usually serve lunch between noon and 2pm and dinner between 7.30-10pm. It is not always easy to find something between those two meal times, as the "non-stop" restaurant is still a rarity in the provinces. However, a hungry traveller can usually get a sandwich in a café, and ordinary hot dishes may be available in a *brasserie*.

A TYPICAL FRENCH MENU

La Carte	The Menu
ENTRÉES	STARTERS
Crudités	Raw vegetable salad
Terrine de lapin	Rabbit terrine (pâté)
Frisée aux lardons	Curly lettuce with bacon bits
Escargots	Snails
Salade au crottin de Chavignol	Goats cheese on a bed of lettuce
PLATS (VIANDES)	MAIN COURSES (MEAT)
Bavette à l'échalote	Sirloin with shallots
Faux filet au poivre	Sirloin with pepper sauce
Pavé de rumsteck	Thick rump steak
Côtes d'agneau	Lamb chops
Filet mignon de porc	Pork fillet
Blanquette de veau	Veal in cream sauce
Nos viandes sont garnies	Our meat dishes are served with vegetables
PLATS (POISSONS, VOLAILLE)	MAIN COURSES (FISH, FOWL)
Filets de sole	Sole fillets
Dorade aux herbes	Sea bream with herbs
Saumon grillé	Grilled salmon
Truite meunière	Trout fried in butter
Magret de canard	Duck breast
Poulet rôti	Roast chicken
FROMAGE	CHEESE
DESSERTS	DESSERTS
Tarte aux pommes	Apple pie
Crème caramel	Cooled baked custard with caramel sauce
Sorbet: trois parfums	Sherbet/sorbet: choose 3 flavours
BOISSONS	BEVERAGES
Bière	Beer
Eau minérale (gazeuse)	(Sparkling) mineral water
Une carafe d'eau	A carafe of tap water (no charge)
Vin rouge, vin blanc, rosé	Red wine, white wine, rosé
Jus de fruit	Fruit juice
MENU ENFANT	CHILDREN'S MENU
Jambon	Ham
Steak haché	Minced beef
Frites	French fried potatoes

For information on local specialities, turn to page

For information on local specialities, turn to page

Basic information

Electricity

The electric current is 220 volts. Circular two-pin plugs are the rule. Adapters and converters (for hairdryers, for example) should be bought before you leave home; they are on sale in most airports. If you have a rechargeable device (video camera, portable computer, battery recharger), read the instructions carefully or contact the manufacturer or shop. Sometimes these items only require a plug adapter, in other cases you must use a voltage converter as well or risk ruining your device.

Post and telephone

Main post offices open Monday to Friday 8am to 7pm, Saturday 8am to noon. Smaller branch post offices generally close at lunchtime between noon and 2pm and at 4pm.

Postage via air mail:

> UK: letter (20g) 0.46€
>
> North America: letter (20g) 0.67€
>
> Australia and NZ: letter (20g) 0.79€

Stamps are also available from newsagents and *bureaux de tabac*. Stamp collectors should ask for *timbres de collection* in any post office.

Public Telephones – Most public phones in France use pre-paid phone cards *(télécartes)*, rather than coins. Some telephone booths accept credit cards (Visa,

Mastercard/Eurocard). *Télécartes* (50 or 120 units) can be bought in post offices, branches of France Télécom, *bureaux de tabac* (cafés that sell cigarettes) and newsagents and can be used to make calls in France and abroad. Calls can be received at phone boxes where the blue bell sign is shown; the phone will not ring, so keep your eye on the little message screen.

National calls – French telephone numbers have 10 digits. Paris and Paris region numbers begin with 01; 02 in northwest France; 03 in northeast France; 04 in southeast France and Corsica; 05 in southwest France.

International calls – To call France from abroad, dial the country code (0033) + 9-digit number (omit the initial 0). When calling abroad from France dial 00, then dial the country code followed by the area code and number of your correspondent.

International dialling codes (00 + code):

Australia	☎ 61
Canada	☎ 1
Eire	☎ 353
New Zealand	☎ 64
United Kingdom	☎ 44
United States	☎ 1

To use your **personal calling card** dial:

AT&T	☎ 0-800 99 00 11
MCI	☎ 0-800 99 00 19
Sprint.	☎ 0-800 99 00 87
Canada Direct .	☎ 0-800 99 00 16

Emergency numbers:

Police:	17
Fire *(Pompiers)*:	18
SAMU (Paramedics):	15

International Information: US/Canada: 00 33 12 11
International operator: 00 33 12 + country code
Local directory assistance: 12

Minitel – France Télécom operates a system offering directory enquiries (free of charge up to 3min), travel and entertainment reservations, and other services (cost per minute varies). These small computer-like terminals can be found in some post offices, hotels and France Télécom agencies and in many French homes. 3614 PAGES E is the code for **directory assistance in English** (turn on the unit, dial 3614, hit the *connexion* button when you get the tone, type in "PAGES E", and follow the instructions on the screen). **Cellular phones** in France have numbers which begin with 06. Two-watt (lighter, shorter reach) and eight-watt models are on the market, using the Itinéris (France Télécom) or SFR network. *Mobicartes* are pre-paid phone cards that fit into mobile units. Cell phone rentals (delivery or airport pickup provided):

Rent a Cell Express	☎ 01 53 93 78 00, Fax 01 53 93 78 09
A.L.T. Rent A Phone	☎ 01 48 00 06 60, E-mail mailto:altloc@jve.fr

Notes and Coins

The euro banknotes were designed by Robert Kalinan, an Austrian artist. His designs were inspired by the theme "Ages and styles of European Architecture". Windows and gateways feature on the front of the banknotes, bridges feature on the reverse, symbolising the European spirit of openness and co-operation.

The images are stylised representations of the typical architectural style of each period, rather than specific structures.

Classical

Baroque and Rococo

Romanesque

19C iron and glass

Gothic

Renaissance

20C modern

Euro coins have one face common to all 12 countries in the European single currency area or "Eurozone" (currently Austria, Belgium, Finland, France, Germany, Greece, Ireland, Italy, Luxembourg, The Netherlands, Portugal and Spain) and a reverse side specific to each country, created by their own national artists.

Euro banknotes look the same throughout the Eurozone. All Euro banknotes and coins can be used anywhere in this area.

Conversion Tables

Weights and measures

1 kilogram (kg)	2.2 pounds (lb)	2.2 pounds
1 metric ton (tn)	1.1 tons	1.1 tons

to convert kilograms to pounds, multiply by 2.2

1 litre (l)	2.1 pints (pt)	1.8 pints
1 litre	0.3 gallon (gal)	0.2 gallon

to convert litres to gallons, multiply by 0.26 (US) or 0.22 (UK)

1 hectare (ha)	2.5 acres	2.5 acres
1 square kilometre (km²)	0.4 square miles (sq mi)	0.4 square miles

to convert hectares to acres, multiply by 2.4

1 centimetre (cm)	0.4 inches (in)	0.4 inches
1 metre (m)	3.3 feet (ft) - 39.4 inches - 1.1 yards (yd)	
1 kilometre (km)	0.6 miles (mi)	0.6 miles

to convert metres to feet, multiply by 3.28 . kilometres to miles, multiply by 0.6

Clothing

Women

	EU	US	UK	
Shoes	35	4	2½	
	36	5	3½	
	37	6	4½	
	38	7	5½	
	39	8	6½	
	40	9	7½	
	41	10	8½	
Dresses & Suits	36	4	8	
	38	6	10	
	40	8	12	
	42	12	14	
	44	14	16	
	46	16	18	
Blouses & sweaters	36	08	30	
	38	10	32	
	40	12	34	
	42	14	36	
	44	16	38	
	46	18	40	

Men

EU	US	UK	
40	7½	7	Shoes
41	8½	8	
42	9½	9	
43	10½	10	
44	11½	11	
45	12½	12	
46	13½	13	
46	36	36	Suits
48	38	38	
50	40	40	
52	42	42	
54	44	44	
56	46	48	
37	14½	14.5	Shirts
38	15	15	
39	15½	15½	
40	15¾	15¾	
41	16	16	
42	16½	16½	

Sizes often vary depending on the designer. These equivalents are given for guidance only.

Speed

kph	10	30	50	70	80	90	100	110	120	130
mph	6	19	31	43	50	56	62	68	75	81

Temperature

Celsius (°C)	0°	5°	10°	15°	20°	25°	30°	40°	60°	80°	100°
Fahrenheit (°F)	32°	41°	50°	59°	68°	77°	86°	104°	140°	176°	212°

To convert Celsius into Fahrenheit, multiply °C by 9, divide by 5, and add 32.
To convert Fahrenheit into Celsius, subtract 32 from °F, multiply by 5, and divide by 9.

Canyoning

Sports and recreation

Safety in the Mountains

Mountain areas are potentially dangerous, even for the most experienced enthusiasts. Avalanches, falling rocks, bad weather, fog, treacherous terrain and snowfields, icy water, loss of one's bearings and wrong assessment of distances are the dangers threatening mountaineers, skiers and hikers.

DRIVING IN MOUNTAIN AREAS

Unaccustomed drivers may be overawed by the experience and it is essential to take certain precautions. Cars must be in good working order (brakes and tyres particularly) and drivers must abide rigorously by the highway code. For instance, horns must be sounded on twisting roads with reduced visibility and along narrow roads and cars going downhill must give way to those climbing. When climbing continuously, it is advisable to watch the oil and cooling liquid levels. In addition, it is recommended to avoid driving in bad weather, getting caught by nightfall, stopping beneath a cliff (falling rocks are frequent) or leaving the car unattended in an isolated spot (danger of theft).

Tricky scenic roads – Michelin maps on a scale of 1:200 000 show very narrow roads where passing is difficult or impossible), unusually steep ones, difficult or dangerous sections, tunnels and the altitude of major passes.

Snow cover – Maps nos 916, 919 and 989 on a scale of 1:1 000 000 show major roads which are regularly blocked by snow with their probable closing dates and those which are cleared within 24 hours. Access roads to resorts are normally cleared daily.

A FEW WORDS OF ADVICE

Advice given to off-piste skiers also applies to hikers and mountaineers. However, a prolonged stay above 3 000m/9 842ft calls for special precautions. Atmospheric pressure is one third lower and the heart beats faster to compensate for the lack of oxygen. It takes roughly a week to get used to it as the production of red cells in the blood is intensified so that as much oxygen can be carried as at lower altitudes.

The main dangers are the following. **Mountain sickness** or hypoxaemia (symptoms: digestive problems, breathing difficulty, headache) which can normally be treated with appropriate medicine that tourists are advised to take with them; the more serious cases (pulmonary oedema) have to be treated in hospital. **Hypothermia** is also a danger in mountain areas for people caught by a sudden change in the weather such as fog, for instance, which always brings a cold snap. **Frostbite** is less obvious as symptoms appear progressively: loss of feeling in the hands and feet, numbness and paleness of the skin. The danger lies in the wrong treatment being applied on the spot: never try to heat up the affected part of the body, by whatever means, unless you can keep it warm until the doctor arrives, as a new attack of frostbite on a partially rewarmed limb would cause even more damage.

Accidents can be avoided or their consequences lessened by following these simple rules; it is also recommended never to go hiking or mountaineering on your own, and to let someone know of your planned itinerary and when you intend to return.

Weather forecast – Up-to-date recorded information about regional weather is available to hikers (for telephone numbers, see Tourist information). In addition, more specific information can be obtained:
- Five-day forecast in high-mountain areas: ☎ 08 36 68 04 04;
- Risk of avalanche: ☎ 08 36 68 10 20.

Avalanches – Whether they happen naturally or are started by passing skiers, they represent a permanent danger which must not be dismissed lightly. **Bulletins Neige et Avalanche** (BNA), posted in every resort and hiking base, warn of the risks that must be taken into consideration by anyone planning an excursion. A new more precise scale of potential risks has been devised for the benefit of those who practise off-piste skiing, cross-country skiing or snowshoeing.

Avalanche-risk scale

1 – **Low:** snow cover is stable and there are only rare avalanches on very steep slopes.

2 – **Limited:** snow cover is again stable but avalanches may be started in specific areas by an excessive number of skiers or hikers.

3 – **Likely:** snow cover is only moderately stable and avalanches may be started in many places by individuals; avalanches are also likely to start naturally as for 4 on the scale.

4 – **Very likely:** snow cover is fairly unstable on all steep slopes and avalanches are very likely to occur, set off by skiers or hikers, or even spontaneously.

5 – **Extremely likely:** snow cover is very unstable following a heavy snow fall and major avalanches will occur even on gentle slopes.

This is only a general guideline which needs to be supplemented with more precise information concerning the planned itinerary. In addition, it is advisable to be fairly flexibl and evaluate the risks incurred in each case.

Warning signs and flags for the benefit of skiers

1 – NO We do not need any help.

2 – YES We are calling for help.

3 – Risk of avalanche in all areas.

4 – Risk of avalanche in certain areas.

Lightning – Violent gusts of wind are the warning signs of an imminent thunderstorm which brings with it the danger of being struck by lightning. Avoid walking along ridges taking shelter beneath overhanging rocks or isolated trees, at the entrance of caves o hollows in the rock and near metallic fences. Do not carry large metallic objects such a an ice-axe and crampons. Do not huddle under a metallic-framed shelter. Stand mor than 15 metres/yards from any high point (rock or tree) and adopt a crouching position, keeping your hands and any bare parts of your body away from the surface of the rock. Before lightning strikes, the atmosphere often becomes electrified and a sound lik the humming of a swarm of bees can sometimes be heard, well known to mountain dwellers. Finally, remember that a car provides a safe shelter during a storm as it make an excellent Faraday cage.

Assistance – Contact the **gendarmerie** who will get their own rescue service to deal with the problem or will call on the local rescue teams.

Who pays for it? – The cost can be very high, especially if a rescue helicopter is calle out, and the person rescued or his family are normally expected to pay. It is therefor advisable to take out insurance to cover such risks.

Skiing

The Alps are the ideal area for winter sports, an environment in which new ways o getting across snowfields are tested and existing techniques perfected.

Downhill skiing – This is the most popular form of skiing, available in all the Alpine resorts. The French champion Émile Allais devised its present form in 1931.

Cross-country or Nordic skiing – This type of skiing is ideal on fairly level terrain; skis ar long and narrow, boots are low and fixed at the point only. Since 1968, cross-country skiing is one of the Olympic events. There are marked tracks of various lengths in most resorts. In addition, most resorts provide specially marked areas for cross-country skiers in the lowe parts of ski slopes. This form of skiing can be practised at any age, each skier going at hi own pace. The **Vercors** region is particularly suitable for cross-country skiing, with specia markings, mountain refuges and shelters. Information is available from the Parc nature régional du Vercors. The **Parc naturel régional du Queyras**, which combined with the Guisane val ley boasts some of the best cross-country skiing in the south, offers similar facilities.

Off-piste skiing – This is intended for very experienced skiers who ski outside markec runs at their own risk. The presence and advice of a guide or instructor with a comprehensive knowledge of dangerous areas is highly recommended. Some resorts have off-piste areas which are unmarked but patrolled. For those with the necessary confidence, mono-skiing, with both feet on a single ski, is a great test of skill and balance.

Ski touring – This form of skiing is suitable for experienced skiers with plenty of stamina as it combines the technique of cross-country skiing for uphill sections and that of offpiste skiing for downhill sections. Skiers should be accompanied by a qualified guide and special equipment is necessary: skis fitted with seal skins for climbing. There are several famous itineraries across the Alps: the **Grande Traversée des Alpes** (GTA) which follows footpath GR 5 from Lake Geneva to the Mediterranean, the **Chamonix-Zermatt**, the **Dômes de la Vanoise**, the **Haut-Beaufortain** and other itineraries in the Haute-Provence region For more information, contact CIMES GTA, 7 rue Voltaire, 38000 Grenoble ☎ 04 76 42 45 90 or Minitel **3615 CIMES**.

Snowboarding – This increasingly popular sport, now an Olympic event in its own right is practised without sticks on steep slopes, with snowboarders usually enjoying going over snow mounds.

Mogul skiing – This acrobatic form of skiing has also become an Olympic event; it consists of skiing down very bumpy runs and is a good way of getting used to off-piste skiing.

Special courses are organised in all the resorts to introduce amateurs to these various forms of "skiing", as well as snow-scooter training. Sledge racing and skijörring, which involves being pulled along on skis by sled dogs, are also gaining in popularity.

Winter sport resorts

See the Places to Stay map at the beginning of the guide and the table of resorts below. All the resorts mentioned offer accommodation listed in The Red Guide France.

The Alps boast a great variety of resorts. Beside internationally famous resorts such as Tignes, Val d'Isère, Courchevel and Chamonix, there are a great number of more modest ones which have retained their village character and attract a family clientele. Skiing resorts have changed over the past decades as skiing itself has developed. The first ones evolved from existing traditional villages or small towns, such as Morzine or Megève; the second generation of resorts, including Val d'Isère, L'Alpe-d'Huez, Les Deux-alpes, moved to high pastures in search of good skiing slopes. The post-war period saw the blossoming of planned resorts like Courchevel, Chamrousse, Tignes and the latest resorts, such as Les Arc, Avoriaz, Les Ménuires, Val-Thorens and Flaine, all of which were designed by a single property developer. Ski-lifts reach higher and higher, extending the resorts' skiing areas which are often linked. In some cases (L'Alpe-d'Huez, Val d'Isère, Tignes, Les Deux-Alpes, Val-Thorens), they reach so high that the snow cover holds throughout the summer making all-year skiing possible.

Summer skiing resorts – Five resorts offer summer skiing as well as more traditional summer activities:
- **L'Alpe-d'Huez** – July to mid-August on the Sarennes Glacier (3 000m/9 842ft).
- **Les Deux-Alpes** – mid-June to early September on the Mont-de-Lans Glacier (3 420m/11 220ft).
- **La Plagne** – July to August on the Bellecôte Glacier (3 416m/11 207ft).
- **Tignes** – July to August on the Grande Motte Glacier (3 430m/11 253ft).
- **Val-Thorens** – July to August on the Péclet Glacier (3 400m/11 155ft).

Linked skiing areas – A number of individual resorts have joined together to form extensive ski areas.

Espace Killy – Tignes et Val-d'Isère.

Les Trois Vallées – Les Ménuires, Courchevel, Val-Thorens, La Tania, Méribel and St-Martin-de-Belleville.

L'Espace Les Arcs – Les Arcs, La Plagne and Peisey-Nancroix.

L'Espace Cristal – Crest-Voland, Cohennoz and Les Saisies.

Le Super Grand Large – Le Corbier, La Toussuire, St-Jean-d'Arves and St-Sorlin-d'Arves.

Les Portes du Soleil – Abondance, Avoriaz, La Chapelle, Châtel, Les Gets, Montriond and Morzine.

Évasion Mont-Blanc – Combloux, Megève, St-Gervais and St-Nicolas-de-Véroce.

Le Grand Massif – Les Carroz-d'Arâches, Flaine, Morillon, Samoëns and Sixt.

La Carte Blanche – Flumet, Notre-Dame-de-Bellecombe and Praz-sur-Arly.

La Grande Plagne – All resorts in the La Plagne complex.

Les Grandes Rousses – L'Alpe-d'Huez, Auris-en-Oisans, Oz, Vaujany and Villard-Reculas.

Hiking

Hiking is the best way to explore mountain areas and discover the finest scenery. Footpaths are extensively described in this guide and three types of hike are identified. **Rambles** are, in principle, suitable for anyone, including children. **Day hikes** require more stamina and some prior training for a walking time exceeding 4hr and a difference in altitude of 700m/2 297ft. A few more demanding **itineraries for experienced hikers** are also

Val Thorens - one of the great French resorts

S. Sauvignier/MICHELIN

described including extremely steep or vertiginous sections which do not howeve
require any specialised mountaineering knowledge: these are worth the extra physice
effort for the exceptional panoramas. Before leaving, always get the latest weather fore
cast and make sure that the length of the hike is compatible with the time of departure
In mountain areas, the estimated length of an excursion is calculated according to th
difference in altitude: 300m/984ft per hour going up and 500m/1 640ft going dowr
excluding stops.

Leave early in the morning if you can, so that all the climbing can be done during th
cool hours of the day and you stand a better chance of observing the fauna.

Whatever the type of hike, you should carry with you a map on a scale of 1:25 000 c
1:50 000, 1 or 2 litres of water per person, energy-building food, waterproof clothing
a pullover, sunglasses, sun cream and a first-aid kit. You should also wear mountai
boots and carry a pair of binoculars to spot distant peaks and observe the fauna (avoi
wearing brightly coloured clothes, moving too abruptly and being too noisy for fear c
frightening the animals away).

Mountain-refuge bookings – Refuges are now equipped with radio-telephones (number
available at tourist offices) and booking is now compulsory during the summer seasor
Hikers arriving without a booking should not therefore count on finding a bed for the nigh

Long-distance footpaths (GR) – Many footpaths marked in red and white run through th
Alps. Accompanying booklets or "topo-guides" give small maps, detailed itineraries, accom
modation information (refuges and lodges), and useful advice (also Minitel **3615 RANDO**).

GR 5 goes across the Alps from Lake Geneva to Nice, following the high Alps and cross
ing other footpaths on its way.

The **TMB** (Tour du Mont Blanc) goes round the massif, entering Switzerland and Italy
Allow eight days.

GR 55 runs through the Parc national de la Vanoise.

GR 54 "Tour de l'Oisans" goes round the Parc national des Écrins and the Oisans regior

GR 58 enables hikers to explore the Queyras region (numerous refuges and lodges).

GR 56 goes through the Ubaye region.

Other footpaths run through the Préalpes, or Alpine foothills.

GR 96 goes through the Chablais, the Aravis and the Bauges massifs.

GR 9, 91, 93 and 95 criss-cross the Vercors.

GR 93 continues across the Dévoluy and GR 94 runs through the Buëch, Bochaine and
Baronnies regions.

GR 6 "Alpes-Océan" links the Ubaye and Forcalquier Regions via Sisteron.

GR 4 "Méditerranée-Océan" goes right through Haute-Provence via Entrevaux
Castellane and Moustiers-Ste-Marie.

In addition, there are numerous local footpaths offering interesting hikes or linking
main itineraries. Shorter routes, known as **Sentiers de Petite Randonnée**, or **PR**, are markec
in yellow.

Useful addresses – Topo-guides are published by the Fédération française de la ran
donnée pédestre, Comité national des sentiers de Grande Randonnée, 14 rue Riquet
75019 Paris, ☎ 01 44 89 93 93. www.ffrp.asso.fr

A very comprehensive hiking guide is published by the Comité régional de tourisme
Rhône-Alpes, 104 route de Paris, 69260 Charbonnières-les-Bains, ☎ 04 72 59 21 59
In the Alps, contact CIMES, 7 rue Voltaire, 38000 Grenoble, ☎ 04 76 42 45 90
Association randonnée en Savoie, 4 rue du Château, 73000 Chambéry, ☎ 04 79 75 02 01
ADRI, 19 rue du Docteur-Honnorat, 04000 Digne-les-Bains, ☎ 04 92 31 07 01
(Haute-Provence region); Comité départemental de randonnée pédestre des Hautes
Alpes, 7 rue du Four-Neuf, 05000 Gap, ☎ 04 92 53 65 11.

Mountaineering

The Alps are one of the major mountaineering regions of the world.

Techniques and equipment have greatly improved over the past decades and
moutaineering has become a popular sport practised nowadays by an increasing num
ber of enthusiasts who look for ever greater difficulties, essentially in the Mont-Blanc
Écrins and Vanoise massifs, using nearby resorts as their base: Chamonix, St-Gervais
les-Bains, Pralognan-la-Vanoise, Bourg-d'Oisans (La Bérarde) and La Grave are the main
starting points of mountaineering expeditions. Climbers in search of greater technica
challenges have developed free-climbing, which uses equipment for safety alone, anc
solo climbing, which abandons climbing apparatus altogether.

Guides usually belong to a *"compagnie"*, the most famous being that of Chamonix
(☎ 04 50 53 00 88) which was founded in 1823.

Useful addresses – Club alpin français, 24 rue de Laumière, 75019 Paris, ☎ 01 53 72
87 13.

Fédération française de la montagne et de l'escalade, 10 quai de la Marne, 75019 Paris,
☎ 01 40 18 75 50.

Rock-climbing – Rock-climbing schools offer beginners the chance to learn basic tech
niques with qualified instructors (half-day, day or progressive courses). Information is
available at tourist offices and guides offices. The main rock-climbing areas are listed below.

– Maurienne region – **Aussois,** where several international competitions have been held, has some ten sites for all levels; apply to the guides office, ☎ 04 79 20 32 48.
– Vercors – The **Presles** Cliffs offer a variety of itineraries; information available at the guides office in Pont-en-Royans, ☎ 04 76 36 10 92.
– Briançonnais – Some ten sites for all levels; apply to the guides office in Briançon and l'Argentière-la-Bessée. For special beginners' courses apply to the guides office, 05240 La Salle-les-Alpes, ☎ 04 92 24 75 90.
– Vallouise region – Courses of varying difficulty (some suitable for children); apply to the guides office in Vallouise and Ailefroide, ☎ 04 92 23 32 02.
– Les Baronnies – Information and a list of guides is available at the Tourist office in Orpierre.
– Alpes-de-Haute-Provence – This area has a choice of sites suitable for beginners accompanied by instructors. **Annot**: contact Association "Vive les gestes", ☎ 04 92 83 35 17; **Chabrières**: contact the Club alpin in Digne, centre Desmichel, ☎ 04 92 32 32 98; Méolans: contact the Club alpin in Barcelonnette, ☎ 04 92 81 28 23; Quinson: club d'escalade de Quinson.
– Gorges du Verdon – La Palud-sur-Verdon: contact the regional rock-climbing centre at the town hall or at the Tourist office in season; Castellane: contact Verdon-Accueil, ☎ 04 92 83 67 36.

Via ferrata – *Via ferrata* climbing, which is a cross between mountaineering and hiking has become increasingly popular in the past few years.
These rock-climbing courses fitted with metal rungs and cables originated in the Dolomites during the First World War; they were planned by the Italian army and only discovered by the public in the 1950s. The first *via ferrata* courses were set up in the Briançon region at the beginning of the 1980s. A few well-equipped courses are mentioned in this guide. Basic equipment includes a harness, a helmet and two ropes (preferably with a fall absorber) to secure oneself to the cable which runs the whole length of the course. It is imperative that inexperienced climbers should be accompanied by a guide or join a group. Below are some useful contacts:
– **Presles**: 200m/656ft-high cliff, mostly easy but with two short abseiling sections. Contact the guides office in Pont-en-Royans, ☎ 04 76 36 10 92.
– **St-Christophe-en-Oisans**: easy course; difference in height 200m. Contact the guides office in La Bérarde.
– **St-Jean-de-Maurienne**: Mont Vernier: start from Pontamafrey, difference in altitude 280m/919ft. Croix des Têtes: start from La Raie car park in St-Julien-Mont-Denis; difficult course demanding good physical fitness. Contact the guides office in St-Jean-de-Maurienne, 76 rue Joseph-Perret, ☎ 04 79 59 90 80.
– **Aussois**: Via ferrata du Diable; contact the guides office, ☎ 04 79 20 32 48.
– **Valloire**: Via ferrata de Poingt-Ravier (1 644m/5 394ft); start from the tennis courts on the left bank of the Valloirette and Via ferrata du Rocher St-Pierre: start from the Borgé car park on the Route du Galibier; difficult course. Contact the guides office in Valloire, ☎ 04 79 83 35 03.
– **Val d'Isère**: Via ferrata des Plates de la Daille (excellent equipment).
– **Chamonix**: the Balcon de la Mer de Glace course is one of the most thrilling but is only suitable for experienced climbers.
There are other *via ferrata* courses in Courchevel and La Norma.
– **Briançon**: the Croix de Toulouse *via ferrata* offers superb views of the old town and the surrounding fortifications. Start from Place du Champ-de-Mars, difference in altitude 400m/1 312ft, allow 4hr. Contact the guides office, ☎ 04 92 20 15 73.
– L'Argentière-la-Bessée: the *via ferrata* at **Les Vigneaux** is the most popular in the area; it is moderately difficult and offers impressive bird's-eye views. Difference in altitude 400m/1 312ft, 200m/656ft vertical, 3hr there and back. Contact "Azimut" guides ☎ 04 92 23 04 51.

The *via ferrata* at Les Vigneaux

– **Freissinières**, near L'Argentière-la-Bessée, is the oldest *via ferrata* in France; moderately difficult, 3hr there and back.
– **L'Aiguillette du Lauzet** in the Guisane Valley offers views of the Écrins Massif; contact the guides office in Serre-Chevalier. Start from Pont de l'Alpe, car park off N°91. Difference in altitude 600m/1 969ft, 6km/3.7mi course including 1.5km/0.9mi on the vertical face of the Aiguillette. 6hr there and back ☎ 04 92 24 75 90.
– **St-Ours**: Via ferrata de l'Aiguille de Luce; Start from St-Ours car park; difficult course with over-hanging sections. Difference in altitude 400m/1 312ft, 5hr there and back; return by abseiling or by a longer return route. A leaflet is available at the Tourist office in Barcelonnette; contact the guides office of the Ubaye region, place des Sept-Portes, Barcelonnette, ☎ 04 92 81 04 71.
– **Motte-du-Caire** near Sisteron *(see SISTERON)* Via Ferrata de la Grande Fistoire

Ruisseling – This winter sport could be described as ice-climbing since those who prac-tise it use rock-climbing techniques and equipment to climb up frozen waterfalls and mountain streams. Contact the guides office in Aussois and Val Cenis.

Canyoning

A good knowledge of potholing, diving and rock-climbing techniques is necessary to abseil or jump down tumultuous mountain streams and to follow their course through narrow gorges *(clues)* and down steep waterfalls. The magic appeal of this sport lies in the variety of the terrain, in the sunlight playing on the foaming water, or in the contrast between the dense veg-etation and the bare rocks heated by the sun. Summer is the best period to practise canyoning: the water temperature is bearable and the rivers are not so high. However, the weather fore-cast plays a crucial role when it comes to deciding whether to go canyoning or not, as a storm upriver can make it dangerous to go through a gorge and cause basins to fill up with alluvial sediments. In any case, it is preferable to leave early in the morning (storms often occur during the afternoon) to allow oneself time to overcome any unforeseen minor problems. A begin-ners' course does not exceed 2km/1.2mi and is supervised by instructors. Later on it is essential to go canyoning with a qualified instructor, who can evaluate the state of a stream and has a good knowledge of local weather conditions. The main canyoning areas are the Vallée d'Abondance in Haute-Savoie, La Norma and Val Fréjus ("Indiana Jones" course) in the Haute-Maurienne, the Canyon des Écouges and Gorges du Furon in the Vercors, the Ubaye Valley between Les Thuiles and Le Lauzet, in particular the Ravin de Sauze, the upper Var and Cians valleys, and, of course, the Verdon (Ravin du Four near Beauvezer). The Vallon du Fournel (Briançonnais) and the Vallon du Pas de La Tour (Ubaye) are best for beginners. Remember that, in spite of appearances, *clues* are no less dangerous in summer, when the river's flow is slower, than at other times. Long, narrow ravines, sometimes with no way out to higher ground, can be filled by a rush of water if a sudden cloudburst swells the river. Respect for the natural environment in the region's otherwise impassable gorges is more essential than ever.
The Conseil Général des Alpes Maritimes produces a guide to the most suitable gorges which offers some useful advice for canyoners (Clues et Canyons, from the Plan Départemental de Randonée, BP3007, 06201, Nice, Cedex 3).

Cycling and mountain biking

The Route des Cols (Galibier, Croix de Fer, Iseran, Lautaret, Izoard etc) was made famous by the Tour de France and in summer many cycle and mountain bike races take place throughout the region, in particular in the area around Vars, which plays host to the "Six jours de Vars", an annual week-long cycling event.
IGN maps with cycling itineraries are available and many lodges *(gîtes d'étape)* offer budget accommodation. Tourist offices have lists of establishments providing a rental service.
Mountain biking is extremely popular as it can be practised almost anywhere, in par-ticular along forest roads, mule tracks, cross-country skiing tracks and even downhill runs (in Montgenèvre and the Queyras Massif for instance). Some areas offer a choice of marked itineraries (Aussois, Bourg-St-Maurice, Parc naturel régional du Vercors).
Mountain biking itineraries are available locally from the **Maisons** (information centres) **du Parc régional du Vercors**, from **ADRI**, 19 rue du Docteur-Honnorat, 04000 Digne-les-Bains, ☎ 04 92 31 07 01, and from the regional centres of the **Fédération française de cyclotourisme**, 8 rue Jean-Marie Jégo, 75013 Paris, ☎ 01 44 16 88 88.
Hautes-Alpes: Comité Départemental de Cyclotourisme FFCT, M J-Pierre Giraud, 6 rue Robespierre, 05400 Veynes, ☎ 04 92 58 18 87.
Alpes-de-Haute-Provence: Comité Départemental des Alpes-de-Haute-Provence, M Gérard Meunier, 04510 Le Chaffaut, ☎ 04 92 34 66 46.
Var: Comité Départemental de Cyclotourisme, rue Emile-Olivier, L'Héliante, 83000 Toulon, ☎ 04 94 36 04 09.

White-water sports

White-water sports are increasingly popular, particularly in the Alps which offer a dense network of rivers and streams, pleasant summer temperatures and many outdoor leisure parks where it is possible to discover and practise these activities, for which special equipment is available.
In every area, the Comité départemental de tourisme *(see Tourist information)* has a list of the various organisations providing group activities. Below is a selection.

White-water rafting on the Haute-Isère

Haute-Savoie – In Thonon, Les Dranses, AN Rafting, ☎ 04 50 71 89 15; in Passy, Eldorado Rafting, ☎ 04 50 78 18 76.
Isère – Vénéon Eaux Vives, 38250 St-Christophe-en-Oisans, ☎ 04 76 80 23 99; Oisans Eaux Vives, Bois de Gauthier, 38520 Bourg-d'Oisans, ☎ 04 76 80 02 83.
Savoie – In Bourg-St-Maurice, Base Internationale d'Eaux Vives, ☎ 04 79 07 33 20; in Mâcot-la-Plagne, AN Rafting, ☎ 04 79 09 72 79. Other centres in Brides-les-Bains (Oxygène Aventures) and Centron (France Raft).
Hautes-Alpes – In Briançon, Eaux Vives Loisirs, Central Parc, ☎ 04 92 20 17 56; in Les Vigneaux, Base Ecrins Eaux Vives ☎ 04 92 23 11 94.
Alpes-de-Haute-Provence – In Le Martinet, Base de loisirs d'eaux vives, AN Rafting, ☎ 04 92 85 54 90, www.an-rafting.com; in Entrevaux, Base Sport et Nature, ☎ 04 93 05 42 45.
For general information, contact: Association Alpes-de-Haute-Provence Eau Vive, Hôtel du département, 13 rue Dr Romieu, BP 216, 04003 Digne-les-Bains, ☎ 04 92 32 29 79.

Rafting – This is the easiest of all the white-water sports. It consists in going down impetuous rivers in groups of six to eight persons, aboard inflatable rubber rafts manoeuvred with paddles and controlled from the rear by an instructor/cox. The technique is simple and team spirit is the key to success. Isothermal and shockproof equipment is provided by the club organising the trip. The level of difficulty is graded from I to VI (easy to virtually impossible). Beginners and amateurs who have not acquired a solid technique are advised not to attempt any difficulty rated above III. Remember to book in advance.
The Alps are the ideal area for rafting, preferably during the thaw (April to June) and in summer along rivers which maintain a constant flow. Among the rivers particularly suitable for rafting are the upper Isère (between Bourg-St-Maurice and Centron, grade III), the Doron de Bozel in the Vanoise region (between Brides-les-Bains and Moûtiers, grades IV and V), the Giffre and the Dranses de Savoie. The Rabioux, a tributary of the Durance, is internationally famous as a proving ground for experts.

Canoeing and kayaking – Canoes, originally from Canada, are manoeuvred with a simple paddle. They are ideal for family trips along rivers.
In kayaks (of Eskimo origin) on the other hand, paddlers use a double-bladed paddle. There are canoeing-kayaking schools in white-water sports centres throughout the Alps and touring takes place on the lakes and the lower courses of most rivers: the Giffre, Chéran, Arly, Doron de Bozel, Guiers Vif and Guiers Mort, Isère, Ubaye, Verdon, Clarée, Guisane, Gyronde, Biaisse, Durance, Guil, Buëch, Méouge, Drac, Souloise and Severaisse.
The Fédération française de canoë-kayak, 87 quai de la Marne, 94340 Joinville-le-Pont cedex, ☎ 01 45 11 08 50 (also on Minitel **3615 CANOPLUS**), publishes an annual guide called *Vacances en canoë-kayak* as well as maps of suitable rivers. Alternatively, the following groups may be able to help:
Club canoë-kayak Alpes-Durance – rue Faure-du-Serre, BP 41 05000 Gap, ☎ 0492534294
Comité départemental de canoë-kayak – 22bis boulevard Bellevue, 05000 Gap, ☎ 04 92 51 36 30
Canoë-kayak de Briançon - Les Alberts, 05100 Briançon, ☎ 04 92 20 53 44

There are also canoeing and kayaking clubs in Aiguilles, Ventavon, Vallouise and Face-en-Champsaur.

Hydrospeed – Anyone wishing to try swimming down mountain streams must know how to swim with flippers and be in top physical condition. Swimmers wear a wet suit and a helmet and lie on a very tough streamlined float, the hydrospeed.

Further information is available from the Association française de Nage en Eaux Vives, 229 avenue Jean-Jaurès, 92140 Clamart, ☎ 0140 95 03 49.

Caving and potholing

This activity requires thorough training if participants wish to explore caves left in their natural state. However, several sites are accessible to amateurs on the condition that they are accompanied by instructors from potholing clubs.
The necessary equipment is sophisticated: reinforced suit, rock-climbing equipment, inflatable dinghy, helmet, waterproof bag, carbide and halogen lamps. The main risk comes from sudden spates which are difficult to forecast as they can be caused by storms occurring miles away.
Fédération française de spéléologie, 130 rue St-Maur, 75011 Paris, ☎ 01 43 57 56 54.
École française de Spéléologie, 28 rue Delondine, 69002 Lyon, ☎ 04 72 56 09 63.

Vercors Massif – This is one of the best areas for potholing: there are more than 1 500 caves or entrances marking the beginning of itineraries, often situated along hiking itin-eraries. It is therefore essential to remain cautious particularly when attempting an unplanned exploration.
The following sites offer the opportunity to spend a day discovering underground exploration: the Goule Blanche and Goule Noire, the Grotte de Bournillon, the Scialet de Malaterre (near Villard-de-Lans), the Trou qui souffle (dry cave) near Méaudre, the Grotte de la Cheminée and the Scialets d'Herbouvilly.
The **Grotte du Gournier** (above the Grotte de Choranche) is particularly good for super-vised beginners; the passage allows them to practise a number of different techniques while moving horizontally through a fossil cave. Only experienced potholers may ven-ture beyond the fossil gallery. The whole network covers a distance of 18km/11.2mi.
To discover potholing in the Vercors Massif, contact the Maison de l'aventure, 26420 La Chapelle-en-Vercors, ☎ 04 75 48 22 38 and Dimension 4, 38000 Villard-de-Lans, ☎ 04 76 95 00 81.

Savoie – There are more than 2 000 caves listed in the area; the temperature inside these caves remains constant throughout the year, around 4°C/39°F. The highest chasms are situated in the Vanoise Massif, at Pralognan and Tignes (3 000m/9 842m) whereas the Gouffre Jean-Bernard in Haute-Savoie holds the depth record (-1 600m/5 249ft).

The most extensive Alpine chasm (58km/36mi) is situated under the Alpette, in the **Chartreuse Massif**.

Riding

There are many riding centres throughout Savoie, Dauphiné and Haute-Provence and numerous touring itineraries – from one-day treks to week-long excursions – identi-fied along the way by orange markings. In addition, tours for beginners and experienced riders are organised by the *associations régionales de tourisme équestre* (ARTE).

or experienced riders wishing to organise their own tours, there are *relais d'étapes équestres* (riding lodges) looked after by the FRETE (Fédération des relais d'étapes de tourisme équestre), same address as the Fédération de tourisme équestre, 170 quai de Stalingrad, 92130 Issy-les-Moulineaux, ☎ 01 40 93 01 77.

A brochure called Tourisme et loisirs équestres en France is published annually by the Délégation nationale au tourisme équestre (DNTE), 30 avenue d'Iéna, 75116 Paris, ☎ 01 53 67 44 44.

Further information is available from:

Alpes-Maritimes – Association régionale du tourisme équestre en PACA, 19 boulevard Victor-Hugo, 06130 Grasse, ☎ 04 92 42 62 98.

Isère – Association Rhône-Alpes pour le Tourisme Equestre (ARATE), Maison du Tourisme, 14 rue de la République, BP227, 38019 Grenoble, ☎ 04 76 44 56 18.

Hiking with a pack donkey

Rest your shoulders for a while and hire a real beast of burden for a day or up to a week. This extra member of the family can carry a 40kg/88lb pack and trots along willingly at a pace of 4kph/2.5mph, whatever the terrain. Farms providing the animals, the equipment and the necessary information for a successful tour can be found in Thorens-Glières, Les Carroz, St-Sigismond, St-Martin-en-Vercors, St-Martin-le-Vinoux, Guillaumes, Seyne-les-Alpes and Val-des-Près. A national donkey association, based in Eourres (where else!) and Cours, also runs a website, available in English.

Fédération nationale "âne et randonnées", Le Pré du Meinge, 26560 Eourres, ☎ 04 92 65 09 07, Fax 04 92 65 22 52 or Ladevèze 46090 Cours ☎ 04 65 31 42 79. www.ane-et-rando.com

Angling

Trout is the prize catch in mountain areas; it can be caught with live insects or larvae (in mountain streams with steep banks) or with artificial flies and a rod and reel in wider streams and mountain lakes. Other common fish found in Alpine streams and lakes are salmon, char, pike, carp and perch.

In France, fishing permits are only available to members of a local angling club; tourists must generally pay for a year's club membership, although day permits may be available in some areas. Seasons vary according to species and the type of water being fished. Any catches under the permitted size (50cm/19.7in for pike and 23cm/9.1in for trout) must be released at once.

Special regulations apply to fishing in some of the large lakes:

Lac du Bourget – White-fish angling along the shore is only allowed near harbours (Aix-les-Bains, St-Innocent) but it is possible to hire a boat and get a special permit to fish for trout and char with a dragnet.

Tarentaise region – Upstream of Albertville, angling for trout is the norm and it is still possible to select a quiet spot along the River Isère. Lower down, barbels and chars can be caught as well.

Lac de Serre-Ponçon – Special regulations apply; contact local angling associations in Savines, Chorges or Embrun.

Lac de Ste-Croix-du-Verdon – Closed to anglers from the beginning of September.

Useful addresses

Conseil supérieur de la pêche, 134 avenue Malakoff, 75016 Paris, ☎ 01 45 02 20 20.
Isère: Fédération départementale du pêche et de protection du milieu aquatique (PPMA), rue du Palais, 38000 Grenoble, ☎ 04 76 44 28 39.
Haute-Savoie: Fédération PPMA, 1 rue de l'Industrie, 74000 Annecy, ☎ 04 50 45 26 90.
Savoie: Fédération PPMA, 73230 St-Alban-Leysse, ☎ 04 79 85 89 36.
Drôme: Fédération pour la Pêche de la Drôme, 50 chemin de Laprat, BP309, 26003 Valence, ☎ 04 75 78 14 40.
Hautes-Alpes: Fédération pour la Pêche des Hautes-Alpes, 2 rue Cadet-de-Charance, 05000 Gap, ☎ 04 92 53 54 71.
Alpes-de-Haute-Provence: Fédération pour la Pêche des Alpes-de-Haute-Provence, Étoiles des Alpes, Bât. B, Traverse les Eaux Chaudes, 04000 Digne-les-Bains, ☎ 04 92 32 25 40.

Circling dots and darts gliding slowly over the valleys are a common sight in the Frenc Alps, proof of the popularity of gliding and powered flight.

Fédération française de vol libre, 4 rue de Suisse, 06000 Nice, ☎ 04 97 03 82 82

Fédération française de planeur ultra-léger motorisé, 96bis rue Marc-Sangnier, 94700 Maisons Alfort, ☎ 01 49 81 74 50.

Paragliding – This summer sport, which began in Haute-Savoie in 1978, does no require any special training and has now spread to winter sports resorts where par ticipants are equipped with skis. Many summer resorts with easy access to nearb summits offer various possibilities of practising this popular sport and of joinin training courses. Les Saisies, Signal de Bisanne, L'Alpe-d'Huez and St-Hilaire-du Touvet are among the best, but **Chamonix** is still one of the main paragliding centres

A. de Valroger/MICHELIN

Paragliding

particularly favourable condition enabled a team of paragliders to cove a distance of 160km/99mi. There i restricted access to the slopes of Mor Blanc in July and August (École d parapente de Chamonix, Parapent Azur, immeuble Le Mommery, impasse de Primavères, ☎ 04 50 53 5(14, parazur@club-internet.fr). The **Vercors** is also one of the favourite area of paragliding enthusiasts. Tw remarkable sites are worth men tioning: the Cornafion, nea Villard-de-Lans (500m/1 640ft flights access forbidden in May and June fo the protection of the fauna); and th Moucherotte (landing in Lans-en Vercors). For all-level courses, contact Dimension 4 in Villard-de-Lans ☎ 04 76 95 00 81 and Fun Fly in Lans en-Vercors.

Haute-Provence is also an ideal are for practising paragliding. The national centre is located in Saint Auban-sur-Durance and there ar many schools in the area includin the École de parapente du Queyras 05350 Château-Ville-Vieille, ☎ 04 92 46 77 51 and the Aéroclub de Sisteron, Aérodrome de Vaumeilh, 04200 Sisteron ☎ 04 92 62 17 45. In order to avoid accidents and disappointments, it is recommended to register with a recog nised school. A list is available from the Fédération française de vol libre (*see above*, also www.ffvl.fr on Minitel: **3615 FFVL**). Courses, usually lasting a week, are followed by some 20 flights monitored from the ground by an instructor.

A brochure entitled **Parapente** is published by the Comité régional de tourisme.

Gliding – The French Alps, where many altitude records have been set, regularly enjoy perfect climatic and atmospheric conditions for gliding, so St-Auban-sur Durance was a logical choice for the national gliding centre.

Hang-gliding – This "older", marginally more dangerous sport requires greater tech nical knowledge and training. The FFVL *(see above)* offer further information.

Ballooning – A few resorts organise hot-air balloon trips all year round; Les Saisies, Corrençon and Villard-de-Lans and Sisteron. Tourist information offices will supply details and addresses.

Something different...

Visitors willing to take their time have the opportunity to travel routes that will help them to discover the wealth of a region and its traditional life.

Themed itineraries

Chemins du Baroque – Some 60 churches and chapels in the Tarentaise and Maurienne regions were selected for their characteristic Baroque style. It is recommended to start in Moûtiers or Lanslebourg. There are guided tours in some places and day tours are organised. Two Baroque centres offer information and displays about the various sites:
The **Fondation pour l'action culturelle internationale en montagne** (Facim), Hôtel du département, 73018 Chambéry cedex, ☎ 04 79 96 74 19, offers 19 half-day hikes and drives with commentary as well as 13 suggestions for unaccompanied tours.
Espace baroque Maurienne, Lanslebourg, ☎ 04 79 05 90 42.

Route historique Stendhal – A marked itinerary links places where the writer Henri Beyle – known to the world as Stendhal – spent his childhood and those locations which were to inspire him. In Grenoble these include the flat where he was born, the Café de la Table Ronde, one of the oldest cafés in France, where he would quite often be seen, the Maison Stendhal (which belonged to his grandfather, Dr Gagnon), the Musée Stendhal and the municipal library where his works are kept. For detailed information, contact the tourist office in Grenoble.

Route des ducs de Savoie – This itinerary includes several prestigious "châteaux" which belonged to the House of Savoie: Ripaille, Thorens-Glières, Menthon, Clermont, Annecy, Chambéry, as well as the Abbaye royale de Hautecombe. The Caisse nationale des monuments historiques et des sites (CNMHS) publishes a small pamphlet listing the castles and residences with their opening times.

Route historique des Dauphins – This itinerary, compiled by the CNMHS, takes the visitor to a number of historic residences in the Isère, including the châteaux of Touvet, Château-Bayard, Vizille, Sassenage and Longpra. Further information is available from the Comité départemental du Tourisme in Grenoble.

The Vaudois – An historic route leads from Luberon, a stronghold of this medieval movement persecuted for their religious practices, across the Durance valley to Vallouise (*see VALLOUISE*).

In Vauban's footsteps – The comprehensive defence system designed by Vauban during Louis XIV's reign is unique in the history of military architecture. Some of these former strategic sites can now be visited: citadels in Mont-Dauphin and Briançon, the castle in Château-Queyras, the citadel in Seyne-les-Alpes and the two forts in Colmars-les-Alpes are the finest examples of Vauban's work.
Later military fortifications are also open to the public: 18C works are centred round Briançon whereas 19C defences are situated further afield. A fort by Maginot, known as Janus, can be visited by appointment. For detailed information, contact the tourist office in Briançon.
The upper Ubaye Valley also boasts several defence works, among them Fort de Tournoux, Fort de Roche-Lacroix and the St-Ours Fortifications. Visits are organised by the tourist office in Barcelonnette.

In Jean Giono's footsteps – The Jean Giono centre at Manosque organises literary walks during the summer season, including accommodation in traditional *mas* (farmsteads) in the Contadour region and explanations of Giono's texts. ☎ 04 92 70 52 54.

Route des campaniles – Wrought-iron campaniles form part of the Haute-Provence scenery. There are a number of 100km/62mi-long itineraries to follow in the Digne, Forcalquier and Manosque regions. The most remarkable campaniles are in Les Mées, Lurs, St-Michel-l'Observatoire, Manosque, Allemagne-en-Provence and Estoublon. For detailed information, contact the Comité départemental du Tourisme.

Routes des cadrans solaires – There are detailed itineraries and brochures with a sundial theme in three areas of the Hautes-Alpes region.

Sundial in Ubaye

How to tell the time by looking at a sundial

A vertical sundial consists of a panel, usually facing south, and of a metal rod, or gnomon, representing the Earth's axis. Its length must not extend the shadow beyond the panel at the time of the summer solstice and be sufficient for the shadow to be visible at the time of the winter solstice. Reading the time on a sundial is relatively easy but the conversion into accepted, "normal" time is rather involved and requires three factors to be taken into account: the longitude which, in the south of France results in a 20 to 30min difference from Paris; real time (solar time) and average time (24-hour day) corresponding to the variation in the Earth's rotating speed (in summer, it can vary from + 3min to – 6min); and finally, the difference between summer and winter time.

The **Briançonnais** offers a variety of mostly 18C or contemporary sundials; there are 20 of them in Briançon alone as well as very original ones in the villages of Prelles, Puy-St-Vincent, Les Alberts, Val-des-Prés, Plampinet, La Salle-les-Alpes and Névache.
The **Vallouise** Valley has a choice of sundials mainly by Zarbula.
In the Queyras, sundials are often decorated with exotic birds; they were designed by Zarbula or other artists influenced by him.
There are also interesting sundials in the **Bochaine** to the west and in the **Ubaye** Valley to the south; contact the Maison de la Vallée in Barcelonnette.

Route des fruits et des vins – This itinerary stretching from the shores of the Serre-Ponçon Lake to Sisteron has opportunities for tastings *(dégustations)* in various wine and fruit cooperatives, according to the season. The Comité départemental du Tourisme in Gap will be happy to provide a list of orchards and wine cellars in Chorges, Espinasses, Tallard, Théus, Laragne and many other villages.

Route de l'Olivier – A number of routes in the Bouches-du-Rhône and Drôme *départements* are devoted to the symbol of Provence and Provençal cuisine, the olive. An itinerary around les Barronies and the Plateau de Valensole takes in mills where oil is produced and sold as well as restaurants which make a point of using local produce. Further information is available from the Comité économique de l'Olivier, 22 rue Henri-Pontier, 13626 Aix-en-Provence Cedex 1, ☎ 04 42 23 01 92

On the water

Several large lakes situated in shallow valleys, such as the Lac du Bourget, Lac d'Annecy, Lac Léman (Lake Geneva) and Lac d'Aiguebelette offer a wide range of outdoor activities (sailing, water-skiing, diving, wind-surfing etc). The mildness of the climate is underlined by the presence of vineyards and olive groves.

Lake Geneva cruises – There are 41 landing stages round the lake, along the French and Swiss shores. During the season, from May to September, there are numerous possibilities for boat trips: a daily direct link Évian-Lausanne (35min), daily 3hr cruises round the Haut-Lac and a complete tour of the lake (10hr); *(see Admission times and charges)*.
In July and August, there is a regular service (20min) between **Yvoire** and **Nyon** in Switzerland several times a day and at night. In June and September, times are different. Information from the Compagnie générale de navigation sur le Lac Léman in Nyon and the tourist office in Yvoire.
Several clubs offer **yachting facilities and sailing courses:** Société nautique du Léman, port de Rives, 74200 Thonon-les-Bains, ☎ 04 50 71 07 29 and Cercle de la voile d'Évian, port des Mouettes, 74500 Évian-les-Bains, ☎ 04 50 75 06 46.
There is a colourful gathering of yachts on the lake in mid-June, called the Bol d'or de Genève.

Lac du Bourget – The largest natural lake in France also offers a variety of water-based activities. Cruises starting from the Grand Port in Aix-les-Bains, from Portout-Chanaz or from Le Bourget-du-Lac include a choice of trips from a 1hr tour of the lake to a day trip to the Savière Canal and the River Rhône. Contact the tourist office in Aix-les-Bains and the Compagnie des bateaux du lac du Bourget, Grand Port, 73100 Aix-les-Bains, ☎ 04 79 88 92 09.
The lake is exposed to high winds and sailing conditions are similar to those encountered at sea, and ideal for the practice of funboards. There are also several sailing clubs in Aix-les-Bains and Le Bourget-du-Lac.

Lac d'Annecy – The superb scenery is the major attraction of the lake. There is a tour of the lake starting from the Thiou pier in Annecy and cruises are organised by the Compagnie des bateaux d'Annecy, 2 place aux Bois, 74000 Annecy, ☎ 04 50 51 08 40. The best period to sail on the lake is from March to early November. **Sailing courses** are organised by various clubs including Base nautique des Marquisats in Annecy, ☎ 04 50 45 48 39 and Cercle de la voile in Sévrier, ☎ 04 50 52 40 04.

Lac du Monteynard – In high season, the cruises on this charming lake on the edge of the Parc régional du Vercors also take in the breathtaking gorges of the Drac and the Ebron, which can only be seen from the water. Ask about sailing times of La Mira, 38650 Treffort ☎ 04 76 34 14 56.

Lac d'Esparron-du-Verdon – Cruises start from Gréoux-les-Bains in season. For information and reservations, contact the town's tourist information office.

Tourist trains

Circuit touristique du Léman – The Rive-Bleue-Express follows the shores of Lake Geneva from Évian to Le Bouveret in Switzerland, a distance of some 20km/12mi. The steam trains run from late June to September on some weekdays and every weekend. Information from the tourist office in Évian; tickets can be bought at the railway stations in Évian and Le Bouvet.

From Vallorcine to Émosson – This is an extension to the Émosson Dam of the international railway line from Chamonix to Martigny via Vallorcine. The trip offers beautiful views of the north face of Mont Blanc. From Châtelard-Village, a funicular in three sections climbs to 1 961m/6 434ft in 13min. The first section is the steepest in Europe with a gradient of 87%. There is a daily service from mid-June to mid-September. Return fare: 33SF; it is possible to buy a one-way ticket and come down on foot in 2hr 30min. Information from the tourist office in Chamonix and the railway station in Martigny (Switzerland), ☎ 00 41 26 68 12 36

Chemin de fer de la Mure – The 30km/19mi itinerary of this former mining railway between St-Georges-de-Commiers and La Mure includes an impressive number of engineering works and offers exceptional views of the Gorges du Drac. Today, it is powered by electric engines dating from the 1930s *(see Lacs de LAFFREY)*.

Chemin de fer de la Provence – The famous **Train des Pignes** – so-called because the old steam locomotives used to burn pine cones – links Nice and Digne-les-Bains, covering a distance of 150km/93mi via Puget-Théniers, Entrevaux, Annot and St-André-les-Alpes, along a route which once continued to Toulon on the coast.

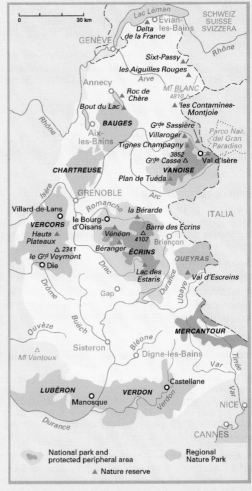

The line, built between 1890 and 1911, includes some 60 metal bridges, viaducts, tunnels and other daring works of engineering. A three-hour journey through five mountain valleys opens up a world of magnificent landscapes, dotted with hilltop villages. Steam trains run on the section between Puget-Théniers and Annot in season. The line allows access all year round to the Lac de Castillon, the Gorges du Verdon and skiing resorts of the Alpes-Maritimes region. Designated stopping points, in addition to the stations, allow walkers to strike off into open countryside and rejoin the train further along the line.

In winter the **Train des Neiges** runs daily to the resorts in the Val d'Allos.

Information from Gare du Sud, 4 bis rue Alfred-Binet, 06000 Nice, ☎ 04 93 82 10 17; Gare des CP, avenue P.-Semard 04000 Digne-les-Bains, ☎ 04 92 31 01 58.

National park and protected peripheral area

Regional Nature Park

▲ Nature reserve

Industrial sites

These sites, some still operational, some now preserved as cultural monuments, offer an insight into traditional and contemporary industries.

Caves de la Chartreuse – The famous liqueur distillery; 10 boulevard Kofler, 38500 Voiron, ☎ 04 76 05 81 77 *(see Massif de la CHARTREUSE)*.

Coopérative laitière du Beaufortain – Co-operative dairy; 73270 Beaufort, ☎ 04 79 38 33 62 *(see BEAUFORT)*.

Eaux minérales d'Évian – Mineral water bottling plant *(See ÉVIAN-LES-BAINS)*.

Centre scientifique et technique de Grenoble – Tours and temporary exhibitions in a science and technology centre; La Casemate, 1 place Laurent, Grenoble ☎ 04 76 44 30 79

Musée Opinel – Museum devoted to the Opinel knife *(See ST-JEAN-DE-MAURIENNE)*.

Barrage de Monteynard – Hydroelectric dam; 38650 Sinard, ☎ 04 76 34 26 00.

Hydrelec – Energy museum; 38114 Allemont ☎ 04 76 80 78 00 *(see Route de la CROIX DE FER)*.

La Mine-Image – Coal mine; 38770 La Motte d'Aveillans *(see Lacs de LAFFREY)*.

Centrale hydroélectrique de La Bâthie (beneath the Roselend Dam) – Hydroelectricity generator; 73540 La Bâthie, ☎ 04 79 31 06 60.

For nature-lovers

A number of organisations offer natural history excursions in the Alps; a list of locations is available from UNCPIE, 2 rue Washington, 75008 Paris ☎ 01 45 63 63 67. Summer in the parc national du Mercantour sees the start of a season of themed nature walks in the upper Var valley, shedding new light on its populations of birds, ibexes and marmots. For more information on the walks, which take place every Thursday, contact the Maison du Parc in Valberg ☎ 04 93 02 58 23.

The Réserve géologique de Haute-Provence in Digne also organises weekly tours, which aim to teach visitors to "read" the environment and understand the processes that formed it. Further details are available from the Réserve géologique de Haute-Provence, ☎ 04 92 31 51 31.

The clear skies of the southern mountains are perfect for **astronomy**. The observatory at St-Véran will be happy to provide details of the numerous local organisations which run beginners' courses. Observatoire de Chateau Renard, La Ville, 05350 St-Véran, ☎ 04 92 45 85 44

Across the Border

Switzerland

USEFUL INFORMATION

Bordering Lake Geneva are the cantons of Vaud and Valais and the prosperous, international city of Geneva, all within easy reach of Haute-Savoie. The **Green Guide Switzerland**, the **Michelin Hotel and Restaurant Guide Switzerland** and **Michelin Map 927** provide all the information you need for a weekend break or a longer stay.

Swiss Tourist Offices

Canada: 926 The East Mall, Etobipoke, Toronto, Ontario M9B 6K1 ☎ 416 695 2090

United Kingdom: Swiss Centre, Swiss Court, London W1V 8EE ☎ 020 7734 1921

United States: Swiss Centre, 608 Fifth Avenue, New York City, NY 10020 ☎ 212 757 5944

Internet: www.MySwitzerland.com

FORMALITIES

For a stay of less than three months, citizens of an EU member state require a valid ID card (or in the case of UK visitors, a passport). Travellers from outside the European Union must be in possession of a passport. When travelling by car, drivers should be prepared to present a driving license, international driving permit and car registration papers. Motorcyclists will require the same documents and must wear helmets when on the road. Owners of pets brought into the country will be required to prove that the animal has been vaccinated against rabies in the past year, but more than a month before their entry into Switzerland.

EXCURSIONS

Vallorcine to Émosson – Travellers may like to continue the route from Chamonix to Vallorcine as far as Martigny and then on to the Émosson Dam *(see Green Guide Switzerland)*; the approach to the lake offers a superb view of the north face of Mont Blanc. From the resort of Châtellard-

Village at the bottom of the valley, a three-stage cable car trip takes visitors to a height of 1 961m in 13min. The first section is the steepest in Europe, rising at a dizzying gradient of 87%. The cable car runs daily from mid-June to mid-September; a round-trip ticket costs 33 SFr. Experienced walkers can return on foot in about 2hr 30min. For further information contact the tourist office in Chamony and at the station in Martigny (Switzerland), ☎ 0041/266 812 36.

On the water – Avoid the traffic jams and take to the water for a cruise across Lake Geneva. The Compagnie Générale de Navigation (☎ 0041/848 811 848) offers regular sailings from Geneva, Vevey, Nyon and its headquarters in Lausanne.

Italy

USEFUL INFORMATION

Italian State Tourist Office – ENIT (Ente Nazionale Italiano per il Turismo)

Canada: 175 Bloor Street, Suite 907 South Tower, Toronto M4W 3R8

United Kingdom: 1 Princes Street, London W1B 2AY ☎ 020°7408 1254; 24-hour brochure request line ☎ 09065 508 925 (calls charged at premium rate).

United States: 630 Fifth Avenue, Suite 1565, New York City, NY 10111 ☎ 212°245°4822, 12400 Wiltshire Boulevard, Suite 550, Los Angeles, CA 90025 ☎ 310°820°1898

Internet: www.enit.it, www.discoveritalia.com, www.initaly.com, www.governo.it

The **Green Guide Italy, The Michelin Hotel and Restaurant Guide** and **Michelin Map 428 Italy North West** provide further in-depth information on the western Italian Alps and the north-west coast.

The Mont Blanc Tunnel

Val d'Aoste – *After the tunnel, continue on the A 5 or follow the S 26 towards Turin (see Massif du MONT-BLANC).* The valley of the Dora Baltea and its tributaries is surrounded by the highest peaks of the French and Swiss Alps, including the Matterhorn, Mont-Blanc, Monte Rosa, Grand Combin, Dent Hérens, Gran Paradiso and Grande Sassière. Countless excursions by car and cable car or on foot, quiet valleys, picturesque villages and above all the superb **views★★★** make the Aosta valley one of northern Italy's most popular holiday destinations.

An agreement dating back to 1948 guarantees considerable autonomy for a region where many locals still speak a Provençal dialect and official documents are written in French as well as Italian. Aosta, the capital, has preserved relics from Roman and Medieval times.

Courmayeur※※Well-known to skiers and climbers, this resort on the French border makes an excellent base for excursions. Take the cable car through the Mont Blanc massif *(starting from La Palud, see Massif du Mont-Blanc,)* or drive to Val Veney, Val Ferret, Testa d'Arp or Col du Petit-St-Bernard, a vital alpine pass since Roman times.

Parco Nazionale del Gran Paradiso★★ – Roads over the Nivolet pass and through the valleys of Rhemes, Savarenche, Cogne and Locano lead into this national park, the habitat of rare alpine plants and some of the last free-roaming European ibexes.

Via the Tunnel de Fréjus

Susa★ – *Via A 32.* Marking the intersection of the two main roads to France, the "gateway to Italy" lies at the foot of a colossal massif, crowned by the Rocciamelone (3 538m/11 608ft). Besides its best-known landmark, the 4C **Savoy Door★** (Porta Savoia), the town also boasts a fine **Romanesque campanile** on the south side of the Gothic **cathedral** and the elegant **Arco di Augusto★**, the oldest monument in the city (8C BC).

Further along the road to Turin, perched high on a hill, stands the Benedictine **abbey Sacra di San Michele★★★** *(A 32 then S 25).* The great staircase leads up to the **Zodiac Door** with its decorated capitals and pilasters. The Romanesque-Gothic abbey church, built on top of the rocky eminence, has fine 16C frescoes. From the esplanade there is a lovely **view★★★** of the Alps, the Dora Valley, the Po and Turin plains.

Crafts and gastronomy

Woodcarving and painting – The **Queyras** is undoubtedly the most famous of Alpine regions for the skill of its woodcarvers. The Maison de l'Artisanat, 05350 Ville-Vieille, ☎ 04 92 46 75 06 has a fine selection of wooden objects as well as other handicraft samples. Arvieux on the other hand is famous for its traditional toys, on sale at a local cooperative: L'Alpin chez soi, 05350 Arvieux, ☎ 04 92 46 73 86.

A Queyras speciality

Objects and furniture made by craftsmen from the Queyras region are not usually painted or varnished (although the wood is sometimes stained) and have to meet with five criteria to be granted the Queyras seal of origin:
– the article must be made in the region by a local craftsman;
– it must be made entirely of solid pine;
– it must be decorated with traditional carved motifs from the Queyras region;
– the parts must be joined with pegs and dovetailed and no part can be factory-turned;
– at least one fifth of the surface of the object or piece of furniture must be carved.

Tartiflette alfresco

Wood painting is the speciality of the **Chartreuse** region, in the area of Entremont-le-Vieux.

Earthenware and santons – These are the speciality of the **Haute-Provence** region. **Faïences de Moustiers** are world-famous, but there are other earthenware workshops in Barcelonnette, Reillanne and St-Michel-l'Observatoire. Fine pottery is manufactured in the nearby towns of Forcalquier and Castellane. **Santons** (human and animal figures which make up a Provençal Christmas crib) are handmade and painted in Riez, Gréoux-les-Bains, Champtercier, Volx and Manosque.

Gastronomy – Cheese and wine in the north and olive oil and honey in the south are the main Alpine specialities.

Cheeses – Below are the addresses of some places where it is possible to watch cheese being made.

Cheese-lovers should make time for a visit to a Savoyard dairy like the one in St-François-de-Longchamp, where it is possible to watch Beaufort being made in high-pasture chalets at the Col de la Madeleine. Visitors can also look around the Cave coopérative du val d'Aillon (Tomme des Bauges) and the Cave coopérative du Beaufort, ☎ 04 79 07 08 28 (Beaufort cheese). Among the other varieties to bear the Appelation d'Origine Controlée or AOC, at once the designation of a local product and a confirmation of quality, are Abondance from the val d'Abondance, Tomme de Savoie, Bleu de Termignon and Reblochon from Savoie. This last is also one of the main ingredients of Savoie's most famous dish, *tartiflette*, a rich potato bake made with onion, crème fraîche, bacon and local white wine.

Wines – Two itineraries offer the opportunity of discovering and tasting wines from Savoie: the "red itinerary" starts from Chambéry and goes through the Combe de Savoie via Apremont, Montmélian and Challes-les-Eaux; the "blue itinerary" skirts the shores of the Lac du Bourget. Below are some useful addresses:

– Coopératives des vins de Savoie in Ruffieux, ☎ 04 79 54 51 08.

– Coopératives viticoles de Cruet, ☎ 04 79 84 28 52.

– Comité interprofessionel des vins de Savoie, 3 rue du Château, 73000 Chambéry, ☎ 04 79 33 44 16, has a list of cooperatives where tasting is available.

The French shores of Lake Geneva produce a white wine called Roussette de Savoie which is very palatable served with fried fish; several local inns have it on their menu, particularly in Excevenex, Port de Séchex, Corzent and Amphion-les-Bains. Die is known for its sparkling *Clairette de Die*, made from a blend of Clairette and Muscat grapes. From the north come powerful liqueurs like *Chartreuse*, *Cherry-Rocher* and aperitifs such as *Chambérysette* and *Vermouth*. *Génépi*, a gold-coloured aperitif, is distilled in the Ubaye and can be found in Barcelonnette or in Forcalquier, which is perhaps better known for its aniseed-flavoured *pastis* and the now rare *vin cuit de Noël*, a dark amber-coloured wine which is traditionally enjoyed at Christmas.

Olive oil – The production is concentrated in the Alpes-de-Haute-Provence *département*; the Moulin de l'Olivette, place de l'Olivette in Manosque, ☎ 04 92 72 00 99, produces and sells high-quality olive oil and suggests ways of using it. There are other mills in Oraison (Moulin Paschetta) and Peyrus (Moulin Mardaric).

Honey – The Haute-Provence region produces large quantities of honey from a whole variety of plants; lavender honey comes essentially from the Alpes-de-Haute-Provence *département*. Honey from Savoie (miel de Savoie) is produced between July and September; Vercors honey comes from around the regional park. There are two official seals of origin, namely "miel de lavande" and "miel toutes fleurs de Provence". The Maison du miel et de l'abeille in Riez *(for the address, see Admission times and charges)* offers an introduction to bee-keeping. Several bee-keepers in the area sell their product in towns like Castellane, Château-Queyras, Molines-en-Queyras, St-Véran (Maison du miel, ☎ 04 92 45 82 47) and Aiguilles (la Miellerie de la Vignette, ☎ 04 92 46 77 97).

As well as the famous exports listed above, you may be lucky enough to find some lesser-known specialities of the Alps. Look out for **croquants de Queyras**, little crunchy honey and almond cakes, and **confiture de genièvre**, a juniper conserve sold in the markets of the Ubaye. Other treats include **biscuits de Savoie**, **rissoles aux poires** (pastry filled with pears), pralines known as **cloches** or **roseaux d'Annecy** and **sabayon**, a sweet egg cream which takes its name and inspiration from the Italian *zabaglione*.

Calendar of events

55

Pont de Cervières	Dance of the Swords *"Bacchu Ber"* (16 August)
Thorens-Glières	Procession of floats with singing and dancing (First Saturday after 15 August)
Val d'Isère	International All-Terrain Driving Festival (mid-August)
Aix-les-Bains	Flower Festival (Third weekend in August)
Chamrousse	Lumberjack Contest
Tignes	Lake Festival
Châtel	Pasture Festival (Third Sunday in August)
La Rosière	Shepherd's Festival (*"La Fête des Bergers"*; third Sunday in August)
Flumet	Coach and cart festival (*"Fête de l'Attelage de Val-d'Arly"*; last Sunday in August)

Moustiers-Ste-Marie	Feast of "Diane" (First week of September)

Digne-les-Bains	International Accordion Festival
Forcalquier, Valensole . . . . **and other towns**	Story-telling Festival, *"Oralies de Haute Provence"*; (mid-October) ☎ 04 92 74 85 55
Chambéry	Cartoon Festival

Isola	Chestnut Festival

Autrans	International Film Festival on the theme of "ice and snow" (Early December)

Traditional festivals and specialist fairs

Forcalquier	Pottery and Craft Fair (End of April)
Forcalquier	Crafts Fair

Annot	Crafts Fair (13 August)
Aiguilles	Wool Fair (7 August)
Barcelonnette	Themed Fairs (4, 18 August)
Buis-les-Baronnies	Foire au Tilleul (Lime-blossom market; first Wednesday in July)
Castellane	Crafts Fairs (10 July, 28 August)
Colmars	Wool Fair (20 August)
Digne-les-Bains	Lavender Fair (End of August)
Flumet	Junk market (First Sunday in July), Mule market (First Tuesday in August)
Forcalquier	Crafts Fair (17 August)
Gap	Crafts Fair (12 July)
Gréoux-les-Bains	Crafts Fair (13 and 27 July, 10 and 24 August)
Jausiers	Leather Fair (28 July), Pottery Fair (9 August)
Manosque	Crafts Fairs (Thursdays)
Moustiers-Ste-Marie	Regional Fair (16 August)
Puy-St-Vincent	Wool Fair (6 August)
St-Étienne-les-Orgues	Herb Fair (14 July)
St-Firmin	Leather and Wood Fair (15 July)
St-Paul-sur-Ubaye	Farming Fair (13 August)
Seyne	Mule market (2 August)
Sisteron	Regional Fair (26 August)
Valensole	Santons Fair (Second half of July)
Venosc	Wool Market (Third Sunday in August)

Barcelonnette	Craft and Farm Fair (1 September)
Lagrand	Turkey Fair (9 September)
Volx	Craft Fair (mid-September)
Corps	Wool Fair (17 and 18 September)
Seyne	Donkey Market (21 September)

Arèches-Beaufort	*Salon des sites remarquables du goût*; (exhibition of regional gastronomy)

Thoard	Wool Fair (4 December)
Champtercier	Santons Fair (First week in December)

Sporting events

Avoriaz	Alpine skiing World Championships

Courchevel	Several ski shows

January	
Les Ménuires	Alpes Quad Trophy
Megève	International snow polo competition (Second half of January)

Mid-January	
Autrans	*"Foulée blanche"* (cross-country skiing across the Vercors Plateau)

Late January	
Chamonix.	Alberg-Kandahar (downhill race)
Megève	Sledge racing

18 to 21 March	
Arèches-Beaufort	Pierra-Menta-Tivoly (high-level skiing-mountaineering competition)

Late March	
La Clusaz	Telemark Championship

Early July	
Les Gets.	"Free-Raid" Mountain bike race

1st weekend July	
Châtel	Paragliding Competition

Early August	
Valloire	Traditional mountain competitions

Mid-August	
Haute-Maurienne	Tran'Maurienne-Vanoise (mountain bike competition in the upper Arc Valley)

December	
Val-Thorens	Andros Trophy (snow and ice-driving competitions; First week of December) "Boarderweek" (International Snowboarding; mid-December)
Forcalquier.	International hot-air ballooning competition

Further reading

History

First Lady of Versailles; Mary Adelaide of Savoy, Dauphine of France – Lucy Norton

Princesse of Versailles: The Life of Marie Adelaide of Savoy – Charles Elliott

The Eagles of Savoy: The House of Savoy in Thirteenth Century Europe – Eugene L Cox

Victor Amadeus II: Absolutism in the Savoyard State, 1675-1730 – Geoffrey Symcox

Tears of Glory: The Betrayal of Vercors, 1944 – Michael Pearson

Mountaineering and skiing

Mont Blanc: Discovery and Conquest of the Giant of the Alps – Stefano Ardito

The Mont Blanc Massif: The 100 Finest Routes – Gaston Rebuffat

Savage Snows: The Story of Mont Blanc – Walt Unsworth

The Alpine 4000m Peaks by the Classic Routes: A Guide for Mountaineers – Richard Goedeke, translated by Hill Neate

Walking in the French Alps: GR5 – Martin Collins

A History of Mountain Climbing – Roger Frison-Roche

These more general titles may also be of interest:

Killing Dragons – the Conquest of the Alps – Fergus Fleming

How the English made the Alps – Jim Ring

Films and the French Alps

Most of the recommended films are in English but a few of the better known French ones have been included. Local locations and settings are given.

The Eagle with the Two Heads (1948) – Jean Cocteau; Vizille

La Bride sue le Cou (1961) – Roger Vadim; St-Nizier-du-Moucherotte

Murmur of the Heart (1971) – Louis Malle; Aix-les-Bains

Allons z'enfants (1980) – Yves Boisset; Curial district in Chambéry

The Woman Next Door (1981) – François Truffaut; Grenoble

Louis: Enfant Roi (1993) – Roger Planchon; Baroque chapel in the Musée Dauphinois in Grenoble

Les Marmottes (1993) – Elie Chouraqui; Chamonix

Le Parfum d'Yvonne (1994) Patrice Leconte; a passionate liaison in a luxury hotel in Evian on the banks of Lake Geneva

Rien ne vas plus (1997) – Claude Chabrol; Aix-les-Bains

Haute-Savoie, village of Combloux

Introduction

Landscapes

The mountain range of the Alps – the highest in Europe – stretches along a curved line from Nice on the Mediterranean coast to Vienna in Austria covering a distance of 1 200km/750mi. The French Alps extend from Lake Geneva to the Mediterranean, a distance of 370km/230mi, and they are over 200km/125mi wide at their widest point, between the Rhône Valley and the Italian Piedmont. The highest peak, Mont Blanc, rises to 4 807m/15 771ft, but the altitude gradually decreases towards the south and the range is easily accessible through a series of deep wide valleys.

The region is famed for magnificent views which appear to change with every bend of the steep, winding roads. It is an area full of contrasts from the colourful shores of Lake Geneva to the glaciers of Mont Blanc, the chalk cliffs of Vercors and the dry Mediterranean landscapes of Haute-Provence.

Geologists divide the French Alps into four main areas:

– The **Préalpes**, or Alpine foothills, consisting almost entirely of limestone rocks formed during the Secondary Era, except in the Chablais area.

– The **Alpine trench** *(sillon alpin)*, a depression cut through marl, lying at the foot of the central massifs.

– The **central massifs** *(massifs centraux)*, consisting of very old and extremely hard crystalline rocks. The tectonic upheavals of the Tertiary Era folded the ancient land mass *(see below)*, creating "needles" and high peaks, which are the highest of the whole Alpine range. From north to south, these massifs are: the Mont-Blanc, the Belledonne, the Grandes Rousses, the Écrins and the Mercantour.

– The **intra-Alpine zone**, forming the axis of the Alps. It consists of sedimentary rocks transformed and folded by the violent upheavals which took place in the area. It includes the Vanoise, the Briançonnais and the Queyras as well as the upper valleys of the Tarentaise, the Maurienne and the Ubaye.

FORMATION OF THE ALPS

Among the "younger" of the Earth's mountains, formed at roughly the same time as the Pyrenees, the Carpathians, the Caucasus and the Himalayas, the Alps are also one of the most geographically complex ranges. Long before the folding of the peaks some 65 million years ago, and the erosion by water, wind and ice which continues to this day, powerful forces were at work beneath the surface.

During the **Paleozoic Era**, which began 570 million years ago, Hercynian mountains, similar to the Vosges, the Massif Central and the Massif Armoricain, appeared where the central massifs now stand. This folding was followed by considerable erosion and, by the end of the Primary Era, the Alps looked much like Brittany today. The luxuriant vegetation, stimulated by the hot and humid climate, produced a considerable amount of plant deposits which are the origin of several coalfields at La Mure and in the Briançonnais.

The **Mesozoic Era** began approximately 245 million years ago. Following the subsidence of the whole region, a vast marine depression was formed where the high Alps now stand. Deposits of limestone and sand (which were transformed into sandstone when compressed) as well as clay (which under high pressure often flaked into shale) piled up on the old foundation of crystalline rocks. The climate was uniform; forests consisted of pines, oaks, walnut trees, eucalyptus and palm trees. Huge reptiles such as dinosaurs roamed the earth and the first birds appeared.

The **Cenozoic Era**, which began 65 million years ago, saw the formation of the high range of mountains as we know them. Under pressure from the east, on the Italian side, huge layers began to slide westwards forming the Briançonnais and the Vanoise. During the second half of the Tertiary Era, the old foundation rose in turn to form the Mont-Blanc, Écrins and Mercantour massifs. Various theories have been devised to explain this phenomenon. The concept of plate tectonics describes the earth's crust as consisting of a number of rigid plates moving in relation to one another and causing what is known as 'continental drift'. Situated at the boundary of the African and European plates, the Alps folded, according to this theory, like putty pressed between one's fingers. Following this tectonic upheaval, the sedimentary deposits left behind during the Secondary Era drifted down the slopes and came up against the edge of the Dauphiné. As a result, the pliable layers of sediments folded, creating the Préalpes. A depression appeared between the crystalline massifs and the Préalpes, which eventually became the Alpine trench through the work of erosion. To this north-south uplifting was added, in the southern part of the Alps, an east-west folding of Pyrenean origin which explains the complicated structure of this particular region. The Tertiary Era also saw the accumulation of sand deposits which were later transformed into sandstone in the Champsaur and Annot areas or into flysch (alternate strata of coarse and fine sandstone) in the Ubaye Valley.

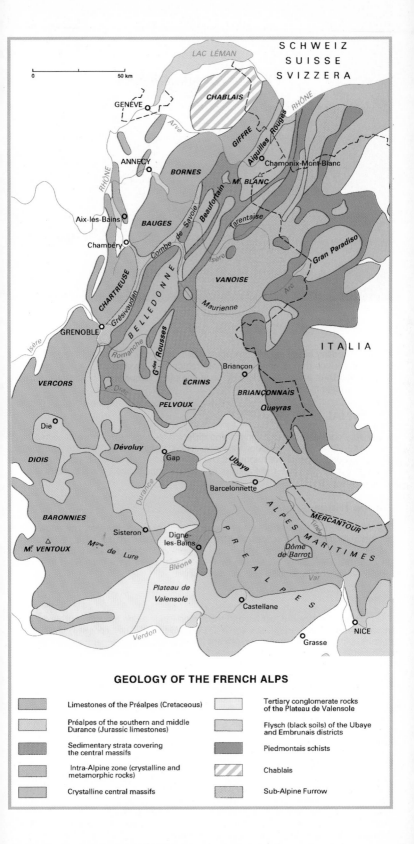

GEOLOGY OF THE FRENCH ALPS

Limestones of the Préalpes (Cretaceous)	Tertiary conglomerate rocks of the Plateau de Valensole
Préalpes of the southern and middle Durance (Jurassic limestones)	Flysch (black soils) of the Ubaye and Embrunais districts
Sedimentary strata covering the central massifs	Piedmontais schists
Intra-Alpine zone (crystalline and metamorphic rocks)	Chablais
Crystalline central massifs	Sub-Alpine Furrow

Préalpes de Digne

A general cooling of the earth's atmosphere over the last 2 million years caused a series of glacial periods during which the whole region was covered with a huge mantle of ice. Erosion then worked relentlessly on a complete remodelling of the Alps into the mountain range it is today.

REGIONAL LANDSCAPES

These vary considerably according to the different geological structure of each area. It seems therefore logical to adopt the geologists' division of the Alps into four distinct parts preceded by what we might call the Alpine fringe. Listed from west to east and south to north, they are: the Préalpes, the Alpine trench, the central massifs and the intra-Alpine zone.

Alpine fringe

The Albanais, the Geneva area and the Bornes Plateau situated on the edge of the northern Alps offer landscapes of green rolling hills dominated by a few moderate mountain ranges such as the **Salève** south of Geneva and the **Mont du Chat** near the Lac du Bourget. The basins left behind by retreating glaciers have been filled in by deep lakes: the Lac d'Aiguebelette and Lac du Bourget.

Préalpes

The northern Préalpes lie just beyond the Alpine fringe along a north-south axis, forming a barrier which rarely rises above 2 000m/6 561ft. They consist of five distinct massifs carved out of limestone (except for the Chablais), separated by the *clues*, (transverse valleys) of the Arve, Annecy, Chambéry and Grenoble.
Overlooking Lake Geneva and drained by the three Dranse rivers, the **Chablais** is backed by the **Giffre** with its lively winter resorts, Samoëns and Flaine.
The **Bornes** Massif, flanked by the **Chaîne des Aravis** in the east, is drained by several rivers including the Fier; La Clusaz is an important ski resort.
Further south, the **Bauges** Massif offers pleasant pastoral landscapes where small ski resorts are developing.
The **Chartreuse** Massif stands like an imposing limestone fortress; features include high cliffs, deep gorges, valleys with pastures and magnificent dense forests on the well-watered slopes.
The **Vercors** is the largest of the Préalpes massifs; within its impressive outer ramparts, this natural citadel offers beautiful forest and pastoral landscapes, as well as striking gorges and popular resorts such as Villard-de-Lans.
The southern Préalpes spread over a vast area along a curved line in a northwest-south-east direction. The Durance Valley divides them into two groups:
West of the river, on the Dauphiné side, is the wild and austere **Dévoluy,** with its cliffs and bare summits below which sheep and cattle graze.

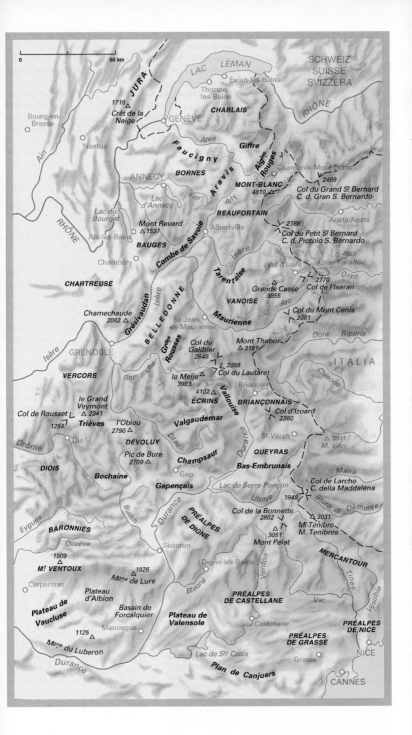

The wooded **Bochaine** marks the transition between north and south whereas the **Diois** and **Baronnies** already offer typical southern landscapes where the Alpine and Pyrenean folds mingle in conflicting directions. To the south, the limestone massif of **Mont Ventoux** stands alone, towering 1 909m/6 263ft above the Avignon Basin.

East of the Durance, the relief becomes more intricate, without any apparent plan; the mountain ranges of the **Préalpes de Digne** and **Préalpes de Castellane** are cut crosswise by deep wild gorges, known as *clues*, guarded by picturesque towns like Sisteron, Digne and Castellane. These areas are the least populated of the Alpine region: owing to strict conservation regulations, the slopes have retained their varied vegetation, but the summits are mostly bare.

Lying between the River Verdon and River Var, the **Préalpes de Grasse** rise to an altitude varying between 1 100m/3 609ft and 1 600m/5 250ft.

The **Préalpes de Nice** are deeply cut in a north-south direction by rivers (Var, Tinée, Vésubie) which make their way to the sea through impressive gorges overlooked by villages perched high above the river beds.

Lying between the Préalpes, the **Plateau de Valensole** occupies the former delta of the River Durance filled in by an accumulation of rocks from nearby mountains. These rocks and pebbles, bound together by a kind of natural cement, form a conglomerate which has been carved by erosion into the famous **Pénitents des Mées** *(see Vallée de la Moyenne DURANCE)*. Further east, there are several limestone plateaux through which streams penetrate and disappear into sink-holes. Spectacular gorges have been carved out by the River Verdon and River Artuby.

Alpine trench

In the northern Alps, the **Bassin de Sallanches** and the **Val d'Arly** form, together with the depression of the **Combe de Savoie** and **Grésivaudan**, a wide longitudinal plain into which open the upper valley of the River Isère (Tarentaise) and the valleys of the Arc (Maurienne) and of the Romanche (Oisans). Owing to the means of communication provided by this internal plain, to the fertile soil which favours rich crops (maize, tobacco, vines) and to the availability of hydroelectric power, the Alpine trench has become one of the most prosperous areas of the whole region.

In the southern Alps, a similar depression cut through marl runs along the foot of the Écrins, Briançonnais and Queyras massifs; the River Durance and its tributaries flow through this relatively flat area partly flooded by the artificial Lac de Serre-Ponçon. Some strange rock formations, carved out of ancient moraines, can be seen in this region. They stand like groups of columns and are known as **Demoiselles coiffées** (capped maidens) because they are crowned by a piece of hard rock *(see Barrage et lac de SERRE-PONÇON)*. Between Sisteron and Manosque, the fertile Durance Valley brings Provence, its typical vegetation and orchards to the heart of the southern Alps.

Central massifs

This central mountain range includes **Mont-Blanc**, the **Aiguilles Rouges**, the **Beaufortain**, the **Belledonne**, the **Grandes Rousses**, the **Écrins-Pelvoux** and, in the south, the **Mercantour**. Together, these massifs form the high Alps, consisting of hard crystalline rocks, which were uplifted during the Tertiary Era while their sedimentary cover was removed. Austere and impressive, they are well known among mountaineers who like to cross the glaciers and climb the needles and snow-capped peaks. The Beaufortain is the only massif to have retained its layers of schist: it offers pleasant pastoral landscapes scattered with wooden chalets. Beautiful lakes have filled in the basins left by the glaciers.

La Clarée Valley

M. Blanchard/MARCO POLO

Intra-Alpine zone

Situated between the central massifs and the Italian border, the **Vanoise** Massif and the **Briançonnais-Queyras** Massif also belong to the high Alps but they consist of a mixture of schist and metamorphic crystalline rocks. Valleys are deep and slopes are covered with pastures. Thanks to its mild, sunny climate and snow-covered slopes, the Vanoise (which has the Tarentaise and Maurienne as natural boundaries and includes the Parc national de la Vanoise) has recently acquired the highest concentration of winter resorts in the French Alps including Val-d'Isère, Tignes, Courchevel, La Plagne, Méribel-les-Allues and Les Arcs.

The Briançonnais-Queyras Massif has a more complicated relief due to the diversity of its rock structure: sandstone, limestone and schist carried over from the Italian side as a result of overthrust. Its characteristic southern light, blue skies and generous sun make this area one of the healthiest in Europe, which explains the rapid development of summer and winter tourism centred round high villages such as St-Véran (2 040m/6 693ft).

The **Gap, Embrun** and **Ubaye** districts, lying between the high Alps and the Préalpes, offer a mosaic of heights, small basins and wide valleys carved out of layers of "black soil", or flysch in the case of the Ubaye.

ALPINE RELIEF

The slow but irresistible action of glaciers, rivers, rain and frost has completely remodelled the Alps over thousands of years into the mountain range it is today.

The action of the glaciers – Around 10 000 years ago, glaciers covered the whole Alpine range and spread over the adjacent flat areas as far as the region of Lyon. Some of these "solid rivers" were huge, reaching thicknesses of 1 100m/3 609ft in the Grésivaudan for instance. They scooped out cirques with steep back walls and dug U-shaped valleys characterised by successive narrowings and widenings and a series of steps, with tributary valleys "hanging" over the main ones.

Alpine glaciers today – Since the beginning of the 20C, Alpine glaciers have been consistently receding because they are not being sufficiently renewed, and today they only cover an area of 400km≤ /154sq mi; four fifths of them are in Savoie (Mont-Blanc and Vanoise), the remainder being in the Écrins Massif.

The Mer de Glace is a very good example of a "valley glacier". Moving downstream, we find in succession a **névé**, an expanse of snow not yet turned into ice, and a **glacial "tongue"** cut by deep crevasses. Level changes are marked by jumbled piles known as **séracs**; accumulations of debris carried down by the glacier are called **lateral moraine** when deposited on the edges, **terminal moraine** when deposited at the end and **medial moraine** when deposited between two joining glaciers. Alpine glaciers move at a speed of 70m/230ft per year.

Erosion by water – When the ice mantle disappeared, mountain streams and rivers began to smooth out the relief. Connecting gorges opened up the "bolts" and joined the floor of a "hanging" valley to that of the main valley. The gorges of the Diosaz and of the Doron de Champagny are good examples of this kind of defile through which roads are built as a last resort.

There are gorges of another kind, mainly in the Préalpes, which cut across the axis of the folds: they are called **cluses** (transverse valleys). They are often the only means of communication between the mountain and the lower areas, since roads have been carved out of the rock face in the Défilé de Pierre-Châtel or the Gorges de Guiers for instance. The most active mountain streams deposit debris they have been carrying when they reach the bottom of the main valley and their accumulation at the foot of the slopes forms alluvial cones which obstruct the valleys.

STREAMS AND RIVERS

The southern Alps have three distinct river networks: in the centre the Durance and its tributaries, in the east the Var which gathers water streaming down the Alpes Maritimes, and in the west the tributaries of the Rhône.

Mediterranean rivers are particularly interesting because they behave like real mountain streams: during the summer, they are reduced to a trickle of water owing to the absence of rain and intensive evaporation. But in spring and autumn, violent rain storms or sudden thaws fill up the river beds so suddenly that the flow of foaming water tumbles down at the speed of a galloping horse. For instance, the rate of flow of the River Var varies from 17m/600cu ft per second to 5 000m/176 575cu ft per second. The Durance, Verdon, Aigues and Ouvèze rivers are equally capricious. However, the Durance and Verdon have been harnessed by dams (Serre-Ponçon across the Durance, Castillon and Ste-Croix across the Verdon) and canals. The impressive gorges dug by these rivers (Grand Canyon du Verdon, Gorges du Cians) are one of the main attractions of Haute-Provence.

Underground streams forming mysterious hydrographic networks sometimes reappear further on; streams from the Montagne de Lure, for instance, feed the famous resurgent spring of Fontaine-de-Vaucluse *(see The Green Guide Provence: FONTAINE-DE-VAUCLUSE)*.

ALPINE CLIMATE

The Alpine range is divided into two distinct climatic regions: the northern Alps which are subject to west winds off the Atlantic and the southern Alps which enjoy a Mediterranean climate. The separation between these two regions follows a line drawn from west to east between the following mountain passes: Col de Rousset, Col de la Croix Haute, Col du Lautaret and Col du Galibier.

Rainfall over the **northern Alps** is abundant all year round and temperatures are low. The Préalpes and central massifs get the brunt of the rainy weather. The intra-Alpine zone, protected by these barriers, is drier and sunnier; snow remains on the slopes longer. However, many factors such as altitude, aspect and the general direction of the various ranges and valleys, contribute to create a great variety of local climates.

Pointe de l'Échelle and Lac Blanc in the Massif de la Vanoise

Altitude – Temperatures fall rapidly as the altitude increases (roughly 0.5°C/1°F every 100m/328ft); interestingly, this phenomenon can be reversed in winter, during periods of settled weather, as cold, heavier air slips down the slopes and accumulates in the valleys and the warm air rises.

Aspect – South-facing slopes, called **"adrets"**, enjoy more sunshine than north-facing slopes called **"ubacs"**, usually covered with forests and on which snow holds better.

Relief – It has an influence on rainfall and wind direction; rain and snow fall more generously on the first heights in their path and on slopes exposed to the wind. Winds generally blow along wide valleys, particularly during the warm season when, towards midday, warm air rises from the valleys and causes clouds to form round the summits. This is a sign of continuing fine weather. Later on in the day, the process is reversed and a cold mountain breeze blows down into the valleys. Heights usually attract storms which are often violent and spectacular.

The climate enjoyed by the **southern Alps** displays typical Mediterranean features: a good deal of sunshine, dry weather, clear skies, the absence of mist or fog, rare yet abundant precipitation and the famous *mistral* wind. In winter there is a fair amount of snow and plenty of fine weather in which to enjoy it. Spring is characterised by a short rainy spell while the mistral blows hard from the southwest. Summer is hot and dry over the whole of Haute-Provence and the air filled with the delicate scent of lavender and thyme. Nearer the summits, temperatures are more moderate. In the autumn, violent storms are succeeded by sunny spells, the air is pure and the light ideal for discovering the beauty of nature.

Flora

In mountain areas, the pattern of vegetation is not only influenced by the climate and the type of soil, but depends also on aspect and altitude which defines a succession of vertical stages. This staging is modified by man who has done much to alter original landscapes. South-facing slopes *(adrets)*, which offer the best conditions for settlement and agriculture, have been the most subject to deforestation, whereas northern slopes *(ubacs)*, often uninhabited, have retained their trees which thrive in the prevailing wetter conditions; a pattern seen at its best in valleys running from east to west.

Slopes are usually farmed up to an altitude of about 1 500m/5 000ft; above this there is a belt of conifer forest. From around 2 200m/7 000ft upwards, the trees give way to Alpine pastures with their rich mixture of wild grasses and Alpine flora. Above 3 000m/10 000ft, bare rock prevails, with mosses and lichens clinging to it in places.

TREES

The Alps are famous for their vast forests of conifers. Old **fir trees** have broad crowns with flattened points looking like storks' nests. The bark is greyish; the cones, standing up like candles, break up when ripe and shed their scales. The soft needles are lined up like the teeth of a comb (hence the name *sapin pectiné*) and have a double white line on their inner surface (hence the name *sapin argenté* – silver fir). The **spruce** is the most

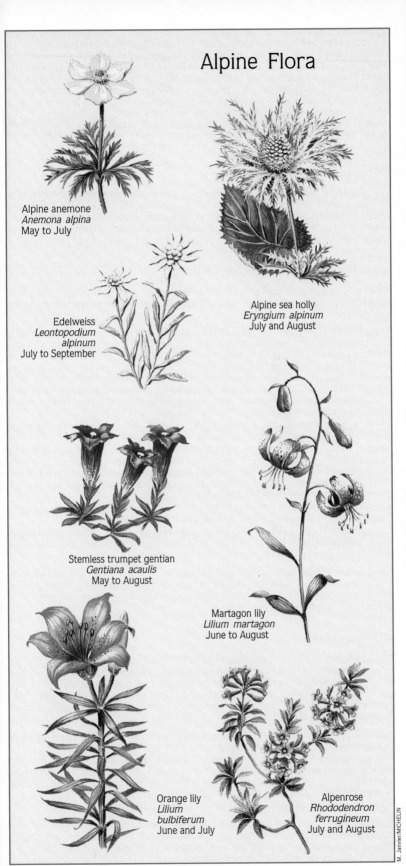

Alpine Flora

Alpine anemone
Anemona alpina
May to July

Alpine sea holly
Eryngium alpinum
July and August

Edelweiss
*Leontopodium
alpinum*
July to September

Stemless trumpet gentian
Gentiana acaulis
May to August

Martagon lily
Lilium martagon
June to August

Orange lily
*Lilium
bulbiferum*
June and July

Alpenrose
*Rhododendron
ferrugineum*
July and August

M. Janvier/MICHELIN

commonly found tree on north-facing slopes. It has a pointed, spindle-shaped crest and drooping branches, and its reddish bark becomes deeply fissured with age. It has sharp needles and its hanging cones fall to the ground in one piece when ripe. The only conifer in the French Alps to shed its leaves in winter, the **larch** is commonly found growing on south-facing slopes, particularly in the *"Alpes sèches"* (dry Alps). The cones are quite small. The delicate, light-green foliage casts relatively little shade, thus favouring the growth of grass, one of the attractive features of larch woods. The many species of **pine** all have needles growing in tufts of two to five encased in scaly sheaths. The cones have hard rough scales. The forest pine, with its tall slender trunk, grows in considerable numbers in the southern Alps, usually on the *adrets* (sunny slopes).

Deciduous trees

The grey-trunk beech prevails in the Préalpes up to an altitude of 800m/2 625ft. With its thick boughs it provides shade for many rare plants: Turk's-cap lily, belladonna or deadly nightshade, medicinal speedwell and many more. Among other deciduous trees, there are alders, maples, birches, service trees, willows and laburnums with their lovely clusters of yellow flowers.

MEDITERRANEAN VEGETATION

Trees and xerophilous plants (adapted to extremely dry conditions) require mild temperatures which do not fall below 4°C/39°F during the coldest month of the year.

Trees – Several varieties of oaks and pines, as well as almond trees and the typically Provençal cypresses and olive trees grow in the southern Alps, either in cultivated areas or scattered on dry, rocky moors known as *garrigues*. Such landscapes can be seen in the Durance Valley, on the southern slopes of Mont Ventoux or the Montagne de Lure and in the Baronnies and Diois areas. Further north, above 600-800m/1 968-2 625ft, forests of white oaks, forest pines and beeches prevail, particularly on north-facing slopes. Such forests often alternate with heaths where gorse, box and lavender grow.

The evergreen **holm oak** has a short, thick-set trunk with a wide-spreading dome and fine, dark green leaves. It grows on arid calcareous soil at less than 328m/1 000ft; in stunted form, it is a characteristic element of the *garrigues (see below)*.

The deciduous **downy** or **white oak**, so-called because the undersides of the leaves are covered with dense short white hairs, requires more water than the evergreen oak. It is found in valleys and on the more humid mountain slopes.

The **Aleppo pine**, one of the Mediterranean species of pine trees, has a light, graceful foliage and a trunk covered with grey bark which twists as it grows.

The outline of the dark **cypress**, a coniferous evergreen, marks the Mediterranean landscape with its tapered form pointing towards the sky, while the common **almond tree** delights the eye with its lovely early spring pink blossoms.

Garrigues – This word is used to describe vast expanses of rocky limestone moors. Vegetation is sparse, consisting mostly of holm oaks, stunted downy oaks, thistles, gorse and cistus as well as lavender, thyme and rosemary interspersed with short dry grass which provides pasture for flocks of sheep.

ALPINE FLORA

The name "Alpine" is normally used to describe those plants which grow above the tree line. Because of the short growing season (July and August), these hardy and mostly small species flower early, while the disproportionate development and colouring of the flowers is the result of exposure to intense ultraviolet light. Their resistance to drought is often their main characteristic; many have woolly leaf surfaces and thick, water-retaining leaves.

Remote origins – Most Alpine plants originated elsewhere. The dandelion and the centaury are among those which came from the lower mountains and plains but adapted to the harsher conditions at high altitude; others come from the Mediterranean area, like the pink and the narcissus, from the Arctic (buttercup, white poppy) or from Asia like the primula and even that most emblematic Alpine flower, the edelweiss. The few truly indigenous species such as columbine and valerian managed to survive the Quaternary glaciations.

Suitable sites – Mountain plants do not grow at random: some need an alkaline soil, others prefer an acid soil; some flourish on scree, in a cleft in the rock or in a bog. Each type of site has its specific plant species or combination of species – always the same – which is able to thrive in the given conditions.

Fauna

Above the tree line, at high altitudes, animals have learnt how to adapt to the special conditions of a harsh environment, in which it is only possible to survive by building up one's defences against the cold, the snow and the lack of food. Some animals are protected against the cold by their thick coat or plumage, others such as the marmot hibernate below ground, solving at the same time the problem of food shortage. The blue hare and the snow-partridge, which are the favourite game of foxes and birds of prey, make themselves inconspicuous by changing colour with the seasons. In winter, large herbivores like the ibex and the chamois make their way down to the forests in search of food and shelter. In addition to this struggle for life, these animals must contend with man's expansion into their habitat; most of the shy, rarer species seem doomed to extinction in the near future except in conservation areas within the nature parks.

Mammals – The **ibex** is a stocky wild goat with a pair of easily recognisable curved, ridged horns which can be more than a metre long; this peaceful animal enjoys basking in the sun. Males sometimes gather in flocks of more than 50. When snow begins to fall, they join up with the females who are smaller and shier. The males then fight for the females and the clatter of their horns knocking echoes throughout the mountains. The measures undertaken by the Parc national de la Vanoise to protect the species have ensured its survival.

The graceful silhouette of the nimble **chamois** can be seen high up on the steep rocky peaks capped with snow all year round. The "Alpine antelope" has a tough reddish brown coat, thicker and darker in winter, with a black line on its back. Its small head is surmounted by curved slender dark horns. This extremely strong animal jumps from one rock to the next and climbs the steepest passages; its thin, strong legs and its special hooves explain its extraordinary agility. It lives in groups of between three and 20 head, led by a male goat. A chamois can weigh as much as 50kg/110lb (half the weight of an ibex). In summer it feeds on grass, whereas in winter it goes down to the forest and nibbles at the bark of trees.

The short-eared **blue hare** lives in the very high Alpine pastures and is very difficult to observe owing to its scarcity and above all its ability to change colour with the seasons in order to blend in better with its surroundings. Pure white in winter, it thus becomes greyish in summer.

The reddish brown summer coat of the **stoat** becomes white in winter apart from a thin tuft of black hair at the end of its tail. This small carnivorous mammal lives among stones or near chalets.

You may need binoculars, and a stroke of luck, to catch a glimpse of a solitary **lynx**, stalking the slopes at sunset in search of birds, marmots, chamois and small deer. Virtually extinct in the region by the beginning of the 20C, this wild cat has returned to the woods of Savoie from Switzerland.

The **Corsican moufflon** is a large wild sheep, living in flocks led by the older males. Originally from Asia, but particularly well adapted to the Mediterranean climate and vegetation, it has been introduced into the Mercantour and Queyras nature parks. Males are easily identified by their thick scroll-shaped horns.

One of the most retiring creatures in the mountains is the snow-mouse, which can live at an altitude of 4 000m/13 123ft.

Butterflies and moths – There are more than 1 300 different species of butterflies and moths in the Alpes-de-Haute-Provence *département* alone and more than 600 species in the area around Digne (there is an exceptionally fine collection of lepidoptera in the local museum), among them some 180 butterflies which represent three quarters of the total butterfly population of France. Among the most remarkable species are the Swallowtail butterfly, the Parnassius and, smaller but also rarer, the Diana and the Proserpina, the Jason, the Vanessas and the Érèbiae (including the Scipio, presently becoming extinct) which hover over lavender fields. The destruction of the traditional environment and the development of industries in the area are responsible for numerous species becoming extinct every year.

Birds of Prey – **Golden eagles** can be seen throughout the Alps, circling above their territory, which can cover most of a valley. Breeding pairs remain together for life, rearing their young in eyries on the side of inaccessible cliff faces. Eagles prey on marmots in summer and feed off ibex carcasses when food becomes short in winter. The reintroduction of the **bearded vulture**, which soars on wings 2.80m/9ft long from tip to tip, has been a great success story *(see BEUIL)*. A scavenger of carrion, it generally stays close to herds of cattle.

Alpine Fauna

Black grouse

Chamois

Ibex

Salamander

Tengmalm's owl

Moufflon

Bearded vulture

Local economy

For hundreds of years, Alpine economy was based on agriculture and handicraft until the region witnessed two economic revolutions: the first, which happened as a result of the discovery of hydroelectric power, led to the industrialisation and urbanisation of the valleys; the second, which was the rapid development of tourism, led to drastic changes in high mountain landscapes. These two phenomena, however, saved the region from the population drift to the cities, which threatened its future prosperity. Today, the northern Alps are already a very dynamic region with important towns such as Grenoble and Annecy, whereas the southern Alps are changing at a slower pace and still retain a strong traditional economy centred on small and medium-sized towns such as Briançon, Sisteron and Digne.

AGRICULTURE

Forestry and cattle farming have always been the mainstays of rural life in the Alps, where a trend towards specialisation is spreading. Orchards and nut groves dot the landscape and the broad valleys of the Combe de Savoie and Grésivaudan are given over to cereals, as are the Gapençais, Embrunais, Buëch valley and Plateau de Valensole to the south.

Cattle – In mountainous regions, south-facing slopes are generally devoted to pastures and farming whereas north-facing slopes are covered with forests. In the Alps this pattern has been significantly altered as arable land was gradually turned into pastureland, although cereal farming is developing in the southern Alps. On the other hand, seasonal migrations from the villages to high mountain pastures, once an important event in the farming year, are becoming less common owing to a shortage of cowherds. Cattle are now kept near the villages, which makes it easier to collect and sell dairy produce.

Alpine cattle are famous for their sturdiness and ability to walk long distances, which enables them to adapt to the difficult physical and climatic conditions of their natural environment. In the Préalpes, the predominant breeds originate from Abondance and Villars-de-Lans. The short-legged **Abondance**, valued for its long lifespan, has a reddish-brown hide with white patches. The **Villarde** of the Vercors was once reared as a working animal, then declined with the spread of industry before being reintroduced and is now bred for both milk and beef. A high milk yield is the main advantage of the reddish-coloured **Montbéliardes**, introduced from the Jura and, like the distinctive, black and white Holsteins, increasingly taking the place of the local breeds. In the high mountain areas, the most common breed is known as **Tarine**, for the simple reason that it originates from the Tarentaise region.

In many areas, especially on the steeper slopes, farmers still make hay by hand, scything grasses and binding up bales. In the northern massifs, milk is essentially used to make various kinds of cheese in the *fruitières* (cheese cooperatives): Reblochon from the Bormes, Vacherin from the Bauges, Beaufort from the Beaufortain, Tomme from Savoie, Bleu de Sassenage and St-Marcellin from Dauphiné.

Pig farming is developing in cheese-producing areas: by-products from cheese-making, especially Reblochon, are used to feed pigs, which explains why most cheese cooperatives keep a lot of pigs as a sideline.

Sheep – Sheep farming is one of the main economic activities of the Alpes du Sud and Haute-Provence *départements*. These specialise in the production of lambs fattened quickly and sold when they reach the age of three months. In summer, the resident population is joined by sheep migrating from lower Provence in search of greener grass. This migration, known as **transhumance**, begins around Midsummer's Day and ends around Michaelmas at the end of September. Unfortunately, it is no longer as

Montbéliarde

Tarentaise

Abondance

picturesque as it used to be when shepherds, donkeys, goats and sheep travelled for days through many villages before reaching the Vercors or the upper valley of the Durance. Nowadays, 200 000 head travel every year by special trucks or trains.

At the end of their journey, the sheep are gathered in flocks numbering between 300 and 4 000 head and taken by shepherds to high pastures rented by the farmers who own the sheep. These pastures can be communal or privately owned and their use is strictly regulated.

Sheep from Haute-Provence do not migrate since they can roam freely over vast areas during the warm season and take shelter in large sheds known as *jas* when winter approaches.

Forestry – In recent years, the policy of reafforestation, which is intensive in some areas, has been helped by the restrained use of high pastures and the discontinuation of mowing at high altitude. In fact, forests now cover more than a third of all usable land, and even half in the Préalpes and the northern Alps. They are essentially made up of conifers (fir trees and spruce), and of deciduous trees at low altitude; more than half the forested areas belong to municipalities or private owners. The rest belongs to the state and is administered by the Office National des Forêts (Forestry Commission).

Even though the northern Préalpes boast some splendid specimens of beech, which thrive in humid countries, forests of conifers predominate as in the rest of the Alpine region. Spruce is the most common conifer of the Salève, Faucigny, Aravis and Bauges areas, whereas fir trees grow most happily in the Chartreuse, Vercors, Beaufortain, Maurienne, and Grésivaudan, as well as in the Diois and Préalpes de Digne; in the high mountain areas of the southern Alps, such as the Briançonnais, Queyras, Embrunais, Ubaye and Mercantour areas, there are mixed forests of fir trees, spruce and larch.

Many Alpine areas owe their prosperity to their forests; some have retained the traditional practice of *"affouage"*, which consists in allotting a certain quantity of wood to each household within the precinct of a given municipality. Forestry development has become easier through the improvement of forest tracks and the use of chain saws as well as towlines when access is particularly difficult. Wood is essentially used as timber or sold to sawmills and paper mills. Quantities are indicated in cubic metres. One cubic metre (35.3cu ft) of spruce can be converted into 800m^2/957sq yd of paper or 24 000 ordinary newspaper pages.

Whole areas of Haute-Provence have been reafforested since the middle of the 19C and forests, which are now protected, are not used for industrial purposes.

Lavender and lavandin – The delicate scent of lavender is characteristic of Haute-Provence. At the beginning of this century, the picking of the flowers of this wild plant, which grows at an altitude of between 600m/1 968ft and 1 400m/4 593ft on the southern slopes of Mont Ventoux and the Montagne de Lure, represented an extra income. Then, when it became necessary to replace cereal crops, lavender was cultivated on the plateaux and high slopes. Well adapted to the climate and calcareous soils of Provence, this plant helped many farmers to survive when they were about to give up. Land which had not been ploughed for 20 years was suddenly covered with numerous green bushes with mauve flowers giving off a delightful fragrance in July.

Later on, *lavandin*, a more productive but less fragrant hybrid, was cultivated on the lower slopes and in the valleys between 400m/1 312ft and 700m/2 297ft. Superb fields of *lavandin* can be spotted on the Plateau de Valensole and along the road from Digne to Gréoux-les-Bains. The harvest takes place from July to September according to the region: most of the picking is now mechanised but the inaccessible or closely planted older fields are still picked by hand. After drying for two to three days, the picked lavender is sent to a distillery equipped with a traditional still.

Each complete operation lasts 30min: 1 000kg/2 205lb of picked lavender are needed to produce 5-10kg/11-22lb of lavender essence or 25-40kg/55-88lb of *lavandin* essence. Lavender essence is reserved for the perfume and cosmetic industries, whereas *lavandin* essence is used to give a pleasant smell to detergents and cleaning products. Lavender flowers can also be dried and placed in scent bags.

The annual production for the whole of Provence varies from 30t to 40t of lavender essence and from 800t to 900t of *lavandin* essence.

Olive trees and olive oil – Olive groves traditionally mark the northern boundaries of the Mediterranean region. The production of olive oil, which represents more than two thirds of the national output, comes mainly from the Alpes-de-Haute-Provence and the Luberon area. Following the hard winter of 1956, when almost a quarter of the olive trees growing in the Baronnies area died, olive groves were renewed with hardier species. There are many varieties and the flavour of the fruit varies accordingly; the type of soil and picking time are also very important; tradition demands that several varieties should grow in the same olive grove. The harvest begins as early as the end of August, depending on the area. Olives are picked by hand when they are intended to be eaten whole or shaken down into nets with a pole and then sent to the mill. Olives from Nyons *(tanches)* are at present the only ones to have been granted an AOC (Appellation d'Origine Contrôlée) seal of origin. Picked when ripe (black) and preserved in brine, they are a delicacy.

Truffles – The truffle, or *rabasse* in Provençal, is an edible, subterranean fungus which develops from the mycelium, a network of filaments invisible to the naked eye. They live symbiotically with the root of the downy oak, known in Provence as the white oak. These small stunted oaks are planted in fields called *truffières*. The most productive of these are situated below 500m/1 640ft, but there are a few up to an altitude of 1 000m/3 281ft. The Vaucluse *département* is the main producing area of the Mediterranean region, followed by the Luberon, Riez and Forcalquier areas as well as the upper valley of the River Var. Truffles, known as the "black gold" of Haute-Provence, are harvested from mid-October to mid-March, when they are ripe and odorous. Pigs are traditionally used to sniff out truffles, but they are being replaced by dogs, easier to train and less greedy. Once the animal has found a truffle (sometimes buried as deep as 25cm/10in), it is carefully dug up by hand. A white variety of truffle, which is harvested between May and mid-July mainly in the upper valley of the River Var, is used as a flavouring in cooking. This less highly prized variety is known as a *truffe blanche de St Jean* or by its Provençal name, *mayenque*.

HYDROELECTRIC POWER AND INDUSTRY

In the French Alps, industries were at first intended to satisfy local needs, but then they undertook to work for the rest of the country and even for the export trade. This led to the development of clock factories in Cluses, of several silk factories, subsidiaries of the textile industries in Lyon, of paper mills in Dauphiné, supplied with wood from the forests of the Chartreuse and the Vercors, of cement factories in the Préalpes, of glove factories in Grenoble and of steel foundries in Ugine.

Hydroelectric power – Known as *houille blanche* (literally white coal), this was the fuel which drove Alpine industry forward. During the late 1860s, a factory owner of the Grésivaudan region, called Amable Matussière, who wished to increase the driving power of his mills, called on two engineers, Fredet and **Aristide Bergès**. The latter deserves credit for having harnessed the first 200m/656ft waterfall at Lancey in 1869. At first, the power of the turbines was used mechanically, but by 1870 the invention of the dynamo by Gramme, followed by the building of the first power lines on an industrial scale (the first line dates from 1883), made the new power stations switch to the production of electricity.

The Alpine relief lends itself to the production of hydroelectricity: the combination of high mountain ranges and deep valleys creates numerous waterfalls. Engineers began by using waterfalls with a low rate of flow, situated high above the main valleys. They then tapped the main valley rivers, which had a much higher rate of flow, thus creating a concentration of industries along these valleys (valley of the River Isère, known as Tarentaise, Arc Valley, known as Maurienne, Romanche Valley). During the 1950s, engineers conceived complex projects embracing whole massifs and involving water storage. The flow of water, channelled through miles of tunnels and sometimes diverted from the natural river basin, is collected in huge reservoirs like that formed by the Tignes and Roselend dams or ducted into neighbouring, more deeply cleft valleys (Isère-Arc bypass)

Today, most of the turbines are connected to alternators, which are in turn linked to the EDF (Électricité de France) network.

There are basically four main types of dam. **Gravity dams** withstand water pressure by their weight alone. They are triangular in section with an almost vertical upstream face and a back sloping at about 50°; examples include Chambon and Bissorte. **Arch dams,** graceful and economic in design, have a curved structure with its convex side upstream which transfers the pressure of water laterally to the steep sides of the gorge, as at Tignes, le Sautet, St-Pierre and Monteynard. **Buttressed dams** are used when the width of the dam does not allow the use of an arch; they are a combination of gravity and arch dams and can be seen at Girotte, Plan d'Amont and Roselend. **Riprap dykes** are found at La Sassière, Mont-Cenis and Grand-Maison.

Industry and water power – Electrometallurgy and electrochemistry were the two industries which benefited most from the use of hydroelectricity. They settled near the power stations built by the industrialists themselves, but the cost of transport of raw materials is such a handicap in the mountains that factories are compelled to turn to more and more complex products, which are rare and expensive, such as certain steel alloys. Nowadays, electrochemical factories are huge complexes producing detergents, weedkillers and solvents. The future belongs to specialised processing industries; firms now choose to settle in *cluses* (transverse valleys) near large, well-located towns such as Annecy, Chambéry and Grenoble, with Grenoble's reputation for high-tech engineering training often tipping the scale. **Mechanical engineering** and **electrical engineering** have become vital aspects of the industrial landscape of the Alps, while the traditional clock industry is still going strong in Annemasse.

Historical table and notes

Events in italics indicate milestones in history

The Celts and the Romans

6-5C BC	The Celts progressively occupy the whole Alpine region; the powerful Allobrogi settle in the area situated between the River Rhône and River Isère.
218	Hannibal crosses the Alps in spite of the Alloborgi's attempt to stop him.
125-122	The Romans conquer southern Gaul.
121	The Allobrogi finally acknowledge Roman superiority.
1C BC	During the reign of Augustus, the whole Alpine region is pacified.
End of 2C AD	The first Christian communities expand in spite of persecution.
4C	Christianity gets a firm hold on the region and bishoprics are founded.
313	*Proclamation of the edict of Milan, through which Constantine grants religious freedom to the Christians.*
476	*Fall of the Roman Empire.*

The Franks and the kingdom of Burgundy

534-36	The Franks seize Burgundy and invade Provence.
800	*Charlemagne becomes Emperor of the West.*
8C	Franks and Arabs devastate Provence.
987	*Hugues Capet is crowned King of France.*
10C	Provence becomes part of the kingdom of Burgundy. The Saracens are repelled.
1032	The kingdom of Burgundy is annexed by the Holy Roman Empire. At the same time, the archbishop of Vienne splits his huge territory into two: the future Savoie to the north and the future Dauphiné to the south.

Savoie, Dauphiné and Provence

11-12C	Expansion of the three provinces. The dynasty of the Count of Savoie becomes the guardian of the Alpine passes. The ruler of Dauphiné adopts the title of "Dauphin" and the Count of Provence Raimond Bérenger V inherits the County of Forcalquier which is thereafter united with Provence.
	Building of abbeys and monasteries throughout the land.
	St Bruno founds the Carthusian Order and monastery.
1209	*Albigensian Crusade led by Simon de Montfort.*
1232	Chambéry becomes capital of Savoie
1268	The Dauphin Guigues VII marries the daughter of the Count of Savoie.
1270	*Death of King St Louis of France, who was married to the daughter of the Count of Provence.*
1337-1453	*Hundred Years War.*
14C	Savoie becomes a powerful feudal state under Amadeus VI, VII and VIII.
1349	Dauphin Humbert II, being in political and financial difficulties, negotiates the sale of Dauphiné to the King of France. It is decided that the heir to the throne of France will, from then on, bear the title of "Dauphin" *(see GRENOBLE).*
1416	Savoie becomes a dukedom.
1419	Unification of Savoie and Piedmont.
1447	Dauphin Louis II (the future King Louis XI) settles on his domains, puts an end to the feudal system and creates the Parliament of Grenoble.

C. de Torquat/PIX

Seal of Amadeus VI

Italian Wars and Wars of Religion

1461-83	*Louis XI's reign. The king inherits Savoie in 1481*
1488	Crusade against Vaudois heretics in the Alpine valleys.
1489-1564	Life of Guillaume Farel, a native of Gap, who preaches the Reformation.
1492	*Christopher Columbus discovers America.*
1494-1559	The Italian Wars reveal the strategic importance of the Dauphiné passes.
1536	With the help of the Swiss cantons, François I invades Savoie which remains under French rule for 23 years.
1559	Treaty of Cateau-Cambrésis: Savoie is returned to the Duke of Savoie who transfers his capital from Chambéry to Turin.
1543-1626	Life of Lesdiguières, the protestant governor of Dauphiné, who fights the Duke of Savoie.
1562-98	Fierce fighting between Catholics and Protestants: Sisteron, Castellane and Seyne are besieged; armies of the rival factions clash at Allemagne-en-Provence
1589	*Beginning of Henri IV's reign.*
1598	*End of the Wars of Religion; Edict of Nantes: Protestants obtain the freedom of worship and guaranteed strongholds.*
17C	Savoie is occupied several times by French troops.
1628	Dauphiné loses its autonomy.

From Louis XIV to the Revolution

1643-1715	*Louis XIV's reign.*
1685	*Revocation of the Edict of Nantes: Protestants flee the country.*
1692	The Duke of Savoie invades the southern Alps. The king sends Vauban to the area in order to build fortresses and strengthen existing ones (Briançon, Mont-Dauphin, Sisteron and Colmars).
1707	Invasion of Provence by Prince Eugène of Savoie.
1713	Treaty of Utrecht: Dauphiné and Provence expand; France loses part of the Briançonnais but receives the Ubaye region in compensation.
1736	Jean-Jacques Rousseau settles in Les Charmettes near Chambéry.
1740-48	War of the Austrian Succession. Eastern Provence is invaded by Austrian and Sardinian troops; Savoie is occupied by the Spaniards, France's allies. The treaty of Aix-la-Chapelle ends the war and the Spaniards have to give up Savoie.
1774	*Beginning of the reign of Louis XVI, deposed by the revolution less than 20 years later.*
1786	Balmat and Paccard are the first Alpinists to climb Mont Blanc.
1788	Reaction in Grenoble and Vizille to the closure of the local *parlements* foreshadows the Revolution.
1789	*Bastille day signals the start of the French Revolution; départements are created the following year.*
1791	Dauphiné is divided into three *départements*: Isère, Drôme and Hautes-Alpes.
1792	French revolutionary troops occupy Savoie which becomes the "Mont-Blanc *département*".
1793	Creation of the "Alpes-Maritimes *département*" (returned to the kingdom of Sardinia in 1814).

19C

1811	The Route du Mont-Cenis is built by order of Napoleon I.
1815	By the treaty of Paris, Savoie is given back to King Victor-Emmanuel I of Sardinia. Napoleon I, returning from exile on Elba, lands in Golfe-Juan on the Mediterranean coast and crosses the southern Alps to Grenoble.
1852	*Napoleon III becomes Emperor of France.*
1858	Napoleon III meets the Italian statesman Cavour in Plombières (Vosges region): they agree that France shall help the King of Sardinia to drive the Austrians out of Italy; in exchange, France is to receive Nice and Savoie.
April 1860	A plebiscite is organised in Savoie: an overwhelming majority vote in favour of the union with France. The new province is divided into two *départements*: Savoie and Haute-Savoie.
1869	Aristide Bergès harnesses the first high waterfall in Lancey thus becoming the "father" of hydroelectric power.
1870	*Proclamation of the Third Republic on 4 September.*
1872	Inauguration of the Fréjus railway tunnel.
1878	Mountaineer Henri Duhamel takes to the slopes of Chamrousse on skis.
End of the 19C	Acceleration of the population drift from the mountains to the towns.

1924	First Winter Olympic Games held in Chamonix.
June 1940	The advancing German army is temporarily halted by the River Isère. Italian attacks are repelled by border garrisons.
1944	Fierce fighting in the Vercors: Dauphiné is one of the main strongholds of the Resistance. One of the underground fighters' most heroic feats takes place on the Plateau des Glières *(see THORENS-GLIÈRES)*.
1945	The Resistance liberates the Ubaye region.
1947	The Treaty of Paris alters the Franco-Italian border in favour of France who receives the Vallée Étroite *(see Le BRIANÇONNAIS)*.
1955	Cable-cars make the high peaks accessible to everyone.
1955-1967	Construction of the huge Serre-Ponçon Dam.
1962	Signing of the Accords d'Évian (Treaty of Évian, *see ÉVIAN-LES-BAINS*)
1963	Creation of the Parc national de la Vanoise, the first French national park.
1965	Inauguration of the Mont Blanc road tunnel.
1968	10th Winter Olympics held in Grenoble.
1980	Inauguration of the Fréjus road tunnel, over 100 years after the opening of the railway tunnel.
1992	16th Winter Olympic Games held in Albertville.
1995	Creation of the Parc naturel régional de Chartreuse.
1996	Creation of the Parc naturel régional du massif des Bauges.
1999	Fire in the Mont Blanc tunnel claims 41 lives.

THE HOUSE OF SAVOIE

The House of Savoie was the oldest reigning dynasty in Europe: it began with the feudal lord Humbert "White Hands", who became count of Savoie in 1034 and ended with the last king of Italy, Umberto II, Victor-Emmanuel III's son, who abdicated in 1946. For nine centuries, the House of Savoie ruled over Savoie when it was a county, then a duchy; it governed Piedmont from 1429 onwards, Sardinia from 1720 and finally provided Italy's monarchs from 1861 to 1946.

How counts became dukes – Their role as "gatekeepers" of the Alps gave the counts and later the dukes of Savoie exceptional power. Owing to its strategic position, Savoie was constantly coveted by its neighbours to the point that its history amounts to a string of successive occupations, each followed by a treaty returning it to its rightful owner.
During the Middle Ages, three of Savoie's rulers, Amadeus VI, VII and VIII, gave the region unprecedented ascendency; their court, held in Chambéry, rivalled in splendour those of the most important sovereigns of Europe. The most illustrious, **Amadeus VIII**, was the first to bear the title of Duke of Savoie and at the end of his life was elected as the last Antipope under the name of Felix V.
In the 16C, the Treaty of Cateau-Cambrésis freed Savoie from French domination which had lasted 23 years. **Duke Emmanuel-Philibert** reorganised his domains and moved his capital from Chambéry to Turin, which was less easily accessible to French monarchs. His wish to expand on the Italian side of the Alps was accomplished during the reign of Victor-Amadeus II, who gained the kingdom of Sicily by the Treaty of Utrecht, then promptly exchanged it for Sardinia and became the king of that region.

Union with France – The people of Savoie were tired of their government which they ironically called *"il Buon Governo"*. Moreover, they were worried by Cavour's anticlerical policy and turned towards France for help. Napoleon III and Cavour met in Plombières in 1858 and decided that, in exchange for France's help against Austrian occupation, Italy would relinquish Nice and Savoie if the populations concerned agreed. This led to the plebiscite of April 1860: by 130 533 votes to 235, the people of Savoie overwhelmingly agreed to become French.

Famous natives of the Alps

SCHOLARS AND WRITERS

Savoie, which has only belonged to France for just over 100 years, was, strangely enough, the cradle of the French language; the Savoyard humanist **Guillaume Fichet** (1433-78) who set up the first printing press in Paris. Almost two centuries later, in 1606, the first French Academy was founded in Annecy; one of its founders was **Saint François de Sales** (1567-1622), who inspired religious life in his native Savoie and whose works contributed to the blossoming of the French language *(see ANNECY)*.

One of the prominent early figures of the southern Alps was another humanist **Guillaume Farel** (1489-1565), a native of the Gap area, who preached the Reformation with Calvin in Geneva. At the same time, Occitan was the dominant language of the southern Alps as indeed of the whole of southern France and, although its official use was discontinued in the 16C, it continued to be spoken by the people for another three centuries.

Champtercier, in the hills above Digne, was the birthplace of Pierre Gassendi (1592-1655), a philosopher, mathematician and scientist who rose to prominence in the 17C. During the late 18C and early 19C, the brothers **Joseph** (1753-1821) and **Xavier** (1763-1852) **de Maistre** rejected the ideals of the French Revolution and supported absolute monarchy.

However, the most famous man of letters of the Alpine region was undoubtedly the novelist **Henri Beyle** (1783-1842), a native of Grenoble, better known by his pseudonym **Stendhal**. Besides his masterpieces, *Le Rouge et le Noir* (1830) and *La Chartreuse de Parme* (1839), he wrote numerous studies, including *De l'amour* (1822), in which he analysed love from a psychological as well as a historical and social point of view, and several volumes of autobiography, including *Vie d'Henry Brulard* in which he depicted his childhood and adolescent years in Grenoble.

Stendhal

V. d'Amboise/PIX

The 19C also saw the birth of the **Félibrige** movement, a revival of the Occitan language and of Provençal traditions under the leadership of **Frédéric Mistral** (1830-1914). One of his disciples, **Paul Arène** (1853-96), a native of Sisteron, wrote tales and poems both in French and Occitan. Better known was **Jean Giono** (1895-1970), born in Manosque, who celebrated Haute-Provence and its country folk in works such as *Regain* (1930) and *Jean le Bleu* (1932). His contemporary, **Alexandre Arnoux** (1884-1973), also chose Haute-Provence as the setting for most of his works *(Haute-Provence, Rhône mon fleuve)*.

SOLDIERS AND POLITICIANS

Born in Grésivaudan, **Bayard** (1476-1524), known as "*le chevalier sans peur et sans reproche*" ("the knight who is fearless and above reproach") has gone down in history as the model soldier of his time. He had the honour of knighting King François I after the battle of Marignan in 1515. **François de Bonne de Lesdiguières** (1543-1626) led the Huguenots from Dauphiné during the Wars of Religion and was given command of the armed forces of his native region by King Henri IV, which led him to fight against the Duke of Savoie. He was the last Constable of France before Richelieu abolished the title in 1627.

In 1788, two natives of Grenoble, judge **Jean-Joseph Mounier** and barrister **Antoine Barnave**, led the peaceful protest of the Assemblée de Vizille which paved the way for the French Revolution a year later. Another native of Grenoble, **Casimir Perier**, was prime minister of France in 1831-32, during the reign of King Louis-Philippe. His grandson was President of the French Republic in 1894-95.

SCIENTISTS AND INVENTORS

Among her famous sons, Savoie counts the mathematician **Gaspard Monge** (1746-1818), who devised "descriptive geometry" at the age of 19 and later was one of the initiators of the École Polytechnique where he taught, and the chemist **Claude Louis Berthollet** (1748-1822), who discovered the whitening properties of chlorine, widely used in the manufacture of linen. Dauphiné on the other hand prides itself on having had several inventors such as **Vaucanson** (1709-82), who built automata and partly mechanised the silk industry, and **Xavier Jouvin** (1800-44), who devised a system of classifying hand sizes and invented a machine for cutting gloves to these sizes.

ABC of architecture

Religious architecture

SISTERON – Ground plan of the Église Notre-Dame (12-15C)

The early Romanesque style from northern Italy is characterised by a chancel with three capital apsidal chapels and a single nave. The basilical plan has no transept.

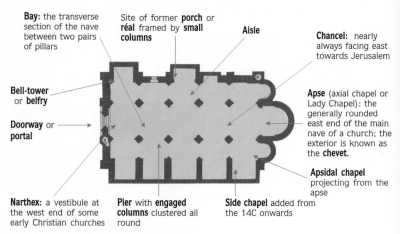

Bay: the transverse section of the nave between two pairs of pillars

Site of former **porch** or **réal** framed by **small columns**

Aisle

Chancel: nearly always facing east towards Jerusalem

Bell-tower or **belfry**

Doorway or **portal**

Apse (axial chapel or Lady Chapel): the generally rounded east end of the main nave of a church; the exterior is known as the **chevet**.

Apsidal chapel projecting from the apse

Narthex: a vestibule at the west end of some early Christian churches

Pier with **engaged columns** clustered all round

Side chapel added from the 14C onwards

Cross-section of a church

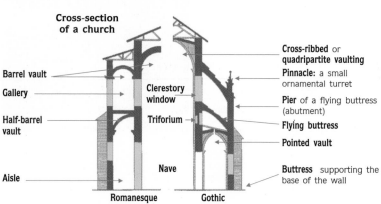

Barrel vault

Gallery

Half-barrel vault

Aisle

Clerestory window

Triforium

Nave

Romanesque

Cross-ribbed or quadripartite vaulting

Pinnacle: a small ornamental turret

Pier of a flying buttress (abutment)

Flying buttress

Pointed vault

Buttress supporting the base of the wall

Gothic

GANAGOBIE – Doorway of the Abbey Church (12C)

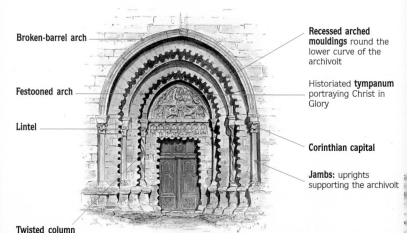

Broken-barrel arch

Festooned arch

Lintel

Twisted column

Recessed arched mouldings round the lower curve of the archivolt

Historiated **tympanum** portraying Christ in Glory

Corinthian capital

Jambs: uprights supporting the archivolt

EMBRUN – Porch (14C) of the Cathédrale Notre-Dame

This highly ornamented and elegant feature, usually found on the north side of a church, is common in northern Italy.

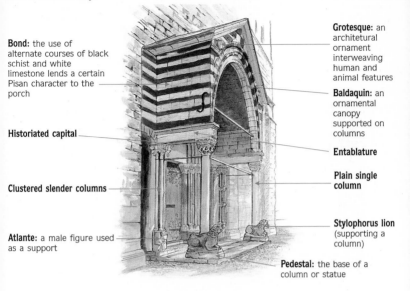

Bond: the use of alternate courses of black schist and white limestone lends a certain Pisan character to the porch

Historiated capital

Clustered slender columns

Atlante: a male figure used as a support

Grotesque: an architetural ornament interweaving human and animal features

Baldaquin: an ornamental canopy supported on columns

Entablature

Plain single column

Stylophorus lion (supporting a column)

Pedestal: the base of a column or statue

EMBRUN – Chancel and crossing of the Cathédrale Notre-Dame (12-13C)

The Romanesque parts (barrel-vaulted aisles and apse) blend harmoniously with the pointed vaulting of the Gothic nave

Corbelled **base** supporting the weight of the pipes

Stop: a set of organ pipes

Great organ case: the wooden frame encasing the mechanism

Clerestory window

Diagonal

Section of **vaulting** between ribs

Transverse arch used to reinforce the vaulting

Keystone

Gallery: a balcony providing room for members of the congregation

Triumphal arch: the large arch separating the nave from the chancel

Oven-vaulted apse

Main arch separating the nave from the aisles

Engaged column

Backing **pilaster** against which a column rests

R. Corbel/MICHELIN

ARVIEUX – Nave of Renaissance church (16C) with Baroque altarpiece

Cornice: the third or upper part of an entablature resting on a frieze

Frieze: a decorative band near the top of an interior wall below the cornice

Entablature: it comprises the architrave, the frieze and the cornice.

Corner piece: the wall section situated between the arch and its frame

Attic: the top part of a structure designed to make it more impressive

Altarpiece

Coffer: a sunken panel in a vault or ceiling

Pilaster: an engaged rectangular column

Agrafe: an ornamental element in the form of a mascaron placed on the keystone

NÉVACHE – Baroque altarpiece from the Église St-Marcellin-et-St-Antoine (15-17C)

Modillion: a small console supporting a cornice

Crowning piece

Scroll

Armature: a frame of metal bars supporting and protecting a window

Cartouche: an ornamental tablet often inscribed or decorated

Composite capital combining elements from different classical orders

Saddle-bars fixed into the masonry to maintain stained-glass panels in place

Twisted columns decorated with vine branches

Foliated scrolls: a kind of ornamentation depicting foliage

Niche: recess in a wall, usually meant to contain a statue

Altas

Altascloth

Predella: the bottom tier of an altarpiece divided into several panels

Palaces and Castles

GRENOBLE – Façade of the Palais de Justice (16C)

The doorway and chapel of the former palace of the Dauphiné Parliament date from the Late Gothic. The main part of the edifice bearing the Renaissance imprint contrasts with the plainer left-hand extremity which is more recent.

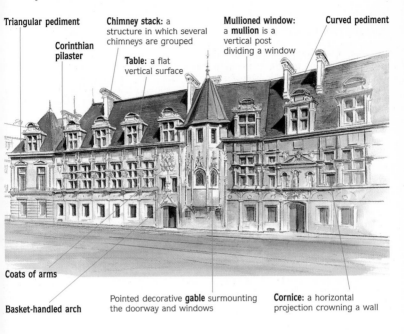

Triangular pediment

Corinthian pilaster

Chimney stack: a structure in which several chimneys are grouped

Table: a flat vertical surface

Mullioned window: a **mullion** is a vertical post dividing a window

Curved pediment

Coats of arms

Basket-handled arch

Pointed decorative **gable** surmounting the doorway and windows

Cornice: a horizontal projection crowning a wall

ST-GEOIRE-EN-VALDAINE – Château de Longpra (18C)

This former fortified castle, turned into a residential castle in the 18C, has very steep roofs well-suited to the hard winters of the Dauphiné region.

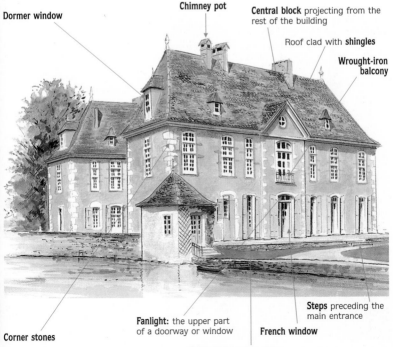

Dormer window

Chimney pot

Central block projecting from the rest of the building

Roof clad with **shingles**

Wrought-iron balcony

Corner stones

Fanlight: the upper part of a doorway or window

French window

Stone base of the edifice

Steps preceding the main entrance

Art and architecture in the Alps

RELIGIOUS ART

Churches and chapels - In the north of the region, churches and chapels are small but solidly built on steep slopes or summits where their thick stone walls, pierced by small windows, have been braving the bad weather for centuries, their wide roof structures forming an awning to protect the most exposed façades. In Savoie, churches are surmounted by characteristic steeples swelling out into onion shapes, whereas in Dauphiné, stone spires are topped by pyramids. The names of these humble churches built by thrifty peasants are evocative: Notre-Dame-de-Tout-Secours (Our Lady of All Assistance), Notre-Dame-des-Neiges (Our Lady of the Snows).

In the south, the majority of churches date from the Romanesque period. The main features of the **Early Romanesque** style, imported from Italy, are the simple plan, massive appearance and rustic aspect of the buildings. Moderate in size, these churches were designed without a transept and with a single nave with narrow openings, surmounted by barrel vaulting or a strong timber frame and ending with an oven-vaulted apse. The best examples of this early style, in which a minimum of decoration was used, are the Église St-Donat, the crypt of Notre-Dame-du-Dromon and of the Prieuré de Vilhosc near Sisteron. The **Late Romanesque** style flourished during the 12C and 13C, introducing a new harmony between spaces, openings and curves as well as the general use of more refined building stones. However, in spite of gaining in height, churches retained their rustic look while the influence from Lombardy and Piedmont could still be felt, particularly in the Briançonnais, Queyras, Ubaye and Embrun regions. Designed like basilicas, these churches were adorned with baldaquined porches, often supported by squatting lions as in Embrun, Guillestre, St-Véran and La Salle. The slender steeples were surmounted by four-sided pyramids. Exterior ornamentation remained sober owing to the use of hard limestone, difficult to carve. Interior decoration was also rare, with one exception however, the Monastère de Ganagobie which has a beautifully carved pediment and remarkable mosaics. On the other hand, the stylistic simplicity of the Abbaye de Boscodon bears evidence of the primitive Cistercian influence.

The Romanesque style lasted into the 13C and 14C with the building of the Église Notre-Dame in Forcalquier, of the Église St-Sauveur in Manosque and of the churches in Seyne-les-Alpes and Bayons.

The **Gothic** style had only a limited impact on the region and is best represented by the cathedrals built in Embrun and Forcalquier.

Belfry of Notre-Dame-de-Bellecombe

The only worthy example of the **Baroque** architectural style in the southern Alps is the Église Notre-Dame de Briançon, built between 1703 and 1718. However there is a wealth of Baroque ornamentation, such as wreathed columns, carved pulpits, organ cases, altarpieces and recessed statues all richly painted and gilt.

In the north, on the other hand, particularly in Savoie, many churches were built or decorated at the time of the Counter-Reformation (a movement which, during the 16C and 17C, tried to counteract Protestant austerity with an abundance of ornamentation, concentrating mainly on decorative altarpiece and pulpit designs). Artists mostly came from Italy. The best examples of this rich style are Notre-Dame-de-la-Gorge and the church of Champagny-en-Vanoise, and in the Maurienne and Tarentaise areas, Baroque trails (*"les Chemins du Baroque"*) have been specially designed to enable visitors to discover this unique heritage (*see Practical information*).

Murals – Pilgrims and travellers crossing the Alps in the 14C and 15C decorated churches and chapels with bright frescoes in a naive style. These illustrated the life of Jesus (Chapelle St-Antoine in Bessans, Chapelle de Puy-Chalvin and Chapelle de Prelles, to name a few) and various saints (the most popular being Christopher, patron saint of travellers and St Sebastian, who cures the plague), as well as many episodes from the Old and New Testaments.

An equally popular theme was that contrasting the **"virtues"**, represented by beautiful young maidens, and the **"vices"**, riding various symbolical animals. In most cases, the connection is still clear to modern eyes, such as pride riding a lion, anger on the back of a leopard and laziness mounted on a donkey, but a few, such as the badger of avarice, hardly have the same powerful associations today. The corresponding punishments for these deadly sins were depicted with great realism and, for that reason, they have generally disappeared. The most common technique was tempera painting which used an emulsion of pigment mixed with egg, glue and casein. In the Alpes-Maritimes region, the name of some of the artists who painted these murals are known, for instance **Canavesio** in St-Étienne-de-Tinée, **Andrea de Cella** in Roure. From the mid 15C to the mid 16C, a Gothic school of painting, based in the Comté de Nice, produced some remarkable pictures such as the altarpiece by **Louis Bréa** which decorates the church in the tiny village of Lieuche.

Crosses and oratories – Discreet and humble, dotted along paths and on the edge of precipices, crosses and oratories represented an art form which expressed the religious fervour of mountain folk and travellers having to face a hostile natural environment. Oratories were originally mere heaps of stones known as "Montjoie", sometimes with pre-Christian origins, but they gradually became larger, were surmounted by crosses and included a recess which sheltered a small statue. Crosses were erected in the most dangerous places, in order to comfort passers-by. The most remarkable of these, which are situated in the Queyras, bear the symbols of Christ's Passion and are known as *"croix de la Passion"*.

CASTLES AND FORTS

Feudal castles – These, or what is left of them, usually draw the visitors' attention because of the sheer beauty of their ruins standing in picturesque surroundings in isolated spots or overlooking ancient villages. Very few of them offer any real architectural interest, either through their style or state of preservation. Particularly noteworthy, however, are the Château de Simiane and its famous rotunda, dating from the 12C and 13C, the Château de Bargème, dating from the 13C, and the Château de Montmaur, dating from the 14C. Many castles, such as those of Montbrun-les-Bains and Tallard, were seriously damaged during the Wars of Religion, which were particularly violent in that area. Some castles were entirely rebuilt during the 17C and 18C, while sometimes retaining part of their former structure: such is the case of the castles of Gréoux-les-Bains, Esparron-du-Verdon and Château-Queyras.

Fortifications – Towns had, since Antiquity, been protected by walls which often had to be rebuilt or consolidated during the Middle Ages and even later, until the reign of Louis XIV, owing to constant border conflicts. Embrun has retained a 12C tower and Sisteron still boasts four 14C towers and a citadel dating from the end of the 16C. However, most of the border fortifications were built by Vauban who, from 1693 onwards, endeavoured to "enclose" Haut-Dauphiné.

Sébastien le Prestre de Vauban (1633-1707) took his inspiration from his predecessors, in particular Jean Errard (1554-1610) who is believed to have rebuilt the Sisteron fortifications and wrote a treatise on fortifications published in 1600. Having observed the numerous sieges which took place during his lifetime, Vauban was able to evolve a series of new types of fortifications, well adapted to the local terrain. In his opinion, Dauphiné was not sufficiently well protected by the natural barrier of the Alps which could be crossed at certain times of the year. He therefore studied in great detail the advantages and drawbacks of natural sites such as peaks, passes and valleys in order to choose the best position for his defences.

He protected gun-sites from enemy fire by means of armoured casings, shielded gunners and soldiers, and made an exact science of defensive features like fortified gates and broken-line walls. The results of his ingenuity can be seen in Briançon, Mont-Dauphin, Château-Queyras, Colmars and Entrevaux, fortresses which were still being used in the 19C. Vauban was equally aware of the aesthetic aspect of his works and of its importance, making skilful use of local materials like the pink marble in Mont-Dauphin, which blend well with the landscape.

Residential chateaux – They first appeared in the 16C, when former castles were often remodelled and a Renaissance building was added to the existing structure (Allemagne-en-Provence, Château-Arnoux and Tallard).

During the 17C and 18C, the chateaux lost their military aspect, which gave way to comfort and attractive features. There are practically no constructions of this type in the area with the exception of the Château de Sauvan, designed by Jean-Baptiste Franque in 1719, which is a real gem. The Château de Malijai is another example of the classical style in the region.

Traces from the past – Most ancient villages, especially in the southern Alps, have retained a wealth of details from the main architectural styles of the past: Romanesque vaults, cellars and doorways; Gothic arches and twin openings; Renaissance lintels, carved jambs decorated with acanthus leaves, mullioned windows and elegant wrought iron; 17C pediments and bosses; 19C neo-Classical buildings and various other imitations.

TRADITIONAL ARCHITECTURE

Houses

In the Savoie and Dauphiné mountains, rural dwellings are in harmony with the harsh conditions of the natural environment: isolation, bad weather and intense cold. Houses are therefore stocky with a minimum of openings. A lot of space is set aside for storage: a wood shed, larders for cheese and charcuterie and barns for hay and grain, often situated above the living area to insulate it from the cold.

All the houses have balconies, known as *solerets*, which enable their occupants to take advantage of the slightest ray of sun; protected by overhanging roofs, these balconies are also used for drying clothes as well as wood for winter use etc.

In areas where snow is abundant, roofs are of prime importance and are always very large, overhanging all round to protect the houses and their immediate surroundings. They are either steep and smooth in order to allow the snow to slide off easily or almost flat in order to allow the snow to form a protective layer against the cold.

In forested areas, timber is the most common building material; in former days, trees were selected on north-facing slopes where they grow more slowly and their wood is therefore harder.

Villages are often situated halfway up south-facing mountain slopes with all the houses facing the sun. In flat areas and on plateaus, houses are usually grouped round the church.

In Haute-Provence on the other hand, where climatic conditions are milder in spite of strong winds and a marked contrast between summer and winter, stone and tiles are the traditional building materials. Villages are built on dry rocky south-facing slopes their houses nestling round the shaded square with the café, church and town hall nearby.

Préalpes de Savoie – In the forested areas of the Chablais, Aravis and Bauges mountains, the most traditional type of house is the wooden chalet built on a stone base with an overhanging roof covered with wood or slate and balconies all round. The living quarters for people and animals as well as the storage space are on the ground floor whereas the barn is on the upper floor.

Préalpes du Dauphiné – In the Chartreuse area, large stone-built farmhouses are surrounded by various outbuildings. In the Vercors area, on the other hand, stone-built gabled houses, two or three storeys high, have everything under one roof.

Oisans region – In this high mountain area, houses are very rustic in appearance and their rather flat roofs are covered with heavy slabs of schist, known as *lauzes*, although these are now often replaced by slates or corrugated metal. Openings are small and often arched.

Beaufortain, Tarentaise and Maurienne regions – In forested areas, houses have wooden façades and flat roofs covered with wood. Wherever scree-covered slopes predominate, houses are stone built with wooden balconies, few small openings and flat roofs covered with *lauzes*, which retain a thick layer of snow in winter. Some of these houses consist of a single room.

Briançonnais and Vallouise regions – This is an area of scattered stone-built houses: the animals' stalls are on the lower level behind a line of stone arches, the living area, entirely surrounded by wooden balconies, is on the intermediate level and the barn, directly accessible from the rear, on the upper level. The roof is usually covered with slates.

Queyras region – Built of stone and wood, the houses of this area are highly original *(see ST-VÉRAN)*. The ground floor, which includes the living area and stalls, is stone-built and surmounted by several wooden storeys used for drying and storage. The roofs, overhanging on the balconies, are covered with wood or *lauzes*.

House from the Maurienne region

House from the Vercors region

R. Corbel/MICHELIN

Embrunais and Ubaye regions – This area, which marks the transition between the high mountains and Haute-Provence, offers great architectural variety. Houses are rectangular and stocky, stone built with wooden balconies; the steep four-sided roofs are covered with slates. The interior plan is simple: the kitchen and animals' stalls are at ground level, the bedroom and threshing floor above and the barn at the top of the house. In Guillestre, families would move down to the warmer ground floor to live with the animals.

Haute-Provence – Village houses, often built of irregular stones and several storeys high, have a Mediterranean look about them, owing to their rounded tiles covering the roofs and forming under the eaves a decorative frieze known as a *génoise*. Isolated houses, called *granges*, are generally larger, but still fairly high, and surrounded by out-buildings. Outside walls are coated with roughcast and, inside, floors are usually covered with terracotta tiles. A dovecote can be seen nearby. Lower wooden houses with thatched and slate roofs can still be seen to the east near Mercantour.

Hilltop villages

These hilltop villages and small towns (Sisteron, Forcalquier, Digne) contain an amazing number of dwellings within a relatively small area enclosed by a wall.
Their origin is thought to go back to the 10C Arab invasions. In fact, the inhabitants of the region deliberately chose to build their villages on high ground, between the vineyards (which have now disappeared) and other crops. These villages are situated high above the surrounding countryside, on the edge of plateaux or on top of rocky peaks to which they cling. Built of local stone, they almost blend with the background and look very picturesque.
The steep and twisting streets or lanes are only for pedestrians; they are paved or simply stony, interrupted now and then by flights of steps and often spanned by arches. In some cases, the ground floor of the houses consists of rows of arcades which protect passers-by from the sun and rain. Tiny shaded squares are adorned with attractive fountains and sometimes with a belfry surmounted by a wrought-iron campanile. The high, narrow houses huddle together round the church or the castle which dominates them.
Seen from above, their bright tiled roofs appear to be tangled in a confused mass. Old studded doors, bronze door knockers and carved lintels show that these were once the residences of the local nobility and wealthy middle class. Very often, these small villages are still enclosed within their walls, the fortified gate still being the only entrance.
During the 19C and 20C, villages moved down into the valleys as peasants chose to live in the middle of their land where they built their farmhouses, known as *mas* in Provence. However, places like Montbrun-les-Bains, Lurs, Banon, Bargème, Brantes, Valensole, Auvare, Simiane-la-Rotonde and St-Auban-sur-l'Ouvèze still remind visitors of the old Provençal way of life.

Dovecotes and bories

There are many **dovecotes** in the southern Alps, particularly in the Diois, Baronnies and Forcalquier areas: pigeons were a precious source of food and their droppings were used as fertilizer for the kitchen garden. There were two basic styles: some dovecotes formed part of a larger structure including a shed and hen house on the lower level; others were separate buildings raised on pillars. The latter were subject to tax. In some cases, the holes through which the birds had access to their nests were often cut in the shape of diamonds, stars or hearts.
The drystone huts known as **bories** are typical of the Forcalquier area. Their use was never clearly defined and at various times most probably served as sheep pens, tool sheds, shepherds' huts or other temporary dwellings. Whether round or square, they only have one opening, the door. They were built of 10-15cm/4-6in-thick limestone slabs, layered up into distinctive false corbelled vaulting: as the walls were built up, each stone course was laid to overhang the preceding one so that finally the small opening at the top could be closed simply by placing one slab over it. The interior was lined with earth or mortar. Much larger than *bories* are the **jas**, similar drystone constructions covered with *lauzes* and used as sheep pens.

Manosque-St-Sauveur

Quinson

Allemagne-en-Provence

Campaniles

These metal structures, which can either be simple cages containing a bell, or intricate wrought-iron masterpieces, form part of the Provençal skyline. In this part of the world, campaniles were designed to withstand the assaults of the powerful mistral better than the traditional limestone belfries and today they can be seen on top of church towers, town gates and other public buildings.

Generations of craftsmen have toiled to produce elaborate wrought-iron works, onion or pyramid-shaped, spherical or cylindrical. Most remarkable are those on the tower of the Église St-Sauveur in Manosque, the clock tower in Sisteron, the church tower in Mane and that of the Chapelle St-Jean in Forcalquier, not forgetting the lace-like onion-shaped structure surmounting the Soubeyran gate in Manosque.

Sundials

In the southern Alps, from the Briançonnais to the Vallée de la Tinée, numerous buildings, houses, churches and public buildings are decorated with colourful sundials appreciated by lovers of popular art and photographers alike. Considered as a kind of homage to the sun, so omnipresent in this region, these dials, dating mostly from the 18C and 19C, were the work of travelling artists, very often natives of Piedmont like Jean-François Zarbula who travelled the length and breadth of the region for 40 years making many sundials on his way and decorating them with colourful exotic birds. The sundial makers had to be familiar not only with the art of setting up a dial, but also with the art of fresco painting. **Decorations** are often naive yet charming, dials being set within a round, square or oval frame and surrounded by motifs depicting aspects of nature such as flowers, birds, the sky, the sun or the moon. The most elaborate of these sundials include some Baroque features: *trompe-l'œil* decoration, fake marble, scrolls, shells, foliage, fake pilasters; the best example of this type of work can be seen on the towers of the Collégiale Notre-Dame in Briançon.

Briançonnais façades

ottos are equally interesting; often written in Latin, sometimes in French, they xpress the passing of time: 'Passers-by, remember as you go past that everything asses as I pass' (Villard-St-Pancrace); or death: 'All the hours wound, the last one Ils'; or the sun: 'Without the sun I am nothing, but you, without God, are powerless' (Val-des-Prés). These mottos, which often make an attempt at moralising, remind us at that we must make good use of our time: 'May no hour go by that you would wish to prget', 'Mortal, do you know what my purpose is? To count the hours that you waste' (Fouillouse).

CONTEMPORARY ARCHITECTURE

uring the past few years, the economic expansion of the Alps, the rapid evelopment of the towns and the advent and growth of winter sports resorts ave created a real need for public and residential buildings. Today the Alps ank as one of the most prominent French regions in the field of modern archi- ecture.

hurches – The first modern art edifice built in the Alps was the Église Notre- ame-de-Toute-Grâce on the Plateau d'Assy. Its completion in 1950 marked a turn- g point. Designed by **Novarina**, who was responsible for many buildings in the lps, it had no revolutionary feature but, for the first time in the history of con- emporary religious art, great artists were commissioned to decorate the church. nnecy, Aix-les-Bains, Grenoble and L'Alpe-d'Huez all followed the trend for mod- rn churches and chapels.

ublic buildings – Between 1964 and 1970, Grenoble was turned into a vast uilding site in preparation for the Winter Olympic Games. At the same time, an xtensive programme of research into the technical and aesthetic aspects of mod- rn architecture was launched.

rbanisation was not so systematic in other Alpine cities; however, there were ome modern achievements such as the sports complex in Chamonix, the 1aison des Arts et Loisirs (Arts and Entertainment Building) in Thonon, the alais de Justice (Law Courts) in Annecy, the Maison de la Culture (Cultural entre) in Chambéry, the Dôme in Albertville and Grenoble Museum to name nly a few.

Vinter sports resorts – Rapidly developing resorts tended to follow the gen- ral trends of modern urban architecture and serve the demand for comfort nd organised entertainment, a combination which was bound to produce its hare of functional, unremarkable buildings, yet some of these new creations roved highly original: for instance Avoriaz with its strange, rock-like build- gs or the triple pyramid of La Plagne, both controversial but defining proj- cts.

Traditions and folklore

n spite of harsh living conditions, the Alps have always been densely populated, vith a well-structured social life following the rhythm of the seasons and strongly ttached to its traditions, each valley having its own customs, dialect and cos- ume.

RADITIONAL LIFE

raditional life in the Alps was regulated in two ways: by the main events of life (birth, narriage and death) and by the impact of the seasons on the environment.

Birth – A mother's first visit after the birth of her child was to the local church to xpress her gratitude to God, but before the end of her confinement, tradition emanded that she eat several dozen eggs, which the child's godmother would bring o her. Children were christened very soon after being born.

Marriage – Many rituals were linked to marriage: in some areas, young maidens rayed to the local saint to provide a husband for them, in Entrevaux, girls would nake a clay figure of the ideal partner. There were also all kinds of symbolic cus- oms before a wedding: in the Embrunais area, the young man would offer his ancée some jewellery on the Sunday preceding the ceremony. In the Hautes-Alpes egion, a young man who married someone from another village had to cross a sym- olic barrier, usually a ribbon or a decorated log, on the day of the wedding, vhereas a young maiden in the same situation had to buy a round of drinks for the oung men of her village in order to make amends for not having chosen one of hem. After the wedding, the locals played a variety of tricks on the young couple hroughout the wedding night.

The frontière: a traditional regional headdress

Funerals – When a death occurred, the whole village would take turns to watch over the body while members of local brotherhoods sang the *De profundis* and *Miserere*. A funeral banquet inevitably took place after the funeral. In high mountain areas it was impossible to bury the dead in winter because the ground was frozen, so the bodies were kept covered with snow, on the roof of the house, until the thaw came.

The seasons – In the Alps, the year was divided in two: summertime during which people worked in the fields and looked after the animals, and wintertime, when all outdoor activity ceased.

Summer was a particularly busy time because the haymaking and harvesting season was short. Bread was made once a year by the whole village, the large loaves having to last the whole year; only with the introduction of the potato in the 18C was the fear of food shortages at the end of a hard winter diminished. Cattle and sheep farming were the main sources of wealth; the herds were taken from the stables to the summer pastures where they were looked after on a private or collective basis.

In winter, village folk usually stayed at home and lived on what had been stored during the summer: wood for heating, bread, dry vegetables, smoked meat, charcuterie and cheese. Men would repair their tools and make furniture and other objects such as toys while women were busy at their spinning-wheels. Many men however left their home to wander from region to region, selling the seeds of Alpine plants and herbs, sweeping chimneys, or finding temporary employment in the valleys as masons and builders. The Queyras and Briançonnais regions even had a reputation for "exporting" wandering schoolmasters, hired by villages for their food and lodging and a small wage. Those travellers who could read and write wore a feather in their cap, teachers of arithmetic wore two and the few who could teach Latin proudly added a third. Many of the mountain-dwellers left their homes for good and settled in the towns. Today, the men and women who remained find winter employment in the numerous sports resorts.

COSTUMES

A shawl, an embroidered bodice and belt, and an apron brightened up the long black skirt women wore, and still do on festive occasions. In St-Colomban-des-Villars, the number of blue stripes sewn onto the dress indicated the size of the dowry which a husband would receive, allowing bachelors to plan the most advantageous match. Headdresses were extremely varied and consisted of a lace or linen bonnet decorated with ribbons and worn under a felt or straw hat. Most remarkable of all was the **frontière**: worn by women from the Tarentaise area, it was richly adorned with gold and silver braid and had three points framing the face like a helmet. Gold belts and necklaces were the most popular pieces of jewellery; in some areas, women wore a **ferrure**, a gold cross and heart hanging round their neck from a black velvet ribbon, as a token from their betrothed.

Men's costumes were simpler, consisting of a loosely fitting jacket of dark ordinary cloth, a pair of black trousers, a white shirt with a touch of lace around the collar, a black tie and wide woollen belt, not forgetting a large felt hat.

LEGENDS

The mystery surrounding the mountains was the source of many legends and tales recounted at village gatherings during the long winter evenings.

The devil of Bessans – For all his proverbial cunning, the devil was outwitted by a native of Bessans who sold his soul to him in exchange for supernatural powers. As death drew close, the man went to see the Pope in Rome and asked for his pardon. He obtained it on the condition that he would hear mass in Bessans, Milan and St Peter's in Rome on the same day. He therefore used the powers he still had to get from one place to the next in a flash. Since then, the men of Bessans have been carving devils.

St John's fingers – In the 6C, St Thècle, a native of Valloire, dreamt that she saw St John the Baptist blessing Christ with three fingers as he baptised him. It is said that the saint's six-year search for those three fingers ended in Alexandria on the grave of St John, where they suddenly appeared. She took them back to her local diocese, a town which was later called St-Jean-de-Maurienne, where the relic is still kept.

The seven wonders of Dauphiné – These seven wonders, which are the pride of the people of Dauphiné, are sites or monuments steeped in mystery and strange myths: **Mont Aiguille**, known as the mount Olympus of Dauphiné, is a kind of "table mountain" dominating the Vercors, once believed by local people to be inhabited by angels and supernatural animals. Fairies were thought to live in the **Grottes de Sassenage** near Grenoble, but it was the devil who haunted the **"fontaine ardente"** near the Col de l'Arzelier. Between Grenoble and St-Nizier, a ruined keep still bears the name of **"Tour sans venin"** because, according to the legend, no snake can get near it since the lord of the castle brought back some magic earth from the crusades. Candidates for the remaining wonders include the remarkable **Pont de Claix**, built by Lesdiguières, the **Grottes de la Balme** and the **Pierre Percée**, a rock shaped like an arch.

Ancient beliefs from Haute-Provence – Legend has it that fairies live in the rocks overlooking Moustiers-Ste-Marie. On the other hand, the people of Arvieux *(see Le QUEYRAS)* were, for a long time, divided into two groups: the *"gens du Renom"*, who were thought to have gained their wealth through a deal with the devil, and the *"gens de la Belle"*, who invented all sorts of rituals to protect themselves from the evil influence of the former, marriage between the two groups being, of course, strictly forbidden.

FESTIVALS

Paganism and Christian belief were often combined in the many traditional feasts of the Alpine communities, where religious fervour was mixed with superstition. Nowadays, however, these events have become merry folk festivals. Most villages still celebrate the feast-day of their own patron saints as well as various events linked with work in the fields, not forgetting pilgrimages which are still popular. The religious side of these festivals consists of a procession followed by mass or a benediction. Non-religious events also form part of the festivities, among them the Provençal *bravade*, which is a kind of mock battle organised by the local youth; in Riez, it traditionally pitted the bourgeoisie, in the role of the Christians, against the craftsmen, posing as the Saracens. The sword dance, performed in Pont-de-Cervières every year on 16 August, features young men representing death, the stars and the rising sun. Entrevaux has its feast on Midsummer's Day, when the hero of the day, St John, is carried in effigy from the cathedral to the chapel of St-Jean-du-Désert, 12km/7.5mi out of town and back. In Annot, the winner of the archery contest is named "king for the day".

Every Provençal festival has its costumed musicians, playing the flute and the tambourin. In Moustiers-Ste-Marie, a group of musicians, known as the **Diane**, wakes the community every night around 4am with its lively music, during the nine days of the Moustiers festival.

Wedding chest from Queyras

HANDICRAFT

Woodwork

The densely forested Alps have, for centuries, produced enough wood to keep local craftsmen busy during the winter evenings, thus maintaining a strong wood-carving tradition which blossomed between the 17C and 19C, particularly in the Maurienne and Queyras areas.

These regions have retained some splendid samples of this popular art including furniture and other objects made by the local farmers out of larch or walnut wood.

Wood-carving in Maurienne – The Maurienne region was famous for its carved religious furnishings and objects: pulpits, altars, statues. Bessans was well known as early as the 17C for the skill of its craftsmen. One of them, Étienne Vincendet, who lived in the 19C, was the first craftsman to carve the famous "devils".

Chests and toys from Queyras – Wedding chests are an ancient speciality of the Queyras region. Carved out of larch with chisels and gouges, they are made up of four panels and a lid. Inside, there is often a small compartment meant for silverware and precious objects. The best samples of these chests have remarkable carvings on their front panels. Geometric motifs (rosettes) were first drawn with the help of a pair of compasses, whereas other motifs (interlacing, palmettes, hearts, foliage and arabesques) were copied from Gothic motifs or inspired by the Renaissance style and leather objects from Cordoba. The wood was carved with a knife; this took a very long time. Some chests bear a mark indicating when it was made and by whom.

The people from Queyras made numerous other pieces of furniture which testify to their considerable woodworking skills, as well as a wealth of objects for daily use such as spinning-wheels, lace hoops, bread seals (which enabled a housewife to distinguish her own bread baked in the communal oven), butter-boards, and boxes of all shapes and sizes.

Traditional toys, which used to be so popular, have practically disappeared except in La Chalp where, in 1919, a Swiss vicar had the good idea of encouraging the local production of wooden toys in order to slow down the drift from the land to the towns. Small characters, animals and pieces of dolls' furniture are cut out of thin planks of wood and then assembled and painted by hand in the craftsmen' homes.

Provençal furniture – In Haute-Provence, furniture is mainly made of walnut and more or less decorated according to the prosperity of the area. In addition to chests, tables and beds, there are large dresser cupboards, *crédences* and kneading-troughs.

The dresser cupboard has two double doors separated by two drawers. This massive piece of furniture is sometimes decorated with foliage, grotesque and diamond motifs. A *crédence* is a kind of sideboard with two drawers, sometimes with an added crockery shelf. The kneading-trough or bread box was the most common piece of furniture; often placed on top of a low cupboard, it was used to store food.

Moustiers earthenware

Manufacturing technique – The word faïence, which means earthenware in French, comes from the name of an Italian town, Faenza, already renowned for its earthenware production before the 15C. The earthenware tradition in Moustiers could never have developed without the town's plentiful supplies of clay, water and wood, but the turning point came in the 17C, when a monk brought back from Italy the secret process of earthenware making. Manufacture stopped altogether in 1873 and though later revived in the 1920s, now only serves the tourist trade.

There are several manufacturing stages. A kind of paste made of a mixture of clay, sand and chalk is moulded into shape then dried and fired in an oven at a temperature of about 1 000°C/1 832°F. This "terracotta", which is hard and porous, is then dipped into tin oxide, forming an enamel, and slightly fired again. The artist then paints his motifs on the object, using metal oxide colours. Another high temperature (850°C/1 562°F to 950°C/1 742°F) firing session follows. With this method, the choice of colours used is limited to those able to withstand such high temperatures. There is, however, another method, which allows the use of a wider choice of colours: the earthenware object is fired before being painted the artist then applies the colours mixed with certain chemicals which act as a fixative, then the object is fired a second time at a lower temperature of around 400°C/752°F.

There are four main types of faïence:

- the blue monochrome earthenware (1680-1730), influenced by the Nevers and Rouen traditions,
- the Bérain decoration (early 18C) named after the artist who introduced new motifs,
- the refined polychrome decoration imported from Spain in 1738,
- the *"petit feu"* (low temperature) decoration (late 18C), with bright colours.

'Santons"

They are the symbol of Provençal handicraft. These small earthenware figures, intended to represent the villagers of Bethlehem at the time of Christ's birth, are in fact typical Provençal villagers dressed in regional costume and representing 19C village trades. There is a famous annual fair *(foire aux santons)* in the village of **Champtercier**, near Digne.

Food and drink in the Alps

Alpine cuisine owes more to the quality and freshness of local produce than to the complexity of its recipes. Cheese from the rich Alpine pastures, fish from the lakes and rivers, mushrooms from the forests, crayfish from the mountain streams, game (thrush patés from Provence are delicious!), potatoes and fruit form the basis of most Alpine dishes, served with wine from Savoie or Provence. As for Provençal cuisine, its main characteristic is the generous use of garlic and olive oil, the latter replacing the butter so liberally used in the north.

REGIONAL PRODUCE

Fish – Fish from the lakes and mountain streams are a must in any gastronomic menu: arctic char, pike and trout are prepared in many different ways: meunière (dipped in flour and slowly fried in butter), poached, in butter sauce or braised.

Meat – Beef from Dauphiné is particularly famous; it is delicious served *en daube* (stewed) with herbs from Provence. Lamb from the Sisteron area is said to be more tender and savoury than anywhere else and there is a whole range of charcuterie available, such as ham cured with herbs and spices from the Mont Ventoux region, known as **jambon aux aromates de Ventoux**. Rabbit is appreciated by gourmets, particularly **lapin en cabessol**, stuffed and cooked in a white wine sauce.

Cheeses – Made from cow's, ewe's or goat's milk, cheeses vary a great deal according to the manufacturing process. Alpine pastures of the Beaufortain and Tarentaise areas produce **Beaufort**, one of the tastiest kinds of Gruyère, whereas **Reblochon**, an Alpine farmhouse cheese, is a speciality of the Aravis. Among the wide selection of Tommes – the name means "cheese" in Savoyard dialect – available in the northern Alps, **"Tomme de Savoie"** is the best known. **Tome des Bauges** – always written with a single "m" – is also deservedly famous. The small **Saint-Marcellin** is the most popular cheese of the lower Dauphiné area. Originally made from pure goat's milk, it is now processed from mixed goat's and cow's milk. **Bleu de Sassenage** includes ewe's milk as well. Several regional dishes are based on these tasty cheeses, one of the most famous being the **fondue savoyarde**, which successfully combines Gruyère cheese with the local dry white wine. In the southern Alps, **Picodon** from the Diois area is a sharp goat's cheese matured for at least three months, while **Banon** is a rustic, strong-tasting cheese from the Montagne de Lure.

Herbs – Either growing wild or cultivated on sunny slopes, herbs are essential ingredients of Alpine cuisine, especially in Haute-Provence. The general term *"herbes de Provence"* includes **savory** *(sarriette)* used in the making of goat's and ewe's milk cheeses, **thyme** *(thym)* used to flavour vegetables and grilled meat or fish, **basil** *(basilic)*, **sage** *(sauge)*, **wild thyme** *(serpolet)*, **rosemary** *(romarin)* which helps the digestion, **tarragon** *(estragon)*, **juniper berries** *(genièvre)*, used in the preparation of game dishes, **marjoram** *(marjolaine)* and **fennel** *(fenouil)*. The secret of tasty cooking lies in the subtle combination of these herbs.

SPECIALITIES AND RECIPES

Gratins – The universally known **gratin dauphinois** is a delicious mixture of sliced potatoes, eggs and milk; **gratin savoyard**, topped with Tomme de Savoie is a similar dish in which milk is replaced by broth. Few people know, however, that there are numerous other kinds of gratins made with pumpkin, courgette, spinach, beans, millet and crayfish tails, this last being an outstanding delicacy.

Tarte au Beaufort – This tart is filled with fresh cream mixed with Beaufort cheese and served hot.

Toasts savoyards – This delicious snack is made from creamy Reblochon mixed with peeled walnuts and spread on toasted rye bread.

Tartiflette – Cut a whole Reblochon cheese in thin slices, having first removed the rind. In a flat dish, arrange alternate layers of sliced potatoes and Reblochon; add chopped garlic, herbs, salt and pepper. Cook in the oven for 30min, adding fresh cream 5min before the time is up. Serve with smoked charcuterie and a dry white wine from Savoie. To make a **pela**, two halves of Reblochon, rind side up, are allowed to melt into a mixture of diced potato, onion and bacon.

Tourte de veau – This pie from the Ubaye region is filled with pieces of shoulder of veal marinated in onion and garlic and covered with bone jelly. It can be eaten hot or cold.

Raïoles – A favourite dish to the north of Annot, these "ravioli" from Haute-Provence are stuffed with a paste made from dried walnuts and saffron and served with spinach and pumpkin.

Aïoli – This is a rich mayonnaise made with olive oil and flavoured with plenty of crushed garlic, intended to be served with hors-d'œuvre, poached fish and various other dishes.

Fougasse – This kind of flat bread dough cooked in olive oil and topped with crushed anchovies is sold in most baker's shops in Haute-Provence and served as a snack or hors-d'œuvre. Its big brother, the **pompe à huile**, was traditionally served on Christmas Eve with liqueur wine.

Desserts – In Savoie, strawberries, raspberries and bilberries are used to make delicious tarts; **gâteau de Savoie**, on the other hand, is a light sponge cake unlike the rich **walnut cake** from the Grenoble region.

Fruit is abundant in the southern Alps, particularly in the Durance Valley. Plums are the most popular filling of the traditional tart, known as *tourte*, which rounds off many family meals.

Thirteen desserts – Traditionally served for Christmas, in honour of Christ and the 12 apostles, these desserts include raisins, dried figs, several kinds of nuts, apples, pears, nougat (made from honey), prunes stuffed with marzipan, melons and dry cakes flavoured with orange blossom.

Lou Pastelou – This speciality of Haute-Provence, a heavy pie made with chopped walnuts and sugar, originally became popular as a way of using up the little nut pieces left over from oil pressing.

WINES AND LIQUEURS

Vines have been growing in Savoie since Roman times and wine-growing is today one of the most dynamic activities of the region; this is a remarkable feat considering the drawbacks of the local climate. In fact vines grow in areas enjoying a microclimate (south-facing slopes up to an altitude of 500m/1 640ft or on lake shores) and where the soil is well drained and stony (moraines). There are several types of local vines; one of these, the **Mondeuse**, with its

Chartreuse Distillery, Voiron

delicate strawberry, blackcurrant and bilberry bouquet, produces one of the best red wines of the region, which matures very well. According to a local saying, "September makes the wine", for this month is generally mild, sunny and dry. The area produces light, dry white wines, which must be drunk while they are still young.

White wines from **Seyssel** and **Crépy** (on the shores of Lake Geneva), both A.O.C. (Appellation d'Origine Contrôlée, guaranteeing the quality) are fruity and go well with fish; they are at their best when they are between two and four years old.

The label "Vins de Savoie" includes several wines from the Massif des Bauges; Abymes, St-Badolph, Chignin, Apremont, Cruet, Azye, an extra dry sparkling wine from the banks of the Arve, as well as reds from Chautagne on the Lac du Bourget, and Arbin, where the *mondeuse* grows.

Wines designated "Roussette de Savoie" are light, dry whites with a fruity taste; 'rangy and Marestel are two names you may see.

The wine production of Haute-Provence has considerably declined and there are now fewer quality wines. However, two A.O.C. *(see above)* wines are among the most palatable: Côtes du Ventoux from the Bédoin area *(see The Green Guide Provence)* and Côte du Lubéron, from the mountainous area of the Luberon *(see The Green Guide Provence)*. On the southern border of Haute-Provence, there are some excellent rosé wines, and to the north of the region, the famous Clairette de Die is one of the great French sparkling wines, made from a mixture of *clairette* and muscat grapes by the same method as Champagne.

Among the **liqueurs** produced in the northern and southern Alps, Chartreuse, known as the "elixir of life" is undoubtedly the most famous; its formula, dating from the 16C, includes the essence of 130 different plants to which are added alcohol distilled from wine and honey.

Others include gentian liqueur, marc brandy from Savoie, "Origan du Comtat", made from herbs from the slopes of Mont Ventoux.

Moustiers-Ste-Marie

Sights

ABONDANCE ★

Population 1 294
Michelin map 328 N3 and 224 fold 9
Local map see THONON-LES-BAINS

The massive buildings of the Abbaye d'Abondance bear witness to the past vitality of one of the most important monasteries in the Alps. The village, which developed in the Val d'Abondance below the abbey, is a winter sports centre as well as a pleasant summer and health resort producing an excellent cheese similar to Tomme de Savoie.

Nearby sights: AVORIAZ, CHÂTEL, EVIAN-LES-BAINS, MORZINE, THONON-LES-BAINS, YVOIRE

Frescoes in the abbey cloisters

★ ABBEY 1hr

During the Middle Ages, the Abbaye d'Abondance had a major religious and cultural impact on the northern Alps under the rule of the Augustinian order. A branch of the Cistercian order took over in 1607 and remained here until 1761.

Cloisters ⊙ – There are only two galleries left, dating from the 14C. The Porte de la Vierge (the Virgin Mary's door), which gave access to the church, is richly decorated, although badly damaged, with a Virgin and Child on the tympanum and graceful statues on either side. Surprisingly fresh, sometimes naive, the **frescoes★★** decorating the cloisters depict scenes from the life of Christ and of the Virgin Mary; they are believed to have been painted by Giacomo Jacquerio of Piedmont between 1410 and 1420. *The Wedding at Cana* is particularly remarkable with a wealth of details of daily life in Savoie in the 15C.

Church ⊙ – The five bays of the 13C nave and the aisles were destroyed by successive fires. Two bays were rebuilt in the 19C, the remainder of the church is original. The chancel paintings by Vicario date from 1846. Note the fine 15C abbot's seat.

Museum of Religious Art ⊙ – Part of the abbey buildings house an important collection of religious vestments, paintings, statues, silver and gold plate and 15C manuscripts. The chapter-house has been reconstructed.

EXCURSION

Les Plagnes – *5.5km/3.4mi southeast. Cross the Dranse d'Abondance and turn left before a saw-mill towards Charmy-l'Adroit and Les Plagnes.*

The road reveals the bottom of the valley dotted with large chalets and dominated by the Pic de la Corne and the Roc de Tavaneuse. Beyond a hamlet called Sur-la-Ravine, it dips into the forested upper Malève Valley and reaches Les Plagnes de Charmy, within sight of the Pointe de Chavache, in front of a lake framed by wooded slopes.

La Chapelle-d'Abondance – *6km/3.7mi northeast on D 22* At the foot of the Mont de Grange and the Cornettes de Bises, this is a charming family resort where the typical regional houses, with wooden façades and carved open-work balustrades, are reminiscent of Swiss chalets across the border. The 18C church, decorated in Baroque style, has an elegant onion-shaped spire. Every year in January, a cross-country skiing race over a distance of 35km/21.7mi starts here; there are fine cross-country tracks towards Châtel and Abondance.

B + B in the valley

BUDGET

Chambre d'hôte Champfleury – *74360 Richebourg – 3km/2mi NE of Abondance towards Châtel on D 22* – ☎ *04 50 73 03 00* – ✉ – *5rms: 24.39/38.11€ – main meal 12.20€.* At the heart of the Abondance valley, this chalet typical of the Savoie region has been completely renovated and offers five cosy, well-furnished rooms. Choose between south-facing with a balcony or north-facing with a terrace.

HIKES

Start from La Chapelle d'Abondance; both climbs are relatively easy, even for less experienced hikers.

Les Cornettes de Bises – *Allow 3hr. It is advisable to carry identity papers since the itinerary skirts the Swiss border. From the village centre, walk north to the Chalets de Chevenne, then continue to climb alongside the stream to the Col de Vernaz on the Swiss border. Follow the ridge to the Chalets de la Callaz, then start the last climb to the summit* (alt 2 432m/7 979ft).

🚶 The splendid **panorama★★★** extends over the whole lake and the Alps from Mont Blanc to the Bernese Oberland.

Mont de Grange – *Allow 3hr 30min. Cross the Dranse and walk south along the path leading to the Chalets du Follière.*

🚶 The Alpine flora is particularly varied and chamois can be seen on the rocks high above the valley. The ascent starts at the end of the Chemine coomb; from the summit (alt 2 433m/7 982ft) there is a striking **view★★** of the Val d'Abondance and the shores of Lake Geneva. You may be lucky enough to spot some chamois on the rocks above the valley.

Beyond La Chapelle-d'Abondance, the peaks, pastures and forests of the vast Châtel Basin offer some of the best landscapes in the Haut Chablais.

ABRIÈS ★

Population 370
Michelin map 334 J4 and 224 fold 43
Local map see Le QUEYRAS

One of the oldest resorts in Haut-Queyras, this village is, depending on the season, the starting point of excursions, hikes, climbing or cross-country skiing expeditions in the peaks along the Italian border and in the nature reserve of the Guil valley. Abriès also draws visitors to its colourful market, held every Wednesday.

Nearby sights: BRIANÇON, BRIANÇONNAIS, GUILLESTRE, MOLINES-EN-QUEYRAS, MONT-DAUPHIN, Le QUEYRAS, ST-VÉRAN, VARS

WALKING ABOUT

A calvary including 14 Stations of the Cross overlooks the village to the west. The **church** is surmounted by a steeple with an octagonal spire; its churchyard and porch were destroyed by the flood of 1728. The sundial bears the inscription: *Il est plus tard que vous ne croyez,* "It is later than you think".

Trail of the inscribed stones – This interesting trail, lined with inscribed stones illustrating the history of Abriès, is complemented with a brochure published by the Parc naturel régional du Queyras, available at the tourist office.

The hamlets of Valpreveyre – **Valpreveyre** can be reached by following the Bouchet mountain stream and turning right at Le Roux *(6km/3.7mi on the D441)*; the road is rough but offers beautiful views of neighbouring peaks and goes past authentic old hamlets.

MODERATE

Chalet de Ségure – *05460 Ristolas –
4km/2.5mi SE of Abriès on D 947 –* ☎ *04 92
46 71 30 – closed 1 Apr-25 May and 24 Sept-
21 Dec –* ◘ *– 10rms: 41.16€ –* 😋 *6.10€ –
12.20/18.29€.* This family-run hotel in a peaceful village on the edge of the Queyras regional park takes good care of its guests. Its pleasant rooms are furnished in a style typical of the local mountain region. Meals are served in the evenings and to hotel guests only.

HIKES

★ **Walk to La Colette de
Jilly** (Alt 2 467m/8 094ft)
Take the Jilly chair-lift ⊙
*on the way out of Abriès
towards Ristolas.*
🏃 From the station
(2 150m/7 054ft), a path
(with red and white markings of trail GR 58) climbs
steeply to La Colette
de Jilly *(45min)* then
on to the Jilly Peak

(2 467m/8 094ft), offering **panoramic views★** of the Tête du Pelvas, Bric Bouchet, Grand Queyron, Pic Ségure and Pic du Fond de Peynin.

★★ **Hiking round the Bric Bouchet** (2 997m/9 833ft) **via Italy** *About 8hr; one night
in the Lago Verde (Italy) mountain refuge.*
🏃 Marked itinerary with possible alternatives from Abriès or Valpreveyre. Here are two of them: the shorter and more demanding one, suitable for long-distance skiing in winter, leads to the border pass of Valpreveyre with close views of the Bric Bouchet; then on to the Lago Verde refuge where the two alternatives meet. The longer one offers better views of the various landscapes from Valpreveyre through the hamlet of Le Roux to the border pass of **Abriès** or **St-Martin** (2 657m/8 717ft) during an easy 4hr walk. Superb **view★★** of the **Val Germanisca** (Italy) and the Bric Bouchet Summit. The Lago Verde refuge (2 583m/8 474ft) is an hour further on, along the well-marked path. The **Grand Queyron** Peak (3 060m/10 039ft) stands out to the north. From the refuge, **Prali** and its ethnological museum can be reached in 2hr 30min. *Continue along
the path until it reaches a resurfaced road. Turn left here and follow the track along the river
which leads to the first houses of Pomieri.* There is a way back from Prali through the Col de la Croix or the Col d'Urine *(see below)* over two or three days, with overnight stops in Villanova or at the Jervis refuge (at Col de la Croix).

★★ **Col de la Croix and Col d'Urine via Ciabot del Pra (Italy)**
Two days' walk and a night spent in the Jervis refuge.
From La Monta, a 2hr walk to the Col de la Croix; follow path GR 58; note the old border stone with a fleur-de-lis on the French side. The Jervis refuge is a 1hr 30min walk further on; the footpath goes down to Ciabot del Pra *(food available in season
at the inn and Jervis refuge)*. Continue northwards to reach the **Col d'Urine** in about 3hr. The imposing **Tête du Pelvas** (2 929m/9 610ft) towers over the pass and the small valley which prolongs it to the west and leads to the valley of Valpreveyre *(2hr walk
from the pass)*. Trail GR 58B takes you back to Abriès in 30min.

★★ MOUNTAIN BIKE TOURS

The most interesting itineraries start on D 947 with the section Abriès-La Monta and diverge beyond that point. There is a one-day excursion to the Col de la Croix (2 298m/7 539ft) and a longer and more fascinating one to the Val Pellice and the **Barbara-Lowrie refuge** (1 753m/5 751ft) with an impressive climb to the Col du Baracun (2 380m/7 808ft) before the final descent towards the refuge.

AIX-LES-BAINS ♨♨

Population 25 732
Michelin map 333 I3 and 224 fold 18
Local map see Lac du BOURGET

Aix-les-Bains lies at the foot of Mont Revard, on the eastern shore of the Lac du Bourget. This well-known spa, which specialises in the treatment of rheumatism and respiratory ailments, is also one of the best-appointed tourist centres in the Alps, with lively streets, splendid palace hotels near the baths and attractive lake shores.
Nearby Sights: ANNECY, Lac d'ANNECY, L'ALBANAIS, Les BAUGES, Lac du BOURGET, CHAMBÉRY

BACKGROUND

Taking the waters: a fashionable pastime – Aix's health-giving waters have been famous for almost 2 000 years. The Romans excelled in the art of hydropathy and the baths were at once a social club, a casino and a fitness club. The name of the town comes from *Aquae Gratianae*, "the waters of Emperor Gratianus".
During the Middle Ages, the baths were severely neglected. Taking the waters became fashionable again in the 16C, but the first real establishment dating from the 18C was only equipped with showers. The treatment offered became more

Eating out

BUDGET

Brasserie de la Poste – *32 av. Victoria* – ☎ *04 79 35 00 65* – *closed Mon* – *12.20/25.92€*. This family-run establishment has won a loyal local clientele. The menu offers classic brasserie fare at reasonable prices and more sophisticated cuisine à la carte in a setting free of frills.

MODERATE

Les Platanes – *173 av. du Petit-Port* – ☎ *04 79 61 40 54* – *closed 6 Nov-1 Mar and Sun evening except Jul-Aug* – *16.16/36.59€*. This Mecca for jazz enthusiasts is on the shores of the lake. Patrons can dine to the rhythm of mini-concerts on Fridays or enjoy the performance of a jazz pianist on Saturdays. In good weather there is a pleasant terrace in the shade of plane trees. Children's menu and some rooms available.

Lille – *Pl. É-Herriot* – ☎ *04 79 63 40 00* – *closed Oct-Apr* – *22.11€*. Not far from the Lac du Bourget and its large harbour, guests here can sample the delights of the water or relax in the shade of the plane trees on the terrace. This establishment also has a pizzeria, the Café de la Marine. Some rooms available.

Where to stay

BUDGET

Hôtel La Croix du Sud – *3 r. du Dr-Duvernay* – ☎ *04 79 35 05 87* – *closed end Oct-beg Apr* – *16rms: 22.87/36.59€* - ☐ *5.03€*. This little pink building in the bend of one of the quiet streets in the town centre draws people taking the waters. The modestly furnished rooms are spotlessly clean and Madame la Patronne waits on guests hand and foot. A small garden courtyard adds a certain charm to the place.

MODERATE

Hôtel Palais des Fleurs – *17 r. Isaline* – ☎ *04 79 88 35 08* – *closed 30 Nov-1 Feb* – ☐ – *40rms: 49.39/67.99€* - ☐ *8.38€* – *restaurant 20.58/24.39€*. Whether you are here to see the sights, take the waters or attend a seminar, this quiet hotel near the centre of town and the baths offers a chance to relax in its heated swimming pool, open all year round. There are two dining rooms, one of which boasts contemporary style decor overlooking the swimming pool.

Hôtel Astoria – *Pl. des Thermes* – ☎ *04 79 35 12 28* – *closed Dec* – *135rms: 53.36/77.75€* - ☐ *8.40€* – *restaurant 20.60/25€*. This superbly restored Belle Époque mansion opposite the Baths gives an impression of the former splendours of Aix-les-Bains. The splendid atrium opens onto six floors of rooms which are spacious and comfortable, as well as the restaurant with its mezzanine and the magnificent lounges. Menu for hotel guests only.

Hôtel Le Manoir – *37 r. Georges-1ᵉʳ* – ☎ *04 79 61 44 00* – ☐ – *73rms: 60/136€* - ☐ *9€* – *restaurant 22.60/54€*. This manor house on the hillside above Aix-les-Bains occupies a quiet location amid a delightful garden with trees and flowering plants. The terrace is ideal for surveying the charm of the scene from the moment the sun rises. Inside, the decor is rustic in style. Indoor swimming pool.

On the town

Baccara – *18 r. du Casino* – ☎ *04 79 35 16 16* – *Tues-Wed 10pm-2am, Thu 4pm-2am, Fri 5pm-8pm and 10pm-3am, weekends 4pm-8pm and 10pm-3am.* This tea-dance room inside the Casino will delight practitioners of the cha-cha-cha and other old-fashioned dance steps. There are dancing competitions and numerous themed nights.

Casino "Grand Cercle" – *200 r. du Casino* – ☎ *04 79 35 16 16* – *grand-cercle@icrtec.net* – *daily*. This splendid example of 19C spa architecture has housed many a crowned head of state, from Victor Emmanuel II of Sardinia to Empress Elisabeth of Austria ("Sissi"). Some opulent interior design survives from this era, including the Italian theatre and the Salviati room with its magnificent ceilings adorned with mosaics. In this luxurious setting, guests may enjoy chancing their fortune at roulette or blackjack, or less glamorously at one of the games arcade-style slot machines.

Colisée – *200 r. du Casino* – ☎ *04 79 35 16 16* – *grand-cercle@icrtec.net* – *daily 7pm-1am*. You do not have to have lost a fortune at roulette to savour the sophisticated atmosphere of this piano bar located inside Aix casino.

AIX-LES-BAINS

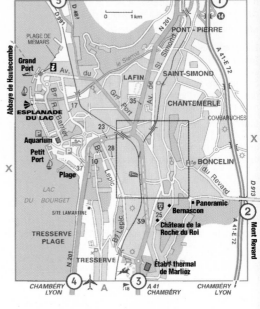

sophisticated in the 19C with the introduction of the steam bath and shower-massage, a technique brought back from Egypt by Napoleon's doctors, which is still the great speciality of the spa.

The splendour of Aix-les-Bains at the turn of the century – The expansion of the spa town, which began in 1860, reached its peak during the Belle Époque. Luxury hotels were built in order to attract the aristocracy and the crowned heads of Europe: the "Victoria", for instance, welcomed Queen Victoria on three separate occasions, whereas the Splendide and the Excelsior counted among their guests a maharajah from India, the emperor of Brazil and Empress Elizabeth ("Sissi") of Austria. Most of the buildings in the spa town were designed by an architect from Lyon, Jules Pin the Elder (1850-1934), whose masterpiece was undoubtedly the Château de la Roche du Roi.

After the Second World War, most of these magnificent hotels could not adapt to the new type of clientele and had to close down for economic reasons; some of them were turned into apartments.

THE SPA TOWN

The life of the spa town is concentrated round the baths, the municipal park with its vast open-air theatre, the Palais de Savoie and the new casino, as well as along the lake with its beach and marinas. Rue de Genève, rue du Casino and adjacent streets form the shopping centre of the town.

Treatment – The baths, which are open all year round, are supplied by two hot springs, the sulphur spring and the alum spring; showers and the *bouillon*, a bath at exactly 42°C, are the main treatments. There are four specialised pools for the treatment of rheumatism. Cold water from the St-Simon spring is used for drinking.

To the south, the **Établissement thermal de Marlioz** (Marlioz baths), situated in a peaceful shaded park, treats disorders of the respiratory system. Several crowned heads of Europe, including Queen Victoria, have benefited from this treatment in the past.

WALKING ABOUT

The Lake Shore

Follow avenue du Grand-Port and leave Aix by ⑤ on the town plan, heading towards Culoz. At the port, turn left onto Boulevard Robert-Barrier.

Grand Port – Boat trips ⟁ to Le Bourget-du-Lac, the Abbaye de Hautecombe and the Rhône leave from this pier *(see above)*.

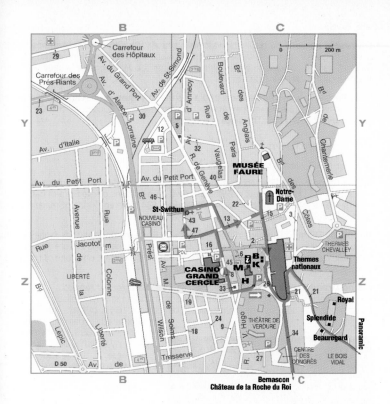

La Rotonde – *7 sq. Jean-Moulin* – ☎ *04 79 35 00 60 – Apr-Oct: daily 9am-midnight; rest of the year: daily except Mon and Sun evening – closed in Feb.* The terrace overlooking a peaceful square with flowering plants is a popular feature here.

Les Platanes – *Av. du Petit-Port* – ☎ *04 79 61 40 54 – daily except Wed. noon-3pm, 7pm-2am – closed Nov-Feb.* Bar-restaurant where themed evenings are put on at the end of the week: jazz concerts on Fri and cabaret (variety) on Sat.

Murphy's – *R. Haldiman – daily from 6pm.* This trendy pub within the casino offers pool and darts as a good alternative to roulette and blackjack. Wide selection of beers and whiskies.

Shopping

Chocolaterie-confiserie La Royale – *2 r. Albert-1ᵉʳ* – ☎ *04 79 35 08 84 – Mon-Sat 8.30am-12.30pm, 2.30pm-7.30pm – closed 1st fortnight in Feb.* This confectioner and chocolate maker offers a variety of home-made specialities with fanciful names, such as the Rocher de la Dent du Chat, Glaçons du Revard and Perles du Lac.

La Ferme Savoyarde – *12 r. de Genève* – ☎ *04 79 88 10 14 – Mon-Sat 8am-12.30pm, 3pm-7.30pm; Sun 9am-noon – closed for a fortnight in Jan.* This farm is devoted to making and selling local produce: Savoie wines, cheeses, preserves and smoked or cured meats.

Les Artisanales – *Quai Jean-Baptiste-Charcot – May-Sept: Wed 5pm-10pm.* Local craftspeople and producers sell their wares here: cheeses and smoked or cured meats, plus leather goods and *objets* and tools fashioned in wood.

★ **Esplanade du bord du lac** – This vast open space (10ha/25 acres) is equipped with children's games and is suitable for picnics. A shaded alleyway skirting the Lac du Bourget calls for pleasant walks within sight of the Hautecombe Abbey and the steep slopes of the Dent du Chat.

Petit Port – This is a fishing port and a marina. An **aquarium** ⊘, containing around 50 fresh water species in their natural environment, is housed in the Centre of Hydrobiological Studies. The **beach** is just beyond.

The Roman Town

Begin at the Tourist Information Office

Arc de Campanus – Erected by a member of the "Pompeia" family, this arch stood 9m/30ft high in the centre of the Roman town. The remains of the Roman baths can only give a rough idea of their former splendour (24 different kinds of marble were used to decorate them).

Temple de Diane – This remarkable rectangular Roman monument, its stones set in place without mortar, now houses the Museum of Archaeology. Note the classic Italianate façade on the former **Grand Hôtel** (1853) on the corner, once one of the most prestigious addresses in town.

★ **Casino Grand Cercle** – *West of the town hall, across place du Revard.*
Despite a series of renovation projects, this stylish casino still symbolises the golden age of Aix's high society. The main building dates from 1849, but it is the elegantly decorated gaming rooms, opened in 1883, which are particularly worth a visit. The finest of these is the grand **Salle des Jeux★**, with allegorical figures intricately depicted on a vast, brightly coloured mosaic ceiling. Sarah Bernhardt was one of the many great actresses to perform at the casino's **theatre**, decorated in Belle-Époque style.

Casino d'Aix-les-Bains

Mosaic in the Salle de Jeux

Turn left into rue Casino, then left again on to rue Victoria and follow rue du Temple to St Swithun's church.

St Swithun – Built in 1869, thanks to donations from the English community, this Anglican church bears witness to the resort's British connections and the lasting popularity of "taking the cure".

Turn right into rue de Genève, then follow rue Dacquin to the left.

Église Notre-Dame – Twelve 17C paintings representing the Apostles are displayed in the chancel of this Byzantine-style church.

Return to the Thermes nationaux and head uphill along rue Georges I.

For the hotel developers of the Belle-Époque, this area, overlooking the town, was the most sought-after of all. Visitors strolling through streets can still admire the façades of some of the prestigious symbols of a bygone era: the **Splendide**, the **Royal** and the **Excelsior**, rue Georges I, the **Bernascon** and the fairy-tale **Château de la Roche du Roi** on the way to the Établissement thermal de Marlioz.

SIGHTS

★ **Musée Faure** ⊘ – In 1942, Dr Faure bequeathed to the town a rare collection of paintings and sculptures including a large number of works by the Impressionists and their predecessors, Corot, Jongkind and Boudin. Note in particular *Mauve Dancers* by Degas, the *Seine at Argenteuil* by Sisley, *Ferryboat in Bonnières* by Cézanne and works by Vuillard and Pissarro.
The collection of sculptures is also rich in works by Carpeaux and Rodin, including a series of bronze, marble and terracotta sculptures forming part of his project entitled *The Doorway to Hell*, inspired by Dante's *Divine Comedy*. The last floor houses furniture and objects recreating Lamartine's surroundings in the Perrier boarding house, which is no longer there.

Thermes nationaux ⊘ –
Inaugurated in 1864, the baths were enlarged by the addition of the Nouveaux Thermes in 1934, modernised in 1972; these are open to visitors. A vast room in the basement contains the **Roman remains** of a *caldarium* (hot bath) and of a circular pool. A 98m/322ft-long gallery gives access to the **caves** where one of the sulphur springs can be seen.

In 1816, Aix-les-Bains was the setting of one of the most famous love stories in French literature, between the Romantic poet **Alphonse de Lamartine** and Julie Charles who died a year later and inspired the moving lines of *Le Lac*.

Musée lapidaire ⊘ – *Access through the Tourist Information Centre*. Stone fragments, ceramics, glassware and coins dating from the Gallo-Roman period. Remarkable male bust, probably of a Roman emperor.

Hôtel de ville – This restored château, once home to the Marquis of Aix, lends a Savoyard look to the spa district. The elegant **staircase★** was built during the early Renaissance period, with stones from the Roman monuments.

EXCURSIONS

★★**Lac du Bourget** – *See Lac du BOURGET*.

★★**Abbaye royale de Hautecombe** – A regular **ferry service** *(see boats trips above)* links the Grand Port and the abbey which can also be reached by driving round the lake *(see Lac du BOURGET: 1 Round tour of the lake)*.

★★**Circuit de la Chambotte** ⊘ – *36km/22.4mi – about 2hr 30min. Leave Aix by ① on the town plan and N 201. Turn left at La Biolle along D 991ᴮ; turn left in St-Germain and left again at La Chambotte past a small chapel.*

★★**View from the Restaurant de la Chambotte** – Splendid **view** over the Lac du Bourget and the mountains lining its shores; in the distance, one can see the Allevard, Grande-Chartreuse and southern Jura massifs.

Return to La Chambotte and follow D 991ᴮ to Chaudieu.

This road offers good bird's-eye views of the northern extremity of the lake and of the Marais de Chautagne (Chautagne marshland).

From Chaudieu, return to Aix by the lakeside road described under Lac du BOURGET.

★★**Mont Revard** – Alt 1 537m/5 043ft. Drive along the road to Le Revard until you reach the former cable-car station. The **panorama★★★** is splendid: to the west, there is an aerial view of the Lac du Bourget, the Dent du Chat, the Rhône like a shiny ribbon in the distance and Aix-les-Bains in the foreground; to the east, there is a fine vista of Mont Blanc behind a series of forested heights.

Beyond the Col de la Cluse, the **view★** embraces the whole verdant Albanais depression and the heights of the southern Jura in the distance. Further down, the Lac du Bourget comes into view.

Pleasant rural landscapes unfold between Trévignin and Aix-les-Bains *(reached by D 913)*.

L'ALBANAIS★

Michelin map 333 I/J6 and 244 fold 18

The Albanais depression, between the Lac du Bourget and the Lac d'Annecy and framed by the Gros Foug, Revard and Semnoz mountains, is a rich agricultural region which once specialised in tobacco-growing and not only connects Aix-les-Bains and Annecy but also gives access to the Jura mountain range via Bellegarde and to Switzerland via Geneva.

Nearby Sights: AIX-LES-BAINS, ANNECY, Lac d'ANNECY, Les BAUGES, Lac du BOURGET, CHAMBÉRY, THORENS-GLIÈRES

EXCURSIONS

Vallée du Chéran – *40km/25mi – allow half a day*

Rumilly – This former stronghold at the confluence of two mountain streams is the capital of the Albanais region, a lively market town and industrial centre. The old town, nestling round the "Halle aux Blés" (corn exchange, rebuilt in 1869), includes a few interesting 16C and 17C buildings, in particular round **place de l'Hôtel-de-Ville** with its graceful fountain. Also worth visiting are the **Église Ste-Agathe** with its Tuscan-style façade and the part-13C **Chapelle Notre-Dame-de-l'Aumône** ⊘ on the bank of the Chéran. The **Musée de l'Albanais** ⊘ *(avenue Gantin)*, housed in a former tobacco factory, deals with local history from the 17C onwards.

Eating out

MODERATE

Rôtisserie du Fier – *In the Val du Fier – 74910 Seyssel – 3km/2mi S of Seyssel on D 991 and D 14 – ☎ 04 50 59 21 64 – closed Tue and Wed during the school holidays in Feb and autumn (around 1st Nov) – 16.77/39.64€.* This romantic location makes the ideal setting for the simple, wholesome and excellent cooking using mainly fresh ingredients. On sunny days, tables are set in the garden along the tree-lined river bank.

Where to stay

BUDGET

Camping Le Chéran – *74540 Cusy – 7.5km/5mi S of Alby-sur-Chéran on D 63 and D 3 – ☎ 04 50 52 52 06 – open Apr-Sept – reservations recommended – 26 pitches: 10.98€ – catering available on site.* For those who love peace and solitude, this campsite is the answer; at the end of a steep and narrow track, it occupies a beautiful unspoiled natural setting on the river bank. It is well kept and offers friendly service and a small restaurant with local fare.

MODERATE

Gîte rural du Château de Lupigny – *74150 Boussy – 7km/4mi N of Alby-sur-Chéran towards Rumilly on D 31 – ☎ 04 50 01 12 01 – ✉ – 1 gîte 1/7 persons: weekly 304.90/558.42€.* At the tip of a rocky pinnacle stands a fortified building that once served as a watchtower. Guests can choose to stay in the gîte or the comfortable guest room. Anyone with an eye for fine architecture should take a moment to admire the 15C spiral staircase.

Chambre d'hôte La Ferme sur les Bois – *Le Biolley – 74150 Vaulx – 10km/6mi NE of Rumilly on D 3 – ☎ 04 50 60 54 50 – http://perso.wanadoo.fr/annecy-attelage – closed 1 Nov-Easter – ✉ – 4rms: 39.64/45.73€ – restaurant 15.24€.* This former farmhouse has been completely renovated and now features fine rooms with colourful rustic furnishings. Guests can enjoy the comfort of sitting round the open fire in the evenings. Weather permitting, there are trips around the estate in a horse-drawn cart.

Sport and leisure

A particularly exciting experience is **canoeing in the Chéran gorge** down as far as Rumilly. Book during season at the Club Alpes-Sports-Nature-Takamaka, 17 Faubourg Ste-Claire, 74000 Annecy, ☎ 04 50 45 60 61.

Leave Rumilly by D 3 going south.

★ **Alby-sur-Chéran** – This picturesque village was an important shoemaking centre housing no fewer than 200 craftsmen in the 19C. The charming triangular **place du Trophée★**, situated in the old part of Alby, is surrounded by medieval arcaded workshops, which have been tastefully restored. The **Musée de la Cordonnerie** ⊙, located inside the town hall, is devoted to the shoemaking industry. The Église Notre-Dame-de-Plainpalais (1954) has a remarkable stained-glass wall.

Leave Alby by D 3 towards Le Châtelard.

The road offers fine views of the Chéran. Beyond Cusy, where the route bears left, the Bauges Massif bars the horizon to the south. Another left turn leads to the **Pont de l'Abîme** *(see Les BAUGES)* which spans the Chéran, 94m/308ft above the river bed in a spectacular **setting★** including, to the northeast, the imposing rocky peaks of the **Tours St-Jacques**.

It is possible to drive on to the Vallon de Bellevaux along D 911 (see Les BAUGES). Alternatively, drive north on the D 5 to Gruffy after crossing the Chéran.

Musée de la Nature ⊙ – In Gruffy at the Guevin farm as you enter the village. The museum gives a good idea of traditional life in Savoie by means of the reconstruction of a 19C farm, a mountain chalet and the cheesemaking process.

Continue towards Viuz-la-Chiésaz; the dark silhouette of the **Crêt de Châtillon** (1 699m/5 574ft), the highest peak of the Semnoz Mountain, towers over the village. Roads D 141, D 241 and D 41 lead to the summit *(see Lac d'ANNECY: Excursion* ③ *).*

Drive west along D 38 to Marcellaz-Albanais.

Marcellaz-Albanais – *Go through the village towards Rumilly and turn right.*

Musée "l'Art de l'enfance" ⊙ – 🖾 This is a real treasure cave for children with magic lanterns, optical illusions, games and ancient toys.

Place du Trophée in Alby-sur-Chéran

★ **Val du Fier** *42km/26mi – allow 2 hr*

Leave Rumilly by D 31 across the Pont Édouard-André towards Lornay.

At first the road follows the Fier, then crosses it before reaching the hilltop village of Clermont.

Château de Clermont ⊙ – Built straight onto the rock at the end of the 16C, this palace in Italian Renaissance style consists of three 2-storey wings, an imposing gateway and two square towers. The gallery on the south wing offers a fine view across the Albanais.

Return to St-André along D 31 and turn right just before the factory.

★ **Val du Fier** – This is a typical transverse valley hidden under greenery, seen at its best in the late-afternoon light. The road goes through several narrow defiles including two tunnels. Just before the last tunnel, a path on the left leads to a gate barring the entrance to the **Voie romaine du Val du Fier** (Val du Fier Roman road), part of the road which, in the 1C AD, linked the Albanais region and the Rhône Valley.

Return to Rumilly via Val-de-Fier and Vallières.

From Vallières it is possible to make an interesting detour to **Vaulx** *(follow D 14 to Hauteville and D 3 to Vaulx)* and stroll through the wooded **Jardins secrets** ⊙, a pleasant succession of small gardens with fountains, pergolas and patios, which feel more Andalucian than alpine.

ALBERTVILLE

Population 17 340
Michelin map 333 L3 and 244 folds 19 and 20
Local ap see BEAUFORT

Lying at the entrance of the Arly Valley, Albertville is the converging point of several scenic roads leading to the Beaufortain and Tarentaise areas. Conflans, perched on a rocky spur overlooking the confluence of the River Isère and River Arly, was the economic centre until eclipsed by its former satellite in the 18C; the old town is well worth visiting.

Nearby Sights: ANNECY, Lac d'ANNECY, Massif des ARAVIS, Les BAUGES, BEAUFORT, La Vallée des BELLEVILLE, Route de la MADELEINE, MEGÈVE, La TARENTAISE

SIGHTS

The Olympic City

In 1992, Albertville hosted the opening and closing ceremonies of the 16th Winter Olympic Games while events took place in nearby resorts. It was the third time since 1924 that the games had been held in the French Alps.

Olympic venues – The venue where the opening and closing ceremonies were staged is now a sports and leisure park where major events are held.

Eating out

MODERATE

La Tour de Pacoret – *73460 Grésy-sur-Isère – 14km/9mi SO of Albertville on N 90 then D 201 via Frontenex – ☎ 04 79 37 91 59 – closed end Oct-beginning of May, Tues except evening in Jul-Aug, Mon in Oct and Tue – 19.06/45.73€.* This squat old watchtower retains its fine original façade with its narrow apertures. It occupies an outstanding site on a rocky promontory between the valley and the mountains, which is worth a detour in itself. The sumptuously decorated rooms contrast with the austerity of the setting.

Where to stay

MODERATE

Hôtel Le Roma – *Rte de Chambéry – 4km/2.5mi SO of Alberville – ☎ 04 79 37 15 56 – 🅿 – 134rms: 45.73/80.80€ - ☲ 8.38€ – restaurant 19.51/27.75€.* This is a vast hotel complex near the bypass. The swimming pool, gym and tennis court lend it a holiday atmosphere. There is a pizzeria and a more classic restaurant, La Montgolfière. The rooms are all comfortable, but those that have been restored have the edge.

The **Halle olympique** (Olympic stadium) is a training centre for the French ice-hockey team as well as a public ice-skating rink and a venue for the European Ice-skating Championship.

The **Anneau de vitesse** (Speed rink) has become a sports stadium hosting regional competitions.

The **Maison des 16ᵉˢ Jeux olympiques** (16th Olympic Games Centre ⊘) houses an exhibition devoted to the 1992 Olympic Games with audio-visual support.

Le Dôme – Designed by Jean-Jacques Moisseau, this new cultural centre stands on place de l'Europe and comprises a theatre, a multimedia reference library and a cinema with a panoramic screen.

★ Conflans *allow 45min*

Drive north across the pont des Adoubes and up the montée Adolphe-Hugues; leave the car in the car park on the right; continue on foot as indicated below.

Château Manuel de Locatel ⊘ – This 16C castle, recently restored, overlooks the new town of Albertville. Note the 17C ceiling painted by an Italian artist.

Conflans

Porte de Savoie – Before going through the gate, admire the lovely **view**★ of the building dominated by the slender Tour Ramus and of the charming 18C fountain.

Rue Gabriel-Pérouse – This is the former "Grande-Rue" (High Street), lined with medieval workshops still occupied by craftsmen.

Turn left to go up to the church.

Church – This hall-church is in authentic 18C style; the nave, which consists of four bays, is prolonged by a chancel with a flat east end. The carved **pulpit**, dating from 1718, is remarkable; note also the baptismal font and the retable over the high altar.

Return to rue Gabriel-Pérouse, which leads to the Grande Place.

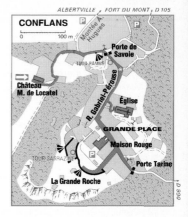

★ **Grande Place** – A lovely 18C fountain decorates the centre of this picturesque square, lined on one side with a 14C brick building, known as **Maison rouge** ⊙, which houses the municipal **museum**. This offers reconstructions of Savoyard homes, local religious statues, regional furniture, traditional tools and weapons and local documents.

The **Porte Tarine** has kept watch over the town and the route de la Tarentaise since the 14C.

La Grande Roche – This terraced area shaded by ancient lime trees, overlooks the confluence of the River Isère and River Arly, offering fine views of the Combe de Savoie depression with the rocky peaks of the Chartreuse Massif in the distance.

EXCURSION

★★ Route du Fort du Mont *29km/18mi – about 1hr 30min*

From the Porte de Savoie in Conflans, drive along D 105. (Snow may block this steeply rising road between December and April).

The road climbs continuously, soon offering a panoramic view of the Doron and Arly valleys with the pyramid-like Mont Charvin in the distance to the north.
Higher up, a wide bend forms a good **belvedere** over the Basse Tarentaise Valley which narrows between Feissons and Aigueblanche.
Continue past the Fort du Mont to the second hairpin bend at les Croix (two chalets stand nearby - alt 1 120m/3 675ft). There are fine **views**★★ of pastures in the foreground, the Combe de Savoie, through which flows the River Isère, and the Mont Blanc Massif.

Return by the forest road on the left towards Molliessoulaz. From Molliessoulaz, a path leads down into the Doron Valley and joins up with D 925 which takes you back to Albertville.

Route du Col de Tamié *40km/25mi – allow 2hr*

From Albertville to Faverges – *D 104 towards Faverges.* The Col de Tamié between the Massif des Bauges and the Dent de Cons links the area around Annecy to the Combe de Savoie and the Tarentaise. The road winds upwards towards the Col de Ramaz and a view of the Combe de Savoie. *Turn onto the first road on the right; follow the sign for "Plateau des Teppes".*

★ **Plateau des Teppes** – Beyond la Ramaz there is a fine view of the Abbaye de Tamié. *Park the car on the second bend and continue on foot along the path to your right (15min there and back).* Climb to the top of a small rise beyond the wood for a delightful **view**★ of Albertville.

Return to the Col de Ramaz and continue towards Col de Tamié.

Below the Fort de Tamié, a fine, extended **view**★ opens up just before the pass: Abbeville at the confluence of the Arly and the Isère. The abbey comes into view immediately on the other side of the Col de Tamié.

Abbaye de Tamié – *Only the church is open to the public.* Founded in 1132 and rebuilt at the end of the 17C, the abbey stood empty for 70 years until, in 1861, a Cistercian community settled here. The monks make a famous cheese, known simply as Tamié; an audio-visual presentation gives a flavour of everyday life at the abbey.

Continue towards Faverges. The road runs around part of the Sambuy, which can be reached by chair-lift from Vargnoz. *(See Lac d'ANNECY, ②)*

Faverges – *(see Lac d'ANNECY, ①)*

ALLEVARD♨

Population 3 081
Michelin map 333 J5 and 244 fold 29
Local maps see below and Le GRÉSIVAUDAN

Allevard, lying in the green Bréda Valley, at an altitude of 475m/1 558ft, is the starting point for numerous excursions. The jagged ridges of the Allevard Massif (highest peak: Puy Gris, 2 908m/9 541ft), which are covered with snow for the greatest part of the year, give the whole area a genuine Alpine atmosphere. The vast forests of conifers covering the lower slopes from 1 500m/4 921ft are the main attraction of mountain resorts of the upper Bréda Valley such as Le Curtillard.

Nearby Sights: Les BAUGES, CHAMBÉRY, Massif de CHAMROUSSE, Massif de la CHARTREUSE, Le GRÉSIVAUDAN, ST-PIERRE-DE-CHARTREUSE

BACKGROUND

The **Chaîne de Belledonne**, which forms part of the central massifs *(see Introduction: Formation of the Alps)*, overlooks the Isère Valley from Allevard to the Croix de Chamrousse towering above Grenoble. Its highest point is the Rocher Blanc (2 928m/9 606ft), and it only includes two small glaciers.

Allevard established itself as a local iron smelting centre as early as the 13C, and although the industry has long since moved on, a museum, a themed walk and the remains of the smelting-houses are reminders of the town's metalworking past.

It was after an earthquake in 1791 that the Allevardins discovered the local "black water" and its curative properties: the natural traces of carbon and sulphur compounds aid the treatment of respiratory complaints. The baths, a striking architectural mix of the classical and the oriental, are the centre of a popular spa resort.

EXCURSIONS

★★① **Route du Collet** *10km/6.2mi – about 30min – see local map*

Leave Allevard by D 525ᴬ to Fond-de-France. Turn left after 1.4km/0.9mi onto D 109.

Hairpin bends afford a series of glimpses of Allevard and its immediate surroundings, of the Veyton and Gleyzin valleys separated by the Pic de Gleyzin and finally of the upper Bréda Valley. As the road reaches the winter sports resort of **Le Collet d'Allevard** (1 450m/4 757ft), it reveals a vast panoramic view embracing the Vercors, Chartreuse and Bauges massifs as well as the Grésivaudan, Chambéry and Combe de Savoie depressions. The view is even better 3km/1.9mi further on from the summit of **Grand Collet** (1 920m/6 299ft), which can be reached by chair-lift.

② **Chartreuse de St-Hugon**

8.5km/5.3mi, then 1hr there and back on foot – see local map

Leave Allevard by D 525 north, turn right onto D 209 then right again after the bridge across the Buisson.

The road gives panoramic views of the Combe de Savoie and Massif des Bauges before following the Bens Valley.

In the Buddhist centre at Chartreuse de St-Hugon

After 6.5km/4mi, ignore D 109 on your right and park the car near the St-Hugon forest lodge

🚶 *1hr there and back. Continue on foot along the forest track for 1.5km/0.9mi then, near a corrugated iron hut, turn left onto a path leading down to Pont Sarret (boots may be needed after a thaw or heavy rain).*

Pont Sarret – This bridge spans the Bens in a pleasant forest setting with the foaming torrent below.

Cross the bridge and follow the path uphill on the opposite bank of the Bens.

Chartreuse de St-Hugon ⊙ – Nothing remains of the Carthusian monastery founded in the 12C except a 17C building with a Gothic-style pediment surmounted by a wrought-iron fan light, now occupied by a Buddhist centre, the most important of its kind in Europe; the Dalai Lama visited it several times.

Continue along the path and bear left at the fork.

Pont du Diable – The engraved stone on this 200-year-old bridge used to mark the border between France and Piedmont.

Cross the bridge to rejoin the road and return to the lodge on the right.

★ ③ Vallée des Huiles

50km/31mi round tour – about 2hr 30min – see local map

Leave Allevard by D 525 north then bear right on D 925 towards Albertville.

La Rochette – The cardboard factories of this industrial town and tourist centre are among the largest in Europe.

Drive east towards Étable for 1km/0.6mi and turn right.

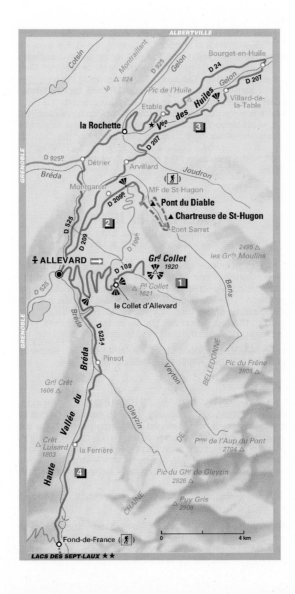

The road climbs through the upper Gelon Valley, known as the Vallée des Huiles, along the cultivated slope of the valley which contrasts with the forested slope opposite. Upstream from Étable stands the solitary Pic de l'Huile which gave its name to the whole valley; "Huile" is derived from a local form of the word *aiguille*, or needle.

Continue on the D 24 towards to Bourget-en-Huile and turn left along D 207 towards Allevard.

After crossing the Gelon, the road winds along the forested slope of the valley. Just beyond Villard there is a fine view of the basin of La Rochette and the lower Bréda Valley leading to the Grésivaudan. Woods give way to pastures dotted with walnuts and chestnuts as one approaches the lovely village of Arvillard.

Return to Allevard along D 209.

HIKE

4 **Haute Vallée du Bréda** *17km/10.6mi – about 30min – see local map*

Follow D 525ᴬ to Fond-de-France.

This excursion through restful landscapes is popular with tourists taking the waters in Allevard. **Fond-de-France** (alt 1 089m/3 573ft) is the ideal starting point for mountain hikes.

** **Hike to the Lacs des Sept-Laux** *– Leave the car in Fond-de-France in front of the Sept-Laux hotel. This trip is suitable for experienced hikers: 3hr 45min climb; 1 150m/3 773ft difference in altitude; it is advisable to wear mountain boots.*
Most of the walk is through woodland *(follow the yellow and then yellow and red markings)*. At the halfway mark, take the less demanding Sentier des deux Ruisseaux track. Beyond the Lac Noir *(2hr 30min walk)* the hike is easier and quite pleasant, as the path skirts several **glacial lakes, Lac Carré, Lac de la Motte, Lac de Cottepens** and **Lac du Cos**★★. *Walk along the Lac de Cottepens towards the Col des Sept-Laux; bear left where you see yellow, white and red markings on a rock.* A steep path, not easy to spot, leads through pastureland and rocks up to a mound overlooking the small Lac Blanc and affording a stunning **panorama**★★★ of the Sept-Laux, of the Eau d'Olle Valley and of numerous peaks and ridges all around. Walkers with energy to spare can follow the path along the edge of the pasture for a further 10min to a mountain lake.

L'ALPE-D'HUEZ✳✳

Michelin map 333 J7 and 244 fold 40
Local map see Bassin du BOURG-D'OISANS

L'Alpe-d'Huez, lying at an altitude of 1 860m/6 102ft, more than 1 000m/3 281ft above the Bourg-d'Oisans Valley, is one of the most attractive winter sports resorts in the French Alps. In summer, L'Alpe-d'Huez is the starting point of fascinating **hikes** and mountaineering expeditions in the Massif des Grandes Rousses, and the end of one of the most famously gruelling climbs of the Tour de France cycle race, with 21 numbered hairpin bends leading up to the top. The resort comprises numerous large chalet-style hotels close to the swimming-pool and the summer pastures.

Nearby Sights: Le BOURG-D'OISANS, Massif de CHAMROUSSE, Route de la CROIX-DE-FER, Route du GALIBIER, La GRAVE, L'OISANS, Le VALBONNAIS

THE RESORT

Ski area – L'Alpe-d'Huez (1 120-3 330m/ 3 675-10 925ft) is the most important ski resort in Dauphiné. Although its ski area is not so extensive as that of other resorts in the Tarentaise region, it has developed considerably and there are now more than 100 Alpine ski runs including 10 black pistes, plus 6 cross-country runs. The spectacular course of some of these attracts daring skiers. The main attraction of L'Alpe-d'Huez is that it is linked with nearby resorts: Villard-Reculas, Auris-en-Oisans, Oz-en-Oisans and Vaujany. In July, the Sarennes Glacier provides a thrilling black piste when snow cover is adequate.

SIGHTS

Musée d'Huez et de l'Oisans ⊘ *– Route de la Poste.* This municipal museum displays objects discovered since 1977 on the **Brandes** archaeological site (near the airfield). The remains of a 13C-14C silver mine were unearthed. There are also exhibits concerning traditional life in the Oisans area, local fauna and flora.

Centre Notre-Dame-des-Neiges – The modern rotunda-like building (1970), surmounted by a spiral roof, houses a meeting centre and a crypt which serves as a parish church and a concert venue ⊙. Twelve decorative windows represent scenes from St Mark's Gospel. The organ is particularly noteworthy.

★**Route de Villars-Reculas** – *4km/2.5mi along D 211ᴮ – local map see Bassin du BOURG-D'OISANS.* This steep road offers bird's-eye views of the Bassin du Bourg-d'Oisans below.

Eating out

EXPENSIVE

La Cabane du Poutat – *Access on foot (40min) from the Marmottes cable-car station – 38750 L'Alpe-d'Huez – ☎ 04 76 80 42 88 – closed May-Nov – reservations compulsory in the evenings – 42.69/48.78€.* A good breath of fresh air is guaranteed in this chalet-restaurant at 2 100m/6 890ft on the pistes. It can also be accessed in the evening via snow-scooter or snowcat ("ratrak"). An à la carte selection of regional specialities is served on the terrace in the middle of the ski slopes or in the wood-panelled dining room.

Where to stay

EXPENSIVE

Le Mariandre – *Pl. Paganon – 38750 L'Alpe-d'Huez – ☎ 04 76 80 66 03 – closed 29 Apr-30 Jun and Sept-Nov – ▣ – 26rms: from 73.94€ - ⊑ 9.91€ – restaurant 20.58/36.59€.* You are at the heart of the resort here, within yards of the ski lifts. The atmosphere in this chalet is cosy, with a lounge, fireplace and library. Several of the rooms face south and have a terrace with the obligatory mountain view! Simple fare.

Hôtel Au Chamois d'Or – *Rd-pt des Pistes – 38750 L'Alpe-d'Huez – ☎ 04 76 80 31 32 – closed 22 Apr-19 Dec – ▣ – 44rms: from 201.23€ - ⊑ 12.96€ – restaurant 35.83/44.21€.* This imposing chalet with the modern façade is located at the highest point of the resort, overlooking the Pic du lac Blanc and Grandes Rousses slopes. After exerting yourself on your skis you can relax on the south-facing terrace with a view of the Oisans glaciers or in the lounge with its pleasant mountain chalet decor.

HIKES

★★★**Pic du Lac Blanc** ⊙ – *Access is by means of two successive gondola rides followed by a cable car ride.* The **Dôme des Petites Rousses★★** can be reached from the Lac Blanc (▨ *1hr there and back*.)

★★★**Pic du Lac Blanc** – Alt 3 323m/10 902ft. *As you come out of the cable-car (viewing table), there is a sweeping* view, *from left to right, of Les Deux-Alpes, Lac* Lauvitel, Mont Ventoux (in the distance), L'Alpe-d'Huez (below), Le Taillefer, as well as the Belledonne and Chartreuse massifs. *Go to the main platform and climb on to a mound (viewing table).* The **panoramic view★★** is even wider, with Pic Bayle in the foreground and, in the distance, the heights of the Maurienne and the peaks of the Vanoise and Écrins massifs.

★**La Grande Sure** ⊙ **(or Le Signal)** – Alt 2 114m/6 936ft. *Access by the Grande Sure chairlift in winter and on foot (▨2hr there and back) in summer.* Extensive **views** of the Grandes Rousses range, the Oisans region, the Taillefer Mountain and the Belledonne range.

★**Lac Besson** – *6.5km/4mi by the road leading to Col de Poutran in the north.* The road winds through pastures, reaches Col de Poutran and L'Alpe-d'Huez basin and, beyond, a high plateau dotted with glacial lakes. From Lac Besson, the most picturesque of these lakes, it is possible to climb on foot up to a ridge which reveals **Lac Noir** below in wild surroundings. A path *(30min there and back)* goes round the lake, offering more impressive views.

ANNECY★★★

Conurbation 136 815   -
Michelin map 328 J5 and 244 folds 18 and 19
Local maps see Lac d'ANNECY and Massif des ARAVIS

Annecy lies on the shores of the Lac d'Annecy, water and mountains blending admirably to form one of the most remarkable landscapes in the French Alps, equally unforgettable in summer and winter: there is a fine overall view from the height crowned by the castle and overlooking the town

If the shores of the lake, the River Thiou and the Vassé canal have earned it the nickname of "the Venice of Savoie", the colourful streets of Old Annecy have a Piedmontese air; a charming combination which perhaps explains why the Annéciens seem to understand the art of living well.

Nearby sights: L'ALBANAIS, ALBERTVILLE, AIX-LES-BAINS, Lac d'ANNECY, Massif des ARAVIS, Les BAUGES, Lac du BOURGET, CHAMBÉRY, La CLUSAZ, La ROCHE-SUR-FORON, THORENS-GLIÈRES

HISTORICAL NOTES

Beginnings – The site was occupied as far back as prehistoric times (a lake settlement stood where the harbour is now situated). The town, which owes its name to a Roman villa, Villa Aniciaca, developed round its castle from the 12C onwards under the name of Annecy-le-Neuf, to distinguish it from the neighbouring Gallo-Roman city of Annecy-le-Vieux. It gained in importance in the 16C when it replaced Geneva as the regional capital.

Humanist and spiritual father – The outstanding religious and literary figure of Annecy is **François de Sales** (1567-1622). Born in the nearby Château de Sales *(see THORENS-GLIÈRES)*, he studied law before being ordained in Annecy at the age of 26. His reputation as a gifted preacher and a vigorous denouncer of Calvinism soon spread all over France; de Sales was created bishop of Geneva but could not hope to hold sway in the heartland of the Reformation and based himelf in Annecy. In 1608, François de Sales published his *Introduction à la vie dévote* (Introduction to a Life of Piety). His belief that man could live a pious life without withdrawing from the secular world met with such success that forty editions were sold in the author's lifetime. Having perceived the usefulness of a congregation devoted to the poor and the sick, he met Jeanne de Chantal, the ancestor of Madame de Sévigné, who later founded the first Convent of the Visitation of the Virgin. François de Sales was canonised in 1665 and **Jeanne de Chantal** in 1767. Their relics are kept in the basilica of the Visitation.

Jean-Jacques the proselyte – In 1728, the sixteen year-old **Jean-Jacques Rousseau**, ill-treated by his employer, fled from his home town, Geneva, to Annecy; there he was dazzled and disarmed by **Madame de Warens**, who had been asked to convert him to Catholicism. Her task was easy for he was 'sure that a religion preached by such a missionary could not fail to lead him to Paradise'. Readers of the *Confessions* can see the place where they first met in the Ancien Palais Épiscopal.

★★ THE LAKESHORE *2hr*

Leave the car in the car park of Centre Bonlieu or on place de l'Hôtel-de-ville. From Quai Eustache-Chappuis on the Canal du Vassé or place de la Libération head towards avenue d'Albigny.

Centre Bonlieu – This cultural centre, designed in 1981 by Novarina, houses the Maison du Tourisme, the library, the theatre and several shops.

Avenue d'Albigny – This royal avenue, lined with hundred-year-old plane trees, crosses the common where the townspeople used to take a stroll. The concrete and glass law courts (1978), built by Novarina, stand to the left.

Walk across the Champ de Mars to the viewing table by the lake.

There is an extensive **view★** of the Grand Lac framed by mountains, with Mont Veyrier and the Crêt du Maure in the foreground.

Parc de l'Impérial – *follow ② on the map.* Shaded by beautiful trees, this pleasant park (2ha/ 5 acres) at the east end of Avenue d'Abigny takes its name from a former luxury hotel, now the conference centre. Work up a sweat in the largest sports centre on the lake or relax to the sound of birdsong at the aviary.

Return to the town along the lake shore.

Pont des Amours – The bridge spans the Canal du Vassé, offering lovely views of the shaded canal one way, dotted with small crafts, and of the wooded Île des Cygnes the other way.

Eating out

MODERATE

Le Fréti – *12 r. Ste-Claire* – ☎ *04 50 51 29 52* – *closed Mon except school holidays* – *16.77/22.87€*. This establishment at the heart of the old town is above the arcades and the family-run cheese-making business, from which issue mouth-watering specialities and the scent of raclettes, fondues and tartiflettes to tempt food-lovers. Simple decor. Summer terrace.

Le Chalet Savoyard – Le Matafan – *Quai de l'Évêché* – ☎ *04 50 45 53 87* – *closed Sun from 1 May-15 Sept and Mon from 15 Sept-30 Apr* – *18.29/30.49€*. Picture this: in summer, you're on the terrace of this canal-side restaurant enjoying the fresh air and elegant ballet of the swans... in winter, you are cosily installed in the warm decor of the interior amid a variety of antiques, knick-knacks and hunting trophies.

Brasserie St-Maurice – *7 r. Collège-Chapuisien* – ☎ *04 50 51 24 49* – *closed Sun* – *21.04/39.64€*. This house dates from 1675 and now houses a restaurant. Practically as soon as the sun has risen, regulars and tourists settle themselves on the terrace. The dining room is on the first floor and features stone and wood-panelled decor. Cuisine is contemporary with Provençal overtones.

Auberge de Savoie – *1 pl. St-François-de-Sales* – ☎ *04 50 45 03 05* – *closed 1-10 Jan, 18-26 Apr, Tue evening and Wed except Jul-Aug* – *22.56/41.92€*. The windows of this inn overlook a charming paved square opposite the Palais de l'Isle. The sophistication of the contemporary decor in the old inn building is complemented by a menu specialising in fish and seafood.

L'Atelier Gourmand – *2 r. St-Maurice* – ☎ *04 50 51 19 71* – *closed 2-10 Jan, 27 Aug-5 Sept, Sun and Mon* - *29.73/44.97€*. Visitors here can feast their eyes as well as their palate. The owner, a painter in his day, puts up an impressive performance as chef, producing mouth-watering French cuisine. The tastefully decorated dining room is hung with Italian inspired paintings.

Where to stay

BUDGET

Chambre d'hôte Au Gîte Savoisien – *98 rte de Corbier* – *74650 Chavanod* – *6km/4mi SE of Annecy on D 16 towards Rumilly, Le Corbier's village* – ☎ *04 50 69 02 95* – *http://ourworld.compuserve.com/homepages/gite-savoisien* – ⊠ – *reservation recommended* – *4rms* ⌖ *36.59/42.69€* – *restaurant 15.24€*. This old farm on the slopes above Annecy in the village centre has been converted into guestrooms and a gîte and offers simple and comfortable accommodation. In summer, guests can relax and sunbathe in the garden with a view of the mountains, or join in a local game of pétanque.

MODERATE

Hôtel Kyriad – *1 fg des Balmettes* – ☎ *04 50 45 04 12* – *24rms: 45.43/54.58* ⌖ *5.79€*. Part of this modern hotel at the entrance to the pedestrian zone in the shopping district of the old town occupies a 16C building. Service is attentive. Public car park nearby.

Les Terrasses – *15 r. L.-Chaumontel* – ☎ *04 50 57 08 98* – 🄿 – *20rms: 57.93€* - ⌖ *16.10€* – *restaurant 12.96€*. This new hotel is located in a quiet district quite near the station. Its rooms are furnished in pale wood. The restaurant offers a single menu which is changed every day. On fine days, patrons can eat on the terrace in the sun, or in the peace and quiet of the garden. Prices are very reasonable out of season.

Hôtel Marquisats – *6 chemin Colmyr* – ☎ *04 50 51 52 34* – 🄿 – *22rms: 60.98/91.47€* - ⌖ *8.38€*. This old residential building with the pink façade in a cul-de-sac slightly out of town is a peaceful place to stay. Some of its rooms overlook the lake, others the forest. They are modern and comfortably furnished. Warm welcome.

EXPENSIVE

L'Impérial Palace – *32 av. d'Albigny* – ☎ *04 50 09 30 00* – 🄿 – *91rms: from 167.69€* - ⌖ *24.39€* – *restaurant 26.73/74.70€*. This palace on the lake shore boasts contemporary decor and a fine 1900 façade, vast luxurious rooms, attentive service and a casino. In short it is a dream world! We recommend dining on the terrace or having a drink by the open fireplace.

On the town

Au Chardon d'Écosse – *10 r. Vaugelas* – ☎ *04 50 51 24 31* – *daily 6pm-4am.* This bar has wood panelling and the atmosphere of a pub. It gets very lively at the end of office hours and when the shops close. Numerous locals come here for their aperitif or finish off their evening with one of the house cocktails, to the mellow strains of jazz music.

Au Fidèle Berger – *2 r. Royale* – ☎ *04 50 45 00 32* – *Tues-Sat 8.45am-7.15pm; Wed 10am-7.15pm – closed for a week in Nov.* This comfortable salon de thé attracts a chic clientele to sample its home-baked pastries and sip delicately at a cup of tea or coffee. Foodies will find it hard to resist following their example once they have seen the display window with its tantalising chocolate fountain.

BHV (Brasserie de l'Hôtel de Ville) – *Pl. de l'Hôtel-de-Ville* – ☎ *04 50 45 83 01* – *daily 11am-2am.* This popular address is on the edge of the old town opposite the landing stage. Local residents and tourists compete for a seat on the terrace, while night owls jostle shoulders in the lively evening events held at the end of the week.

Café des Arts – *4 passage de l'Isle* – ☎ *04 50 51 56 40* – *winter: daily from 9.30am; summer: daily 8.30am-2am.* This café with its slightly retro charm is located in the courtyard of the old prison, providing an oasis of calm at the heart of the old town. There are cartoon strips available to read free of charge, and a pleasant terrace in summer.

Pub Médiéval – *14 r. Perrière* – ☎ *04 50 51 27 06* – *daily 2pm-3am in winter; 11am-3am in summer.* The medieval style trappings, with weapons, armour and tartans in different Scottish clan colours, are supposed to evoke the Celtic atmosphere of the Arthurian legend. In the evening, there is often quite a scrum to get to the bar, so elbows at the ready! Summer terrace.

L'Auberge du Lac – *Le port* – *74290 Veyrier-du-Lac* – ☎ *04 50 60 10 15* – *daily from 8am – closed Dec, Jan and Feb.* This well reputed establishment boasts a magnificent terrace at the water's edge, opposite a stunning backdrop.

Show time

Dinecitta – *Rte Nationale* – *74320 Sévrier* – *towards Albertville* – ☎ *04 50 52 41 00* – *daily 8.30pm-4am.* Small Far West town setting with waiting staff dressed up as cowboys, with regular cabaret evenings alternating variety acts with an orchestra playing dance numbers. A DJ takes up the reins until 4am.

Shopping

Marché de la rue Ste-Claire – *R. Ste-Claire* – *Sun morning.* This market, considered to be one of the finest in France, is held in the historic town centre of Annecy and draws record crowds in the summer season. Cheese market every Tues.

Sport

For a beginner's course in canyoning or rock-climbing, contact the **Bureau des guides**, Centre Bonlieu, ☎ 04 50 45 00 33. The Club nautique de Doussard (☎ 04 50 44 81 45) offers a choice of water sports as does the Ski club nautique in Sévrier. The Col de la Forclaz is the favourite haunt of paragliders (first flight from the "Chalet du Mini-golf" in Montmin).

Rental of sports equipment – "Locasport", 37 avenue de Loverchy, in Annecy and "Ogier Sports" in La Clusaz.

Bathing in the lake – Many beaches *(free or with admission charge)* line the shores of the lake: "Plage d'Albigny" *(admission charge)*, "Plage des Marquisats" and "Plage du Petit Port" *(free)* in Annecy.

★ **Jardins de l'Europe** – These gardens, which used to form an island, were joined to the town and laid out as an arboretum with a variety of species from Europe, America and Asia including several huge **sequoias** and a ginkgo biloba, also called "maidenhair tree". From the harbour along the Thiou there are interesting views of the massive castle.

Walk to place de l'Hôtel-de-ville and continue on foot through Old Annecy.

★★ **OLD ANNECY** *1hr 30min – see plan*

The old part of town has been largely pedestrianised and renovated during the last few decades. Note the arcaded houses and Italian-style wells. A colourful market *(wide choice of regional cheeses)*, held on Tuesday, Friday and Sunday mornings, brings life to rue de la République and rue Ste-Claire.

Start from place de l'Hôtel-de-ville and walk across quai E.-Chappuis.

Église St-Maurice – The church was built in the 15C with a large overhanging roof in typical regional style. Inside, the vast Gothic nave, traditional in churches with a Dominican connection, is flanked with side chapels built by aristocratic families or guilds, whose arms and emblems are displayed. The town's tailors, for example, marked their chapel, the second on the right, with a pair of scissors. Note in particular a 16C fresco of the Assumption near the pulpit and, in the chancel, a fine **Deposition**★ by Pieter Pourbus the Elder and a remarkable **mural painting** in *grisaille* dating from 1458.

Walk towards the river past the Église St-François.

Église St-François – St François de Sales and St Jeanne de Chantal were originally buried in this Baroque-fronted 17C church which once belonged to the order they founded; grilles in the transepts still mark the places where they were originally laid to rest. The Église St-François is now the parish church of the Italian community.

Cross the bridge over the River Thiou, which is the natural outlet of the lake.

Pont sur le Thiou – The picturesque **Palais de l'Isle★★** standing in the middle of the river offers the most famous **view★★** of Old Annecy.

Continue along rue Perrière.

Rue Perrière – The houses are built over a row of arcades.

Turn right, then right again and cross the Thiou once more.

From the bridge, enjoy a lovely view of the houses lining the river bank. The entrance of the Palais de l'Isle is on the right.

★ **Palais de l'Isle** ⊙ – This monument has become a local emblem. Built on an island in the 12C, when Annecy was little more than a market town, the palace was used in turn as the Count of Geneva's residence, the mint, the law courts and a fearsome prison, which it remained until 1870, resuming that grim role for a time during the Second World War.

It now houses the **Musée de l'Histoire d'Annecy**, illustrating the town's prestigious past and the history of Savoie; the cells, kitchen and prison are open to visitors.

Turn left along quai de l'Isle, cross the Pont Morens and turn right.

★ **Rue Ste-Claire** – The high street of Old Annecy is lined with arcaded houses. The 16C mansion at **no 18** has a particular link to the bishopric of St François de Sales. Thirty years before Richelieu's Académie Française was inaugurated, de Sales became the co-founder of the Académie Florimontane, a literary institution intended to promote the public good, influence opinion and spread the cult of beauty. The society still meets to this day.
On the corner of rue de la République stands a former convent of St Clare which became known as the **"Manufacture"** when it was turned into a spinning mill in 1805. The whole area has been tastefully renovated and pedestrianised; the lively placette Ste-Claire and place Volland contrast with the peaceful quai des Clarisses.

Turn back at the Porte Ste-Claire and walk along rue de la République to rue Jean-Jacques-Rousseau.

Ancien palais épiscopal – It was built in 1784, on the site of Madame de Warens' house; a bust of Rousseau stands in the courtyard. St François de Sales wrote his famous *Introduction à la vie dévote* (Introduction to a Life of Piety) in the 16C **Maison Lambert**, at no 15 rue Jean-Jacques-Rousseau.

Cathédrale St-Pierre – Built in the 16C with a Renaissance façade and a Gothic interior, it became the cathedral of Bishop François de Sales. Jean-Jacques Rousseau sang in the choir and played the flute in the cathedral.

Turn left onto rue Filaterie lined with imposing arcades.

Continuing past the Église Notre-Dame-de-Liesse with its tower which leans slightly, one reaches rue du Pâquier, also lined with arcades; the 17C Hôtel de Sales, decorated with sculptures illustrating the Seasons, is at no 12.

Turn right onto quai E-Chappuis to return to place de l'Hôtel-de-ville.

★ MUSÉE-CHÂTEAU D'ANNECY ⊘

Access by car via chemin de la Tour la Reine, or on foot, up the castle ramp or the steep hill starting to rise from rue Ste-Claire.
This handsomely restored former residence of the lords of Geneva, from a junior branch of the House of Savoie, dates from the 12C to the 16C. The castle was damaged by fire several times, abandoned in the 17C then used as a garrison before being restored with the help of public funds. There is a fine view of the clustered roofs of the old town and its four church steeples and, beyond them, the modern town.

The old town

To the right of the entrance stands the massive 12C Tour de la Reine, with 4m/13ft-thick walls; this is the oldest part of the castle. From the centre of the courtyard, one faces the austere living quarters of the Logis Vieux (14C-15C), with its stair turret and deep well; to the left is the early Renaissance façade of the Logis Nemours (16C) and to the right the late-16C **Logis Neuf**, which housed the garrison of the castle. At the end of the courtyard are the recently restored 15C Logis and **Tour Perrière**, which house the **Observatoire régional des lacs alpins** ⊘, illustrating the various aspects of mountain lakes including the effects of pollution on the fauna and displaying archaeological finds. In the **Salle des fresques**, on the top level, fragments of 15C murals give a good idea of what the medieval castle was like.

From the terrace, there is a good overall view of Old Annecy and of the modern town beyond.

The Logis Vieux and the Logis Nemours house an interesting **regional museum** on three floors linked by a spiral staircase. Note the remarkable fireplaces facing each other in the vast kitchen, the splendid guardroom with its rows of columns and the great hall. There are collections of contemporary art, carved glass and popular art including pottery, earthenware, glassware and furniture.

Revival of the ecosystem of the Lac d'Annecy

In spite of the many mountain streams which flow into it, the fairly shallow lake (30-45m/98-148ft deep) had lost most of its bird population by the end of the 1960s as pollution from hotels along the shores and from motor boats had upset its fragile ecosystem. The local municipalities clubbed together to build an impressive network of underwater drainpipes leading to an ultra-modern filtering plant.

This action, combined with collective awareness of the dangers of pollution, led to the lake waters becoming pure again. Char and trout have come back and swans are nesting in the reeds once more.

The **Réserve naturelle du Bout-du-Lac**, situated at the western end of the lake, shelters reptiles, ducks, swans and beavers.

ADDITIONAL SIGHTS

Conservatoire d'Art et d'Histoire de la Haute-Savoie ⊘ – This art and history museum, situated just south of the castle, is housed in a fine 17C building in Sardinian style. The collections include numerous paintings and engravings depicting landscapes of Haute-Savoie, as well as 18C and 19C paintings.

Basilique de la Visitation ⊘ – The church of the Couvent de la Visitation stands on the slopes of Crêt du Maure, affording a vast open vista of Annecy and the western Préalpes. The richly decorated interior of the 1930 building with its sturdy grey-marble pillars attracts many pilgrims, particularly for the feast-day of St François on 24 January and in August. The relics of St François de Sales and St Jeanne de Chantal are displayed at the end of the aisles; the stained-glass windows illustrate the life of the patron saints of Annecy as does the small **museum** adjoining the church on the right. The church has a peal of 38 bells.

Basilique St-Joseph-des-Fins ⊘ – Designed by the Benedictine architect Dom Bellot just before the Second World War, this church is plain outside with a few regional features such as its onion-shaped spire and large steep roof. By contrast, there is a wealth of interior decoration illustrating many teachings from the Bible (chancel, high altar, stained glass, baptistery, triumphal arch). Note the lovely 15C Virgin Mary in a side chapel and the 15C Christ in the baptistery.

Parc de l'Impérial – This park, situated at the eastern end of avenue d'Albigny and covering an area of 2ha/5 acres shaded by beautiful trees, includes an aviary, a sports centre and a former hotel turned into a conference centre.

★★★**Lake cruises** ⊘ – The Compagnie des bateaux d'Annecy organises various trips on the lake aboard their launches with stops in several ports: Veyrier, Menthon, Duingt, St-Jorioz and Sévrier. The *Libellule*, a panoramic boat with a capacity of 600 passengers, offers lunch-cruise and dinner-show combinations; departure from the pier along the Thiou in Annecy.

EXCURSION

★★**Gorges du Fier and Château de Montrottier**
20km/12.4mi – about 2hr 30min.

Leave Annecy by N 508; 3km further on, beyond the motorway underpass, turn left on D 14. Turn left again past the Église de Lovagny along D 64 and drive down a steep hill.

★★ **Gorges du Fier** ⊙ – Visitors can walk along galleries clinging to the sheer walls of the gorge; sunlight plays through the foliage which forms an arched roof over the narrow defile. Beyond the exit and a cluster of beeches, there is a belvedere on a rocky promontory which affords a good view of the "Mer de Rochers" (sea of rocks), an impressive heap of boulders piled on top of one another.

Drive back to the D 116 junction and turn left then right up the path leading to the Château de Montrottier.

★ **Château de Montrottier** ⊙ – The castle stands on an isolated mound between the Fier and its former bed, known as the "Grande Fosse". Built between the 13C and the 16C, it is a fine specimen of Savoyard military architecture; a 36m/118ft-tall round keep towers over it. The castle houses important **collections**★ bequeathed in 1916 by the former owner to the Académie Florimontane: weaponry, earthenware, porcelain, ceramics, ivory from the Far East, antique furniture, statuettes and four 16C bronze reliefs by Peter and Hans Vischer of Nuremberg.

In fine weather, it is worth climbing the 86 steps up to the crenellated walk at the top of the castle; a panoramic view of nearby peaks stretches away to Mont Blanc in the distance.

Go back to D 116 and turn right towards Corbier.

The road runs along the cliff for a short while then rapidly leads down to the river and crosses it. After a steep climb through a small wood, one is rewarded by a magnificent view of the castle and the valley below.

In Corbier, take D 16 to the left towards Annecy.

The Gorges du Fier

G. Sommer/EXPLORER

Les Ponts de la Caille

4km/2.5mi south of Cruseilles. From Annecy, take the N 201 towards Cruseilles.

The two very different bridges spanning side by side the gorge of the Usses, 150m/492ft above the river bed, form a fascinating **picture**★.

Pont Charles-Albert – This suspension bridge, commissioned in 1838 by Charles-Albert de Sardaigne, is no longer in use.

Pont moderne – The "new" bridge, inaugurated in 1928, consists of a single arch with a 138m/453ft span, one of the largest non-reinforced concrete arches of its kind.

Lac d'ANNECY★★★
Michelin map 328 J5 and 244 folds 18 and 19 - Local map see p

The Lac d'Annecy is the jewel of the Savoie region. The snow-capped peaks of the Tournette (2 351m/7 713ft), the pointed needles of the Dents de Lanfon or the elegant curves of the Montagne d'Entrevernes towering above its deep blue waters form one of the most attractive Alpine landscapes, discovered barely 100 years ago by artists and writers. A tour of the lake by boat or car enables one to appreciate the full beauty of this impressive lake setting.

Nearby sights: L'ALBANAIS, ALBERTVILLE, AIX-LES-BAINS, ANNECY, Massif des ARAVIS, Les BAUGES, Lac du BOURGET, CHAMBÉRY, La CLUSAZ, La ROCHE-SUR-FORON, THORENS-GLIÈRES

Eating out

BUDGET

Auberge des Dents de Lanfon – *74290 Col de Bluffy – 11km/7mi SE of Annecy on D 16 then D 909 –* ☎ *04 50 02 82 51 – closed 2-23 Jan, 9-18 May, 12-19 Nov, Sun evening out of season and Mon – 15.55/32.01€.* This simple establishment at the roadside is run by a young couple. Generous portions of local fare are served in a typically regional setting featuring wood, painted pottery and other homely items. There are some small rooms in case of emergency.

Super Panorama – *Rte du Semnoz – 74000 Annecy – 3.5km/2mi SE of Annecy on D 41 and a forest road –* ☎ *04 50 45 34 86 – closed 31 Dec-6 Feb, Mon evening and Tues – 16.77/39.64€.* This small spartan restaurant hidden away in the forest offers a magnificent view of the lake and mountains. Nature lovers in search of solitude will be well catered for here at a modest cost, but at a fairly basic level of comfort. Five rooms.

MODERATE

Tournette-Plage – *20 prom. des Seines – Les Avollions – 74320 Sévrier –* ☎ *04 50 52 40 48 – closed Jan, Feb, Sun evening and Mon except Jul-Aug – 15.55/27.44€.* The terrace at this restaurant on the shores of the lake offers a splendid view of the Dents de Lanfon from the pleasant shade of the plane trees. People come here in droves to have lunch at weekends, on foot or by boat (there is a landing stage), so it is best to book in advance.

Bistrot du Port – *At the port – 74320 Sévrier –* ☎ *04 50 52 45 00 – closed Oct-Feb and Mon except Jul-Aug – 21.04€.* There is a real holiday atmosphere in this restaurant-grill with its rotunda and decor on a maritime theme. The terrace overlooks a marina on the lake and offers a view of the mountains. Lake fish and grilled meats feature on the menu which includes several fixed price options and a children's menu.

Au Gay Séjour – *74210 Faverges –* ☎ *04 50 44 52 52 – closed 11 Nov-18 Dec, Sun evening and Mon from Sept-Jun except public holidays – 22.87/64.03€.* This family chalet offers the chance of an enjoyable and peaceful break. Decor and facilities are simple, very well kept and clean. Local cooking is served in a small neat dining room with a pleasant view from the windows. Warm welcome guaranteed.

EXPENSIVE

Auberge de l'Éridan – *13 vieille rte des Pensières – 74290 Veyrier-du-Lac –* ☎ *04 50 60 24 00 – closed 16 Nov-3 May, Wed lunchtime, Thu lunchtime, Mon and Tues – 137.20/213.43€.* This fine residence with elegant antique local furniture lands guests truly in the lap of luxury, with sumptuous rooms, perfect peace, a superb terrace with a lake view and of course proprietor Marc Veyrat's celebrated cooking, famous for his use of spices, herbs and mountain plants.

Where to stay

BUDGET

Chambre d'hôte Le Corti – *30 imp. des Hirondelles – near the town hall – 74210 Doussard –* ☎ *04 50 44 34 76 – closed Oct-Jan –* ⊅ *– 3rms: 22.11/30.49€ – restaurant 11.43€.* Having walked round the lake or gone on a mountain ramble, guests here will be delighted to rest in the peace and quiet of one of the small rooms with sloping ceilings in this country house or in the gîte. There is one small snag: the bathrooms are on the landing. The garden has a small vegetable patch.

MODERATE

Hôtel La Châtaigneraie – *74210 Chaparon – 4km/2.5mi S of Duingt on N 508 then B-road towards Lathuile –* ☎ *04 50 44 30 67 – closed 2 Nov-31 Jan, Sun evening and Mon except May-Sept –* 🅿 *– 25rms:*

The view from Col de la Forclaz

56.41/73.18€ - ☐ 8.38€ – restaurant 17.99/37.35€. Ideal for taking the air at the foot of the mountains. A swimming pool and tennis court offer alternative entertainment for those not content to relax in the shade of the trees. The neat and tidy rooms are well equipped. The cuisine features local produce and is served on the terrace in summer months. Attentive service.

Hôtel Les Grillons *– 74290 Angon – 2km/1mi S of Talloires on D 909' – ☎ 04 50 60 70 31 – closed 16 Nov-31 Mar – ◻ – 30rms: 68.60/83.85€ - ☐ 7.62€ – restaurant 21.34/38.11€.* This hotel boasts a vast swimming pool built a few years ago as a major enhancement to the garden of this large building with the atmosphere of a boarding house. Food is served outside if the weather permits.

Hôtel Marceau *– in Marceau-Dessus – 74210 Doussard – 2km/1mi W of Doussard on a B-road – ☎ 04 50 44 30 11 – ◻ – 16rms:70.13/109.76€ - ☐ 58.38€.* This large peaceful hotel provides the opportunity to savour the natural surroundings. Some of the rooms, which are all spacious enough, overlook the lake, while the others overlook a pleasant garden. The decor is stylish if slightly dated.

BACKGROUND

The lake – The picturesque vistas afforded by the lake are largely due to its twisting contours. The Lac d'Annecy consists of two depressions originally separated at the straits overlooked by Duingt Castle. Smaller (2 800ha/6 919 acres) and less deep (40m/131ft on average) than the Lac du Bourget, it is fed by several streams and a powerful underwater spring, the **Boubioz**, located 250m offshore from La Puya. The main outlet of the lake is the Thiou which flows through Annecy and into the Fier.

The steep wooded slopes of the Petit Lac in the south offer a more austere aspect than the more accessible shores of the Grand Lac in the north, dotted with villages and hamlets surrounded by vineyards and clusters of trees. A state-of-the-art purification plant near Annecy has so improved the water quality that fish and breeding pairs of swans have returned to the lake. Pollan is often found on local menus, but gourmets prefer arctic char, trout, perch and carp.

EXCURSIONS

★★ ☐ The West Shore from Annecy to Faverges

38km/23.6mi – about 1hr 30min – see local map

This itinerary, which runs in an almost straight line from Annecy to Faverges, makes a delightful **day trip★★**. The drive along the shore and through the Parc régional des Bauges from Sévrier to Faverges offers lovely views of the lake, of the heights of the Tournette and of the jagged peaks of the Dents de Lanfon. A cycle track runs above, along part of the same route, between Letraz and Chaparon.

Leave Annecy by N 508, ③ on the town plan.

The road skirts the promontory of La Puya, offering good views of Mont Veyrier in the foreground and the Parmelan, Tournette and Dents de Lanfon beyond.

Sévrier – This resort lies on the very edge of the lake, overlooked by the church occupying a prominent position.

Écomusée du Costume savoyard ⊙ – Opposite the church, housed in the former girls' school. Reconstructions of scenes of traditional life in Savoie and explanations of needlework techniques help to demonstrate the amazing variety of costumes between the 18C and the 20C.

★ **Musée de la Cloche** ⊙ – *N 508, on the way out of Sévrier.*

This museum, the work of the **Paccard bell-foundry**, explains the manufacturing process and traces the history of this ancient craft through a collection of bells dating from the 14C to the 19C; other exhibits include tuning forks, which were of prime importance in the making of peals. The "Savoyarde" now in the Sacré-Cœur Basilica in Paris, the "Jeanne d'Arc" in Rouen Cathedral and the mighty 42t "World Peace Bell", cast for the millennium celebrations in Newport, Kentucky, were all made in Annecy.

Between Sévrier and Duingt the road turns away inland. The Château de Duingt is linked to the shore by a drawbridge.

★ **Duingt** – Situated at the narrowest part of the lake which marks the separation between the Grand Lac and the Petit Lac, this pleasant summer resort has retained its rustic Savoyard character. The **castle** *(not open to the public)* has been keeping watch on the narrows from a tiny wooded island since the 11C. It was restored in the 17C and 19C and, like the Château d'Héré just south of Duingt, it once belonged to the De Sales family. Further on, the road skirts the steep and more austere shores of the Petit Lac.

At Doussard, follow the road leading through the Combe d'Ire for 6km/3.7mi.

★ **Combe d'Ire** – This deep wooded furrow overlooked by the Montagne de Charbon, through which runs a rushing stream, used to be one of the wildest and most mysterious Alpine valleys; the last bear was killed in 1893. It is now part of the **Réserve cynégétique des Bauges** (Les Bauges game reserve), rich in chamois, roe-deer, black grouse, rock-partridge, marmots and moufflons.

Rejoin N 508 and turn right to Faverges.

The road goes through the marshy valley of the River Eau Morte, offering closer views of the Bauges Massif and the jagged crest of its highest peak, the Arcalod (2 217m/7 274ft).

Faverges – Situated at an important crossroads, between the Chaîne des Aravis and the Massif des Bauges, this large village is overlooked by the 13C round keep of its castle; traditional industries include prefabricated wooden chalets, mechanical engineering, household appliances and luxury goods.

★★★2 **Route de la Forclaz**

FROM FAVERGES TO ANNECY 40km/25mi – *about 1hr 45min – see local map*

The road climbs up through the fine Alpine valley of Montmin, beneath the escarpments of the Tournette, to the Col de la Forclaz and its beautiful view of the lake.

Grotte and Cascade de Seythenex ⊘ – *2km/1.2mi south of Faverges then right; path signposted "Grottes de Seythenex".*
Several footbridges lead to the top of the waterfall which drops 30m/98ft through a narrow crack into a picturesque wooded vale. It is possible to walk along the former underground river bed which testifies to the power of water erosion. An exhibition shows how craftsmen use water power in their workshops, sawmills and oil-mills

Turn right at Seythenex and follow the road to Vargnoz.

★ **Montagne de la Sambuy** – The **Seythenex chair-lift** ⊘ leads to the Favre refuge (alt 1 820m/5 971ft) affording a fine **view** of the Belledonne range to the south, the Aravis Massif and Lac d'Annecy to the north, the Mont-Blanc Massif to the northeast and the Vanoise glaciers to the southeast.

Return to Faverges and drive north along D 12.

Viuz – This hamlet is within sight of the snow-capped summit of Mont Blanc. Next to the church and its 12C Romanesque apse, a small **Musée archéologique** ⊘ houses a collection of Gallo-Roman objects found locally, including a remarkable cauldron of the 3C, an amber necklace and numerous Roman coins.

Continue on D 282 to Vesonne. The gradient reaches 13% on certain stretches; please drive with extra care and concentration.

The climb from Vesonne to Montmin reveals panoramic views of the Massif des Bauges to the south, including some of its highest summits, the Belle Étoile, the Dent de Cons, Sambuy and Arcalod, and of the Tournette to the north.

Montmin – Set in pastoral surroundings, this attractive resort is the ideal starting point for mountain expeditions, such as the ascent of the Tournette.

From Le Villard, the road climbs to the Col de la Forclaz through pastures and picturesque hamlets.

★★ **Col de la Forclaz** – Alt 1 150m/3 772ft. From the belvedere on the left there is a bird's-eye view of the Lac d'Annecy; note the shallow bank just off Duingt, occupied by lake-dwellings in prehistoric times, which casts a yellowish shadow on the deep blue waters of the lake.

Follow a path on the right, which goes up to a small café, known as La Pricaz, then turn left to reach the belvedere (15min there and back).

Fine panoramic view of the summits of the Bauges Massif, rising to the peak of the Arcalod. If this spectacular view makes you want to take to the air, certified hang-gliding instructors will take you on an unforgettable two-person flight. For more information, ask at La Pricaz or call ☎ 04 50 64 41 11.

The steep drop from the Col de la Forclaz to Rovagny reveals more beautiful views of the Bauges, the Semnoz, the curve of the Grand Lac and Annecy nestling on its shores.
Further on, the Ermitage de St-Germain overlooks a narrow wooded valley.

★ Ermitage de St-Germain – *From D 42, 15min there and back up a steep footpath starting on the left of the first tunnel (on the way down).*
This is a centre of local pilgrimage, particularly on Whit Monday; otherwise, the place is a charming and quiet retreat. According to tradition, St Germain, the first abbot of the Abbaye de Talloires, retired to a grotto in the small escarpment overlooking the road. The splendid **landscape** formed by the chapel and its ancient lime tree with Talloires Bay, the Duingt narrows and the Bauges mountain range in the background also attracted St François de Sales *(see ANNECY)*, who planned to retire here.
There is a wider **panorama** of the Grand Lac and the surrounding mountains from the **Belvédère de la Vierge★** *(15min there and back along a steep footpath skirting the cemetery)*. Go back to the tunnel entrance and start walking along the second path on the left: the view of Talloires Bay is magnificent.

Talloires – One of the area's best-loved resorts, with a beach and water sports centre, Talloires lies in beautiful **surroundings★★**, with the harbour nestling inside a rounded bay, sheltered by the cliffs of the Roc de Chère opposite the wooded promontory of Duingt Castle.

Past the junction with the direct road to Annecy, D 909ᴬ, the Château de Menthon comes into view, higher up on the right.

★ Menthon-St-Bernard – This is a pleasant family resort on the shores of the Lac d'Annecy. The **Château de Menthon** ☉★ *(2km/1.2mi climb by D 969 starting from the church)* was the birthplace of St Bernard de Menthon, who founded the Grand-St-Bernard hospice. The present 13C and 15C château, crowned with turrets, has the picture-perfect look of a fairytale castle. Don't miss the beautiful **view★** of the lake from the terrace.
The **Roc de Chère★** *(2hr there and back on foot)*, a wooded promontory separating Menthon-St-Bernard and Talloires, shelters a **nature reserve** covering 68ha/168 acres with interesting species of Mediterranean and Northern flora. The **view** extends across the Petit Lac to the Tournette and the Bauges mountain range, with Duingt Castle in the foreground.

Veyrier – There is a lovely view of the Grand Lac from the garden behind the town hall *(opposite the church)*; the view stretches from south east to north east, from the glaciers of the Vanoise to the peaks of the Salève and Voirons.

★★ Mont Veyrier – *1km/0.6mi, then 5hr there and back on foot. Leave Veyrier by the Route du Mont Veyrier, turn left into the Route de la Combe. Leave the car at the end of the road and follow the Sentier du Col des Contrebandiers which leads to the summit of Mont Baron.* From the viewing table, there is a bird's-eye **view** of the Lac d'Annecy, framed by mountains on all sides. In fine weather, the view extends southeast to the glaciers of the Vanoise Massif and northeast as far as Lake Geneva.

From Chavoire onwards, the road widens, affording a good overall view of Annecy overlooked by the Basilique de la Visitation and the castle.

Talloires

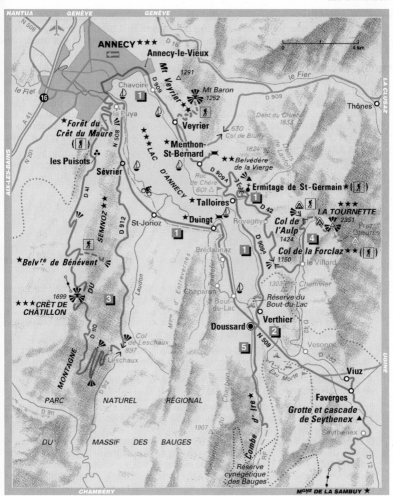

★★ ③ The Semnoz

ROUND TOUR FROM ANNECY *52km/32mi – about 2hr – see local map*

The Semnoz is a picturesque wooded ridge stretching from the Crêt du Maure, a forested area ideal for walking, to the Crêt de Châtillon, its highest peak.

The road leading to the summit can be blocked by snow from November to May, but it is usually cleared by Whitsun.

★★★**Annecy** – *See ANNECY.*

D 41 from Annecy rises quickly towards the Crêt de Châtillon.

★**Forêt du Crêt du Maure** – This vast wooded area, which is to a large extent the result of 19C reafforestation, is criss-crossed by footpaths leading to numerous belvederes and includes a few pens for marmots, deer, roe-deer and reindeer along D 41.

From the Semnoz road, follow a path which starts at the second hairpin bend after entering the forest, by a reservoir.

The Chalet Super-Panorama offers one of the loveliest **views★★** of the lake.

Les Puisots – The old hamlet, burnt down in 1944 (memorial), was replaced by the chalets of a *centre aéré* (outdoor centre) for children and a public park.
The road goes through the forest, offering a few glimpses of the Albanais depression.

Follow the forest road leading to the Belvédère de Bénévent. Leave the car in a bend on the left and follow a footpath on the right.

★**Belvédère de Bénévent** – **View** of the Tournette and the Duingt narrows. The peaks of Le Beaufortain are just visible on the horizon between the Tournette and the Dent de Cons.

Return to D 41.

The landscape changes to stony pastures dotted with blue gentians in early summer. The climb becomes more pronounced and, after a right bend, a vast mountain panorama opens out in front of your eyes.

★★★**Crêt de Châtillon** – *15min there and back on foot. Leave the car at the end of the road and walk up through pastureland to the summit where a tall cross and a viewing table stand.*
The **panoramic view** embraces some of the most famous summits of the western Alps: Haut-Faucigny, Mont Blanc, Vanoise, Écrins, Aiguilles d'Arves and Viso massifs.
The road goes down to the Col de Leschaux through a pine forest and continues in a series of hairpin bends along the steep slopes of the Semnoz, offering fine views of the surrounding mountains.

From the Col de Leschaux, return to Annecy by D 912 and N 508 via Sévrier.

HIKES

★Belvédère de la Tournette

FROM ANNECY – HIKE FROM THE CHALET DE L'AULP
35km/22mi – allow 2hr – see local map

Leave Annecy by ③ *on the town plan, follow D 909 to Menthon-St-Bernard then D 42 towards the Col de la Forclaz.*

Route du Col de l'Aulp – *3.5km/2.2mi from Le Villard* – This forest road goes past Le Villard then climbs between steep wooded slopes, revealing the chalk cliffs of the Tournette on the right. The road gives way to a track which leads to the Col de l'Aulp (1 424m/4 672ft) just below the Tournette: from the mound situated behind the chalet, there is a lovely **view** of part of the Lac d'Annecy.

The road continues to the Chalet-Buvette de l'Aulp (1 424m/4 672ft) at the foot of the Tournette. There is a particularly good view of the lake from a little rise beyond the kiosk.

A stony, badly maintained road provides the only other access to the Chalet-Buvette de l'Aulp. From here, the only way up is on foot.

From the Chalet de l'Aulp to the Refuge de la Tournette – *2hr there and back on foot; difference in altitude 350m/1 148ft. You will need a good pair of binoculars to watch the ibexes roaming around.*
🚶 A marked path rises to the east of the pass then skirts the limestone cliffs overlooking the Cirque du Casset. From the viewing table near the Refuge de la Tournette (alt 1 774m/5 820ft), there is a splendid **panorama**★★ of the western shore of the lake overlooked by the Semnoz. Climbing to the summit of the Tournette requires good experience of hiking through rocky terrain; however, no special equipment is necessary as there are handrails and ladders along the way. One of the finest **panoramas**★★★ of the northern Alps unfolds from the summit (alt 2 351m/7 713ft).
Experienced walkers with the necessary stamina and provisions can follow the east face of the Tournette to the Praz Dzeures refuge. *(Check opening times before departure. Walking map recommended).*

ANNOT★

Population 988
Michelin map 334 I9 and 245 fold 23

This small town, lying on the banks of the River Vaire, 700m/2 297ft above sea level, is the oldest settlement in the valley, developing as a stopping point on the Roman road which linked Digne and Nice along the line of today's N°202. Annot is surrounded by picturesque rocks, known as **grès d'Annot**. These sandstone formations, which were sculpted by erosion into strange shapes and natural arches, make for interesting walks around the town and earned Annot the nickname "the painters' paradise".

Nearby Sights: BEUIL, CASTELLANE, Gorges du CIANS, CLUES DE HAUTE-PROVENCE, COLMARS, Val d'ENTRAUNES, ENTREVAUX, Route NAPOLÉON, PUGET-THÉNIERS, ST-JULIEN-DU-VERDON

★OLD TOWN

The old town looks quaint with its steep twisting lanes, its arcades, its arched alleyways and its leaning houses. The **Cours Provençal** is the centre of activity, a typical southern avenue lined with splendid old plane trees. For a good overall view, walk along rue Basse then **Grande-Rue** leading through a fortified gate to the church. On the way, note the 16C-18C carved doorways and the **Maison des Arcades**, a fine 17C mansion.

Where to stay and Eating out

MODERATE

Hôtel de L'Avenue – ☎ *04 92 83 22 07 – closed 2 Nov-31 Mar – 11rms: 48.78€ - ⛌ 6.10€ – restaurant 13.72/22.87€.* This house with its green shutters looks very welcoming. The terrace on the small street is shaded by trees. Service is warm and friendly; rooms are simple and decorated in pastel shades. As far as the cooking is concerned, the meals here are mouth-watering!

The Romanesque **church** has an unusual raised east end designed as a defensive tower, a lovely Renaissance steeple, as well as a 17C aisle and adjoining chapel. Walk under a gateway onto rue des Vallasses where there is a wash-house opposite the Tour du Peintre (Artist's Tower). Rue Notre-Dame on the left leads back to Grande-Rue.

Les Grès d'Annot – These rock formations are a paradise for amateur and professional climbers alike. Others will be content to take a leisurely walk to the **Rochers de la gare** along a trail marked "Chemin des Grès" and to watch the climbers' progress. The vegetation seems to bind the rocks together and sometimes literally grows out of the blocks, which have been given appropriate names: you may be able to make out the camel, the stem, the zodiac, the face and the king's bedroom. It is worth walking as far as the Arches de Portettes.

> The Whitsun parade, known as the *Bravade*, for which the townspeople dress in uniforms of Napoleon's grenadiers, commemorates the return of local troops from defeat at the hands of the British and Prussians at Waterloo. In the years of the Restoration that followed, the songs and regalia of the procession came to symbolise the old soldiers' resentment of Louis XVIII and Charles X and their nostalgia for their exiled emperor.

Chapelle Notre-Dame de Vers-la-Ville – *20min there and back on foot. From the Cours, follow the street to the right of the fountain then the chemin de Vers-la-Ville.* This path is lined with the Stations of the Cross. The 12C chapel is surrounded by rocks piled on one another, contributing to a good overall **view** of the village and its mountain setting.

EXCURSION

Route du Col de la Colle St-Michel

FROM ANNOT TO COLMARS *46km/29mi – around 1hr*

Head north from Annot by D 908

Le Fugeret – The village lies in a green depression on the left bank of the Vaire. Note the charming 18C humpback bridge spanning the stream with its single 14m/46ft arch. The slopes of the valley offer a landscape of scattered sandstone rocks and clumps of walnut, chestnut and pine trees, as well as lavender fields.

★ **Méailles** – This hilltop village is built on a limestone ridge overlooking the left bank of the Vaire. The small church has Gothic features and contains an interesting altarpiece depicting *The Virgin and Child* (early 16C) as well as several 17C paintings.

On the way down, there is a marked contrast between the forested slopes and the barren limestone layer overlooking the valley dotted with picturesque villages; the Digne-Nice railway line is a showpiece of civil engineering skills.

Beyond the pass, turn left onto D 32 towards Peyresq.

Peyresq – This old shepherds' village lies in a very picturesque **setting**★ overlooking the source of the Vaire and was restored by a group of Belgian students to house an international cultural and artistic university centre; it has retained a 15C mansion and a 13C Romanesque church.

Return to the D 908

Col de la Colle St-Michel – Alt 1 431m/4 695ft. The pass offers a soothing landscape of green pastures. In winter, it is a cross-country skiing centre with tuition and 50km/31mi of tracks available.

HIKE

Grotte de Méailles – *From Méailles, drive towards La Combe and park the car in the first major bend on the right. Wear non-slip shoes and carry several torches. Allow 4hr there and back for a short exploration of the cave entrance. Visitors are asked not to break stalactites or frighten bats.*

🚶 From the parking area, a well-marked path leads north across a ravine then climbs in a landscape of scrub dotted with cairns. The two entrances of the cave are situated beyond the ridge, about 10m/11yd apart. The main gallery slopes gently down 150m/164yd to a stream and a vast chamber partitioned by numerous concretions. *There are other chambers further on, but some are difficult to negotiate and beginners should stop here.*

The incline of the cave follows that of the geological strata, thus offering potholers the rare opportunity to progress without using the karstic network. Potholing enthusiasts who are aware of the risks and take the necessary precautions will enjoy exploring this cave without special equipment.

Massif des ARAVIS★★

Michelin map 333: L-2 to M-3 and 244 folds 8,9,19 and 20

The natural boundaries of the Massif des Aravis, which forms part of the western Préalpes, are the Lac d'Annecy Basin, the valleys of the River Arly and River Arve and the Bornes depression. The rocky Chaîne du Bargy and Massif du Jallouvre form the horizon to the north and the mighty barrier of the **Chaîne des Aravis** stretches between the Val d'Arly and Vallée de Thônes (highest peak: Pointe Percée at 2 752m/9 029ft), continued to the north by the **Chaîne du Reposoir**.

Reblochon country – The Vallée de Thônes, lying at the heart of the Aravis region, has been the home of Reblochon since the 13C. After maturing in the high Alpine pastures, this strong creamy cheese made from the unpasteurised milk of Abondance, Tarentaise and Holstein cows is sold in the market towns of Thônes and Le Grand-Bornand.

Nearby sights: ALBERTVILLE, ANNECY, Lac d'ANNECY, BEAUFORT, La CLUSAZ, CLUSES, Les CONTAMINES-MONTJOIE, Route des GRANDES ALPES, MEGÈVE, La ROCHE-SUR-FORON, ST-GERVAIS-LES-BAINS, Bassin de SALLANCHES, THORENS-GLIÈRES

BACKGROUND

Like the other massifs of the Préalpes, the Chartreuse, Bauges and Vercors, the Massif des Aravis is surrounded by high limestone peaks. Two powerful streams, the Fier and the Borne, cut through the massif by way of some long and narrow gorges such as the **Défilé de Dingy** (Fier), the **Défilé des Étroits** and **Gorge des Éveaux** (Borne). Between the Fier and the Borne, the **Parmelan** (alt 1 832m/6 010ft), whose its tall cliffs stretch across the Annecy landscape, is the favourite goal of mountain hikers. Visitors to the area in January should look out for the famous dog-sled race known as the "Grand Pia".

EXCURSIONS

1 Route de La Clusaz

FROM ANNECY TO LA CLUSAZ *41km/25.5mi – about 1hr – see local map*

The road rises above the lake then goes through the wooded valleys of the River Fier and River Nom, beneath the towering cliffs of the Parmelan Massif. Between Veyrier and the Col de Bluffy there are open views of the Grand Lac and, in the distance, of the Sambuy and Charbon mountains

★★★**Annecy** – *See ANNECY.*

Leave Annecy by D 909 to La Clusaz.

At first the wide road follows the contour of the lake, revealing the Semnoz and Entrevernes mountains on the opposite shore.

Veyrier – *See Lac d'ANNECY,* 2.

From the Col de Bluffy to the bridge at Alex, the road leads down into the Fier Valley and through the Défilé de Dingy. Further upstream, one can see the **Cascade de Morette** (waterfall) on the opposite slope.

Cimetière des Glières – The cemetery, situated on the right of the road, contains the graves of 105 Resistance fighters of the Plateau des Glières *(see THORENS-GLIÈRES)*. An inscription relates the different stages of the operation.

The **Musée de la Résistance** ⊙ in Haute-Savoie, housed in a reconstructed 18C chalet on the right of the cemetery, illustrates in detail the successive episodes of the fierce fighting that took place on the plateau. There is also a memorial to those deported during the Second World War.

★ **Thônes** – Nestling below the cliffs of the Roche de Thônes, at the confluence of the River Fier and River Nom, this market town is the ideal starting point for mountain excursions. The Forêt du Mont is the favourite haunt of ramblers and the slopes of Mont Lachat attract amateur botanists looking for edelweiss.

The 17C **church** ⊙ stands on the main square lined with old arcaded houses. The elegant onion-shaped steeple surmounted by a slender spire (42m/138ft), and the interior decoration are in typical Baroque style. Note the high-altar retable (1721), the carved figurines of the 17C altarpiece to the left of the chancel and the wood-work including 18C stalls.

The first floor of the **musée du pays de Thônes** ⊙ is devoted to the history of the area, which remained loyal to the King during the revolution. The second floor covers local arts and crafts; exhibits include a 15C *Pietà*.

Until the beginning of the 20C, there were many water-mills and sawmills along the Mainant Valley. The Étouvières sawmill has found a new role as an **Écomusée du Bois** ⊙ *(3km/1.9mi west of the town centre)* devoted to timber working in the Thônes region.

Drive south on D 12 then take the first left (D 16).

The road follows the **Vallée de Manigod**★★, the name given to the upper Fier Valley. The slopes are planted with fir trees alternating with orchards and dotted with old chalets.

Les clefs – The church built on a wooded height overlooking the Fier forms a charming picture beneath the steep cliffs of the Tournette.
The road rises further still, to Col de la Croix-Fry.

Col de la Croix-Fry – The pass is equipped with ski lifts. The vast **panorama**★ includes the whole Aravis range. On the way down, the transverse valleys of La Clusaz (River Nom) and Les Étroits (River Borne) appear successively.

D 909 leads to La Clusaz.

✳✳ **La Clusaz** – *See La CLUSAZ.*

② Route de La Colombière

FROM LA CLUSAZ TO CLUSES *40km/25mi – about 1hr 30min – see local map The Col de Colombière is blocked by snow from late November to late May.*

Linking the Thônes and Arve valleys, this route offers a succession of contrasting landscapes from the austere upper valley of the River Chinaillon to the delightful Vallée du Reposoir beyond the Col de la Colombière.

North of La Clusaz, the road follows the wooded valley of the River Nom.

St-Jean-de-Sixt – This peaceful resort lies on the edge of the Nom and Borne valleys, at the heart of the Aravis Massif.

Follow D 4 towards Le Grand-Bornand.

✳ **Le Grand-Bornand** – The pleasant, sunny home town of Reblochon cheese *(market on Wednesdays)* is also a winter sports resort, with an annexe at Le Chinaillon *(6km/3.7mi higher up)*, and a good place to start excursions to Pointe Percée via Le Bouchet.

The road continues up to Pont de Venay, past Le Chinaillon, in a series of hairpin bends offering fine **views** of the Tournette and the high peaks of the Aravis range.

Le Chinaillon – The ski resort nestles round the old village, close to the ski slopes of Mont Lachat de Châtillon.
Beyond the Pont de Venay, the landscape becomes wilder as the rocky escarpments of the Jallouvre Massif replace the Alpine pastures.

Col de la Colombière – Alt 1 613m/5 292ft. The view extends to the northeast towards the limestone heights of the Faucigny, Les Dents Blanches and Les Avoudrues. On the way down to Le Reposoir, the green summits and rocky peaks of the Chaîne du Reposoir come into view and the roofs of the Chartreuse du Reposoir can be seen in the foreground, below the village.

From Le Reposoir, take a narrow road to the Chartreuse.

Chartreuse du Reposoir – This monastery, in typical Carthusian style, was founded in 1151 and restored in the 17C. Abandoned by the order of St Bruno in 1904, it is now home to a community of Carmelite nuns.

From Le Reposoir to Cluses, the road overlooks the wooded gorge of the Foron before reaching the orchards of the Arve Valley and Cluses.

Cluses – *See CLUSES*

③ Vallée du Borne

FROM LA CLUSAZ TO BON-NEVILLE *40km/25mi – about 1hr 15min – see local map*

This pleasant itinerary follows the Borne Valley through two picturesque gorges.

St-Jean-de-Sixt – *See ② above.*

★ **Défilé des Étroits** – The River Borne cuts crosswise through the limestone range to form this narrow gorge which the road follows beneath impressive cliffs.

Entremont – As the valley widens, the village comes into view amid lush meadows. In the church, remodelled several times, there is an interesting **treasury** ⊙, in particular a gilt wood reliquary dating from the 12C.

The road continues through a pleasant pastoral landscape with the Jallouvre Massif looming in the distance (highest peak, 2 408m/7 900ft).

Le Petit-Bornand-les-Glières – This small summer resort, set in restful surroundings, is the ideal starting point for a trip to the Plateau des Glières *(2km/1.2mi south of the village, at Essert, a forest road leads to the plateau).*

Take the signposted road to the left of the town hall.

Route de Paradis – The breathtaking climb up the steep slopes of the Jallouvre offers bird's-eye views of the lower and upper Borne Valley *(for the best views, stop at Puze and again at a crossroads, 2.5km/1.5mi further on).*

The road ends at the Paradis ski centre with stunning **views**★ of the Rochers de Leschaux and the funnel-shaped chasm below.

Return to Le Petit-Bornand and continue on D 12 towards Bonneville.

★ **Gorge des Éveaux** – The road follows the Borne through another transverse valley which narrows considerably, the stream running below at the bottom of the gorge.

The road crosses the Borne in St-Pierre-en-Faucigny and reaches the River Arve in Bonneville.

Bonneville – *See La ROCHE-SUR-THORON, ③.*

④ Route des Aravis

FROM LA CLUSAZ TO FLUMET *19km/11.8mi – about 1hr – see local map*

This is one of the best-known itineraries in the Savoie Alps, its greatest attraction being the view of Mont Blanc from the Col des Aravis, particularly late in the afternoon *(the pass can be obstructed by snow from*

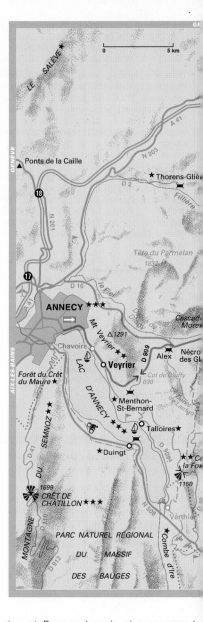

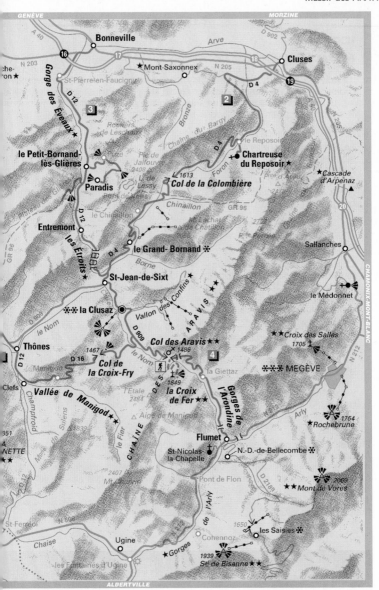

December to April). The road climbs to the pass in a succession of hairpin bends, beneath the escarpments of the Étale. Mont Blanc suddenly appears as one reaches the pass, a particularly impressive sight in the late afternoon sunlight.

★★ **Col des Aravis** – Alt 1 498m/4 915ft. A small chapel dedicated to St Ann stands amid pastures overlooked by the impressive cliffs of the Étale, with the Porte des Aravis on the opposite side. The **view** finally extends over the whole Massif du Mont-Blanc, from Aiguille Verte in the north to Mont Tondu in the south, with the Tête du Torraz in the foreground. The slopes are covered with wild violets and gentians at the end of May and with alpenroses in early summer.

★★ **La Croix de Fer** – *2hr there and back on foot. Follow the path (chemin du Chalet du Curé) starting from the restaurant and leading to the Croix de Fer.*

🚶 The **panorama** is even more impressive here than from the pass, extending beyond Mont Blanc south to the Vanoise glaciers.

Gorges de l'Arondine – On the way down from the pass, the road goes through deeply cut gorges, where slate used to be extracted at the beginning of the 20C.

Eating out

BUDGET

Auberge de la Gloriette – *2 rte d'Annecy – 74230 Thônes – ☎ 04 50 02 98 16 – closed 26 Mar-2 Apr, 18-25 Jun, 17-24 Sept, 1-15 Dec Sun evening and Mon – 14.48/36.59€.* In this neat and tidy local-style house, one of the two dining rooms features the interior decor of an old chalet, like those used when spending the summer season with the animals in the mountain pastures. "Gloriette" was the name given to the shop at the back of the old bakery.

MODERATE

La Ferme de Lormay – *74450 Grand-Bornand – 7km/4mi from Le Grand Bornand towards the Bouchet valley and Route des Troncs – ☎ 04 50 02 24 29 – closed 1 May-20 Jun, 10 Sept-20 Dec at lunchtime on weekdays in winter and on Tues in summer – ⌿ – 25.92/33.54€.* Do not miss a stopover in this farm at the "back of beyond", built in 1786. There is a friendly welcome. Sausages and ham hang drying above the hearth. Meals served here are generous and authentic.

Where to stay

BUDGET

Chambre d'hôte La Passerelle – *Near the church – 74450 St-Jean-de-Sixt – ☎ 04 50 02 24 33 – ⌿ – 4rms ⌚ 30.49/45.73€.* This new chalet, built behind the church next to the traditional family farm, opens onto a large field with a view of the Mont de l'Étale in the background. The four rooms are comfortable, well lit and have wood panelling.

Hôtel La Vieille Ferme – *74230 Manigod – 10km/6mi NE of Manigod toward the Croix Fry and Merdassier passes (on D 160) – ☎ 04 50 02 41 49 – closed 20 Apr-1 Jun, 30 Oct-20 Dec and Wed out of season – ◻ – 6rms: 30.49/45.73€ ⌚ 5.34€ – restaurant 15.24/22.87€.* At the heart of the summer pastures, this old mountain farm is located at the foot of the ski slopes in winter. Rooms are modern and appealing, while the restaurant is more typical of the region with wood fittings. There is a fabulous view of Mont Charin and La Tournette from the terrace.

Flumet – This large village, situated at the confluence of the River Arly and River Arondine and at the intersection of the Val d'Arly, Col des Saisies and Col des Aravis roads, is very busy in season. It is a pleasant summer resort offering walks through forested areas on the road to Notre-Dame-de-Bellecombe. It is also a lively winter resort linked to the nearby village of **St-Nicolas-la-Chapelle**.

The bridge which spans the Arly 60m/197ft above the river bed opens the way to the picturesque village of Notre-Dame-de-Bellecombe.

High pasture on the Col d'Aravis

Les ARCS⁎⁎

Michelin map 333 N4 or 244 fold 21
Local map see Massif de la VANOISE

This resort, which is one of the most important ski centres in the Alps, includes Arc 1600, Arc 1800 and Arc 2000. In addition, Arc 1800 is linked by ski runs in winter and by road in summer to Vallandry and **Peisey-Nancroix**, situated in a forested area on the edge of the Parc national de la Vanoise.

Les Arcs is also famous for its **Kilomètre lancé** (speed-skiing) competitions carried out with special equipment. The track, which has a 77% gradient, was used for the 1992 Winter Olympic Games, when the record speed of 229.299kph/142.5mph was reached.

Nearby Sights: BEAUFORT, BOURG-ST-MAURICE, CHAMPAGNY-EN-VANOISE, COURCHEVEL, Route des GRANDES ALPES, La PLAGNE, La TARENTAISE, TIGNES, VAL-D'ISÈRE, MASSIF de la VANOISE

THE RESORTS

The three resorts are modern and functional, but their architectural style blends reasonably well with the landscape owing to the extensive use of wood.

Arc 1600 (or Arc Pierre Blanche) – Access is by the **Arc-en-ciel** ⊘ funicular; *7min, starting point behind the station*. This resort is known for its traditional family atmosphere. There is a lovely **view⋆** of Bourg-St-Maurice, the Beaufortain and Mont Blanc.

Arc 1800 – South of Arc 1600; this resort occupies a fine position overlooking the Isère Valley and offering **panoramic views⋆** of the Beaufortain, Mont-Blanc and Bellecôte massifs as well as the Haute Tarentaise Valley.

Arc 2000 – More recent and remote than the other two, this high-mountain resort, lying just beneath the Aiguille Rouge, attracts advanced skiers.

Where to stay

MODERATE

Village Club du Soleil – *73700 Les Arcs 1800 – ☏ 04 79 04 09 09 – closed 2 May-15 Jun and 2 Sept-14 Dec –* ☐ *– 137 apartments: 2/6 persons, weekly full board 388.74/818.65€.* This modern hotel-club offers guests an all-inclusive package. A room with a balcony for admiring the view of the valley or of Mont Blanc, a children's club, a gym, skiing equipment and fees, plus dining and entertainment on site make for a carefree holiday.

Ski area – It is on the whole not so vast as that of Les Trois Vallées, but extremely varied. The ski slopes of Arc 1600 and Arc 1800 offer few difficult passages except in the Deux Têtes area. Skiing above Arc 2000, on the other hand, is more than satisfying for advanced skiers: the Dou de l'Homme chair-lift, Grand Col ski lift and Aiguille Rouge cable car give access to 10 black runs which are technically very demanding.

Peisey-Vallandry⁎ is also made up of three resorts: Nancroix, a favourite with Nordic skiers, Plan Peisey, best known for its downhill runs, at the foot of the Aiguille Grive and the newer Vallandry. The area is linked to Les Arcs, La Plagne, the Espace Killy and les Trois Vallées.

HIKES

The beautiful panoramas more than make up for the unattractive aspect of the ski area in summer.

⋆⋆⋆**Aiguille Rouge** ⊘ – Alt 3 227m/10 587ft. *From the main square in Arc 2000, a path leads to the Dou de l'Homme chairlift, followed by the Aiguille Rouge cable car. Go to the viewing table. Mountain boots and sunglasses are recommended.*
Enjoy the stunning close-up view of Mont Pourri and, further away, of the Sommet de Bellecôte and Les Trois Vallées. One can spot in the distance the Belledonne and Lauzière ranges as well as the Aravis Massif to the west, the Mont Blanc Massif to the north and the summits marking the Italian and Swiss borders to the east.

Take the cable car back and either go down by chairlift, or head downhill on foot to the lovely **Lac Marlou** *(be sure to ask the* pisteurs *about the risk of avalanches).*

⋆⋆ **Télécabine le Transarc** ⊘ – *Access from Arc 1800*. The gondola passes over the Col du Grand Renard and reaches the foot of the Aiguille Grive at an altitude of 2 600m/8 530ft. There are good views of the Aiguille Rouge, Mont Pourri, Grande Motte de Tignes and the impressive ridge of Bellecôte, as well as the Mont Blanc and Beaufortain massifs to the north.

Numerous possibilities of hikes of varying levels of difficulty. Some itineraries are described below.

★★★ Aiguille Grive – Alt 2 732m/8 963ft.

🚶 *Experienced hikers, who do not suffer from vertigo, can reach the summit in about 30min up very steep slopes. The ascent should only be attempted in dry weather.*

From the viewing table, there is a stunning **view★★★** of the Vanoise Massif.

★★ Refuge du Mont Pourri *(3hr)*.

🚶 A relatively untaxing round tour on the edge of the Parc de la Vanoise, via Col de la Chal, Mont Pourri mountain refuge and the Lac des Moutons.

It is also possible to take a trip to the Aiguille Rouge from the highest point reached by the Transarc. The walk to the Dou de l'Homme chairlift takes under 1hr; take the cable car up and down the Aiguille Rouge, then continue on foot to Lac Marlou and return to the Transarc.

★ Télésiège de la Cachette ⊘ – Alt 2 160m/7 087ft. *Access from Arc 1600.*
Fine views of the Isère Valley, Bourg-St-Maurice and Mont Blanc.

★★ Hike to L'Arpette – From the top of the chairlift, go right to join a path which climbs alongside the Arpette chairlift and leads to the Col des Frettes. Once there, take a path to the left which leads to L'Arpette (alt 2 413m/7 917ft), a hang-gliding and paragliding take-off point. Splendid **views★★** of La Plagne, Les Arcs and the main peaks of the Haute Tarentaise.

EXCURSIONS

✳ Peisey-Nancroix

South of Arc 1800 (Forest road to Vallandry, D 226)

The villages of Peisey and Nancroix, linked to form one resort overlooking the upper Isère Valley, are fine mountaineering and skiing centres. Branching off N 90, the road leading to Peisey-Nancroix goes up the wooded **Vallée du Ponturin★**; to the northwest, there is a view of the Roignais summits, the isolated Pierre Menta and the rocky barrier of the Grande Parei. Peisey's church with its slender steeple makes a lovely picture against the Bellecôte or Roignais massifs.

Local traditions are very much alive in the area: the *"frontière"*, a headdress worn by women from the Tarentaise region, can be seen on Sundays and feast days, especially on 15 August, the Feast of the Assumption.

Cirque de la Gura – *Beyond Nancroix the D 87 runs along the banks of the fast-flowing Ponturin to a pleasant valley of green fields and larches. To the right, a road once led to the mining academy, founded by Napoleon in the days when Peisey was known for its silver-rich lead ore.*

*The road leads to the **Rosuel** refuge and stops in front of the imposing cirque with Mont Pourri rising above it and cascades rushing down its rock face. Beyond this high ridge, the Parc National de la Vanoise begins.*

★★ Hike to Lac de la Plagne

🚶 *Start from Rosuel – 2hr 30min on the way up. Difference in altitude: 650m/2 133ft. Follow footpath GR 5 as far as the bridge over the Ponturin, then continue along the left side of the river. A path on the right bank leads down to the lake in 1 hr 45 min. From there, it is possible to rejoin GR 5 which leads to the Col du Palet (about 4hr return).*

ARGENTIÈRE***

Michelin map 328 O5 and 244 fold 21- 8km/5mi north of Chamonix
Local map see Massif du MONT-BLANC

rgentière is the highest (1 252m/4 108ft) resort in the Chamonix Valley; with its nnexes of Montroc-le-Planet and Le Tour, it forms an excellent holiday and moun-ineering centre offering a wide choice of expeditions to the Massif du Mont-Blanc nd Massif des Aiguilles Rouges. The relatively gentle slopes of the upper Arve Valley rovide pleasant walks through a fringe of larch woods.

he Argentière Glacier is hardly visible from the village; note, however, the morainal ebris forming a bulge round the rock surface once covered by the top end of the lacier and, higher up, the vertical walls of the U-shaped valley which the Ice Age lacier would have filled completely.

legend in the French Alps, Armand Charlet (1900-75), a native of Argentière, was eld to be the king of mountain guides until the early 1960s. He set a record, which as never been equalled, by climbing the Aiguille Verte (4 121m/13 520ft) more han 100 times.

djacent Sights: CHAMONIX-MONT-BLANC, Les CONTAMINES-MONTJOIE, Les OUCHES, Massif du MONT-BLANC, MEGÈVE, SAINT-GERVAIS-LES BAINS, Bassin e SALLANCHES

THE RESORT

Ski area – The Grands-Montets ski slopes are among the finest and most famous in Europe. Argentière is a real paradise for experienced skiers: their length, their gradient, the quality of the snow and the splendid landscapes account for their popularity, but the runs rarely seem overcrowded. The Point de Vue black run, which starts from the Aiguille des Grands-Montets and stretches over 5.2km/3.2mi, is an exceptional downhill run offering unforgettable views of the Argentière Glacier, Aiguille Verte and Aiguille du Chardonnet. The Chamois run along the Combe de la Pendant is also worth mentioning. These runs are only suitable for experienced skiers. Others will find easier runs along the Bochard and Marmottons chairlifts. As for hikers, a special trail linking the Plan Joran and Pendant plateaux is at their sole disposal.

Where to stay

IODERATE

lôtel Les Becs Rouges – *74400 Montroc-le-Planet – 2km/1mi NE f Argentière on N 506 then a B-road – ☎ 04 50 54 01 00 – closed 1 Nov-5 Dec – P – 24rms: 80.04/102.90€ - ☕ 12.96€ – restaurant 8.20/44.97€.* Whether staying in summer or winter, guests here can sample the delights of nature. A panoramic terrace adjoins a summer garden vith a view of the Mont-Blanc range: we recommend the rooms with a balony. The Danish team will conjure up original little specialities for guests at heir request.

XPENSIVE

hambre d'hôte La Ferme d'Elisa – *394 chemin de la Rosière – ☎ 04 50 54)0 17 – www.helisa-ski.com – 4rms: from 160.07€ - ☕ 12.20€.* The Maison 'Elisa is a charming place! It is located off the beaten track and boasts an eleant lounge, a fine terrace and well-kept rooms in which to recover from the ay's exertions. Breakfast is served in the "pêle", the old living room of the summer pasture farmhouse.

HIKES

**Aiguille des Grands-Montets Alt 3 295m/10 810ft

Access by the Lognan and Grands-Montets cable-cars ⓥ. About 2hr 30min return. From the last platform, climb to the viewing table (120 steep steps).

The **panorama***** is breathtaking. The view extends to the Argentière Glacier over which tower the Aiguille du Chardonnet and Aiguille d'Argentière to the north, Mont Dolent to the east, Aiguille Verte and Les Drus to the south, with the Aiguille du Midi, Mont Blanc and Dôme du Goûter further away. Slightly to the west, there is a fine view of the Chamonix Valley as far as Les Houches with the Aravis range in the distance.

*Hikes to the Col de Balme

Le Tour – *3km/1.8mi northeast of Argentière.* This pleasant village lies just below the Tour Glacier which, in summer, reveals many crumbling seracs *(for general information on glaciers see Introduction: Alpine relief)*. The resort

Argentière Glacier

is the starting point for easy hikes to the Col de Balme during the warm season and, in winter, the ski area is ideal for beginners and intermediate skiers owing to its gentle slopes, the quality of its snow and the amount of sunshine.

★★ Col de Balme – Alt 2 204m/7 231ft. *Access all year round by the **Col de Balme gondola** ⊙. Allow 10min to walk from the lift to the pass.*
The **view★★** extends northeast to the Swiss Alps and southwest to the Chamonix Valley surrounded by the Aiguille Verte, Mont Blanc and the Aiguilles Rouges massif. Food and drink is available in several places. At the beginning of July, when the herds go up to the high pastures, bovine tempers fray in the rush to the green grass on the other side ...

★ Aiguillette des Posettes – Alt 2 201m/7 221ft. *Hiking enthusiasts can prolong the excursion to the Col de Balme by coming down via the Tour du Mont-Blanc - Col des Posettes alternative, climbing alongside the Aiguillette ski lift. From the top of the ski lift, there is a 10min ascent to the summit.*
A fine **view** can be had of the Col de Balme, the Aiguille du Tour and glacier of the same name, Argentière and Grands-Montets, the Aiguille Verte, Aiguilles Rouges and Émosson Dam.

★★★ Réserve naturelle des Aiguilles-Rouge

3km/1.8mi north of Argentière on N 506. This nature reserve, situated between Argentière and Vallorcine and covering an area of 3 300ha/8 155 acres at an altitude of 1 200m/3 937ft to 2 995m/9 826ft, offers a selection of high-altitude mountain landscapes within sight of the magnificent Massif du Mont-Blanc.
The **chalet d'accueil** (Information Centre ⊙) situated on the Col des Montets (alt 1 471m/4 826ft), presents exhibitions, slide shows and video films about the fauna, flora and geology of the cristalline massifs. The laboratory downstairs presents the habitats and food chains of local species in a series of taxidermy displays and shows how plants and insects are studied.
An **ecological discovery trail**, which follows the old stagecoach route from Chamonix to Martigny, enables nature lovers to discover the remarkable diversity of high-altitude flora and fauna *(guide for sale at the chalet)* over a distance of 2km/1.2mi. The nature reserve is inhabited by ibexes, chamois, blue hares and black salamanders. More than 500 species of plants have been identified.
The itinerary is split into some 15 numbered sections, each concentrating on a different ecosystem: from peat bogs and alder plantations to avalanche corridors and scree slopes. In addition, there are beautiful views of the Tour and Argentière glaciers.

L'ARGENTIÈRE-LA-BESSÉE

Population 2 312
Michelin map 334 H4 and 244 fold 42
Local map see Le BRIANÇONNAIS

This industrial centre, which owes its name to ancient silver-lead mines, lies at the confluence of the Rivers Gyronde and River Durance. In summer, sports enthusiasts make straight for its nearby canyoning and rock-climbing sites.

Nearby Sights: BRIANÇON, Le BRIANÇONNAIS, CEILLAC, EMBRUN, Vallée de FREISSINIÈRES, Route des GRANDES ALPES, GUILLESTRE, MONT-DAUPHIN, MONTGENÈVRE, Le QUEYRAS, SERRE-CHEVALIER, La VALLOUISE, VARS

L'ARGENTIÈRE-ÉGLISE

The old district of L'Argentière-Église, 2km/1.2mi from N 94, has retained its rustic character. Arriving from Briançon, turn right, cross the Durance then turn left towards the industrial zone and drive beyond the railway line.

Chapelle St-Jean ⊘ – This chapel, one of the few Romanesque buildings (12C) in the Hautes-Alpes region, was founded by the Knights Hospitallers on the road to Italy. Note the carved capitals decorated with plant motifs and geometric patterns.

Church ⊘ – It dates from the 15C; the exterior is decorated with **murals** (1516) depicting the vices and the virtues *(See ABC of ARCHITECTURE)*, while the door is adorned with a splendid 16C wrought-iron bolt representing a chimera's head.

ADDITIONAL SIGHTS

Musée des Mines d'argent ⊘ – In what was once the farmhouse of the Château St Jean, this museum retraces the evolution of silver mining which used to be the most important economic activity of the valley.

Vallon du Fournel – *Leave L'Argentière on D 423 up the narrow Fournel Valley (access not allowed in winter). Walking shoes recommended.*
Drive up to L'Eychaillon from where there is a fine view of the Gorges du Fournel and the ruins of the medieval castle. Leave the car and walk down the miners' path to the bottom of the gorge. Silver mining had its heyday in the 19C, when up to 500 miners were employed. The mines closed down in 1908.

Anciennes mines d'argent ⊘ – Archeological finds have revealed mining activity in the area going back to the 12C *(The mines can be cold and the pathways uneven in places; warm clothing and sturdy shoes recommended.)*

Réserve biologique des Deslioures ⊘ – One of the aims of this nature reserve, which forms part of the Parc national des Écrins, is the preservation of a thistle-like plant known as **Alpine sea holly**.

MOUNTAINEERING ACTIVITIES

★ **Via Ferrata des Vigneaux** – *Situated at the end of the village of Vigneaux, on D 4 to Prelles; rock-climbing enthusiasts are advised to refer to the Practical information chapter.* This is the most popular "via ferrata" in the Briançonnais region; it is less crowded in the early morning or late afternoon. There are two courses to choose from on the Falaise de la Balme, which is almost 200m/656ft high. Spectators will need binoculars to track the climbers to the top.

Via Ferrata des Gorges de la Durance – *D 994 towards Vallouise; at La Bâtie des Vigneaux turn right towards Barri and follow the signs. Not recommended for children, even under adult supervision.* Allow about 4hr to complete this new rock-climbing course, which should only be attempted by those with a sound knowledge of freeclimbing techniques.

Canyon du Fournel – *Follow D 423 towards the silver mines. The canyoning course is situated upriver from the rock-climbing school (leave the car there). Note that the Canyon is located below a hydroelectric station. Follow the instructions posted at the start of the course and listen for the warning siren that signals the opening of the dam.* The canyon is fully equipped and the site is one of the most popular among those wishing to be introduced to **canyoning**. However, those who wish to do the course unaccompanied when the water level is low are advised to ask about meteorological conditions at the guides' office in Argentière.

AURON✳

St Denis; fresco in the Chapelle St-Érige, Auron

On top of a sunny plateau at an altitude of 1 608m/5 276ft, with Las Donnas (2 474m/8 117ft) towering above, this former hamlet, once the granary of St-Étienne-de-Tinée, has become a lively summer resort and winter sports centre. Auron is only an hour away from Nice and its sunny skies, sledge rides and attractive pistes draw visitors from along the Côte d'Azur.

The village is named after a 6C bishop of Gap called Aurigius, who became a saint; according to legend, he was being chased by highway robbers on his way back from Rome, when his horse saved him by jumping in one single leap from the River Tinée to Auron 500m/1 640ft above.

Adjacent Sights: BEUIL, Route de la BONNETTE, ISOLA 2000, SAINT-ÉTIENNE-DE-TINÉE, VAL D'ENTRAUNES, Vallée de la TINÉE

SIGHTS

Chapelle St-Érige ⊘ – This Romanesque chapel dedicated to Aurigius has a single nave with a double apse, which is covered with a larch framework carved with notched motifs. The rich **decoration**★ painted in tempera dates from 1451.
Between the two apses, a recess surmounted by a canopy is covered with paintings illustrating the life of Mary Magdalene. In one image, covered only by her long, flowing golden hair, she is borne up to heaven by two angels. On the canopy she is depicted in a meadow, preaching to a congregation of Provençal farmers. An older fresco showing the angel Gabriel, part of an Annunciation scene, is believed to date from the 13C.

On the town

Les Enfants Terribles – *Pl. Centrale – Open daily 10pm-2.30am – closed May-Jun and Sept-Nov.* If you want to dance, there is only one venue in the whole of the resort: Les Enfants Terribles goes its own sweet way and offers something for everyone in a highly varied musical programme including rock, soul, funk, techno, afro and more.

On the left-hand wall, a huge St Christopher holds Jesus as a child.
From outside, there is a fine **view**★ of the mountains all round.

★★ **Las Donnas** – A cable car ⊘ in two sections takes visitors up to 2 256m/7 402ft in 7min, close to the summit of Las Donnas. Panoramic **view** of the upper Tinée Valley and summits on the Franco-Italian border.

AUSSOIS *

Population 628
Michelin map 333 N6 and 244 fold 32
Local map see La MAURIENNE or Massif de la VANOISE

Set in **fine surroundings★** at an altitude of 1 500m/4 921ft, beneath the towering summits of the Rateau d'Aussois and Dent Parrachée, this charming old village of Aussois lies on the doorstep of the Parc national de la Vanoise *(see Massif de la VANOISE).* Aussois enjoys a remarkable amount of sunshine and offers numerous hikes and mountain bike trails for summer visitors.

Nearby sights: BESSANS, BONNEVAL-SUR-ARC, Route du GALIBIER, Route des GRANDES ALPES, Route de l'ISERAN, La HAUTE MAURIENNE, MODANE, Route du MONT-CENIS, ST-JEAN-DE-MAURIENNE, VAL-D'ISÈRE, Massif de la VANOISE

THE RESORT

Ski area – The south-facing ski area, which reaches an altitude of 2 750m/9 022ft and has reliable equipment, is popular with intermediate skiers and family parties. Snow conditions on the slopes situated above 2 000m/6 562ft are usually good until April. For cross-country skiers, there are 35km/21.7mi of trails available between Aussois and Sardières.

The 17C **church** still has its original rood beam and Gothic fonts instead of a stoup

WALKS AND HIKES

★**Télésiège le Grand Jeu** – The chairlift reaches 2 150m/7 054ft. Views across the Arc Valley towards the summits of Longe-Côte, the Aiguille de Scolette and the Pointe de la Norma with the massif du Thabor in the distance. Climb alongside the Eterlou chairlift for more panoramic views: Rateau d'Aussois, artificial lakes of the Plan d'Amont and Plan d'Aval. From there, the Plan Sec mountain refuge is accessible in dry weather. In winter it is possible to reach the foot of Dent Parrachée by the Bellecôte chairlift: **views★★** of the Haute Maurienne northern slopes, with Grande Ruine and the Meije to the southwest.

★★**Walk to Fond d'Aussois** – *6km/3.7mi drive from the Maison d'Aussois.* The route leads to the Plan d'Aval Dam *(stop to admire the view at the first car park),* then along an unsurfaced road to the Plan d'Amont Dam. *Park the car and continue on foot. 3hr 30min there and back.*
🚶 The footpath skirts the lake shore then leads to the Fond d'Aussois refuge. View of the glacial cirque beneath Dent Parrachée.

★★**Hike to the Col d'Aussois** – *Access from the Fond d'Aussois refuge – 4hr there and back. Difference in altitude: 700m/2 297ft – Should only be attempted in dry weather and not before the end of July. Mountain boots are essential.*
🚶 For superb views all round, experienced hikers can climb to the **Pointe de l'Observatoire** (3 015m/9 892ft).

AVORIAZ ★★

Population 5 016
Michelin map 328 N3 and 244 fold 10 - 14km/8.7mi east of Morzine
Local map see THONON-LES-BAINS
Accessible by cable-car from a station 4.5km/2.8mi from Morzine

Established in 1966, Avoriaz is a modern resort situated at an altitude of 1 800m/5 906ft. Its original and uniform architectural style – buildings clad with wood, looking like huge rocks – blends well with the surroundings. Private motor vehicles are banned from the centre and replaced by sledges.

Nearby Sights: ABONDANCE, CHÂTEL, CLUSES, ÉVIAN-LES-BAINS, Les GETS, MORZINE, SAMOËNS, SIXT-FER-À-CHEVAL, THONON-LES-BAINS, YVOIRE

THE RESORT

Ski area – Avoriaz enjoys excellent snow conditions and a favourable position at the heart of the vast Portes du Soleildd ski area, which includes 12 French and Swiss winter resorts between Lake Geneva and Mont Blanc with an impressive total of 650km/404mi of ski slopes. However, in order to take full advantage of the area, it is necessary for the snow to be plentiful at low altitudes (all the resorts, except Avoriaz, are barely above 1 000m/3 281ft).
The Avoriaz ski slopes are ideal for intermediate skiing; the ski runs leading to Les Lindarets offer pleasant skiing through the forest. Advanced skiers can take the Combe chairlift which gives access to four black runs, including the Combe-du-Machon. There are also ski lifts to the Châtel and Morzine areas and, in Switzerland, to the resorts of Champéry and Les Crosets.

Avoriaz

The "Brasilia of the Alps"

The striking modern architecture of Avoriaz couldn't fail to catch the imagination of the public and the press, who soon dubbed the new town "Brasilia des Neiges" drawing a parallel with Brazil's state-of-the-art capital. The irregular contours of the first hotel, Les Dromonts, were designed to blend in with the rugged landscape, and subsequent developers followed architect Jaques Labro's lead with jutting façades overlaid with sequoia. Even if the look isn't to everyone's taste, the resort's facilities have made it a firm favourite with skiers.

The **Festival du film de demain** (Tomorrow's Film Festival), following the Festival du Fantastique (Supernatural Film Festival) created in 1973, takes place every year in January and attracts enthusiasts from all over the world.

* **Télésiège du Choucas** ⊙ – *From the top of the chairlift, go to the Pas de Chavanette on the left (arrival point of two ski lifts).* View of the Swiss Alps and Avoriaz.

EXCURSION

In summer, it is well worth exploring the surrounding area along D 338 to Morzine. After 1km/0.6mi, the **Chapelle d'Avoriaz**, designed by Novarina, appears on the right and there is a fine view of the Lac d'Avoriaz. The road then overlooks the Vallon des Ardoisières with the snow-capped Hautforts Summit (2 466m/8 090ft) in the distance. After running for a while along a ledge covered with pastures and dotted in summer with colourful pansies and gentians, the road reaches the resort of **Super-Morzine** (view of Mont Blanc) then runs down towards Morzine.

Eating out

MODERATE

Le Bistro – *Pl. Centrale, near the tourist office* – ☎ 04 50 74 14 08 – *closed May, Jun, Sept-Nov* – 16.01/25.76€. Why not travel here by sleigh? Seated around a large friendly table, or in a more peaceful corner, guests can sample specialities such as fondue or stone-grilled meats. At lunchtime, take your pick from the hors d'œuvre buffet and carvery.

Where to stay

EXPENSIVE

Hôtel de la Falaise – *Quartier de la Falaise* – ☎ 04 50 74 26 00 – *closed 23 Apr-23 Dec* – 47rms. half-board: 123.48€. For those who love wide open spaces and peace and quiet. All the rooms here have south-facing balconies. Food is served at the La Chapka restaurant, tastefully decorated in the local style, with carved wooden furniture, benches covered in red velvet etc.

BARCELONNETTE ★

Population 2 976
Michelin map 334 H6 and 245 fold 10 - Local map L'UBAYE

arcelonnette lies at the heart of the Ubaye Valley amid orchards and lush meadows.
his little Mediterranean-style town is one of the administrative centres of the Alpes-de-
aute-Provence *département*.

earby Sights: Route de la BONNETTE, PRA-LOUP, Lac de SERRE-PONÇON, L'UBAYE,
AL d'ALLOS

BACKGROUND

A troubled past – Founded in 1231 by the count of Barcelona and Provence under
the name of Barcelone, the town, and the Ubaye region with it, first belonged
to the House of Savoie then to France in 1713, when it was exchanged for
part of Dauphiné under the Treaty of Utrecht. Soon afterwards, the townspeople
asked to join the Parlement de Provence and the town took the name of
Barcelonnette.

Public figures born in the town include **JA Manuel** (1775-1827), a member of parliament during the reign of Charles X (1824-1830) who was thrown out of the House
for having criticised the King's policy, and **Paul Reynaud** (1878-1966), who resigned
as prime minister of France in 1940 and was replaced by Marshal Pétain. Sent to
prison, he was deported to Germany in 1942 but was able to resume his political
career at the end of the war.

The "Barcelonnettes" in Mexico

It all started in Jausiers *(9km/5.6mi northeast of Barcelonnette)* in 1805,
when two brothers, Jacques and Marc-Antoine Arnaud decided to leave the
family business and try their luck in America. In Mexico, Marc-Antoine opened
a fabric store known as "El cajon de ropas de las Siete Puertas" (a craft centre
in Barcelonnette now bears the same name). The success of the business was
such that by 1893 there were more than 100 fabric stores in Mexico owned
by natives of the Ubaye region. Some tried their hand at other businesses
(paper, breweries and finance, including the London and Mexico Bank which
was empowered to print money!).

The 1910 Mexican revolution followed by the First World War put an end to
the flow of emigrants which, however, started again in 1930 and finally
stopped in 1950. Most of the emigrants were country folk who, except for
the Arnaud brothers, eventually returned to their native country and built
sumptuous villas to mark their success in the New World.

Set amid spacious parks, these opulent houses built between 1880 and 1930
testify to the spectacular success of their owners. Architectural styles vary
considerably and denote various influences; Italian, Tyrolean, Baroque, but
certainly not Mexican. There are two fine examples along avenue des Trois-
Frères-Arnaud and avenue Antoine-Signoret and several along avenue de la
Libération. One of the last to be built was the Villa Bleue (1931), avenue
Porfirio-Diaz, which is decorated with an impressive monochrome stained
glass depicting the owner's Mexican textile factories.

WALKING AROUND THE TOWN

Place Manuel – This vast open space at the heart of the grid-like former *bastide*
(walled town in southern France) is surrounded by colourful buildings and pavement
cafés full of holidaymakers. Note the **fountain** with a medallion of JA Manuel by David
d'Angers and the **Tour Cardinalis** (15C), the former bell-tower of a Dominican convent
which once stood here.

Villa la Sapinière – Housed in one of the most splendid Mexican villas, the **Musée de
la Vallée** ⊘ illustrates the history of the Ubaye Valley with an Iron-Age burial rites, the
charter of the town dating from 1231, an 18C map showing the chequered layout
of the town and various objects connected with agriculture and handicraft in the
19C.

During the season, the ground floor houses the **Maison du Parc national du Mercantour** ⊘
where information about guided **themed hikes** ⊘ is available.

Cemetery – Situated at the end of allée des Rosiers, it houses a fascinating array of
funeral monuments erected by the emigrants after their return: temples, mau-
soleums, chapels in stone and Carrara marble were, for the most part, the work of
Italian artists.

Eating out

MODERATE

La Mangeoire Gourmande – *Pl. des Quatre-Vents, near the church* – ☎ *04 9 81 01 61 – closed 6 Nov-1 Jan, Mon and Tue* Oct-Jun – 24.39/32.01€. Guests her are seated in the 17C vaulted stable room, complete with original manger. The blue painted furniture matches the Provençal colours of the decor. From the kitche which opens onto the dining room, issues a selection of dishes designed to appe to current tastes.

Where to stay

MODERATE

Hôtel Pyjama – *Super-Sauze – 10km/6mi SE of Barcelonnette on D 900 an D 209* – ☎ *04 92 81 12 00 – closed 21 May-14 Jun and 14 Sept-19 Dec* – 🅿 *10rms: 51.83/100.62€* - 🍽 *6.86€*. After a day's skiing, slip into your pyjama here... and enjoy the total peace and quiet of this hotel set amid the larches Some rooms are fitted with spacious mezzanines to accommodate families.

Hôtel Azteca – *3 r. F.-Arnaud* – ☎ *04 92 81 46 36* – *closed 4-3 Nov* – 🅿 – *27rms: 54.88/76.22€* - 🍽 *7.62€*. The Azteca is furnished and fit ted with items from Mexico, in memory of people from this area who emigrate there in 1820. Whether in the old villa or the recently built annexe, all room with a balcony face the mountains, a peaceful stay is guaranteed.

Alp'Hôtel – *04400 Sauze* – ☎ *04 92 81 05 04 – closed 1 Apr-31 May an 2 Oct-19 Dec* – 🅿 – *24rms: 70.13/76.22€* 🍽 *7.62€ – restaurar 15.24/29.73€*. This hotel near the ski slopes but off the beaten track offers complete fitness programme along with accommodation. If in a group or with family, ask for one of the four apartments fitted with their own kitchen.

On the town

Place Manuel – *Pl. Manuel* – This lively square has a friendly atmosphere largel due to the small bandstand on which local groups frequently perform. It is line with numerous bars with terraces.

Sport

Maison du Rafting – *Four à Chaux-Pont du Martinet* – ☎ *04 92 85 53 99 – ope daily 9am-8pm – closed Oct-Mar*. This rafting centre has an annexe at Barcelonnett and a base camp at Méloans. It has a dozen qualified guides, all expert in mountai sports (cross-country cycling, climbing, hiking), and of course river sports (white water rafting, canoeing etc). Visitors are well supervised and can choose the leve that suits them best (sporting, recreational or family).

EXCURSIONS

Église de St-Pons – *2km/1.2mi northwest*. The interesting church, which forme part of a Benedictine monastery, has retained some Romanesque features (west doorway, chancel and apse). The two doorways are remarkable; their arches are dec orated with mouldings and supported by columns with a frieze at the top. Note in particular the naive style of the frieze on the 12C west doorway. The 15C **south door way★** is more richly decorated although the style remains naive; the themes illustrate are all connected with death since this door used to give access to the cemetery. On the left embrasure are a Crucifixion and a figure resurrected from a tomb; beneat the arch is an image of the Magi.

✷ **Le Sauze and Super-Sauze** – *4km/2.4mi southeast*. Situated at an altitude o 1 380m/4 528ft, Le Sauze is one of the oldest winter sports resorts in the Alps, dating from the 1930s and linked to the recent Super-Sauze (alt 1 700m/5 577ft) by road (6km/3.6mi) and **cable-car** ⊙. There is a wide choice of summer hikes an mountain expeditions to the nearby Chapeau de Gendarme and Pain de Sucre.
The two resorts are well known for their family atmosphere, their generous sunshine and the gentle gradient of their slopes, offering numerous cross-country skiing pos-sibilities. Artistic and acrobatic skiing are also specialities here.
The **Col de Fours** (2 314m/7 592ft), accessible via the **Télésiège de la Rente** and a short walk, offers a panoramic **view★** of Barcelonnette and the surrounding area. On the other side of the pass, the path joins up with the road leading to the Col de la Cayolle *(see Route de la CAYOLLE)*.

✷ **Pra-Loup** – *8.5km/5.3mi southwest*. See PRA-LOUP

HIKES

★ **Chapeau du Gendarme** – *(4hr 30min there and back)*
From the Raquette car park in Super-Sauze a marked path follows the ski runs then goes through the woods to a stream *(where hikers are advised to fill up with water)*. The path continues alongside the stream before heading due west to a ridge. Follow the ridge towards the southwest then go round a rock spur and join up with another trail at Collet du Quieron. Continue south towards the east face of the **Chapeau de Gendarme★★** and take the steep, right-hand fork to the Col de Gyp, where there is a fine **view★** of the Vallée de Bachelard. At the summit (2 685m/8 809ft), a splendid **view★★** takes in the Barcelonnette Basin and the **Gorges du Bachelard★**.

★ **Vallon du Riou Bourdoux** – *3hr from the Le Tréou car park. From Barcelonnette, follow D 900 towards Gap then turn right onto D 609 to La Frâche. Pass the aerodrome and, leaving the access road to La Frâche on your left, cross the Riou Bourdoux and continue along the forest road.* The road runs past devices designed to hold back the black mud from which the torrent takes its name. The unpredictable character of the Riou Bourdoux led to the building of some of the most important dams in Europe at that time. Completed in 1880, after 14 long years of construction, these feats of engineering minimised the devastating effects of the floods and retained the alluvial deposits.

Stop by the Tréou forest lodge and follow the marked path.

🚶 The walk to the mountain stream and a good **view** of the dam leads past a number of information panels which explain how the torrent was tamed. In a small coppice are the ruins of the abandoned village of Cervière; the cemetery cross stands as a reminder of this once important centre.

★ **Col de la Pare** – *4hr 30min there and back from Les Dalis car park; difference in altitude 800m/2 625ft. For the section to Le Tréou see above.* To the right, the trail marked "Col de la Pare" leads through a forest of larch and pine trees to a cottage, the gîte de la Pare (45min). Beyond the cottage, a path goes up to an altitude of 2 000m/6 562ft, above which there is no vegetation, and continues along the scree-covered slopes to the Col de la Pare (2 655m/8 711ft), overlooked by the Grande Épervière (2 884m/9 462ft), with the impressive Grand Bérard (3 048m/10 000ft) further away to the north. There is a fine **view★** of the Barcelonnette Basin and of the surrounding mountains. The fauna in this area is protected so that discreet and patient visitors may be rewarded with the sight of moufflons frisking about.

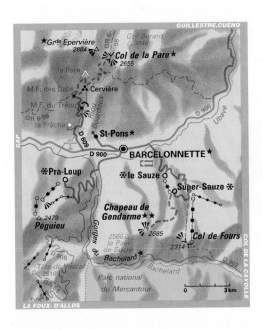

BARGÈME★

Population 115
Michelin map 340 O3, 114 fold 10 and 245 fold 35

In a beautiful **setting★** a few miles northeast of Comps-sur-Artuby, this hilltop village the highest municipality of the Var *département* (1 097m/3 599ft). The church, th ruined walls and the towers of the castle can be seen from a long way off. In the last fe years, the village has regained its old-world charm through a programme of extensiv restoration work.

Nearby sights: CASTELLANE, MOUSTIERS-STE-MARIE, Route NAPOLEON, ST-JULIEN DE-VERDON, Lac de STE-CROIX, Grand Canyon du VERDON

A WALK THROUGH THE VILLAGE

Motor vehicles are banned from the village.

Walk through the "Porte de Garde", one of the two 14C fortified gates still standing The narrow streets, linked by alleyways and arched passages, are lined with ol houses brightened up by colourful hollyhocks.

Église Saint-Nicholas ⊙ – The stone-built 11C Romanesque church has an oven vaulted apse. Note in particular the **Retable de saint Sébastien★**, an altarpiece in carve wood.

Castle – *Restoration work in progress.* Dating from the 13C, it comprised four roun towers, a square keep and a main courtyard. Although the building is in ruins, it layout is revealed by the remaining stairs, chimneys and windows.
From the castle, the **view★** extends to the Malay and Lachens mountains and, beyond to the Préalpes de Grasse, Canjuers Plateau and Maures Massif.

Chapelle Notre-Dame-des-Sept-Douleurs – Facing the castle, this small building, i typical local style with awning and wooden railings, was built during the Wars o Religion to atone for the murder of young nobleman Antoine de Pontevès, stabbe at the church altar during mass in the blood-feud that had claimed the lives of hi father and grandfather.

Les BAUGES★

Michelin map 333 J7 to K16 and 244 fold 18

The Massif des Bauges stands like a powerful citadel between the Annecy and Chambér valleys. In spite of its impressive outer defences (Dent du Nivolet towering abov Chambéry, Mont Revard above Aix-les-Bains and the Montagne du Charbon above th Lac d'Annecy), the centre of the range, through which flows the Chéran, offers gentl modelled Alpine landscapes and forested slopes.

Adjacent Sights: AIX-LES-BAINS, L'ALBANAIS, ALBERTVILLE, ALLEVARD, ANNECY, La d'ANNECY, Lac du BOURGET, CHAMBÉRY, Massif de la CHARTREUSE, Le GRÉSIVAUDAN

HIGHLIGHT

The **Réserve nationale des Bauges** created in 1950, stretches over 5 500ha/13 591 acres and is home to 600 chamois and 300 moufflons. The conservation programme of the area was completed in 1995 by the creation of the **Parc naturel régional du massif des Bauges** which covers over 80 000ha/197 684 acres from the Lac d'Annecy in the north, Val d'Isère in the east, the *cluses* (transverse valleys) of Chambéry to the south and the hills of the Albanais to the west. Within the park, small, well-defined areas still bear the economic and cultural imprint of the religious orders which, in times past, were focal points of economic life.

The Réserve cygétique des Bauges (National Game and Wildlife Preserve of the Bauges) in the upper valley of the river Chéran contains more than 1 000 chamois as well as numerous moufflons, roe-deer and black grouse.

EXCURSIONS

1 A Tour of the Two Lakes

FROM CHAMBÉRY TO ANNECY *68km/42.3mi – about 2hr – see local map*

From Chambéry take N 6 towards Albertville then, at the intersection of N 512 and N 6, turn onto the N 512 and then immediately afterwards onto the D 11 towards "Curienne".

Where to stay

BUDGET

Camping Les Cyclamens – *Rte du Champet – 73630 Le Châtelard – ☎ 04 79 54 80 19 – open 15 May-16 Sept – ✍ – reservations recommended – 33 pitches: 9.76€*. Drive past a housing estate to get to this small family camp-site kept in impeccable condition by a father and son team. The pitches are on a smooth lawn and have plenty of shade. There is a play area for children. Tennis and half-court tennis facilities 500yd away.

MODERATE

Chambre d'hôte La Grangerie – *Les Ginets – 73340 Aillon-le-Jeune – 4km/2.5mi from the resort towards les Ginets – ☎ 04 79 54 64 71 – www.lagrangerie.fr.st – closed 15 Jun-7 Jul – ✍ – 4rms: 39.64€ – main meal 9.76€*. A few hairpin bends above the village stands this old converted farm, with blackened beams and an open fire. Its windows overlook the Les Bauges range. Guests are given a warm welcome here. In winter skis can be put on as soon as you go out of the main door.

Beyond Leysse, there is a clear view of the Chambéry Valley and the Combe de Savoie-Grésivaudan meeting at right angles with the jagged silhouette of the Allevard Massif in the background.

From Le Boyat, follow the lane to Montmerlet. Continue on foot (45min return).

★ **Mont-St-Michel** – *Head uphill on the path to the right.* There is a choice of several itineraries, some easier than others; the most pleasant of them, beginning on the right as you go into the wood, leads to the Chapelle du Mont St-Michel. From the top, there is a bird's-eye **view** of the Chambéry Valley, of the town and of Challes below, with the snow-capped peaks of the Belledonne range in the distance. The Lac du Bourget is partly visible to the northwest, with the Mont du Chat towering above.

From Le Boyat to the Col des Prés, the view extends north to the Mont de Margeriaz and south to the Chambéry Basin overlooked by Mont Granier. The pastures around the **Col des Prés** (alt 1 135m/3 724ft) are dotted with a profusion of buttercups and daffodils.

> **Nature Notes**
>
> Notice how the predominant tree species varies according to the aspect of the slopes. Oaks and boxtrees flourish on the dry, rocky hillsides while fir trees prefer the moisture of the valleys. You may also come across a variety of Mediterranean maple, which thrives in hot, dry weather.

Aillon-le-Jeune – Situated at the relatively low altitude of 1 000m/3 281ft, this winter sports resort has spread its chalets all over the valley.

The road then follows the Aillon Valley with the grass-covered Grand Colombier (2 043m/6 703ft) and the more arid Dent de Rossanaz (1 891m/6 204ft) on the right. Beyond Le Cimeteret, the **Lescheraines** Basin comes into view: Le Châtelard village *(see below)* lies on the opposite bank of the Chéran backed by the Charbon Massif with the Pécloz summit (2 197m/7 208ft) in the distance.

★ **Pont du Diable** – *Follow the road to the Col de Leschaux for 600m/656yd; leave the car near two chalets facing each other and follow the marked path on the right; it goes round a private house to reach the wood and the bridge (15min there and back on foot).*
A small bridge spans the foaming Bellecombe mountain stream. This place is the main starting point of hikes in the area.

Between **Col de Leschaux** and Sévrier, there are fine **vistas★** of the "Grand" Lac d'Annecy, overlooked by the Château de Menthon and framed by Mont Veyrier, the Dents de Lanfon and the Tournette, and lower down, of the picturesque Roc de Chère facing the Château de Duingt at the narrowest part of the lake.

Sévrier – See Lac d'ANNECY, ⊡.

2km/1.2mi before reaching Annecy, the road comes close to the lake as it goes round the Puya promontory.

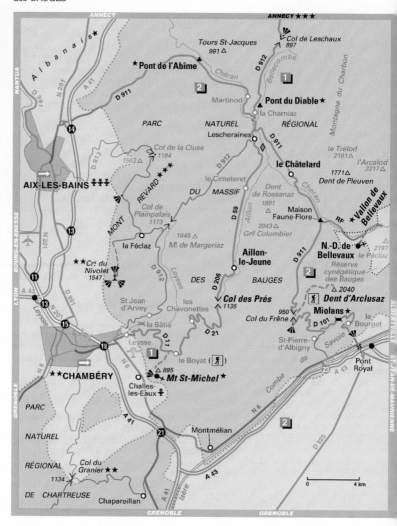

② From the Pont de l'Abîme to the Pont Royal

FROM AIX-LES-BAINS TO CHAMBÉRY *104km/65mi – around 3hr – see local map*

★ **Pont de l'Abîme** – The bridge spans the gorge through which flows the Chéran, 94m/103yd above the river bed. A spectacular **view**★ includes the peaks of the **Tours St-Jaques**.

From the Pont de l'Abîme to La Charniaz, D 911 follows the narrow Chéran Valley, affording views of the Montagne du Charbon and then, just before La Charniaz, of the summits enclosing the upper Chéran Valley. The road then goes through the Lescheraines Basin, where several routes intersect.

Le Châtelard – The village lies on either side of a wooded ridge once crowned by a castle, which separates the wide and open Lescheraines Basin from the more austere upper Chéran Valley. The administrative centre of the Parc naturel régional du massif des Bauges is here.

Beyond Le Châtelard, landscapes are definitely more Alpine with the impressive silhouette of the Dent de Pleuven (1 771m/5 810ft) towering over the valley and the Arcalod (2 217m/7 274ft) looming in the distance.

On reaching École, turn onto the Route de Jarsy at the church then follow the forest road through the Vallon de Bellevaux.

★ **Vallon de Bellevaux** – Turn right immediately after a bridge over the Chéran and continue to follow the stream through its wooded upper valley, one of the narrowest in the Alps. About 1.5km/0.9mi after the roundabout, the road leads to the meadows of Orgeval.

Turn back at the end of the road.

Chapelle Notre-Dame de Bellevaux – *On the way back, leave the car on the car park of the Office National des Forêts then take the narrow path on the left to a plantation of young trees*. A small oratory marks the place where the Bellevaux monastery once stood. Further up, in a clearing, stands the **Chapelle Notre-Dame de Bellevaux**, known as the Sainte Fontaine, an old place of popular pilgrimage on Whit Monday. There is a refreshing spring nearby.

Hike to Dent d'Arclusaz

Château de Miolans

Allow an entire day: 2hr 30min there, 3hr back plus breaks. Not recommended in poor weather conditions. Remember to take sufficient water for a day's walking, as there are no sources of drinking water along the route. Follow the marked path from the Col du Frêne. From the **Col du Frêne** *and on the way down to* St-Pierre-d'Albigny there are splendid **vistas**★ of the Combe de Savoie, through which flows the River Isère.

★**Château de Miolans** ⊙ – The castle occupies a commanding **position**★★ on an isolated rock spur overlooking the Combe de Savoie; it is one of the finest examples of medieval military architecture in the Savoie region. From 923 to 1523 the castle was the seat of the lords of Miolans before it was inherited by the dukes of Savoie and converted into a state prison (1559-1792).

Leave the car in the car park, 100m/110yd out of Miolans village, and enter the castle through the gates; allow 1hr.

Fine panoramic **view**★ extending to the Chartreuse and Belledonne ranges.
The square **keep**, flanked by four turrets, is the most characteristic part of the castle. From the top of the **Tour St-Pierre** there is an even more breathtaking view★★ – you may be able to make out Mont Blanc in the distance. In the garden, narrow steps lead down to the secret dungeons known as **oubliettes**; equally interesting is the **Souterrain de défense**★, a kind of underground watch-path with loopholes covering the access ramp to the castle.

Narrow twisting lanes link the Château de Miolans to the Pont Royal. Return to Chambéry by the A 43 motorway.

BEAUFORT★★

Population 1 985
Michelin map 333 D6 and 244 fold 20

Set in pleasant meadows which provide rich grazing for its dairy herds, the village of Beaufort is best known for the cheese that bears its name. The smooth contours of the slopes favour cross-country ski runs and several winter sports resorts have developed in the area, namely Arèches, Les Saisies, Val-Joly and Queige-Molliessoulaz.

Nearby Sights: ALBERTVILLE, Massif des ARAVIS, Les ARCS, BOURG-ST-MAURICE, Route des GRANDES ALPES, MEGÈVE, La TARENTAISE

HIGHLIGHT

★★**Beaufortain** – Bounded by the Val d'Arly, Val Montjoie and Tarentaise, the Beaufortain forms part of the central massif in the same way as the Massif du Mont-Blanc, but barely rises to 3 000m/9 843ft (Aiguille du Grand Fond: alt 2 889m/9 478ft) and displays neither glaciers nor peaks with sharp outlines, apart from the Pierra Menta monolith. On the other hand, the Beaufortain offers visitors an unbroken belt of forest (lower Doron Valley) and pastoral landscapes likely to appeal to those who prefer mountains of medium height.

Searching for water power – The Beaufortain region is an intensively exploited source of water power. The **Lac de la Girotte** *(2hr 30min there and back on foot from the Belleville power station to the end of the road running through the Hauteluce Valley)* was the first reservoir to be utilised (1923). The lake helped to provide the supply of water to seven power stations along the River Dorinet and River Doron.

Its capacity was doubled following the building of a damin 1946-48. An additional supply of water from the Tré-la-Tête glacier compensated for the seasonal shortage of water. It was channelled to the lake via a tunnel beneath the glacier.

The building of the Roselend Dam was an even more daring technical achievement. Its supply of water comes along 40km/25mi of tunnels from the Doron Valley and from tributaries of the River Isère. The water then drops from a height of 1 200m/3 937ft to the Bathie power station in the Basse Tarentaise region. The production of electricity totals 982 million kWh. There are additional reservoirs at St-Guérin and La Gittaz nearby.

SIGHTS

Between Villard and Beaufort, the valley widens below the impressive mass of the Montagne d'Outray, guarded by the ruined tower of the **Château de Beaufort**. The V-shaped gorge known as Défilé d'Entreroches can be seen beyond Beaufort. The **church** offers a typical example of Savoyard decoration, with its rood beam, altars in carved gilded wood and a remarkable pulpit dating from 1722.

NEARBY SIGHTS

★★ **Signal de Bisanne** – *In Villard-sur-Doron, take the road signposted "Signal de Bisanne" (13km/8mi).*The twisting road overlooks the Doron Valley. From the top (1 939m/6 362ft), the splendid **panorama** extends all around to the Combe de Savoie, the Aravis mountains, the Beaufortain and Mont Blanc massifs. Access *is also possible from Les Saisies, see* **2**.

Défilé d'Entreroches – *Leave Beaufort by the D 295. Park the car 1km/0.6mi beyond Beaufort, near the first bridge over the Doron.* The raging mountain torrent has carved interesting rock formations in this gorge.

EXCURSIONS

★★ **1 Route du Cormet de Roselend**

FROM BEAUFORT TO BOURG-ST-MAURICE *45km/28mi – about 3hrs - see local map*

Leave Beaufort by the D 218 heading south towards Arèches.

Arèches – Surrounded by gentle slopes ideal for skiing, Arèches is today one of the most typical winter resorts of the Beaufortain region.

The Lac de Roselend

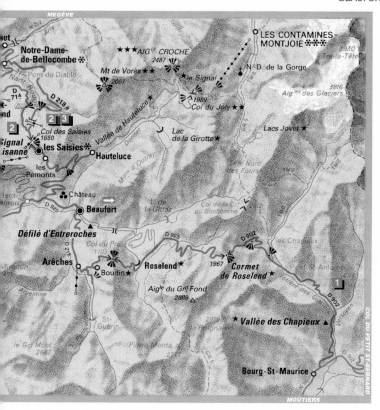

The Route du Col du Pré continues to the left, passing the village of Boudin.

★ **Boudin** – From the road leading to the St-Guérin Dam, there is a fine overall view of this characteristic Alpine village with its large chalets rising in tiers.

Barrage de Roselend – The buttressed dam rests against a natural arch obstructing the gorge of the River Doron. The **artificial lake★** and its austere surroundings come into view on the way down from the Col du Pré. Past a belvedere, the road follows the top of the dam then skirts the edge of the lake which flooded the village of Roselend (the chapel is a copy of the old church) and begins its final climb. The view extends westwards to Mont Mirantin and Grand Mont (2 687m/8 816ft), two of the best-known summits of the Beaufortain.

★ **Cormet de Roselend** – This depression, stretching over several kilometres, links the Roselend and Chapieux valleys at an altitude of more than 1 900m/6 234ft, in a landscape of remote treeless pastures, dotted with rocks and a few rustic shelters. From the small mound on the right, surmounted by a cross, there is a wide **view★** of the surrounding summits towering over the Chapieux Valley, including the Aiguille du Grand Fond (2 889m/9 478ft), the highest of them all.
The drive down from Cormet offers a glimpse of the Aiguille des Glaciers (3 816m/12 520ft), the most southern peak of the Mont Blanc Massif. Road D 902 continues past the village of Les Chapieux, partly destroyed in 1944, towards Bourg-St-Maurice.

★ **Vallée des Chapieux** – This is the meeting point of two mountain streams, the Versoyen and the Torrent des Glaciers. Beyond Bonneval, the road follows the deep forested valley of the Versoyen until it reaches a rock spur crowned with a ruined tower. There are fine views of the Haute Tarentaise just before the road veers to the right towards Bourg-St-Maurice.

★ ② Route des Saisies

FROM FLUMET TO BEAUFORT *41km/25.5mi – about 1hr 30min – see local map*

Flumet – *See Massif des ARAVIS* ④.

The road starts climbing through a forest of fir trees; view of the Aiguille Verte and Mont Blanc just before the last hairpin bend.

147

Beaufort cheese

It takes 10l/2.2gal of milk from cows of the Tarine and Abondance breeds, processed through 10 different stages, to make 1kg/2.2lb of cheese. Copper vats with a capacity of 4 000l of milk can produce eight rounds of Beaufort.

The first stage is called **emprésurage**, during which rennet is added to the heated milk; the curd is then allowed to harden and the cheese is constantly heated and mixed. During the fourth stage, it is poured into moulds known as **cloches de soutirage** from which rounds of cheese later emerge pressed between wooden hoops and covered with linen. **Pressage** and **retournement** give the cheese a denser and firmer aspect. **Saumurage** comes next, causing the crust to form. The long maturing process can then start: over six months, the 40kg/88lb rounds of cheese are salted, rubbed with linen and turned over twice a week in damp cellars kept at a constant temperature of 10°C/50°F.

Notre-Dame-de-Bellecombe – This is the most popular of the Val d'Arly ski resorts.

Turn right onto D 71 (liable to be blocked by snow from late November to April).

Crest-Voland – This typical Savoyard village is a peaceful summer and winter resort; linked by ski lifts to the nearby resort of Les Saisies under the name of **Espace Cristal**, it offers a wide choice of skiing, including cross-country skiing. It is well known to advanced skiers for its treacherous black run nicknamed "the kamikaze". There are numerous possibilities for summer hiking, in particular to Le Cernix, Cohennoz or Les Saisies, and of travelling on snowshoes through the surrounding snowfields in winter.

Eating out

MODERATE

La Ferme de Victorine – *Le Planay – 73590 Notre-Dame-de-Bellecombe – ☎ 04 79 31 63 46 – closed 25 Jun-5 Jul, 12 Nov-15 Dec, Sun evening and Mon Apr-Jun and Sept-Nov – 21.04/35.06€.* The proprietor has transformed his grandmother's farm into a restaurant. The bay window of the bar overlooks cattle feeding peacefully in the cowshed. Local specialities are served by staff dressed in regional costume.

Where to stay

BUDGET

Hôtel Grand Mont – *Rte de Grand-Mont – 73270 Arêches – ☎ 04 79 38 33 36 – closed 24 Apr-8 May, 1 Oct-8 Nov and Sat out of season – 13rms 39.64€/48.78€ - ☐ 7.32€ – restaurant 17.53P/18.29€.* This is a good family establishment at the heart of the village. The house in traditional local style is well kept and welcomes its patrons as friends. Accommodation is simple but neat. The dining room is charming and the regularly renovated rooms beyond reproach.

MODERATE

Auberge du Poncellamont – *L'Illaz – 73270 Arêches – ☎ 04 79 38 10 23 – closed 16 Apr-27 May, 1 Oct-21 Dec, Sun evening and Wed except school holidays – ☐ – 14rms: 48.78/51.83€ - ☐ 6.40€ – restaurant 14.94/25.92€.* This recently built house typical of the Savoie region is slightly out of town near the departure point for the ski slopes. Its façade is bright with flowers in summer, and more sober in appearance in winter. It is furnished in a simple rustic style and its fairly plain rooms are well kept and comfortable.

Hôtel Caprice des Neiges – *Rte des Saisies – 73590 Crest-Voland – 6.5km/4m S of Flumet on D 71ᴮ then D 218ᴮ – ☎ 04 79 31 62 95 – closed 21 Apr-19 Jun and 16 Sept-14 Dec – ☐ – 16rms: 51.83/68.60€ - ☐ 5.79 € – restaurant 14.48/19.82€.* This appealing chalet at the foot of the ski slopes is typical of the Savoie region and a perfect place to stay for nature lovers in summer and winter alike, whether in search of sport or relaxation. Its attributes include a terrace and a flower garden, as well as tennis and miniature golf facilities, cosy panelled rooms and local cooking.

Return to Notre-Dame-de-Bellecombe.

The next part of the journey to the Col des Saisies offers wide vistas of the Aravis mountains extending to Pointe Percée, their highest peak (2 752m/9 029ft).

❋ **Les Saisies** – This winter sports resort was founded in 1963 near the **Col des Saisies** (alt 1 633m/5 358ft) on typical Alpine pastureland belonging to nearby villages in characteristic pastoral surroundings. All the cross-country skiing events of the 1992 Winter Olympics took place in Les Saisies which is today the main Alpine centre for that sport. It is also the home town of **Frank Piccard** who became a double Olympic champion in Calgary in 1988.
From the pass and from **Les Pémonts** village, there are wide **views★** of the Beaufortain mountains.
The road then runs along the green **Vallée de Hauteluce★**.

Hauteluce – This sunny summer and winter resort offers visitors the lovely picture of its graceful onion-shaped spire in the foreground and Mont Blanc in the distance, seen through the Col du Joly in the upper part of the valley.
The **écomusée** ⊘, situated at the heart of the village, organises exhibitions on traditional life and development projects concerning the Beaufortain region.
Before reaching Beaufort, note the tower of the ruined castle perched on a wooded height.

③ The Arly and Doron Gorges

FROM BEAUFORT 72km

Leave Beaufort by the D 925 and follow the D 218 towards Hauteluce.

The drive over the Col des Saisies to Notre-Dame-de-Bellecombe includes some fine views of the Massif des Aravis. Just after Notre-Dame de Bellecombe, the wide-reaching view takes in the Arly valley.

Notre-Dame-de-Bellecombe – *see* ② *above*

Flumet – *see Massif des ARAVIS* ④

Beyond Flumet and the Pont de Flon, lies the Arondine basin through which the tributary flows before joining the Arly. The prettiest view is that of St-Nicholas-la-Chapelle with its attractive onion spire and the picturesque landscape around it.

Turn right onto the D 109 at the Pont de Flon.

Between the bridge and Le Château, the road climbs the steep, terraced slopes of Héry, with impressive views of the Gorges d'Arly and the little village of Cohennoz on the opposite side. Just before the road turns sharply to the north there is a place to park and a **viewpoint★**. The Dent de Cons rises above the factory chimneys of the Ugine valley, and in the far distance, beyond the Combe de Savoie, the snow-capped peaks of the Massif d'Allevard are visible until late in the year.

Ugine – The old town, its houses clustered around the church, looks down towards the steelworks at **Les Fontaines-d'Ugine**.

Drive back to the Gorges d'Arly and turn right onto the D 67 towards Queige and the Col de Forclaz.

The road winds its way uphill giving views of the Arly valley and the end of the Massif d'Aravis to the west.

Housed in the 13C Château de Crest-Crechel, the **Musée des Arts et Traditions populaires du Val d'Arly** ⊘ displays furniture, tools and costumes from the region.

The road continues past the ruined fortresses of Barrioz and Cornillon to **Queige**, a small village on the right bank of the river Doron, which the road follows to Beaufort. The section between Venthon and Villard runs through thick forest, although the Roche Pourrie and the summit of the Mirantin (2 461m) are visible near Queige power station.

La vallée des BELLEVILLE✳✳✳

Michelin map 333 M5 and 244 fold 31
Local map see Massif de la VANOISE

This huge area covering 23 000ha/56 835 acres (Bella Villa means large estate in Latin) lies between the Tarentaise and the Maurienne on the western edge of the Massif de la Vanoise. St-Martin-de-Belleville became an important tourist centre with the creation of the Les Ménuires (1964) and Val-Thorens (1972) resorts. Its vast and splendid **ski area** forms the main part of **Les Trois Vallées**✳✳✳ *(see Massif de la VANOISE)*. Besides its 120 marked ski runs, the valley has retained large areas in their natural state, which make it one of the most attractive areas in Europe for off-piste skiing.

In summer, the valley is ideal for **walking** and **hiking** (180km/112mi of footpaths and trails). Furthermore, the wealth of traditional villages in the area and the 36 churches and chapels, most of them Baroque, cannot fail to attract visitors who appreciate the cultural aspect of tourism. **Circuits sur les chemins du Baroque** (tours along Baroque trails, *see Practical information*) are organised to help visitors who wish to discover the historic heritage of the valley.

Nearby Sights: ALBERTVILLE, BOURG-ST-MAURICE, CHAMPAGNY-EN-VANOISE, COURCHEVEL, Route de la MADELEINE, MÉRIBEL, LA PLAGNE, PRALOGNAN-LA-VANOISE, La TARENTAISE, Massif de la VANOISE.

VILLAGES OF THE LOWER VALLEY

The deep valley is dotted with clumps of deciduous trees.

St-Jean-de-Belleville – Rebuilt after a major fire, the village has retained a richly decorated church (Baroque altarpiece by Todescoz and imposing altarpiece over the high altar in early Empire style, beginning of the 19C). From St-Jean, there is an interesting detour through the **Nant Brun Valley**.

St-Martin-de-Belleville – Alt 1 400m/4 593ft. This charming old village has some gentle sunny slopes linked by chair-lift to those of Méribel and Les Ménuires. In summer there are numerous possibilities of hikes in the surrounding area as well as concerts in the churches.

The stocky **Église St-Martin** surmounted by a Lombard-style steeple, is characteristic of 17C-18C hall-churches. 1km/0.6mi south, along the road to Les Ménuires, stands the **Chapelle Notre-Dame-de-Vie**. This 17C edifice, crowned with a cupola and surmounted by a slender steeple, is an important place of pilgrimage (15 August and first Sunday in September) set in pastoral surroundings. Its remarkable **altarpiece★**, dedicated to the Virgin Mary, was carved in arolla pine by J.-M. Molino. A profusion of decoration includes the paintings of the Trinity and the Blessed Virgin which adorn the cupola, attributed to the school of Nicolas Oudéard.

★**Salins-les-Thermes via D 96** – *Narrow road safe in summer and dry weather only.* This itinerary offers picturesque views of the villages.

Notre-Dame-de-Vie, St-Martin-de-Belleville

WINTER RESORTS OF THE UPPER VALLEY

Beyond the Chapelle Notre-Dame-de-Vie, the slopes become smooth and moderately steep; Les Menuires can be seen in the distance, with Pointe de la Masse and Cime de Caron *(both accessible by cable-car)* towering over the resort.

** **Les Menuires** – This modern resort consists of seven sites spread over 2km/1.2mi at an altitude varying between 1 780m/5 840ft and 1 950m/6 365ft. The two main sites (La Croisette and Les Bruyères) are practical and pleasant at the same time; the skiing area is nearby and there is a large shopping centre. Recent landscaping and tree-planting projects, and a return to a more rural style of architecture, have succeeded in softening the resort's functional edges.

Ski area – Enjoying a fair amount of sunshine, Les Ménuires is appreciated by advanced skiers for its demanding ski runs (the Pylônes, Dame Blanche and Rocher Noir). The off-piste area is easily accessible and skiing facilities are extended over the whole ski area of Les Trois Vallées. There are some 30km/18.6mi of cross-country skiing tracks, which are particularly fine between Le Bettaix and Le Châtelard.

In winter, guided excursions are available for ski-trekking enthusiasts, and in summer a wide choice of activities is provided.

** **Mont de la Chambre** – Alt 2 850m/9 350ft. *From La Croisette, take the gondola then walk up to the summit, which is only a few minutes away*. The fine panorama includes Mont Blanc, the Vallée de Méribel, the Val-Thorens and Vanoise glaciers.
🚶 It is possible to walk back to Les Ménuires *(2hr)*.

** **Val-Thorens** – In winter, the car-free village has parking available outside with shuttle services to the centre. The highest ski resort in Europe, set in magnificent surroundings, it is overlooked by the Aiguille de Péclet (3 561m/11 683ft) and bounded by three glaciers marking the limits of the Parc national de la Vanoise. The barren landscape does not entice hikers but attracts rock-climbers instead.

Ski area – Situated between 1 800m/5 905ft and 3 300m/10 827ft and covered with snow from November to May, Val-Thorens is a skiers' paradise: snowfields all round, crisp mountain air, breathtaking views of the Mont Blanc, Vanoise and Écrins massifs, famous ski runs including the Combe de Caron and access in 20min to the ski areas of Mont de la Chambre and Mont Vallon de Méribel. Inaugurated in 1996, the Orelle gondola takes skiers from the Maurienne Valley up to the Val-Thorens ski area in 20min. In July, several pistes are available on the Glacier de Péclet.

There is a wide choice of après-ski activities in a complex extending over 9 000m²/10 764sq yd. Childcare facilities include the Village d'Enfants-Académie des Neiges, created and run by the ski champion Marielle Goitschel *(see VAL D'ISÈRE)* who shares her love of the mountains with the children.

** **Cime de Caron** – Alt 3 198m/10 492ft. *Access by the* **Caïrn and Caron gondolas** ⊙ *followed by the* **Caron cable car** ⊙ *(minimum 2hr there and back)*.
The summit can then be reached in 5min. The extraordinary **panorama**★★★ unfolding from the viewing table embraces practically the whole of the French Alps, in particular the imposing summits of the **Mont Blanc**, **Vanoise**, **Queyras** and **Écrins** massifs to the northeast and south, the **Belledonne** and **Aravis** ranges to the west and northwest with the Jura mountains on the horizon.

* **Glacier de Péclet** – *Access by* **Funitel** ⊙ *(twin-cable cable car)*. Close-up view of the glacier and the Cime de Caron. Advanced skiers can, in summer and autumn, take the 3 300m chairlift to the summit *(caution is advisable at the summit)* from which there is a splendid **panorama**★★★ of the Mont Blanc and Vanoise massifs.

HIKES

A map of the local footpaths is available from the tourist office. The various summits in the surrounding area can all be spotted from the Cime de Caron and Pointe de la Masse viewing tables; it is well worth making the ascents at the beginning of a stay to take in an overall view of the region.
There are pleasant walks for inexperienced hikers to the **Lac du Lou** *(2hr 30min there and back from Les Bruyères)* and **Hameau de la Gitte**★ *(1hr 45min there and back from Villaranger)*. The following hikes are suitable for experienced hikers. Note that, in an effort to preserve the natural habitat of the 250 ibexes and 400 chamois, tourist infrastructure in the area has been kept to a minimum; maintained hiking paths are a rarity, and even these must be followed without the usual signs and markings.

** **La Croix Jean-Claude** – *4hr 30min. Difference in altitude: about 600m/1 968ft. Just before Béranger, take a path on the right to the hamlet of Les Dogettes; turn right towards two small mountains (the Fleurettes); continue to the spring and beyond to the ridge separating the Belleville and Allues valleys; turn left to Croix Jean-Claude and Dos de Crêt Voland (2 092m/6 864ft).*

Eating out

BUDGET

La Bergerie – *Immeuble 3 Vallées – 73440 Val-Thorens – ☎ 04 79 00 77 18 – closed 9 May-12 Jul and 25 Aug-19 Nov – 22.87/30.49€*. This little restaurant furnished in local style is tucked inside a modern building. It has old farming implements on the walls and is decorated in classic Savoyard style. The cooking, popular with neighbourhood gourmets, is also inspired by local tradition. There is a livelier atmosphere in the evenings.

MODERATE

Bar de la Marine – *73440 Val-Thorens – ☎ 04 79 00 03 12 – closed beginning May-beginning Dec – ✗ – 19.82€*. A strange name for a restaurant in the mountains! This is the place to eat, however, when on the ski slopes. It is above the Cascade cable-car. The cooking is revitalising and some fine specialities are served here, such as pot-au-feu, which are perfect after a hungry day on the slopes.

Le Sherpa – *73440 Val-Thorens – ☎ 04 79 00 00 70 – closed 3 May-29 Nov – 22.11/25.92€*. This hotel-restaurant built in the 1970s lies slightly out of the town centre and is very peaceful. It has comfortable rooms overlooking the mountains through French windows. The atmosphere is friendly and ideal for families.

La Bouitte – *73440 St-Marcel – 2km/1mi SE of St-Martin-de-Belleville on a B-road – ☎ 04 79 08 96 77 – closed 2 May-30 Jun and 1 Sept-14 Dec – 23.63/79.27€*. If you're starting to feel a little peckish, put on your skis and treat yourself to a bite to eat on the terrace of this chalet-restaurant. Charming dining room with rustic style decor.

Le Bellevillois – *73440 Val-Thorens – ☎ 04 79 00 04 33 – 27.44/56.36€*. This is the "classy" restaurant in Val Thorens hotel and is only open in the evenings. It has whitewashed walls, terracotta floor tiles and wooden furniture, and all the ingredients of a grand dinner venue. The menu is contemporary.

Where to stay

EXPENSIVE

Le Val Thorens – *73440 Val-Thorens – ☎ 04 79 00 04 33 – closed 4 May-30 Nov – 80rms: from 162.36€ - ☲ 10.67€ – restaurant 12.20/27.44€*. This 1980s hotel at the centre of the resort has a stylish air with its wood-panelled façade. It offers opulent comfort, without ostentatious luxury, and draws a loyal clientele of regulars. Its three restaurants include Le Bellevillois, listed above, and La Fondue.

L'Ours Blanc – *73440 Roberty 2000 – 1.5km/1mi SE of Les Ménuires – ☎ 04 79 00 61 66 – closed 24 Apr-30 Nov – ▣ – 49rms: from 111.29€ - ☲ 9.91€ – restaurant 27.44/44.21€*. This large chalet in a village above Les Ménuires has a magnificent site: on the side of the ski slopes, all its windows overlook snow-capped mountains. Besides the view, the modern rooms all offer the perfect peace and quiet of the mountains.

🔼 Magnificent **view★★** of the Belleville villages, Méribel, the Vanoise, La Plagne and Mont Blanc. The path reaches the Roc de la Lune *(signposted "Col de la Lune")*. The walk down to Béranger offers fine views of the villages.

★★★**Crève Tête** – *Alt 2 342m/7 684ft. Take a small road starting in a bend preceding Fontaine-le-Puits; it leads to the Col de la Coche and to the dam of the same name (alt 1 400m/4 593ft). A rough road on the left leads directly to the Pas de Pierre Larron. If you do not wish to take it, park your car at the end of the dam and walk along the Darbellaz path to the Pas de Pierre Larron in 1hr 30min.*

🔼 From the **Pas de Pierre Larron**, the **view★** extends to the valley of the River Isère and Mont Blanc. Go to the refuge on the left. A steeper and more demanding path leads to the summit *(2hr)* offering superb **views★★★** *(see VAL MOREL)*.

★★**Pointe de la Masse and tour of the lakes** – *Take the gondola to La Masse. From the first section, allow 5hr for the whole itinerary. Less experienced hikers are advised to skip the ascent of the Masse (in this case allow 3hr 30min). The tour includes Lac Longet, the Pointe de la Masse, Lac Noir, Lac Crintallia and Le Teurre.*

Val-Thorens, Europe's highest winter sports resort

From the viewing table at the top of La Masse (2 804m/9 200ft), there is a splendid **panorama★★** of the Écrins, Grandes Rousses, Belledonne ranges, Mont Blanc, the Vanoise and the Vallée des Encombres immediately below.

Vallée des Encombres – The village of **Le Châtelard**, near St-Martin, lies at the entrance to this secluded 14km/8.7mi-long valley. Tourist facilities have been limited in order to preserve the exceptionally rich alpine fauna. There are fine guided hikes *(ask at Les Ménuires)* to the **Petit Col des Encombres★★** (alt 2 342m/7 684ft) and the **Grand Perron des Encombres★★★** (alt 2 825m/9 268ft) offering impressive views of the Maurienne Valley and Écrins Massif.

BESSANS✳

Population 311

Michelin map 333 O6 and 244 fold 33 - Local map see La MAURIENNE

Bessans lies in a small valley enclosed by high summits, at the heart of the traditional Maurienne region. Some of the land belonging to the municipality forms part of the Parc national de la Vanoise *(see Introduction: Nature parks and reserves)*.
The old village was largely destroyed by fire in 1944 and most of modern-day Bessans dates from after the Second World War. However, a strong sense of history still survives in a village which has retained its ancient traditions (the local costume is still worn on festive occasions) and a reputation for decorative woodcarving. This cottage industry has been a speciality of the area since Renaissance times and is now exclusively devoted to the production of the famous **diables de Bessans**, little wooden devil figurines with their origins in local legend *(see Introduction;Traditions and Folklore)*.

Nearby Sights: AUSSOIS, BONNEVAL-SUR-ARC, Route des GRANDES ALPES, Route de l'ISERAN, La Haute MAURIENNE, MODANE, Route du MONT-CENIS, TIGNES, VAL D'ISÈRE, Massif de la VANOISE

SKI RESORT

Ski area – The resort offers more than 80km/49.7mi of cross-country trails. Its superb snow coverage at a moderate altitude of 1 700m/5 577ft offers fine ski treks during the greater part of the season.

Satan as a souvenir? – For an unusual gift, try the shop in rue St-Esprit (of all places), where the devil makes work for idle hands. The huge range of handcrafted figures combines fine workmanship and diabolical inspiration!...Contact Georges Personnaz, ☎ 04 79 05 95 49

The devil's in the detail: a finely carved souvenir from the village

SIGHTS

Church ⊙ – It contains many 17C statues and an altarpiece by Clappier, one of the famous sculptors from Bessans. There is also a very expressive Crucifixion and a remarkable **Ecce Homo**.

Chapelle St-Antoine ⊙ – *Access through the cemetery, opposite the side door of the church.* Although still used for services, the chapel is now a museum.
Built in the 14C and restored in the 19C, the building is decorated outside with murals in poor condition, depicting the virtues and the vices. Inside, the **paintings★** illustrating the life of Jesus Christ are believed to date from the 15C. The chapel also contains statues carved by local sculptors between the 17C and the 19C including several representations of Christ at the time of the Passion and St Anthony with his bell (hermits used bells in the past to frighten evil spirits away). The Renaissance coffered ceiling, decorated with stars, dates from 1526.

★★ VALLÉE D'AVÉROLE

At the time of the Renaissance, Italian artists came through this valley, dotted with chapels and pastoral villages, characteristic of the Haute Maurienne (La Goula, Vincendières, Avérole). Visitors must leave their car in the car park located 0.5km/0.3mi before Vincendières and continue on foot to Avérole *(45min there and back)*: view of the Pointe de Charbonnel (south) and the Albaron (north).

★★**Refuge d'Avérole** – Alt 2 210m/7 250ft. *Easy hike from Avérole, the only steep climb coming at the very end (2hr 15min there and back); difference in altitude: 200m/656ft.*
⚐ Beautiful mountain setting with glaciers, waterfalls and the Bessanese summit (3 592m/11 785ft) in the foreground.

BEUIL★

Population 334
Michelin map 115 fold 4, 341 C3 and 245 fold 24

Clinging to a steep, south-facing slope of the upper valley of the River Cians and overlooked by Mont Mounier (2 817m/9 242ft), Beuil owes much to its charming **setting★**. An elegant church steeple, surrounded by snowfields or a lilac haze of lavender, stands at the centre of this pleasant summer and winter resort, best explored on a mountain hike, a rafting excursion, a skiing trip, or a walk through narrow, medieval streets with a Provençal atmosphere.

Nearby Sights: ANNOT, AURON, BARCELONNETTE, Route de la BONETTE, Gorges du CIANS, Val d'ENTRAUNES, ENTREVAUX, Route des GRANDES ALPES, ISOLA 2000, PUGET-THÉNIERS, ST-ÉTIENNE-DE-TINÉE, VILLARS-SUR-VAR.

THE RESORT

Ski area – Lovers of winter sports have been meeting in Beuil-les-Launes, the oldest resort in the Mediterranean Alps, since 1910 and the architecture remains true to its turn-of-the-century style. Pistes with generous snow cover offer something for beginners as well as black-run experts and cross-country skiers.

In spite of being only an hour from the coast, Valberg (see below) also enjoys good snow conditions on slopes from 1 500-2 066m/4 921-6 778ft. Linked to Beuil, its 50 runs, some provided with floodlights for night skiing, welcome snowboarders, ski-jumpers and other daredevils drawn by the speed-skiing along the Kilometre Lancé run *(see also VARS)*. Cross-country skiers have 40km/25mi of trails at their disposal.

SIGHTS

Church – Rebuilt in the 17C, it has retained a 15C Romanesque bell-tower and some fine **paintings★**: on the right there is an Adoration of the Magi by an artist from the Veronese School and, further along, fragments of an altarpiece

(St. Lucia) and a predella. The high-altar retable in Primitive style has 16 panels and, on the left, there is a predella illustrating Christ rising from the tomb as well as the panel of an altarpiece depicting St Catherine of Sienna.

Chapelle des Pénitents-Blancs ⏱ – This Renaissance chapel was built with stones from Grimaldi Castle, once the seat of a powerful dynasty whose territorial claims to the area from the 14C to the 17C set them in constant conflict with the treacherous dukes of Savoie. The façade decorated in *trompe-l'œil* was recently restored by Guy Ceppa.

EXCURSIONS

⋆ Route du Col de Valberg

20km/12.4mi west along D 28 – about 45min, not including walks.

This road links the **Gorges du Cians** *(see Gorges du CIANS)* and the **Gorges Daluis** *(see VAL D'ENTRUANES)* via the Valberg Pass.

⁑ **Valberg** – Lying amid larch forests and green pastures, Valberg is a sunny summer and winter resort created in 1935 at an altitude of 1 669m/5 476ft. It is only 80km/50mi away from the Mediterranean coast and is the starting point for round tours of the Gorges du Cians and Gorges du Daluis as well as hikes to Mont Mounier (alt 2 817m/9 242ft). Behind the simple façade of the mountain church, the **Chapelle Notre-Dame-des-Neiges**, is a more elaborate **interior⋆**, a fine example of modern religious art. The coffered ceiling, like the upturned hull of a boat, combines depictions of the Virgin Mary with brightly coloured images of skiers and alpine flowers.

Croix de Valberg – *45 min there and back on foot. Start from the Col du Sapet road and continue along a steep path.* The cross, which is made with wooden skis, is lit at night. The **panorama⋆⋆** reaches from the Grand Coyer to Mont Pelat , and from Mont Mounier to the Mercantour.

On the way down from the Col de Valberg to Guillaumes, the road offers a succession of picturesque **views**. There is a striking contrast between the forested north-facing slope and the vineyards, orchards and wheat fields on the cultivated southern side.

Follow the D 28 directly to Guillaumes or take the D 29 via Péone, some 8km/5mi away

⋆⋆ **Péone** – The tall houses of this ancient village nestle at the foot of the **dolomitic peaks⋆** which are one of the natural attractions of the pretty **surroundings⋆**. Several Catalan families settled here in the 13C and the inhabitants have kept the nickname "Catalans". A stroll through the maze of narrow streets and stepped lanes takes one past beautiful doorways, windows and trompe-l'œil façades to the charming place Thomas-Guérin with its sundial and carved doorways. The Promenade des Demoiselles leads to the **Cheminées de calcaire⋆**, striking rock formations which resemble petrified flames.

Guillaumes – See Val d'ENTRAUNES.

⋆ Route du Col de la Couillole

Col de la Couillole – 1 678m/5 505ft. Extended view on either side of the pass. This is the popular rendezvous and vantage point of fans of the Monte-Carlo Rally. The road winds up to the pass, within sight of the Gorges du Cians and the village of Beuil, amid spruce and larch woods.

⋆ **Roubion** – This village, perched on top of a red-schist ridge, at an altitude of 1 300m/4 265ft, forms a striking **picture⋆⋆**. It has retained part of its 12C fortifications, some old houses, a belfry carved out of rock and the 18C Fontaine du Mouton on the village square.
The **church** dates from the 18C, apart from the crenellated Romanesque bell-tower. The interior decoration is interesting; particularly noteworthy are a 15C Virgin in one of the south side chapels and a 15C Crucifixion in the chapel on the left of the chancel. From the main square, a **tunnel** leads through the rock to **Vignols**, a pretty mountain village with some well-preserved farmhouses. To the right of the church, follow a little passageway to a fine **viewpoint** looking down into the Vionène valley; a narrow street, with tufts of lavender sprouting here and there, leads back to the entrance to the village.

Chapelle St-Sébastien ⏱⋆ – *Right towards St-Sauveur-de-Tinée, then right again down a small road leading down the hill.* Situated below the village, this rustic 16C chapel is decorated with murals: symbolic images of the virtues and vices and 12 panels relating the legend of St Sebastian with captions in Old Provençal. Outside, there is a representation of St Michael slaying the dragon.

The return of the "bone breaker"

The **bearded vulture**, the largest Alpine bird with an impressive 2.80m/9ft wing span, is typical of Europe's endangered species. Decimated throughout the Alpine region during the 19C, it survived in the Pyrenees and in Corsica. This vulture has a strange lifestyle: it flies over almost inaccessible high pastures and feeds on dead chamois and ewes, ripping off large bones from their carcasses and dropping them from a great height onto the rocks below in order to break them, hence its nickname. In 1993, the Parc national du Mercantour and the Parco Naturale delle Alpi Marittime joined forces to attempt the reintroduction of the bearded vulture into the area. The operation was highly successful. Young birds (90 days old) are placed in caves and usually fly away 30 days later. However, it takes eight years for the vultures to be fully grown and they have a life expectancy of 40 years.

To date, five bearded vultures have been reintroduced into the southern Alps and a total of 70 into the whole Alpine range stretching from Austria to France, as part of a unique international programme.

The road follows the raging torrent of the Vionène and continues through a **landscape★** where red schist provides the predominant colour.

Turn left onto the D 130 towards Roure

★ **Roure** – Lying at the heart of a beautiful mountain setting, this ancient village has retained a wealth of interesting 17C and 18C domestic architecture. The houses are partly built of red schist and their roofs are covered with red-schist slabs *(lauzes)*. Some of them still have walls made of roughly hewn larch trunks.

The Baroque **church** ⊙, rebuilt in the 18C, contains some fine works of art: the 16C **St-Laurent altarpiece★**, richly coloured in green and red against a gold background, is framed by twisted columns and surmounted by a representation of the Entombment. The **Chapelle St-Bernard-et-St-Sébastien** ⊙★ is decorated with remarkably well-preserved naive frescoes by Andrea de Cella depicting the life of St Bernard of Menthon and of St Sebastian, famous for his healing powers against plague and cholera. The friezes separating the panels date from the Renaissance.

The nearby **Arboretum** planted by botanist Marcel Kroenlein has brought together specimens of mountain trees from around the world.

Return to D 30

The road runs down to the Tinée Valley and the village of St-Sauveur in a series of tight hairpin bends, through a landscape of schist and patchy forest, its wild beauty enhanced by the contrasting colours of the rocks.

St-Sauveur-sur-Tinée – *see Vallée de la TINÉE, Excursions*

Route de la BONETTE★★

Michelin map 334 I6 and 245 folds 10, 23 and 24

This road stretches from the Ubaye Valley to Nice via the Vallée de la Tinée covering a distance of some 150km/93mi. Several military constructions along the route are a reminder of its long-standing strategic importance. The present road, built in 1963-64, goes through part of the Parc national du Mercantour and over the Col de la Bonette, which makes it the highest road in France.

Nearby Sights: AURON, BARCELONNETTE, BEUIL, ISOLA 2000, PRA-LOUP, ST-ÉTIENNE-LA-TINÉE, Vallée de la TINÉE, L'UBAYE, VAL D'ALLOS

EXCURSIONS

★★★Cime de la Bonette

BARCELONNETTE TO ST-ÉTIENNE-DE-TINÉE *64km/40mi – about 3hr*

This twisting road is blocked by snow from November to the end of June.

★ **Barcelonnette** – See BARCELONNETTE.
From Barcelonnette, follow D 900 towards Italy.

Jausiers – See L'UBAYE: ②.
Coming out of Jausiers, turn right towards Nice.

The road climbs towards **Le Restefond** in a series of hairpin bends offering lovely views of the Ubaye Valley. Between the Casernes de Restefond, a complex fortified by Maginot in 1931, and St-Étienne-de-Tinée, 18 special viewing tables set along the road explain the main features of the landscape.

The road continues to climb past the **Col de la Bonette** (2 715m/8 907ft) to an altitude of **2 802m/9 193ft** before skirting round the foot of the Cime de la Bonette. It is one of the highest altitudes reached by a European road.

★★★ **Cime de la Bonette** – Alt 2 862m/9 390ft. *From the highest point of the road, 30min there and back on foot. Viewing table.* The breathtaking **panorama** embraces most of the mountain ranges of the southern Alps: the Queyras (Font Sancte), Monte Viso and the Ubaye (Brec de Chambeyron and Tête de Moïse) to the north, the Pelvoux to the northwest; then the upper Verdon (Grande Séolane and Mont Pelat) and the southern Alps to the west, the Préalpes de Digne to the south and the Corborant and Argentera to the east. A special viewing table explains the formation of the Alps.

On its way down, the road reaches the ruins of the **Camp des Fourches**, a large encampment occupied until the end of the Second World War by a battalion of *chasseurs alpins* (mountain troops). From there, a path leads in 5min to the Col des Fourches which affords a superb **view**★ of the vast cirque of Salso Moreno, close to the Italian border *(viewing table with explanations on local geology).*

Hike to Pas de la Cavale★★, **Hike to the Lacs de Vens**★★★ – *See ST-ÉTIENNE-DE-TINÉE.*

Only 3km/1.8mi beyond Le Pra, one can see the Vens waterfall on the left. As the road runs down into the valley, the short grass of the high pastures gives way to a larch forest.

At Pont-Haut, turn right onto D 63 to St-Dalmas.

★ **St-Dalmas-le-Selvage** – St-Dalmas, situated at the top of the upper Tinée Valley, is the highest village of the Alpes-Maritimes *département*. The tall, Lombard-style steeple of the village **church**⊙, built in neo-Romanesque style and covered with larch shingles, stand out against the splendid wild setting of the Jalorgues Valley. The west front is decorated with *trompe-l'œil* **paintings**: one of these which St Dalmas, a 3C martyr who preached the gospel in the Alps. Inside, notice the fine 16C altarpiece and several interesting paintings.

The narrow streets are lined with stocky houses built of dark schist, covered with shingles and adorned with numerous sundials.

★ **Col de la Moutière** – *12km northwest along a narrow road.* The road offers bird's-eye views of the village and goes through a splendid larch wood, known as the Bois de Sestrière. Beyond the refuge of the same name, the road enters the central zone of the Parc national du Mercantour. Colonies of marmots can be observed near the pass situated below the Cime de la Bonette.

From St-Dalmas, return to D 2205 and turn right to St-Étienne-de-Tinée.

The road follows a stream through an impressive gorge.

★ **St-Étienne-de-Tinée** – *See ST-ÉTIENNE-DE-TINÉE.*

View of the Pas de la Cavale from the Col des Fourches

BONNEVAL-SUR-ARC★★

Population 216
Michelin map 333 P5 and 244 fold 33
Local maps see Route de l'ISERAN and La MAURIENNE

Situated beneath the Col de l'Iseran, in the imposing cirque where the Arc has its source, the highest municipality of the Maurienne region has retained the charming character of its old village. In summer, it is an excursion centre offering many itineraries within the Parc national de la Vanoise as well as a mountaineering centre organising fascinating expeditions to the border massifs of the Levanna, Ciamarella and Albaron.

Nearby Sights: AUSSIOS, BESSANS, Route des GRANDES ALPES, Route de l'ISERAN, La Haute MAURIENNE, MODANE, Route du MONT-CENIS, TIGNES, VAL-D'ISÈRE, Massif de la VANOISE

THE RESORT AND OLD VILLAGE

Ski area – Most of the tourist facilities can be found in the hamlet of Tralenta, 500m/0.3mi from the village. There are 10 ski lifts for a ski area of moderate size but of good quality. Winter sports are practised here from December to May between 1 800m/5 905ft and 3 000m/9 843ft on some of the best snow in the French Alps. Beginners and intermediate skiers enjoy the Moulinet ski lift, close to the Vallonet Glacier. Advanced skiers on the other hand take the 3 000 ski lift to the foot of **Pointe d'Andagne** from where there is a magnificent **view★★** of the Haute Maurienne (Bessans below, Pointe de Ronce on the left and the rocky ridges of the Vanoise on the right) with the Meije and Aiguilles d'Arves in the background. In summer, skiers make for the **Glacier du Grand Pissaillas**, which can be reached from the Col de l'Iseran.

★★ **The old village** – Bonneval has made a point of preserving the character of its old streets and houses by burying electric and telephone cables and banning individual television aerials and satellite dishes, as well as cars which are kept outside the village.
Visitors can therefore walk safely and undisturbed through the narrow streets lined with stone houses, covered with rust-coloured *lauzes* (slabs of schist) and adorned with wooden balconies where dry cow-dung, still used as fuel, is sometimes stored.
At the heart of the village, a large old chalet known as **La Grande Maison** houses a butcher's and a baker's.
On the way out of the village, past the 17C church, there is a **fromagerie** ⊙ (cheese dairy) where local cheeses are made, including Beaufort, Emmental, Tomme and Mont Séti.

L'Écot – This hamlet, which lies in imposing and austere surroundings, more than 2 000m/6 562ft up, has retained its old stone houses and 12C Chapelle Ste-Marguerite. Once extremely remote, it is today a favourite tourist destination.

Eating out

MODERATE

Auberge Le Pré Catin – ☎ 04 79 05 95 07 – *closed 1 May-22 Jun, 24 Sept-20 Dec, Tue lunchtime, Wed lunchtime in winter, Sun evening and Mon – 22.11/24.39€.* This stone chalet at the entrance to the village offers a lip-smacking opportunity to sample hearty local cuisine. Meats grilled over an open fire are served on rough wooden tables which complement the typically regional decor very well.

Where to stay

BUDGET

Hôtel La Bergerie – ☎ 04 79 05 94 97 – *closed 25 Apr-14 Jun and 1 Oct-21 Dec* – 🅿 – *22rms: 38.11/48.78€ -* ☕ *7.01€ – restaurant 11.28/21.65€.* The main attraction of this 1970s building is its site, opposite the ski slopes, with peace and quiet guaranteed. As far as the food is concerned, local dishes predominate. The rooms are comfortable and fitted out in wood.

MODERATE

À la Pastourelle – ☎ 04 79 05 81 56 – *closed 20-30 May and school holidays around 1 Nov* – 12rms: 44.21/51.83€ - ☕ 5.34€ – restaurant 10.52/12.96€. This hotel/restaurant blends in perfectly with the style of the old village with its stone slab roof and stone walls. The rooms are painted in typical local style and are very cosy. The restaurant-crêperie is welcoming. Note the stone walls and small vault in the dining room.

HIKES

Bonneval is the ideal starting point for **walks** and **hikes** through the Parc national de la Vanoise and the conservation area of **Les Évettes** which offer hikers 120km/74.6mi of way-marked footpaths.

Bonneval-sur-Arc

★ **Refuge du Criou** – Alt 2 050m/6 727ft. *Access: in winter by the Vallonet chairlift, in summer on foot in 30min.* View of the seracs of the Glacier du Vallonet and Glacier des Sources de l'Arc and of the Col de l'Iseran road.

★★ **Le Carro refuge** – Alt 2 760m/9 055ft. *From L'Écot, 3hr 15min on the way up (steep climb); 2hr on the way down. It is also possible to take the scenic path from the Pont de l'Oulietta (alt 2 480m/8 136ft) on the Col de l'Iseran road; this itinerary is long (4hr), but easy and extremely rewarding.*
↗ Fine **views**★★ of the Albaron and of the Sources de l'Arc, Évettes and Vallonet glaciers. From the refuge, one can admire the Lac Noir and the Lac Blanc.

★★ **Les Évettes refuge** – Alt 2 615m/8 579ft. *From L'Écot, 1hr 45min on the way up, 1hr on the way down.*
↗ The steep climb affords views of L'Écot and Bonneval. From the refuge, the **panorama**★★ is splendid: the Glacier des Évettes and the Albaron are reflected in the still waters of the Lacs des Pareis. The Glacier du Grand Méan and Glacier du Mulinet can be seen beyond the refuge. It is possible to make a detour to the **Cascade de la Reculaz**★ *(1hr there and back).* When you reach the waterfall, cross the little bridge and go to the left past the waterfall. The view is quite impressive *(but not suitable for anyone liable to feel dizzy).*

★ **Walk to the Chalets de la Duis** – *From L'Écot: 2hr there and back. Very easy walk.*
↗ Family outing along a broad path in an idyllic setting of green pastures overlooked by fine glaciers.

Le BOURG-D'OISANS
Population 2 984
Michelin map 333 J7 and 244 fold 40
Local maps see Bassin du BOURG-D'OISANS and L'OISANS

Le Bourg-d'Oisans ("Le Bourg" for short) is the modest capital of the Oisans region and one of the most successful tourist resorts in Dauphiné. Its position at the junction of a number of valleys has always made it a natural meeting point and fairs, markets and numerous shops ensure that it remains lively all year round.
Some local names testify that, during the Middle Ages, a group of Saracens colonised the area.

Nearby Sights: L'ALPE-D'HUEZ, Les DEUX-ALPES, Massif de CHAMROUSSE, Route de la CROIX-DE-FER, Route du GALIBIER, La GRAVE, Lacs de LAFFREY, L'OISANS, Le VAL-BONNAIS, VIZILLE

SIGHTS

★ **Musée des Minéraux et de la Faune des Alpes** ⊘ – Housed in one of the aisles of the church, the museum displays a permanent collection of minerals particularly rich in quartz, as well as excellent temporary exhibitions. Alpine fauna are also represented and a palaeontology section has a collection of fossils dating back to the time of the Alpine geological upheavals.

★ **Cascade de Sarennes** – *1km/0.6mi to the northeast, then 15min there and back on foot. Leave Le Bourg on the road to Briançon; 800m/0.5mi further on, turn left onto D 211 towards L'Alpe-d'Huez and park the car just before the bridge over the Sarennes; continue on foot along the path on the right.* The triple waterfall of this tributary of the Romanche is very impressive in springtime.

Belvedere – *45min there and back on foot along the shaded alleyway beyond the church.* From the platform built at the highest point of the walk, there is a fairly clear view of the Bassin du Bourg-d'Oisans, of the Grandes Rousses mountain range and of the first peaks rising south of the River Vénéon.

EXCURSIONS

★★ Corniches du Bassin d'Oisans

1 FROM LE BOURG-D'OISANS TO L'ALPE-D'HUEZ

4km/8.7mi – about 30min – see local map

From Le Bourg-d'Oisans, follow the Briançon road then turn left to L'Alpe-d'Huez.

The road climbs in a series of hairpin bends, affording lovely vistas of the Romanche and Vénéon valleys and, in the distance, the Rochail Massif and Villard-Notre-Dame Glacier. Just before the attractive old village of **Huez**, perched on the hillside, there is a good view of the remote upper Sarennes Valley. As the road reaches L'Alpe-d'Huez, the Meije suddenly appears above the vast white-capped Mont-de-Lans Glacier. The narrow road, cut into the cliff face, makes for one of the most impressive drives in the French Alps

★★ **L'Alpe-d'Huez** – *See L'ALPE-D'HUEZ.*

2 FROM LE BOURG-D'OISANS TO THE VALBONNAIS *29km/18mi – about 1hr – see local map*

This interesting itinerary links the Bourg-d'Oisans Basin and the Valbonnais via the Col d'Ornon, following the course of the River Lignarre and River Malsanne.

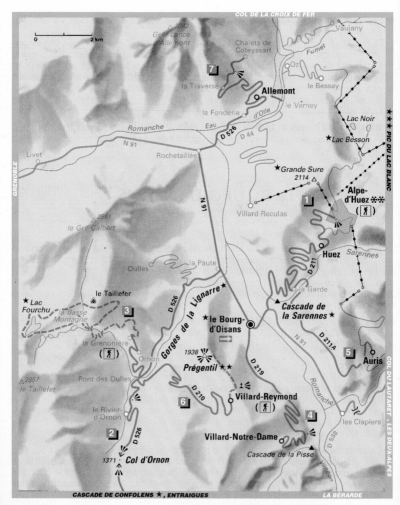

From Le Bourg-d'Oisans take N 91 towards Grenoble. Turn left at La Paute onto D 526.

★ **Gorges de la Lignarre** – The river has dug its way through schist (slate used to be quarried here). From Le Rivier, there is a fine view of the Belledonne and Grandes Rousses ranges to the north.

Col d'Ornon – Alt 1 367m/4 485ft. The pass crosses a barren stony landscape. The road follows the narrow valley of the rushing River Malsanne.

At Le Périer, turn left towards the Cascade de Confolens. Leave the car at the entrance to the Parc national des Écrins and continue on foot.

★ **Cascade de Confolens** – *2hr there and back.*
🚶 The path on the left leads to the 70m/230ft-high waterfall, set in lovely surroundings.
On the way down to Entraigues, there are fine **views★** of Mont Aiguille to the southwest, across the River Drac.

Entraigues – *See Le VALBONNAIS, Excursions*

★ ③ **FROM LE BOURG-D'OISANS TO THE REFUGE DE TAILLEFER AND LAC FOURCHU** *14km/8.7mi drive then 3hr on foot – difference in altitude: 800m/2 625ft*

From Le Bourg d'Oisans take N 91 to Grenoble; at La Paute turn left onto D 526 (see drive ② above). At Pont-des-Oulles, turn right to Ornon and La Grenonière.

🚶 Beyond the Parc des Écrins information panel *(on a bend)* the road is unsurfaced. Park here and continue on this road for 200m/219yd, take a path on the right which leads to La Basse-Montagne, a 20min walk.

From La Basse-Montagne, allow 2hr for experienced hikers. Leave the stream on your left and follow the path (red markings) through the woods. After 1hr the path, meandering through pastures, reaches the Taillefer refuge.

From the ledge (2 000m/6 562ft) there is a fine view of the Taillefer Massif and the Lignarre Valley, while behind the building you can see L'Alpe-d'Huez and the Grandes Rousses Massif.

Continue westwards to reach the Lac Fourchu in 45min along an easier path.

In spring and summer, the peaceful shores of the lake (2 060m/6 759ft) are dotted with wild flowers, rhododendron bushes, clusters of houseleek and columbine. There is a succession of small lakes lower down.

It is possible to go straight back via the Lac de la Vache and La Basse-Montagne.

★★ PETITES ROUTES DES "VILLAGES-TERRASSES"

These itineraries leading to villages perched on heights overlooking the Bassin du Bourg-d'Oisans follow very narrow cliff roads where vehicles can only pass one another at specified points. With the exception of drive ⑦ they all require experience of driving on mountain roads and must not be attempted by beginners.

★★ ④ **Route de Villard-Notre-Dame** – *From Le Bourg-d'Oisans, 9km/5.6mi – about 1hr. The road has a 10% gradient and must be avoided during or after a rainy period; dangerous gulley across the road at the start.*
This cliff road offers fine views of some wild mountain landscapes and of a remote but picturesque village at the end.
The best view is on a bend, 8km/5mi from Le Bourg-d'Oisans, and includes the lower Vénéon Valley with the Aiguille du Plat-de-la-Selle in the distance and a succession of waterfalls in the foreground.

★★ ⑤ **Route d'Auris** – *From La Garde (on the way to L'Alpe-d'Huez), 8km - about 45min. Follow D 211ᴬ towards Le Freney.*
This itinerary is interesting for its bird's-eye views of the Bassin du Bourg-d'Oisans (sheer drop of some 500m/1 640ft).

★ ⑥ **Route de Villard-Reymond**. *From Le Bourg-d'Oisans, drive north along N 91, turn left onto D 526 to Pont-des-Oulles then left onto D 210 for 8km/5mi.*
The road runs upriver along a tributary of the Lignarre.

Villard-Reymond – This hamlet, lying in lovely surroundings, is now a health resort. Walk to the cross at the Col de Saulude *(15min there and back)* and admire the **view★** of the village of Auris, of L'Alpe-d'Huez and the Belledonne range.

★★ **Prégentil** – *1hr 30min there and back on foot from Villard-Reymond (northwest).*
🚶 From the summit (alt 1 938m/6 358ft), there is a sweeping view of the high mountains surrounding the Bassin du Bourg-d'Oisans.

★ ⑦ **Route de la Traverse d'Allemont** – *From Le Bourg-d'Oisans, take N 91 towards Grenoble, turn right onto D 526 to La Fonderie d'Allemont. 6.5km/4mi – about 30min.*

From there, take D 43 to Allemont, turn left onto Route de la Traverse; shortly before this hamlet, turn right onto a forest road; after 6km/3.7mi, leave the car beyond a bend (parking); walk 100m/109yd along the path which starts at the bend.

From that point, there is a splendid **view★** of the patchwork of fields in the northern, well-cultivated part of the Bassin du Bourg-d'Oisans and of the mountains that surround it.

Return to the car and drive for another 200m/219yd.

On the right, there is a **panorama★★** of Le Bessey village and the Dôme des Petites Rousses as well as the Col de la Croix-de-Fer and Lac Noir, with the Belledonne and Taillefer massifs forming the horizon to the north and south.

Drive on for another 300m/328yd.

There is a clear view of the Grandes Rousses massif and the Combe d'Olle.

Lac du BOURGET★★

Michelin map 333 H/I and 244 folds 17 and 18

Enclosed within its impressive mountain setting, the Lac du Bourget has been the most famous French lake ever since the Romantic poets, headed by Lamartine, celebrated the changing colour of its waters and the wild beauty of its steep shores.

Nearby Sights: AIX-LES-BAINS, L'ALBANAIS, ANNECY, Lac d'ANNECY, Les BAUGES, CHAMBÉRY, Massif de la CHARTREUSE

BACKGROUND

The Lac du Bourget is the largest (4 500ha/11 120 acres) natural lake in France – with the exception of five vast expanses of water lying just inland from the Atlantic Ocean and the Mediterranean – and also the deepest (145m/476ft). Unlike the Lac d'Annecy, it has never been known to freeze in winter. Windstorms can be extremely violent. Like Lake Geneva, it has been part of an ongoing clean-up project in recent years and the waters abound in fish.

The lake used to extend northwards to the Grand Colombier Mountain and was supplied directly by the Rhône. Today, it is separated from the river by the Chautagne marsh; it is however still linked to the Rhône by the 3km/1.8mi-long Savières Canal. La Chambotte offers the most impressive view of the lake.

EXCURSIONS

★★① Round tour of the Lake

STARTING FROM AIX-LES-BAINS – *87km/54mi – about 3hr 30min*

The road overlooking the western shore of the lake clings to the steep slopes of the Mont du Chat and the Mont de la Charvaz, offering superb vistas.
On the east side, the road runs close to the lake at the foot of the cliffs of the Mont de Corsuet, revealing the changing moods of the lake.

Leave Aix by ④ on the town plan, N 201 towards Chambéry.

The road, skirting the foot of Tresserve hill, a sought-after residential area, follows the low-lying shore, quite busy until Terre-Nue.

Le Bourget-du-Lac – This lakeside town, once linked by steamers to Lyon via the Canal de Savières and the Rhône, is now an expanding holiday resort with a harbour and a beach along the Lac du Bourget.
Built on an ancient religious site, the **church** ⊘ was remodelled in the 15C and partly rebuilt in the 19C. Inside, the **frieze★** running round the walls of the apse is a 13C masterpiece. Note also the 15C font.
The **Château-Prieuré** ⊘ adjacent to the church *(entry through the arched doorway)* was built in the 11C then remodelled in the 13C and 15C. The tour includes the refectory, the kitchen, the chapel from which a staircase leads to an oratory opening on to the chancel of the church, and the library with its ceiling lined with Cordoba leather. The 15C cloisters consist of two superposed galleries; the Gothic vaulting is particularly impressive on the lower level. The attractive gardens, illuminated in season, are decorated with fountains and yew trees trimmed to look like chess pieces.

Château Thomas II – *near the mouth of the Leysse.* The hunting lodge of the Dukes of Savoie was the scene of diplomatic and dynastic intrigue until the 15C.

Continue along N 504; at the second intersection signposted Bourdeau, turn left onto D 914 signposted Abbaye de Hautecombe.

Eating out

BUDGET

Auberge de Savières – *73310 Chanaz* – ☎ *04 79 54 56 16* – *closed 18 Dec-15 Mar, Tue evening and Wed except from 12 Jul-1 Sept* – *12.20/30.49€*. Some people moor their boats opposite this inn after a trip along the Savières canal. Others might like to take the pleasant boat trip on offer here, before sitting down to family recipes by the side of the canal.

Les Oliviers – *In Brison village* – *73100 Brison-St-Innocent* – *6km/4mi N of Aix-les-Bains on D 48 and D 991* – ☎ *04 79 54 21 81* – *closed 10 Jan-10 Feb, and Tue except 15 Jun-15 Sept* – *13.72/27.44€*. This establishment has been lent a new lease of life by the arrival of its new chef. His contemporary cuisine can be enjoyed in the dining room, heated by an open fire in winter, or on the terrace under the shade of tall trees in summer.

La Cerisaie – *618 rte des Tournelles* – *73370 Les Catons* – *2.5km/1.5mi Ne of Le Bourget-du-Lac on D 42* – ☎ *04 79 25 01 29* – *closed 1-8 Jan, 25 Oct-25 Nov, Sun evening and Wed except Jul-Aug* – *14.94/34.30€*. A small chalet in a peaceful natural setting overlooking the lake and with a fabulous view of the mountains: this is the idyllic setting for simple comfort in a friendly family atmosphere. The terrace is very popular on fine days. Seven small rooms.

MODERATE

La Grange à Sel – *La Croix Verte* – *73370 Le Bourget-du-Lac* – ☎ *04 79 25 02 66* – *closed 1-20 Jan, 1 Mar-5 May, Sun evening and Wed* – *29.73/60.98€*. This old salt store has a vine growing over its façade, a tree-lined terrace and a flower garden. Inside, old stones and beams are left bare, there is an open fire and small lounges. The chef will delight food-lovers with his specialities in terms of quality and quantity.

Auberge Lamartine – *Rte du Tunnel du Chat* – *73370 Le Bourget-du-Lac* – *3.5km/2mi N of Le Bourget on N 504* – ☎ *04 79 25 01 03* – *closed mid Dec-mid Jan, Tue lunchtime Sept-Jun, Sun evening and Mon* – *33.54/62.50€*. Let your gaze drift across the water as you savour a meal full of sophistication and character. This well-reputed establishment has a dining room on two levels overlooking the Lac du Bourget. Warm decor with discreet furnishings and soft lighting.

EXPENSIVE

Bateau Ivre – *Rte du Tunnel du Chat* – *73370 Le Bourget-du-Lac* – *2km/1mi N of Le Bourget on N 504* – ☎ *04 79 25 00 23* – *closed beginning Nov-beginning May, Mon lunchtime and Tue lunchtime* – *57.93/105.19€*. Dine in the magnificent setting of the Hôtel Ombremont's restaurant, which enjoys a good reputation in the region. Weather permitting, prolong this unique experience after dark by spending some time on the wooden terrace above the lake ringed with lights. Fish from the local lakes are a speciality.

Where to stay

MODERATE

Hôtel du Port – *553 bd du Lac* – *73370 Le Bourget-du-Lac* – ☎ *04 79 25 00 21* – *closed 15 Dec-1 Feb* – 🅿 – *23rms: 50.31/54.88€* - ⌷ *6.40€* – *restaurant 17.84/35.06€*. This 1970s hotel facing the lake offers a pleasant view from the terrace and most of the rooms. The dining room is decorated in the style of a ship's cabin and makes a great port in a storm when the weather is bad. Ask for rooms with a lake view!

EXPENSIVE

Hôtel Ombremont – *Rte du Tunnel du Chat* – *73370 Le Bourget-du-Lac* – *2km/1mi N of Le Bourget on N 504* – ☎ *04 79 25 00 23* – *closed 4 Nov-3 May* – 🅿 – *12rms: from 141.78€*. This majestic residence dating from the early 20C overlooks the lake from its park with century-old trees. The idyllic view of the mountains from the terrace or the edge of the swimming pool is unforgettable. Spacious luxurious rooms with corner baths.

The road rises above the lake towards the Col du Chat; from the second hairpin bend, there is a fine **panorama★** of the Chambéry depression separating the Bauges (Mont Revard) and the Chartreuse (Mont Granier) massifs, with the indented Massif d'Allevard in the distance.

Chapelle Notre-Dame-de-l'Étoile – *15min there and back on foot. The signposted path starts on a bend of D 914.* From the platform in front of the church, there is a fine overall **view★★** of the lake and its frame of mountains including the Grand Colombier, the Semnoz and Mont Revard. The road runs along a ledge and the lake ceases to be visible.

Bifurcation d'Ontex – From this intersection, there is a view of Hautecombe Abbey. The road goes down towards the north end of the lake, where the Château de Châtillon stands on a wooded promontory; on the opposite shore, the Restaurant de la Chambotte occupies a prominent position.

Turn right onto D 18 to the Abbaye royale de Hautecombe.

★ **Abbaye royale de Hautecombe** – The abbey stands on a promontory jutting out into the lake. It is the burial place of many members of the House of Savoie including **Béatrix de Savoie**, whose ambitions for her four daughters were more than fulfilled when three of them became queens (of England, France and the Two-Sicilies) and the fourth one, empress of Germany. The last king of Italy, **Umberto II**, was buried in Hautecombe in 1983. During the 19C, the **church** ⊙ was entirely restored in neo-Gothic style by artists from Piedmont, which explains the profusion of ornamentation. The 16C former doorway, situated on the left-hand side, is in striking contrast with the highly decorated façade. The interior is also profusely adorned: there are paintings by Gonin and Vacca over the vaulting as well as 300 statues in marble, stone or gilded wood and low-relief sculptures decorating the funeral monuments of the princes of Savoie. Some statues, carved out of Carrara marble, are remarkable, in particular a **Pietà★** by Benoît Cacciatori. Among the restored paintings from the 14C to the 16C is an Annunciation by Defendente Ferrari. Near the landing-stage, the **grange batelière** (water barn), built by Cistercian monks in the 12C, was designed to store goods reaching the abbey by boat; the barrel-vaulted lower part comprises a wet dock and a dry dock.

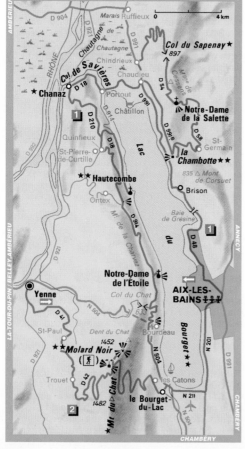

Return to D 914 as far as Quinfieux and take D 210 to the left towards Chanaz.

Chanaz – Situated on the banks of the Canal de Savières, a once busy commercial route, this lively old border town found a new purpose when the canal was opened to pleasure boats. There is an interesting oil-mill still producing walnut oil. The 17C **Maison de Boignes**, easily identified by its two entrances, is now the town hall.

From Chanaz, drive along D 18 towards Aix-les-Bains.

Canal de Savières – This 4km/2.4mi canal connects the waters of the Lac du Bourget to the Rhône and acts as a "safety valve" when, after the spring thaw or the heavy autumn rains, the flow is reversed and the river overflows into the lake. A major trade route until the 19C, the canal was also the easiest way for the dukes of Savoie to travel from Chambéry to Lyon.

The Canal de Savières

The road crosses the Canal de Savières at Portout, then runs through marshland to Chaudieu.

Turn left onto D 991 then right at Chindrieux towards the Col de Sapenay.

The narrow twisting road affords lovely views of the Lac du Bourget, the Abbaye de Hautecombe and the Dent du Chat summit, with the Rhône Valley to the north, guarded by the impressive Grand Colombier.

★**Col du Sapenay** – Alt 897m/2 943ft. The road goes through a mountain landscape of fir trees and pastures.

Chapelle Notre-Dame de la Salette – From this high point in the Montagne de Cessens, the **view**★ extends over the Albanais depression to the east.

At St-Germain, turn onto D 991[B], then turn left in La Chambotte past a small chapel.

★★**View from the Restaurant de la Chambotte** – *See AIX-LES-BAINS: Excursions.*

Beyond La Chambotte, the road goes down to Chaudieu, offering fine views of the Lac du Bourget.

In Chaudieu turn left onto D 991.

From then on, the road skirts the edge of the lake; good views of the Dent du Chat and the Abbaye de Hautecombe on the opposite shore. Just beyond **Brison-les-Oliviers**, a fishing village with a strong wine-growing tradition, the road runs close to the shores of the lovely Baie de Grésine and on to Aix-les-Bains.

✠✠ **Aix-les-Bains** – *See AIX-LES-BAINS.*

② Route du Mont du Chat

FROM YENNE TO LE BOURGET-DU-LAC – *34km/21mi – about 2hr – see local map*

Yenne – The small capital of the Bugey Savoyard region occupies a favourable position at the entrance of the Défilé de Pierre-Châtel, through which the Rhône forces its way out of the Alps.
The west doorway of the 12C-15C **church** has retained some fine Romanesque capitals; inside, the **stalls**★ dating from the 15C are delicately carved with Flamboyant motifs and decorated with the twinned royal arms of France and Savoie. The sacristy contains a fine Christian tombstone from the 6C.
The town centre offers pleasant walks through its streets lined with old houses.

From Yenne take D 41 (which branches off D 921 to the left); from St-Paul continue south on D 41 past Trouet, then turn left onto D 42 to the Lac du Bourget.

★**Mont du Chat** – A television relay pylon (alt 1 504m/4 934ft) stands some 50m/55yd south of the pass. Fine **view** of Aix-les-Bains and the lake from the platform below (1 470m/4 823ft).

★★**Molard Noir** – *1hr there and back on foot from Mont du Chat.*
▧ Follow the ridge to the north, through the woods; from the clifftop on the west side, a fine stretch of the Rhône Valley can be seen from the Défilé de Pierre-Châtel north to the Grand Colombier. The top of Molard Noir (alt 1 452m/4 764ft, viewing tables) offers a vast **panorama** of Mont Revard and, beyond, of Aiguilles de Chamonix, Mont Blanc, the Vanoise Massif, the Belledonne range and Mont Granier.
On the east side, the road meanders through the woods.

Continue on D 42 to Le Bourget-du-Lac.

BOURG-ST-MAURICE

Population 6 747
Michelin map 333 N4 and 244 fold 21
Local maps see Le BEAUFORTAIN and Massif de la VANOISE

Bourg-St-Maurice is situated at the heart of the Haute Tarentaise region and occupies a commanding position at the intersection of the upper Isère Valley, the Chapieux Valley and the road leading to Italy via the Col du Petit-St-Bernard.

For this reason, "Le Bourg", as the locals call it, is the ideal starting point for driving tours in the area.

The **"Fête des Edelweiss"** *(see Calendar of events)*, which takes place in July, is an international folk festival showing off the picturesque costumes of the Tarentaise and Aosta valleys.

In winter, ski enthusiasts can enjoy the sophisticated equipment of the fine resort of Les Arcs, while in summer white-water sports are extremely popular and numerous canoeing competitions take place on the River Isère.

Nearby Sights: Les ARCS, BEAUFORT, La Vallée des BELLEVILLE, Route des GRANDES ALPES, Route de l'ISERAN, La PLAGNE, La TARENTAISE, TIGNES, VAL-D'ISÈRE, Massif de la VANOISE

MUSEUM

Musée des Minéraux et Faune de l'Alpe ⊘ – *Avenue du Général-Leclerc*. Fine crystals in their natural setting.

EXCURSIONS

Chapelle de Vulmix – *4km/2.5mi south*. This simple chapel, restored in the 17C, contains splendid 15C **frescoes★** depicting the life of St Grat, known as the protector of crops; the legend begins on the south wall.

Hauteville-Gondon – *4km/2.5mi from Bourg-St-Maurice, drive along D 90 towards Aime then follow D 220.*

Musée du Costume ⊘ – Housed in the former presbytery, this museum illustrates the diversity of local costumes during the 19C and early 20C and displays specimens of the *frontière (see Introduction: Traditions and folklore)*, a headdress which became the symbol of Savoie.

Église St-Martin – Built in the 17C, the church is richly decorated in Baroque style, with several 18C altarpieces including the fine polychrome retable over the high altar framing an illustration of St Martin's legend.

★★★ **Les Arcs** – *Take N 90 from the north-east exit of Bourg-St-Maurice and turn right almost immediately onto D 119. Arc 1600: 12km/7.5mi (or funicular during the season), Arc 1800: 15km/9.3mi, Arc 2000: 26km/16.2mi (see Les ARCS).*

★★Route du Petit-St-Bernard

31km/19.3mi – about 1hr 15min – local map see Massif de la VANOISE

This former international trade and military route today has a major tourist appeal as part of the famous "Tour du Mont Blanc". The road leading to the pass on

Fr. Isler/MICHELIN

The altar of Église St-Martin, Hauteville-Gondon

the French side, built during the reign of Napoleon III, has a 5% gradient as it climbs above the Isère Valley from 904m/2 966ft (at Séez) to 2 188m/7 178ft.

The pass is usually blocked by snow from the end of October to the end of May.
From Bourg-St-Maurice, take N 90 towards Val d'Isère and Italy.

Séez – This ancient village, situated on the old Roman road, was named Séez because it stood close to the sixth milestone between Lyon and Milan. It grew prosperous in the 19C through its woollen-cloth industry, an activity which has recently picked up again after a long period of decline. The Baroque **Église St-Pierre** contains a splendid altarpiece by Fodéré, a local artist, and the 15C recumbent figure of a knight in armour to the left of the entrance.

Bear left as you leave Séez.

The road climbs in a series of impressive hairpin bends with Mont Pourri towering above to the south, offering views of the Moyenne Tarentaise to the southeast, and then of the upper Isère Valley towards the snow-capped peaks which divide the Haute-Tarentaise from the Haute-Maurienne.

✳ **La Rosière 1850** – This pleasant resort, situated, as the name suggests, at an altitude of 1 850m/6 070ft, overlooks the Tarentaise from a superb commanding position.
Its ski slopes offer good snow coverage and plenty of sunshine within a vast international skiing area linked to the Italian resort of La Thuile. The Roc Noir, Traversette and Belvédère summits, the ski runs of San Bernardo and La Tour, afford splendid **views**★ of Mont Blanc and a **viewpoint** offers an impressive panorama including the Rocher de Bellevarde, the dam at Tignes and Mont Pourri (3 779m/12 398).
In summer, La Rosière is a peaceful holiday resort offering a wide choice of excursions. There are kennels breeding the famous St Bernard dogs nearby.

★ **Col du Petit-St-Bernard** – Fierce fighting during the Second World War caused great damage to the hospice believed to have been founded by **St Bernard de Menthon** (923-1008), whose statue stands in front of the buildings. The institution provided shelter for travellers facing terrible snowstorms. Further on stands the Colonne de Joux, originally surmounted by a statue of Jupiter (Jovis), which, so the story goes, was torn down by St Bernard himself. A statue of the saint, commissioned by a benefactor of the hospice, replaced it at the end of the 19C.
The **view**★ to the right of the Hotel de Lancebranlette extends to Mont Ouille, with the Italian slope of Mont Blanc to the right.
The **Jardin botanique La Chanousia** is a late 19C botanical garden, neglected after the Second World War and recently replanted, containing about 1 000 species of Alpine plants.

HIKE

★★★**Lancebranlette**

4hr there and back on foot by a mountain path which is often in poor condition at the beginning of summer. Mountain boots are recommended. Detailed information is available at the Chalet de Lancebranlette.
🔼 From the chalet, climb the northwest slope of the pass towards an indented crest on the left. An isolated building halfway up the slope is a useful landmark to aim for. Once you reach a vast cirque in a landscape of screes and pastures, keep going left to join the path which winds all the way up to the summit (2 928m/9 606ft). Vast **panorama** including the Italian side of Mont Blanc *(viewing table)*.

BRIANÇON★★

Population 10 737
Michelin map 334 H3 and 244 folds 42 and 43
Local map see Le BRIANÇONNAIS

Europe's highest town (1 321m/4 334ft) occupies a strategic position at the intersection of the Guisane, Durance, Cerveyrette and Clarée valleys, close to the Montgenèvre Pass leading to Italy. This explains the number of strongholds surrounding the town. The old fortified town or **Ville Haute**, surrounded by a ring of forts planned by Vauban, Louis XIV's military engineer, has retained its steep, narrow streets, but the forbidding setting which once deterred enemies now draws tourists and skiers. Briançon, which has had a military skiing school since 1904, forms part of the winter sports complex of **Serre-Chevalier** *(see SERRE-CHEVALIER)* .

Nearby Sights: ABRIÈS, L'ARGENTIÈRE-LA-BESSÉE, Le BRIANÇONNAIS, CEILLAC, Vallée de FREISSINIÈRES, Route du GALIBIER, Route des GRANDES ALPES, La GRAVE, GUILLESTRE, MOLINES-EN-QUEYRAS, MONT-DAUPHIN, MONT-GENÈVRE, L'OISANS, Le QUEYRAS, ST-VÉRAN, SERRE-CHEVALIER, La VALLOUISE, VARS

Eating out

BUDGET

Le Rustique *– 36 r. du Pont-d'Asfeld –* ☎ *04 92 21 00 10 – closed 20-30 Jun, 20 Nov-10 Dec, Tue lunchtime and Mon except public holidays – 15.09/23.17€.* This pretty house with its coloured façade is as rustic as its name suggests. Inside the dining room is white with a vaulted ceiling and old wooden floor and adorned with traditional farming implements and an old sleigh. Local specialities include the famous fondue.

MODERATE

Le Péché Gourmand *– 2 rte de Gap –* ☎ *04 92 21 33 21 – closed Mon – 20.58/37.35€.* Is it a sin to love food? It depends on your beliefs. While reflecting on this, perhaps, in this old house on the banks of the Guisane, note that the cuisine here is modern and sophisticated and makes use of good ingredients.

Menus Vauban – A local tourist office initiative encourages the town's restaurants to put forgotten dishes from the age of Louis XIV back on the dinner table. Look for Vauban's name on the menu and sample revived and updated recipes from the turn of the 18C.

Where to stay

MODERATE

Hôtel Vauban *– 13 av. du Gén.-de-Gaulle –* ☎ *04 92 21 12 11 – closed 5 Nov-20 Dec –* ▣ *–38rms: 60.98/70.13€ -* ☞ *5.49 € – restaurant 18.29/26.68€.* This modern town-centre hotel with its small tree-filled park on the banks of the Durance is a haven of peace in the middle of urban hubbub. Its rooms are comfortable, if a little dated, and the food is traditional and served in generous portions.

On the town

Eden bar *– 29 r. Centrale –* ☎ *04 92 21 17 70 – Mon-Fri 6am-1am, Sat-Sun 6am-2am.* Whatever the time, whatever the season, this is the local people's favourite bar! Entertainment is brisk beneath the roof of this little mountain "chalet". In summer there are two concerts a week on the terrace. The highlight of the season is the "mussels and chips" evening, which draws more than 500 people! In winter, revellers vie with each other in games of table-football, pool and karaoke.

Tucson café *– 6 r. du Gén.-Barbot –* ☎ *04 92 20 34 89 – Mon-Fri 11am-1am, Sat-Sun 11am-2am.* This bar with its trendy atmosphere has the decor of the Wild West, recalling a famous Arizona town, with cowboys and Indians getting along amiably. In summer and winter there are rock and blues concerts to enhance the spirit of the venue. Every Tue evening, tomahawks are sharpened for the karaoke evening.

Sport

Bureau des Guides de Briançon *– Parc Chancel –* ☎ *04 92 20 15 73 – bgb05@club-internet.fr – Jul-Aug: daily 9.30am-7pm, Sept-Jun 5pm-7pm.* For the last twenty-five years a team composed of keen enthusiasts has done its utmost to ensure that visitors enjoy the delights of the mountains in complete safety. They do this regardless of the season: rock-climbing, mountaineering, canyoning, hiking and paragliding are on offer in the summer; excursions on skis, snowshoes and off-piste are on the menu in winter.

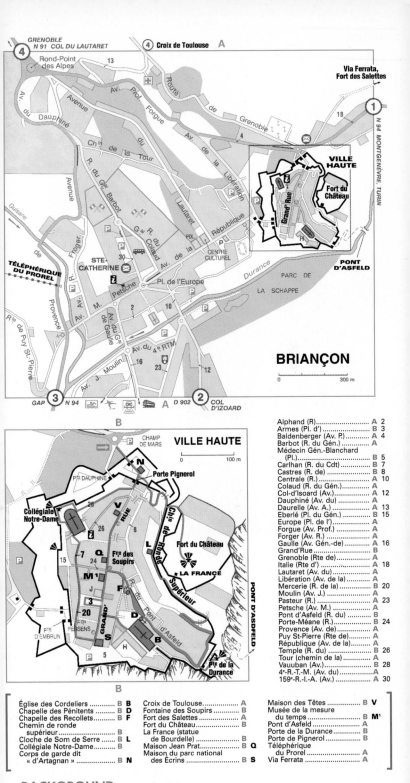

BRIANÇON

VILLE HAUTE

BACKGROUND

The capital of the Briançonnais region – In accordance with the **Grande Charte** granted to them in 1343 and later confirmed by the kings of France, 52 municipalities of the Briançonnais region, situated on either side of the border with Italy, formed a kind of free state with Briançon as their capital. One of the privileges of the *Escartons*, as they were known, was to fix and levy their own taxes. Thirty-two of these municipalities became Italian under the Treaty of Utrecht signed in 1713.

A military town – The rock, which towers over the Durance, was fortified in turn by the Celts and the Romans and again during the Middle Ages. The fortifications were strengthened in 1590 by the Huguenot commander Lesdiguières, and a second wall was erected in 1690. However, after a fire destroyed most of the town in 1692, Louis XIV asked Vauban to rebuild the fortifications as war had broken out between France and Savoie. Vauban undertook the building of a ring of forts which was completed almost 200 years later. After Napoleon's defeat at Waterloo in 1815, Briançon was besieged by allied forces but held out until peace was signed under the Treaty of Paris several months later.

★★ VILLE HAUTE *1hr 30min – Car park on the Champ de Mars*

The walled city is accessible through four gates: Porte Pignerol to the north, Porte d'Embrun to the southwest, Porte de la Durance to the east and Porte Dauphine (recently opened to ease the flow of traffic).

It is divided into four districts by the intersection of Grand-Rue and rue Porte-Méane, which leads into rue du Pont-d'Asfeld: Quartier du Temple grouped round the

The Porte d'Embrun
and Briançon's formidable defences

Collégiale Notre-Dame, Quartier Mercerie with place d'Armes in its centre, which was the commercial and administrative district, the residential district of the Grand Caire to the northeast, and Quartier de Roche which was centred on the various monasteries including the Récollets and Pénitents. Two steep streets running through the town, known as *gargouilles*, have a fast-flowing stream in the middle, which provided a ready supply of water for fighting fires. There is a good view of the old town from the upper battlements.

Porte Pignerol – As was usual in the 18C, the gate comprises several separate defences. The outer gate, rebuilt in the 19C, bears an inscription recalling the 1815 siege. The guardhouse, known as "D'Artagnan", houses temporary **exhibitions** ⊘ in summer. Next come the drawbridge, a gate reinforced by a portcullis and another gate decorated with a splendid frontispiece. A vaulted passage gives access to the walled town. Exhibitions devoted to "Three hundred years of military architecture" are held in the building adjacent to Porte Pignerol.

Follow the road to the left of the gate

★**Chemin de ronde supérieur** – This upper line of defence overlooks the roofs of the walled city with the towers of the Collégiale Notre-Dame rising above. It skirts the **Fort du château** ⊘ in front of which towers a 9m/30ft-high statue of **"France"**★ by Bourdelle, originally intended to stand on the spot where American troops first set foot on French soil during the First World War and rescued from store-room obscurity in 1933. The **Som de Serre bell**, used in the past to sound the alarm, hangs in the small tower to on the left.

Continue along the road which leads down to the town.

The terrace of the **Porte de la Durance** offers a charming **view**★ of the Durance valley and the bridge.

★**Pont-d'Asfeld** – This single-arched bridge spanning the Durance 56m/184ft above the river bed was built in 1729-31 by military engineers headed by Asfeld, Vauban's successor, in order to link the town with the Fort des Trois Têtes.

Turn onto the rue du Pont-d'Asfeld.

It leads to the "religious" district. Look first for the fine restored steeple of the **Chapelle des Pénitents**, badly damaged by fire in 1988 and, for the most part, sadly neglected since; a little further on stands the **Chapelle des Récollets** ⊘, which houses art exhibitions in summer.

Turn left onto the Grande Gargouille.

★ **Grande Gargouille or Grand-Rue** – This is the main shopping street of the walled town, very lively in summer on either side of its fast-flowing central stream. Going down the street, note the Fontaine Persens on your right and the beautiful doorway of no 64, dating from 1714. The **Fontaine François I**, named after the French king who made a present to the town of the elephants' heads decorating the fountain, stands under an archway on a street corner. The **Maison de Jean Prat**, at no 37 across the street, has a fine Renaissance front decorated with masks and statues (St John the Evangelist with two angels). The **Maison des Têtes** at no 13 was decorated at the turn of the century with figures in regional costume representing the owner's family.

At no 47 stands the **Musée de la Mesure du Temps** ⊘, the converted stable in which a private collection of over 200 clocks and other timepieces are on permanent display. The water clocks even allow you to hear time passing drop by drop.

Place d'Armes – Its brightly coloured façades and pavement cafés give this former market square linking the Grande Gargouille and Petite Gargouille a southern atmosphere; it is decorated with two **sundials**. The left-hand one, painted in the 18C on the front of the former prison, bears the simple inscription "Life slips by like a shadow", whereas the right-hand one, which adorns the 19C law courts bears the more elaborate inscription 'From sunrise to sunset, this fleeting shadow rules simultaneously over the work of Themis (the goddess of justice) and of Mars (the god of war)'. The central well, dug on the orders of Vauban, stood the city in good stead during the siege of 1815. A street to the left leads to the former Cordelier monastery (now the town hall) and to its **church** ⊘, currently undergoing renovation work, with an imposing façade decorated with Lombard arcading.

Return to the Grande Gargouille

Maison du Parc national des Écrins ⊘ – The National Park office is based in an imaginatively converted 18C military hospital, where a permanent exhibition presents the flora and fauna of the area and the history of skiing in agreeably unstuffy style.

Head towards the Porte d'Embrun and turn right onto the Petite Gargouille (rue de la Mercerie).

Petite Gargouille – A narrow street of tall, rather austere façades, offset by some fine decorative ironwork on the doors.

Collégiale Notre-Dame – Built during the early 18C to a plan reworked by Vauban, this imposing edifice has a remarkable façade flanked by two high towers decorated with sundials. The left-hand one, dating from 1719, is in Baroque style; it is one of the finest painted sundials in the Alps. The stone lions placed in front of the doorway belonged to a church demolished in 1692, and now provide tourists with a much-needed spot to rest their legs. The **viewing table★** situated behind the church offers a good view of the three tiers of fortifications built in to the terrain, of the modern town below, of the Fort des Salettes to the north with the Croix de Toulouse above it, of the mountains framing the Briançon Basin and of the Montgenèvre Pass to the east.

The fortress and the Massif des Écrins

★★ Croix de Toulouse *8.5km/5.3mi – about 1hr*

Leave Briançon by④ on the town plan (Route de Grenoble) and turn left onto D 232ᵀ towards the Croix de Toulouse. The narrow road rises through pine trees in a series of hairpin bends. Carry on along the unsurfaced part and leave the car near a block-house.

It is also possible to reach the Croix de Toulouse on foot *(2hr there and back)* from the Fort des Salettes. A well-marked path runs along the cliffside offering fine views. The Croix de Toulouse (alt 1 962m/6 437ft) is a rock spur situated at the end of a ridge separating the Guisane and Clarée valleys and towering over Briançon. From the viewing table, the **view** extends on one side to the walled town, with its ring of forts and the Durance Valley in the distance, and takes in the whole Guisane Valley up to the Col du Lautaret on the other side.

Round tour via Puy-St-André and Puy-St-Pierre

15km/9.3mi – about 1hr

From Briançon, drive southwest towards Puy-St-Pierre on the road between ③ and ④.

The small road rises quickly above the Durance Valley. Beyond the village of **Puy-St-André**, it affords interesting **views** of the Condamine and Écrins massifs.

Puy-Chalvin – The 16C **Chapelle Ste-Lucie** ⊘ standing in the heart of this hamlet is covered with murals inside and outside. The front is decorated with panels, separated by interlaced motifs, illustrating scenes from the Passion and representing various saints. Inside, the paintings in naive style depict scenes from the life of Christ.

Return to Puy-St-André and drive to Puy-St-Pierre along D 335.

Puy-St-Pierre – Almost completely destroyed during the Second World War, this hamlet has retained a church standing on the edge of a cliff and offering a splendid **panorama★★** of Briançon and the Durance Valley. At night, the floodlit church can be seen clearly from the Ste-Catherine district in Briançon.

The history of irrigation and the techniques of modern hydro-engineering are revealed in the open-air **Musée de Plein Air sur les Canaux d'Irrigation** ⊘, near the "Serre che soleil" path.

Continue along D 335 then D 35 to return to Briançon.

HIKES

★ Fort des Salettes

From the Champ de Mars – 45min there and back on foot – along the chemin des Salettes.

🔲 Designed by Vauban in 1692, the fort was not built until a year after his death in 1707 and was remodelled during the 19C. It was intended to guard the access to Briançon from Montgenèvre and Italy. Its small keep standing in the middle of a courtyard is surrounded by bastions linked to it by underground passages.

From the platform in front of the fort, there is an interesting **view★** of the walled town and its ring of forts.

★ Le Prorel ⊘

Start from the cable-car station in the Ste-Catherine district. The journey is in two sections and it is possible to do part of the journey or take a one-way ticket only. Be prepared to face strong, cold winds blowing continuously at the top.

On the way up, there are superb views of the summit (2 566m/8 419ft). There are numerous possibilities for fine walks to the surrounding heights offering magnificent **panoramic views★★**. You can go back down towards Chantemerle or Puy-St-Pierre (via the Chapelle Notre-Dame-des-Neiges).

Chapelle Notre-Dame-des-Neiges – Alt 2 292m/7 520ft. *15min on foot; marked path*. This small chapel decorated with ex-votos can be reached from the cable-car station; it offers a fine view of the Serre-Chevalier Valley.

It is possible to return to Briançon along the marked path running through the high pastures (about 2hr 30min).

Via ferrata at the Croix de Toulouse – The path leading to the foot of the cliff starts between two cafés opposite the Champ de Mars car park (15min walk). The course ends just east of the Croix de Toulouse and it is possible to go back along the chemin des Salettes. Ask at the **Bureau des Guides** for further information.

Le BRIANÇONNAIS★★

Michelin map 334 H3 and 244 folds 42 and 43

The geography of the Briançonnais is marked by striking contrasts which Vauban described in the following terms: "The area includes mountains reaching for the sky and valleys sinking to incredible depths". In the centre of the area lies Briançon at the intersection of four valleys. During the Middle Ages, the communities of these valleys formed a kind of federation under the terms of the Grande Charte *(see BRIANÇON)*. The large stone-built houses, decorated with arcades and columns, testify to the fact that the inhabitants were relatively well off.

The region is well known for its southern mountain climate, clear skies, unmistakable light, and good snow coverage which encouraged the early development of important ski resorts such as Montgenèvre and Serre-Chevalier.

Nearby Sights: ABRIÈS, L'ARGENTIÈRE-La-BESSÉE, BRIANÇON, CEILLAC, Vallée des FREISSINIÈRES, Route du GALIBIER, Route des GRANDES ALPES, La GRAVE, GUILLESTRE, MOLINES-EN-QUEYRAS, MONT-DAUPHIN, MONTGENÈVRE, L'OISANS, ST-VERAN, SERRE-CHEVALIER, La VALLOUISE, VARS

EXCURSIONS

★① Vallée de la Guisane

FROM COL DE LAUTARET TO BRIANÇON *32km/20mi – about 1hr*

This wide valley, linking the *départements* of Isère and Hautes-Alpes, has acquired a high reputation for cross-country skiing, ski-trekking and on-piste skiing within the **Serre-Chevalier** winter sports complex. *See SERRE-CHEVALIER*

★★ **Col du Lautaret** – *See L'OISANS ② and SERRE-CHEVALIER: HIKES.*

The imposing mass of the Meije glaciers comes into view soon after the Col du Lautaret. The road goes through a wide valley, relatively arid except for the larch forest covering the north-facing slope *(ubac)*. On the way down from the pass, road N 91 skirts the barren slopes of the **Grand Galibier** (alt 3 229m/10 594ft). The pyramid-shaped Grand Pic de Rochebrune can be seen in the distance, down the valley beyond Briançon. The valley then widens and villages begin to appear.

Le Casset – The elegant steeple rises above the steep roofs of this hamlet dwarfed by the mighty Glacier du Casset. The Parc national des Écrins information centre is open in summer *(See SERRE-CHEVALIER: HIKES)*.

★ **Le Monêtier-les-Bains** – *See SERRE-CHEVALIER.*

In Villeneuve, turn left onto the road leading to La Salle-les-Alpes.

La Salle-les-Alpes – The road rising just above Chapelle Ste-Lucie leads to the centre of the old town and one of the most beautiful churches in the Briançonnais. **L'Église St-Marcellin** ⊘★ has a Romanesque bell-tower (13C-14C) from an earlier building, an elegant, canopied south porch and a late Gothic nave with quadripartite vaulting. A gilded chancel altarpiece, which dates from the 17C and depicts the Virgin and Child, is framed by Baroque ornamentation including twisted columns and recesses. The lectern and pulpit are the work of local artists. On a terrace stands the **Chapelle St-Barthélemy** ⊘★: frescoes represent episodes from the lives of the saints, and there is an attractive **view★** of the valley

In Chantemerle, take D 234ᵀ up to the Col de Granon, 12km/7.5mi away

The road climbs up the arid slopes overlooking the left bank of the River Guisane, offering broad views of the Briançonnais mountains and Écrins Massif.

★★ **Col de Granon** – *Leave the car beyond the barracks and climb to a viewing table on the right.* From here, the **panorama** unfolds in front of your eyes, including the Briançon mountains and the Massif des Écrins

Go back along D 234ᵀ and take a detour through the old village of St-Chaffrey before rejoining N 91.

★★ **Briançon** – *See BRIANÇON.*

★★② Vallée de la Clarée

FROM BRIANÇON TO THE CHALETS DE LAVAL

30km/18.6mi – about 2hr, not including walks – see local map

This picturesque valley owes its name to the clear waters of the mountain stream running through it. Its slopes being unsuitable for ski lifts, it has retained its lovely villages, its hamlets, its houses covered with larch shingles and decorated with sundials and its churches adorned with fine murals.

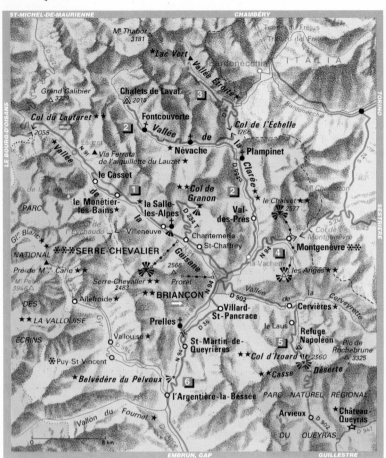

Landscapes change considerably as one drives up the long and narrow valley, fresh and pleasantly wooded at first, then more open and also more densely populated beyond Plampinet, when it suddenly veers to the left. The upper part again becomes narrower as the Clarée comes cascading down among woods of larch trees against the austere landscape formed by a vast glacial cirque crowned by Mont Thabor.

★★ Briançon – *See BRIANÇON – tour of the town: 1hr 30min*

Leave Briançon by ① on the town plan, (N 94 towards Montgenèvre). At la Vachette turn left onto the D 994 and into the Vallée de la Clarée.

The road overlooks the narrow valley of the River Durance and the Pont d'Asfeld with the Chalvet Summit towering above the Clarée Valley.

In La Vachette, bear left along D 994ᴳ, which goes up the Clarée Valley.

Shortly beyond La Vachette, the road reaches the confluence of the River Durance and River Clarée. The mighty river of the southern Alps looks very disappointing compared to its tributary, the Clarée, which the road follows from that point.

Val-des-Prés – Lovely village with typical houses resting on an arcaded base. The **church** has an imposing square bell-tower with two tiers of Romanesque arcading and a large portico in characteristic regional style.
The road follows the Clarée among pine trees through one of the most attractive parts of the valley.

Plampinet – Situated at the top of the village, the **Église St-Sébastien** ⊘ is a solid building, characteristic of mountain architecture, decorated with a fine sundial. The richly decorated interior comes as a surprise. The **murals★**, dating from 1530, which are probably the work of an artist from Piedmont, are remarkable for their lively details and warm colours (ochre, dark red and brown). Note in particular 19 scenes depicting the Passion in the bay preceding the chancel and an illustration of the Annunciation on the arch separating the nave and the chancel.

The **Chapelle Notre-Dame-des-Grâces** ⊙ has also retained a set of 16C **murals★**, slightly older than those of the church, illustrating the virtues and the vices. Kneeling women symbolising the virtues are placed above the seven deadly sins mounted on various animals. Other figures in the paintings include St Odile, the blind patron Saint of Alsace.

The valley becomes more open beyond Plampinet. The road leading to the Vallée Étroite *(see below)* starts on the right between Plampinet and Névache.

★ **Névache** – The church of the *"ville haute"*, **L'Église St-Marcellin et St-Antoine** ⊙ ★ was built in 1490 to make good a vow made on pilgrimage by Charles VIII. The site chosen was that of the castle. The 11C tower was retained as the base of the steeple. A representation of the Annunciation decorates the tympanum of the west doorway, in green and pink marble. The wooden doors are beautifully carved with scenes of the Deposition and interlaced Gothic motifs. There is a similar doorway on the south side.
Inside, there is a fine Baroque **altarpiece** in gilded larch wood decorated with 15 statues. The **treasury**, exhibited in the cell of the former castle, includes an 11C copper pyx inlaid with enamel.
The gallery dates from the 16C.
Beyond Névache, the road crosses an area of high pastures brightened by several cascading streams and a carpet of wild flowers in early summer.
Along the way, note the picturesque shingle roofs of the Chalets de Fontcouverte (1 857m/6 093ft) and its lovely **chapel**. The Cascade de Fontcouverte is nearby.

Chalets de Laval – The road ends here (alt 2 015m/6 611ft). This is the starting point for several mountain excursions such as the ascent of Mont Thabor.

★ **Hike to Lac de Laramont and Lac du Serpent** – *From the chalets at Fontcouverte continue on the D 301 to La Fruitière. Difference in altitude: 500m/1 640ft to Lac de Laramont, 700m/2 297ft to Lac du Serpent*
🚶 The path rises gently to the refuge de Ricou, surrounded by small chalets. A winding path continues past the refuge and joins GR 57, which leads to Lac Laramon (2 359m/7 740ft). From the shores of the lake, lined with wild flowers in spring, a fine **panorama★★** includes the Massif des Écrins. Lac du Serpent (2 448m/8 031ft) lies due east.

★ ③ Vallée Étroite

17 km/10.6mi – about 2hr

The road leading to the Vallée Étroite, which crosses to the Italian side, is open from mid-June to mid-November exclusively to private cars.

Between Plampinet and Névache, turn right onto D 1 towards the Col de l'Échelle.

Col de l'Échelle – Alt 1 766m/5 794ft. This is the lowest border pass in the western Alps. On the Italian side, the road goes down steeply towards the Bardonecchia Valley, with views of the Vallée Étroite and Mont Thabor.

★ **Vallée Étroite** – This valley, which was Italian territory from the Treaty of Utrecht in 1713 until 1947, still retains its signposting in Italian, although it is now part of the municipality of Névache, the largest in the Hautes-Alpes *département*. It is similar to the Vallée de la Clarée but on a smaller scale, with larch trees growing among scree-covered slopes.

★ **Lac Vert** – *1hr there and back on foot. Leave the car at the CAF refuge and continue along the road until you reach the signpost* "Lago Verde". *Follow the path.*
🚶 The small lake suddenly appears framed by larch trees; its colour is due to the profusion of green algae that it contains and its clear, icy water.

④ Route de Montgenèvre

FROM BRIANÇON TO MONTGENÈVRE *12km/7.5mi – about 30min*

Leave Briançon by ① *on the town plan, N 94.*

The road overlooks the deep valley of the River Durance. Leaving the Clarée Valley road to its right, the N 94 rises rapidly, offering glimpses of the Briançon Basin and the Clarée Valley. As Montgenèvre gets nearer, pine trees give way to a forest of larches.

★★ **Montgenèvre** – *See MONTGENÈVRE.*

★★ ⑤ Route du Col de L'Izoard

FROM BRIANÇON TO CHÂTEAU-QUEYRAS *38km/24mi – allow 1hr 45min*

The Col d'Izoard is usually obstructed by snow from October to June.

★★ Briançon – *See BRIANÇON*

Between Briançon and Cervières, the itinerary follows the cliff road through the Gorges de la Cerveyrette.

Cervières – This village, damaged during the Second World War, has nevertheless retained a 15C church and a few traditional houses including the 18C **Maison Faure Vincent Dubois** ⊘★

From Cervières, a 10km/6.2mi-long road, partly surfaced, runs through the lovely **Vallée de la Cerveyrette**.

Large stone-and-wood chalets covered with larch shingles form a succession of hamlets scattered over pastures and woodland.

Drive out of Cervières, stop the car and turn round to see the top of the Barre des Écrins (alt 4 102m/13 458ft) through the lower Cerveyrette Valley.

As the road winds up past **Le Laus** towards the pass along the River Izoard, the **Pic de Rochebrune**, one of the familiar silhouettes of the Briançonnais's landscapes, appears on the left.

Refuge Napoléon – It was erected in 1858 with funds bequeathed by Napoleon (*see ROUTE NAPOLÉON*).

★★ Col d'Izoard – Alt 2 360m/ 7 743ft. This is the highest point of the Route des Grandes Alpes south of the Col du Galibier. There is a

> ### The Refuges
>
> Heartened by the enthusiastic welcome in Gap on his return from Elba, a grateful Napoleon bequeathed funds to build refuges on the most dangerous mountain passes. Construction began 40 years later at the Col de Manse, Col d'Izoard, Col de Lautaret, Col de Vars and Col du Noyer. Two further refuges at Col de la Croix and Col Agnel have now fallen into disrepair, and the site at Col du Noyer is now a hotel.

memorial dedicated to Alpine forces who contributed to the construction of many mountain roads. A small **museum** ⊘, situated at the pass itself, is devoted to the **Tour de France** cycle race which goes across the Col d'Izoard.

Go up (15min there and back on foot) to the viewing panels overlooking the road. The superb **panorama** includes, to the north, the Briançonnais mountains with Mont Thabor in the background, and, to the south, the heights of the Queyras region, the Pic des Houerts, Pic de la Font Sancte and Chambeyron Massif.

★★ Casse Déserte – The road goes through a strange desolate landscape: jagged rocks, gullied slopes and screes.The ragged spires, towering over the Col de l'Izoard road, are due to a local geological phenomenon causing layers of ground limestone and gypsum to be bonded into a yellowish conglomerate, known as *cargneule*. The

Casse Déserte

hardest blocks of this conglomerate are less eroded than the rest and form groups of "needles". Two plaques commemorate two heroes of the Tour de France: the Italian Fausto Coppi, who won the race in 1952 and the Frenchman Louison Bobet who won it in 1953, 1954 and 1955.

Arvieux – *See Le QUEYRAS.*

The site of Château-Queyras comes into view as soon as the road reaches the narrow Guil Valley.

★ **Château-Queyras** – *See CHÂTEAU-QUEYRAS.*

⑥ Haute Durance

FROM BRIANÇON TO L'ARGENTIÈRE-LA-BESSÉE *17km/10.6mi – about 1hr*

Leave Briançon by ③ on the town plan (N 94), then turn left and cross the Durance towards Villard-St-Pancrace.

Villard-St-Pancrace – Note the fine houses in typical Briançonnais style. The 15C **church** has two beautiful south doorways with triple arches resting on slender columns. The artist's signature (1542 J Ristolani) can be seen on the left-hand jamb of the right-hand doorway. A sundial bears the Latin inscription: 'They (the hours) all wound, the last one kills'.
Next to the church stands the 17C **Chapelle des Pénitents**, and on a hilltop the **Chapelle St-Pancrace★** ⊙, which contains 15C murals.

Drive through the old village of Villard-St-Pancrace and continue along D 36 to rejoin N 94.

Prelles – The **Chapelle St-Jacques** ⊙, situated in the high street, has retained some 15C **murals★**; in the oven-vaulted chancel, there is a Christ in Glory inside a mandorla with the 12 apostles lined up beneath. The arch separating the nave and the chancel is decorated with an illustration of the Annunciation. Scenes depicting the life of pilgrims on their way to Santiago de Compostela can be seen on the left-hand wall of the nave.

Rejoin N 94 and drive south.

Between Prelles and Queyrières, the road clings to the cliffside above the gorge through which flows the River Durance.

St-Martin-de-Queyrières – The church standing on the roadside has a high steeple, typical of the Embrun region, and two doorways.

Queyrières – This village, backing onto a rock, is characteristic of the Briançonnais area.

★ **Belvédère du Pelvoux** – A viewing table placed near the road helps to locate the main summits of the Écrins Massif, which can be seen through the valley of the lower Vallouise.

L'Argentière-la-Bessée – *See L'ARGENTIÈRE-LA-BESSÉE*

Pays du BUËCH★
Michelin map 334 C5 to C6 and 245 fold 6

Much travelled but little explored, this depression of the Préalpes du Sud opens the way to the main Alpine winter route *(N 75)* and to the railway line from Grenoble to Marseille via the Col de la Croix Haute. The area enjoys a Mediterranean climate, although pastures and fir forests still predominate as far south as St-Julien-en-Beauchêne; the Col de la Croix-Haute marks a sort of climatic boundary, where the green north gives way to the dry bare landscape of the Southern Alps. The area is also known as "la Bochaine".

Nearby Sights: BUIS-LES-BARONNIES, Le CHAMPSAUR, DIE, Le DÉVOLUY, GAP, MONT-MAUR, Route NAPOLÉON, SISTERON, Le TRIÈVES

VALLÉE DU BUËCH

From Lus-la-Croix-Haute to Serres *43km/27mi – about 2hr*

Lus-la-Croix-Haute – Lying at the centre of a wide Alpine basin through which flows the Buëch, at an altitude of 1 030m/3 379ft, Lus-la-Croix-Haute is the highest resort of the Pays du Buëch.

From the Grande-Place in Lus, drive east along D 505.

★ **Vallon de la Jarjatte** – The road follows the upper Buëch Valley, with forested slopes on either side.

Eating out

MODERATE

La Sérafine – *Les Paroirs* – *05400 Veynes* – *2km/1mi E of Veynes on the Ga*[...]*road then a B road* – ☎ *04 92 58 06 00* – *closed 5-20 Mar, 3-18 Sept, Mon an*[...]*Tue* – *reservations compulsory* – *35.83€*. This 18C building provides a home from-home at the heart of this hamlet. Safely ensconced within its stone walls warmed by the open fire or seated on the terrace, guests can discover the delight[...]of Madame the proprietor's cooking and Monsieur the proprietor's wine cellar.

On approaching the ski resort of La Jarjatte, there are impressive **views★★** of th[...]indented silhouettes of the Aiguilles framed by the Vachères (2 400m/7 874ft) an[...]Tête de Garnesier (2 368m/8 769ft). The head of the valley forms a cirque in[...]setting of dark escarpments towering over a dense fir forest.

Return to N 75.

The road follows each bank of the Buëch in turn. The wide river bed is overlooked b[...]the jagged peaks of the Diois, known as *"serres"*; the wooded slopes of Montagn[...]Durbonas can be seen on the left as the road reaches the village of **St-Julien-en-Beauchêne**[...]Beyond St-Julien, the landscape becomes more arid, and deep gullies run down th[...]mountain slopes, with a few pines and oaks dotted about; rocky peaks are now an[...]then surmounted by ruined castles such as the 12C fortress of La Rochette.

Veynes – Owing to its position on the main Gap-Die route, this former stronghol[...]suffered much at the hands of the Huguenots and of the duke of Savoie's troups[...]From 1894 onwards, it gradually became a major railway junction with lines t[...]Grenoble, Marseille, Briançon and Valence, as well as an industrial centre; the town[...]**Écomusée** ⊘ remembers the life and work of the railwaymen. Today, Veynes ha[...]turned to tourism instead; known for its colourful façades and sunny enough fo[...]some homes to be heated by solar power, the town is the perfect place to start hike[...]and pony-treks through the south Buëch region. The Base nautique des Isles (wate[...]sports park) provides plenty of summer activities.

Aspres-sur-Buëch – This lively town lies at the intersection of N 75 an[...]D 993/D 994 linking Die and Gap, and in a picturesque mountain setting (goo[...]overall **view** from the former castle mound crowned with a war memorial).
The **church** has an interesting Romanesque doorway bearing statues of Chris[...]between Mary and St John the Baptist (unfortunately mutilated).
Beyond the Pont de la Barque, at the confluence of the Buëch and Petit Buëch, a nar[...]rowing of the valley hides the village of Serres.

★ **Serres** – The picturesque old village, an attractive maze of narrow lanes and covere[...]passageways, clings to a pointed rock above the River Buëch. From the arcade[...]square, walk up to the old high street where the **town hall** stands, Lesdiguières' forme[...]residence (17C porch and fine 16C vaulting inside). *Turn back and walk eastward*[...]*along the high street, now* **rue Henri-Peuzin**.

Snow in Provence? Serres in the winter sun.

Note on the right the bell-tower surmounted by a wrought iron belfry and several carved doorways along the street, in particular **no 56**. The **Maison de Lesdiguières** (no 39) with a fine Renaissance façade and attractive stucco work inside, is open to the public free of charge. The Romanesque **church** was remodelled in the 14C; the south side is the most interesting with its six **funerary recesses** and two beautifully carved doors. Opposite the church, a passageway leads to the former **Jewish quarter**

notable for its high-fronted houses, sometimes six storeys tall and backing on to the square. In 1576 Serres became the property of the **Duc de Lesdiguières** and a safe haven for Huguenots (Protestants), no doubt reassured by the new ducal armouries established in the town. On the death of Henri IV, however, the Wars of Religion flared up once again. Richelieu ordered the destruction of the citadel in 1633 and the Huguenots were either converted to Catholicism or driven into exile.

> ### Sundials in the Pays du Buëch
>
> This tour through the valleys of the Buëch region leads to the discovery of an interesting collection of sundials showing the diversity of local pictorial art during the 18C and 19C. In **St-Julien-en-Beauchêne**, the Durbon forest lodge (a former Carthusian monastery) is decorated with two 18C sundials. In **Aspres-sur-Buëch**, a contemporary sundial, made according to traditional techniques, adorns the town hall. At the **Col de Cabre**, near La Beaume, a sundial has been carved in the rock at the western exit of the tunnel. The primary school in **Serres** also has its sundial, showing the sun's trajectory and the position of the equinox *(see Practical information)*.

Hikes

★**Montagne de Céüse** – This table mountain offers interesting hikes from different starting points.

🚶 *From Veynes: take D 20 towards Châteauneuf d'Oze heading north, then turn left at the intersection onto the forest road leading to the Col des Guérins.*
Footpath GR 94 skirts the east side of the isolated mountain to reach Manteyer on the northeast slope.

From the Céüse 2000 resort: take the track which starts opposite Hôtel Gaillard, climb as far as the ledge then follow the steep course of the Marseillais ski lift to the top. Go up towards the Torrent chairlift until you reach a signpost. A path leads to the Pic de Céüse which reveals a splendid **view**★★ of the Massif de Bure and Massif des Écrins to the north and of the Ubaye to the east. It is possible to return via the west side, skirting the top of the rock-climbing course, going down through the Vallon d'Aiguebelle and then following the signs.

★★ **Pic de Bure** – *See MONTMAUR, Hike*

BUIS-LES-BARONNIES★
Population 2 030
Michelin map 332 E8 and 245 folds 17 and 18

Between the ridge of Les Baronnies and the distant silhouette of Mont Ventoux, this little town on the Ouvèze looks south in more ways than one. Vines, olives, apricots and almonds flourish in the valley and fields of lavender *(see Introduction)* supply many family-run distilleries. The clink of pastis glasses on the café terrace and the click of boules announce your arrival in the south.
80% of France's lime blossom tea – tilleul or tilhotou to the locals – comes from this area; on the first Wednesday in July, traders gather along the river bank for the **Foire au Tilleul**★, the largest market of its kind in Europe.

Nearby sights: Pays du BUËCH, MONTBRUN-LES-BAINS, Route NAPOLÉON, SISTERON

WALKING ABOUT

★**The Old Town** *1hr*

Esplanade – This alleyway, shaded by plane trees, runs along the Ouvèze, where the town walls once stood; it is a typical Provençal *cours* (avenue), particularly lively on market days *(Wednesday mornings)*. Across the river, the Rocher St-Julien, a popular challenge for rock-climbers, rises to a height of 767m/2 516ft.

Place du Marché – This "square", looking more like a wide street, is lined with slightly pointed stone arcades dating from the 15C.

The Place du Marché

Rue de la Conche – The shopping street has retained a few fine doorways.

Turn left onto rue de la Commune.

Former Dominican monastery – The recently restored 16C building has been turned into holiday accommodation. Note the staircase and the cloisters.

Walk past a gate on the left and through a vaulted passageway called rue de la Cour-du-Roi-Dauphin.

Church ⊘ – Burnt down during the Wars of Religion and rebuilt in the 17C, it contains wood carvings and stalls from the former Dominican church.

Walk along the left side of the church.

Former Ursuline convent – Founded in the 17C, it is now a cultural centre. The only original feature left is the fine Renaissance doorway of the former chapel, which today houses the library.

Walk past the east end of the church to avenue Aristide-Briand and return to the Esplanade, then go to the embankment on the right bank of the river.

The **Tour de Saffre** (12C) is the only part of the town walls still standing.

Eating out

BUDGET

La Scala – *7 allée des Platanes* – ☎ *04 75 28 01 05* – *closed mid Nov-mid Jan, Wed evening out of season and Thu except evening in Jul-Aug* – *13.72/17.53€* France and Italy meet on the fixed price and à la carte menus of this restaurant. There is no pizza, however, as there are plenty of other options to choose from in the peninsula's gastronomic repertoire. You can eat in the dining room or on the terrace in the shade of the plane trees.

Where to stay

BUDGET

Camping Les Éphélides – *1.4km/1mi SO of Buis on Av. de Rieuchaud, along the Ouvèze* – ☎ *04 75 28 10 15* – *open 21 May-2 Sept* – *reservations recommended* – *40 pitches: 12.04€* – *Food service*. There is a warm welcome from the owner of this campsite tucked into a hollow in the Ouvèze valley, on the banks of the river. Swimming pool. Chalets, bungalows and caravans for hire.

Hôtel Les Arcades Le Lion d'Or – *Pl. du Marché* – ☎ *04 75 28 11 31* – *arcadulion@aol.com* – *closed 15 Dec-1 Feb* – *15rms: 32.01/39.64€* – ⌒ *4.57€*. The house with a pretty coloured façade dating from 1661 stands on the market square with its arcades. Tucked away at the back is a delightful enclosed garden ideal for whiling away some time. The small renovated rooms are colourfully decorated and come at a very reasonable price.

ALONG THE OUVÈZE

Pierrelongue – Perched on a rocky knoll overlooking the village, the **church**, built at the end of the 19C, looks totally out of place in this attractive setting.

Mollans-sur-Ouvèze – This small "border" town is the gateway to the Baronnies region, and the beginning of the Dauphiné region is symbolised by the dolphin on the elegant 18C fountain. The bridge across the Ouvèze links the *basse ville*, with its 18C covered wash-house, and the *haute ville* with its belfry crowning an old round tower; opposite stands a small chapel projecting over the Ouvèze. From there, a walk through the narrow streets of the "high town" leads to the church and a large square keep, which is all that remains of the castle.

Entrechaux – This village, formerly the possession of the Bishops of Vaison, is overlooked by the ruins of its castle, which include a 20m/66ft-high keep.

EXCURSIONS

★ ① Les Baronnies du Buis

ROUND TOUR FROM BUIS-LES-BARONNIES

97km – allow 3hr – see local map

This relatively low range (1 757m/5 764ft) of the Préalpes du Sud stretches from west to east, its limestone ridge being separated by the upper valleys of the River Eygues and River Ouvèze. Mountain streams have cut deep furrows in the hillsides, sculpting a barren landscape, characteristic of the area, while orchards and vineyards cover the lower slopes.

From Buis-les-Baronnies drive northeast along D 546.

The road follows the Ouvèze amid olive groves and goes through the picturesque **Gorges d'Ubrieux**.

Turn left onto D 108 and drive up to the Col d'Ey.

Olive trees, pines and broom grow on south-facing slopes. Fine views of the Ouvèze Valley and Mont Ventoux.

Col d'Ey – Alt 718m/2 356ft. From the pass, flanked by the Montagne de Montlaud to the east and the Montagne de Linceuil to the west, the view extends to the Ennuye Valley and the Montagne de Buisseron.

Take D 528 left to Rochebrune.

Rochebrune – The village stretches over a rock spur; its only street leads to a round tower (all that remains of the 13C castle) and to the 12C church remodelled in the 15C. Fine **view** of the Ennuye Valley.

Return to D 108 and turn left.

Ste-Jalle – The **old town**★ has retained part of its walls and two of its gates. One of these is surmounted by the Chapelle des Pénitents (17C). The **castle** consists of a massive square keep (12C-13C), a round tower with Renaissance windows, and living quarters (17C-18C) looking more like a large house.
The size of its bell-tower spoils the otherwise fine proportions of the 12C Romanesque church of **Notre-Dame-de-Beauvert**. The unusual carved **doorway** has a tympanum depicting a rooster and three figures of a farmer, a lord and a troubadour representing the different social classes. A large transept separates the barrel-vaulted nave from the three semicircular apsidal chapels. The oven-vaulted axial chapel is decorated with very simple arcading.

Follow the River Ennuye along D 64 then turn right onto D 94 after Curnier.

The road runs through the pleasant valley of the River Eygues, planted with vines, peach, cherry and olive trees.

Sahune – The old village lies on the left bank of the Eygues. Beyond Sahune, the road makes its way through the deep **Gorges de l'Eygues**★; note the regular layers of the rock face and the foaming waterfall on the left.

St-May – This village is perched on a promontory overlooking the gorge. Beyond St-May, the Eygues flows between brightly coloured limestone cliffs.

Turn right onto D 162.

The road rises through orchards to the **Col de Soubeyrand** (alt 994m/3 261ft) set among fir trees. On the way down from the pass, firs give way to oaks and the view extends to Mont Ventoux.

Go through St-Sauveur-Gouvernet and turn left onto D 64, then right onto D 546.

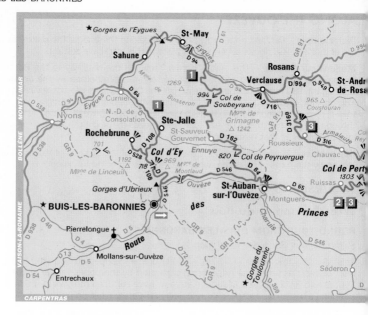

☑ Route des Princes d'Orange

BUIS-LES-BARONNIES TO EYGUIANS *63km/39mi – allow 3hr – see local map*

From the 14C to the 18C, this road gained strategic importance as a link between the Principality of Orange and Orpierre; both were territories of the house of Orange Nassau, whose descendants are now the Dutch royal family.

On leaving Buis-les-Baronnies, the D 546 crosses the **Gorges d'Ubrieux**.

St-Auban-sur-l'Ouvèze – Built on a rocky promontory at the confluence of the River Ouvèze and River Charuis, this old village has retained part of its former defences. From place Péquin, at the top of the village, there is a fine view of the surrounding area dotted with many farms. There is a wide choice of hikes in and around a beautiful chestnut grove. The area's economic life is centred round medicinal (lime, sage and camomile) as well as aromatic plants.

Beyond St-Auban, follow D 65 via the Col de Perty.

The road goes through Montguers (note the charming isolated chapel on the plateau then rises in a series of hairpin bends through a wild landscape, offering **views** of the whole Baronnies area.

★★**Col de Perty** – Alt 1 303m/4 275ft. A path to the right leads to the viewing table *(10min return on foot)*. Splendid panorama of the Durance Valley and the southern Alps to the east, of the Ouvèze Valley and the Mont-Ventoux Massif to the west. The road continues along the Céans Valley.

Orpierre – This mountain village at the bottom of the Céans Valley became the seat of a barony belonging to the prince of Orange in the 13C, rising in prominence as a Protestant centre under the house of Nassau before declining after the Revocation of the Edict of Nantes and being ceded to the French crown in 1713. For all its political changes, Orpierre has retained its pleasant **old centre★** with some fine Renaissance doorways along the **Grand-Rue** and the narrow passages known as *"drailles"* linking its picturesque old streets.

The cliffs overlooking the village offer many marked and suitably equipped itineraries for **rock-climbing** enthusiasts (Quiquillon, Falaise de Quatre heures Cascade de Belleric – level 5 to 6a).

Show time

Le Canard en bois – *Le Village* – *26510 Montréal-les-Sources* – *5km/3mi E of Sahune on D 205.* – ☎ *04 75 27 42 04* – *Fri or Sat every fortnight, telephone to find out dates.* This cabaret in a woodland setting is dedicated to French chanson, theatre and acoustic music. At the end of performances, proprietor Marcel Moratal serves liberal quantities of wine and patrons strike up discussion with each other and with the performers.

Beyond Orpierre and several gorges, the Céans Valley suddenly widens as the river joins the Buëch and the Blaisance.

Lagrand – Of the important monastery which flourished here in medieval times, only the **church** remains; this well-preserved Romanesque building has a large nave, covered with broken barrel vaulting, ending with a pentagonal apse set within a rectangular east end. Inside, the only decorations are floral motifs carved on the capitals. Note the gilded wood tabernacle in a recess on the right-hand side. The west doorway has been heavily restored. The south side used to open onto the cloister and the monastery buildings. Note the funeral recesses near the base.

The town hall at the entrance of the old village is a fine 18C building characteristic of Provençal country houses of that period.

Eyguians – It is here that the Route des Princes d'Orange reaches the Buëch Valley.

③ Le Pays de Rosans

FROM BUIS-LES-BARONNIES TO ST-ANDRÉ-DE-ROSANS *95km – around 3hr*

For Buis-les-Baronnies to Orpierre see ② above

From Orpierre, drive west along D 30 then turn right onto D 130.

The road follows the St-Cyrice Valley, then goes through a forest as it climbs to the Col du Reychasset; beyond the pass, there is a fine **view** of the Armalauze Valley.

Take D 316 on the left, then D 316ᵉ through Chauvac and Roussieux .

Good **views** of the pyramid-shaped Coustouran Summit (965m/3 166ft).

Take the D 116 to Verclause.

Verclause – This old fortified village was a fief of the Dauphin in the 13C. The ruins of its castle and chapel stand on a promontory offering a lovely **view★** of the Eygues Valley and the Montagne de la Clavelière.

Turn right on to the D 94 and D 994.

Rosans – The most westerly village in the Hautes-Alpes has a true Provençal atmosphere. Its narrow streets wind round the hill in a spiral to the imposing 13C keep.

St-André-de-Rosans – One of the most important Cluniac monasteries in Haute-Provence was founded here in the 10C; it was destroyed during the Wars of Religion, leaving behind the ruins of a vast 12C **church**, including the walls of the nave and an apsidal chapel with traces of a rich decoration inspired by Antique art.

CASTELLANE★

Population 1 508
Michelin map 334 H9 and 245 fold 35
Local maps see Grand Canyon du VERDON

This tourist centre, located at the intersection of the Route Napoléon and the Route du Haut-Verdon, close to the famous canyon, lies at the foot of a 184m/604ft-high limestone cliff in one of the most striking **settings★** of the Haute-Provence region. First, an ancient fort occupied the top of the cliff; then a Roman town, **Petra Castellana**, was built in the valley below and surrounded with fortifications in the 14C, the remains of which are still visible today

Nearby Sights: ANNOT, BARGÈME, CLUES DE HAUTE-PROVENCE, DIGNE-LES-BAINS, ENTREVAUX, MOUSTIERS-STE-MARIE, Route NAPOLÉON, RIEZ, ST-JULIEN-DU-VERDON, Lac de STE-CROIX, Plateau de VALENSOLE, Grand Canyon du VERDON

SIGHTS

Place Marcel-Sauvaire – This central square, a useful central parking spot, is decorated with arcades and a fountain and lined with hotels, cafés, shops and administrative buildings.
In rue Nationale nearby, no 34, which welcomed Napoleon on his way back from Elba in March 1815, houses the small **Ethnological Museum** .

CASTELLANE

Fontaine aux lions .... **B**
Musée ethnologique
(Ancienne
sous-préfecture) .... **M**

N 85 DIGNE-LES-B., GRENOBLE
D 955 BARRAGE DE CASTILLON

Fortifications – Several sections of the walls built in 1359 are still standing: the **Tour Pentagonale** and two complete gates, the **Tour de l'Horloge** surmounted by a wrought iron campanile (near the Tourist Information Centre) and the **Porte de l'Annonciade**. There is a good overall view of the walls and Tour Pentagonale from chemin du Roc off boulevard St-Michel.

Old town – Situated north of place Marcel-Sauvaire, the old town includes some picturesque twisting lanes and a lovely **Fontaine aux Lions** along rue du Mitan.

Eating out

BUDGET

La Main à la Pâte – *R. de la Fontaine* – ☎ *04 92 83 61 16 - jn.rispaud@wanadoo.fr – closed 15 Dec-15 Feb, Tue in Jul-Aug and Wed Sept-Jun – 15.24/24.39€*. Salads and pizzas feature prominently on the menu of this establishment in a narrow street in the old town. There is a relaxed atmosphere in the two dining rooms with their warm Provençal decor.

MODERATE

Auberge du Teillon – *6km/4mi SE of Castellane on N 85* – ☎ *04 92 83 60 88 - closed 15 Dec-10 Mar, Sun evening Oct-Easter and Mon except Jul-Aug – 17.53/36.59€*. If you miss this inn beside the Route Napoléon, do a U-turn! This is a stop not to be missed. The menus are truly mouth-watering and the regional fare sophisticated and imaginative. Some rooms available.

Where to stay

MODERATE

Nouvel Hôtel du Commerce – *Pl. de l'Église* – ☎ *04 92 83 61 00 – closed 16 Oct-28 Feb* – 🅿 *– 40rms: 42.69/60.98€* - 🍽 *6.86€ – restaurant 18.29/42.69€*. Ask for the older rooms in this hotel on the village square, as they have a stronger appeal. Do not fail to sample the Provençal-inspired cuisine. There is a pleasant terrace beneath the trees.

On the town

Le Glacier – *Pl. de la Fontaine* – ☎ *04 92 83 62 88 – Open daily 8am-2am*. Winter or summer, this welcoming bar is always buzzing. In fine weather, you will have to fight for your place on the terrace on a small square. At the first sign of a nip in the air, people flock to the karaoke evenings and concerts (Wed and Sun). Good selection of beers and ice cream.

Place Marcel-Sauvaire – *Pl. Marcel-Sauvaire* – This is a must for those who decide to stop in Castellane. There are parking spaces in the shade, a big advantage in hot weather, and one or two bars where visitors can quench their thirst.

Sport

Swimming pool (Piscine) – *Rte de Robion* – ☎ *04 92 83 60 22 – daily noon-6pm except Jul-Aug 10am-7pm – closed beginning Feb-end Jun*. Picture the beauty of the mountains and the pleasures of bathing united under a sunny sky! This is what is on offer at Castellane swimming pool (three heated pools) for the delight of holiday-makers, and especially children who never tire of its water chutes.

Église St-Victor ⊙ – This 12C Romanesque church has a remarkable Lombard tower with rough-hewn stones, originally part of the old city walls, at its corners and wide openings with rounded arches. Inside, the quadripartite vaulting and the oven-vaulted apse are characteristic of the transition between the Romanesque and Gothic styles. The walnut decoration of the chancel and the baldaquin surmounting the high altar date from the 18C.

La Maison des Sirènes ⊙ – Between the town hall and the post office stands a museum run by the Réserve Géologique de Haute-Provence and devoted to manatees or sea cows, the aquatic mammals of the order *Sirenia* which once inspired sailor's tales of mermaids.

Porte de l'Horloge and Notre-Dame-du-Roc

WALKS

Vallée des Sirènes fossiles – *Take the N 85 from Digne. After 6km park the car at Col de Lèques, on the right after the campsite.* A half-hour walk through woodland and lavender leads to the "valley of the sea cows", where a unique collection of over a hundred Sirenia fossil remains is now protected by a museum.

Chapelle Notre-Dame-du-Roc – *1hr there and back on foot.*
🚶 Pleasant **walk★** offering a fine overall view of Castellane nestling at the foot of its rock. A path starting behind the church joins up with a wider one; turn right. This path, lined with the Stations of the Cross, rises rapidly over the roofs of the town and the machicolated Tour Pentagonale. Some ruined walls on the left are all that remain of the feudal village.
The chapel, surmounted by a tall statue of the Virgin Mary, dates from 1703; it stands on top of the cliff, 180m/590ft above the bed of the River Verdon and is a popular place of pilgrimage (note the large number of ex-votos).
From the terrace, the **view★★** extends over the town, the 17C bridge spanning the river, the Castellane Basin surrounded by mountains and the beginning of the Gorges du Verdon.

EXCURSIONS

★**Chapelle St-Thyrse** ⊙ – *7km/4.3mi south on D 102 towards Robion; take great care because of the narrowness of the access road.*
The picturesque road rises from the gorge to the plateau where the recently restored 12C Romanesque **chapel** stands in a remarkable **setting★**. The interior is decorated with blind arcading in the oven-vaulted apse and along the north and west walls of the nave. The 3-tiered steeple is characteristic of early Romanesque style.

★★**Grand Canyon du Verdon** – *See Grand Canyon du VERDON.*

★**Lacs de Castillon et Chaudanne** – *See ST-JULIEN-DU-VERDON.*

CEILLAC★

Population 276
Michelin map 334 I4 and 245 fold 10
Local map see Le QUEYRAS

Located at an altitude of 1 650m/5 413ft, at the confluence of two mountain streams, this lovely village has survived fire, flood and the demands of modern life and retained its unspoilt, traditional character; visitors expecting casinos and theme parks should look elsewhere. One of the most attractive winter sports resorts in the Hautes-Alpes *département*, adapting its lifestyle and activities to the seasons, Ceillac is a perfect starting point for walks along the GR 5 and GR 58. Anglers, mountain-bikers and paragliders will be in their element. Others come for the climbing, riding or just to admire the beautiful **countryside★**.

Nearby Sights: L'ARGENTIÈRE-LA-BESSÉE, BRIANÇON, Le BRIANÇONNAIS, EMBRUN, Vallée de FREISSINIÈRES, GUILLESTRE, MOLINES-EN-QUEYRAS, MONT-DAUPHIN, Le QUEYRAS, ST-VÉRAN, Lac de SERRE-PONÇON, VARS

Where to stay and Eating out

MODERATE

Hôtel La Cascade – *2km/1mi SE of Ceillac, at the foot of Mélezet* – ☎ *04 92 45 05 92 – closed 6 Apr-31 May and 10 Sept-21 Dec –* ▣ *– 23rms: 42.69/62.50€ - ⌑ 6.86€ – restaurant 11.43/19.82€*. Get away from it all to the bright and simple rooms of this mountain inn. There is nothing here but unspoilt nature, green or white depending on the season, stretching away as far as the eye can see and encompassing forest, Alpine meadows, lakes and mountain summits.

THE RESORT

The Alpine **ski area** is no extensive but has severa good points in its favour beautiful surroundings good snow coverage (owing to the altitude, a north facing aspect and goo upkeep of the slopes) a reasonable gradien (800m/2 625ft) and variety The ski area, ideal for begin ners and experienced skier alike, appeals to anyone pre ferring the charm of the environment to the qualit

and number of facilities. There are interesting possibilities for ski-trekking toward Col Girardin and the Cristillan Valley.

The more extensive cross-country skiing area offers 50km/31mi of good quality trails

★ **Église St-Sébastien** ☉ – The chancel is embellished by 16C murals with, in the centre, Christ in red inside a mandorla.

The **Chapelle des Pénitents** ☉, adjacent to the church, is now a museum of religious ar containing statues, altarpieces, sacred receptacles and paintings, and also houses a small exhibition on the flood of 1957.

HIKES

Dogs must always be kept on a lead for the protection of cattle and wildlife.

★ **Vallon du Mélezet** – *It is possible to drive upstream for 5km/3mi.*
🔼 This picturesque valley, dotted with tastefully restored hamlets, has forested slopes rising above 2 000m/6 562ft, the towering Font Sancte (3 387m/11 112ft) on the right and a waterfall known as the **Cascade de la Pisse**.

★★ **Lac Ste-Anne** – *Alt 2 415m/7 923ft. 2hr 15min there and back on foot. Park the car at the end of the Vallon du Mélezet road (1 967m/6 453ft).*
Pleasant hike through a fine larch forest and across pastures. The deep blue-green waters of the Lac Ste-Anne are held in place by a moraine deposited by a former glacier. The reflection of the Pic de la Font Sancte adds to the beauty of the landscape. A small chapel stands by the lake (pilgrimage on 26 July).

CÉRESTE✳

Population 1000
Michelin map 334 B9 and 245 fold 32

This little village in sun-bleached stone, a maze of pleasant streets behind the remains of its old medieval walls, lies between the pays d'Apt and the pays de Forcalquier. In May, fields of spring flowers make the drive down from the Prieuré de Carluc through the Vallon du Nid d'Amour even more charming.

Nearby Sights: Vallée de la Moyenne DURANCE, FORCALQUIER, Monastère de GANAGOBIE, GRÉOUX-LES-BAINS, MANE, MANOSQUE, Plateau de VALENSOLE

SIGHTS

The square – The village square at the top of the town once led up to the door of a church, before the Cérestins converted it into a barn; the arched Romanesque porch still survives.

Church – The broad façade and the elegant wrought-iron decoration around the bell are both typically Provençal; the lawned courtyard lends a further southern note.

Where to stay and Eating out

BUDGET

Hôtel L'Aiguebelle – *Pl. de la République* – ☎ *04 92 79 00 91 – closed 16 Nov-14 Feb and Mon except Jul-Aug – 17rms: 28.97/50.31€ - ⌑ 5.79€ – restaurant 13.57/33.54€*. Take a break in this unpretentious hotel at the heart of the village. The rooms are plain and well lit, the cooking is regional, without frills, but tasty and served in generous portions at a very reasonable price.

Nid d'Amour – Below the village on the banks of the Encrème, this "love-nest" is actually a vaulted stone wash-house fed by two natural springs: cool and refreshing on hot summer days. *Beware of falling rocks.*

EXCURSIONS

Dogs must always be kept on a leash for the protection of cattle and wildlife.

Pont Romain – *Head towards Forcalquier, then turn left onto Avenue du Pont-Romain.* The old Roman bridge spanning the Encrème is on the right.

Tour d'Embarbe – *Follow the road to Apt for 2km/1.2mi, then turn left just before the river.* This forbidding stone tower has kept watch over the road since the 12C. Its massive 2m/6.56ft thick walls are broken only by the narrowest arrow slits off a spiral staircase.

Prieuré de Carluc ⊘ – *Follow the N 100 towards Forcalquier for 5km/3mi, then follow the signposted road to the left.* Only ruins remain of this 12C monastery, affiliated to the abbey of Montmajeur, which would once have dominated the hollow known as the Ravin de Cure. One of the three churches at the site has stood the test of time, thanks largely to its nave carved into the face of the cliff. The animal and plant motifs on the capitals are still visible, as are a caryatid, straining under the weight, and a pair of well-fattened doves. To the left is a mysterious gallery, also hollowed out of the rock, which would have led through to a second church. The traces of tombs indicate that this was once an important place of burial and of veneration, made all the more sacred by the presence of saintly relics.

Vallée de l'Encrème – The Encrème and its tributaries support a protected population of otters. Branches bitten to a point are the sign that Europe's largest rodents have been hard at work: their dams across the river have submerged openings but remain dry inside.

CHAMBÉRY★★

Population 55 786
Michelin map 333 I4 and 244 fold 29
Local maps see and Les BAUGES

Captured by François°I, then retaken by the Duchy a generation later, Chambéry ha
always mirrored the changing fortunes of France and Savoie. The town was until th
16C the capital of a sovereign state and remains the centre of the Savoyard heartland
its well-restored old centre having regained something its past splendour.
The town developed in the narrowest part of the depression lying between the Bauges an
Chartreuse massifs, close to the three main nature parks in the Alps: Parc national de l
Vanoise, Parc naturel régional de Chartreuse and Parc naturel régional du massif des Bauges

Nearby Sights: AIX-LES-BAINS, L'ALBANAIS, ALLEVARD, ANNECY, Lac d'ANNECY, Le
BAUGES, Lac du BOURGET, Massif de la CHARTREUSE, GRENOBLE, Le GRÉSIVAUDAN
St-PIERRE-DE-CHARTREUSE

BACKGROUND

The capital of Savoie – Chambéry became the capital of the counts of Savoie i
1232. At that time, it was only a large village defended by a fortress. The expansion
of the town is due to the prosperity of the House of Savoie and to the efforts of th
three Amédées. **Amédée VI (Count of Savoie, 1343-83)** was known as "the Green Count
because of the colours he wore when taking part in tournaments. A brave knight and
a clever statesman, he extended his domains towards Switzerland and Italy and too
part in a crusade against the Turks. The fact that his armour was always covered wit
blood during the course of a battle earned **Amédée VII (Count of Savoie, 1383-91)** the nick
name "the Red Count". **Amédée VIII (Duke of Savoie, 1391-1434)**, the "Duke-pope", wa
made duke by the emperor of the Holy Roman Empire and acquired the Geneva and
Piedmont provinces. At the height of his fame he retired to the castle-monastery o
Ripaille, then played the role of anti-pope for 10 years during the Great Schism
before returning to his monastery as a simple monk.
After the three Amédées, Savoie went into decline until its prestige and influence
were restored by **Emmanuel-Philibert** who made Turin the capital of Savoie, Chambéry
remaining the seat of Justice of the duchy. Chambery's most famous son of the 19C
was **Benoît de Boigne** (1751-1830), a rich merchant's son whose picaresque adven
tures saw him enlist in the French guard corps before joining a Greek regiment and
then seeing service with the Egyptian and Indian armies. A maharajah who recog
nised his military talents named him governor of a vast territory on the subcontinent
After the prince's death, the by now fabulously wealthy General de Boigne returned
to Europe, married in London and settled in Chambéry, where his public works and
charitable projects earned him the nickname "*le munificent*" ("the generous one")
Made president of the *département* by Napoleon and an aide-de-camp by Louis XVIII
he ended his days as a count, elevated to the nobility by the King of Sardinia.

★★ OLD TOWN   *4hr walk including a tour of the castle*

A **small train** ⊙ takes tourists round the pedestrianised historic centre during the
summer season. Many blind walls are decorated with impressive *trompe-l'œil* paintings by local artists; particularly fine examples can be found at the covered market
and on the corner of the Théâtre Charles-Dullin.

Start from the Fontaine des Éléphants and follow the itinerary marked on the plan.

Fontaine des Éléphants - Chambéry's most famous monument was erected in 1838
to celebrate **Général Comte de Boigne** (1751-1830), the town's great benefactor. The
elephants are a reminder of his time spent in India.

Follow boulevard du Théâtre.

Théâtre Charles-Dullin – Rebuilt following a fire which seriously damaged it in the
19C, the theatre is named after the famous actor-director from Savoie. It has retained
the original stage curtain painted by Louis Vacca in 1824, depicting *Orpheus' visit to
the Underworld*;

*Continue along boulevard du Théâtre, which becomes rue Ducis after the Musée
Savoisien. Turn right onto the rue de la Croix-d'Or and right again down passage
Métropole, which leads to the cathedral.*

★ Cathédrale métropolitaine ⊙ St-François-de-Sales – Known as "Métropole", the
former church of the Franciscan monastery founded in the 13C, dates from the 15C
and the 16C, when the Franciscan order was at its height. It became a metropolitan
cathedral in 1817. The late-15C west front is remarkable with its Flamboyant-Gothic
decoration and early-17C wooden doors. The interior is surprisingly vast and the
single vaulting over the aisle and side chapel is noteworthy; it was intended to compensate for the instability of the terrain. In 1835, the church was decorated in
trompe-l'œil by Vicario who used the neo-Gothic style in fashion at the time.

Eating out

BUDGET

La Table de Marie – *193 r. de la Croix-d'Or – ☎ 04 79 85 99 76 – closed 8-21 May, 19-26 Nov, Sun evening and Mon lunchtime – 12.20/22.11€.* This listed building features a fine 16C door which opens onto two adorable little rustic dining rooms decorated with antiques. Meals are simple and typical of the region. The vaulting in the first room dates from the 14C. Warm welcome.

Le Café Chabert – *41 r. Basse-du-Château – ☎ 04 79 33 20 35 – closed 15-31 May, Sat evening, Mon evening and Sun except in summer – 13.26/16.77€.* As you walk through the town, take a stroll down the 14C rue Basse du Château. In summer the tables spill onto the pedestrian street. Daily changing menus offer good value for money.

MODERATE

Le Tonneau – *2 r. St-Antoine – ☎ 04 79 33 78 26 – closed Sun evening in Jul-Aug and Mon – 18.29/38.11€.* This lively brasserie is a popular local eatery. In a retro setting with carved wood features, the service is friendly, the atmosphere friendly and the fixed price menus good value. There is also a children's menu.

Aux Piétons – *30 pl. Monge – ☎ 04 79 85 03 81 – closed Tue evening and Sun - 22.87/38.11€.* At the gates of the old town, several small rooms have been done up to look like old streets with paving on the floor, a pavement and guardrails. Occasional "café théâtre" show on the first floor. Friendly atmosphere.

Where to stay

MODERATE

Art Hôtel – *154 r. du Sommeiller – ☎ 04 79 62 37 26 – ▣ – 36rms: 38.87/44.97€ - ☕ 5.34€.* This hotel is near the station and a stone's throw from the old town and its shopping districts. It offers contemporary comfort and is fully sound-proofed. The breakfast buffet gets the day off to a good start.

Hôtel des Princes – *4 r. Boigne – ☎ 04 79 33 45 36 – 45rms: 51.83/59.46€ ☕ 6.10€.* This small hotel makes a good place to stay. It is well located at the entrance to the old town, and has been renovated throughout. It offers a warm welcome and has a friendly atmosphere and fresh decor. Good value for money.

EXPENSIVE

Hôtel Mercure – *183 pl. de la Gare – ☎ 04 79 62 10 11 – ▣ – 81rms: from 114.34€ - ☕ 9.91€.* This hotel opposite the station is easy to get to and functional. Its rooms are spacious and fitted with sound-proofing and air-conditioning. The original architecture of the façade distinguishes it from other hotels in this chain.

On the town

Café de l'Horloge – *107 pl. St-Léger – ☎ 04 79 33 39 26 – Tue-Sun 7.30am-1am – closed in Nov.* This café is right in the centre of the old town, in a pedestrianised shopping area, and has a terrace which is hard to resist. There is an impressive choice of beers (200) and whiskies (30).

Café de Lyon – *Pl. Monge – ☎ 04 79 75 19 40 – daily 6am-midnight.* This café has preserved its retro character over the years and its decor features old items such as Seltzer water bottles, yellowing posters and an accordion... If you are here in time for aperitifs, order the speciality of the house: a "chambérien", or happy mixture of vermouth and Chambérysette (a sweet strawberry flavoured fruit vermouth).

Café du Théâtre – *Pl. du Théâtre – ☎ 04 79 33 16 53 – daily 7am-1am – closed for a fortnight in Oct and a week in Feb.* Local intellectuals and theatre lovers meet here after performances at the Théâtre Dullin (Oct-end Apr only, for practical reasons). Those who want to see and be seen compete for a place on the terrace.

La Transat – *29 pl. Monge – ☎ 04 79 33 37 81 – Mon-Sat 7am-1.30am. Concerts Thu and Fri.* This Irish-style pub is particularly lively and popular on concert evenings. Guinness flows in rivers and the atmosphere is buzzing. A big screen shows video-clips and sports events.

Le Flore – *1 r. Denfert-Rochereau – ☎ 04 79 33 41 39 – Mon-Thu 7am-10pm, Fri-Sat 7am-1.30am.* Clearly less well known than its Parisian namesake, this is nonetheles one of the liveliest cafés in town thanks to a clientele made up of cinema lovers who enthusiastically frequent the Carré Curial complex.

O'Cardinal's – *Pl. Métropole* – ☎ *04 79 85 53 40* – *Mon 2pm-1.30am, Tue-Sa 7.30am-1.30am.* This little pub with unpretentious decor boasts one of the most agreeable terraces in town. The journalists from the Dauphiné Libéré have made it their regular drinking haunt and discuss the latest local stories at "l'heure de l'apéro", or after-work drinks.

Shopping

La Régence – *20 r. d'Italie* – ☎ *04 79 33 36 77* – *Mon-Sat 7.30am-noon, 2pm 7.15pm, Sun 8am-12.30pm.* This chocolate-maker and salon de thé is famous for its specialities, notably the "Flocons de neige des Alpes" (Alpine snowflakes)

The base of the 13C steeple, the only remainder of the original church, houses the cathedral **treasury** ⊘: note in particular an ivory **diptych★** from the 10C, a 13C enamel pyx, a carved-wood representation of the Nativity and a 15C Flemish painting.

Walk back to rue de la Croix-d'Or.

Rue de la Croix-d'Or – This street, lined with old mansions, was the most aristocratic avenue in Chambéry. The **Hôtel de Châteauneuf** at no 18 was built by an ironmaster in the 17C (remarkable **wrought-iron work★** in the courtyard). The **Hôtel des Marches et de Bellegarde** at no 13 opposite, has a lovely façade dating from 1788. Napoleon stayed here in 1805; Pope Pius VII had been imprisoned here on the Emperor's orders the year before. Walk along the driveway to admire the staircase.

★ **Place St-Léger** – This vast oblong area was rebuilt and pedestrianised at the end of the 1970s. It was paved with pink porphyry, adorned with fountains and lamp-posts and its façades were restored and painted in warm colours; lined with numerous pavement cafés, it is the ideal place to stop for a drink.

Rue Basse-du-Château – Picturesque footbridge-gallery and old workshops; note in particular the 15C shop at no 56 and the little 16C tower on the Hôtel du Chabod (no 76). The street leads to the castle

Place du Château – Overlooked by the castle, the square is framed by the fine 18C Hôtel de Montfalcon, an Italian-style palace, and the 17C **Hôtel Favre de Marnix**. A statue of the brothers **Joseph-Marie and Xavier Maistre** *(see Introduction: Famous natives of the Alps)* stands in the centre.

★ **Château** ⊘ – This former residence of the counts and dukes of Savoie and occasional home to the kings of Sardinia was rebuilt in the 14C-15C and partly destroyed by two fires in the 18C, after which a royal palace – now the Préfecture – was built.

Follow the ramp which passes beneath the former Porterie (lodge) and leads to the courtyard surrounded by the Sainte-Chapelle and the préfecture.

Tour Trésorerie - 14C. Local history and family tree of the House of Savoie.

Salles basses – 14C. A monumental staircase leads to these barrel-vaulted rooms with 3m/10ft-thick walls, used as a chapel and a crypt and later as an arsenal.

★ **Sainte-Chapelle** – The east end of the 15C Flamboyant-Gothic chapel is surrounded by a watch-path. The Baroque façade dates from the 17C. The building was named Sainte-Chapelle when the Holy Shroud was deposited inside in 1502 (later transferred to Turin; a replica is exhibited). The 16C stained-glass windows are remarkable. There are traces of *trompe-l'œil* frescoes (1836) by the Piedmontese artist Vicario. The large tapestry showing the arms of Savoyard towns was made to celebrate the union of Savoie and France.

Numerous historic weddings were celebrated inside, including that of Charlotte of Savoie and Louis XI and Alphonse de Lamartine and his English wife, Miss Birch.

A **peal of 70 bells** ⊘, made by the Paccard bell-foundry in Sévrier *(see Lac d'ANNECY)*, was placed inside the Tour Yolande in 1993.

*Near the **Tour Demi-Ronde**, go down the steps leading to place Maché.*

Fr. Isler/MICHELIN

Italian influences: the arcades in rue Boigne

CHAMBÉRY

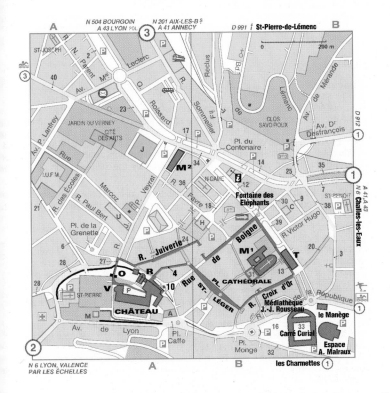

Musée des Beaux-Arts	A **M²**	Portail St-Dominique	A **O**	Théâtre Charles-Dullin	B **T**
Musée Savoisien................	B **M¹**	Sainte-Chapelle	A **R**	Tour Demi-Ronde	A **V**

Go through the 15C Flamboyant archway of the **Portail St-Dominique**, part of a Dominican monastery re-erected here in 1892.

From place Maché, start back towards the castle and turn left onto rue Juiverie.

Rue Juiverie – Bankers and money changers used to live in this street, recently pedestrianised. Look inside the courtyard of no 60.

Continue along the narrow rue de Lans leading to place de l'Hôtel-de-Ville.

Walk along the covered passage on the right (nos 5 and 6 place de l'Hôtel-de-Ville), one of the many **"allées"** in the old town.

Rue de Boigne – Designed by Général de Boigne and lined with arcades as is customary across the Alps, its orderly yet lively atmosphere makes this one of the town's most characteristic streets. It leads back to the Fontaine des Éléphants.

QUARTIER CURIAL

Most of the buildings in this important military district, dating from the Napoleonic period, were restored when the army left in the 1970s.

Carré Curial – *The courtyard is open to the public.* These former barracks, built in 1802 and modelled on the Hôtel des Invalides in Paris, have retained their original plan and have been refitted to house shops and offices.

Espace André-Malraux – Designed by Mario Botta, this house of culture containing a 900-seat theatre, audio-visual rooms and exhibition areas, stands next to the Carré Curial.

Centre de congrès "le Manège" – The former riding school of the Sard *carabinier* is a harmonious blend of traditional military architecture and modern design. A transparent peristyle has been added.

Médiathèque Jean-Jacques-Rousseau – Designed by Aurelio Galfetti (1993), the building is crowned by a panoramic glass roof. Its unusual shape – and Arthur Rimbaud's poem "*Bâteau-Ivre*" – gave rise to its local nickname, the "*Bâteau-Livre*" or "Book-boat".

SIGHTS

★ **Musée savoisien** ⊙ – This museum is housed in a former Franciscan monastery, later used as the archbishop's residence; the 13C, 15C and 17C buildings, surrounding vast cloisters, contain an important collection of prehistoric and Gallo-Roman exhibits on the ground floor. The upstairs galleries are devoted to religious (mainly medieval) art and coins from Savoie. A fine collection of Primitive Savoyard paintings is being restored. There is also a set of non-religious late-13C murals. The ethnographical section displays an excellent collection of objects illustrating traditional crafts, agriculture, daily life and popular art. The role played by the Savoie region during the Second World War is also explained.

★ **Musée des Beaux-Arts** ⊙ – Temporary exhibitions are held on the ground floor, in the vaulted room where the people of Chambéry voted for the union with France, and on the first floor.
The second floor is devoted to Italian painting: works by Primitive Sienese artists (altarpiece by Bartolo di Fredi), Renaissance paintings (*Portrait of a Young Man*, attributed to Paolo Uccello) and works from the 17C and the 18C (Florentine and Neapolitan schools in particular). The 19C is represented by two major trends, neo-Classicism and Realism. Still-life painting, northern schools and regional painting are also represented.

Église St-Pierre-de-Lémenc ⊙ – *To the north of the town*. The church stands on the site of an ancient Roman settlement; the priory to which it belonged was one of the liveliest religious centres in medieval times. The small rotunda is a remainder of the first church; once believed to be a Carolingian baptistry, it has now been identified as a reliquary chapel from the 11C.
The chancel of the **crypt**★ was built in the 15C as a base for the Gothic church above. It contains a Deposition of the same period, mutilated during the Revolution.

AROUND CHAMBÉRY

Les Charmettes ⊙ – *2km/1.2mi south. Leave Chambéry along rue Michaud. At the first major junction out of town, follow D 4 then drive straight on along the narrow surfaced alleyway leading to Les Charmettes. Stop by the former chapel below the house.*
The country house of Madame de Warens, who converted the Calvinist Jean-Jaques Rousseau to Catholicism, now belongs to the town of Chambéry. The charming De Warens captivated the young philosopher who described his stay here from 1736 to 1742 as "a time of happiness and innocence" in his *Confessions*. The careful restoration has preserved the 18C furnishings: on the ground floor, the dining room has *trompe-l'œil* decoration and the music room recalls Rousseau's musical career. On the first floor are the rooms occupied by Rousseau and Madame de Warens preceded by an oratory.
The terraced garden, containing plants which were popular in the 18C, overlooks the Chambéry Valley with the Dent du Nivolet in the distance.

✢ **Challes-les-Eaux** – *6km/3.6mi southeast. From Chambéry, drive east along avenue Dr-Desfrançois, N 512, which veers southeast and joins N 6.*
This little spa town specialises in the treatment of gynaecological and respiratory diseases. The spring waters are cold and contain a high concentration of sulphur. The casino and the baths, in late-19C style, are pleasantly situated in a shaded park east of N 6. The former 17C castle is now a hotel.

★ **Mont St-Michel** – *9.5km/6mi east, then 1hr there and back on foot. Drive 1km south of Challes along N 6, turn left then left again onto D 21; at the Boyat junction, turn left then left again towards Montmerlet; leave the car near the hamlet (parking) and take the footpath on the right.*
There is a choice of several itineraries; as you go into the wood, the footpath on the right leads to the Chapelle du Mont St-Michel. Note the variety of tree species according to the aspect of the slopes. From the top, there is a bird's-eye **view** of the

Chambéry depression, of the town and of Challes below, with the snow-capped peaks of the Belledonne range in the distance. The Lac du Bourget is partly visible to the northwest, with the Mont du Chat towering above.

★ **Lac d'Aiguebelette** – The lake is easily accessible from Lyon via the Lyon-Chambéry motorway. This attractive triangular expanse of water dotted with two islets (a chapel stands on one of them), covers an area of 550ha/1 359 acres; its unpolluted waters are 71m/233ft deep in parts. The steep and forested eastern shore contrasts with the more accessible western and southern shores

Lac d'Aiguebelette

where leisure activities are concentrated: fishing, swimming, boating and pedalo rides. Marked footpaths offer interesting hikes in the surrounding area.

Montmélian – This ancient, rapidly expanding little town, with a growing reputation as a centre of local viticulture, surrounds its rocky knoll, on which one of the most powerful strongholds in Europe once stood. The top of the rock *(accessible by a ramp signposted* "le fort"*)*, clear of any fortification since the fort was dismantled in 1706 on the orders of Louis XIV, is now occupied by a platform decorated with flowers which offers a lovely **panorama**★★ of the Isère Valley and of the Alps as far as Mont Blanc. Another rock to the northwest has been nicknamed "La Savoyarde" because its silhouette suggests a woman's head wearing the regional headdress *(see Introduction: Traditions and folklore)*. One reminder of Montmélian's past as a fortified town is the **Pont Cuénot**, whose ten arches have spanned the Isère since the 17C; for many years the only way to enter the town was by the bridge. Although the **Maison du Gouverneur** was remodelled in the 18C, it is not difficult to make out its Renaissance origins.

Combe de Savoie – Combe de Savoie is the name given to the northern section of the *sillon alpin* (Alpine trench), which includes the Isère Valley between Albertville and the Chambéry depression. Unlike the Grésivaudan to the south, it is an area exclusively devoted to agriculture. Villages, occupying sunny positions at the foot of the Bauges mountains between Montmélian and Mercury, are either lost among orchards or surrounded by fields of maize and tobacco or by famous vineyards; this is the main wine-growing area in Savoie. The best overall view of the Combe de Savoie can be enjoyed from the Rocher de Montmélian. Moreover, the roads leading to the Fort du Mont, Col du Frêne and Col de Tamié offer bird's-eye views of the depression. The most impressive sight in the area is the "eyrie" at Miolans *(see Les BAUGES, ②)*

Eating out

MODERATE

La Combe "Chez Michelon" – *73610 La Combe – 4km/2.5mi N d'Aiguebelette on D 41 – ☎ 04 79 36 05 02 – closed 2 Nov-5 Dec, Mon evening and Tue – 28.20/36.59€.* This restaurant stands in splendid isolation between the mountains and the forest, with its large bay windows overlooking the Lac d'Aiguebelette. In summer, meals are served on the terrace in the shade of chestnut trees that are centuries old. This is a good family address, without fuss or pretension, that also offers one or two rooms.

Where to stay

MODERATE

Hôtel St-Alban-Plage – *73610 St-Alban-de-Montbel – 1.5km/1mi NE of St-Alban on D 921 – ☎ 04 79 36 02 05 – closed Nov-Easter – ◘ – 16rms: 39.64/64.03€ - ☺ 6.10€.* The decor of this hotel is heavily frilled and furbelowed, having been renovated with great recourse to draperies, lace and little bows. There is a private beach below the hotel which enables guests to make the most of the lake. This is truly a chocolate-box establishment…

Hike

★★ Croix de Nivolet 48km/30mi – allow 2hr

Leave Chambéry by the D 912 heading east, then follow signs to "Massif des Bauges

Between Villaret and St-Jean-d'Arvey the road rises steeply beneath the cliffs of tw mountains, Mont Peney and the Dent de Nivolet, crowned by a monumental cros which is illuminated at night. After a glimpse of the Château de la Bâthie and, on th other side, the wooded gorges of the Bout-du-Monde, literally the End of the World a series of tight bends leads to an impressive view of the Chambéry valley and Mon Granier. From St-Jean-d'Arvey to Plainpalais, the road runs along the top of th Leysse valley, until the river vanishes into a fissure in the rock just after Les Déserts Ahead are the escarpments of Mont de Margeriaz.

La Féclaz – This important centre of cross-country skiing is popular with the inhab itants of Lyon and Chambéry.

2hr there and back on foot; park the car at the start of the chairlift.

⬛ Follow the yellow-marked footpath *(no 2)* to the Chalet du Sire and continu through the woods. From the top of the Dent de Nivolet there is a superb **view★★** c the Lac du Bourget and of the mountain ranges as far as Mont Blanc in the east.

EXCURSION

★ Route de l'Épine 85km/53mi – *allow one day*

Roads between Chambéry and the Lac d'Aiguebelette are busy on Sundays durin the holiday season. The Col de l'Épine is blocked by snow from November to April.

Leave Chambéry by *the N 6, then turn right onto D 916.*

★★ Panorama – Between St-Sulpice and the pass, the road offers glimpses of Mon Revard with its cable-car station, and of the Dent du Nivolet surmounted by a hug cross; beneath them lie Aix-les-Bains, its lake and the Chambéry conurbation. Th parapet on the last bend before the pass makes a good viewpoint.

Col de l'Épine – Alt 987m/3 238ft. The pass may take its name from a thorn believed to be from Christ's crown of thorns, which was venerated in Nances Castle nearby Beyond the pass, the cliff road offers bird's-eye views of the Lac d'Aiguebelette over looked by the sparsely forested escarpments of Mont Grelle, with the Chartreus summits in the background and the Vercors cliffs still further away.

Leave Novalaise by the D 916 to the west.

The road follows the line of the massif to Col de la Crusille (573m/1 880ft), then run parallel to a small tributary of the Rhône as far as **St-Genix-sur-Guiers**, once on th border between Savoie and France. Convenient motorway connections to Lyon an Chambéry have boosted its growth as a popular holiday town.

Continue west on the D 914 for 3km/1.9mi.

Aoste – This busy market town with a thriving food-processing industry was, i Roman times, an independent town *(vicus)* run by its own council, controlling th traffic between the main city of Vienne *(south of Lyon)* to Italy via the Petit-St

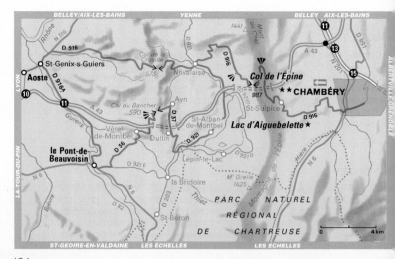

Bernard Pass. Aoste, named after Emperor Augustus, owed its importance to its production of pottery and ceramics, some of which have been found as far away as Germany and the British Isles; the recently reorganised **Musée archéologique** ⊙ illustrates life in Aoste under the Roman occupation. Note in particular a **"crossroads altar"** surmounted by a roof with four recesses intended for the deities of travelling. Social life in the Gallo-Roman city is also clearly explained, covering religious rituals (the goddess of Abundance is particularly attractive), domestic life (reconstruction of a kitchen) and crafts (model of potters' workshops and a rich collection

Roman glass from the workshops at Aoste

of **ceramics★**). Walk south across N 516 towards the retirement home; a remarkably well-preserved **pottery kiln** can be seen *in situ* under a concrete awning and behind glass, about 10m/11yd left of the entrance.

Return to St-Genix-sur-Guiers and turn onto the D 916 to Le-Pont-de-Beauvoisin.

The road now heads upstream along the course of the Guiers, a tributary of the Rhône which once formed the Franco-savoyard frontier and now marks the boundary of the *département* of Isère.

Le Pont-de-Beauvoisin – This small town is at the centre of an important tobacco-growing area, its other main economic activity being the manufacture of furniture. From the border **bridge** spanning the Guiers, there is a pleasant view of the river lined with fine old houses over which towers the steeple of the Église des Carmes.

Take the D 36 north towards Dullin.

The prospect from the road, which runs right along the edge of the slope, stretches as far as the Petit Bugey. The **view★** to the left just as the road enters the Col du Banchet is the best of many between Vérel-de-Montbel and Ayn.

It is worth making a detour to **St-Geoire-en-Valdaine** *(14km/8.7mi to the south along D 82)* to see the 12C-15C **church**, which contains a set of magnificent Renaissance **stalls★** decorated with caricatures and, on the edge of the town, the **Château de Longpra** ⊙, the 18C residence of a former member of the Grenoble Parliament, which boasts some remarkable interior decoration, in particular in the chapel and the dining room.

From Ayn take the D 37 towards Lac d'Aiguebelette.

The road leads to the plateau around Dullin which is planted with tobacco, nut trees and cereal crops, before running alongside the western shore of the Lac d'Aiguebelette between St-Alban-de-Montbel and Novalaise.

From Novalaise follow the road back to Chambéry.

CHAMONIX-MONT-BLANC***

Population 9 830
Michelin map 328 O5 and 244 fold 21
Local map see Massif du MONT-BLANC and below

Already the French mountaineering capital thanks to its Compagnie des Guides, Chamonix has also become one of the best equipped ski resorts in the Alps.

The development of the town as a skiing destination, which began when the first Winter Olympic Games were held here in 1924, has been helped since 1965 by the direct link to the Val d'Aoste provided by the Mont Blanc tunnel; the Italian resort of Courmayeur is only 20 minutes away.

Today, the Chamonix Valley looks like a built-up area, offering a mixture of architectural styles and incessant traffic going through during the high season. Hardly beautiful in itself, its main attraction lies in its magnificent landscapes, lively atmosphere and numerous opportunities for practising sports and cultural events (Semaines musicales du Mont-Blanc). Lovers of peace and nature are advised to avoid school holidays.

Nearby Sights: ARGENTIÈRE, Les CONTAMINES-MONTJOIE, Les HOUCHES, MEGÈVE, Massif du MONT-BLANC, ST-GERVAIS-LES-BAINS, Bassin des SALLANCHES

THE RESORT

Rue du Dr-Paccard, extended by rue Joseph-Vallot, is the town's main artery. The short rue de l'Église, perpendicular to it, leads to the church at the heart of the old town and to the **Maison de la Montagne**, which houses the offices of the Compagnie des Guides. In the opposite direction, avenue Michel-Croz leads past the **statue** of Docteur Michel Gabriel Paccard *(see Massif du MONT-BLANC)* to the station and the newer districts of Chamonix lying on the left bank of the Arve.

The controversial concrete buildings of the Bouchet sports centre and of place du Mont-Blanc stand on this side of the river.

A **bronze sculpture** by Salmson, depicting the naturalist Horace Bénédict de Saussure and the mountain guide Balmat admiring Mont Blanc *(see Massif du MONT-BLANC)* decorates the widened Pont de Cour.

The Compagnie des Guides

Founded in 1821 in order to try and control the access to Mont Blanc, it originally comprised 34 guides, all natives of Chamonix. At the time, the person in charge was chosen by the Sard government. In 1995, 150 guides listed in the Compagnie's books took care of an average of 10 000 clients a year. The most popular excursions offered by the guides are the TMB (Tour of Mont Blanc with overnight stops in refuges) and the ascent of Mont Blanc in small groups (10hr hard-going trek). In winter, skiing down the Vallée Blanche with a guide is an unforgettable memory for any experienced skier. Charges for the various excursions are available at the Compagnie's offices in Chamonix (☎ 04 50 53 00 88, www.cieguides-chamonix.com), in Argentière, in Les Houches and in Servoz.

Every summer, the *fête des guides*, which takes place on 15 August, gathers mountain lovers for a charitable cause.

Musée alpin ⊘ – The Association des Amis du Vieux Chamonix (Friends of Old Chamonix Association) is in charge of this museum housed in the former Chamonix-Palace hotel, which illustrates the history of the Chamonix Valley, daily life in the 19C, the conquest of Alpine summits, scientific experiments on Mont Blanc and the beginnings of skiing in the valley.

There are documents and photographs of famous ascents, old mountaineering equipment, costumes, regional tools as well as 18C and 19C prints and old posters of the valley.

EXCURSIONS

Viewpoints accessible by cable car

The following excursions to the nearby peaks involve a series of cable-car journeys. Although the rides and the views are breathtaking, the mounting cost of cable car trips can get fairly steep. Double-check the prices in the *Admission Times and Charges* section and be sure to reserve places in advance, particularly in high season.

***Aiguille du Midi** ⊘ – *minimum 2hr there and back by cable-car.*

CHAMONIX-MONT-BLANC

The Aiguille du Midi cable-car, suspended part of the time 500m/1 640ft above ground, and the daring gondola which continues the trip towards the Col du Géant, together form the most thrilling attraction in the French Alps.

★★ **Plan de l'Aiguille** – Alt 2 310m/7 579ft. This midway stop, situated at the foot of the jagged Aiguilles de Chamonix, is the starting point for easy walks. Good view of the upper parts of the Mont-Blanc Massif.

The Mer de Glace

★★★ **Aiguille du Midi** - *Piton Nord:* alt 3 800m/12 467ft. The upper station is separated from the highest point – Piton Central – by an abyss spanned by a footbridge. From the viewing platform, there is a bird's-eye **view** of the Chamonix Valley 2 800m/9 186ft below. The indented Aiguilles de Chamonix appear slightly lower and the most remarkable peaks to be seen are the Aiguille Verte, Grandes Jorasses and Aiguille du Géant overlooking the snowfields of the Col du Géant.

Piton Central (accessible by **lift** ⊘ *):* alt 3 842m/12 605ft. There is a totally clear **view** of the snow-capped peaks of Mont Blanc and of the dark rock face of the Aiguilles. Mont Rose and Mont Cervin can be seen in the distance.

Before returning to the cable car, venture through the galleries dug at the base of the Piton Nord: one of them leads to a platform facing Mont Blanc; the other – used by skiers intending to ski down the **Vallée Blanche** ⊘ – to the gondola station *(Aiguille du Midi to Pointe Helbronner, see Massif du MONT-BLANC).*

★★★ **Le Brévent** ⊘ – Alt 2 526m/8 287ft. *1hr 30min there and back by gondola to Planpraz and then cable car.* **Planpraz★★** relay station (Alt 2 062m/6 765ft) offers a splendid view of the Aiguilles de Chamonix.

The Montenvers rack-railway

This picturesque train, which enables non-mountaineers to experience the feel of high mountains and glaciers, gets its name from the viewpoint at the end of the line. In a mere 5km/3mi, there is a drop of 870m/2 854ft between the upper and lower stations.

The service ran in summer from 1908 onwards, the train being pulled by a Swiss steam engine which negotiated slopes with a 20% gradient with the help of a rack; the ascent lasted approximately 1hr at an average speed of 6kph/3.7mph. Since 1993, the line has been modernised with protection against avalanches and more powerful engines are now used, so that the service runs all year round and trains have a top speed of 20kph/12.4mph.

J.-L. Gallo/MICHELIN

From the Brévent summit *(viewing table)*, the **panorama** extends over the whole French side of the Mont-Blanc Massif, including the Aiguille du Midi and the Chamonix Valley.

★ **La Flégère** ⊙ – Alt 1 894m/6 168ft. *Access by cable car, starting from Les Praz.* From the viewing table, there is an impressive **view** of the Aiguille Verte and the Grandes Jorasses summits closing off the Mer de Glace depression.
A gondola service links La Flégère and **l'Index** ⊙ (alt 2 385m/7 825ft), from the top of which the **view** embraces the whole Mont Blanc Massif from the Aiguille du Tour to the Aiguille du Goûter.

★★ Mer de Glace via the Montenvers mountain railway ⊙

Lowest altitude of the glacier: 1 700m/5 577ft. *1hr 30min there and back including a 45min journey by rack railway.*
🗓 From the upper station at the top of the **Montenvers** (alt 1 913m/6 276ft), there is the famous **panorama★★★**, a natural wonder comprising the **Mer de Glace** and two impressive "needles", **Aiguille du Dru** and **Aiguille Verte** with the **Grandes Jorasses** in the background. *Viewing table in front of the Hôtel du Montenvers.*
An annexe of the **Musée alpin** ⊙, housed in the former Hôtel du Montenvers (1840), contains documents relating to the Mer de Glace and the Montenvers rack railway.
It is possible to visit an **ice cave** ⊙ freshly dug every year through the Mer de Glace. A **gondola** ⊙ leads to it from the Montenvers upper station. In summer access is also possible along a footpath starting to the right of the station, which also leads to the **Rock-crystal Gallery** ⊙ lower down on the right. The site of the cave changes every year. The glacier moves at a faster pace in the middle (90m/98.4yd per year) than on the sides (45m/49.2yd per year), so that the main chamber moves forward more quickly than the entrance tunnel. When the glacier slips over a rock, the surface cracks open and crevasses split the ice to a great depth, whereas when the glacier goes over a depression, crevasses tend to close up again. It is for this reason that the cave is always dug where the ice covers a depression.

Before leaving

– Take warm clothing with you as the weather is unpredictable at high altitude;
– Even when going on easy hikes, wear mountain boots and sunglasses;
– Several cable-car rides involve a sudden huge change in altitude; do not rush to the top when you arrive, but take it easy: one ought to be able to hold a conversation whilst climbing;
– The less daring will find that midway cable-car stations offer interesting viewpoints;
– Food and drink are available at the Planpraz and Brévent stations and there are restaurants at the Aiguille du Midi, Brévent and Flégère top stations;
– Dogs are not usually allowed, particularly when the itinerary goes through a nature reserve.
Advice concerning excursions to the **Aiguille du Midi** and the **Vallée Blanche**:
– During peak periods, departure times are fixed and passengers are given a numbered boarding card: it is imperative to abide by these regulations.
On arrival at the Piton Nord, it is advisable to go over the footbridge in order to gain access to the Piton Central and Mont Blanc terrace which ought to be seen first. The Piton Nord can be visited before returning to Chamonix. Access to the Helbronner gondola is via the Vallée Blanche gallery, on the left after the footbridge. The ice tunnel is reserved for suitably equipped mountaineers.

The Chamonix Valley can undoubtedly boast the most remarkable **ski area** in Haute-Savoie, for it offers some of the finest runs to be found anywhere, combining length, gradient and unsurpassed mountain scenery. In order to make the most of this incomparable ski area without encountering long queues at the lifts, it is advisable to avoid school holidays and weekends.
The ski area spreads over several massifs linked by shuttle services: the Brévent and Aiguille du Midi to Chamonix, the Flégère to Les Praz, the Grands-Montets to Argentière and the Balme to Le Tour. Snow cover is usually excellent above 1 900m/6 234ft (on the second section of each massif), but is often insufficient to allow skiers to ski right down to the bottom of the valley (return by cable-car is provided for). Experienced skiers favour such runs as the **Charles Bozon**, the Combe de la Charlanon and Col Cornu (Brévent area), the Pylônes and Pic Janvier (Flégère area) and above all the second section of the **Grands-Montets★★★** *(see ARGENTIÈRE)*. Off-piste itineraries, to be ventured only with a guide, are exceptional, in particular the famous **Vallée Blanche★★★** (20km/12.4mi downhill run with a 2 800m/9 186ft drop from Aiguille du Midi). Inexperienced skiers feel particularly at ease in the Balme area, where slopes are moderate and snow plentiful. There are also some fairly easy runs in Planpraz and La Flégère. Note that the **Mont Blanc Skipass** covers 13 resorts in the Mont Blanc area (including Megève, Les Contamines, St-Gervais...) and the Chamski pass gives access to all the ski lifts in the Chamonix-Mont Blanc area. In summer, the Aiguille du Midi cable car enables enthusiasts to ski down the glacial valley known as the Vallée Blanche. Cross-country skiing is practised between Chamonix and Argentière, at the bottom of the valley.

★★★**Crossing the Mont Blanc Massif** *1 day there and back – see Massif du MONT-BLANC,* **5** *.*

Hikers with high-altitude mountain experience can make their way up the Mer de Glace along the Balcon de la Mer de Glace *via ferrata* and admire the superb view. *(Information available from the Guides de Chamonix office).*

WALKS AND HIKES

There are numerous possibilities for hikers along 200km/125mi of marked footpaths. The *Carte des Promenades d'été en montagne* published by the tourist office in Chamonix suggests a wide choice of itineraries of all levels of difficulty. Ascents which are reserved for specialists and require special equipment as well as the presence of qualified guides are not dealt with in this guide.

★★★**Short tour of Mont Blanc** – *4-day round tour – see Massif du MONT-BLANC.*

★★**Lac Blanc** – *Alt 2 352m/7 717ft. From Les Praz, take the cable car to La Flégère then the gondola to L'Index. 1hr 15min on foot to the lake. Walk back directly to La Flégère in 1hr. Mountain boots essential (for crossing névés and walking along the stony path).*
Sweeping view from left to right of the Tour Glacier, Aiguille du Chardonnet, Aiguille d'Argentière and glacier of the same name, Grands-Montets, Aiguille Verte, Mer de Glace, Grandes Jorasses, Aiguille du Géant, Aiguille du Midi and Mont Blanc. The lovely shimmering colours of the lake waters look best at the end of July.

Eating out

BUDGET

La Bergerie – *232 av. Michel-Croz* – ☎ *04 50 53 45 04* – *closed Tue out of season* – *15.09/19.06€*. The decor features traditional local farming equipment. Hearty grills prepared over an open wood fire. Regional dishes are also on offer, and there is a peaceful shady terrace for summer days.

La Calèche – *18 r. du Dr-Paccard* – ☎ *04 50 55 94 68* – *closed 15 Nov-1 Dec* – *15.09/24.24€*. This restaurant at the heart of the resort resembles a museum or bric-à-brac fair, with a variety of antique and old-fashioned articles, copper pots, bells and old skis displayed all around the dining room. The waiting staff are dressed in traditional local costume, and a folk group puts on a show once a week.

L'Impossible – *9 chemin du Cry* – ☎ *04 50 53 20 36* – *closed Nov, Tue evening in May-Jun and Sept-Oct, and lunchtime* – *15.09/26.22€*. This typical local farm dating from 1754 has preserved its original character with beamed ceiling and the traditional fireplace under the roof truss on the first floor. The proprietor uses this to prepare his local specialities and grilled meats.

MODERATE

Le 3842 – *At the summit of Aiguille du Midi – by cable car* – ☎ *04 50 55 82 23* – *closed 1 Nov-15 Dec and evening* – *22.87/32.01€*. After travelling up in the cable-car and negotiating a series of galleries and footbridges, patrons sit down to dine at 3 842m/12 600ft above sea level. The narrow windows don't make the most of the view, but this is a small price to pay for eating more or less on the rooftop of Europe!

Maison Carrier – *Rte du Bouchet* – ☎ *04 50 53 00 03* – *closed 5-15 Jun, 12 Nov-13 Dec, Tue lunchtime and Mon except 10 Jul-31 Aug and public holidays* – *23.63/38.87€*. Treat yourself to a foodie's feast in this local restaurant on the premises of Hameau Albert 1. One of the dining rooms is an authentic farm room dating from 1794. The cooking is typical of the rural mountain region, and traditional meat dishes are grilled over a large central open fireplace.

Le Panoramic – *Summit of Le Brévent – by cable car and cable way* – ☎ *04 50 53 44 11* – *closed 20 Apr-15 Jun, 1 Oct-15 Dec and evening* – *23.63€*. A place on the terrace here makes you feel as if you are suspended in mid-air... There is a breathtaking view of Mont-Blanc, the Aiguille du Midi and the Bossons glacier. The menu features local cuisine, with tea and coffee breaks in the sunshine; life as it should be!

La Cabane – *At Praz-de-Chamonix golf course* – *2.5km/1.5mi NE of Chamonix on N 506* – ☎ *04 50 53 23 27* – *closed 1-14 May, 5 Nov-15 Dec and Mon evening* – *24.24/41.01€*. This "hut" on Chamonix golf course recreates a friendly Scandinavian atmosphere in a vast room with exposed wooden beams and logs. Traditional fare served in generous portions.

Where to stay

BUDGET

Camping La Mer de Glace – *At Les Praz-de-Chamonix* – *2.5km/1.5mi NE of Chamonix on N 506* – ☎ *04 50 53 08 63* – *open 12 May-Sept* – ✄ – *150 pitches: 16.31€*. This is indisputably the best campsite in the valley. The various buildings, designed as chalets, blend harmoniously into an unspoiled natural setting. There is no entertainment, so as not to disturb the peace and quiet of the valley. Simple clean accommodation.

Hôtel Arveyron – *Rte du Bouchet* – *2km/1mi NE of Chamonix on N 506* – ☎ *04 50 53 18 29* – *closed 16 Apr-1 Jun and 21 Sept-20 Dec* – ▣ – *31rms: 32.78/52.59€* - ☲ *7.62€* – *restaurant 13/17.50€*. Make the most of the garden shaded by cherry trees and breathe in the pure mountain air in full view of the Mont Blanc range. Guests here are pampered, either tucked up snugly in wood-panelled rooms or at table over homely local cooking. Good value for money.

MODERATE

Chambre d'hôte La Girandole – *46 chemin de la Persévérance* – *1.5km/1mi NW of town centre towards Le Brévent cable-car and the Route des Moussoux* – ☎ *04 50 53 37 58* – *closed May and Nov* – ✄ – *3rms: 44.21/53.36€*. A journey more resembling a treasure hunt brings you to this typical local chalet off the beaten track. It sits in a remarkable landscape, and the windows of its fine timber-panelled lounge overlook Mont-Blanc, the Aiguille du Midi and the Aiguille Verte. Warm welcome.

Hôtel Beausoleil – *Le Lavancher – 6km/4mi NE of Chamonix on N 506 then B road –* ☎ *04 50 54 00 78 – closed 21 Sept-19 Dec –* 🅿 *– 15rms: 76.22/89.94€ -* ☕ *7.32€ – restaurant 11.89/22.87€.* 5min from town, this is an ideal resting place. The hotel occupies a homely mountain chalet with a flower garden where guests can go for a walk on grass or snow, depending on the season, and make use of a private tennis court. This genuine mountain establishment offers traditional regional fare.

Hôtel Aiguille du Midi – *479 chemin Napoléon – 74400 Bossons – 3.5km/2mi SW of Chamonix on N 506 –* ☎ *04 50 53 00 65 – closed 19 Apr-21 May and 21 Sept-19 Dec –* 🅿 *– 40rms:48.78/71.65€ –* ☕ *8.69€ – restaurant 19.51/35.83€.* This typical regional hotel is located in the middle of the valley. Don't forget your tennis rackets and swimming costumes! Courts and pool are within yards of your room. Meals are served on the terrace and then it is time to relax in the flower garden. Sauna and spa bath help restore guests' well-being.

EXPENSIVE

Hôtel Hermitage-Paccard – *R. des Cristalliers –* ☎ *04 50 53 13 87 – closed 17 Apr-15 Jun and 17 Sept-21 Dec -* 🅿 *– 27rms: from 74.70€ -* ☕ *8.69€ – restaurant 21.19€.* This hotel away from the city centre occupies a peaceful natural setting. The garden is the ideal place to take a break between rambles and there are also the options of having a meal there, or spending some time in the gym.

Hameau Albert 1 – *119 imp. Montenvers –* ☎ *04 50 53 05 09 – closed 8-23 May and end Oct-5 Dec –* 🅿 *– 27rms: from 149.40€ -* ☕ *14.48€ – restaurant 38.11/106.71€.* This is an authentic local hamlet (luxury version!), consisting of the Hôtel-restaurant Albert 1 and individual chalets constructed in traditional style in the middle of a park and garden. Spacious sophisticated rooms blend granite, terracotta, and woodwork in larch, arolla and pine. Swimming pool and gym.

On the town

Bar du Plan de l'Aiguille – *Le Plan de l'Aiguille –* ☎ *06 85 17 31 25 – http://plandelaiguille.free.fr – Apr-Nov: access possible using the Aiguille du Midi cable car.* This modest bar at the foot of the Aiguille du Midi, in a magnificent site 2 317m/7 601ft above sea level makes a pleasant place to stop for rambling enthusiasts.

L'M – *R. Joseph-Vallot –* ☎ *04 50 53 00 11 – Daily 7am-midnight.* One of Chamonix's finest terraces with picture-postcard views. Glass in hand, admire the Aiguilles de l'M, de Charmoz, de Blaitière, du Plan and du Midi.

La Terrasse Le Grand Café – *43 pl. Balmat –* ☎ *04 50 53 09 95 – open daily 10am-2am.* This hundred-year-old establishment in fact houses two: La Terrasse, on the ground floor and very popular in fine weather; and Le Grand Café on the first floor with Art Nouveau decor and bay windows with a view of Mont Blanc.

Shopping

Ancey – *3 pl. Saussure –* ☎ *04 50 53 09 79 – Daily 8am-8pm; Jul-Aug 8.15am-10pm.* This chocolate-maker enjoys a good reputation and offers a number of mouth-watering specialities: Chamoniardises (praline-nougat), Galets de Chamonix (noisette with cocoa butter) and excellent fruit jellies.

Le Refuge Payot – *166 r. Vallot –* ☎ *04 50 53 18 71 – open daily 8.15am-8pm.* This boutique is well stocked with local specialities of all kinds: charcuterie (bilberry sausage), cheeses (Fromage d'Abondance), jams (milk jam), wines from Savoie, confectionery and ready-cooked local dishes to take away.

★★ **Walk from La Flégère to Planpraz** – *Take a bus to Les Praz, then the cable car to La Flégère. From there, about 2hr on foot to Planpraz. Take the gondola back to Chamonix.*
🔃 This pleasant, relatively easy walk forms the central part of the Grand Balcon Sud itinerary linking the Col des Montets and Les Houches. The footpath, lined with rhododendrons, offers uninterrupted views of the Mont-Blanc Massif.

★ **Hike from the Plan de l'Aiguille to the Montenvers** – *about 2hr 15min on foot.*
🔃 Overall views of the valley, from Les Houches to Argentière, and Aiguilles Rouges in particular. Towards the end, take the path on the left leading to the Mer de Glace.

CHAMPAGNY-EN-VANOISE✳✳

Michelin map 333 N and 244 folds 31 and 32
Local map see Massif de la VANOISE

This unpretentious village, situated at an altitude of 1 250m/4 101ft, beneath the impressive **Grand Bec** (3 403m/11 165ft) and opposite Courchevel, has retained its traditional character in spite of its recent expansion as a tourist resort.

Nearby Sights: Les ARCS, La Vallée des BELLEVILLE, COURCHEVEL, MÉRIBEL, La PLAGNE, PRALOGNAN-LA-VANOISE, La TARENTAISE, Massif de la VANOISE

THE RESORT

The pleasant and sunny **ski area** is linked to that of La Plagne by gondola and chairlift. The Borselliers and Rossa ski lifts lead to ideal runs for beginners and intermediate skiers. When snow cover is adequate, the **Mont de la Guerre red run**, with its 1 250m/4 101ft drop, offers splendid views of the Courchevel and Pralognan snowfields. Owing to its beautiful surroundings, Champagny-le-Haut has fine cross-country skiing trails, although it is not very sunny at the beginning of winter.

Church ⊙ – Erected at the top of a mound in 1250 and rebuilt in 1648, the church contains a remarkable **altarpiece✳** (1710) dedicated to the Virgin Mary, by Clérant, a sculptor from Chambéry. The altar front representing the Christ child surrounded by angels is in similar style.

EXCURSIONS

✳ **Télécabine de Champagny** ⊙ – Alt 1 968m/6 457ft. The gondola journey reveals the Courchevel ski area overlooked by the Saulire Summit and the Aiguille du Fruit with, in the background, the Péclet, Polset and Grand-bec peaks and the Vanoise glaciers. From the upper station, skiers or hikers, according to the season, can go on up to the terrace of the restaurant at the top of the Borselliers ski lift (alt 2 109m/6 919ft, viewing table). The **view✳** extends to the Grande Casse, Aiguille de l'Épena, Grande Glière, Pointe de Méribel summits and to the area of Les Trois Vallées.

✳✳ **Champagny-le-Haut** – The narrow road, sometimes literally hewn out of the rock, overlooks the Gorges de Champagny and leads into the austere basin of Champagny-le-Haut. Note the **Cascade de la Chiserette** on the left, just before the village of the same name. Beyond Chiserette, there is a view of the Grande Motte Glacier with the Grande Casse Peak on the right.

🚶 The Porte du Parc du Bois refuge houses an information centre about the Vanoise Massif and is the starting point of a **sentier-découverte** (discovery trail) dotted with information panels explaining the various features of the landscape (1hr 30min walk on flat ground).

HIKES

Champagny is a popular starting point for walks in summer. (The Information office will supply itineraries). From La Plagne, the main paths lead to Mont Jovet, la Grande Rochette and the Col de la Chiaupe, connected by cable car to the Bellecôte glacier. The most beautiful walks, however, start above Champagny-le-Haut in the parc de la Vanoise.

🚶 Begin early at Laisonnay-d'en-Bas (1 559m/5 115ft): from there, various trails lead to the **Col du Palet✳✳** (7hr 30min there and back, see TIGNES), **Col de la Grassaz** (7hr there and back) and **Col du Plan Séry** (5hr 30min there and back). Hikers, who need to be in top physical condition for these long excursions, are rewarded with magnificent views of the Grand Bec, Grande Motte and Grande Casse summits.

Where to stay and Eating out

EXPENSIVE

Hôtel L'Ancolie – Le Crey – ☎ 04 79 55 05 00 – closed 18 Apr-15 Jun and 3 Sept-16 Dec – 🅿 – 31rms: from 82.32€ - ☐ 8.38€ – restaurant 16.77/19.06€. The mountainside chalet above the resort boasts a fine summer swimming pool and a panoramic terrace with a view of the Vanoise slopes. Rooms are spacious and decorated in cherry wood. Simple local cuisine.

Le CHAMPSAUR★

Michelin map 334 E4 to F4, 244 folds 40 and 41
and 245 folds 7 and 8

The Champsaur is the area surrounding the upper Drac Valley upriver from Corps. Lying at altitudes often higher than 1 000m/3 281ft – similar to those of the Chamonix Valley – this region offers rural landscapes of a kind quite unknown in the northern Alps. The most impressive bird's eye views are from the Col du Noyer when coming from Dévoluy. Several winter sports resorts have developed in the Champsaur area: Orcières-Merlette, Ancelle, St-Michel-de-Chaillol, St-Léger-les-Mélèzes and Laye.

Nearby Sights: Pays du BUËCH, Le DÉVOLUY, GAP, Lacs de LAFFREY, MONTMAUR, Route NAPOLÉON, Lac de SERRE-PONÇON, Le VALBONNAIS, Le VALGAUDEMAR

EXCURSIONS

★① Drac Noir

FROM COL DE MANSE TO ORCIÈRES *66km/41mi – about 2hr 30min (not including tours from Orcières-Merlette)*

Col de Manse – The pass links the Gap Basin and Drac Valley in a landscape of high pastures. Refuge Napoléon *(see Le BRIANÇONNAIS, ⑤)*.

Follow D 13 towards Ancelle.

The road offers a pleasant drive through pastures, with lovely glimpses of the upper Drac Valley, and then through larch woods down to the bottom of the valley.

In Pont-du-Fossé, turn right onto D 944 then turn left in Pont-de-Corbière.

The old mill in Pont-du-Fossé has been converted into the **Musée des Arts et Traditions du Champsaur** ⊙, displaying tools and other everyday objects from the rural life of days gone by.

Between the Pont de Corbière and Orcières the road folows the course of the Drac Noir. Larches and firs grow along the northern slopes of the valley, which becomes increasingly mountainous.

> ## Where to stay and Eating out
>
> ### MODERATE
>
> **Hôtel Les Gardettes** – *05170 Orcières* – ☎ *04 92 55 71 11 – closed 2 May-14 Jun and 16 Sept-30 Nov –* 🅿 *– 15rms: 56.41/68.60€ -* 🍽 *6.10€ – restaurant 11.89/26.68€.* This typical mountain inn situated on the slopes above the resort has a friendly atmosphere. Rooms are small and have sloping roofs on the second floor. The cooking strikes the same simple rustic note.

Orcières – This south-facing village is the starting point of pleasant forest walks. On the way out towards Prapic, note how the walls of the houses in Montcheny are adorned with *"pétètes"*, decorative little heads which are unique to the Champsaur.

* **Orcières-Merlette** – *5km/3mi from Orcières.* Orcières-Merlette occupies a promontory overlooking the village of Orcières at the heart of the Champsaur Valley, between the Oisans and Dévoluy regions, in an austere high-mountain setting. Created in 1962 at an altitude of 1 860m/6 102ft, it has become one of the best equipped ski resorts of the Hautes-Alpes.There is an outdoor leisure centre along the Drac for summer holidaying, and the **Parc national des Écrins** offers numerous hikes.

Ski area – Spread over three distinct areas (Drouvet, Lac des Estaris and Méollion), the resort is well adapted to average skiers with a difference in altitude of 800m/2 625ft and 46 runs, but not really suitable for beginners (no real green run) and too restricted for advanced skiers. Snowboarders can try out their jumps in the Funpark.

The cross-country ski area includes two 5km/3mi trails on the Roches Rousses and Jujal plateaux (alt 2 200m/7 218ft, accessible by chair-lift) and 25km of tracks at the bottom of the valley (alt 1 450m/4 757ft). When snow cover conditions are good, cross-country skiers can ski along 100km/66mi of tracks linking the valleys. Orcières-Merlette is a family resort enjoying 300 days of sunshine a year and offering a wide choice of après-ski activities. The **Palais des sports** has a swimming pool, ice-skating rink, fitness club and bowling alley.

From Orcières-Merlette it is possible to take a diversion via Drouvet and walk from there to the Grand Lac des Estaris

★★ **Drouvet** ⊙ – Alt 2 655m/8 711ft. *Gondola ride in two sections.*
Panoramic view★★ of the southern peaks of the Écrins Massif to the north, the Vieux Chaillol and Gap region to the west, the resort of Merlette in the foreground to the south, the Pic de la Font Sancte in the distance to the east.

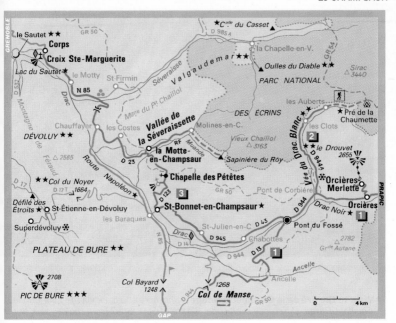

★ **Grand Lac des Estaris** – Alt 2 558m/8 392ft. *1hr on foot from the Drouvet Summit along a stony path. Mountain boots recommended.*
Beautiful mountain lake. The journey back to Merlette takes 1hr 30min without stopping. There are several lakes along the way.
Experienced hikers can continue from the Lac des Estaris to the Col de Freissinières, or the **Col de Prelles**★★, from where there is a beautiful view of the Pelvoux Massif and Ailefroide summit *(45min climb in each case).*

Follow the road to Prapic from Orcières-Merlette.

Prapic – This hamlet, situated at the bottom of the valley in a splendid mountain setting, has retained its heritage of traditional houses; a small **museum** ⊙ contains a reconstructed interior with furniture, clothes, tools and even newspapers. There are numerous opportunities for drives and walks.

Poet's grave – *1hr there and back; easy walk.* This walk through a lovely dale leads to a rock beneath which is the grave of a local poet, Joseph Reymond.

★★ ② Drac Blanc

FROM PONT DU FOSSÉ TO CHAMPOLÉON AND LES AUBERTS

From Pont-de-Corbière (after Pont-du-Fossé) turn left onto the D 944 to Champoleon.

The Vallée du Drac Blanc, also known as the Drac de Champoléon Valley, is remarkably wild and desolate.

Where to stay and Eating out

BUDGET

Chambre d'hôte Les Chemins Verts – *05500 Buissard – 1km/0.5mi E of St-Julien-de-Champsaur on D 15 – ☎ 04 92 50 57 57 – ☐ – 4rms: 33.54/41.16€ – main meal 11.43€.* Try a higher altitude! This charming, restored farmhouse stands 1 200m/3 936ft above sea level. There is a view of the Drac valley and the mountains. Rooms have white walls. Pleasant lounge, panoramic terrace and warm welcome. Gîte available.

MODERATE

Hôtel de la Poste – *05170 Orcières – ☎ 04 92 55 70 04 – closed Nov – 21 rms: 44.21/51.83€ - ☐ 5.34€ – restaurant 13.72/24.39€.* This inn stands at the entrance to the Parc national des Écrins, on the road through the village, and its renovated rooms provide a welcome port in a storm. The cooking is simple and local.

From peaceful meander to furious torrent: the Drac is known for its devastating flash-floods

★ **Walk to the Pré de la Chaumette refuge** – *3hr there and back via the Tour du Vieux Chaillol GR trail. Difference in altitude: 320m/1 050ft. Start from the car park at the end of the road, near Les Auberts bridge. Follow the footpath starting just before the second bridge. This very pleasant walk is suitable for everyone.* The path follows the valley planted with beeches and larches, beneath wild cliffs and waterfalls, before reaching the Pré de la Chaumette where the refuge is located.
It is possible to return to the car park via the path on the other bank.

③ The Lower Drac

FROM PONT-DU-FOSSÉ TO CORPS *60km – allow 2hr – see local map*

Between Pont-du-Fossé and St-Bonnet *(via D 43, D 945 and D 215)*, the road follows the Drac which meanders along its stony bed.

★ **St-Bonnet-en-Champsaur** – This small town which, in 1543, was the birthplace of the Duc de **Lesdiguières**, has retained its medieval appearance and narrow streets. A few art craftworkers have settled in the town. There is a 16C covered market in place Grenette.

From St-Bonnet, follow D 23 towards Bénévent, turn right then left at the signpost "Cimetière".

A small road leads to a chapel surrounded by its cemetery and to the Trois Croix view-point offering a wide **panorama**★ of the St-Bonnet Valley overlooked by the Dévoluy.

Continue until you reach L'Auberie.

Chapelle des Pétètes – The name means "dolls' chapel". The façade has numerous small recesses sheltering naive statuettes sculpted between 1730 and 1741 by Jacques Pascal, the carpenter who also carved the cross in front of the porch. No one can be sure whether Pascal himself invented this local art form or whether the distinctive figures with roughly shaped bodies, expressive faces and wrought-iron eyes are part of a much older tradition. Inside, the leather-covered altar comes from the chapel of Lesdiguières' former castle.

La Motte-en-Champsaur – Picturesque village with fine stone houses covered with roof shingles.

Take the forest road leading to Molines-en-Champsaur along the Séveraissette.

★ **Vallée de la Séveraissette** – The little road follows the green, narrow valley to the tiny village of Molines at the entrance of the Parc national des Écrins. Possible hike to the Sapinière du Roy *(2hr 30min there and back)*.

Return to La Motte-en-Champsaur and turn right to Chauffayer and N 85.

Between Chauffayer and Le Motty, the Route Napoléon makes a detour into the lower Séveraisse Valley guarded by the ruined 15C Château de St-Firmin. In the distance looms the pyramid-shaped **Pic d'Olan** (alt 3 564m/11 693ft).
Beyond Le Motty, there are bird's-eye views of the artificial Lac du Sautet, which blends well with its mountain setting.

Croix-Ste-Marguerite – Lovely view of the Lac du Sautet and Obiou Summit.

Corps – *See Le DÉVOLUY,* ②.

Massif de CHAMROUSSE★★

Michelin map 333 I7 and 244 fold 39 and 40

The summits of the Chamrousse Massif, which are the last important heights at the southwest tip of the Belledonne range, are the favourite haunt of skiers from Grenoble. The area has been so extensively equipped with access roads and a large-capacity cable car to the Croix de Chamrousse viewpoint that the former Olympic venue has become a sought-after tourist centre in summer as well as in winter.
In the valley below, the spa town of Uriage and the nearby village of St-Martin are pleasant holiday resorts.

Nearby Sights: ALLEVARD, L'ALPE-D'HUEZ, Le BOURG-D'OISANS, Massif de la CHAR-TREUSE, Route de la CROIX-DE-FER, GRENOBLE, Le GRÉSIVAUDAN, Lacs de LAFFREY, Route NAPOLÉON, ST-PIERRE-DE-CHARTREUSE, Le TRIÈVES, Le VALBONNAIS, Le VERCORS, VILLARD-DE-LANS, VIZILLE

THE SPA TOWN AND THE SKI RESORT

✢ **Uriage-les-Bains** – Known for its waters since the 1820s, Uriage-les-Bains lies in a green, sheltered valley, at the foot of the Belledonne mountain range. The baths, the casino, hotels and villas are scattered over a 200ha/494-acre park. The isotonic waters, containing sodium chloride and sulphur, are used in the treatment of skin diseases, chronic rheumatism as well as ear, nose and throat complaints.

✳ **Chamrousse** – This large ski centre above the Grenoble plain is actually made up of two sites, **Recoin de Chamrousse** (1 650m/5 413ft) and **Roche-Beranger** (1 750m/5 741ft). Originally a popular destination for visitors to the spa, who travelled up to enjoy the pure mountain air, Chamrousse became more widely known as a venue in the 1968 Winter Olympics.

TOUR *39km/24.2mi – see also local map Le GRÉSIVAUDAN*

This tour runs in a curve from Chamrousse to the Uriage spa.

D 111 climbs steeply into the **Forêt de Prémol★**, where deciduous trees are gradually replaced by firs and spruce. In spite of the abundant vegetation, it is possible to catch glimpses of the Vercors and Chartreuse Massifs.

Ancienne chartreuse de Prémol – The only remaining building of this former Carthusian monastery has been turned into a forest lodge. The vast clearing is the ideal place for a pause.

Beyond the Col Luitel, the road continues to climb in a series of hairpin bends, reaching its highest point at the Highways Department chalet, where the snow-ploughs are kept and which controls the various means of access to Roche-Béranger.

★ **Réserve naturelle du Luitel** ⊘ – *From Uriage-les-Bains follow D 111 towards Chamrousse and turn right onto the forest road signposted "Col du Luitel". The road skirts the lake before reaching the beginning of the nature trails. Car park near the Information Centre.*
This nature reserve, the oldest in France, covers 18ha/44 acres of peat bog, a unique ecosystem which developed in a depression of glacial origin.
Marked footpaths and platforms on duckboards enable visitors to observe peat bog vegetation. The "lawns" on the lake shores are in fact carpets of moss floating on water. Pine trees take root in the peat but as soon as they reach a height of 3m/10ft they topple over into the lake. The flora includes rare species such as carnivorous plants (sundew, bladderwort, butterwort) and orchids.

★★ **Croix de Chamrousse** ⊘ – Alt 2 257m/7 405ft. *1hr there and back including a 10min cable-car ride.*
🔲 The upper cable-car station, close to a television relay, is only a few steps away from the base of the cross, a splendid viewpoint affording a vast **panorama★★** *(viewing panels)*: the Drac Valley, Grenoble Basin and Grésivaudan depression over which tower the Chartreuse and Bauges massifs. In fine weather, the view extends as far as the Cévennes range.

Road D 111 continues beyond Chamrousse on its way down through the St-Martin forest, offering **glimpses★** of the Vercors Massif and Grenoble. Just as the road leaves the forest, there is a fine **view★** of the Uriage valley
The road then goes down into the valley past the 13C-14C castle, which once belonged to the Bayard family, and reaches **Uriage.**

Massif de la CHARTREUSE★★
Michelin map 333 H5 and 244 folds 28 and 29

The Grande Chartreuse is a famous monastery; it is also the well-defined mountain range known simply as the Chartreuse, where the monks of the order of St Bruno have built their retreat, cut off from the world by narrow gorges, striking limestone summits and impenetrable forests.

From a geological point of view, the Chartreuse Massif contains three of the most extensive networks of underground galleries and caves in the Alps: the Alpe (nearly 30 access points for a 50km/31mi network), Dent de Crolles (60km/37.3mi network, well known to potholers) and Granier. A great many bones of prehistoric bears, recently discovered in a cave, have given this site a new scientific value.

Nearby Sights: ALLEVARD, Les BAUGES, Lac du BOURGET, CHAMBÉRY, Massif de CHAMROUSSE, GRENOBLE, Le GRÉSIVAUDAN, Lacs de LAFFREY, Route NAPOLÉON, ST-PIERRE-DE-CHARTREUSE, Le VERCORS, VILLARD-DE-LANS, VIZILLE

BACKGROUND

A geological wonder - Cretaceous limestone was the basic ingredient of the geological formation of the Chartreuse Massif; 200-300m/656-984ft thick on average, it folded and split alternately. Tall cliffs cut through its thickness show thin layers of marl forming horizontal grassy outcrops, or **sangles**, suspended above vertical drops.

Parc natural régional de Chartreuse - Founded in 1995 and covering a total of 63 000ha/155 676 acres, the park includes 46 municipalities from the Isère and Savoie *départements*. Within its boundaries areas of biological importance are protected from development, waterways are managed and the environment of the high plateaux is preserved with a view to having these areas designated as nature reserves. The park is also responsible for projects such as the marking of five cultural hiking tours and the promotion of "gentle tourism" based on activities like hiking, free-flying and rock-climbing.

High rainfall and intense sunshine have helped to create a great variety of natural environments including vast forests, damp areas and pastureland. Each supports its own flora and fauna; as well as the eagle owl, the park's emblem, the Chartreuse is home to the black grouse, the pigmy owl and the rare Tengmalm's owl, while golden eagles and peregrine falcons can be seen near the numerous cliffs.

EXCURSIONS

★★ 1 Col de Porte and Route du Désert

FROM GRENOBLE *79km/49.1mi – about 4hr – see local map*

Head north from Grenoble via La Tronche, then follow the D 512.

The road from La Tronche to the Col de Vence climbs in hairpin bends along the slopes of Mont St-Eynard (alt 1 379m/4 524ft), offering bird's-eye views of the Grésivaudan depression and Grenoble with remarkable **vistas★★** of the Belledonne range, the Taillefer, Thabor and Obiou summits as well as part of the Vercors.

Le Sappey-en-Chartreuse – This friendly, high altitude resort nestles in a sunny basin with forested slopes, overlooked by the imposing Chamechaude Peak.

From Sappey to the Col de Porte, the road follows the Sappey and Sarcenas valleys with the indented Casque de Néron in the background.

Col de Porte – This important pass is overlooked by the tilted limestone shelf of Chamechaude, looking like a huge lectern.

At the Col de Porte, take D 57⁰ on the left towards Charmant Som.

★★★ Charmant Som – The road rises steeply *(14% maximum)* through a forest scarred with rocky ridges, which becomes thinner before giving way to pastures. Stop on the edge of the Charmant Som Plateau (alt 1 654m/5 427ft) and take a look at the **panorama**.

Leave the car at Bergeries and continue on foot. 1hr there and back.

🚶 From the summit (alt 1 867m/6 125ft), there is an interesting **panorama**. Walk to the edge of the escarpment in order to get an overall view of the **setting★** of the Grande Chartreuse Monastery.

Return to the Col de Porte. Continue with particular care as this route is often used by timber trucks.

The road meanders through the woods and across clearings, offering closer views of the extremity of the Chamechaude shelf.

Eating out

BUDGET

Chalet Hôtel Le Cucheron – *38380 St-Pierre-de-Charteuse – 3.5km/2mi N of St-Pierre-de-Chartreuse on D 512 –* ☎ *04 76 88 62 06 – closed 15 Oct-25 Dec, Sun evening and Mon except school holidays – 15.09/25.92€.* Nature lovers will find the necessary peace and quiet for a good night's sleep in this little hotel between the Chartreuse and Entremonts valleys. This simple stopover among the pine trees is peaceful and ideal for those on a limited budget. Half-board option.

MODERATE

Le Pudding – *Pl. de l'Église – 38700 Le Sappey-en-Chartreuse –* ☎ *04 76 88 80 26 – closed 2-12 Jan, 3-28 Sept, Sun evening, Tue lunchtime and Mon – 22.11/60.22€.* Contrary to appearances, this small restaurant with the welcoming façade does not serve English food, but French, and original and well-cooked to boot! The charming dining room opens onto a courtyard full of flowers in summer; ask for a table outside if the weather is fine.

Where to stay

BUDGET

Chambre d'hôte Le Gîte du Chant de l'Eau – *Mollard-Giroud, near the town hall – 38700 Le Sappey-en-Chartreuse –* ☎ *04 76 88 83 16 – closed 14 Apr-2 May –* ⌇ *– 5rms: 32.01/41.16€ – main meal 13.72€.* This converted barn restored in traditional style, has a large well-lit living room. One charming feature is that books and binoculars are put at guests' disposal for discovering the surrounding countryside.

MODERATE

Hôtel des Skieurs – *R. Giroudon – 38700 Le Sappey-en-Chartreuse –* ☎ *04 76 88 82 76 – closed Apr, Nov, Dec, Sun evening and Mon –* ▣ *– 18rms: 47.26€ -* ⌸ *6.10€ – restaurant 19.82/38.11€.* This typical local dwelling allows guests to experience the mountains at their own pace. From here you can go on a ramble, sightsee in the region or stretch out in the sun by the pool. You will be made welcome amid the pale wood decor, by the open fireplace or on the restaurant's terrace.

✳ **St-Pierre-de-Chartreuse** – *See ST-PIERRE-DE-CHARTREUSE.*

Turn back and follow the "Route du Désert" (D 520³, to St-Laurent-du-Pont).

★★ **Belvédère des Sangles** – *4km/2.4mi on foot from the Valombré bridge. See* ② *below and ST-PIERRE-DE-CHARTREUSE.*

Porte de l'Enclos – The valley seems completely enclosed by high cliffs. This was the upstream entrance of the "Désert" and the beginning of the wooded **Gorges du Guiers Mort**★★ overlooked by long limestone ridges. This is the famous **Route du Désert** which, in the 16C, bordered the grounds of the Carthusian monastery. The area was celebrated by Chateaubriand, Lamartine and Dumas.

View from the summit of the Charmant Som with the Grand Som to the left and Mont Blanc in the distance

At the St-Pierre bridge, take the road on the right to La Correrie (one way only).

La Correrie – In a clearing with a view of the Charmant Som, this annexe of the monastery housed the lay brothers of the order and also served as the monks' infirmary. The **Musée de la Grande Chartreuse** ⏱★ introduces the history of the order and the life of the monks with an audio-visual show. Be sure to see the reconstructions of the cloisters and a monk's cell.

★**Couvent de la Grande Chartreuse** – Founded in 1084, this monastery was destroyed and rebuilt many times; an avalanche buried the original building in 1132, only for fires to damage its replacement. The present buildings date from 1676 and cannot be visited as la Grande Chartreuse is still the mother house of the Carthusian order. The monks have been forced to leave on two occasions: during the Revolution and then in 1901, only returning after the outbreak of the Second World War. The distillery which produces the famous green or yellow Chartreuse liqueur is now in Voiron *(see below)*.

Return to the Route du Désert.

The road goes downhill through three successive tunnels; note the strange limestone needle, known as the **Pic de l'Œillette**, standing 40m/131ft high on the roadside.

Pont St-Bruno – This imposing structure has a single arch spanning the Guiers Mort 42m/138ft above the river bed.

Leave the car on the left bank and walk down (15min there and back) to the old bridge once used by the Carthusian monks.

The mountain stream disappears into potholes and flows under a boulder stuck in the gorge and forming a natural bridge *(viewpoint; keep a close watch on children)*.

Fourvoirie – This place name *(forata via)* is a reminder that, at the beginning of the 16C, the Carthusian monks hewed a passage through the rock which later became a road. Guarded by a fortified gate, now gone, it marked the downstream entrance of the Grande Chartreuse estate.

St-Laurent-du-Pont – This lively tourist centre was formerly know as St-Laurent-du-Désert.

Défilé du Grand Crossey – This wooded transverse valley is hemmed in by high limestone cliffs. The eastern end of the gorge, where the steep slopes of the Sûre rise to almost 1 500m/4 921ft, is particularly striking at sunset.

Voiron – This busy trading centre, situated on the edge of the Chartreuse Massif, is known for its skiing equipment: the town where the famous Rossignol brand was born in 1905 now accounts for 65% of the total French production of competition skis.

Église St-Bruno – The majestic steeple of this neo-Gothic church is visible for miles around and would not disgrace a cathedral. This local landmark was designed by Eugène Viollet-le-Duc

★**Chartreuse cellars** ⏱ – *Boulevard Edgar-Kofler.* The formula of the elixir of life was given to the Carthusian monks in 1605; from this

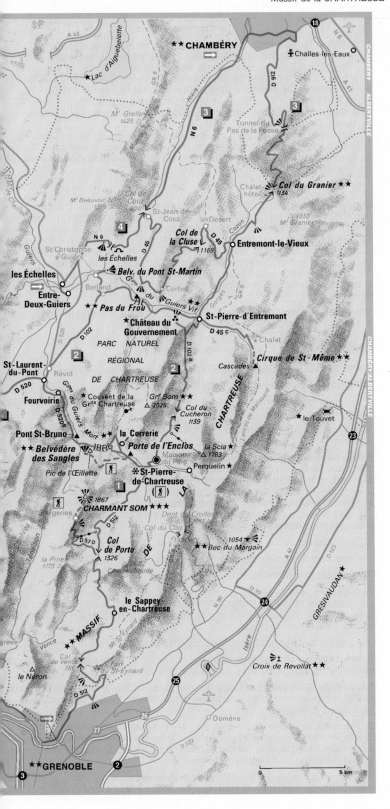

★★ CHAMBÉRY

Challes-les-Eaux

Lac d'Aiguebelette

Col du Granier ★★
Chalet-hôtel 1134

Col de la Cluse
1169

Entremont-le-Vieux

St-Jean-de-Couz

le Désert

Belv. du Pont St-Martin

les Échelles

les Échelles

St-Christophe-s-Guiers

Entre-Deux-Guiers

Berland

★★ Pas du Frou

★ Château du Gouvernement

Guiers Vif

St-Pierre-d'Entremont

Cirque de St-Même ★★

Chalet

Cascades

PARC NATUREL

RÉGIONAL

St-Laurent-du-Pont

Révol

Fourvoirie

DE CHARTREUSE

Couvent de la Grde Chartreuse
△ 2026

Gde Som ★★

Col du Cucheron 1139

le Touvet

Pont St-Bruno

★★ ★ la Correrie

Porte de l'Enclos

la Scia
△ 1783

Perquelin ★

★★ Belvédère des Sangles

Maison du Parc

Pic de l'Œillette

✳ St-Pierre-de-Chartreuse

1867

CHARMANT SOM ★★★

Bergeries

Dent de Crolles

Col du Coq

Col de Porte 1326

1054
★★ Bec du Margain

la Pinéa 1773

Coq-chaude

le Sappey-en-Chartreuse

GRÉSIVAUDAN

★★ MASSIF

Mt St-Eynard

le Néron

Col de Vence 788

Fort du St-Eynard

Croix de Revollat ★★

D 512

Domène

★★ GRENOBLE

0   5 km

The Carthusian order

In 1084, the bishop of Grenoble had a vision warning him of the arrival of seven travellers who wished to lead a solitary life. He took them to the "Désert" de Chartreuse where **St Bruno** founded the order of the same name. In the 12C, one of his successors laid down the Carthusian rule which has never been altered since. The order developed and included up to 200 monasteries at the time of the Renaissance. Today their number is reduced to just 17 throughout the world plus five convents of Carthusian nuns.

Carthusian monks and nuns observe vows of solitude and silence, dividing their days between work and prayer. Their cells open onto the cloisters. They meet only three times a day in church, share the Sunday meal and take a walk together through the woods once a week.

---

elixir (71° proof), which is still made today, they later created the Chartreuse Verte (55° proof), the Chartreuse Jaune (40° proof), a Génépi (absinthe, 40° proof), the Eau de noix des Pères Chartreux (23° proof) and fruit liqueurs (21° proof): raspberry, bilberry, wild blackberry and blackcurrant. The distilling and maturing take place in Voiron, as a visit to the cellars reveals, but the selection and preparation involving 130 different plants remain a secret. There are exhibitions and slide shows as well as a video made by the monks themselves, about the various stages needed to produce the famous **Chartreuse** liqueur.

Between Voiron and Grenoble the N 75 follows the course of the Isère, running along the southern boundary of the park.

★★ ② The Heart of the Chartreuse Massif

FROM ST-PIERRE-DE-CHARTREUSE *50km/31.1mi – allow 4hr – see local map*

❋ **St-Pierre-de-Chartreuse** – *See ST-PIERRE-DE-CHARTREUSE.*

From St-Pierre-de-Chartreuse follow the Route du Désert (D 520) towards St-Laurent.

The section from St-Pierre-de-Chartreuse to St-Laurent is described in ① above.

★★ **Belvédère des Sangles** – *4km/2.4mi on foot. Leave the car beyond the bridge on the Guiers Mort, then cross back and take the Valombré Forest road.*
 ⬧ It leads to the lovely **Prairie de Valombré** which offers the nicest **view★** of the Grande Chartreuse Monastery, framed by the escarpments of the Grand Som on the right and the forested ridges of the Aliénard on the left.
The road ends at a roundabout. From there, a path climbs up to the **viewpoint** overlooking the wooded gorge of the Guiers Mort.

Leave St-Laurent by the D 520 as far as Le Révol, then follow D 102.

The road rises to a small plateau occupied by the village of Berland.

Take a small road to the north.

Belvédère du pont St-Martin – *5min there and back on foot.* Beyond St-Christophe-sur-Guiers, just before the bridge over road D 46, a path on the right follows the left bank of the Guiers Vif and leads to a viewpoint 30m/98ft above the stream, which affords a lovely view of the gorge.

It is possible to come back along the footpath which crosses the old bridge.

Between Berland and St-Pierre-d'Entremont, the road follows the impressive **Gorges du Guiers Vif★★** with two striking narrow sections, one of which is the "Frou"

★★ **Pas du Frou** – This overhang, clinging to the 150m/492ft-high cliff, is the most spectacular section of road in the Chartreuse. "Frou" means "awful" or "frightening" in local dialect *(viewpoint).*

St-Pierre-d'Entremont – 459 villagers live in the Isère *département* and 295 in Savoie. From an administrative point of view, there are two villages separated by the stream which used to mark the border between France and Savoie. The village is also a good starting point for walks in the area.

A short detour leads to the **Château du Gouvernement★** *(3km/1.8mi). Head south towards the Col du Cucheron, turn right just before a bridge onto D 102[8] then take a sharp right again 1.5km/0.9mi further on.* The ruins of the castle stand on a grassy height which offers a lovely **view★** over St-Pierre-d'Entremont and the surrounding area.

Return to St-Pierre-d'Entremont and continue along D 45ᴱ to the Cirque de St-Même chalet.

★★ **Cirque de St-Même** – The Guiers Vif springs out of a limestone cliff rising to 400m/1 312ft and forms two splendid waterfalls.

Return to St-Pierre-d'Entremont and drive south on D 102.

This road forms part of the main route from Chambéry to Grenoble which avoids the Guiers gorges. Driving along this stretch is less demanding, and the landscape takes on a gentler character. The crests of the Lances de Malissard appear on the approach to the Col du Cucheron, and on the way down the peaks of Chamchaude and the Col de Porte come into view.

※ **St-Pierre-de-Chartreuse** – *see ST-PIERRE-DE-CHARTREUSE*

★★ ③ **Route des Trois Cols**

FROM CHAMBÉRY TO COL DE LA CLUSE OVER COL DE COUZ AND COL DU GRANIER
54km/33.6mi – about 2hr

Leave Chambéry by Route des Échelles (N 6) heading towards Col de Couz; the road soon enters the Park. Turn left at Col du Couz and head left through St-Jean-de-Couz, then follow the D 45.

Beyond Col des Égaux the road runs above Les Échelles basin, then above the Gorges du Guiers Vif. Excellent **view★** of the Pas du Frou *(see ② above)*.
Outside Corbel, by a wayside cross, there is a good view of the Guiers Vif valley as it opens out; on the opposite side are the hamlets of La Ruchère. Corbel stands at the entrance to another very picturesque valley, out of which the D 45 climbs steeply.

Col de la Cluse – 1 169m/3 835ft. This pass, often pleasantly cool compared to the sunny Entremonts Valley, is the ideal place for a short pause.

Head down in the direction of Le Désert to Entremont-le-Vieux.

Entremont-le-Vieux – The route follows the Gorges d'Entremont, hardly wide enough at times for the road and the Cozon mountain stream. Beyond Entremont-le-Vieux the D 912 leads to the Col du Granier with the mighty Mont Granier above it.

★★ **Col du Granier** – Alt 1 134m/3 729ft. This pass, over which tower the impressive cliffs of Mont Granier (alt 1 933m/6 342ft), opens the way to the Chartreuse Massif from Chambéry.
In 1248 a massive landslide buried many villages, killing 5 000 people and forming a huge pile of rocks at the foot of the mountain. Today, the **Abymes de Myans** is an area covered with vines and dotted with small lakes.
From the terrace of the chalet-style hotel, there are open **vistas★★** of the Combe de Savoie, the Bauges Massif, Belledonne range and Mont Blanc in the distance.

On the way down from the pass to Chambéry, there is a **sweeping view★★** of the Chambéry depression and the Lac du Bourget from the exit of the Pas de la Fosse tunnel.

★★ ④ **Route du Col de la Cluse**

FROM LES ÉCHELLES TO COL DE LA CLUSE *30km/18.6mi – allow 2hr*

Les Échelles-entre-Deux-Guiers – This lively tourist centre was formed by combining Les Échelles in Savoie with the neighbouring village of Entre-Deux-Guiers, lying across the Guiers Vif in the Isère *département*. In the 13C Béatrix de Savoie, countess of Provence, settled here, living in the building which is now the town hall. The village's mountain stream, once the Franco-Savoyard border, joins the Guiers Mort downstream from Les Échelles to form the River Guiers which flows through the impressive wooded Gorges de Chailles.

Follow the N 6 for 4km/2.5mi towards Chambéry

Grottes des Échelles ⊙ – *Leave the car at the exit of the Échelles tunnel.* The two caves have historic connections with the **Route royale Sarde** and with the legendary smuggler **Mandrin** (1724-55); the public enemy no 1 of his day is reputed to have used the lower cave as a hideout. The gorge separating them is a caved-in natural tunnel which used to be the only through way between the Couz Valley and the Échelles Basin. The steepness of the Roman road was eased in medieval times by a succession of steps (or *échelles* in French), which were levelled in the 17C to allow vehicles through (monument near the lower cave). Napoleon had the tunnel dug; it was completed in 1813.

The **tour of the caves** ⊙ starts from the inn situated on the N 6 at the eastern exit *(on the Chambéry side)* of the tunnel. The **upper cave** consists of a corridor splitting into two; the left-hand gallery leads to several chambers linked by narrow, strangely eroded corridors. A 220m/240yd-long footbridge clinging to the rock face runs along halfway up the lower cave known as **Grand Goulet★**. From the south exit, there is a lovely **view★** of Chartreuse Valley overlooked by the Grand Som and Sûre summits.

Continue along the N 6 to Chambéry: the route is described in **3** *above.*

Vines at the foot of Mont Granier

CHÂTEL★★
Population 1 190
Michelin map 328 O3 and 244 fold 10

The most popular, and at 1 235m/4 052ft also the highest Chablais ski resort owes much to a beautiful **setting★**. The massive rock face of the Cornettes de Bises (2 432m/7 979ft) towers on the horizon across the Swiss border; to the southeast lies the Dranse valley, with wooded hills on one side and the Cascade de l'Essert on the other. The vast snowfields of Portes du Soleil are within easy reach and in summer the forests and fields are perfect for walks.

Nearby Sights: ABONDANCE, AVORIAZ, ÉVIAN-LES-BAINS, MORZINE, THONON-LES-BAINS, YVOIRE

THE SKI RESORT

The pistes of Super-Chatel extend over the Morcan and Linga massifs, which are linked by a shuttle service and form part of the Franco-Swiss **Portes du Soleil**★★, an area boasting over 650km/404mi of pistes. Torgon and Morgins are accessible from Morclan; more experienced skiers may prefer the massif de Linga with the Les Renards black run and easy connections to the slopes of Avoriaz by the Col de Bassachaux.

EXCURSIONS

Where to stay

BUDGET

Gîte de séjour Le P'tit Cornillon – *L'Essert, near the Linga cable car* – ☎ *04 50 81 35 49 – closed Jun and 15 Sept-15 Dec –* ⬚ *– 32 persons; per night/per person: 21.34/22.87€.* This chalet with its clean functional rooms is located opposite the Linga ski slopes in as yet unspoiled surroundings. Breakfast included. Half-board option. Basic gîte.

Whether exploring by car or on foot, the countless routes through the countryside around Châtel may leave you spoiled for choice: over 300km of paths link the twelve Portes du Soleil resorts.

★★ **Pic de Morclan** – *Access by the* **Super-Châtel gondola** ⊙ *up to an altitude of 1 650m/5 413ft. The summit is reached on foot; allow 1hr 30min there and back.*

◫ From the summit (alt 1 970m/6 463ft) the **panorama** includes the Cornettes de Bises and Mont de Grange to the west and the Diablerets and jagged Dents du Midi on the Swiss side. It is possible to walk along the ridge to the Pointe des Ombrieux or to the Swiss *Lac du Goleit (from the La Conche cable-car station)*.

★★**Tête du Linga** – Alt 2 127m/6 978ft. *Skiers have access by the Linga 1 cable car and Linga 2 chairlift. On arrival, go to the top of the Combes chairlift and climb to the summit in a few minutes.* Splendid panorama of Morgins below, overlooked by the Dents du Midi.

★**Pas de Morgins** – Alt 1 371m/4 4981ft. The small lake lying at the heart of this forested area forms a picturesque landscape with the jagged heights of the Dents du Midi (Swiss Alps) in the background

Gorges du CIANS ★★★

Michelin map 341 C4 and 245 fold 24

The gorges of the Cians, a tributary of the River Var, are among the most beautiful in the Alps. In order to negotiate a drop of 1 600m/5 249ft over a distance of only 25km/15.5mi, the Cians has hewn its way through a narrow cleft, sculpting the rocks in the process. The superb sheer cliffs vary in appearance according to the terrain, the lower gorge being cut through limestone and the upper gorge through red schist.

Nearby Sights: ANNOT, AURON, BEUIL, CLUES DE HAUTE-PROVENCE, Val d'ENTRAUNES, ENTREVAUX, Route des GRANDES ALPES, ISOLA 2000, PUGET-THE-NIERS, ST-ÉTIENNE-LA-TINÉE, Vallée de la TINÉE, VILLARS-SUR-VAR

EXCURSION

From Touët-sur-Var to Beuil *38km/23.6mi – about 2hr*

★**Touët-sur-Var** – Tall and narrow houses, backing onto the rocky slope, line the partly roofed over streets of this picturesque village overlooking the Var Valley. Nearly all the houses have a south-facing galleried loft, known as the *soleilloir*, used for drying figs. The recently restored 17C parish **church** is decorated with numerous paintings and altarpieces. It is curiously built over an arch spanning a mountain stream, which is visible through a small opening in the floor of the nave.

Eating out

MODERATE

Auberge des Chasseurs – 06710 Touët-sur-Var – ☎ 04 93 05 71 11 – closed 15 Jan-5 Feb, 15 Nov-5 Dec and Tue – 15.09/29.73€. This village inn offers classic tasty regional cuisine. Pleasant terrace surrounded by greenery.

From Touët, drive west along N 202.

The chapel on the left-hand side of road, Notre-Dame-du-Cians, dates from the 12C.

Turn right onto D 28.

★★**Gorges inférieures du Cians** – Water oozes from every crack in the spiky rock face. The road makes its way through the tortuous gorge.

Turn right onto D 128, which rises sharply; caution is recommended.

Lieuche – Black schist forms the impressive **setting★** of this tiny mountain village. The unassuming **church** houses the **Retable de l'Annonciation★**, one of Louis Bréa's earliest works, set in carved and gilded wood panelling (17C). From the church terrace there is an overall **view★** of the Gorges du Cians, overlooked by the Dôme de Barrot, and part of the Var Valley.

Return to D 28, turn right then 1km/0.6mi further on left onto D 228.

The road climbs above the Cians Valley, revealing an impressive landscape.

Rigaud – This hilltop village overlooking the Cians Valley nestles below the ruins of its medieval Templar fortress in a very attractive **setting★**; there is a fine panoramic view from a spot near place de la Mairie.
The fortified parish **church**, decorated in Baroque style, houses several 17C paintings including a Deposition over the high altar, a panelled naive painting dating from 1626 *(on the left)* and a Virgin with Child.

Return to D 28 and turn left.

Touët-sur-Var

***Gorges supérieures du Cians** – At the entrance of the gorge, 1.6km/1mi beyond Pra-d'Astier, the road overlooks the confluence of the Cians and the Pierlas, 100m/328ft below, and rises progressively following the mountain stream which drops down to the valley in a series of steps. The steep bright-red rocky slopes, alternately jagged and smooth, contrast with the dark green scanty vegetation. The narrowest passages, known as the **Petite Clue**★★ and the **Grande Clue**★★★, where the road has been hewn out of the rock, are the most picturesque. A tunnel bypasses the Grande Clue which can only be seen on foot *(park before the tunnel)*. The cliff faces are only 1m/3.28ft apart at their narrowest point

Beuil in its striking **setting**★ suddenly appears on a bend.

★**Beuil** – *See BEUIL.*

To the west between Guillaumes and Daluis, the Var has carved out another, almost parallel, valley through the red schist: the Gorges de Daluis *(see Val d'ENTRAUNES, Excursions).*

CLUES DE HAUTE-PROVENCE★★
Michelin map 341 C4 and 245 folds 23, 24, 36 and 37

Only 40km/25mi from the busy coast, rushing rivers have cut their way across the mountains, forming narrow *clues*, the transverse valleys which are typical of this region. In the heart of this mountain mosaic lie hidden villages, each more delightful than the last, set in neat terraced fields or surrounded by untouched nature.

Nearby Sights: ANNOT, CASTELLANE, Gorges du CIANS, ENTREVAUX, Route NAPOLÉON, PUGET-THÉNIERS, ST-JULIEN-DU-VERDON, Vallée de la TINÉE, GRAND CANYON DU VERDON, VILLARS-SUR-VAR

EXCURSIONS

★**1** Clue du Riolan

FROM PUGET-THÉNIERS TO ROQUESTERON *23km/14.3mi – about 1hr*

★**Puget-Théniers** – *See PUGET-THÉNIERS.*

Cross the River Var and follow D 2211ᴬ.

The road rises in wide hairpin bends above Puget-Théniers to the Col de St-Raphaël; beautiful view of Roudoule and the Mercantour region beyond.

La Penne – A square keep overlooks the village clinging to a rocky ridge. Walk up through the pretty streets to a viewpoint and admire the view of the Vallée du Miolan and Montagne du Cheiron.

At Pont des Miolans, take D 17 on the left towards Sigale.

★**Clue du Riolan** – This is an impressive gap cut across the mountain range by a tributary of the Esteron. The overhanging road offers a fine **view** of the gorge and the mountain.

★ **Sigale** – The village stands in a picturesque **setting**★ on top of an escarpment over-looking the confluence of the Riolan and the Esteron, above terraced orchards. A viewing point gives a fine panorama of the surrounding peaks. This former strong-hold has retained two fortified gates, several Gothic houses and a 16C fountain. The 19C clock tower crowning an isolated rock is surmounted by a wrought-iron cam-panile.

Notre-Dame-d'Entrevignes – This 12C **chapel**, situated on the right-hand side of the road to Roquestron, was rebuilt in the 15C and decorated in the 16C with murals illustrating the life of Our Lady, including a pregnant Mary.

Roquesteron – There are houses on both banks of the River Esteron which marked the border between France and Savoie until 1860, when Savoie became part of France. This is the reason why there are two municipalities, Roquesteron in the north and Roquesteron-Grasse in the south, where the 12C Romanesque **church** stands on top of the rocky knoll.

★ 2 Clue d'Aiglun

FROM ROQUESTERON TO THE COL DE BLEINE *33km/20.5mi – about 1hr*

Roquesteron – *See above.*

Between the D 17 junction and Le Mas, the road is very uneven and narrow: passing other vehicles is often tricky and you are recommended to drive cautiously.

Beyond Notre-Dame-d'Entrevignes, follow D 10 on the left.

The bridge over the Riolan offers a lovely **view**★ of the gorge and the splendid emerald-green stream flowing among rocks and disappearing into potholes.

Cascade de Végay – It consists of a succession of fine waterfalls.

Aiglun – This picturesque hilltop village celebrated by Frédéric Mistral, clings to the steep slope of the gorge overlooked by the Cheiron Mountain.

★★ **Clue d'Aiglun** – The road, which crosses the Esteron as it comes out of the gorge, offers a striking view of the most secluded *clue* in the area: only a few metres wide, between 200-400m/656-1 312ft deep and 2km/1.2mi long, it looks like a gully separating the Charamel and St-Martin mountains.

Le Mas – This village, built on the edge of a beak-shaped limestone spur, has a 13C Romanesque **church**. The D 10 meanders along the hillside.

Follow the D 5 on the left as it climbs up the forested slopes to the Col de Bleine.

★★ **Col de Bleine** – Alt 1 439m/4 721ft. Magnificent **view** of the deep Faye Valley, the Harpille Peak (alt 1 686m/5 532ft), the ridge of the Charamel Mountain and the Grandes Alpes du Sud in the distance.

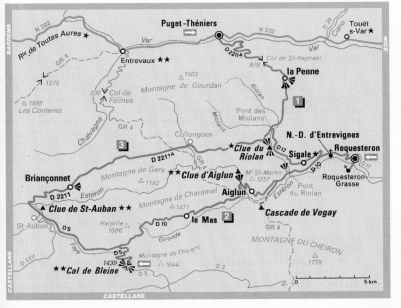

> ### How were the "clues" formed?
>
> In the Mesozoic era, an inland sea formed in the area where the Alps now stand, and a layer of fine calcic deposits covered its bed. 60 million years later, the upheaval which formed the Alps brought these layers of rock to the surface. The surrounding rock was eroded and rivers dug deep paths, which, over the course of millions of years, became the *clues* of today.

★★ ③ Clue de St-Auban

FROM THE COL DE BLEINE TO THE PONT DES MIOLANS *36km/22.4mi – about 1hr*

★★ **Col de Bleine** – *See Clue d'Aiglun.*

5km/3.6mi beyond the pass, keep left on D 5 which runs along the Faye and joins D 2211.

★★ **Clue de St-Auban** – The Esteron, a tributary of the River Var, goes through this impressive gorge with vertical sides hollowed out in places and forming huge caves; the river bed is scattered with boulders marked by deep potholes.

Briançonnet – This tiny village lies in a strange setting, beneath a huge rock. The houses were built with stones from an earlier Roman settlement as the **inscriptions** set in their walls testify. There is a wide **view★** of the Alpine summits from the cemetery adjacent to the east end of the church.

Beyond Briançonnet, the **view** embraces the Montagne de Gars and the Montagne de Charamel on either side of the River Esteron. Soon after Collongues, the Clue d'Aiglun can be seen on the right; further on, the Clue de Riolan appears like a deep gash in the landscape. From the Pont des Miolans, it is possible to return to Puget-Théniers along D 2211ᴬ.

La CLUSAZ★★

Population 1 845
Michelin map 328 L5 and 244 fold 10
Local map see Massif des ARAVIS

The most important resort in the Aravis Massif owes its name to the deep gorge or *clue* through which flows the Nom, situated downstream from the village.
Its large number of pistes and other sports facilities offer something for every taste, in every season.

Nearby Sights: ANNOT, Lac d'ANNECY, Massif des ARAVIS, CLUSES, Route des GRANDES ALPES, MEGÈVE, La ROCHE-SUR-FORON, THORENS-GLIÈRES

Eating out

BUDGET

Le Bercail – *At Crêt-du-Merle – 5km/3mi SE of La Clusaz on D 909 then minor road –* ☎ *04 50 02 43 75 – closed 16 Apr-30 Jun and 1 Sept-14 Dec except weekends between 1 Sept-13 Dec – 9.06/28.97€*. People flock here on foot, on skis or in tracked vehicles, and this former Alpine farmhouse certainly has plenty of charm. Hams hang drying above the fireplace amid old *objets* and wooden furniture, giving the place the air of a mountain refuge. The regional cooking ensures a full house every evening. Children's menu.

MODERATE

Aux Fourneaux de Marie – *La Perrière – top of village –* ☎ *04 50 02 53 27 – closed May, Oct and weekdays in Jun, Sept and Nov – 17.53/22.87€*. Above the resort, on the first floor of a small shopping arcade, the sunny panoramic terrace here gives a view of the Aravis range. In the evening, guests can discover the delights of local specialities in the muted atmosphere of the dining room.

La Table du Berger – *Top of village –* ☎ *04 50 02 60 54 – closed 15 Apr-15 Dec, Mon lunchtime and Tue lunchtime except school holidays – 21.34€*. Behind a timber façade, this restaurant specialising in cheese dishes is run by the son of a cheese-maker from Annecy (it must run in the blood!). Note that the restaurant also serves a few meat dishes. The homely welcome goes well with the simplicity of the setting.

Where to stay

MODERATE

Hôtel La Montagne – *La Perrière – top of village – – ☎ 04 50 63 38 38 – 27rms: 68.60/76.22€ - ⌒ 6.40€ – restaurant 14.94/29.73€*. Geraniums embellish the façade of this large chalet in the summer season. The hotel has been entirely refurbished and is cosy, comfortable and welcoming. Pale wood dominates the decor. The rooms face south, east or west.

EXPENSIVE

Les Chalets de la Serraz – *Rte du col des Aravis – 4km/2.5mi SE of La Clusaz on D 909 – ☎ 04 50 02 48 29 – closed 1-22 May and 1 Oct-8 Nov – ▣ – 7rms: from 129.58€ - ⌒ 10.37€ – restaurant 19.06/28.20€*. At the heart of the summer mountain pastures, this is the place for those who love nature and peace and quiet. The delightful rooms in this genuine setting are furnished with a mixture of old and new. In summer, the swimming pool and terrace are the best places to enjoy the view. There are three independent chalets for hire to families.

Résidence Le Panorama – *La Perrière – top of village – ☎ 04 50 02 42 12 – closed 15 Apr-16 Jun and 15 Sept-22 Dec – ▣ – 19 studios 2/10 persons: per week from 533.57€*. This large 1960s chalet near the centre, slightly higher up, is divided into studios and apartments all facing due south, in full view of the ski slopes and the Aravis range. Sheets and pillowcases provided. Well equipped kitchenettes.

THE RESORT

La Clusaz has been a winter sports destination since the 1920s, and today amateurs of all forms of skiing appreciate the considerable differences in altitude offered by the resort's four neighbouring massifs. The Manigod and Étale massifs offer several runs for intermediate skiers as well as a wide choice of facilities. The Aiguille Massif on the other hand offers advanced skiers a black run (Vraille) and several red runs. Acrobatic ski jumping is also available here. Cross-country skiers have at their disposal 70km/43.5mi of trails, including 12 loops. The ski area is linked to that of Le Grand-Bornand, both areas having a common ski pass under the name of "Aravis".

EXCURSIONS

★★ **Vallée de Manigod** – *See Massif des ARAVIS:* ①.

★ **Vallon des Confins** – *5.5km/3.4mi. Turn left in the wide bend on the way out of La Clusaz towards the Col des Aravis and follow the Chemin du Fernuy*. The road runs along the bottom of the valley then rises rapidly to the Col des Confins, a depression hollowed out by glacial erosion and lying just below the escarpments of the Aravis mountains. Continue along this road beyond the chapel in order to get a clearer view of the Vallon du Bouchet.

La Clusaz

CLUSES

Population 17 711
Michelin map 328 M4 and 244 fold 9

Cluses made its name in the 18C as an important watchmaking centre, and the precision crafting of metal components, which once served this industry, has now taken over as the town's main export. Not that the mountain town is just about business; as a cultural centre it is the ideal starting point for exploring historic Faucigny.

Nearby Sights: Massif des ARAVIS, AVORIAZ, La CLUSAZ, Les GETS, Route des GRANDES ALPES, Les HOUCHES, MEGÈVE, MORZINE, La ROCHE-SUR-FORON, ST-GERVAIS-LES-BAINS, Bassin des SALLANCHES, SAMOËNS, SIXT-FER-A-CHEVAL

BACKGROUND

A Brief History of Timepieces – The painstaking craft of watch– and clock-making has been a local tradition since the 18C, when Clusiens returning from Germany offered their new-found skills to the watchmakers of Geneva. The town's reputation grew, and in an attempt to gain an advantage over their Swiss competitiors, a school of watchmaking, the Ecole nationale d'horlogerie, was founded in Cluses in 1848, continuing its work until 1989.

EXCURSIONS

★★Le Faucigny

This region, which, until the 14C, was a bone of contention between the Dauphins (rulers of Dauphiné) and the counts of Savoie, gets its name from Faucigny Castle whose ruins still stand on a rocky spur overlooking the Arve Valley between Bonneville and Contamine-sur-Arve. The most interesting area from a touristic point of view includes the Arve Valley from Bonneville to Sallanches and the valley of the River Giffre, a tributary of the Arve, which leads to the heart of the Faucigny limestone heights.

1 La Cluse de l'Arve

FROM CLUSES TO FLAINE
28km/17.4mi

From Cluses, drive south along N 205 towards Chamonix.

The road follows the narrow passage between the Chaîne du Reposoir (Pointe d'Areu on the west bank) and the Chaîne des Fiz (Croix de Fer, Tête du Colonney and Aiguilles de Varan on the east bank) through which the Arve flows; the narrowest part lies between Cluses and Magland where the A 40 motorway and N 205 run alongside the railway line.

At Balme, turn left onto D 6 towards Arâches.

The road clings to the cliffside; a sudden widening makes it possible to stop the car *(beware of falling rocks)* and admire the long corridor through which the Arve makes its way from Sallanches to Cluses, with Mont Joly barring the horizon.

Arâches – Small ski resort in a pleasant wooded setting.

Les Carroz-d'Arâches – Ski resort situated on the edge of a plateau overlooking the Cluse de l'Arve.

2km/1.2mi further on, there is a clear view of the nearby Croix de Fer and Grandes Platières summits, with the narrow valley below. The road rises to 1 843m/6 047ft then goes down towards Flaine nestling inside a small basin.

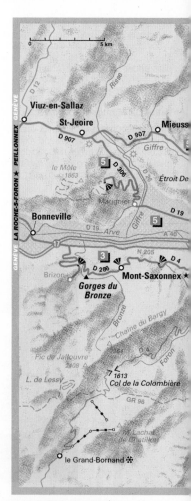

SIGHTS

Only the **church** and the 1674 single-span bridge **(Vieux pont)** have survived from the old Cluses, which was destroyed by fire in 1844. Turin was the inspiration for the new town's grid system, and an Italian style is apparent in its squares and wide, arcaded avenues.

Musée de l'Horlogerie et du Décolletage (Espace Carpano et Pons) ⊘ – This illustrates the technical evolution of time-measuring instruments and includes exhibits such as Louis XIV's one-handed watch, one of Voltaire's desk clocks, marine chronometers, large watch mechanisms and watchmaking tools.

Church – This former monastery chapel dates from the 15C and 17C. It contains a monumental 16C **stoup★** bearing the benefactor's family arms and surmounted by a stone cross. Notice also the 18C Calvary in the chancel and several painted statues of the same period in the nave. A tabernacle in the Chapelle du St-Sacrament on the right represents The Feeding of the Five Thousand.

** **Flaine** – This attractive modern resort lies in a secluded mountain valley at an altitude of 1 600m/5 249ft.

In summer and winter time, life in the car-free resort centres round the Forum, decorated with a polychrome geometric sculpture by Vasarely. Not far from this stands a painted sculpture entitled *Woman's Head*, which is the monumental version (12m/39ft) of an 80cm/32in model made by Picasso in 1957. The homogeneous concrete architecture is the work of Marcel Breuer, a former member of the Bauhaus School, who contributed to the UNESCO building in Paris and to the Whitney Museum of American Art in New York.

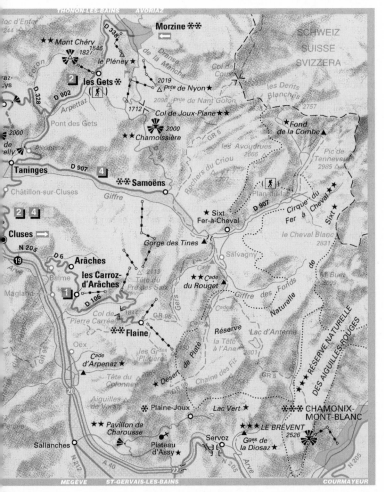

The resort makes use of a vast area, known as "Le Grand Massif", linked to the resorts of Carroz, Morillon, Samoëns and Sixt *(area pass)*. In addition, a remarkable 13km run links Flaine to the latter. Some of the resort's equipment is reserved for snowboarding enthusiasts. The **Téléphérique des Grandes Platières** ⊙ gives access to the **Désert de Platé** overlooked by the Mont Blanc Massif, from the Aiguille Verte to the Aiguille de Bionnassay.

★ 2 Route des Gets

FROM CLUSES TO MORZINE VIA LES GETS *43km/26.7mi*. Itinerary in reverse order, see *MORZINE*, 2.

★ 3 Route de Mont-Saxonnex

FROM CLUSES TO LA-ROCHE-SUR-FORON *36km – allow 1hr 30min*.

Leave Cluses by the D°4 heading south. Itinerary in reverse order from LA-ROCHE-SUR-FORON.

4 The Route du Giffre

FROM CLUSES TO SAMOËNS *21 km. Leave Cluses by the D 902, heading north towards Taninges.*

Immediately after Taninges, the view embraces the huge escarpments of the Rochers du Criou towering over Samoëns and flanked by the Avoudrues Massif, while Mont Buet can be seen in the distance.

The D 907 leads to Samoëns.

★ 5 The lower Vallée du Giffre

FROM CLUSES TO ST-JEOIRE *38km/23mi. Leave Cluses and head north towards Taninges, then take the D 4 on the left to St-Jeoire.*

From Marignier the road follows the fast-flowing Giffre.

Cross the river, ignoring the D 26 on the right, and head into the village.

★ **La Môle viewpoint** – *The road rises steeply; to be avoided after rainfall.* At the north exit, head towards Ossat and follow the road that leads up to the viewpoint, offering a wonderful view of the Giffre valley and the Arve. Mont Saxonnex is visible to the south.

Follow the D 306 until the Giffre joins the Risse.

St-Jeoire – Pleasant holiday resort at the heart of a wooded valley.

The D 907 overlooks the confluence of the River Giffre and River Risse and gives a view of the massif du Reposoir and the Chaîne du Bargy, then goes through a wooded gorge to reach the Mieussy Basin within sight of the snow-capped Mont Buet.

Mieussy – This village is one of the finest sights along the way. The onion-shaped spire of the **church** ⊙ rises into the sky, enhanced by the delightful landscape with its many shades of green.
The Étroit Denté, a short gorge cut through an obstruction of glacial origin, opens into the middle valley of the River Giffre, which widens beyond Taninges.

Taninges – *See MORZINE*, 2.

Itinerary from Taninges to Cluses, see MORZINE, 2.

COLMARS ★

Population 378
Michelin map 334 H7 and 245 fold 22

At the centre of the Haute Vallée du Verdon, the splendid wooded mountain setting of this small walled town, guarded by two forts, makes it a pleasant summer resort (alt 1 250m/4 101ft) and a good cross-country skiing centre in winter. Behind the town walls its pretty streets have kept an almost medieval feel, but in fact their origins are much older: the town took its name from a temple built on a hill to celebrate the Roman god, Mars *(collis Martis)*.

Nearby Sights: ANNOT, BARCELONNETTE, Val d'ENTRAUNES, PRA-LOUP, ST-JULIEN-DU-VERDON, VAL D'ALLOS.

EXPLORING COLMARS

★ **Old town** – Once through the Porte de Savoie or the Porte de France, visitors will appreciate the southern atmosphere pervading the city, as they wander through the narrow streets linked by tiny squares adorned with fountains. The tall houses are built to reach above the parapets to make the most of the sun; straw for animals, and on washing day the family laundry, can be left to dry in the open attics known as "soleil-lados".

The walls – The original **Église St-Martin** ○ was built on the site of the temple of Mars in the 8C; its replacement, a 16C-17C church in Gothic style with Romanesque features, has only one side aisle, built into the town's wall. Colmars was first fortified in the 14C and acquired strategic importance as a border town when Savoie annexed Allos. In 1528, François I strengthened the walls by adding small square towers which can still be seen today in spite of successive fires. The duke of Savoie's declaration of war against France in 1690 brought the French army to the gates of Colmars, but the town narrowly survived the siege which followed. Plans drawn up by Vauban, Louis XIV's military engi-

The fortress watchtower

neer, led to the construction of the forts linked to the town by *caponnières* or covered passages, and to the fortification of the town gates. Visitors can now walk along half the length of the ramparts which were recently restored, much to the disappointment of the locals who are no longer allowed to hang out their washing on this prime drying spot!

Fort de Savoie ○ – Built in 1693-95 at the same time as the Fort de France, this fort comprises two successive enclosures; inside the second one, there are four vaulted rooms which used to house the garrison and where exhibitions are now held. Stairs lead to a round tower and to the vast armoury; note the remarkable roof structure made out of larch wood. The fort is the venue for a folk festival at the end of July and for a series of "medieval days" in the second week of August.

Cascade de la Lance – *40min there and back. Follow the road which starts opposite the church.* A pleasant path leads through pinewoods to the foot of a cliff, then slips through a narrow gorge to reach the waterfall noisily splashing on the rock face.

EXCURSION

★**Haute Vallée du Verdon** *36km/22.4mi – allow 45min*

Leave Colmars by the D 908 heading south. At the approach to Beauvezer turn left towards Villars-Heyssier and continue to the car park.

★**Gorges de St-Pierre** – *1hr 30min on foot there and back.* A marked path leads to the gorge carved by a tributary of the Verdon. The path climbs along the steep sides, offering impressive views of the grey schist and white and ochre limestone lining the gorge.

After **Beauvezer**, a small summer resort in a pleasant, verdant setting, the road follows the bottom of the valley, overlooked in the east by the imposing Grand Coyer (2 693m/8 835ft).

The road, dug deep into the rocky slope, winds upwards from St-Michel-Peyresq. Beyond the Pont de Villaron, D 955 runs between arid mountains where lavender alternates with isolated clumps of trees. The river then flows through a long and narrow transverse valley which opens out into the small St-André-des-Alpes Basin.

St-André-des-Alpes – This village lies at the confluence of the River Issole and River Verdon and at the crossroads of several tourist routes, in a pleasant setting of orchards and lavender fields. It is a fine base for excursions in the surrounding area.

Downstream of St-André, the Lac de Castillon lies at the centre of a scrubland area.

Lac de Castillon – *See ST-JULIEN-DU-VERDON, Excursions*

Les CONTAMINES-MONTJOIE✶✶✶

Population 1 129
Michelin map 328 N6 and 244 fold 21
Local map see Massif du MONT-BLANC

Located at an altitude of 1 164m/3 819ft, at the foot of Mont Joly and the snow-capped Dômes de Miage, Les Contamines is one of the most pleasant and restful holiday resorts in the Mont Blanc Massif. The 18C church with painted façade and overhanging roof is particularly charming.

Nearby Sights: ARGENTIÈRE, CHAMONIX-MONT-BLANC, Les HOUCHES, MEGÈVE, Massif du MONT-BLANC, SAINT-GERVAIS-LES-BAINS, SALLANCHES

SUMMER AND WINTER SPORTS

The ski resort, created in the 1930s, is surrounded by a practically equipped ski area with good snow cover. It aims to attract families looking for moderately difficult ski runs and beautiful scenery such as that of Les Contamines just beneath Mont Blanc. The ski area is linked to that of the Mont d'Arbois. Cross-country skiers can enjoy 30km/18mi of trails.

In summer, the resort is an exceptionally fine **hiking and mountaineering centre**. Major ascents usually start from the Hôtellerie de Tré-la-Tête *(4hr 30min there and back from Cugnon)*, built just below the glacier which feeds the Lac de la Girotte. Hikers will encounter some of the most attractive footpaths in the Alps.
In addition, the village offers visitors the opportunity to take part in various sports and cultural activities and to enjoy the **Base de loisirs du Pontet**, a leisure park surrounding a small lake.

Where to stay

BUDGET

Le Christiania – *593 rte Notre-Dame-de-la-Gorge* – ☎ *04 50 47 02 72* - *closed 16 Apr-19 Jun and 11 Sept-19 Dec* – 🅿 – *14rms: 32.01/68.60€* ☟ *5.95 € – restaurant 16.31€*. There is something for all the family here A. Nursery slope for beginners and children's play area are right by the hotel For adults: a session in the gym or a few lengths of the swimming pool in summer, followed by a drink on the terrace opposite the garden. A simple homely place to stay.

MODERATE

Hôtel Gai Soleil – *288 chemin Loyers* – ☎ *04 50 47 02 94* – *closed 17 Apr 14 Jun and 16 Sept-21 Dec* – 🅿 – *19rms: 45.73/68.60€* - ☟ *6.86€ – restaurant 15.09/22.17€*. This family-friendly house looks almost like a child's drawing with its painted shutters, sloping roof and balconies adorned with flowers in summer. Summer and winter alike the atmosphere is homely and guests are treated as friends. Right in the middle of the resort, it offers well kept rooms peace and quiet and a sunny terrace.

HIKES

★ **Le Signal** ⊙ – Alt 1 850m/6 070ft. *Accessible via the Gorge and Signal gondolas* Splendid view of the Dômes de Miage and Tré-la-Tête Massif as well as of the Chaîne des Fiz further north.

★★ **Walk to the Col du Joly** – Alt 1 989m/6 526ft. *30min easy climb from Le Signal.* 🚶 Superb panorama of the Mont Blanc Massif, the Hauteluce Valley and Lac de la Girotte with the Aravis mountains further away to the northwest.

★★★ **Hike to the Aiguille Croche** – Alt 2 487m/8 159ft. *1hr 30min on foot from the Col du Joly. As the path is very steep, mountain boots are strongly recommended.*
🚶 One's efforts are rewarded by a wide and most beautiful **panorama★★★**, one of the finest in the Alps, which encompasses, in a clockwise direction, the Aiguilles de Chamonix, Aiguille Verte, Aiguille du Midi, Aiguille de Bionassay, Mont Blanc, Mont Pourri, the Grande Motte and Grande Casse glaciers, Pierra Menta, the Écrins massif the Meije, the Mont de Lans and Étendard glaciers, the vast Aravis range, Megève and its mountain airfield.

★★★ **From Aiguille Croche to Mont Joly along the crest path** – *Experienced hikers using a map and leaving early in the morning to make the ascent of the Aiguille Croche, will be able to carry on to Mont Joly (about 2hr).*

🚶 From the path, which is narrow but does not often run along the cliff edge, a succession of splendid views unfold. From Mont Joly *(viewing table, for details see MEGÈVE)*, allow another 2hr to return to Les Contamines. *Turn round towards the Tête de la Combaz and take the path on the left which leads rapidly down to the bottom of the valley. Turn right in Colombaz onto the surfaced road then left 200m/218yd further on.* The path leads to L'Étape from where a gondola takes you down to La Gorge. It is also possible to go back on foot.

★ **Lacs Jovet** – Alt 2 174m/7 133ft. *Difference in altitude: about 1 000m/3 281ft. 5hr on foot there and back from Notre-Dame-de-la-Gorge.*
🚶 This well-marked itinerary, which forms part of the Round Tour of Mont Blanc, goes through the Réserve naturelle des Contamines. Splendid light reflections on the lakes surrounded by Mont Jovet, Mont Tondu, Col du Bonhomme and Aiguilles de la Pennaz.

Notre-Dame-de-la-Gorge – a small classic of the Savoyard Baroque

COURCHEVEL✶✶✶

Michelin map 333 M5 and 244 fold 31
Local map see Massif de la VANOISE

Courchevel is undoubtedly one of the major and most prestigious winter sports resorts in the world. Founded in 1946 by the Conseil général de la Savoie (regional council), it played a leading role in the development of the **Trois Vallées**✶✶✶ complex *(see Massif de la VANOISE)*. Émile Allais, who was the downhill world champion in 1937, was the first to introduce the idea of maintaining and packing down ski runs in French resorts.
Après-ski activities are just as exciting: art exhibitions, classical and jazz concerts, an impressive number of luxury shops, sports centres, fitness clubs, and famous nightclubs. However, Courchevel also owes its reputation to the quality of its hotels and gastronomic restaurants, unrivalled in mountain areas.
Even in summer, when Courchevel changes radically and becomes a peaceful resort, this diversity sets it apart.

Nearby Sights: Les ARCS, La Vallée de BELLEVILLE, CHAMPAGNY-EN-VANOISE, Route de la MADELEINE, MÉRIBEL, PRALOGNAN-LA-VANOISE, La TARENTAISE, Massif de la VANOISE

THE RESORTS

The maintenance and development of the Courchevel ski area is still considered as an example to follow. Snow cover is guaranteed from early December to May, owing to the north-facing aspect of the slopes and an impressive array of more than 500 snow-cannon. The other strong point of the resort is its ski school which employs 480 instructors and ranks first in Europe. There are excellent runs for beginners along the lower sections of the Courchevel 1850 ski lifts (Verdon, Jardin Alpin). Advanced skiers prefer the great Saulire corridor and the Courchevel 1350 area. As for cross-country skiers, they can explore the elaborate network of loops linked to the Méribel network.

There are four resorts situated at altitudes ranging from 1 300m/4 265ft to 1 850m/6 070ft on the slopes of the Vallée de St-Bon, among pastures and wooded areas, in a vast open landscape framed by impressive mountains.

Le Praz or Courchevel 1300 – Alt 1 300m/4 265ft. The 90m/295ft and 120m/394ft ski jumps used during the 1992 Olympic Games are close to the old village. A picturesque 7km/4.3mi-long forest road leads to the recent resort of **La Tania** and to Méribel.

Courchevel 1550 – Family resort situated on a promontory near woodlands.

Eating out

MODERATE

La Fromagerie – *R. des Tovets – 73120 Courchevel 1850 –* ☎ *04 79 08 27 47 – closed 2 May-30 Jun and Sept-Nov – 21.34/35.06€.* Small restaurant at th entrance to the resort offering regional specialities for cheese-lovers. There is a smil ing welcome in a simple, well kept setting. You should sample: Tarte au Beaufor and chicken roasted with thyme served with a Gratin de Crozets (type of pasta).

La Saulire – *Pl. du Rocher – 73120 Courchevel 1850 –* ☎ *04 79 08 07 52 – closed May, Jun and 11 Sept-9 Oct – 25.92/36.59€.* This very central restau rant serves classic cuisine and is almost as famous as the proprietor who opene it over 25 years ago. The dining rooms on two levels are all wood-panelled an decorated with old advertisement posters on the theme of the mountains. Lunc on the terrace.

EXPENSIVE

La Cloche – *Pl. du Rocher – 73120 Courchevel 1850 –* ☎ *04 79 08 31 30 – closed May and Jun and at weekends Sept-Nov – 38.11/53.36€.* There is a appealingly warm atmosphere in this dining room in which tradition is revive The decor is typical of mountain establishments, with pastel colours combine with rough old wooden floorboards and chairs covered with embroidered appliquéed fabric and lamps from the 1930s. Sunny terrace.

Bateau Ivre – *R. Chenus – 73120 Courchevel 1850 –* ☎ *04 79 08 36 88 – closed mid Apr-mid Dec – 59.46/118.91€.* From the roof of the Hôtel L Pomme de Pin, the view from the large bay windows of this "ship" are enchant ing. The proprietor will try to distract you from it with his carefully prepared cui sine using delicate flavours. Access via an outside lift.

Where to stay

MODERATE

Hôtel Chalet Alpin – *R. des Clarines – 73120 Courchevel 1850 –* ☎ *04 79 0 11 42 – closed end Apr-15 Jul and 15 Aug-1 Dec –* 🅿 *– 52 persons, half-boar per night/per person: 69.36€.* This recently restored chalet at the heart of th resort offers the comfort of a mountain inn. The buildings are spick and span There is a warm welcome and homely cooking. Reservations are preferably b the week, half-board, with members of the Club Alpin Français given priority.

EXPENSIVE

Les Peupliers – *73120 Le Praz –* ☎ *04 79 08 41 47 – closed 23 Apr-22 Jun an 16 Oct-9 Dec –* 🅿 *– 33rms: from 91.47€ -* 🍽 *9.15€ – restaurant 25.15€* Tradition is a fine thing... This hotel has passed from father to son since 1938. Th welcoming building stands opposite a small lake and the Olympic ski-jump. Th open fireplace, warm wood-panelling, the gym, rooms generally with a balcony.. all these add up to a homely place to stay with a loyal clientèle of regulars.

On the town

L'Équipe – *73120 Courchevel 1850 – Open daily from 6pm.* The original an quirky decor makes this Courchevel's fashionable place to go. Entertainmen every evening attracts such a crowd that it is sometimes difficult to get to th bar. Guinness and a good cocktail list.

Le Panoramic – *La Saulire – 73120 Courchevel 1850 –* ☎ *04 79 08 00 88 – Open daily 9am-4.45pm mid Dec-Apr, access by La Saulire cable-car.* Open onl during the winter season, this bar-restaurant at high altitude (2 700m/8 860ft offers a fantastic view of some of the highest peaks in the Alps from its terrace

Les Caves de Courchevel – *Immeuble Porte de Courchevel – 73120 Courchevel 1850 –* ☎ *04 79 08 12 74 – Open daily from 11pm in winter.* All the stars i the night sky above Courchevel would lead you to Les Caves, *the* disco not to b missed in this resort. In season its prestigious setting and entertainment attrac a well-heeled crowd of all ages every evening.

Shopping

Monsieur Gilbert-Chapuis – Atelier de menuiserie – *R. Tovets – 7312 Courchevel 1850 –* ☎ *04 79 08 30 21 – daily 7am-9am, 3pm-5pm.* At 85 year of age, this craftsman joiner still displays the same passion for working wit wood. His workshop offers happy chalet owners and other fans of rustic Alpin fittings the chance to buy magnificent wooden *objets* for their homes includin stools, benches and flower tubs.

Moriond or Courchevel 1650 – Sunny resort where urban-style architecture contrasts with traditional chalets.

Courchevel 1850 – With its elaborate ski lift system, Courchevel 1850 is the main resort of the complex as well as the liveliest and the most sought after. There is an impressive **panorama★** of Mont Jovet, the Sommet de Bellecôte and the Grand Bec peaks.

There are luxury hotels and chalets and a mountain airfield *(altiport)* offering sightseeing flights over the Olympic sites and Mont Blanc.

VIEWPOINTS ACCESSIBLE BY GONDOLA

★★**La Saulire** ⊙ – *Access from Courchevel 1850 by the Verdon gondola and the Saulire cable car*. The well-equipped summit links the Courchevel and Méribel valleys and is the starting point of a dozen famous runs. Non-skiers can take a gondola to Méribel or Mottaret and a cable-car to Courchevel.

From the top platform (alt 2 690m/8 825ft), the view embraces the Aiguille du Fruit (alt 3 050m/10 007ft) in the foreground, the Vanoise Massif and glaciers further away, the Péclet-Polset Massif to the south, the Sommet de Bellecôte and Mont Pourri to the north with Mont Blanc on the horizon.

The upper terrace of the Pierre Plates restaurant *(viewing table)*, close to the Méribel gondola station, offers a bird's-eye view of the Allues Valley with, in the distance, the northern part of the Écrins Massif (Mont-de-Lans Glacier and Meije) the Grandes Rousses Massif and the Belledonne range.

Sommet de la Saulire (television relay) – Alt 2 738m/8 983ft. *1hr there and back on foot.*

🚶 This excursion is recommended in summer to tourists familiar with mountain conditions and not likely to feel dizzy. The summit can be reached from the cable-car station, along a wide, 300m/328yd-long path and then a shorter steep lane on the right. Splendid panorama including the Meije, and the Écrins and Vanoise massifs.

★★**Télécabine des Chenus** ⊙ – *Access from Courchevel 1850*. From the upper gondola station, view of the Rocher de la Loze and, further away, of the Croix de Verdon, the Saulire, Aiguille du Fruit and the Vanoise. Skiers can reach the **Col de la Loze★★** (alt 2 305m/7 562ft) for a fine view of the Allues Valley.

★**Mont Bel-Air** ⊙ – Alt 2 050m/6 726ft. *Access from Courchevel 1650 by the Ariondaz gondola*. Fine overall view of the St-Bon Valley, the Sommet de Bellecôte, the Grande Casse and Mont Blanc in the distance. It is possible to return to Courchevel on foot in winter as well as in summer.

HIKES

Courchevel is an ideal **hiking centre**. A map of the area's network of footpaths is available from the tourist office.

★★**Petit Mont Blanc** – Alt 2 677m/8 783ft. *Allow 3hr 30min on the way up and 2hr 15min on the way down. Start from Le Belvédère (Courchevel 1650) or from the top of Mont Bel-Air.*

Lac Merlet

Y. Bontoux

🏔 Walk across the Vallée des Avals then up to the summit via the Col de Saulces. Ver fine **panorama** of the Pralognan Valley framed by the Grande Casse, the Vanoise gla ciers and the Pointe de l'Échelle.

★★ Lacs Merlet – *Alt 2 449m/8 035ft. Ascent: 2hr; start from Mont Bel-air.* 🏔 The posi tion of the lakes at the foot of the Aiguille du Fruit forms a splendid **setting★★**. Go t the upper lake, the deepest of the Vanoise lakes (30m/98ft) and walk along the right hand shore to the end. The Vanoise glaciers and the Aiguille du Rateau are reflecte in the waters, on which drifting ice can be seen almost all year round.

Walk to La Rosière – *Access by car along an unsurfaced forest road starting betwee Courchevel 1650 and Le Belvédère.*
Lovely little lake overlooked by the Dent de Villard. Nature trail introducing a few rar species including columbine and lady's slipper. Continue along the waterfall path.

★ Via ferrata de la Croix de Verdon – *Access by the Verdon gondola and the Saulir cable-car.* This is a remarkable **viewpoint★** (alt 2 739m/8 986ft), reached by climbing route fitted with safety cables and ladder rungs; ideal for thrill-seekers *(se Practical information).*

Route de la CROIX DE FER★★★
Michelin map 333 K6 or 244 folds 29 and 30

This itinerary, and the alternative route which branches off halfway through along th route du col du Glandon link the Romanche Valley, known as L'Oisans, to the Arc Valley also called La Maurienne, and the vallée de l'Eau d'Olle to the Arvan and Glandon Valleys One of the finest drives through the Alps leads through charming, traditional villages not yet overtaken by the pace of modern life, and some stunning landscapes; highlight include the Défilé de Maupas, the Gorges de l'Arvan and a fine view of the three Aiguille. d'Arves from the Col de la Croix de Fer.

Nearby Sights: L'ALPE-D'HUEZ, Le BOURG-D'OISANS, Massif de CHAMROUSSE, Rout du GALIBIER, Route de la MADELEINE, ST-JEAN-DE-MAURIENNE

EXCURSIONS

★★ From Rochetaillée to St-Jean de Maurienne *96km/59.7mi about 4hr*

The road is blocked by snow from November to May between Le Rivier-d'Allemond and the Combe d'Olle.

It is possible to make a round tour of some of the great Alpine passes (**Circuit des Grand Cols★★★**) by extending this itinerary with two more described in this guide: the Rout du Galibier *(see Route du GALIBIER)* and the Col du Lautaret to Le Bourg-d'Oisans *(see L'OISANS,* 2 *)*

Between Rochetaillée and Le Verney, the D 526 follows the green lower Olle Valley known as the *Jardin de l'Oisans.*

Drive along the left bank of the artificial lake and follow signposts to "Centrale d Grand'Maison et Hydrelec".

As you cross the narrow Flumet Valley, you will get a glimpse of the Cascade de la Fare with the Grandes Rousses summits in the background.

★ Hydrelec ⊙ – *The Grand'Maison power station and Oz factory are not open to th public. Leave the car in the visitors' car park area at the entrance of the power statio and walk down the path on the right to Hydrelec.*
The reconstructions and equipment displayed on two levels illustrate the history o hydroelectric power from Chinese waterwheels and the Versailles fountains t modern turbines.

Return to D 526 and follow D 43ᴬ on the right towards Vaujany.

★ Vaujany – This south-facing village lies in a lovely **setting★** on the slopes of the Rissiou facing the Grandes Rousses. From the end of the village, there is a splendid view o the **Cascade de la Fare★** and its spectacular 1 000m/3 281ft drop.
Vaujany is linked by cable car to the Dôme des Rousses (2 805m/9 203ft), via the Alpettes station. From there, it is possible to reach L'Alpe-d'Huez (1 860m/6 102ft)

A road, starting near the cemetery, leads to the Collet de Vaujany.

★★ Collet de Vaujany – Extended view of the west side of the Grandes Rousses, with the Pic de l'Étendard and Lac Blanc.

Return to Le Verney and turn right onto D 526.

The road rises above the stream and crosses many tributaries coming down from the Belledonne mountains. The valley becomes narrower and densely forested.

★ **Défilé de Maupas** – Beyond Le Rivier-d'Allemond, the road makes its way through this deep gorge cluttered with fallen rocks. One of the mountain streams rushing down from the Sept-Laux Massif forms a beautiful waterfall, the Cascade des Sept-Laux, which can be seen from the road.

★★ **Combe d'Olle** – This pasture-covered valley running between huge hilltops was the site chosen by EDF (the French Electricity Board) for the **Barrage de Grand'Maison** on the Eau d'Olle: the dam, its 220ha/544-acre lake and its power stations are linked by a 7km/4.2mi gallery to the lower reservoir (75ha/185 acres) and to the Verney Dam power station in order to insure a production of electricity of a mixed type known as "energy transfer"

At this point the itinerary divides: the alternative route over the Col du Glandon is described at the end of this section.

Beyond the Combe d'Olle, keep to the right along D 926. *The road is blocked by snow between the Combe d'Olle and St-Sorlin-d'Arves from November to May.*

★★ **Col de la Croix de Fer** – Alt 2 068m/6 785ft. *15min there and back on foot.* Climb onto the rocky knoll bearing a commemorative pyramid south of the pass, and turn towards the east for a fine **view** of the Aiguilles d'Arves.

★★ **Hike to the Étendard refuge** – *Allow 3hr 15min there and back on foot from the pass.*
🚶 After climbing for 1hr 50min, one suddenly discovers the refuge lower down on the shores of Lake Bramant, overlooked by the Pic de l'Étendard (3 464m/11 365ft). The Belledonne range, stretching across the horizon to the west, is particularly spectacular at sunset and there is a magnificent **view**★★ of the Vanoise Massif to the northeast with the Mont Blanc Massif in the distance.
The refuge can be reached in 10min. Experienced hikers can walk to the foot of the **St-Sorlin Glacier**, beyond lakes Bramant, Blanc and Tournant *(allow 1 day)*.

Between the Col de la Croix de Fer and St-Sorlin the road offers open views of the upper Arvan Valley, with its vast sloping pastures dotted with hamlets against a background of high peaks and glaciers. The Pic de l'Étendard's glacier, the Glacier du St-Sorlin, is also visible.

St-Sorlin d'Arves – New buildings connected with the nearby ski area somewhat spoil the traditional character of this village.

In Malcrozet, turn left onto D 80 which climbs towards St-Jean-d'Arves.

St-Jean-d'Arves – The church cemetery outside the village overlooks the upper Arvan Valley, offering an extended **view**★ of the snowy peaks of the Grandes Rousses, including the Pic de l'Étendard and the Cimes de la Cochette.

About 2km/1.2mi beyond St-Jean-d'Arves as you go into a bend, note the narrow Entraigues Valley on the right, and further on, as you come out of the tunnel, admire the lovely **picture**★ formed by the hamlet of Montrond with the Aiguilles d'Arves in the background. The road also offers impressive glimpses of the **Gorges de l'Arvan**★ which cuts deep through the schist.

St-Jean-d'Arves and the Massif du Col de la Croix de Fer

Route de la CROIX DE FER

The road joins D 926 just before a tunnel; turn left.

★**Combe Genin** – The late-afternoon light plays on the schist lining the sides of this imposing scree-covered corridor.

Turn back along D 926 to Belleville and take D 80 on the left.

The road crosses the Arvan and climbs above the treeline to the village of Le Mollard with views of the lower Arvan Valley and Combe Genin.

★**Col du Mollard** – There are very attractive **views**★ of the Aiguilles d'Arves and Vanoise summits from the highest point of the road (alt 1 683m/5 522ft).
As you drive west out of Albiez-le-Vieux, the thrilling descent into the Arvan Valley begins, offering breathtaking bird's-eye views. The journey down is less impressive beyond Gevoudaz as the road makes its way to St-Jean-de-Maurienne.

St-Jean-de-Maurienne – *See ST-JEAN-DE-MAURIENNE.*

★**Col du Glandon** *22km/13.7mi – allow 1hr 30min*

This is the most direct route from Le Bourg-d'Oisans or Vizille to the Arc Valley. The road runs through the Glandon Valley, also known as the Vallée des Villards.

Bear left along D 927 after the Combe d'Olle. The road is blocked by snow upstream from St-Colomban-des-Villards from November to early June.

Col de la Croix de Fer and Aiguilles de l'Argentière

★ **Col du Glandon** – Alt
1 924m/6 312ft.
250m/273yd from the
Chalet-Hôtel du Glandon.
The pass, with the
colourful rock formations
of the Aiguilles
d'Argentière above, offers
a splendid **vista** of Mont
Blanc through the Col de
la Madeleine to the northeast. The upper Glandon
Valley affords austere
landscapes of meagre pas-
tures and rocky slopes
brightened by clumps of
red rhododendrons in
early summer.

SUNSHINE

Hôtel Beausoleil – *73530 St-Sorlin-d'Arves –*
☎ *04 79 59 71 42 – closed 21 Apr-30 Jun*
and 1 Sept-18 Dec – 🅿 *– 23rms:*
39.64/53.36€ - 🍽 *6.86€ – restaurant*
15.09/19.82€. This isolated hotel-chalet on
the side of a mountain is a haven of peace
and quiet. The atmosphere is homely and
the proprietor produces a few local specialities in the kitchen to tempt your tastebuds. You can then slumber on his terrace
while the sun is high in the sky, in an idyllic
setting.

Les DEUX-ALPES★★

Michelin map 333 J7 and 244 fold 41

In the heart of the Oisans region, the passion for skiing continues all year round. The
twin resorts of L'Alpe-de-Mont-de-Lans and L'Alpe-de-Venosc, known as "Les Deux-
Alpes", spread their modern residential buildings on a vast saddle covered with
pastures, which connects the Romanche and Vénéon valleys at an altitude of
1 600m/5 249ft.

Nearby Sights: L'ALPE D'HUEZ, Le BOURG D'OISANS, Route du GALIBIER, La GRAVE,
L'OISANS, Le VALBONNAIS

THE RESORT

Ski area – Competent skiers aim for the steep first section and the Tête Moute Summit.
Less experienced skiers prefer the gentle slopes, the excellent snow and magnificent
panoramas of the Mont-de-Lans Glacier, the largest European glacier suitable for
skiing: equipped with a dozen ski lifts, it offers many green and blue runs between
2 800m/9 186ft and 3 568m/11 706ft, the highest altitude of any French pisted
run. This enables intermediate-level skiers to experience the thrill of a
2 000m/6 562ft difference in height on the way back to the resort. The Girose
Glacier, belonging to the ski area of La Grave *(see La GRAVE)*, is easily accessible *(by
tracked vehicle in winter)* from the Dôme de la Lauze Summit; together they form
one of the largest **summer ski** areas *(mid-June to early September)*. Paragliding sites,
a skating rink and a heated open-air pool provide plenty of activity off the slopes;
walkers can head for the old village of Venosc (Télécabine du Super-Venosc, see
L'OISANS, **1**), the La Fée refuge and Le Sapey.

Chapelle St-Benoît – This modern chapel, traditionally built in undressed stone, contains a few original sculptures including the Stations of the Cross.

VIEWPOINTS

★★ **Glacier du Mont-de-Lans** ⊘ – *2hr there and back to the Dôme du Puy Salié and half
a day to the Dôme de Lauze. Climbing boots, sunglasses and binoculars recommended.*
Access by the Jandri Express cable-car from the resort centre, near the tourist office.
There is a cable-car change at 2 600m/8 530ft; the next one takes you up to
3 200m/10 499ft. Fine **view** of the Vercors and Oisans areas.
A diagonal lift and rack railway then lead to the Dôme du Puy Salié
(3 421m/11 224ft). Magnificent **view★★** of the Écrins Massif. Go to the ski lift arrival
point to get a panoramic view of the Vercors, Belledonne range, Grandes Rousses
Massif (L'Alpe-d'Huez resort and Pic du Lac Blanc), Mont-Blanc Massif, the indented
Aiguilles d'Arves and the Vanoise. Mont Ventoux can also be seen in fine weather conditions.
Skiers can take the ski lift to La Lauze and admire the splendid **panorama★★★** of the
Rateau Summit, the Écrins and Soreiller massifs and, further away to the northeast,
of the Péclet, Grande Casse and Mont Pourri summits.

Grotte de glace ⊘ – Several caves, dug through thick ice, are decorated with ice
sculptures.

Non-skiers can also reach the Dôme de la Lauze by tracked minibus. This excursion,
known as the **Croisière Blanche★** is the only one of its kind in France.

Eating out

BUDGET

Bel'Auberge – *1 r. de la Chapelle – 38860 Les Deux-Alpes –* ☎ *04 76 79 57 90 – closed 1 May -23 Jun, 2 Sept-30 Nov and lunchtime in winter –* *16.16/28.97€.* This chalet-inn with finely carved woodwork offers classic rustic cuisine with one or two local specialities, fondues and raclettes. The proprietor, a ski instructor when the fancy takes him, will look after you well in the evening.

MODERATE

Le Panoramic – *Summit of Jandri 2 or Jandri Express 1 cable cars – 38860 Les Deux-Alpes –* ☎ *04 76 79 06 75 – closed beginning May-beginning Dec – reservations essential in the evening – 21.34€.* At 2 600m/8 530ft this chalet is certainly high up! On skis or on foot, come and build up your strength with mountain cooking from the restaurant or toasted sandwiches in the self-service café. The breathtaking view of the Vercors range reaching as far as Mont-Blanc lives up to its billing.

Where to stay

BUDGET

Chambre d'hôte Le Chalet – *3 r. de l'Oisans – 38860 Les Deux-Alpes –* ☎ *04 76 80 51 85 – closed 1 May-24 Jun and Sept-Nov –* ✒ *– 7rms: 27.44/51.83 €.* This large 1960s chalet at the heart of the resort offers the peace and quiet of one of six nicely kept if not altogether inspired rooms. This is a good place for value for money. Pleasant garden in summer.

MODERATE

Hôtel La Belle Étoile – *111 av. de la Muzelle – 38860 Les Deux-Alpes –* ☎ *04 76 80 51 19 – hoteletoil@aol.com – closed 6 May-30 Jun and 5 Sept-5 Dec –* ▣ *– 29rms (breakfast included): 44.21/114.34€.* This hotel near the ski slopes has numerous points in its favour: a spa bath in which to relax after skiing (unless you prefer lounging in front of the open fire!) and in summer a swimming pool, tennis court and garden. Outstanding view of La Muzelle.

Les Mélèzes – *17 rue des Vikings – 38860 Les Deux-Alpes –* ☎ *04 76 80 50 50 – closed 29 Apr-19 Dec –* ▣ *– 32rms: 56.41/76.22€ -* ☕ *8.38€ – restaurant 22.87/36.59€.* Skiers will love this hotel at the foot of the ski slopes! For those who prefer a more leisurely holiday, there is a terrace, or you can choose a room with a balcony from which to watch the more energetic types. Restaurant for hotel patrons only.

EXPENSIVE

Chalet Mounier – *2 r. de la Chapelle – 38860 Les Deux-Alpes –* ☎ *04 76 80 56 90 – closed 21 Apr-29 Jun and 2 Sept-14 Dec –* ▣ *– 44rms: from 82.32€ – restaurant 21.19/48.78€.* Built using a late 19C summer pasture farm as a basis. The friendly atmosphere is enhanced by carved woodwork, fabrics in warm colours and cosy lounges. Good food from the P'tit Polyte. Summer and winter swimming pools and gym.

★ **Croisière Blanche** ⊘ *– It is advisable to get bookings from the tourist office during the season. Departure from the cable car station.* Visitors on foot can reach the **Dôme de la Lauze** by tracked minibus. This excursion offers a unique experience in a high-mountain environment.

★ **Belvédère des Cimes** – *Alt 2 100m/6 890ft. Access via the Cimes chairlift; it leaves from the outskirts of the resort, on the Mont-de-Lans side.*
This viewpoint, situated on the northeast slope of Pied Moutet, offers a fine view of the Romanche Valley and Bourg-d'Oisans Basin.

★ **Belvédère de la Croix** – From the cross standing on top of a grassy knoll, on the way out of the resort on the Alpe-de-Venosc side, one looks down a sheer drop to the bottom of the Vénéon Valley with jackdaws whirling above. The pointed Aiguille de Venosc stands across the river and the Roche de la Muzelle (alt 3 459m/11 348ft), with its characteristic suspended glacier, towers above the whole landscape.

Le DÉVOLUY★★

Michelin map 334 D4, 244 fold 40 and 245 fold 7

This massif, which forms part of the southern Préalpes, offers desolate and sometimes magnificent landscapes. Barren limestone escarpments dominated by the highest peak, the Obiou (nearly 3 000m/9 843ft), surround a central values through which flow the Ribière and the Béoux.
The Dévoluy is riddled with sink-holes known as **"chourums"**, also called *"scialets"* in the Vercors Massif, which are sometimes filled with ice, as in the case of Chourum Martin, south of St-Disdier.
Roads crossing the Dévoluy, particularly the Col du Noyer, run through treeless landscapes, devoid of fertile soil and streams, scorched by the sun and overlooked by jagged peaks with scree-covered slopes.

Nearby Sights: Pays du BUËCH, Le CHAMPSAUR, GAP, Lacs de LAFFREY, MONTMAUR, Route NAPOLÉON, L'OISANS, Lac de SERRE-PONÇON, Le TRIÈVES, Le VALBONNAIS, Le VALGAUDEMAR

EXCURSIONS

★1 Round tour via the Col du Festre and Col du Noyer

STARTING FROM CORPS *81km/50.3mi – about 3hr 30min*

Corps – *See* 2.

From Corps, drive west along D 537. Stop just before the bridge at Lac du Sautet.

It is worth taking a few moments by the shore to admire the Perle de Dévoluy and the reflections of the surrounding mountains.

Continue along the D 537 which now turns to the south.

Try to catch a glimpse of the impressive Obiou, briefly visible to the west beyond Trièves and the Drac Valley.

★ **Défilé de la Souloise** – The road runs between splendid limestone escarpments.

St-Disdier – An isolated 13C church known as **La Mère-Église**, literally "the mother church", can be seen on the slopes overlooking the village to the east; the insignia of the Templars – the sun, the moon and the Maltese cross – are in evidence inside. A music festival is held here every summer.

Col du Festre – Alt 1 441m/4 728ft. Fine views from this pass below the desolate heights of the Montagne d'Aurouze. The road then runs down towards Montmaur along the Béaux Valley *(see MONTMAUR)*.

Turn back and take D 17 on the right.

★ **Col de Rioupes** – This pass offers splendid **views** of a vast ring of barren mountains: Crêtes des Aiguilles, Grand-Ferrand, Obiou and Montagne de Féraud separated by the Col du Noyer from the Montagne d'Aurouze which is riddled with sink-holes.

★ **Défilé des Étroits** – *Stop the car between the two bridges which D 17 crosses.* The road overlooks the River Souloise which has carved a 40-60m/131-197ft deep passage (only 2m/7ft wide in parts) through the rock. The *via ferrata* is guaranteed to set the pulse racing.

The Souloise Valley suddenly widens as the road reaches St-Étienne-en-Dévoluy.

St-Étienne-en-Dévoluy – This green oasis in the barren Dévoluy landscape was once virtually self-sufficient, cut off from the rest of the world until, after 15 long years of work, the connecting road was opened in 1872.

Where to stay and Eating out

MODERATE

Auberge La Neyrette – *05250 St-Disdier* – ☎ *04 92 58 81 17 – closed 15 Nov-15 Dec –* 🅿 *– 12rms: 42.69/60.98€ -* ☕ *6.40€ – restaurant 16.77/33.54€.* Refurbished rooms in a natural setting where guests will be lulled to sleep by the murmuring of the wind and nothing else. An ideal location for exploration on foot or on skis. In fine weather, there is the chance to go trout fishing. On the subject of trout, this inn by the river offers it as an option on all its menus.

Hôtel Les Chardonnelles – *05250 Superdévoluy* – ☎ *04 92 58 86 90 – closed 26 Apr-14 Jun and 16 Sept-14 Dec –* 🅿 *– 40rms: from 57.93€ – restaurant 13.57/27.14€.* The packages offered by this hotel at the foot of the Pic de Bure will interest families and groups. Rooms are plain and comfortable. The cooking is unpretentious. Sauna and heated swimming pool.

* **Superdévoluy** – This sk[...] resort at an altitud[...] of 1 500m/4 921ft [...] interesting from a[...] architectural point o[...] view: all the building[...] are grouped to form[...] a 2-tiered ensembl[...] extending along th[...] slopes of the Montagn[...] d'Aurouze with rows o[...] wooden balconies a[...] facing southwest. The sk[...] **area** between 1 500m[...] 2 510m/4 921ft-8 235f[...] includes a variety of sk[...] runs down the norther[...] slopes of the Sommare[...] and the Pic Ponçon. Th[...] link with the La Joue-du[...] Loup ski area is accessibl[...] to intermediate skiers[...] those with more experi[...] ence prefer the Pierra, Sommarel and Mur red runs. Cross-country skiers have acces[...] to 50km/31mi of marked trails. Superdévoluy is also the place to try your hand a[...] something new, be it slalom, boarder cross, snowscooting (a cross between snow[...] boarding and BMX biking) or even a dog-sled ride.

★★ **Col du Noyer** – *The pass is closed from early November to mid-May.* Both sides o[...] the pass (alt 1 664m/5 459ft – *viewing table 100m/109yd southwest of the forme[...] Refuge Napoléon*), offer beautiful contrasting **landscapes**: the barren ridges of th[...] Dévoluy on one side and, on the other, the broad Drac Valley (Bas-Champsaur) che[...] quered with various crops and framed by the heights of the Vieux-Chaillol Massif an[...] the Gapençais mountains, with the high summits and glaciers of the Écrins Massif i[...] distance.

The road running down towards the River Drac is a test of one's driving skills, par[...] ticularly for the first 5km/3mi. At La Fare-en-Champsaur it joins the Route Napoléo[...] (N 85) which leads back to Corps. Remember the Highway Code rule for narrow[...] mountain roads, which states that unless a car heading uphill is able to pull over int[...] a passing place, drivers travelling downhill should give way to it.

★★ ② Round tour of Lac du Sautet

STARTING FROM CORPS 35km/21.7mi – about 2hr

Corps – Overlooking the Lac du Sautet, the capital of the **Beaumont** region (middle[...] Drac Valley between Corps and the confluence of the Bonne) is a lively summer resor[...] along the famous Route Napoléon *(see ROUTE NAPOLÉON)* and a convenien[...] meeting place for pilgrims on their way to Notre-Dame de la Salette. The Obiou[...] towers over the delightful valley **landscape★★**.

St-Étienne-en-Dévoluy and the Col de Rabou,
the southern boundary of the Dévoluy massif

Follow N 85 south towards Gap[...] and, as you leave Corps, tur[...] right past the petrol station[...] Walk the last 91m/100yd, as it i[...] impossible to turn round furthe[...] on. The small **Chapelle St-Roch** ☉[...] overlooking the lake, has some[...] interesting modern stained[...] glass windows.

Rejoin N 85, which runs above[...] the lake. At Le Motty turn righ[...] towards Ambel along D 217.

The road rises above the south[...] bank of the lake and soon offer[...] views of the Obiou, the Vercors[...] Massif, Corps and the heights o[...] Notre-Dame de la Salette[...] *(beware of falling rocks).*

Beyond Ambel, the road runs[...] above the lower Souloise[...] Valley which forms the other[...]

arm of the lake; the Grand-Ferrand soars straight ahead. The road then runs down to the bottom of the valley; from the bridge over the Souloise there is a view of the Petites Gillardes, resurgent springs from underground water courses which are fed by the *chourums* or sink-holes of the upper plateaux.

1km/0.6mi beyond the bridge, turn right onto D 537.

Past Pellafol, there is a fine view on the right of the promontory crowned by the village of Ambel.

★**Pont du Sautet** – The D 537 crosses the River Drac over this bridge, a daring piece of engineering with a single reinforced-concrete arch spanning 86m/282ft, at a height of 160m/525ft above the water

★★**Barrage du Sautet** – This elegant curved dam, 126m/413ft high, has created a reservoir capable of containing 115 million m³/93 231cu ft of water. The hydroelectric power station further downstream was partly built underground.

An alternative route from Corps 15km/8.7mi – 1hr

Between Corps and the village of La Salette, the road follows the deep, fresh green valley of the Sezia. The road rises rapidly from the village to Notre-Dame de la Salette within sight of the imposing Obiou Peak (2 793m/9 163ft).

Large car park available near the basilica.

★**Notre-Dame de la Salette** – The **basilica** ⏱ stands at an altitude of 1 770m/5 807ft, surrounded by pastures and in a striking mountain **setting**★★. It is the venue of many pilgrimages, particularly on 19 September, the anniversary of the apparition of Our Lady.

> ### The weeping Virgin
>
> In 1846, two local children described how the Virgin Mary appeared to them in the form of a weeping woman and spoke to them at length in regional dialect and in French. After a five-year investigation, the Catholic church acknowledged the statements of the children; a basilica was built and today the sanctuary welcomes over 150 000 pilgrims a year.

Behind the basilica, walk round a mound surmounted by a cross to enjoy a panoramic **view**★ of the Oisans, Dévoluy and Beaumont regions. Walkers can continue to **Mont Gargas** *(Alt 2 207m/7 241ft. 2hr there and back on foot. Climb northwards along marked paths to the Col de l'Éterpat then follow the ridge line to the left).* Vast **panorama**★★ of the Obiou and of the heights south of the Oisans.

HIKES

The Superdévoluy tourist office has published a walking map showing 23 recommended itineraries, plus two topographical maps, one for mountain biking.

★★**Plateau de Bure** – *From Superdévoluy; 4hr there and back, difference in altitude: 550m/1 804ft.*

🚶 At first sight, the giant metal dishes of the Institut de radioastronomie millimétrique, or IRAM *(not open to the public)*, make this radio observatory look more like a sci-fi film set. These parabolic antennae have been listening to the cosmos since 1990, searching the spectrum on a frequency between radio waves and infrared radiation. It may seem an inhospitable place – high winds gust around the summit and temperatures have been known to fall as low as -20°C – but the altitude and dry mountain air make it ideal for observation. At the end of July, Superdévoluy plays host to a festival of astronomy which attracts stargazers from France and beyond.

Join the GR 94 above Superdévoluy. Head out of the larch wood, cross the valley and follow a stony path. This leads to an area of level ground with a spring. After a series of curves the path leads to a narrow passage with a rope to hold on to *(extra care is needed here)*. This is Pic Ponson, the most north-westerly point of the plateau.

Population 4 451
Michelin map 332 F5 and 244 fold 38

Die lies hidden in the hills of the sunny Diois valley, to which it gave its name, overlooke
by the shiny escarpments of the Glandasse range south of the Vercors Massif. The easies
way to get to Die is along the Drôme Valley, but a far more interesting route leads ove
the Col de la Chaudière, Col du Rousset or Col de Menée and down through vineyards
orchards and fields of lavender.

Nearby Sights: Pays du BUËCH, Le VERCORS

BACKGROUND

Die had, by the 2C AD, become an important Gallo-Roman city on the main rout
from Milan to Vienne. Many visitors were attracted by the cult of Cybele, the mothe
of the gods, involving the sacrifice of a bull and a ram, as the sacrificial altars exhib
ited in the museum testify.
During the 3C AD, Die was surrounded by walls and became a Christian city in which th
bishop always played an important role, as in the granting of the town's first charter i
1217; the only one of his successors unwise enough to think of revoking these munic
ipal freedoms was murdered by a furious mob in front of his own cathedral.
In the 16C, the Reformation had a major impact on Die whose churches were a
destroyed, but Louis XIV later reinstated the bishopric.
Today, Die is a small administrative and commercial centre, its most popular expor
being the **"Clairette de Die"** a sweet, sparkling white wine made from Clairette an
Muscat, two famous grape varieties. The drinks traditionally flow in June to celebrat
the *transhumance*, when the flocks are herded up to the summer pastures, and fo
a festival of East-West culture in the same month.

AROUND THE TOWN

Ramparts – Although its towers have long since disappeared, the 3C enclosure
stretching over 2km/1.2mi, is still visible on the northeast side of the town. It is pos
sible to walk along the 3m/10ft-thick walls, built with undressed stone and ancien
reclaimed masonry, from the tourist office to the Porte St-Marcel. Gallo-Roma
objects found on location are now exhibited in the museum.

Eating out

BUDGET

La Petite Auberge – *Av. Sadi-Carnot* – ☎ *04 75 22 05 91 – closed 15 Dec
15 Jan, Sun evening and Wed except Jul-Aug and Mon – 15.24/25.92€. Thi
inn near the station offers guests a friendly welcome in its dining room, on the
veranda or on its shaded terrace. Classic local cuisine. The small, rather old-fash
ioned rooms could be useful if you're really stuck.*

Where to stay

BUDGET

Camping La Pinède – *1.7km/1mi W of Die on D 93 –* ☎ *04 75 22 17 77 –
info@camping-pinede.com – open 25 Apr-15 Sept. –✍ – reservations recommended
– 110 pitches: 21.34€ – catering available on site.* Pitch your tent between the for
est and the mountains, in this well shaded site beneath the pine trees. There are als
chalets on the mountain side overlooking the camp site like a small village. Swimmin
pool with splash basin and tiled terrace. Tennis court and children's play area.

Camping L'Hirondelle de St-Ferréol – *26410 Menglon – 13km/8mi SE of Di
on D 93 as far as Pont-de-Quart then D 539, D 214 and D 140 –* ☎ *04 75 2
82 08 – campinghirondelle@minitel.net – open Apr-Sept – reservation compul
sory – 100 pitches: 14.64€ – catering available on site.* This campsite on the
south Vercors slope offers peace and quiet, spacious pitches between under
growth and sunshine, and a salt-water swimming pool. Visitors can spend thei
time exploring and being sporty in the midst of a spacious natural setting.

MODERATE

Relais de Chamarges – *Rte de Valence –* ☎ *04 75 22 00 95 – closed Jan, Feb
Sun evening and Mon out of season except public holidays –* 🅿 *– 12rms
42.69/44.21€ -* ✍ *6.10€ – restaurant 13.72/41.16€.* This small homely hote
is at the exit to the town, near the road. The rooms are furnished in a fairly plai
way, with no frills, but are spotlessly clean. Shaded terrace to the front and gar
den to the rear of the house, facing the countryside.

Porte St-Marcel – The vaulting of this Roman arched garteway is decorated with interlacing and rosettes; the friezes illustrate chariot racing, dancing and the prosperity of the *pax Romana* symbolized by fruit.

Cathedral – The massive bell-tower is surmounted by a wrought-iron campanile. The south wall and Romanesque porch tower belonged to the original 12C-13C church. Note the capitals of the doorways, which illustrate biblical scenes, including Cain and Abel and Abraham and Isaac on the north side and fighting scenes with mythical beasts to the south and west. Partly destroyed during the Wars of Religion, this church was rebuilt and refurbished in the 17C; particularly noteworthy are the pulpit, the woodwork decorating the chancel, the stalls and the high altar.

Also worth seeing is the Renaissance façade of the Maison de Diane de Poitiers (1499-1566), in rue St-Vincent, next to the cathedral, and the Jesuit chapel, now a Protestant church.

SIGHTS

Hôtel de ville – The building housing the town hall and the law courts is the former bishop's palace, which has retained the 11C **Chapelle St-Nicolas** ⊘. It is paved with a remarkable 12C **mosaic★** representing the universe, with the North Star in the centre, surrounded by the four rivers of the Garden of Eden, and the cardinal points in the corners. The walls of the chapel are decorated with medieval frescoes and 18C hand-painted wallpaper.

Museum ⊘ – Housed in a late-18C mansion, this museum contains interesting local archaeological collections, particularly rich in Gallo-Roman exhibits: sacrificial altars, a 4C Christian sarcophagus etc. One room is devoted to popular art and customs and another one to Romanesque sculptures from the cathedral.

EXCURSIONS

Abbaye de Valcroissant ⊘ – *After 6km/3.7mi along D 93 to Sisteron, take the road on the left.* The road goes upstream through a gorge and reaches a cirque below the cliffs of the Vercors Massif. In 1188, Cistercian monks founded an abbey in this remote place. The church and refectory can only be seen from the outside.

Pontaix – *10km/6.2mi west along D 93 towards Crest.*
This old wine-growing village, backing onto a knoll crowned by a 13C castle, forms the most attractive picture of the middle Drôme Valley. The castle keep stands 70m/230ft above the river. Some houses date back to the 15C and the Protestant church contains 15C and 17C paintings.

Le Claps – *20km/12.4mi southeast along D 93, just beyond Luc-en-Diois.* This pile of rocks is the result of a huge landslide which occurred in the 15C. It formed two natural dams and two lakes which have now dried up. The pile of rocks nearer the railway viaduct is the most impressive. Higher up, at a place known as the **Saut de la Drôme**, the river rushes through a small artificial tunnel and splashes onto the rocks; it is worth stopping for a moment when the river is in spate.

★★THE BEAUTY OF THE DIOIS

Life in the Diois is sustained by the Drôme and its tributaries, including the Bez, the Rif and the Boulc, which cut through an otherwise dry landscape to water the lush valleys. A drive through the narrow gorges leads past clusters of houses, perched high on the hillsides, sometimes at an altitude of over 1 000m/3 281ft. These little villages, their squares shaded by plane trees and their houses decorated with pink and white oleander in typical Provençal style, offer tourists a welcome break between two breathtaking excursions through such impressive landscapes as the Cirque d'Archiane.

① Le Rousset

FROM THE COL DE ROUSSET TO DIE *22km/13.7mi – 1hr*

This route leading from the Vercors to the Diois region illustrates the striking contrast which exists between the northern and southern Alps.

★★**Col de Rousset** – Alt 1 254m/4 114ft. *See Le VERCORS,* ④.

Chamaloc – The mellow-stone houses, roofed with curved tiles, contribute to the Provençal appearance of the village. Between Chamaloc and Die, the **Ferme de Baise** has been turned into the Maison du Parc naturel régional du Vercors and offers visitors an interesting nature trail.

★★ 2 Route de Menée

FROM DIE TO THE COL DE MENÉE

45km/28mi – about 2hr. The pass is usually blocked by snow from December to March. Beware of falling rocks.

From Die, follow D 93 towards Gap.

The road runs through the Die Basin, among vineyards overlooked by the limestone cliffs of the Glandasse Mountain.

In Pont-de-Quart, turn left onto D 539.

★ **Châtillon-en-Diois** – The village has retained its medieval character. An intricate network of streets, narrow lanes and covered passages, known as *viols* in local dialect, surrounds place Reviron overlooked by the clock tower. Cool fountains, flowers, and tiled roofs brighten the grey-limestone buildings.

Turn left onto D 120 towards the Col de Menée. In Menée, take D 224 to Archiane.

★★ **Cirque d'Archiane** – The upper end of the Archiane Valley is barred by escarpments forming a splendid amphitheatre split in two by a huge promontory known as the "Jardin du Roi". The area is ideal for mountaineering and hiking to the high plateaux of the Vercors Massif *(GR 93)*.

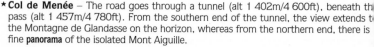

Beyond Les Nonières, the road rises in a succession of hairpin bends; the barren landscape, dotted with clusters of lavende and overlooked by the impressive Rocher de Combau, gradually gives way to pin woods and pastures.

★ **Col de Menée** – The road goes through a tunnel (alt 1 402m/4 600ft), beneath th pass (alt 1 457m/4 780ft). From the southern end of the tunnel, the view extends t the Montagne de Glandasse on the horizon, whereas from the northern end, there is fine **panorama** of the isolated Mont Aiguille.

★ 3 Villages of Yesteryear

FROM CHÂTILLON-EN-DIOIS TO LUS-LA-CROIX-HAUTE

45km/28mi – about 1hr 30min

From Die to Châtillon-en-Diois – *See* 2 *above.*

Châtillon-en-Diois – *see above*

Leave Châtillon-en-Diois along D 539.

The Cirque d'Archiane

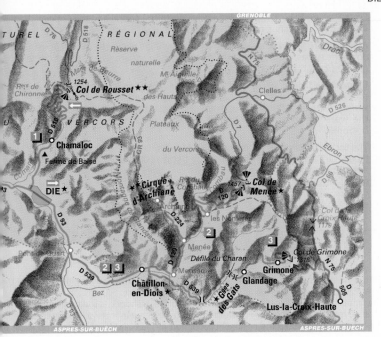

★ Gorges des Gats – Prior to the building of the road in 1865, several fords had to be crossed in order to go up this extremely narrow gorge (only a few metres wide in places) with more than 100m/328ft-high cliffs on either side. Further on, four tunnels negotiate the **Défilé du Charan**.

Glandage and Grimone – The closely grouped houses of these hamlets with large steep roofs, well adapted to heavy snows, give an idea of the hardships of life at high altitude a few generations ago. A group of young people has given new life to these more or less abandoned villages. The church at Glandage is worth a visit.

Beyond Glandage, the southern vegetation gives way to oaks and Austrian pines.

Beyond the **Col de Grimone** (alt 1 318m/4 324ft), the view extends southeast to the Montagne de Garnesier and Crête des Aiguilles.

Drive south on N 75.

Lus-la-Croix-Haute – *See Pays du BUËCH.*

★ ④ Gorges d'Omblèze

FROM DIE *48km/23mi – 2hr 30min*

Leave Die by the D 93 towards Crest then turn right onto D 129 to Ste-Croix.

Ste-Croix – Built on a narrow ridge between the River Drôme and River Sure, the village is overlooked by 13C ruins. In an original spirit of compromise, the **church** is divided into two parts to accommodate both Catholic services (in the transept and apse) and Protestant services (in the nave).

Turn left onto D 172.

The narrow twisting road leads through oak and pine woods to the **Col de la Croix** (alt 745m/2 444ft), then down the Sépie Valley to Beaufort-sur-Gervanne.

Beaufort-sur-Gervanne – The way into Beaufort offers a spectacular view which includes what remains of the fortifications now turned into a pleasant walk. The recently rebuilt church has retained an arcaded bell-tower.

Follow D 70 to Plan-de-Baix.

Plan-de-Baix – Built on a hillside, the village is overlooked by limestone cliffs (Rochers du Vellan), once the site of a Roman settlement. The 12C church has retained its dome on squinches.
The 13C-14C **Château de Montrond**, remodelled many times, towers over the Gervanne Valley.

From Plan-de-Baix, it is possible to drive north to Léoncel and the Col de la Bataill
via the Col de Bacchus *(see Le VERCORS: Route du Col de la Bataille)*.

At first D 578 follows the deep Gervanne Valley, high above the river bed, then it run
down the slopes, planted with box trees and pines, towards the entrance of the gorg
guarded by a towering rock.

Chute de la Druise – *Turn right in Le Moulin-la-Pipe towards Ansage and driv*
for 1km/0.6mi to the car park. 1hr there and back on foot; wear stron
walking shoes and beware of falling rocks. A marked path leads to the top c
the waterfall; from there, another steep and stony path leads down to th
bottom.

The **Gorges d'Omblèze★**, lined by impressive limestone cliffs, start beyond Le Moulin-la
Pipe. The Cascades de la Pissoire fall by the roadside; one of these waterfalls ofte
dries up in summer. Now and then, there are glimpses of the Col de la Bataille to th
north.

DIGNE-LES-BAINS✠✠
Population 16 087
Michelin map 334 F8 and 245 fold 21
Local maps see Préalpes de DIGNE and ROUTE NAPOLÉON

On the Route Napoléon, in a beautiful mountain setting, this town by the banks of th
River Bléone is a sought-after spa resort and tourist centre.
This important Gallo-Roman settlement and medieval bishopric is today the main admin
istrative town of the Alpes-de-Haute-Provence *département*. It is also a lively commercia
town, which centralises the regional production of fruit and lavender; a procession c
flower-covered floats takes place every year in August and a lavender fair is held i
September.
The town's waters have been famous since antiquity, but the spa activities had dwindle
over the centuries until a new building, situated 3km/1.8mi southeast of the centre, wa
inaugurated in 1982; the number of people taking the waters has been growing steadil
ever since.
The most famous son of Digne was **Pierre Gassendi** (1592-1655), the philosopher, math
ematician, astronomer and physicist who greatly admired Galileo and pioneered th
study of astronomical phenomena through a telescope.
The engineer **Alphonse Beau de Rochas** (1815-93) was born in the town. He worked on a
telegraphic link between France and England in the 1850s and later suggested the con
struction of a metal tunnel under the Channel.
The explorer and writer **Alexandra David-Néel** (1868-1969), who, in 1924, was the firs
European woman to enter the capital of Tibet, settled in Digne in 1927 and bequeathed
her house and her collections to the town.

Nearby Sights: CASTELLANE, Préalpes de DIGNE, Vallée de la Moyenne DURANCE
Monastère de GANAGOBIE, Route NAPOLÉON, SEYNE, SISTERON, Plateau de VALENSOLE

WALKING ABOUT

Old town – A network of twisting lanes and stairs surrounds the mound crowned by
the Église St-Jérôme with its characteristic campanile. It is possible to reach th
cathedral by walking up the picturesque Montée St-Charles, which starts on the righ
of rue de l'Hubac. Pedestrian shopping streets at the foot of the mound have beer
renovated and the buildings painted in pleasant pastel colours.
The wide boulevard Gassendi, shaded by plane trees, and place Charles-de-Gaulle are
the liveliest parts of the town. An international **sculpture exhibition** organised in Digne
between 1983 and 1991 revealed several major talents; prize-winning works ir
Carrara marble decorate roundabouts, squares and public gardens; *A list of the*
works displayed is available at the tourist office.

Grande Fontaine – The 19C fountain situated at the end of boulevard Gassendi con
sists of two Doric porticoes perpendicular to one another and limestone concretions
covered with moss.

SIGHTS

★Musée départemental de Digne ⊘ – Founded in 1889 and housed in the former
hospice, it is both a natural history and fine art museum.
A large collection of 19C scientific instruments is displayed in the entrance hall, as a
reminder of the town's association with astronomical studies. Among the most
remarkable exhibits are the **astronomical clock** which tells both the solar and standard
times and gives useful geographical information. It was patented in 1865 after 22
years of research and development.

The natural history collections include minerals, shells, local fossils and butterflies. The first level displays works by 19C Provençal artists: Martin, Mayan, Guindon, Ponson, Nardi and watercolours by Paul Martin, the founder of the museum.

The stock of older works is rich in Italian paintings: the major work is the *Virgin with a Missal* by the 17C Roman artist, **Carlo Maratta**. The Venetian School is represented by *The Allegory of Vice and Virtue* by **Francesco Ruschi**. The Flemish and Dutch schools are illustrated by two portraits by **Frans Pourbus** (1569-1622) and **Van Ravesteyn**. In addition, there is a small but very good collection of Italian and French drawings and pen andwash drawings.

Musée d'Art religieux – This museum, housed in the Chapelle des Pénitents, displays a permanent collection of religious art, presents temporary exhibitions on the subject and shows video films on a range of other topics.

Musée de la Seconde Guerre mondiale – This small museum, situated on place Paradis, is appropriately housed in a former air-raid shelter; exhibits include documents and objects from the period of the Second World War showing the strategic importance of Digne and the damages suffered by the town.

Jardin botanique des Cordeliers – This is a medieval-style garden laid in the grounds of a former Cordelier monastery with medicinal plants, herbs and a vegetable patch.

★ **Ancienne cathédrale Notre-Dame-du-Bourg** – *Access by ① on the town plan.* This vast Provençal Romanesque church, built of blue schist between 1200 and 1330, has an elegant Lombard doorway surmounted by a large rose-window and with crouching lions in front of it. This cathedral was used as a model for other religious architecture in the region *(see SEYNE)*, but was badly damaged in the late 15C, after which orders were given to begin work on a new church, the Église St-Jérome. Excavations beneath the bell-tower have revealed traces of the vast original church, dating from the 5C AD.

There is a faded 14C mural on the inside of the west front depicting the Trinity, and large **painted medallions** in other parts of the church. The nave **murals**, dating from the 15C and 16C, illustrate the Last Judgement *(on the right)*, the Garden of Eden, Hell, the Virtues and the Vices.

DIGNE-LES-BAINS

Eating out

MODERATE

Brasserie La France – *54 bd Gassendi – ☎ 04 92 31 03 70 – closed Sur evening and Mon – 16.01/22.11€*. This brasserie offers a good range o meat and fish dishes in a relaxed setting. At the first sign of sun, patron: leave the banquettes in the dining room to sit on the terrace beneath the plane trees.

L'Origan – *6 r. Pied-de-Ville – ☎ 04 92 31 62 13 – closed 10-24 Feb, 20-2; Dec and Sun – booking essential in season – 17.99/32.78€*. This modest, wel coming restaurant in the pedestrianised centre offers unpretentious, reasonabl) priced local fare. Small veranda overlooking the street and simple rooms.

Where to stay

MODERATE

Hôtel Villa Gaïa – *2km/1mi SW of Digne-les-Bains on N 85 – ☎ 04 92 3. 21 60 – closed 1 Nov-29 Mar – ▣ – 12rms:60.98/83.85€ - ☐ 8.38€ – restau rant 22.87/38.11€*. Looking for somewhere to stay with no frills? This bour geois residence in a large park, below the road, is something of a home from home. Let yourself be pampered and make the most of its perfect peace anc quiet. Tastefully furnished rooms, library, lounge and terrace. Evening meal only reserved for hotel guests.

Tonic Hôtel – *Rte des Thermes – 2km/1mi E of Digne-les-Bains on Av. du 8 May ☎ 04 92 32 20 31 – closed Nov-Mar – 60rms: 62.50/70.13€ - ☐ 7.62€ restaurant 13.72/24.39€*. Treat yourself to a relaxing, restorative stay in thi: contemporary hotel with its harmonious architecture, at the very heart of the Vallon des Sources. Hydromassage and steam baths available in every room Terrace and swimming pool.

On the town

Le Grand Café – *3 bd Gassendi – ☎ 04 92 31 00 05 – Open daily 6.30am-2am* It's a fact: the Grand Café is hugely popular and draws a large clientele. Thi: might be due to the fact that it opens onto Boulevard Gassendi on one side anc Rue du Tampinet on the other. Or perhaps to its lively, switched-on atmosphere You will have to judge for yourself...

Shopping

Faïence d'hier et d'aujourd'hui – *14 r. de Provence – ☎ 04 92 32 34 06 – Tue-Sat 10am-12.15pm, 3pm-7.15pm*. Danielle Blanc-Vatin's work is of the highest standard. Her boutique-workshop is open to visitors, and she can be seen at work making fine pieces of *faïence*, in white or yellow, which she paints by hand.

Rue de l'Hubac and rue Pied de la Ville – *R. de l'Hubac and rue Pied de la Ville* These two arteries lined with clothes boutiques and food stores are the main shopping streets in the old town. Boutique-workshops display the work of one or two craftspeople (*faïence*, wood).

Leisure and sport

Les Ferréols – *Plan d'eau des Ferréols – ☎ 04 92 32 42 02 – May-Jun: Sat-Sun Jul-Aug open daily 11am-7pm – closed Oct-Apr*. This recreation centre on the banks of the Bléone comprises a lake, a miniature golf course, a rock-climbing practice wall, boules pistes and a volleyball court.

The blown and stained glass is the work of Canadian-born artist David Rabinowitch (1943-); his decorative windows vary in shade depending on the position of the viewer. Rabinowitch also produced a series of pieces in copper representing the Word of God in Hebrew, Greek, Latin and French, which can be seen on the floor of the nave.

Alexandra-David-Néel Museum ⊘ - *Access by ② on the town plan. Along the roac to Nice, past the Total petrol station.*
In 1924, Alexandra David-Néel spent months disguised as a Tibetan beggar, her face blackened with soot, in order to cross the Himalayas and reach Tibet and its capita Lhasa, the Forbidden City. On her return, Alexandra David-Néel wrote her mos famous book, *Voyage d'une Parisienne à Lhassa*, translated into English as *M) Journey to Lhasa.*

Tibetan altar in the Musée Alexandra David-Néel

In 1927, David-Néel fell under the spell of the Alpes-de-Haute-Provence region and bought a house in Digne which she called Samten-Dzong (the fortress of meditation). She lived in it between her long travels throughout Asia and filled it with souvenirs from the East; she wrote many books about her unique experiences and bequeathed her house and collections to the town of Digne. A camp-table, camera and Tibetan boots in the hallway are reminders of her travels; lamps, wooden figures and religious wall hangings decorate a small Buddhist temple.

Musée-Promenade St-Benoît ⊘ – *Follow avenue Demontzey and quai St-Benoît, cross the River Bléone and turn left immediately after the bridge; follow the signs to the car park.*
The centre is accessible on foot by the marked path offering fine views of Digne; halfway along, another path branches off along the mediaeval walls. Note the frescoes decorating the façade of the building housing the **Réserve géologique de Haute-Provence**. The building stands on built on tufa, due to the presence of a petrifying waterfall; strange limestone concretions can be seen along the path linking the car park to the centre.

An imaginative synthesis of art and science in the **geological museum** begins with an exhibition of contemporary artwork exploring man's intuitive understanding of the forces of nature and the history of the Earth. An extremely rich geological history is brought to life with film and multimedia, 3-D models and hundreds of fossils: one of the most impressive features shows a model of a 4.5m/15ft-long ichthyosaurus (the original fossil can still be seen *in situ; see Préalpes de DIGNE*, ❶). The aquarium contains nautili and limuli; among the last of the living fossils.

EXCURSIONS

★ **Courbons** – *Leave Digne by* ③ *on the town plan towards Sisteron and turn right before the railway station.*
The narrow twisting road rises rapidly through orchards of almond trees and offers clear **views**★ of the Digne Basin framed by barren mountains and dotted with drystone huts and walls. Irrigation canals are also a reminder of traditional agricultural practices. The village clings to a rocky spur; the lovely 14C church, part Romanesque, part Gothic, stands near the cemetery, shaded by cypresses.

Television relay – *8km/5mi. Leave Digne as for Courbons, drive for 4km/2.5mi and turn right. Follow the signs posted at the beginning of the road.*
A small cedar forest gives way to scrubland brightened with flowers, which is in turn replaced by silent and desolate heights. From the relay station (1 166m/3 825ft), there is an extended **view**★ of the Préalpes de Digne to the north and of the mountains overlooking Grasse and Nice to the east, as well as bird's-eye views of Digne and the Bléone Valley.

★ **St-Michel-de-Cousson** – *11km/6.8mi. Leave Digne by the D 20 leading to Entrages.*
As one drives through the baths complex, the ruins of the Roman baths can be seen below on the right; the road then continues towards the Col de Corobin across a typical landscape of parallel ravines dug by erosion through mountains of black marl known as **robines**. Turn right onto D 120 towards **Entrages**, a charming village overlooking the Eaux-Chaudes Valley. Go through the village and park the car in front of

the heavily restored 17C church. A signpost marks the beginning of the path leading to the Cousson's twin summits *(2hr easy walk; turn left at the Pas d'Entrages)*; from the top of the ridge, there is a lovely view of Entrages.

The **Chapelle Saint-Michel-de-Cousson** stands on top of the cliff above the Asse Valley. Covered with *lauzes* (slabs of schist), it is plainly decorated apart from the fragment of a Merovingian sarcophagus placed above the doorway.

A pilgrimage takes place every year on Whit Monday. There is a splendid overall **view** of the Asse Valley, of the Clue de Chabrières to the south and of the Bléone Valley further west.

It is possible to continue along the path to the main Cousson Summit (1 516m/4 974ft); walk round to the left of it to return to the Pas d'Entrages.

Préalpes de DIGNE

Michelin map 334 E/F/G 7/8 and 245 folds 8,9 and 21

Although the ancient road from Sisteron to Nice once linked the southern Préalpes de Digne to the Roman towns of the Midi, these Provençal mountains lying between the River Durance and River Verdon are the least populated and most desolate in the Alpine region. Gradually left bare as a result of erosion, they were replanted with Austrian pines, larches and forest pines which help to retain the soil they grow on. There are, however, some pastures and cultivated basins. Mountain streams have cut deep into the limestone ridges, creating remote clues (gorges) which testify to the amazingly complex geology of the southern Préalpes.

Nearby Sights: CASTELLANE, DIGNE-LES-BAINS, Vallée de la Moyenne DURANCE, Monastère de GANAGOBIE, Route NAPOLÉON, Lac de SERRE-PONÇON, SEYNE, SISTERON, Plateau de VALENSOLE

HIGHLIGHT

Réserve géologique de Haute-Provence – Founded in 1984, this geological reserve includes 47 municipalities surrounding the town of Digne and covers an area of 1 900km²/734mi².

The protected territory, the largest of its kind in Europe, offers geologists and laymen unique study opportunities, enabling them to follow the evolution of the earth over 300 million years, in particular the succession of upheavals which shaped the region's mountains. The strata of transverse valleys, Verdaches, Chabrières and Péroué, for instance, are like an open book of local geology. Looking at the rough, often barren landscape today, it is hard to believe that the reserve lies in what was a vast "Alpine sea" during the Secondary Era, a natural habitat for fish, molluscs and coral.

Sedimentary deposits were laid during each era. The amount varied considerably, but the density was amazing. Plant deposits inform us about the flora of the Primary Era. Relics of the Secondary Era, characterised by a rich marine life, include the skeleton of a large reptile and numerous ammonite fossils, while the Tertiary Era preserved for us the footprints left by birds combing the shores of the Alpine sea.

The Vélodrome

Twenty sites protected for their exceptional scientific value are scattered over the whole area. Nature study tours led by a geologist are organised during the summer either for a day or a week's hiking or riding, starting in Digne, Castellane or Sisteron. (☎ 04 92 83 19 23).

EXCURSIONS

★① Vallée du Bès

ROUND TOUR STARTING FROM DIGNE *95km/59mi - 3hr on foot excluding visits.*

Digne-les-Bains – *See DIGNE-LES-BAINS.*

Drive north out of Digne-les-Bains along D 900ᴬ, which runs through the Bléone Valley.

★**Dalle à ammonites géantes** – *1km/0.6mi from Digne, on the left of the road.*
This tilted black-limestone slab bears the imprint of 1 553 ammonites, some of them 70cm/28in in diameter, which lived here 200 million years ago.

★**Musée du site de l'Ichtyosaure** – *After driving 8km/5mi north of Digne along D 900ᴬ towards Barles, park the car in the marked car park and continue on foot along the path at the end of the car park. Access: 1hr on foot; walking shoes and water supplies are essential.*
🏃 The path runs along the left bank through a pretty oak wood, past the little waterfalls of the Bélier gorge. The path then climbs the opposite hillside in a series of turns to the Col du Jas. On reaching this broad plateau, turn left and head down to the excavation site where the fossil lies under glass protection.
Ichthyosaurus, a 4.5m/15ft-long, fish-like reptile, swam in the sea which covered the whole region 180 million years ago. Its fossilized skeleton, in remarkable condition, has been left *in situ* under glass. A fresco shows the natural environment of this contemporary of the dinosaurs.

Site du "Vélodrome" – *8km/5mi from the intersection of D 900ᴬ and D 103. Leave the car before the bridge over D 900ᴬ. Follow the path signposted "Serre d'Esclangon". About 2hr on foot.*
🏃 The itinerary goes across an area where the reddish soil contrasts with the black pines growing on it. Keep going left until you breast the first rise and proceed towards the ruins of the village of Esclangon; turn right and aim for the Serre d'Esclangon Summit.
The panorama unfolding to the west reveals one of the finest geological phenomena in the Alps, known as the **"Vélodrome"★**. This huge fan-shaped natural feature is the result, over a period of 16 million years, of the folding of layers of sandstone within a basin subjected to intense compression from the surrounding mountains. Constant erosion gradually dug the Bès Valley and gave the landscape its present appearance.

Empreintes de pattes d'oiseaux – *10km/6.2mi from Digne-les-Bains; the site is signposted and it is possible to park on the left-hand side of D 900ᴬ.* Twenty million years ago, the sea had not yet retreated from the area and birds resembling plovers pecked away at what they could find in the damp sand of the beach. Their footprints are clearly visible in several places and a cast with an explanatory panel is exhibited at the roadside.
Various other geological imprints *(signposted and accompanied by explanatory panels)*, which can be seen on the way to Barles, illustrate the exceptional geological diversity of the region. Note, on the left, the fossilized **imprint of water current** in the sand.

★**Clues de Barles** – The road just gets through these two gorges squeezed alongside the mountain stream. The second gorge is the most impressive: a rocky knoll, obstructing the valley at the end of an extremely narrow passage, outlines its deeply indented silhouette against the sky.
The **plant imprints** visible further on are evidence of what life was like 300 million years ago, when the region enjoyed a tropical climate.

Clue de Verdaches – It is covered with rich green vegetation.

★**Col de Maure** – Alt 1 346m/4 416ft. The pass links the valleys of the River Blanche and River Bès. In summer, these tributaries of the River Durance are reduced to a mere trickle and the arid appearance of their valleys is striking.
The small ski resort of **Grand Puy** close to the pass, in a setting of larch woods and pastures, is a winter annexe of Seyne, situated lower down in the valley.

Seyne – *See SEYNE.*

From Seyne, drive south along D 7.

The road goes through a green valley, then a small forested massif before reaching the pass.

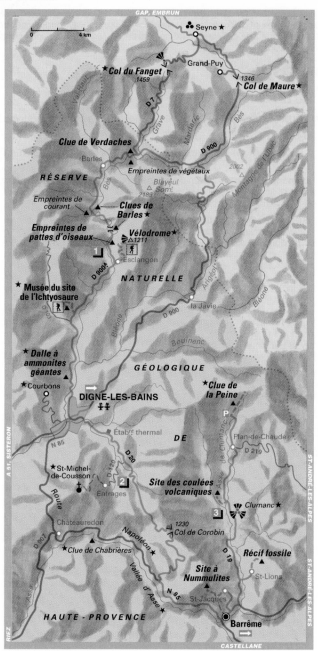

★ **Col du Fanget** – Alt 1 459m/4 787ft. There is a fine **view** to the north with the Blanche Valley in the foreground, flanked on the right by the Dormillouse Summit (2 505m/8 219ft) and Montagne de la Blanche, with the Parpaillon Massif and Gapençais mountains in the distance.

The narrow road joins D 900⁴ near the Clue de Verdaches.

★ 2 Route du Col de Corobin

FROM DIGNE TO BARRÊME *32km along D 20 and N 85 – 1hr*

From Digne, drive along D 20 towards Entrages (see DIGNE-LES-BAINS: Excursions). On the left, there is an ancient farm with a dovecote on either side, where Napoleon is said to have stopped for a meal on his way back from Elba. Further on, the road runs through the Cousson forest, then climbs over the Col de Corobin to join N 85 leading southeast to Barrême.

Barrême is situated at the confluence of the three small Asse valleys: the Asse de Moriez (east), Asse de Blieux (southeast) and Asse de Clumanc (north). Downstream from Barrême, the river is simply called Asse as it flows towards the impressive **Clues de Chabrières★** *(see ROUTE NAPOLÉON).*

③ Asse de Clumanc

FROM BARRÊME TO PLAN-DE-CHAUDE *18km/11.2mi along D 19*

The road closely follows the River Asse de Clumanc from Barrême to Plan-de-Chaude. The valley contains a wealth of fossil-bearing layers which provide an invaluable insight into successive geological upheavals. The sites are listed and marked with explanatory panels.

Site à nummulites de St-Jacques – A path leads in 10min to a site close to the village of St-Jacques, where 40 million-year-old fossils can be seen in limestone strata. *The site can also be reached from Barrême by following the "Voie impériale" footpath (1hr).*

Récif fossile de St-Lions – *Walking shoes recommended. Car park at the entrance to the town.*
🚶 A path leads through brushwood in 30min to a site consisting of a coral reef which used to rest on shingle in this shallow part of the Alpine sea 35 million years ago. Sea urchins and oysters are recognisable in the strata; they were subsequently buried under a layer of clay.

Clumanc – The village houses covered with *lauzes* are spread out along the mountain stream. The Romanesque Église Notre-Dame houses an interesting tabernacle in gilt wood.
A path starting north of the village leads in 10min to the **panorama★** of the castle ruins. The hillside illustrates a period in the formation of the Alps with a mixture of marl and conglomerate rocks, successively folded and eroded.

Site des coulées volcaniques – *Drive to the intersection with D 219, leave the car in the car park in front of the post office and follow the marked footpath for 15min.* This is the only evidence of volcanic activity in the area: following a volcanic eruption which occurred 35 million years ago, lava and ashes settled at the bottom of the Alpine sea and were carried to this place.

★Clue de la Peine – *Leave the car in the parking area near some houses. Follow the path signposted "Clue de la Peine" for 20min.*
🚶 The stream has cut vertically through layers of limestone deposited during the Secondary Era, which folded 60 million years later during the formation of the Alps.

Follow the same itinerary to return to Barrême, or turn left at Plan-de-Chaude on D 219 to Notre-Dame-d'Entraigues, Lambruisse and St-André-des-Alpes.

Vallée de la Moyenne DURANCE★
Michelin map 334 B8 to D11 and 245 folds 20 and 33

The River Durance, which is the last main tributary of the Rhône as it makes its way to the sea, has its source near Briançon and flows along a 324km/201mi course before joining the Rhône. Frédéric Mistral, the famous Provençal poet, used to say: "The mistral (a strong wind blowing down the Rhône Valley), Parliament and the Durance are the curses of Provence". The most unpredictable major river of the southern Alps certainly proved a real threat to local people and, for a long time, defied all attempts to harness it. Since the 1960s, however, the river has become one of the great economic assets of the region, a vital source of urban water supply and hydroelectricity.
South of Sisteron, the Durance enters the Mediterranean Basin. Here, the river bed is less steep and almost 1km/0.6mi wide, the valley broadens and the river flows between stony banks; its rate of flow is regulated by a network of dams and canals built along its course or that of its tributaries. As a result, new ecosystems have been able to flourish in the river valley, for instance wooded areas favourable to the development of animal life including colonies of beavers.

Nearby Sights: CÉRESTE, DIGNE-LES-BAINS, Préalpes de DIGNE, FORCALQUIER, Monastère de GANAGOBIE, GRÉOUX-LES-BAINS, MANE, MANOSQUE, Route NAPOLÉON, RIEZ, SISTERON, Plateau de VALENSOLE

Eating out

MODERATE

Au Goût du Jour – *Chemin du Lac – 04160 Château-Arnoux-St-Auban – ☎ 04 92 64 48 48 – closed Tue lunchtime and Mon Oct-Apr – 13.72/21.34€*. This restaurant is not far (300m/330yd) from Bonne Étape, which is well reputed for the quality of its food, in fact it is its annexe. It offers a simpler menu at a lower price chalked up on a slate. The food caters to modern tastes, as the restaurant's name suggests.

L'Oustaou de la Foun – *04160 Château-Arnoux-St-Auban – 1.5km/1mi N of Château-Arnoux-St-Auban on N 85 – ☎ 04 92 62 65 30 – closed Sun evening and Mon – 19.51/54.58€*. In summer this pretty Provençal house is hidden by trees. Inside, an inventive style of cuisine is served in a vaulted dining room lit by large bay windows. There is also an inviting indoor courtyard with traditional paving stones underfoot.

Where to stay

BUDGET

Chambre d'hôte Campagne du Barri – *04190 Les Mées – 4km/2.5mi S of Les Mées on D 4 – ☎ 04 92 34 36 93 – olgamancin@wanadoo.fr – reservations compulsory in winter – 5rms ☲ 32.01/42.69€ – main meal 15.24€*. This comfortable 18C house has retained traces of its history: the wallpaper in the lounge dates from 1794, and the image on the pediment is a tribute to the republic. Plain rooms with a good view of the mountains and the village.

MODERATE

Hôtel Villiard – *04600 St-Auban – 3.5km/2mi SW of Château-Arnoux-St-Aubin on N 96 – ☎ 04 92 64 17 42 – closed 20 Dec-5 Jan and Sat Oct-Easter – ☐ 20rms: 42.69/64.03€ - ☲ 6.86€*. No need to pay an exorbitant price to be pampered. The hotel tradition is carried on here without frills or fuss, and guests will appreciate the attentive touches offered by this pleasant establishment. Classic rooms that are impeccably well kept.

EXPENSIVE

Hôtel La Bonne Étape – *Chemin du Lac – 04160 Château-Arnoux-St-Auban – ☎ 04 92 64 00 09 – closed 3 Jan-12 Feb, 26 Nov-11 Dec and Mon Oct-Apr – ☐ – 11rms: from 91.47€ - ☲ 13.72€ – restaurant 34.30/90.71€*. This fine residence is an old 18C coaching inn set amid a rolling landscape with the scents of olive trees and cypresses. Cosy rooms with antique furniture. Traditional cooking which enjoys a good reputation. Swimming pool between the mountains and the sky.

EXCURSIONS

① The Valley

FROM SISTERON TO MANOSQUE *74km/46mi – about 3hr*

★★**Sisteron** – *See SISTERON.*

Leave Sisteron by ② on the town plan and drive along N 85.

The road follows the Durance harnessed by the Salignac Dam, passes the mouth of the Jabron winding between the river and the steep edge of the Montagne de Lure and skirts the Lac de l'Escale Dam as it reaches Château-Arnoux.

Château-Arnoux-Saint-Auban – The national gliding centre is nearby and the Festival de jazz des Alpes-de-Haute-Provence takes place in the town. The square 16C **castle**, flanked by round and square towers, is now the town hall and overlooks a garden, arboretum and a keep-fit trail.

2km/1.2mi further on, along N 96, turn right along the road signposted "Route touristique de St-Jean".

★**Belvédère de la chapelle St-Jean** – *15min there and back on foot. Leave the car at the top of the hill (car park near the chapel) and climb along the footpath to a viewing table.*
There is a fine **panoramic view** from west to east of the Montagne de Lure, the Durance Valley, Sisteron, the Lac de l'Escale Dam and the Rochers des Mées.

Return to N 96 and continue south.

Montfort – This hilltop village in a charming **site★** overlooking the Durance is extremely picturesque with its stepped streets, lined with charming old houses, climbing up to the restored 16C castle; there is a fine view of the Durance Valley and Valensole Plateau.

2km/1.2mi further on, turn right onto D 101.

The road follows a wooded vale towards St-Donat.

★**Église St-Donat** – Built in the 11C on the site where St Donat, the religious recluse, had settled in the 6C, the long-neglected church is one of the rare specimens of early Romanesque style in Provence *(restoration work in progress)*.
This vast basilica was intended to contain a great number of pilgrims; three large doors ensured a steady flow of visitors.

Rejoin N 96 and cross it to take D 4ᴬ across the River Durance.

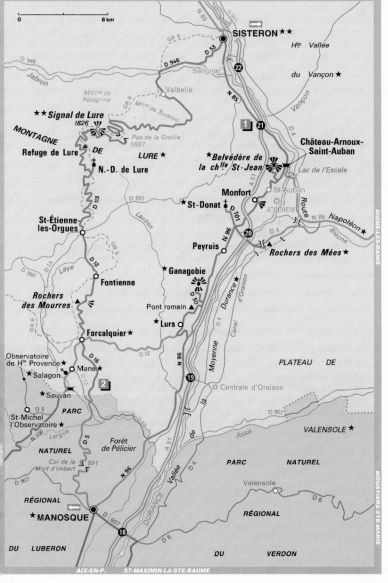

★**Rochers des Mées** – These 100m/328ft-high conglomerate rocks, towering over the village of Les Mées and eroded into strange shapes, are known as the **"Pénitents des Mées"** and make a particularly striking sight when illuminated at night.

Turn left and follow D 101. Return to N 96 and drive towards Manosque.

Peyruis – The old part of the village, once guarded by a drawbridge, is still standing. The 16C church has a six-sided bell-tower, built in tufa, with gargoyles in the shape of a lion's head.

Turn right onto D 30 6km/3.7mi beyond Peyruis.

★**Prieuré de Ganagobie** - *See Prieuré de GANAGOBIE.*

Return to N 96 but take the little road for Lurs just before joining it.

The road follows an ancient Roman road and crosses the Buës over a single-arched **Roman bridge** dating from the 2C AD.

★**Lurs** – This village occupies a remarkable **position★** on top of a rocky spur overlooking the Durance and the area around Forcalquier. Once a medieval stronghold belonging to the bishops of Forcalquier, it was gradually deserted and became derelict until it was "revived" by a group of graphic designers and is today the summer rendezvous of the printing profession through the **Rencontres internationales de Lurs** and a centre of graphic arts.
Go through the clock gate surmounted by a campanile, past the church with its interesting bell tower and along the winding streets lined with bay-windowed houses; there are traces of the old fortifications. Note the **chancellerie des compagnons de Lure**, the rustic open-air theatre, the restored **priory**, now a cultural centre, and the partly rebuilt bishops' castle. Walk round the latter along the **Promenade des Évêques**, lined with 15 oratories dating from 1864, to the Chapelle Notre-Dame-de-Vie offering fine **views** of the Durance and Préalpes de Digne on one side, of the Montagne de Lure and Forcalquier Basin on the other.

A small road south of the village leads to N 96 and to Manosque.

Across the Durance, a canal diverts the flow of the River Bléone and River Durance to the Oraison power station. Beyond the confluence of the Asse and the Durance, the road leaves the bank of the river to reach Manosque.

★**Manosque** – *See MANOSQUE.*

② The Montagne de Lure and the Pays du Contadour

FROM MANOSQUE TO SISTERON

87km/54mi – about 2hr 30min – see local map

From Manosque, drive north along D 5 via the Col de la Mort d'Imbert which offers lovely **views** of Manosque and its surroundings. Turn right onto D 16.

★**Forcalquier** – *See FORCALQUIER.*

Leave Forcalquier along D 12, northwest of the town plan.

Rochers des Mourres – These rock formations, eroded into strange shapes, stand on either side of the road.
On the way to Fontienne, the **view** extends to the Durance Valley on the right.

Fontienne – The small Romanesque chapel of this tiny village, perched on an escarpment, has a belfry-wall with twin openings; the castle goes back to the 13C.

St-Étienne-les-Orgues – This village marks the gateway of the Montagne de Lure. Its past prosperity was based on the production of numerous remedies based on aromatic and medicinal plants, which were sold by pedlars as far away as the Auvergne and Bourgogne regions. The 16C houses have mullioned windows and archivolts over the doorways. The **church** ⊙ has a polygonal chancel and the round towers of the 13C **castle** date from the 18C.

D 113 rises through the sloping lavender fields, then past pines and cedars and into dense forest. Just beyond the Oratoire St-Joseph, a stony road on the right leads to Notre-Dame de Lure.

★**Montagne de Lure** – This impressive ridge, which prolongs Mont Ventoux eastward over a distance of some 30km/19mi, is austere and practically uninhabited; as the altitude rises, holm oaks, scrubland, lavender fields and cedar trees gradually give way to pastures which release a strong scent of aromatic plants. The northern slopes are more densely forested with firs near the summits, replaced by beeches, larches, oaks and black Austrian pines lower down. The arid landscapes of the Montagne de Lure were extensively described by the Provençal writer Jean Giono, a native of Manosque.

The "Pénitents des Mées" – a miracle of geology or theology?

Notre-Dame de Lure ⊘ – The monks of Boscodon Abbey built a modest monastery here in 1165. The only part of this remaining is a large barrel-vaulted room located beneath the small hermitage, a more recent edifice. The abbey church, which became a pilgrims' chapel, has now recovered its original appearance through extensive restoration work.

The oak and three lime trees in front of the chapel are several centuries old.

Return to D 113 and continue upwards.

Refuge de Lure – This small ski centre equipped with a few ski lifts offers a wide **view**. A memorial to the 17C Belgian astronomer, Wendelin, who set up the **first observatory in France**, stands at the roadside 1.5km/0.9mi further on.

Continue for another 3.5km/2.2mi and leave the car on the platform of the telecommunications transmitter. Access is restricted in winter – the road between the Refuge de Lure and Vabelle is usually closed between 15 November and 31 May; enquire in St-Étienne-les-Orgues.

★★ **Signal de Lure** – The mountain's highest summit (1 826m/5 991ft) offers a vast **panorama** of Monte Viso, Mont Pelvoux, the Vercors Massif, the Cévennes range, Mont Ventoux and sometimes the Mediterranean coast. A little further on, to the left, is another good **view**: an opening in the mountains reveals the Jabron Valley.

Beyond the Pas de la Graille, the road goes down through a splendid beech forest to the Jabron Valley overlooked by the steep slopes of the Montagne de Lure.

Follow D 53 to Sisteron.

★★ **Sisteron** – *See SISTERON.*

HIKE

★ **Walk to the Pénitents des Mées** – *3hr on foot. Start from the camp site situated beyond Notre-Dame de la Salette on D 101. Leave the car at the side of the road.*
🅰 Go down to the bottom of the valley and cross the low wall of the second reservoir to reach the north bank. From there, a path, marked in green, winds up *(keep to the right)* to the Forêt des Pénitents which is rich in Mediterranean vegetation (holm oak, Aleppo pine, rock rose, pistachio). As you reach the pass (alt 600m/1 968ft), walk 91m/100yd to the left for striking views of the "Pénitents". Return to the pass and go down to the rocky ridge and the foot of the "Pénitents" *(a few steep sections).* Continue left along the path *(facing the Durance Valley)* until you reach a surfaced road which skirts the old aqueduct and leads to the village of Les Mées. According to local legend, the rocks were formed when a group of monks fell in love with the beautiful Arab girls whom a local lord had brought back from his campaigns against the Saracens. St Donat punished the monks for their sinful lust by turning them into stones as they walked in procession along the Durance.

EMBRUN ★

Population 6 152
Michelin map 334 G5 and 245 fold 9
Local map see Barrage et lac de SERRE-PONÇON

Embrun is picturesquely perched on a rocky ledge, 80m/262ft above the River Durance and the Lac de Serre-Ponçon. Its church, the finest in Dauphiné, testifies to its past influence as a religious centre.

Today, the town is a pleasant summer resort offering a wide choice of water sports on the lake as well as canoeing on the Durance and hiking in the surrounding area. In winter it is a centre of cross-country and Alpine skiing practised on the slopes of Les Orres and near the mountain village of Crévoux.

Nearby Sights: L'ARGENTIÈRE-LA-BESSÉE, BARCELONNETE, CEILLAC, Vallée de FREISSINIÈRES, GAP, Route des GRANDES ALPES, GUILLESTRE, MONT-DAUPHIN Route NAPOLÉON, Le QUEYRAS, Lac de SERRE-PONÇON, SEYNE, L'UBAYE, VAL D'ALLOS, VARS

A RELIGIOUS CENTRE

During the Roman occupation, Embrun was an important town on the way from Briançon to Arles. It later became the main religious centre of the Alpes-Maritimes region and was incorporated into the Holy Roman Empire, the archbishops of Embrun being granted temporal power over the whole region and the right to mint their own coinage.

Eating out

BUDGET

Le Co'case – *Bd Pasteur (pl. du Gén.-Dosse)* – ☎ *04 92 43 06 68 – closed Sept-Jun – 12.96/28.20€.* Fancy a cocktail before you eat? Settle in here and dip into the menu afterwards to read about salads, grilled meats, pancakes and a selection of home-made ice cream to tempt any food-lover. Food is served in a shaded courtyard.

Les Manins – *Hameau des Manins – 05200 St-Sauveur – 8.5km/5mi S of Embrun on N 94. D 40 and D 39A* – ☎ *04 92 43 09 27 – open Jul-Aug and by reservation Sept-Jun* – ⊠ – *7.62/21.34€.* Breathtaking view of the Lac de Serre-Ponçon from the terrace of this mountain chalet. The small charming dining room is entirely panelled in wood. Eclectic cuisine including charcuterie, pizzas, mezes, pancakes and home-made desserts.

Where to stay

BUDGET

Hôtel Notre-Dame – *Av. du Gén.-Nicolas* – ☎ *04 92 43 08 36 – closed 16 Dec-29 Jan, Sun evening and Mon out of season – 14rms: 33.54/45.73€* – ⊽ *5.95€* – *restaurant 16.62/22.71€.* This homely hotel slightly out of the town centre has a small garden to the front which can be used as a terrace in the summer. Rooms are small but comfortable. Traditional fare prepared by the proprietress.

Camping Les Esparons – *05200 Baratier – 4km/2.5mi S of Embrun on N 94 then D 40* – ☎ *04 92 43 02 73 – open 15 Jun-1 Sept* – ⊠ – *reservations recommended – 83 pitches: 10.52€.* Chill out in the shade of an old apple orchard. This simple campsite offers spacious pitches bounded by apple trees. There is a swimming pool, and games for old and young alike. In the village nearby (700m/770yd) there are facilities for tennis and riding.

Camping Le Verger – *05200 Baratier – 4km/2.5mi S of Embrun on N 94 then D 40* – ☎ *04 92 43 15 87 – bresgilbert@minitel.net* – ⊠ – *reservations recommended – 110 pitches: 12.20€ – catering available on site.* Le Verger is a good choice for its selection of chalets in all sizes available for hire, with plenty of room in between them and with an open fire or without. Shaded pitches. Heated swimming pool and children's play area.

MODERATE

Hôtel de la Mairie – *Pl. de la Mairie* – ☎ *04 92 43 20 65 – closed 8-24 May, Oct and Nov – 24rms: 41.16/48.78€* - ⊽ *6.10€ – restaurant 15.24/19.82€.* At the heart of the old town, opposite a stone fountain, stands this pretty old house with pink walls and shutters. It looks most welcoming. Rooms are light and well kept. is tasty and served in generous portions, at a very reasonable price, even à la carte.

Embrun on the cliffs above the Durance

From the 14C onwards, the pilgrimage to Notre-Dame-du-Réal attracted large crowds. The rank of canon conferred on King Louis XI during his visit was passed on to all his successors and is now bestowed on the elected French president.

Owing to its geographical position, Embrun was attacked many times: by the Sarracens, by the Huguenots during the Wars of Religion and by the duke of Savoie, but only the Revolution deprived it of its special religious status.

AROUND THE OLD TOWN

Picturesque squares, brightly painted houses and pretty balconies; bubbling fountains and distant birdsong: it's hard to believe that the austere peaks of the Queyras are only a matter of miles away. The drive down the Durance brings the Mediterranean that much closer.

Place de l'Archevêché – The Belvédère du Roc *(viewing tables)* offers a fine view of the Durance Valley and Morgon Mountain.

The cathedral chapter held meetings in the 13C **Maison des Chanonges** ⊘. It is one of the rare examples of medieval domestic architecture in the area.

Tour Brune ⊘ – This 12C tower is the former keep of the episcopal castle; it now houses a **Musée du Paysage**, devoted to the Parc national des Écrins. There is a fine view from the terrace *(viewing table)*.

Rue de la Liberté and rue Clovis-Hugues – The town's shopping district is very lively in summer. At no 6 rue de la Liberté the governor's palace boasts a beautiful wooden **doorway★** in Renaissance style, surmounted by a lion carved in the round. An old tower still watches over the comings and goings in Place Mazelière. Continue along rue Clovis-Hugues and admire the 12C carved façade between no 29 and no 31. Further on, a beautiful 16C fountain in red marble decorates place St-Marcellin and there are interesting 14C corbelled houses along rue Caffe.

★CATHÉDRALE NOTRE-DAME-DU-RÉAL *45min*

"Réal" is a distortion of *"royal"*. The edifice was built during the transitional period from the Romanesque style to the Gothic style (late 12C, early 13C). Its originality lies in the alternate use of black schist and white limestone. The steeple was rebuilt in the 19C, taking the 14C steeple as a model *(see Introduction: Art and architecture)*.

★ **Portail "le Réal"** – This is a remarkable example of Lombard art. The arch of the doorway is supported by pink marble columns; the front ones stand on two squatting lions. At the back, two slender columns on either side rest on telamones; a small figure, held between the two left-hand ones, is said to be the dean of the cathedral chapter who refused to pay the workers.

Pilgrims prayed in front of *The Adoration of the Magi* which used to decorate the tympanum; the painting is now reproduced as a mosaic inside the cathedral and the tympanum shows Christ surrounded by the symbols of the Evangelists.

Interior ⊘ – The Byzantine influence explains the absence of a transept. The chancel, in pure Romanesque style, was once covered with frescoes. The late-15C organ, bought with a bequest from Louis XI, is one of the oldest in France. Opposite, above the altar, there is a 16C picture depicting the Entombment of Christ.

253

★ **Treasury** ⊘ – It was one of the richest in France before being plundered in the 16C by the duke of Lesdiguières' Protestant troops. However, it still contains an important collection of religious ornaments, paintings, holy receptacles, monstrances, the Embrun Missal and 14C illuminated antiphonaries.

Chapelles des Cordeliers ⊘ – *It houses the tourist office.* The side chapels of the former Franciscan church have survived; they are decorated with recently restored 15C and 16C **murals★**. The second chapel tells the story of St Anthony of Padua, the most famous Franciscan after St Francis himself.

EXCURSIONS

The tourist office sells maps covering the walks described below.

⁎ **Les Orres** – 1 *7km/10.6mi southeast. Leave Embrun along N 94 towards Gap, drive for 2km/1.2mi and turn left onto D 40.* The twisting road follows the Eyssalette Valley and affords lovely views of the northern part of the Lac de Serre-Ponçon. This winter resort (alt 1 600m/5 249ft), created in 1970 and named after the old village on the opposite slope, developed rapidly to form one of the main winter sports resorts of the southern Alps. Les Orres and its annexes of Le Pramouton (Alpine skiing) and Champs-Lacas (cross-country skiing) offer a wide choice of activities including snowmobile, paragliding and snowboarding. There are also numerous summer activities to choose from, including swimming, tennis, trap-shooting, riding and aerial sports. More information is available from www.lesorres.com.

★ **Prelongis and Fontaine chair-lifts** ⊘ – Alt 2 408m/7 900ft. Fine views of the ski slopes running through a larch and pine forest below the Boussolenc Peak. From the top the view encompasses part of the Lac de Serre-Ponçon and the Embrun area.

Crévoux – 1 *3km/8mi. From Embrun, drive east (the road starts in front of a factory) via Coin, then join the route du Col de Parpaillon.* The small mountain village of Crévoux, a popular meeting place for skiers, is enclosed by the slopes of the Méale Mountain and the rocky wall of the St-André Peak, streaming with waterfalls.

The best views around Embrun – The beautiful Lac du Serre-Ponçon is surrounded by peaks which are relatively accessible and offer stunning prospects of the lake and countryside. Among the best are **Mont Guillaume** *(2 550m/8 366ft, 3hr on foot)* which gives views over the Durance and the lake from the mountain chapel at the summit, the **Pic de Morgon** *(2 324m/7 682ft, 2hr 30min, Route du Boscodon from the car park at L'Ours)* with a splendid view of the lake and the **Aiguilles de Chabrières** *(see Lac de SERRE PONÇON, ❷).*

Val d'ENTRAUNES★★

Michelin map 341 A1 to B3 and 245 fold 23

Set in the middle of the **Parc national du Mercantour** ⊘, the Val d'Entraunes is one of the remotest areas of the Alpes-Maritimes *département*, even though the Côte d'Azur lies only 100km/62mi to the southeast.

The D 2202, which follows the upper Var Valley through some deep, narrow passages, is one of the main routes leading from the Alps to the Nice region.
Visitors intending to drive to Puget-Théniers from the Barcelonnette Basin have the choice of two routes: the Route des Grandes Alpes from Barcelonnette to Entraunes *(see Route de la CAYOLLE)*, or the Upper Verdon route via the Col d'Allos to Colmars *(see Route du Col d'ALLOS).* The itineraries below describe the section which will enable motorists to reach the Val d'Entraunes via the Col des Champs.

Nearby Sights: ANNOT, AURON, BARCELONNETTE, BEUIL, Gorges du CIANS, COLMARS, ENTREVAUX, Route des GRANDES ALPES, PRA-LOUP, PUGET-THÉNIERS, Vallée de la TINÉE, L'UBAYE, VAL-D'ALLOS

EXCURSIONS

Haute Vallée du Var

FROM COLMARS TO ST-MARTIN-D'ENTRAUNES *30km/18.6mi – allow 1hr*

The present road was built at the end of the 19C by the chasseurs alpins *(Alpine troops)* and runs alongside a rock face which appears to be about to crumble away at any moment. *The surface is in very poor repair and free-roaming cattle have been known to wander across the road; please drive with extra care.*

Colmars – *See COLMARS.*

From Colmars, D 2 rises in a series of hairpin bends, offering views of the Lance and Upper Verdon valleys, and passes through **La Ratery**, a little summer and winter resort and the starting point for a themed botanical walk.

★**Col des Champs** – Alt 2 045m/6 709ft. The road runs close to the pass at an altitude of 2 095m/6 873ft, through a completely barren landscape, on the border of the Alpes-Maritimes and Alpes-de-Haute-Provence *départements*. Grey and white are the dominant colours of this strange scenery, and the view is limited to the north by the Tête des Muletiers and to the south by the Frema Summit (alt 2 747m/9 012ft).

From the pass, it is possible to walk to **Mont Rénière** *(3hr there and back; starting point: 500m/547yd beyond the pass on the left)*, a comparatively easy climb rewarded by a fine overall view of the Val d'Entraunes.

On the way down from the pass, the stony landscape gives way to a forested area.

Chastelonnette – This small cross-country ski resort, also known as **Val-Pelens** is overlooked by the Aiguilles de Pelens (2 523m/8 278ft).

As the road approaches the hamlet of **Le Monnard**, there is a lovely bird's-eye view of St-Martin-d'Entraunes and the Var Valley. The mountainous area forming the horizon separates the Var and Tinée basins.

St-Martin-d'Entraunes – *See below.*

From Col de la Cayolle to Puget-Théniers

51km/32mi – allow 3hr

Col de la Cayolle – *See Route des GRANDES-ALPES, Excursions.*

Estenc – The chalets of this hamlet stand on a glacial ridge. This is where the Var, the longest river of the Alpes-Maritimes *département*, has its source.

Entraunes – This village lies in a pleasant setting at the confluence of the River Var and River Bourdoux, below the Col de la Cayolle. The church has a strange asymmetrical bell-tower.

La Vierge de la Miséricorde by Francois Bréa, the most famous painter of the Nice Gothic school.

Val d'ENTRAUNES

The **Chapelle St-Sébastien**, situated at the northern end of the village, is worth a visit; frescoes by **Andrea de Cella**, dating from 1516, cover the wall of the apse, forming a kind of Renaissance altarpiece (St Sebastian's martyrdom surmounted by the Crucifixion).

The road runs through an austere mountain landscape; beyond a tunnel, the valley opens out into the St-Martin Basin.

St-Martin-d'Entraunes — The verdant setting of this village perched on a morainic mound offers a contrast with the mostly arid landscapes of the upper Var Valley. The Provençal Romanesque **church** ⊘ has a blind façade and a Gothic side porch bearing emblems which seem to relate it to the Knights Templar. The sundial bears the inscription "The sun guides me, your pastor shows you the way". Inside, there is a fine altarpiece known as the **Retable de la Vierge de Miséricorde★**, by François Bréa, dating from 1555.

3.5km/2.2mi beyond Villeneuve-d'Entraunes, turn left onto D 74 which rises above the Barlatte Valley.

Châteauneuf-d'Entraunes — The village lies in a desolate landscape, above the upper Var Valley. The Baroque church houses an altarpiece in Primitive style (1524), reminiscent of François Bréa's work.

Return to D 2202 and turn left.

Guillaumes — This old fortified village, situated at the confluence of the River Var and River Tuébi, is today a summer resort overlooked by the ruined castle (fine view). A historical pageant takes place every year on 15 August, followed by a pilgrimage to the 18C **Chapelle Notre-Dame-du-Buyei** which stands just beyond the village on the left; inside is a remarkable painting of the fire which devastated Guillaumes in 1682.

Shortly after Guillaumes, the valley narrows into a gorge.

★★**Gorges de Daluis** — This deep, austere gorge, through which flows the River Var, is quite impressive. The cliff road between Guillaumes and Daluis winds its way along the west bank of the upper Var, high above the clear green water of the river. In the narrowest parts, tunnels had to be dug through the rock in order to ease the traffic. It is in those places that the road affords the finest **views★★** of the red-schist gorge dotted with fresh greenery.

A rock in the shape of a female bust seems to guard the downstream entrance of the gorge.

Daluis — Alt 800m/2 625ft. This hilltop village overlooked by the ruins of a castle offers the opportunity of a pleasant break at the exit of the gorge. The **Grotte du Chat** nearby, in which an underground river appears for a distance of more than 720m/787yd, is made up of a series of chambers containing a variety of concretions.

Between Daluis and Entrevaux, the road follows the river which veers left at Pont de Gueydan. The valley narrows once more near Entrevaux.

★**Entrevaux** — *See ENTREVAUX.*

On the way to Puget-Théniers along N 202, there is a lovely **view★★** of Entrevaux.

★**Puget-Théniers** — *See PUGET-THÉNIERS.*

ENTREVAUX★

Population 785
Michelin map 334 I9 and 245 fold 23

Mother Nature and Monsieur de Vauban, the master engineer, both played their part in shaping the town's amazing **setting★★**. Entrevaux lies on the north bank of the River Var, at the foot of a strange rocky spur crowned by a citadel; the closely set houses of the lower town, defended by a wall, seem to have changed little over the centuries. Founded in the 11C, the town was granted its charter in 1542 by King François I in recognition of its defence against the imperial troops of Charles V. When war broke out between France and Savoie in 1690, Vauban, Louis XIV's foremost military architect, linked the castle and the town with a zig-zag fortified wall, built the main gates and set a ring of battlements around the town.

Nearby Sights: ANNOT, BEUIL, CASTELLANE, Gorges du CIANS, CLUES DE HAUTE-PROVENCE, Val d'ENTRAUNES, Route NAPOLÉON, PUGET-THÉNIERS, ST-JULIEN-DU-VERDON, Vallée de la TINÉE, VILLARS-SUR-VAR

The most famous culinary speciality of the town is "secca d'Entrevaux", thin slices of dried beef, sprinkled with olive oil and a squeeze of lemon.

The walled town and citadel of Entrevaux

★THE WALLED TOWN *30min*

Ramparts ⊘ – The drawbridge of the Porte Royale, flanked by two round towers, leads into the town. The guardroom situated beneath the archway houses the tourist office, from where it is possible to walk along the watch-path linking the three fortified gates: Porte de France, Porte Royale and Porte d'Italie. Near the watch-path are the **medieval gardens** ⊘ which contain exotic and medicinal plants, culinary herbs, vegetables and fruit.

Old town – Three main streets: Haute-Rue, Basse-Rue and rue du Marché, go through the town, linked by a network of cool and dark alleyways. Most of the houses date from the 17C and the 18C.

Cathedral ⊘ – Entrevaux was a bishopric from the 12C to the 1789 Revolution. The present church was built between 1610 and 1627 and subsequently incorporated into the ramparts.
The **interior★** contains a wealth of classical and Baroque decoration. The gilt altarpiece of the high altar has a beautiful 17C painting in its centre, depicting the *Assumption of the Virgin Mary* by Mimault. On either side, note the 17C stalls carved by local craftsmen. On the left-hand wall hangs a *Deposition* believed to be by Jouvenet and, opposite, another *Deposition* by Philippe de Champaigne is said to be a gift from Louis XIV. To the left of the entrance, the retable of St John the Baptist, the patron saint of Entrevaux, and the silver bust of the saint are also noteworthy *(see Introduction: Festivals)*.
The 1717 organ by Jean Eustache was recently restored.

SIGHTS

★**Citadel** ⊘ *1hr* – Perched 135m/443ft above the town, the castle is accessible via a rampart following a zigzag course and strengthened by about 20 fortified towers. The rampart rises from the magazine to the entrance of the castle defended by a redoubt with a drawbridge dating from 1693. *The walk to the top takes about 15min.*
The castle buildings are currently being restored, but it is worth climbing up for the remarkable **views★** of the Var Valley and the roofs of Entrevaux.

Musée de la Moto ⊘ – *Rue Sénéquier*. This small museum houses an interesting collection of motorcycles, all of them in working order; the oldest in the collection dates back to 1901.

Moulin à huile et à farine ⊘ – *Near place Moreau, outside the walled town*.
The flow of the River Chalvagne used to drive the oil and flour mills; one of them still produces oil.

ÉVIAN-LES-BAINS✝✝✝

Population 7 273
Michelin map 328 M2 and 244 fold 9 – Local map see THONON-LES-BAINS

Poetically known as the "pearl of Lake Geneva", Évian is remarkably well situated between the lake and the foothills of the Préalpes du Chablais. This famous spa town is also a lakeside and climatic resort, and during the season, a centre of fashionable entertainment whose influence extends all round the lake.

Opulent public buildings and palace hotels nestling amid greenery are characteristic of this international holiday resort, where taking the waters is not the main preoccupation. Every May, the **Rencontres Musicales** festival selects the best classical string quartet from a field of international performers – music lovers take note!

Nearby Sights: ABONDANCE, AVORIAZ, CHÂTEL, MORZINE, THONON-LES-BAINS YVOIRE

THE SPA TOWN

The nearby town of **Amphion-les-Bains** was the first spa resort of the Chablais region, which became fashionable as early as the 17C, when the dukes of Savoie regularly took the waters. The medicinal properties of Évian water were only discovered in 1789, when a gentleman from Auvergne realised it was dissolving the stones he was suffering from. However, Évian remained a small fortified town until 1865 when the lakeside promenade was built, partly over the water, thanks to Baron de Blonay who bequeathed his castle (situated where the casino now stands) to the town.

The treatment – The baths are open from 1 February to the end of November. Évian water, filtered by sand of glacial origin, is cold (11.6°C/52.8°F) and low in minerals. It is used for drinking and for bathing or showering, in the treatment of kidney or digestive complaints and other disorders which respond to hydrotherapy. Bottled Évian water is one of the main French mineral waters.

ALONG THE SHORE AND ON THE WATER

★ **The Promenade** – The attractive lakeside walk is backed by the **Établissement thermal** (the baths), the **Villa Lumière**, now the town hall, and the **Casino**, three remarkable examples of spa-resort architecture of the late 19C and early 20C.

The new baths are situated in the **Parc thermal**. The pump room, designed by Novarina (who is also responsible for the Palais des Congrès), was erected in 1956 and the Espace Thermal in 1983. This is partly built below ground in order to preserve the appearance of the park.

Beyond the harbour where yachts find a mooring and where the lake's pleasure boats come alongside, the **Jardin anglais** offers a view of the Swiss shore. Large hotels are scattered inland on the lower slopes of the Pays Gavot.

★★★ Lac Léman (Lake Geneva)

Lac Léman, which covers 580km²/224sq mi and reaches depths of 310m/1 017ft, is 13 times larger than the Lac du Bourget; it is France's largest lake, even though almost two-thirds of its total area lies over the Swiss border. Shaped like a crescent, it is 72km/44.7mi long and 13km/8mi wide at its widest point; the narrower part between Geneva and Yvoire is known as the Petit Lac, the more open part as the Grand Lac. A natural phenomenon, known as the **"bataillère"** can be observed from the heights overlooking Montreux on the Swiss side and Meillerie on the French side: the muddy waters of the Rhône flowing into the lake seem to be completely absorbed by the lake. In fact, part of the river flow remains at a depth of 20m/66ft until the temperature drops in autumn and the undercurrent of river water blends into the cooling lake.

The areas bordering the lake enjoy a pleasantly mild microclimate: autumn in the Chablais can be glorious, in spite of frequent mist.

★★★ **Boat trips** ⊘ – The boats of the Compagnie Générale de Navigation link the French and Swiss shores of the lake. From Évian, it is also possible to make a round tour of the lake, to cross over to Lausanne-Ouchy or to go on night excursions (see Admission times and charges).

SIGHTS

Exhibition and Information Centre about Évian water ⊘ – The centre is housed in the former pump room (1905) of the **Cachat spring**, an Art Nouveau building surmounted by a cupola. The spring is named after its owner, who improved the installations in 1824.

Church – This church is characteristic of early Gothic style in Savoie (end of 13C). It was remodelled and restored for the last time in 1865; however, it has retained some of its original capitals and a Burgundy-style wooden Madonna carved in low relief. The sculpture, which dates from 1493, can be seen in the side chapel on the right of the chancel.

Évian and Lake Geneva

Villa Lumière ⊘ – Once owned by Antoine Lumière, father of the cinema pioneer, this grand 1896 villa now houses the town hall; the ground-floor rooms and the **grand staircase★** are especially elegant.

Musée Pré-lude – Tools and everyday objects, on display in a converted barn, give an impression of everyday rural life in the Chablais of the 19C.

Monument de la comtesse de Noailles – *Leave Évian by ③ on the town plan, along N 5.* This small rotunda stands at the bottom of a narrow garden, which once belonged to the famous poetess.

Bottling factory ⊘ – This modern bottling factory, set up in Amphion-les-Bains, produces an average of 5 million litres of water per day, the highest output of any mineral water producer.

EXCURSION – *local map see THONON-LES-BAINS p*

★★ ④ Falaises de Meillerie

FROM ÉVIAN TO NOVEL *23km/14.3mi – about 1hr*

This itinerary takes you into the Franco-Swiss border zone *(see Practical information).*

Évian-les-Bains – *See ÉVIAN-LES-BAINS.*

Leave Évian by ① on the town plan, along the lake shore.

The road is lined with imposing properties and passes beneath a gallery linking the Château de Blonay (16C-19C) to the shore. Beyond Lugrin, the road skirts the foot of the Meillerie cliffs within sight of Montreux on the Swiss shore of the lake, over-looked by the Rochers de Naye.

★**Meillerie** – This fishing village, where Rousseau staged some of the action of his *Nouvelle Héloïse* (1764), nestles around its stocky country church (13C steeple) in a charming **setting★** backed by the most impressive cliffs along Lake Geneva.
At the east end of the village, take the path down to the quayside where fishermen's nets are drying.
Beyond Meillerie, the view extends over the eastern part of the lake and the surrounding summits (Tour d'Aï).

St-Gingolph – This border village has two sets of public monuments apart from the church and the cemetery situated on the French side. The river Morge marks the frontier.
In the 18C, St-Gingolph was held to be one of the largest Swiss towns as young men wishing to enrol in the Swiss regiments of Louis XV's royal guard all claimed to be from the Swiss part of the town.

Follow D 30 to Novel.

Novel – Splendid views of Lake Geneva. The village church has a typical Alpine bell-tower.

Eating out

MODERATE

Le Liberté – *Au Casino –* ☎ *04 50 26 87 50 – 17.38€.* This brasserie on the premises of the casino has its sights set on faraway destinations. Its modern decor features brass and wood in a "seaside" atmosphere. It has attracted a fairly trendy following, keen to sample cooking inspired by the four corners of the earth as well as regional specialities.

La Bernolande – *1 pl. du Port –* ☎ *04 50 70 72 60 – closed during school holidays in Feb and around 1 Nov, Thu Sept-Apr and Wed except Jul-Aug – 18.29/25.76€.* If you have luck and fine weather you will be able to admire the view of the lake and the comings and goings of the ferries between Lausanne and Évian. Homely cuisine. Friendly welcome. Expect to be rubbing shoulder to shoulder with your fellow diners!

Aux Ducs de Savoie – *R. du 23 Juillet 1944 – 74500 St-Gingolph –* ☎ *04 50 76 73 09 – closed 29 Jan-13 Feb, school holidays around 1 Nov, Mon and Tue out of season – 25.15/52.59€.* This trim-looking chalet is a food-lover's paradise. It is popular with Swiss clients who cross the border to come here, and will appeal particularly to meat-eaters. In summer, savour the fresh air on the terrace while enjoying a panoramic view of the lake. Rooms available. Children's menu.

Where to stay

BUDGET

Hôtel Terminus – *32 av. de la Gare –* ☎ *04 50 75 15 07 – 14rms: 30.49/45.73€ -* ☐ *4.57€ – restaurant 12.96/25.15€.* You can get off the train and immediately leave your bags in this hotel with its refurbished rooms. Those on the side of the lake have a balcony, but there aren't enough to go round! The little dining room also has a view. A pleasant, unpretentious place to stay.

MODERATE

Hôtel de France – *59 r. Nationale –* ☎ *04 50 75 00 36 – closed 15 Nov-15 Dec – 45rms: 54.88/67.08€ -* ☐ *5.34€.* This hotel in the main pedestrian street in town has a pretty garden growing on the site of the old palace of the Dukes of Savoie, and charming when the weather is fine. The rooms are light and pretty with modern furniture.

EXPENSIVE

Hôtel Royal – ☎ *04 50 26 85 00 – closed 3 Dec-1 Feb –* ☐ *– 130rms: from 350.02€ -* ☐ *17.99€ – restaurant 45.73/79.27€.* The Royal was a favourite of Edward VII, and of the Aga Khan, and measures up to people's fantasies of a great palace. It was built in 1909, and its Belle Époque decor is enhanced by original furniture in the bedrooms. Admire the frescoes in the Café Royal.

On the town

Casino d'Évian – *Quai Baron-de-Blonay –* ☎ *04 50 26 87 87 – www.casino-evian.tm.fr – Coin-operated slot-machines: daily 10am-2am; traditional gambling: 3pm-2am; Liberté bar: noon-2am, and until 3am on Fri and Sat and during summer.* This internationally famous casino offers the classic range of activities to gambling enthusiasts. Once they have made their fortune, they can quench their thirst in the aptly named Jackpot bar or the Liberté, a bar-restaurant-tea room with a terrace overlooking the lake.

L'Embuscade – *82 r. Nationale –* ☎ *04 50 75 02 08 – daily 8am-1am – closed Mon.* This welcoming bar in the centre of town has rustic mountain decor (stone walls and exposed beams). The niches at the back are a good place to lie in wait for friends. There is a modest but decent cocktail menu.

Le Flash – *Pl. Charles-de-Gaulle –* ☎ *04 50 26 87 20 – May-Sept Wed-Sun 11pm-5am; Oct-Apr Thu-Sun – closed in Jan.* The casino disco comprises a dance floor equipped with light shows and lasers flashing in time to the most up-to-the-minute music. Those in search of waltzes, tangos or the paso doble will prefer the tea dances in the casino.

Shopping

La Cave à Paul – *37 r. Nationale –* ☎ *04 50 75 12 47 – open summer: 8.30am-7.30pm; winter: Mon-Sat 8.30am-12.30pm, 2.30pm-7.30pm, Sun 9am-12.30pm.* Wide selection of regional produce includes local *génépi* (wormwood liqueur), fruit liqueurs (raspberry, bilberry), local wines and a speciality of the house: jars of wine preserve *(confit de vin).*

ÉVIAN-LES-BAINS

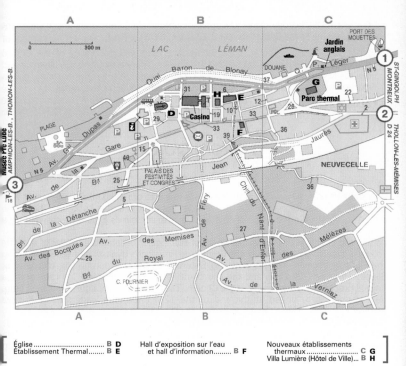

Église .... B D
Établissement Thermal .... B E

Hall d'exposition sur l'eau
et hall d'information .... B F

Nouveaux établissements
thermaux .... C G
Villa Lumière (Hôtel de Ville)... B H

★ 5 Pays Gavot *15km/9.3mi – 1hr 30min.*

The **Pays Gavot**, situated inland from Évian, is a plateau bounded to the south by the Dranse d'Abondance Valley and overlooked in the east by the cliffs of the Pic de Mémise. This open countryside, where woods and pastures predominate, is popular with hikers.

Leave Évian by ② *on the town plan.*

The D 24 rises through a landscape of orchards. Two wide hairpin bends offer fine glimpses of the lake through the woods and give access to Thollon lying beneath the cliffs of the Pic de Mémise.

Thollon-les-Mémises – This resort, which consists of several hamlets overlooking Lake Geneva stretched out 600m/1 968ft below, has become an annexe of Évian, both in summer owing to its fine situation and in winter because of the proximity of the Mémise ski slopes.

★★ Pic de Mémise – Alt 1 677m/5 502ft. *30min there and back on foot.*

The gondola brings visitors up to 1 596m/5 236ft on top of the Mémise cliffs. From there it is possible to reach the cross erected at the highest point and enjoy the **panorama** of the lake and of the Swiss shore from Nyon to Montreux, with the Jura mountains, Vaudois hills and Rochers de Naye in the background.

> The western part of the lake is particularly exposed to winds blowing from the Jura and Alps mountains. The locals give different names to different winds. The *bise*, a northeasterly wind, blows from Switzerland in winter for periods of up to three consecutive days. The *séchard*, an easterly wind blowing along the shore, is appreciated by sailing enthusiasts. The *joran*, a northwesterly wind from the Swiss Jura mountains, brings spectacular storms which create waves several metres high and stops as quickly as it starts. The west wind, which brings rain, is simply called *vent* (wind).

⑥ La Dranse d'Abondance

FROM EVIAN TO ABONDANCE 47km/29mi – allow 2hr

Leave Evian by ② on the town plan and follow D 21 (Route de Thollon)

Bernex – This holiday resort and small mountaineering centre is the starting point of the ascent of the **Dent d'Oche** (alt 2 222m/7 290ft).

From Vacheresse onwards, D 22 follows the deep wooded valley of the Dranse d'Abondance which opens up beyond Abondance. There are quite a few sawmills and chalets in typical local style with large roofs covered with light grey slates, gables marked with a cross and balconies with openwork wooden balustrades.

★ **Abondance** – *See ABONDANCE.*

FORCALQUIER ★

Population 4 302
Michelin map 334 C9 and 245 fold 19

This small Provençal town lies at the heart of a low area of rolling hills, a pretty **site★** bordered by the Montagne de Lure, the River Durance and the Luberon. The town, picturesquely built in the shape of an amphitheatre, surrounds a hill once crowned by a citadel.

At the end of the 11C, the fortified town of Forcalquier became the capital of a *comté* (county) created by a branch of the Comtes de Provence's dynasty and extending along the Durance from Manosque north to Sisteron, Gap and Embrun. The bishopric of Sisteron was split into two and the church of Forcalquier became a "co-cathedral", a unique precedent in the history of the Church. The Comté de Forcalquier and the Comté de Provence were united at the end of the 12C, under the leadership of **Raimond Bérenger V**, the son of the Gersende de Sabran, Duchess of Forcalquier and Alfonso II of Provence. The two territories were eventually bequeathed to the French crown in 1481. Today, Forcalquier is a thriving agricultural and industrial centre and a lively little town where one of the most important markets in the area takes place on Mondays. It is also a busy tourist centre and the starting point for several excursions. In addition, jazz and classical music concerts and localcraft fairs are held every summer *(see Practical information: Calendar of events)*.

Nearby Sights: CÉRESTE, Vallée de la Moyenne DURANCE, Monastère de GANAGOBIE, GRÉOUX-LES-BAINS, MANE, MANOSQUE, MONTBRUN-LES– BAINS, Route NAPOLÉON, RIEZ, SISTERON, Plateau de VALENSOLE

THE OLD TOWN

Église Notre-Dame – This former "co-cathedral" offers an interesting contrast between the Romanesque character of its massive rectangular tower and the slender appearance of its steeple crowned by a lantern. A lofty nave with a roof of broken-barrel vaulting, in typical Provençal Romanesque style, dates from the same period as the transept and the chancel which, built some time before 1217, are the oldest examples of Gothic style in southern France. The aisles were added in the 17C, as was the magnificent organ.

Cité comtale – The **Porte des Cordeliers** gate with its two pointed arches decorated with a torus is all that remains of the town's fortifications and marks the beginning of the medieval town. The narrow streets lined with tall houses were laid out to offer the best protection from the cold north-westerly wind or *mistral*. Many of the houses are in poor repair, but others have kept their paired windows and Gothic, Classical or Renaissance doorways. Walk along rue des Cordeliers leading to rue Passère and rue Bérenger then across place du Palais to Grande-Rue. A lovely 16C **Renaissance fountain**, in the shape of a pyramid crowned by St Michael slaying the dragon, decorates place St-Michel. Rue Mercière leads to place du Bourguet at the heart of the city.

Terrasse Notre-Dame-de-Provence – Rue St-Mary leads up to the site of the citadel where very little remains of the counts of Forcalquier's castle; below are the ruins of a tower which belonged to St Mary's Church, the town's first cathedral. Note the set of **bells** which the ringer plays with his fists *(concert on Sundays at 11.30am)*. A 19C octagonal chapel dedicated to Notre-Dame-de-Provence stands at the top where the splendid **panorama★** embraces the Forcalquier Basin and the surrounding mountains *(viewing table)*; there is a bird's-eye view of the town just below.

★ **Cemetery** – *Leave the town centre north along D 16 and turn left 200m/218yd further on.* A superb central staircase leads to the lower part of the cemetery with its striking clipped yew alleys.

Eating out

BUDGET

L'Aïgo Blanco – *5 pl. Vieille* – ☎ *04 92 75 27 23* – *closed Mon evening and Tue in winter* – *12.81/27.90€*. Behind the church of Notre-Dame, at the heart of the old town, is this eatery renovated in pretty Provençal colours. It offers generous portions of regional fare without any fuss or complication, at very reasonable prices.

MODERATE

Le Lapin Tant Pis – *10 av. St-Promasse* – ☎ *04 92 75 38 88* – *starbrightpacific@libertysurf.fr* – *closed Oct-Mar and lunchtime* – ✍ – *reservations compulsory* – *25.92/30.49€*. This restaurant, which was extremely popular and successful in the old town, has moved to new premises. The dining room is now housed in old stables. The cooking is as good as ever and concentrates on locally grown produce.

Where to stay

BUDGET

Chambre d'hôte Campagne "Le Paradis" – *Rte de Villeneuve on D 16 and D 216* – ☎ *04 92 75 37 33* – ✍ – *4rms: 38.11/44.21€*. Everything evokes the past life of this farm, from the horse's manger to old photos to the barn, so the modern appearance of the guestrooms may come as something of a shock. There is always the option of one of the gîtes decorated in Provençal colours and with traditional furniture.

MODERATE

Auberge Charembeau – *4km/2.5mi E of Forcalquier on N 100 and a minor road* – ☎ *04 92 70 91 70* – *closed 16 Nov-14 Feb.* – 🅿 – *24rms: 50.31/77.75€* - 🛏 *7.17€*. This 18C farm in the middle of seven hectares (17 acres) of fields and hills has been restored in the Provençal tradition and has all sorts of attractive features: comfort, character, greenery, peace and quiet. Unfortunately there is no restaurant here, but there are one or two rooms with kitchen facilities. Swimming pool and tennis court.

Chambre d'hôte Jas des Nevières – *Rte de St-Pierre* – *04300 Pierrerue 6km/4mi E of Forcalquier on D 12 then D 212* – ☎ *04 92 75 24 99* – *http://pro.wanadoo.fr/philippe.duermael* – ✍ – *4rms: 45.73/53.36€*. This old sheep farm in this hamlet has been restored with great care and is now a haven of peace. Rooms are tastefully decorated in an understated style and exude genuine sophistication. The terrace and swimming pool offer the chance to relax to the tune of the cicadas.

SIGHTS

Couvent des Cordeliers ⊘ – Franciscan friars, known as Cordeliers because they wore a knotted cord round the waist, settled in Forcalquier in 1236, probably at the invitation of Raimond Bérenger V. Their monastery, one of the first of its kind in Provence, was occupied until the 18C. The badly damaged 13C and 14C buildings were remarkably well restored in the 1960s.

The cloister was at the centre of the monastery. Several funeral recesses on the southwest and southeast sides were used as graves for the lords of Forcalquier. Note the graceful twin windows framing a Romanesque door on the side of the chapter-house. Part of the buildings can be visited: the library with its original ceiling, the scriptorium, the oratory (15C Virgin Mary with Child) and the refectory divided into three rooms.

Museum ⊘ – Housed in a former 17C convent, the museum contains utensils and decorative objects from the area (old tools, antique furniture, earthenware from Moustiers, Apt and Mane), a fine collection of coins and local archaeological finds.

NEARBY SIGHTS

★ **St-Michel-l'Observatoire** – This pleasant old village built on a hillside is famous for its observatory, whose cupolas shine beneath the clearest skies in France. Narrow streets lead to the elegant, white **Église haute** crowning the hill. From the terrace of this 12C "upper church" there is a fine **view** of the area around Forcalquier, of the Montagne de Lure and of the Luberon. St Peter's Church, the **Église basse** at heart of the village, was built in the 13C and 14C by the counts of Anjou who ruled Provence at the time. The pediment of the doorway is framed by a pointed archivolt. In the apse, there is a beautiful 15C wooden crucifix.

FORCALQUIER

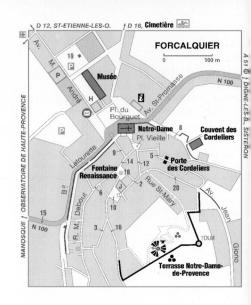

Chapelle St-Paul – *1km/0.6mi south along D 105.* Note the massive columns sur-mounted by Corinthian capitals, which belonged to a 12C priory.

★**Observatoire de Haute-Provence** ⊙ – *North of the village along D 305. Visit: 1hr. Visitors must climb 60 steps.* The location of the observatory in St-Michel was justified by the quality of the air in the Forcalquier region. There are 14 cupolas containing astro-nomical instruments (among the largest in Europe), laboratories, workshops and living quarters. Many astronomers from France and other countries work here.

One of the telescopes, which has a diameter of 1.93m/6.5ft, was built with the latest electronic refinements and allowed researchers to identify the **first planet outside the solar system**. Spectrographs analyse light from the stars, thus establishing their chem-ical components, their temperature and their radial speed. A team of geophysicists is studying the upper strata of the atmosphere by means of laser sounding.

The **Centre d'Astronomie de St-Michel** ⊙ on the Plateau du Moulin à Vent organises themed presentations and night-time observations directed by experts.

From the entrance of the observatory, a path on the right leads to the modest but charming 11C **Chapelle St-Jean-des-Fuzils**, tiled with the traditional schist slabs known as *lauzes*.

EXCURSION

The Montagne de Lure and the Pays de Contadour

FROM FORCALQUIER TO SISTERON *64km/39.8mi – about 2hr – see Vallée de la Moyenne DURANCE.* [2]

Pays de Forcalquier

FROM FORCALQUIER TO BANON – *77km/47.8mi – allow 3hr*

This rich rural area, in striking contrast with the austere surrounding plateaux and Montagne de Lure, is dotted with charming hilltop villages, most facing east or south to shelter from the north-westerly wind.

From Forcalquier, follow N 100 towards Manosque.

★**Mane** – *See MANE.*

Turn onto D 13 then left 4.5km/2.8mi further on towards St-Maime.

St-Maime – A few ruins and the castle chapel overlooking the village are the only remains of the Comtes de Provence's castle, in which the four daughters of Raimond Bérenger V were brought up in the traditional way *(see FORCALQUIER).*

Return to D 13 and cross it to reach Dauphin.

Dauphin – Built on another hilltop facing St-Maime, Dauphin has retained part of its 14C fortifications, its medieval streets and its keep, crowned by a balustrade and a statue of the Virgin Mary; from the top there is a wide open **view** of the surrounding area.

Follow D 5 and cross N 100.

★ **St-Michel-l'Observatoire** – *See above.*

Follow D 105 south.

Chapelle St-Paul – *See above.*

Turn right onto D 205.

Lincel – This village, which nestles in a fold, has retained a small Romanesque church and a castle with a few 16C features.

Cross N 100, continue along D 105, then turn right onto D 907 and left towards Montfuron.

Montfuron – Fine restored **windmill** ⊙. From the village, **view** of the heights of Haute-Provence to the northeast and of the Ste-Victoire Mountain to the southwest.

Return to D 907 and turn left; drive across N 100 and follow D 14.

Reillanne – This village is built on the side of a hill crowned by the 18C Chapelle St-Denis, which replaced the castle; avenue Long-Barri leads past the Portail des Forges (all that remains of the castle) to the viewing table: panoramic **view** of the old village, of the Ste-Victoire Mountain to the south and Luberon to the west.

Continue along D 14 and make a detour to Vachères.

Vachères – This old hilltop village acquired fame when the statue of a Gallo-Roman warrior, now in the Calvet Museum in Avignon, was discovered nearby. The local museum or **Musée communal** ⊙ is housed in the village school; It contains archeological finds going back to prehistoric times, including flint, axes and a copy of the famous **Vachères warrior**, as well as fossils discovered locally.

From Notre-Dame-de-Bellevue on D 14, take a small road to Oppedette.

Oppedette – This tastefully restored hamlet overlooks the Gorges d'Oppedette, 2.5km/1.5mi long and 120m/394ft deep in places, through which flows the Calavon. There is a fine **view★** from the viewpoint near the cemetery; a marked path, starting beneath the viewpoint, leads to the bottom of the gorge.

Continue along D 201 and turn left onto D 18 at Carniol.

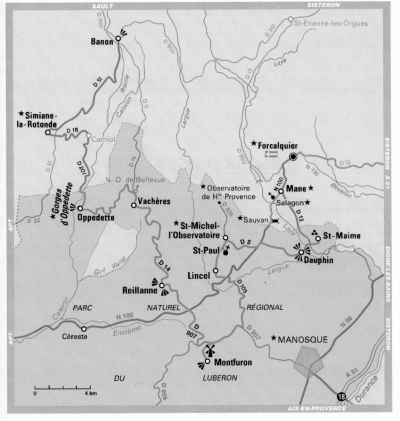

Gargoyle in the Rotonde

★**Simiane-la-Rotonde** – This is one of the loveliest hilltop villages in Haute-Provence; perched on the edge of the Plateau d'Albion, it overlooks vast fields of mauve lavender. Above the tall houses stands the Rotonde, which is all that remains of the castle of the Sault family.

The **Rotonde** ⓒ★ is the late-12C castle keep, of which the glacis is the only part visible from the outside. The interior is on two floors; on the upper level, there are 12 recesses in Rayonnant Gothic style, separated by pilasters with carved capitals, and below, 12 ribs supporting a cupola with central oculus. A festival of ancient music takes place in summer. The houses lining the steep village streets have retained 17C and 18C carved doors. The **church** dates from the 16C, and there is a fine **view** of the Forcalquier region from the covered **market**.

Continue along D 51 to Banon.

Banon – A 14C **fortified gate** and the restored medieval hospital can be seen at the top of the old village, which overlooks the new one; from the east end of the church there is a pleasant **view** of the tiled roofs backed by the Montagne de Lure. A tasty goat's cheese wrapped in chestnut leaves has been named after Banon.

HIKE

★**Gorges d'Oppedette** – *About 3hr on foot from the viewpoint marked by a metal balustrade. Handrails guide visitors through difficult places. It is not advisable to go on this hike after a storm or when the weather is uncertain. There is no water available on the way. Hikers need a good sense of balance.*

🚶 Follow the yellow markings; after three handrail-assisted sections, it is possible to return to the village along the blue-marked path on the left, or to carry on down along the yellow-marked path on the right to the bottom of the gorge dotted with pools (known as *gours*) and potholes. The caves in the cliffsides can be spotted at intervals. Beware of slippery surfaces as you go round the numerous *gours*. The path then runs beneath the bridge carrying the road and climbs up to the end of the gorge. Beyond the bridge, follow the yellow-marked path on the left leading to the GR footpath, which leads through the *garrigue* (scrub) and offers fine views of the gorge. Return to the viewpoint along the surfaced road.

Vallée de FREISSINIÈRES★

Michelin map 334 H4 and 244 fold 42

This small valley, "hanging" 200m/656ft above the River Durance and hidden behind reddish-ochre rocks typical of Mediterranean landscapes, is in fact an Alpine U-shaped valley scoured by a glacier, with a flat floor and contrasting sides: the south-facing *adret* dotted with houses and crops and the north-facing *ubac* covered with larch and pine woods.

The municipality of Freissinières includes 13 hamlets which reflect the importance of sheep-farming in the area: sheep are kept in the vaulted basement of traditional houses, the upper floors being used as living quarters and for storing hay.

Nearby Sights: L'ARGENTIÈRE-LA-BESSÉE, BRIANÇON, Le BRIANÇONNAIS, CEILLAC, EMBRUN, GUILLESTRE, MOLINES-EN-QUEYRAS, MONT-DAUPHIN, MONTGENÈVRE, Le QUEYRAS, SERRE-CHEVALIER, La VALLOUISE, VARS

EXCURSION

From St-Crépin to Dormillouse *25km/15.5mi – about 3hr*

St-Crépin – This village stands on top of a pink marble rock spur barring the Durance Valley. Note the beautiful doorway of the **church** and the bell-tower surmounted by a spire and four corner pinnacles.

Cross the River Durance and follow D 38.

The road rises along a stony slope dotted with juniper bushes and tufts of lavender. Low stone walls are a reminder of the days when these slopes were covered with crops; the view covers the Guillestre Basin and Mont-Dauphin standing on top of its promontory.

★ **Gouffre de Gourfouran** – *30min there and back on foot. Access is difficult and caution is recommended. Leave the car 500m/547yd beyond the hamlet of Le Chambon. Follow the path to a pile of stones. From there, walk across the fields to a rocky promontory overlooking the chasm and the Durance Valley.* The River Biaisse, which flows through the Freissinières Valley, joins the Durance Valley via a 100m/328ft-deep gorge with sheer sides of a striking reddish colour.

In Freissinières, take the road which climbs up the south-facing slope.

From Les Roberts, there is an overall view of the valley blocked by the rocky knoll of Pallon.

Return to D 238

The valley narrows beyond Freissinières. The road leads on through **Les Viollins** (old Protestant church) to the end of the valley, where a number of waterfalls flow together into the Biaisse.

★ **Dormillouse** – *1hr 30min there and back on foot.*
🚶 The path leads to a group of houses, some of which are inhabited in summer. Note the small Protestant church and the restored water-mill *(the path continues to the Col de Freissinières).*

The Rise and Fall of Dormillouse

In winter, Dormillouse has only one resident, yet this valley was once the centre of Protestant life in the area. The remoteness of the valley made it a natural refuge for renegades or dissidents during the long period of religious persecution. Followers of the Waldensian sect, who settled here and in the neighbouring Vallouise *(see La VALLOUISE)* as early as the 13C, were joined by Huguenots in the 16C and the Col de Freissinières became a busy route. In the 19C, **Félix Neff**, a young clergyman from Geneva, came to the area and founded a teachers' training-college in Dormillouse in order to help the local population.

HIKES

★ **Sentier des alpages** – *5hr, no major difficulty; a car is needed to go back. Water is available on the way. Departure from "Champs-Queyras", just before the hamlet of Les Aujards (alt 1 568m/5 144ft). Destination is Dourmillouse (accommodation available).*
🚶 This long hike on the south-facing slope makes use of the old footpaths linking the high-pasture hamlets and overlooking the Fressinières Valley and the River Biaisse. The path climbs to Les Garcines then crosses several streams just above the tree line. Beyond Les Allibrands, the path overlooks the chalets at La Got before reaching Dormillouse. You are likely to see samples of the rich local fauna: chamois, marmots, falcons, black redstarts and – if you are lucky – golden eagles. The itinerary also offers the opportunity of observing the results of the geological upheavals in the area: spectacular folds of sandstone alternating with black schist can clearly be seen from Les Allibrands on the opposite slope.

Grotte des Vaudois and Via ferrata de Freissinières – *Leave the car in the car park at the entrance of Les Roberts. 1hr on foot along a stony steep path.*
🚶 In the 15C, this cave was the refuge of followers of the Waldensian sect, pursued by members of the Inquisition.
The Via ferrata de Freissinières, the oldest in France, is well equipped and safe for beginners, in spite of some vertiginous sections; the course offers aerial views which should delight lovers of heights *(see Practical information: Rock-climbing).*

Route du GALIBIER★★★

Michelin map 333 L7 to M8 and 244 fold 42

This road, one of the most famous in the French Alps, linking the Maurienne (the Arc Valley, *see La MAURIENNE)* and the Briançonnais *(see Le BRIANÇONNAIS)*, offers the possibility of driving through an austere and totally unspoilt mountain area. The panorama unfolding from the Col du Galibier is one of the finest in France, particularly in the early morning or late afternoon.
The itinerary starts with a steep climb from the Arc Valley to the wooded "hanging" valley of the Valloirette, a tributary of the Arc. As the road continues to rise in a series of dizzying curves, the landscape begins to look bleak, then utterly grim. The Écrins Massif comes into view beyond the Col du Galibier, a particularly impressive sight in the first or last hours of daylight.

The Route du Galibier; a real test for the iron men of *"Le Tour"*

The route du Galibier is well known to cyclists as one of the most challenging stages of the Tour de France. This highlight of the sporting calendar, which borders on a national obsession, began in June 1903, with cyclists competing over a six-stage circuit of 2 500km/1 553mi.

Nearby Sights: L'ALPE-D'HUEZ, AUSSIOS, Le BOURG-D'OISANS, BRIANÇON, Le BRIANÇONNAIS, Route de la CROIX-DE-FER, Les DEUX-ALPES, Route DES GRANDES ALPES, La GRAVE, La Haute MAURIENNE, MODANE, L'OISANS, ST-JEAN-DE-MAURIENNE, SERRE-CHEVALIER

EXCURSIONS

From St-Michel-de-Maurienne to the Col Du Lautaret

41km/25.5mi – about 3hr. The Col du Galibier is blocked by snow from October to late May (sometimes until July).

The road rising to the Col du Télégraphe affords views of the escarpments of the Croix des Têtes towering over the narrow basin of St-Michel-de-Maurienne, with the Grand Perron des Encombres (alt 2 825m/9 268ft) behind it and, in the distance, the Péclet-Polset glaciers.

★ **Col du Télégraphe** – Alt 1 566m/5 138ft. *There is a car park.* Climb to the top of the rocky knoll, on the north side, to get a bird's-eye **view** of the Arc Valley. Between the pass and Valloire, the road overlooks the Valloirette rushing through steep gorges towards the River Arc.

✳ **Valloire** – Conveniently situated between the Parc national de la Vanoise and the Parc national des Écrins, Valloire is the main tourist centre of the Maurienne region. It lies at the foot of the Rocher St-Pierre, which partly blocks the Valloirette Valley, and marks the transition between two typical Alpine landscapes: downriver, a wooded coomb and, upriver, a desolate corridor of pastureland with scree-covered slopes. Dating mainly from the 17C, the Baroque **church** ⊘ is one of the most richly decorated in the Savoie region; note in particular the gilded-wood **retable**★★ over the high altar showing St Peter on the right and St Thècle, born in Valloire in the 6C, on the left. The calvary above the vestry door, dating from 1609, is believed to be a copy of Albrecht Dürer's *Christ*.

Beyond Valloire, there are clear views of the barren Grand Galibier Summit. As the road rises from Plan Lachat to the pass, it offers superb views of the Valloirette Valley in the distance.

Valloire is a well-equipped ski resort with a variety of slopes. There is a choice of red and black runs for experienced skiers in the Colérieux, Grandes Drozes and Plan Palais areas. An impressive battery of snow-cannon ensures adequate snow cover in all weather conditions. In addition, there are 40km/25mi of cross-country ski trails and the ski area is linked to that of Valmenier.

★★★ **Col du Galibier** – The road no longer goes through a tunnel but over the pass (alt 2 646m/8 681ft) which is the highest point of the **Route des Grandes Alpes** after the Col de l'Iseran (alt 2 770m/9 088ft). *Leave the car and walk up (15min there and back)*

to the viewing table (alt 2 704m/8 871ft); nearby is an old boundary stone marking the border between France and Savoie. The splendid **panoramic view** includes the Aiguilles d'Arves and Mont Thabor to the north and the glaciers and snow-capped peaks of the Écrins Massif to the south.

At the north end of the old tunnel stands a monument to Henri Desgranges, the chief editor of the sports newspaper *L'Auto* who organised the first Tour de France.

Continue to the Col de Lautaret *(see Oisans, ②)*. There is a magnificent **view★★★** of the Meije and the Glacier de l'Homme (Massif des Ecrins).

HIKE

★★**Pic Blanc du Galibier** – Alt 2 955m/9 695ft. *This 3hr hike is only suitable for experienced hikers. Difference in altitude: 400m/1 312ft; climbing boots recommended.*
🚶 Leave the car at the southern exit of the old tunnel and follow the marked path across the fields, aiming for a round summit on the left which it is advisable to climb on its left side *(steep climb)*: remarkable **panorama★★** of the Meije and Mont Thabor. *People inclined to feel dizzy are advised to turn back here.*

The itinerary continues along a path following the narrow mountain ridge *(dangerous in wet conditions)*. The ascent to the summit of the Pic Blanc du Galibier is very steep but well worth it for the exceptional **panorama★★★**: Pic des Trois Évêchés and Aiguilles d'Arves in the foreground, Mont Thabor and the snow-capped peaks of the Vanoise to the northeast, Mont Blanc and the Grandes Jorasses further away.

On the way back, follow a narrow path on the left leading to the viewing table near the pass, then bear right to return to the car park.

Monastère de GANAGOBIE★
Michelin map 334 D9 and 245 fold 20
Local map see Vallée de la Moyenne DURANCE

The monastery stands on a remarkable site, on top of the Ganagobie Plateau, surrounded by broom, pines, holm oaks and lavender. The thousand year-old building, which was restored and re-inhabited in the 19C, houses one of the finest mosaics in the West.

Nearby Sights: CÉRESTE, DIGNE-LES-BAINS, Préalpes de DIGNE, Vallée de la Moyenne DURANCE, FORCALQUIER, GRÉOUX-LES-BAINS, MANE, MANOSQUE, Route NAPOLÉON, SISTERON, Plateau de VALENSOLE

BACKGROUND

The presence of megaliths shows that the site was already inhabited in prehistoric times. From its medieval past it has retained the traces of a walled village (Villevieille), abandoned in the 15C, the remains of a Carolingian chapel and above all the Monastère de Ganagobie. The bishop of Sisteron was the first to found a community on the site back in the 10C but the present **monastery** was built in the 12C by monks of the Cluniac order. In the 14C, 15 monks worked on the land and in the forest, but 200 years later the buildings were practically abandoned; they were restored in the 17C. Following the 1789 Revolution, the church was saved just in time by the local people who decided to use it as their parish church. Today, the church and the monastery buildings, which are partly used by Benedictine monks, are being restored.

Mosaic from Ganagobie
showing St George slaying the dragon

Lonchamps Delahaye/CNMHS

TOUR ⏱ 30min

Church – The decoration of the **doorway★** is the most noticeable feature of the façade. The pointed arches are separated by stone festoons which also surround the door; on the tympanum, a formal, rather stern Christ in Glory contrasts with the freer representations of the adoring angels and the symbols of the Evangelists. The 12 apostles decorate the lintel.

The single nave, covered with broken barrel vaulting, is prolonged by a double transept and an oven-vaulted central apse. The carved ornamentation is extremely plain since the church was decorated with frescoes (only a few traces remain) as well as polychrome **mosaics★★** in the chancel and transept, which date from the mid-12C and denote a strong Byzantine influence. It is easy to see how the rich tapestries brought back from the Crusades could have provided the inspiration for these designs. Elegant tracery patterns frame a menagerie of mythical animals; note in particular St George slaying the dragon.

WALKING NEARBY

VIEWPOINTS FROM THE PLATEAU

The **Allée des Moines** leads from the left of the church to the edge of the plateau offering an aerial **view★★** of the Durance Valley, the Valensole Plateau and the Préalpes de Digne, with the high Alpine mountains in the distance.

In the opposite direction, the **Allée de Forcalquier** leads to the western edge of the plateau; from this point, the **view★** extends to the Forcalquier Basin and the Montagne de Lure. Megaliths still stand on the left of the path; on the right, hollows cut into the rock mark the site of prehistoric dwellings.

Where to stay and Eating out

MODERATE

Hôtel Le Séminaire – *04700 Lurs – 7km/4mi S of the monastery on D 30 –* ☎ *04 92 79 94 19 – closed Dec, Jan and Mon lunchtime – 16rms: 49.55/68.60€ -* ☕ *8.38€ – restaurant 19.82/30.49€.* This stone building used to be a seminary and now has a pretty garden adjoining it, sloping down to the swimming pool. The rooms are functional and non-smoking only. The food is unpretentious and served in the pleasant vaulted dining room or on the shaded terrace.

GAP★

Population 36 262
Michelin map 334 E5 and 245 fold 7

The liveliest commercial town of the southern Alps lies in a basin, at the heart of wooded farmland and at the intersection of two major roads, the Route Napoléon (Grasse to Grenoble) and D 994 (Valence to Briançon).

There are few architectural traces of Gap's ancient past as the town was destroyed on several occasions, in particular during the Wars of Religion and in 1692 when the troops of Amedée of Savoie laid waste to the centre. However, Gap has retained the general plan of a medieval city with its narrow twisting lanes, now turned into pleasant pedestrian streets with a touch of Mediterranean flair.

The main administrative town of the Hautes-Alpes *département* is also a cathedral town and the headquarters of the Parc national des Écrins. As a tourist centre, it takes advantage of its situation near the Lac de Serre-Ponçon, the cross-country skiing area of Col Bayard and ski resorts such as Orcières-Merlette.

Nearby Sights: Pays du BUËCH, Le CHAMPSAUR, Le DÉVOLUY, EMBRUN, MONTMAUR, Route NAPOLÉON, Lac de SERRE-PONÇON, SISTERON, Le VALGAUDEMAR

WALKING ABOUT

★**The old town** – Few traces of the original medieval architecture remain, but the pattern of streets has changed little over the centuries. The pedestrian area, lined with brightly coloured houses and shopfronts, comes alive with the bustle of shoppers during the Saturday market.

Cathedral – The 19C passion for Historicism was given full rein in this fusion of neo-Romanesque and neo-Gothic styles. Note the use of white, red and grey stone from the area, reminiscent of Embrun's cathedral, and step back to admire the 77m/253ft spire.

Hotel de Ville – The town hall has retained its fine 18C façade, emblazoned with the civic coat of arms.

Eating out

BUDGET

Salon de thé Gondre-L'Ambroisine – *R. du Col.-Roux* – ☎ *04 92 53 74 74* – *closed end Sept-mid Oct, Mon in winter and Sun afternoon in Jul-Aug* – *4.57/12.20€*. This is a mecca for food-lovers who will find it hard to resist the pastries and dainty titbits, generous salads, quiches and puff-pastry slices... All these are served in a freshly refurbished dining room.

Le Tourton des Alpes – *1 r. des Cordiers* – ☎ *04 92 53 90 91* – *12.96/17.53€*. This is a must for discovering a local speciality! *Tourton* is a sort of fritter filled with various ingredients, and this establishment is dedicated to it. So do not hesitate to go down the few steps to take a place at table in this old vaulted cellar.

Laiterie du Col Bayard – *05500 Laye* – *10km/6mi N of Gap by N 85* – ☎ *04 92 50 50 06* – *closed 15 Nov-24 Dec, Tue lunchtime, Wed lunchtime, Thu lunchtime and Mon except school holidays* – *12.96/30.18€*. Go for a bit of a climb! This cheese restaurant is just off the beaten track, and also includes a shop selling local produce and a cheese-making business that can be visited: all this under one roof.

MODERATE

Le Fameux Café du Lycée – *41 bd de la Libération* – ☎ *04 92 51 53 36* – *closed Tue except Jul-Aug* – *20.58/38.11€*. Choose your floor: on the ground floor is a brasserie with ornamental woodwork and family portraits; in the basement is a meeting point for a younger clientele with a commensurately lively, smoky atmosphere; and on the first floor are a couple of lounges. This is a friendly restaurant in which to eat at any time of day or night.

Where to stay

BUDGET

Hôtel de la Paix – *1 pl. F.-Euzières* – ☎ *04 92 51 03 29* – *23rms: 22.87/39.64€* - ⌒ *5.03€*. This homely hotel offers simple well-kept rooms which are in great demand, even those on the fourth floor which do not have their own bathroom. The clientele is largely young people. Friendly welcome.

Hôtel Porte Colombe – *4 pl. F.-Euzières* – ☎ *04 92 51 04 13* – 🅿 – *27rms: 36.59/53.36€* - ⌒ *5.79€* – *restaurant 19.06/33.54€*. This hotel right near the town centre pedestrian zone has fresh-looking soundproofed rooms. The restaurant offers generous portions of well-presented fare, rounded off by delicious desserts. Panoramic terrace on the top floor.

MODERATE

Chambre d'hôte Le Parlement – *At Charance* – *4km/2.5mi NW of Gap on D 994 and a track to the right* – ☎ *04 92 53 94 20* – *bruno.drouillard@wanadoo.fr* – *6rms: 54.88/76.22€*. This house in its leafy setting is really cute. It occupies the outbuildings of the neighbouring château. Large sophisticated rooms, sauna, pool table, swimming pool and children's playroom all add up to a delightful place to stay.

On the town

Place Jean-Marcellin – *Pl. Jean-Marcellin* – Summer and winter alike, Place Marcellin and its numerous bars attract a large throng. Musical entertainment, themed evenings, karaoke and long terraces where you can sit and have a drink. The range of attractions on offer is considerable and makes for an enjoyable evening out.

Show time

Café Musique – *1 r. de la Cathédrale* – ☎ *04 92 52 34 17* – *Thu-Sat 9pm-2am* This café might look fairly commonplace as you come along the Rue de la Cathédrale, but it certainly has some surprises in store for those out for an evening stroll. Every Friday evening there is a concert, usually blues, jazz or rock. There is a café-theatre evening every 4 weeks which generally ends in an enormous karaoke session. The artistic director is none other than the local baker!

Sport

Stade Nautique de Fontreyne – 🖾 – *Rte de Marseille* – ☎ *04 92 51 14 99* – *open daily 10am-7.30pm in summer* This swimming complex has plenty to offer children, happily without neglecting their parents. The kids will love the two pools that are reserved for them, and especially the water chute; the grown-ups can enjoy the Olympic size open-air swimming pool and diving pool. In rainy weather the covered pool comes to the rescue. Tennis and miniature golf by the stadium.

SIGHTS

★ **Musée départemental** ◯ – Situated inside the public gardens of La Pépinière, this museum houses fine archaeological collections and antique earthenware.

Among the local finds in the archaeology section (basement) are a **double bust of Jupiter Ammon★**, the **stele★** of Briançon, a Roman bas-relief from the 2C and some remarkable pieces of **jewellery★** dating from the late Bronze Age.

A whole floor is devoted to fine collections of ceramics, mainly from Manisès (15C-18C), Nevers and Moustiers.

The **display of local ethnography★** illustrates traditional daily life in the Queyras region from the 17C onwards, with carved **furniture★★** and beautifully decorated objects. The third level houses an important collection of European painting from the 14C Italian school to French artists of the 19C. Other rooms are devoted to Alpine fauna, arms and armour and temporary exhibitions.

EXCURSIONS

★ **VIEWS OF GAP** *21km/13mi – about 1hr*

From Gap, drive west along D 994.

★ **Gap basin viewing table** – *1.5km/0.9mi, above a sharp bend to the right.*
Wide **view★** of the Gap Basin, extending to the summits along the Italian border (Brec de Chambeyron) in the east and to the mountains lying south of the Écrins Massif (Vieux Chaillol, Sirac) in the north.

At La Freissinouse, turn left onto D 47 then right beyond the railway line onto D 19 past an artificial lake. Turn left to Pelleautier 2km/1.2mi further on.

Beyond Pelleautier, there is a fine view of the Gap Basin and the Durance Valley.

Continue along D 47 then take N 85 back to Gap.

NOTRE-DAME DU LAUS *23km – about 1hr*

From Gap, drive south towards Valserres then turn left onto D 11 and left again onto D 211. The hamlet of Laus has been a place of pilgrimage since 1664, when a young shepherdess called **Benoîte Rencurel** (1647-1718) had visions of the Virgin Mary. A church was built in 1666 with a chapel marking the spot where the vision appeared.

Les GETS✳

Michelin map 328 N4 and 244 fold 9 – see local map CLUSES

Unswayed by modish Morzine or futuristic Avoriaz, this little village has made it a point of honour to keep its authentic character and its restful, rural way of life. The well-equipped, family-friendly pistes are linked to **Les Portes du Soleil**; cross-country skiers can choose from 6 loops covering 20km/12.4mi in total.

Nearby Sights: AVORIAZ, CLUSES, Route des GRANDES ALPES, MORZINE, La ROCHE-SUR-FORON, Bassin de SALLANCHES, SAMOËNS, SIXT-FER-À-CHEVAL, THONON-LES-BAINS

THE MUSEUM

Musée de la Musique mécanique ◯ – The 16C former "Maison des Soeurs" is now devoted to all forms of mechanical music; an interesting collection includes barrel organs, music boxes, player pianos, gramophones and orchestrions, as well as automata and animated scenes. There are also five reconstructions of environments connected with music: a music room, a fairground, a bistro in 1900, a street and a concert hall.

HIKE

★★ **Mont Chéry** ◯ – Alt 1 827m/5 994ft. *10min gondola and chairlift ride or 2.5km/1.5mi by road to the Col de l'Encrenaz then 1hr 30min there and back on foot.*

▣ A vast **panorama★★** of the limestone Faucigny mountains; the peaks in view are, from left to right, the Pointe de Nantaux, the Hautforts, at 2 464m/8 084ft the highest point in the Chablais, the Dents du Midi, Haut-Faucigny, Ruan, Buet, the Points de Sales with Mont-Blanc beyond, the Désert de Plate *(see CLUSES, ▣)*, Pointe Percée and the Pic de Marcelly.

Route des GRANDES ALPES ★★★

Michelin maps 332, 334, 340, 341 or 244 and 245

The Route des Grandes Alpes is the most renowned of the great routes crossing the French Alps. It links Lake Geneva with the Riviera via a road which follows the line of the peaks, often running alongside the border, and is only fully open at the height of summer. The challenge of crossing the French Alps along their entire length, from Lake Geneva to the Mediterranean, was taken up by the Touring Club de France in 1909. Tremendous difficulties along some sections of the route meant that the project continued for over a quarter of a century.

In 1934, mountain troops opened three passes until then inaccessible to tourists: the Col de la Cayolle, Col de l'Izoard (where an obelisk stands as a reminder of their achievement) and Col de Vars.

In 1937, the President of the Republic inaugurated the completed route from Évian to Nice, a journey which coaches took five whole days to cover.

Nearby Sights: L'ARGENTIÈRE-LA-BESSÉE, Massif des ARAVIS, Les ARCS, AUSSOIS, BARCELONNETTE, BEAUFORT, BESSANS, BEUIL, BONNEVAL-SUR-ARC, BOURG-ST-MAURICE, BRIANÇON, Le BRIANÇONNAIS, Gorges du CIANS, La CLUSAZ, CLUSES, EMBRUN, Val d'ENTRAUNES, Route du GALIBIER, Les GETS, La GRAVE, GUILLESTRE, Route de l'ISERAN, La Haute MAURIENNE, MODANE, MOLINES-EN-QUEYRAS, Route du MONT-CENIS, MONT-DAUPHIN, MORZINE, L'OISANS, Le QUEYRAS, Lac de SERRE-PONÇON, ST-VÉRAN, La TARENTAISE, THONON-LES-BAINS, TIGNES, Vallée de la TINÉE, L'UBAYE, VAL-D'ALLOS, VAL-D'ISÈRE, Massif de la VANOISE, VARS

Two-day itinerary

It is possible to go from Thonon to Menton in two days, by spending a night in Briançon; this, however, is a tiring journey which entails making sacrifices. For instance, it involves leaving out most of the excursions which really make the trip worthwhile, such as Chamonix with the Aiguille du Midi and the Vallée Blanche, or La Grave with the panoramic viewpoint at Le Chazelet… and only allows for carefully timed stops.

Five-day itinerary

- Thonon – Beaufort: *146km/91mi – allow 5hr 30min (tours included)*
- Beaufort – Val-d'Isère: *71km/44mi – allow 3hr (tours included)*
- Val-d'Isère – Briançon: *180km/111mi – allow 7hr 30min (tours included)*
- Briançon – Barcelonnette: *133km/83mi – allow 6hr 30min (tours included)*
- Barcelonnette – Menton: *206km/128mi – allow 6hr (tours included)*

EXCURSIONS

Across the Northern Alps

FROM LAKE GENEVA TO THE COL DU LAUTARET *347km/216mi*

The following route is only open in its entirety in summer. It crosses some of the most famous passes in the French Alps. Picturesque, unspoilt villages are separated by a bleak mountain landscape of exceptional beauty, at its most breathtaking at dawn or sunset.

Follow D 902 from Thonon to Cluses.

‡‡ **Thonon** – *See THONON-LES-BAINS.*

Before leaving Thonon, stop in place du Château to take a last look at Lake Geneva★★★, Lausanne and the Swiss Jura. The damp, beech-lined gorge of the Dranse de Morzine leads into the **Chablais★★**, a pastoral region of the northern Préalpes and the grazing area of the famous Abondance breed of cattle.

✳✳ **Morzine** – *See MORZINE.*

✳ **Les Gets** – *See Les GETS.*

From Tanninges, the road enters the **Faucigny★★** region, an area drained by the River Giffre, with landscapes shaped by glacial moraines through limestone folds.

Cluses – *See CLUSES.*

South of Cluses, the road enters the central massifs of the high Alps.

From Cluses, follow D 4 across the Col de la Colombière (see Massif des ARAVIS).

✳✳ **La Clusaz** – *See La CLUSAZ.*

D 909 from La Clusaz to Flumet is one of the most famous routes in the French Alps. Try to reach the Col des Aravis in the afternoon to enjoy one of the finest views of the Mont Blanc Massif.

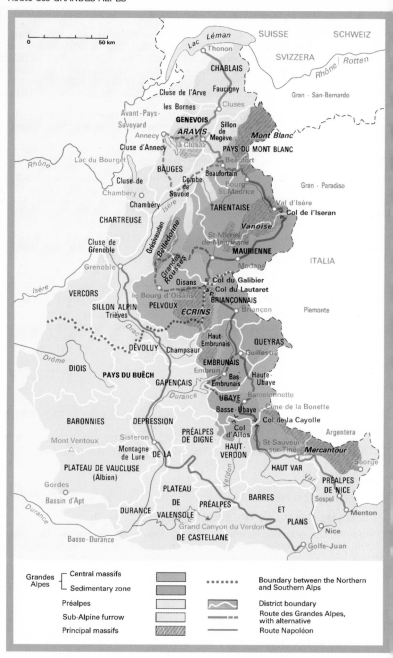

Grandes Alpes	Central massifs			Boundary between the Northern and Southern Alps
	Sedimentary zone			
Préalpes				District boundary
Sub-Alpine furrow				Route des Grandes Alpes, with alternative
Principal massifs				Route Napoléon

Take D 218ᵉ towards the Col des Saisies, via Notre-Dame-de-Bellecombe.

There are glimpses to the right of the Aravis Massif and of the Gorges de l'Arly. The Col des Saisies (1 633m/5 358ft), overlooked by the Signal de Bisanne (1 939m/6 362ft), offers a fine viewpoint of the Beaufortain region.

Beyond Hauteluce, the road runs down to Beaufort, home of the famous Beaufort cheese.

Beaufort – *See BEAUFORT.*

Between Beaufort and Bourg-St-Maurice, the road goes through **Arèches** and the charming hamlet of **Boudin★**, then runs across the top of the Barrage de Roselend and along the **Cormet de Roselend★** depression *(see BEAUFORT* **1***).*

Bourg-St-Maurice – *See BOURG-ST-MAURICE.*

From Bourg-St-Maurice to Val-d'Isère, D 902 climbs in a series of hairpin bends and enters the Haute Tarentaise region.

For the next section of the route to Bonneval-sur-Arc, see Route de l'ISERAN, Excursions.

Beyond Val-d'Isère, the road starts climbing to the Col de l'Iseran, the highest pass along the Route des Grandes Alpes (2 770m/9 088ft), and enters the Parc national de la Vanoise.

★★ **Bonneval-sur-Arc** – *See BONNEVAL-SUR-ARC.*

From Bonneval-sur-Arc to Modane – *56km/34.8mi along D 902 and N 6. See La Haute MAURIENNE, Excursions.*

Continue along the Arc Valley to St-Michel-de-Maurienne (17km/10.6mi). Turn left towards the Col du Galibier via Valloire and continue to the Col du Lautaret.

★★ **Col du Galibier** – Alt 2 646m/ 8 681ft. *See Route du GALIBIER, Excursions.*

The Gorges du Bachelard mark the northern boundary of the Parc du Mercantour

Don't miss the alpine garden at the **Col du Lautaret**★★ (2 057m/6 749ft). Turn right from the pass towards La Grave then left just before the second tunnel to enjoy the lovely panorama of the Meije Massif.

★★ **Oratoire du Chazelet** – *See La GRAVE, Hikes.*

Return to the Col du Lautaret.

Across the Southern Alps

FROM THE COL DU LAUTARET TO THE VALLÉE DE LA TINÉE

Follow N 91 to Briançon, then N 94 to Guillestre.

South of the Col du Lautaret, the road enters the southern Alps. Oaks, ash trees and beeches can be seen along the Guisanne Valley, landscapes become brighter, valleys open out. This is the intra-Alpine zone.

★★ **Briançon** – *See BRIANÇON.*

The road winds its way along the Durance Valley. Layers of marine sediment, shifted from east to west during the formation of the Alps, formed what is known as the **"nappes briançonnaises"** (consisting of schist and flysch). The River Durance has dug

> The Route des Grandes Alpes, which is 684km/425mi from start to finish, crosses 16 mountain passes, including the Col d'Iseran at a height of 2 770m/9 088ft. The altitude difference along the whole of the route is 10 675m/35 023ft.

its way through thick layers of limestone, flowing through a striking gorge (at L'Argentière-la-Bessée) before widening as it reaches the Guillestre Basin.

★ **Mont-Dauphin** – *See MONT-DAUPHIN.*

Guillestre – *See GUILLESTRE.*

This village lies at the exit of the **Combe du Queyras**★★, an impressive canyon through which flows the Guil.

An alternative route links Guillestre and Barcelonnette via Embrun (see Alternative route via the Lac de Serre-Ponçon).

At the intersection with D 902, it is also possible to turn left towards Château-Queyras (see Le QUEYRAS, [1]), eventually reaching St-Véran (15km/9mi east).

★★ **St-Véran** – *See ST-VÉRAN.*

Return to Guillestre by the same route and continue along D 902 towards Vars.

Col de Vars – Alt 2 109m/6 926ft. The pass is the gateway to the Ubaye Valley in an arid landscape of meagre pastures dotted with blocks of sandstone and tiny pools. South of the pass, hamlets scattered across the south-facing slopes live on cattle-farming and handicraft. The upper Ubaye Valley, carved out of black schist, is obstructed by alluvial cones where mountain streams depos debris. Note the strange rock formation of the Colonnes coiffées on the lef just before Les Prats.

The slender octagonal steeple in the village of **St-Paul** signals the beginning of th Haute Ubaye region.

★ **Barcelonnette** – *See BARCELONNETTE.*

The narrow road runs along the bottom of the wild **Gorges du Bachelard★**, then wind round the Mont-Pelat Massif (3 053m/10 016ft), the main summit of the souther Alps.

Great passes of the southern Alps

- Col du Lautaret (2 057m/6 749ft)
- Col de Vars (2 111m/6 926ft)
- Col d'Allos (2 240m/7 349ft)
- Col de la Cayolle (2 326m/7 631ft)
- Col de la Lombarde (2 350m/7 710ft)
- Col d'Izoard (2 360m/7 743ft)
- Col Agnel (2 744m/9 003ft)
- Col de la Bonette (2 715m/8 907ft)

★★**Col de la Cayolle** – A 2 327m/7 635ft.

There are numerous possibil ties for hikes starting fro the pass towards the La d'Allos and Lac des Gare (see Val d'ALLOS and below)

★★**Val d'Entraunes** – The road follows the upper Var Valle lined with schist mountain until **St-Martin-d'Entraunes** where it leaves the high Alp and enters the souther Préalpes. At **Guillaumes**, ignore the road on the right, which runs through the Gorge de Daluis★★ *(see VAL D'ENTRAUNES, Excursions)*, carved out of red porphyry, an turn left towards Beuil. The road rises steadily to the Col de Valberg, affordin varied views of the valley, the forested north-facing side offering a striking con trast with the south-facing slope covered with vineyards and orchards. Beuil lie at the beginning of the **Gorges du Cians★★★** *(see Gorges du CIANS)*, running sout to join the River Var. On the way down to Roubion from the **Col de la Couillole** (a 1 678m/5 505ft; *see BEUIL, Excursions*), the road offers interesting views of th Vionène and Tinée valleys. The beauty of the wild landscape is enhanced by th contrasting colours of the rocks. Beyond **Roubion★**, perched on top of a rocky spu at an altitude of 1 300m/4 265ft, the scenery is marked by red schist and water falls. **Roure★** *(4km/2.5mi along a tiny road on the left, see BEUIL, Excursions)* i another fine village with characteristic architectural features: houses have red schist bases and are covered with *lauzes* (heavy slabs of schist).

The road winds its way alongside the Vionène, to its confluence with the River Tiné in St-Sauveur-sur-Tinée.

St-Sauveur-sur-Tinée – *See Vallée de la TINÉE.*

The road follows the lower Tinée Valley for 4km/2.5mi before veering to the lef towards St-Martin-Vésubie along the Valdeblore Valley. *(For the rest of the itinerary see The Green Guide French Riviera.)*

Alternative route via the Lac de Serre-Ponçon

From Guillestre, it is possible to reach Barcelonnette via Savines-le-Lac and the La de Serre-Ponçon (27km/17mi detour).

★ **Embrun** – *24km/15mi southwest of Guillestre. See EMBRUN.*

Beyond Embrun, the road crosses over to the south bank of the Durance then skirt the Lac de Serre-Ponçon. With its 3 000ha/7 413 acres, this is one of the larges reservoirs in Europe. As you come out of Savines-le-Lac, there is a splendid **view★** o the Dévoluy Massif.

Further on, on the left-hand side of D 954, there is a group of *demoiselle coiffées*, rock columns characteristic of Alpine areas *(see Lac de SERRE-PONÇON Nearby Sights)*. The road then winds round the rocky promontory of Sauze-le-La marking the confluence of the River Durance and River Ubaye.

★ **Barcelonnette** – *See BARCELONNETTE.*

HIKE

★★**Pas du Lausson and Col de la Petite Cayolle** – *4hr there and back on foot. Difference in altitude: 350m/1 148ft. Allow one day in order to derive ful enjoyment from the beautiful landscapes.*

🄰 From the car park at the Col de la Cayolle, walk towards the Pas du Lausson; lovely views of the Val d'Entraunes. Just before reaching the ridge, admire the excep tionally rich flora. From the summit, there is a remarkable **panorama★★**, in particular towards the east and the Lac du Lausson. From the edge of the plateau, it is possible to get a good view of the **Lac d'Allos** and its surroundings *(see VAL D'ALLOS)*.

Go up, on the right, to the **Lac des Garets**; view of the Sommet des Garets and Mont Pelat. After skirting the lake towards the right, one eventually reaches the Col de la Petite Cayolle (2 642m/8 668ft). In clear weather, the view extends to Monte Viso.

Go down on the right to return to the Col de la Cayolle.

La GRAVE**

Michelin map 334 F1 and 244 fold 41 – Local map see L'OISANS

La Grave, which is the main ski resort in Dauphiné, is remarkably **well situated**★★ in the shadow of the Meije, one of the most impressive summits of the Écrins Massif and undoubtedly the most famous as far as mountaineers and tourists are concerned, for its peaks and glaciers offer spectacular views, particularly from the Oratoire du Chazelet. Beside the Meije, there are, in the immediate vicinity of La Grave, no fewer than 50 summits reaching heights ranging from 3 000m/9 843ft to 4 000m/13 123ft, although visitors with less of a head for heights can still enjoy some fine alpine panoramas.

In spite of their tourist appeal, La Grave and its picturesque hamlets have avoided property developers and remained a small family resort with traditional houses.

Nearby Sights: L'ALPE-D'HUEZ, Le BOURG-D'OISANS, BRIANÇON, Le BRIANÇONNAIS, Les DEUX-ALPES, Rout du GALIBIER, Route des GRANDES ALPES, L'OISANS, SERRE-CHEVALIER.

THE VILLAGE AND THE SLOPES

Ski area – In spite of having only a few ski lifts and ski runs, the ski area is nevertheless impressive owing to the difference in altitude (2 150m/7 054ft) between the Dôme de Lauze and La Grave.

Alpine skiing takes place on the slopes of the Meije and, in a more modest way, round Le Chazelet and the Col du Lautaret. There are also 30km/18.6mi of cross-country skiing tracks near Villar d'Arène, on the edge of the Parc national des Écrins. Finally there are numerous possibilities for ski touring *(enquire at the Compagnie des guides de l'Oisans)*.

The cable car leads to two powder runs (Les Vallons de la Meije and Chancel) offering splendid views and the finest snow from late January to mid-May. This high-mountain area, which can be compared to the Chamonix Valley, is only suitable for competent skiers.

Runs on the Girose Glacier, above the cable car's upper station, are accessible in winter and summer to less advanced skiers.

Church – Surrounded by a small cemetery, this charming 12C Romanesque church, with its Lombard-style silhouette, low bell-tower and oven-vaulted apse, blends well into the splendid setting of the resort. Note the 15C font inside.

Next to it stands the 17C **Chapelle des Pénitents** ⊙ with frescoes all over the ceiling.

EXCURSIONS

There is a wide choice of **excursions** at moderate or high altitude. In summer, you need at least four days to explore the surrounding area; the main hiking itineraries lead to the **Plateau d'Emparis** *(starting from Le Chazelet)*, the **Col d'Arsine** *(starting from Pied du Col)* and the **Lac du Goléon** *(accessible from Valfroide)*.

In addition, La Grave is the ideal starting point for drives along the Romanche Valley, to the Col du Lautaret and Col du Galibier and to the resorts of Les Deux-Alpes and Serre-Chevalier.

★★Glaciers de la Meije ⊙ – *Allow one day in order to explore all the possibilities of the site (1hr 10min there and back by cable car).*

The ride is in two sections: the first section leads to the Peyrou d'Amont Plateau (alt 2 400m/7 874ft), the second to the Col des Ruillans (alt 3 200m/10 499ft) on the northwest slopes of the Rateau Summit, offering on the way superb views of the Meije, Rateau and Girose glaciers. The view from the upper station includes the Aiguilles d'Arves due north, Mont Thabor to the northeast with the Vanoise summits in the distance and Mont Blanc further still, the Grandes Rousses and Belledonne mountains to the northwest.

The **Grotte de glace** ⊘, an ice cave decorated with many ice carvings, is easily accessible from the Col de Ruillans.

Several mountain restaurants offer superb panoramas as well as food.

From the Peyron d'Amont station lower down, it is possible to explore the area for half a day or a whole day along marked hiking trails *(ask for map at the tourist office in La Grave)*.

The **Trifides and Lauze ski lifts** offer an even more impressive **panorama★★★** at an altitude of 3 550m/11 647ft, extending as far as the Grand Combin in the Swiss Alps.

Starting from Le Chazelet

View of the Meije Summit
from the Oratoire du Chazelet

★★★**Oratoire du Chazelet** – 6km/3.7mi along D 33 branching off from N 91 to the Col du Lautaret at the exit of the first tunnel. The road goes through the village of **Le Terrasses** with its picturesque church. From the isolated Oratoire du Chazelet, there is a splendid **view** of the Meije Massif *(viewing table higher up, alt 1 834m/6 017ft)*. Continue towards the village famous for its balconied houses. On the way down to the valley, it is possible to stop near the **Chapelle de Ventelon**, which offers another view of the Meije.

★★★ **Hike to the Lac Lérié and Lac Noir** – *3hr there and back. Difference in altitude: 700m/2 297ft. Leave the car at the entrance of Le Chazelet. Go towards the ski lifts at the other end of the village, cross the small bridge and follow footpath GR 54.*

🔼 The Emparis Plateau is reached after climbing for 1hr; from here the walk becomes easier and offers clear views of the Meije.

Another hour's leads to the spot with its height marked 2 300m/7 546ft; turn left at the signpost towards the Lac Lérié. Splendid **view** of the Lautaret road, the Rateau Summit and the vast Girose and Mont-de-Lans glaciers (summer ski area of La Grave and Les Deux-Alpes). Skirt the lake and admire the reflection of the mountains in the water as well as the striking view of the Romanche Valley.

Continue to the right towards the Lac Noir lying in a wild, desolate landscape dotted with edelweiss and gentians.

GRENOBLE ★★

Conurbation 419 334
Michelin map 333 H6 and 244 fold 28

...anding at the confluence of the deep valley of the River Drac and River Isère, ...renoble's reputation as a forward-looking city, as well as the economic and cultural ...pital of the French Alps, has been growing since the Revolution; the dynamism of its ...search centres and the richness of its museums prove that it has lost none of its enthu-...asm for progress.

...earby Sights: CHAMBÉRY, Massif de CHAMROUSSE, Massif de la CHARTREUSE, Le ...RÉSIVAUDAN, Lacs de LAFFREY, Route NAPOLÉON, PONT-EN-ROYANS, ST-PIERRE-...E-CHARTREUSE, Le TRIÈVES, Le VERCORS, VILLARD-DE-LANS, VIZILLE.

HISTORICAL NOTES

Origins – The town, founded by the Gauls at the confluence of the River Drac and River Isère, was fortified by the Romans and given the name of **Gratianopolis** (after Emperor Gratianus) which, in time, became Grenoble. During the Middle Ages, the town was repeatedly flooded by the River Drac, particularly in 1219 when the only bridge and most of the houses were destroyed.

"Dauphins" – In the 11C, the town came under the control of the counts of Albon, whose seat was the Château de Beauvoir on the edge of the Vercors. The English mother of Count Guigues III gave her son the affectionate nickname "Dolphin"; the name, translated into French, came to be the ruler's hereditary title and his territory was known as Dauphiné. **Humbert II**, the last Dauphin, sold the land to the king of France in 1349 and the title was thereafter conferred on the heir to the French throne.

The "Journée des Tuiles" (Day of the Tiles) – On the 7 June 1788, the news spread through Grenoble that the regional *parlements*, or high judicial courts, were to be closed down by order of Louis XVI. The people of Grenoble rebelled against the royal decree, climbed onto the roofs of the buildings and pelted the troops sent to subdue them with heavy tiles. The protest proved successful and the banished members returned to find jubilant crowds lining the streets, yet only three years later, in one of the ironic turns of local history, the *parlement* was dissolved by the leaders of the Revolution without any resistance from the town.

Industrialization – In the 19C, Grenoble developed into a prosperous industrial city. Glove-making, the town's speciality, became mechanised, while coal mines and cement factories changed the landscape of the surrounding area. Later on, paper mills, water power, electrometallurgy and electrochemistry increased the town's prosperity with the contribution of industries related to winter sports (ski lifts).

Grenoble today – The lively **place Grenette** and rue Félix-Poulat, the pedestrian streets of the old town, the many parks and flower gardens, the tree-lined avenues and wide boulevards give Grenoble the "feel of a real town and not that of a large village", as Stendhal once said. There is a new international trade centre, **Europole**, near the railway station. The **University**, founded in 1339 by Humbert II, includes highly spe-cialised institutes of Alpine geography and geology and a centre of nuclear studies. The **Synchrotron**, a particle accelerator with a circumference of 850m/2 788ft standing near the Lyon-Grenoble motorway, symbolizes the dynamic approach of Alpine scientific research. The Winter Olympics of 1968 brought changes to the town's infrastructure and facilities, including a sports hall and a speed-skating rink, but also encouraged new trends in civic architecture.

Maison de la Culture – This imaginatively designed cultural centre, known locally as "*le Cargo*", stands on elegant narrow columns. Black and white surfaces, cylinders and cubes contrast to make a striking modern structure.

Hôtel de ville – The town hall in Parc Paul-Mistral was designed by Novarina in collab-oration with a number of other artists. A marble mosaic by Gianferrari and a bronze by Étienne Hadju decorate the central **patio★**. The Salle des Mariages displays a wall-hanging by Alfred Manessier; a tapestry by Raoul Ubac can be seen in the Salle des Réceptions.

An open-air museum – Grenoble's enthusiasm for modern civic art is on permanent view, as works by contemporary sculptors enliven urban spaces around the town, from the station square (Calder), Parc Paul-Mistral (Apostu, Joseph Wyss) and the Quartier Alpin (Magda Frank) to the Olympic village and the main roads into the centre.

A MOUNTAIN AT THE END OF EVERY STREET

The setting – Stendhal's description of Grenoble sums up the unique charm of the town; the mighty escarpments of the Vercors dominate the skyline to the west, the sheer faces of the Néron and the St-Eynard rise up in the north and to the east stand the dark, often snow-capped peaks of the Belledonne range.

Eating out

BUDGET

Café de la Table Ronde – *7 pl. St-André* – ☎ *04 76 44 51 51* – *closed 31 De* *7 Jan, Sun and public holidays* – *12.20/27.44€*. The reflections of the regular in lively discussion at the bar, elbows on the polished zinc, and photograph signed by Sarah Bernhardt, Raymond Devos and many other stars jostle f place in the huge mirrors on the walls above the moleskin benches. Brasseri style local cooking. The cabaret area claims to be one of the last homes of th classic French chanson. There are concerts on Thu, Fri and Sat.

Bombay – *60 av. Jean-Jaurès* – ☎ *04 76 87 71 80* – *closed 15-31 Aug ar Mon* – *reservations compulsory* – *14.48/19.06€*. It is also possible to trav while seated at a table. Once across the threshold, the tempting smell of Indi spices and the exotic flavours of the food will transport diners to distant clime

Le Provençal – *16 cours St-André* – *38800 Pont-de-Claix* – *8km/5mi S Grenoble on N 75 towards Sisteron* – ☎ *04 76 98 01 16* – *closed 21 Jul-2 Aug, Tue evening, Sun evening and Mon* – *14.48/28.97€*. This restaura behind a privet hedge in the suburbs of Grenoble has a choice of three dinir rooms, one of which is divided with screens, and one is beneath a veranda ope ing out onto a terrace in summer. The proprietress prepares simple tradition dishes in the kitchen using fresh produce.

MODERATE

Le Valgo – *2 r. St-Hugues* – ☎ *04 76 51 38 85* – *closed 3 weeks in Au Christmas-New Year's Day, Tue evening, Wed evening Sun and Mon* – *reserv tions recommended in the evening* – *15.70/19.51€*. This restaurant tucke away in a small street outside the old town is popular with the locals. The fair plain decor is the setting for the authentic traditional local cuisine served in ge erous portions.

À l'Huile d'Olive – *2 r. St-Hugues* – ☎ *04 76 63 12 02* – *closed Sun evenin Tue lunchtime and Mon* – *18.29/39.64€*. At one time operating several mil out of Grenoble the proprietress, Harika, has now set up in business in the ci centre. Her cuisine is still full of the flavours of sunshine. There is no menu her instead she announces the dishes of the day, dictated by what was available the market, as if you were one of her friends.

Ciao a Te – *2 r. de la Paix* – ☎ *04 76 42 54 41* – *closed 22 Jul-12 Aug, F school holidays, Sun and Mon* – *reservations compulsory* – *18.29/30.49€*. Th restaurant in an old part of the city not far from the Musée de Grenoble boas a timber front and hand-painted sign. It serves "fast" cuisine and of course past features prominently on the menu of this popular Italian eatery.

Where to stay

BUDGET

Hôtel Gambetta – *59 bd Gambetta* – ☎ *04 76 87 22 25* – *44rm 33.39/52.59€* - ⌑ *6.10€* – *restaurant 12.96/24.39€*. In spite of the livelines of this district, you will rest undisturbed here. Rooms are well sound-proofe and air-conditioned. Large dining room with pale cherrywood decor.

Hôtel Bellevue – *1 r. de Belgrade* – ☎ *04 76 46 69 34* – *www.hotel-bellevue.fr 37rms: 35.83/44.21€* - ⌑ *4.88€*. This fine building not far from the city cen tre beside the river, offers neat and tidy rooms. Ask for one with a view of th Isère. A few paces away is the cable car up to Fort de la Bastille.

Hôtel Trianon – *3 r. P. Arthaud* – ☎ *04 76 46 21 62* – *closed 4-19 Aug* – ▣ *38rms:36.44/68.60€* - ⌑ *5.79€*. This is a fairly peaceful hotel with one or tw extremely characterful themed rooms: Pastoral, Romantic, Butterfly and Lou XV. Others have a more classic look. Take your pick...

Hôtel Patinoires – *12 r. Marie-Chamoux* – ☎ *04 76 44 43 65* – ▣ – *35rm 39/55€* - ⌑ *6.50€*. This hotel near the Palais des Sports has a modern façac which contrasts with its interior decor, featuring dark wood latticed ceilings, an panelled walls adorned with pictures executed by the proprietor and hunting trc phies. You can take a long lie-in here, as breakfast is served until midday!

On the town

Cybernet Café – *3 r. Bayard* – ☎ *04 76 42 88 98* – *cybernet@neptune.fr Mon-Sat noon-1am*. A total of 13 computer terminals are available. This popu lar café is decorated with old posters and filled with an eclectic miscellany of art cles. Local and national newspapers available.

Brasserie du Téléphérique – Fort-de-la-Bastille – ☏ 04 76 42 87 64 – Mon am-7.30pm, Tue-Sat 9am-11.30pm, Sun 9am-7.30pm – closed in Jan. This tly named brasserie can be accessed using France's first urban cable car and ere is a breathtaking view from its terrace of Grenoble and the surrounding ountains.

Soupe aux Choux-Jazz-club de Grenoble – 7 rte de Lyon – ☏ 04 76 87 5 67 – Tue-Sat 6pm-1am – closed Jul-Aug. This is the only jazz club in enoble and is consequently something of an institution. Jazz groups known all er the world perform here regularly. The rest of the time, local groups show eir skill with tunes such as Can't Get Started or Manhattan.

Tonneau de Diogène – 6 pl. Notre-Dame – ☏ 04 76 42 38 40 – open daily om 8am. Grenoble's only literary café is run by an old professor of philosophy ho organises political and philosophical discussions every Tue and Thu which e highly prized by the Grenoble student fraternity. The café also has its own rary.

s Trois canards – 2 av. Félix-Viallet – ☏ 04 76 87 41 04 – open daily from m. This huge rustic style bar features bare stone walls, beams, mirrors and ge paintings. In the evening there are rock concerts, and some sporting ents are shown on the giant TV screen. Rum enthusiasts should visit the xotic" room.

Shopping

La Noix de Grenoble-Desany – 6 bis pl. Grenette – ☏ 04 76 03 12 20 – on-Sat 9am-7pm. This confectioner-chocolate maker in the city centre offers variety of local specialities, many of which incorporate the famous local wal- ts: Noix de Grenoble, walnut cakes and Galets du Drac.

Salon de thé Burdet – 1 r. de la République – ☏ 04 76 44 26 73 – Mon- t 9am-7pm. Bonnat chocolates are to be found exclusively at this confec- ner-chocolate maker's. Other local specialities are on offer, either for sale or r immediate consumption in the tea room

Panorama from the Fort de la Bastille *1hr*

The fort is accessible by cable car ⊘ or by car; car park next to the lower station.

From the rocky promontory situated on the left as you come out of the upper station, the **view★★** takes in the town, the confluence of the River Isère and River Drac and the transverse section of the Isère Valley framed by the Néron (right) and Moucherotte (left) summits.

Go up to the terrace above the restaurant.

Information panels help visitors to detail the **panorama★★** of mountains unfolding all round: Belledonne, Taillefer, Obiou, Vercors (Grand Veymont and Moucherotte) and even Mont Blanc, which can be seen through the Grésivaudan depression. There is a fine bird's-eye view of Grenoble, the old town and the 19C districts to the south and west, all overlooked by the high-rise tower blocks of the **Île Verte**.

🚶 Two marked paths lead back to town: one goes through the **Parc Guy-Pape** and Jardin des Dauphins *(about 1hr 30min)*, the other follows the **Circuit Léon-Moret** which ends at the Porte St-Laurent near the Église St-Laurent.

From the cable-car station, it is possible to walk towards the heights of Mont Jalla *(1hr)* for an even better panoramic view.

Other marked paths including GTA 2 go through the Bastille area *(specialised topo-graphical guidebooks are available)*.

OLD TOWN *1hr*

Start from place Grenette.

Place Grenette – This lively square lined with shops is one of the favourite haunts of the locals who like to stroll and stop at the pavement cafés. This is also the spot where, on 19 June 1889, to the amazement of the inhabitants and the anger of the local gas companies, six lamps provided the first electric street lighting in the city.

Walk along Grande-Rue.

Grande-Rue – This former Roman road is lined with fine old houses; no 20, facing a Renaissance mansion, is the **Maison Stendhal** ⊘, exhibitions are held in the second-floor flat where Stendhal spent part of his childhood. The two fine courtyards date from the 15C and the 18C.

The Grenoble cable car: an unofficial emblem of the city

Rue J.-J.-Rousseau starts almost opposite; no 14 was Stendhal's birthplace *(not open the public)*.

Return to Grande-Rue.

Several famous natives of Grenoble were born or lived along this street. The Hac workshop, home of the famous family firm of furniture makers, stands on pla Claveyson.

Place St-André – In the centre stands a statue of Bayard, the "knight without fear a above reproach" *(see GRÉSIVAUDAN)*. The appropriately chivalric-sounding Café de Table Ronde (1739) is one of the oldest in France, and yet another address with a cla to literary fame: Stendhal liked to come here to sketch out his first drafts over a drin

★ **Palais de justice** ⊙ – This former palace of the Dauphiné Parliament is the fine building in Grenoble; the left wing is in Flamboyant-Gothic style and the right wi in early Renaissance style. Inside, note the interesting **wood panelling★** and ceilings.

Église St-André – The 13C chapel has a bell-tower surmounted by an octago spire; Bayard's funeral monument (17C) is in the north transept.

Walk round St-André to place d'Agier and go into the Jardin de Ville.

Musée Stendhal ⊙ – Housed in the **Hôtel de Lesdiguières** (late 16C to 18C), which w the town hall until 1967, the museum contains a collection of illustrations relati to the writer and his background *(see Practical information: Themed itineraries).*

Return to place St– André by rue Berlioz and turn right onto rue du Palais.

The place aux Herbes is the oldest square in the city. The streets around nearby r de la Brocherie were once the most sought-after in Grenoble. Some of the arist cratic town houses, or *hôtels*, have retained their Renaissance design; the courtya of the Hôtel de Chasnel at **n°6** is a fine example. Two more inner courts can be se in the parallel rue Chenoise. N°10 dates from the 17C; visitors can catch a glimp of the staircase at **n°8, Hôtel d'Ornacieux**, through the glass panel of the front door.

Place Notre-Dame – Excavations carried out under the cathedral square ha revealed the foundations of the Gallo-Roman walls surrounding Gratianopolis a important paleo-Christian remains; metal markers embedded in the paving of t square follow the outline of the walls. Standing with your back to the cathedral, y will notice a solitary tower, **Tour Clérieux**: it is all that remains of the episcopal buil ings which stood here during the Middle Ages and included three churches: t Cathédrale Notre-Dame, the adjacent Église St-Hugues and the baptistery (destroy in medieval times).

Cathédrale Notre-Dame – Remodelled many times and recently restored to its ori inal aspect, the cathedral has retained some pre-Romanesque features such as t five adjacent naves and the base of the bell-tower; fortunately the cement faça added in the 19C was subsequently removed. In the chancel, note the 14m/45ft-hi ciborium, an impressive example of flamboyant Gothic stonework. The Chapelle S Hugues was once the nave of the 13C Église St-Hugues.

The elegant fountain, known as the fontaine des Trois-Ordres, in the centre of place Notre-Dame takes its name from its three figures who represent the traditional classes of society: the clergy, the nobility and the third estate. The former **bishop's palace** next to the Chapelle St-Hugues now houses the **Musée de l'ancien évêché** *(see below)*.

Walk along **rue Barnave**, lined with charming old town houses. The Gothic **hôtel François Marc** at n°22 dates from 1490; the archway bears a winged lion emblem, the symbol of St Mark the Evangelist. Beyond the door is a courtyard with an elegant spiral staircase.

Follow rue Duclos to rue Raoul-Blanchard.

The former Jesuit college is now the lycée international Stendhal. The walls and staircase were designed to work as a **sundial**, marking the solar and lunar calendars, religious festivals, feast days of the order and the time in the twelve towns in which the Society of Jesus had founded an institution.

Return to place Grenette by rue de la République.

SIGHTS

The Left Bank of the Isère

★**Musée de Grenoble** ⊙ – The new Museum of Fine Arts, inaugurated in 1994, is located along the River Isère, at the heart of the old town. Its architecture is remarkably plain and lighting can be modified according to the works exhibited.
This is one of the most prestigious French regional museums: its collections of paintings from the 16C to the 20C include a particularly rich collection of modern and contemporary art, which is exceptional even by European standards.

16C and 17C painting – Italian painting is represented by Perugino, Tintoretto, Veronese, Carravaggio, Fra Bartolomeo and **Vasari** (*The Holy Family*, in typical Mannerist style). The collection from the 17C French school includes works by **Philippe de Champaigne**, La Tour and Le Lorrain. One of the highlights of the section is a series of pieces by **Zurbarán**: - several paintings which form an altarpiece, originally from the monastery of Jerez de la Frontera.

19C painting – It extends from **neo-Classicism** to **Impressionism** and **Symbolism** and is represented by Ingres, Boudin, Monet, Sisley, Corot, Théodore Rousseau, Gauguin (*Portrait of Madeleine Bernard*) as well as by artists from Grenoble such as Ernest Hébert and **Henri Fantin-Latour**.

20C modern art – Donations and bequests have considerably enriched the museum so that most schools are represented by the most famous artists. **Fauvism** is illustrated by Signac, Vlaminck, Van Dongen and above all **Matisse** (*Interior with aubergines*, 1911); the **Cubist School** is headed by Braque and **Dadaism** is reflected in the works of Picabia *(Idyll)*, Grosz and Ernst. The Paris School is represented by **Chagall** and **Modigliani**. There are important works by **Picasso** and **Léger**. Klee, Miró and Kandinsky lead to **Abstract Art** with later representatives such as Taeuber and Domela.

Contemporary art – All the main trends from 1945 onwards, from **Lyrical Abstract Art** to **New Realism** and **Support-Surface** through **Pop Art** and **Minimalism**, are illustrated by major artists such as Dubuffet, Vasarely, Hartung, Atlan, Brauner *(Woman with a bird)*, Wesselman, Boltanski *(Monument)*, Raysse, Judd and many others.

Antiquities – *In the basement.* The extremely rich collection of **Egyptian antiquities** includes several royal steles, brightly decorated coffins and refined funeral masks.

Tour de l'Isle – Incorporated into the new museum, this medieval tower now houses more than 3 000 drawings including several masterpieces such as a 15C *St Jerome* from northern Italy.

Musée de l'Ancien Évêché – Patrimoines de l'Isère ⊙ – Situated at the heart of the town's historic centre, this interactive museum is housed in the former bishops' palace; it offers an account of the regional heritage through a number of prestigious collections. In the basement, visitors can see *in situ* a paleo-Christian **baptistery**★, one of the oldest of its kind.

Psametik's Sarcophagus (c. 500 BC)

Collection Musée de Grenoble

ST-LAURENT DISTRICT

Situated on the right bank of the River Isère this old district, flanked by the Porte de France to the west and the Porte St-Laurent to the east, is undergoing restoration work.

Access on foot: walk across the footbridge of the Citadelle and take the steps on the left leading to the museum. Access by car: along quai Perrière and rue Maurice-Gignoux.

GRENOBLE

★ **Musée dauphinois** ⊘ – This museum of regional art and traditions is housed in a former 17C convent, the **couvent de la Visitation de Ste-Marie-d'en-Haut**, built on the hillside in lovely surroundings. The tour takes visitors round the cloister, the

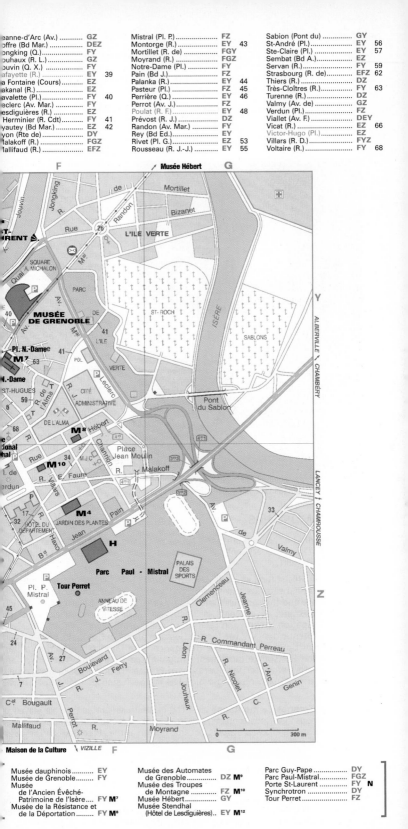

chapter-house and the Baroque chapel. The main rooms, devoted to regional heritage, display a rich collection of furniture and traditional tools. Long-term themed **exhibitions**★★ illustrate various aspects of life in the mountains. The splendid Baroque

chapel★★ from the early 17C is the highlight of the tour and a popular venue for concerts. The murals illustrate the life of St François de Sales and were painted to celebrate his beatification. Note also the trompe-l'oeil painting above the chancel and the remarkable Baroque altarpiece.

★★ Église-musée St-Laurent ⊘ – This building, one of the few of its kind in France, is particularly interesting owing to the extensive excavations which brought to light the numerous additions and alterations made to it. The **St-Oyand Crypt★**, located beneath the east end of the present church, was built in the 6C-7C on the site of a

pagan necropolis (excavation work in progress). This early medieval oratory is richly adorned with Roman and Merovingian decorative motifs skilfully blended with Carolingian elements. The church, surprisingly large by the standards of its time, is entered through the Romanesque porch surmounted by a bell-tower; from the gallery overlooking the nave, there is a fascinating overall view of the different architectural styles. The decoration of the chancel walls and ceiling dates from 1910 before the swastika motif in the design had taken on a political significance. In fact, this 3 000 year-old Hindu ideogram is thought to have represented "the origin of all things" or its literal Sanskrit meaning "well-being", ideas much more in keeping with the surroundings.

Burial site in the Église St-Laurent

THEMED MUSEUMS

Musée Stendhal – The museum in the 18C salons of the **Hôtel de Lesdiguières** (note the fine panelling and parquet) contains a collection of illustrations relating to the writer and his background

★Musée de la Résistance et de la Déportation ⊘ – This ultra-modern museum recreates original settings and sounds and explains the motives of members of the Resistance and the sacrifices entailed by their actions. The intense activity of the local Resistance movements is illustrated by several reconstructions; the German occupation is shown in relation to collaboration and deportation. Note the three authentic doors of the former Gestapo prison in Grenoble, covered with graffiti drawn by members of the Resistance. The importance of the military activity of the Resistance movements (highlighted by a huge relief map) and their preparatory work for the liberation of France are also shown. One room is devoted to the Monaco meeting which led to the fusion of the various movements.

Musée des Troupes de montagne ⊘ – The museum illustrates the role played by mountain troops in various conflicts, in particular the Second World War, when their finest regiment, the *chasseurs alpins*, became known as the "Blue Devils". They were responsible for the promotion of skiing, for improving communications and for ensuring the safety of the local population.

Musée des Rêves mécaniques ⊘ – Hidden at the end of a narrow street, this museum houses a rich collection of automata and music boxes.

Musée d'Histoire naturelle ⊘ – The museum which dates from the 18C is being modernized. The Salle des Eaux Vives on the ground floor contains several aquariums. Exceptionally fine collection of minerals and fossils.

Centre national d'Art contemporain ⊘ – *West of the town centre along cours Berriat (no 155)*. Exhibitions of contemporary art are held inside a former industrial building, known as **Le Magasin**, designed in 1900 by the Eiffel Group.

The "grey gold" of Grenoble

In the 19C, the Grenoble region was the birthplace of the French cement industry based on research carried out by Louis Vicat (1786-1861), who was looking for the lost secret of Roman cement. At the height of its production, natural cement from Dauphiné was exported to New York and South America.

Grenoble has retained several architectural and decorative reminders of this golden age including the neo-Moorish Chapelle Notre-Dame-Réconciliatrice (rue Joseph-Chaurion), the Tour Perret (1925), the former offices of Ciments de la Porte de France (Cours Jean-Jaurès) and the picturesque urinals – no longer in use – along the avenues of the Alpine metropolis.

NEARBY SIGHTS

St Martin-le-Vinoux – **La Casamaure** *13, rue de la Résistance. Northwest of Grenoble towards Voiron.* This 1885 neo-Moorish villa from the heyday of cement construction offers a profusion of Moorish arches and *moucharabies* (window grills) based on designs from a palace in Istanbul.

La Tronche – **Musée Hébert** ⊙ – *Northeast of the Musée de Grenoble, along avenue Randon. Entrance in chemin Hébert.* A vast French-style park is the setting of the former home of the painter Ernest Hébert (1817-1908), a native of Dauphiné, and of the museum devoted to his works.

Lancey – **Musée de la Houille blanche** ⊙ – *16km/10mi. From Grenoble, follow D 523 towards Domène. In Lancey, turn right at the lights towards La Combe-de-Lancey and the paper mills.* The term *houille blanche* (white coal) was coined by **Aristide Bergès** to describe water power. The engineer began building a chute above Lancey in 1869 (completed in 1875) to provide power for the paper mills. Later turbines were introduced. The museum illustrates Aristide Bergès' career and the history of water power in the 19C. His house *(not open to the public)* stands on the left of the entrance; the Art-Nouveau style of the hall is just visible through the window on the ground floor.

Sassenage – *6km/3.7mi west.* The town church is the final resting-place of **François de Bonne de Lesdiguières**, the last Constable of France.

Les Cuves ⊙ – This pair of caves, linked by a waterfall, is one of the "seven natural wonders of Dauphiné". The tour explores a vast underground maze of galleries full of stalactites, stalagmites and fossils and can be combined with a walk along the shady banks of the Furon.

Château ⊙ – Built between 1662 and 1669, this was until recently the seat of the aristocratic Sassenage-Béranger family. According to legend, the local lords could trace their descent back to the beautiful, shape-changing fairy Mélusine, who is represented in relief above the entrance. The elegant château with tall dormer windows stands in a 19C landscaped park *(open to the public)*, below a rocky knoll and its ruined medieval castle. Fine views of the Vercors.

St-Nizier-du-Moucherotte – *15km/9.3mi southwest via Seyssinet. Leave Grenoble by boulevard Vallier and the N 532. Cross the Drac and take the D 106 towards St-Nizier-du-Moucherotte.*

This village, burnt down by the Germans in June 1944 and subsequently rebuilt, occupies a splendid open site on the plateau; it is one of the favourite winter and summer resorts of the residents of Grenoble.

Mémorial du Vercors – *2km/1.2mi by D 106.* This cemetery, containing the graves of 96 members of the Resistance, is situated on the first line of defence attacked by the Germans in July 1944.

Église – Despite extensive restoration work, the church has retained its traditional appearance; it also houses some interesting modern works of art. The stone cross outside dates from 1761.

Walks in the area

★★ **Viewpoint** – A path, starting from the Bel-Ombrage Hotel leads to a viewing table giving extensive views of the Chartreuse, Mont-Blanc, Belledonne and Écrins massifs.

★★ **Sommet du Moucherotte** – *3hr there and back. Start from the car park at the top of the Olympic ski-jump and follow GR 91.* The **vast panorama**★★★ unfolding from the summit includes Mont Blanc when the weather is clear, and at night the view of Grenoble is enchanting.

GRÉOUX-LES-BAINS‡‡

Population 1 921
Michelin map 334 D10 and 245 fold 33

Gréoux has only one spring which releases 2.5 million litres/575 000gal of ho
(37°C/98.6°F), sulphurous water used for the treatment of rheumatism, arthritis an
respiratory complaints. Steles discovered last century, dating from AD 176 and ded
cated to the nymphs of Gréoux, prove that the spa water was already famous in Roma
times. Rediscovered centuries later, the resort became fashionable again during the 190
Today the thriving town, which is favoured for its fine setting and sunny climate, ha
ever more hotels, luxury villas and shops as well as a wider choice of leisure activities.

Nearby Sights: CÉRESTE, Vallée de la Moyenne DURANCE, FORCALQUIER, Monastèr
de GANAGOBIE, MANE, MANOSQUE, MOUSTIERS-STE-MARIE, RIEZ, Lac de STE
CROIX, Plateau de VALENSOLE, Grand Canyon du VERDON

SIGHTS

Santons – traditional Provençal figures
in the Crèche de Haute-Provence

Vieux village – The old villag
centre nestles at the foot of th
castle.

Castle – The former stronghold o
the Knights Templar *(restoratio
work in progress)* overlookin
the village has retained it
massive square keep in th
northwest corner. When festival
are not being staged in th
courtyard *(see Calendar o
events)*, the castle is use
as an exhibition space by loca
artists.

Troglodytic baths – A pool datin
from the 1C AD, found near the sp
centre, shows the importance o
the baths in the Gallo-Roma
period.

Crèche de Haute-Provence ⊘ – 3
avenue des Alpes. Miniatur
village populated by some 300
santons illustrating daily life i
the region at the turn of the
century.

Where to stay and Eating out

MODERATE

Hôtel Villa Castellane – *Av. des Thermes* – ☎ 04 92 78 00 31
hotelcaste@ad.com – *closed end Nov-beginning Mar* – 🅿 – 16rms: 39.64/68.60€
☟ 6.86€ – *restaurant 17.53/24.39€*. At the heart of the spa resort, near the
casino, this old hunting pavilion stands in the centre of a park and houses rooms tha
have been refurbished to a high standard of comfort. There are apartments available
for a longer stay. This is a simple, welcoming establishment. Swimming pool.

Chambre d'hôte Bastide St-Donat – *Rte de Vinon – 4km/2.5mi W of Gréoux o
D 952* – ☎ 04 92 78 01 77 – www.multimania.com/gites04/secteur1/wantzen – *close
Nov-Mar* – ⌷ – 4rms: 42.69/59.46€. The rooms in this fortress are named after flow
ers, and decorated in Provençal colours with antique furniture and hexagonal red tile
on the floors, all of which help one to forget the closeness of the road. The garden is per
fumed with lavender and there is a swimming pool to complete the pleasant scene.

Hôtel La Chêneraie – *Les Hautes Plaines via Av. des Thermes* – ☎ 04 92 78
03 23 – *closed 25 Nov-25 Feb* – 🅿 – 20rms: 45.73/67.08€ - ☟ 7.62€ -
restaurant 15.24/33.54€. This modern hotel on the hillside above town has spa
cious rooms with floral drapes and roughcast walls. The balconies are very pleas
ant in fine weather and overlook a large swimming pool. Simple cooking.

Hôtel Villa Borghèse – *Av. des Thermes* – ☎ 04 92 78 00 91 – *closed 5 Nov
24 Mar* – 🅿 – 66rms: 62.50/105.19€ - ☟ 10.67€ – *restaurant 25.92/35.06€*
This hotel has a plethora of facilities for keeping fit and beautiful: balneotherapy
massages and fitness programmes, not forgetting the swimming pool in a pleas
antly shaded park and the sauna; no excuse for returning home unhealthy after
holidaying here! Comfortable rooms with 1970s decor.

EXCURSIONS

St-Julien-le-Montagnier – *579m/1 900ft 14km/8.7mi south of Gréoux.* Wonderful **view**★ of the Plans de Provence, the Durance Valley, the Plateau de Valensole, Ste-Baume and Ste-Victoire from what used to be the village threshing floor. The square, lantern-shaped bell-tower of the 11C **village church** is a hallmark of traditional Haute-Provence architecture. Inside, a carved, gilded altar from the 17C and a remarkably well-preserved rood beam still survive. The 13C **ramparts** are all that remains of the medieval stronghold. Follow the road to the point where it enters the village; there is a good view of the area from the fortified gate.

Plateau de Valensole – *89km/55.3mi – about 5hr – see Plateau de VALENSOLE*

Plans de Provence – A sea of closely set trees stretches away as far as the eye can see. Here and there, villages set in fields, vineyards and olive groves form little islands.

Le GRÉSIVAUDAN★
Michelin map 333 J5 to J6 and 244 fold 29

The phrase *chevalier sans peur et sans reproche* may sound familiar, but did you know that this "knight without fear and above reproach" first won his spurs in the Isère Valley? This sheltered depression, deeply eroded by Ice Age glaciers, is now the Alps' richest agricultural area; in the 19C, the region pioneered the development of water power for industrial use.

Nearby Sights: ALLEVARD, Les BAUGES, CHAMBÉRY, Massif de la CHAMROUSSE, Massif de la CHARTREUSE, GRENOBLE, ST-PIERRE-DE-CHARTREUSE, VIZILLE.

BACKGROUND

Bayard's youth – Born in the Château de Bayard, near Pontcharra, in 1476, Pierre Terrail belonged to a long line of illustrious soldiers. As a child, he was only interested in riding and soldiering and soon became more skilled than his tutors, honing his skills and courtly graces as the Duke of Savoie's page. The king of France, Charles VIII, brought him to his court and, at the age of 16, Bayard took part in his first tournament, defeating one of the finest jousters in the kingdom. From then on, Bayard shone in a succession of campaigns, his daring feats winning him a reputation as the last embodiment of heroic virtue in the final days of chivalry. King François I, no less an admirer than the rest of Europe's nobility, made him lieutenant-general of Dauphiné in 1515. He died on the battlefield in 1524.

EXCURSIONS

★★ 1 **At the foot of the Chartreuse**
The Valley of a Hundred Châteaux

FROM GRENOBLE TO CHAPAREILLAN – *95km/59mi – about 2hr 30min*

This itinerary which runs along the Plateau des Petites Roches, beneath the impressive Chartreuse Massif, offers constant views of the Belledonne range across the River Isère.

From Grenoble, drive along N 90 towards Chambéry.

In Les Eymes, D 30 starts climbing to the Plateau des Petites Roches, a wide terrace covered with pastures, sheltering beneath the escarpments of the Chartreuse. Mont Blanc can be seen in the distance, to the northeast.

Turn left off D 30, 1km/0.6mi before St-Pancrasse, towards the Col du Coq.

Col du Coq – The road winds along the slopes of the Dent de Crolles offering lovely views of the Isère Valley before reaching the pass (alt 1 434m/4 705ft).

Return to D 30.

St-Pancrasse – The village lies on the very edge of the plateau, beneath the Dent de Crolles.

★★ **Bec du Margain** – *From D 30, 30min there and back on foot.* Leave the car 150m/164yd past the football ground by the tennis courts and follow the path to the right through a pine wood. Walk along the edge of the escarpment to the viewing table situated 800m/2 625ft above the Isère Valley, with a superb **view** of the Vercors, Belledonne, Grandes Rousses, Sept-Laux, Bauges and Mont Blanc massifs.

Where to stay

BUDGET

Camping Les 7 Laux – *38570 Theys – 3.8km/2mi S of Theys. 400m/440yd from the Col des Ayes* – ☎ *04 76 71 02 69 – camping.les7laux@wanadoo.fr – open 15 Jun-15 Sept – reservations recommended – 61 pitches: 11.43€. The main attraction of this campsite near the Col des Ayes pass is its beautiful setting. It is very peaceful and offers the chance to spend a revitalising holiday at the foot of the mountains. Well-kept standard facilities. Swimming pool.*

St-Hilaire-du-Touvet – This small health and ski resort is a great favourite with paragliding and hang-gliding enthusiasts. Since 1924 it has been linked to Montfort on N 90 by the steepest **rack railway** ⊘★ in Europe, which carries 40 people and negotiates a 65% gradient (83% at one point, inside a tunnel) over a distance of 1.5km/0.9mi. From the upper station there is a striking **view★** of the Grand Pic de Belledonne across the valley.

The road continues along the mountainside at the same average altitude of 900m/2 953ft, until the D 282 drops down towards St-Georges and Le-Petit-St-Marcel, where the Combe de Savoie and the peaks of the Bauges come into view. The D 285 carries on to La Palud; from there, it is possible to drive to Chambéry across the Col du Granier.

In La Palud, D 285 turns to the right towards Chapareillan.

Chapareillan – The last Dauphiné village in the Grésivaudan lies just south of the former border between Dauphiné and Savoie at the "Pont-Royal".

The N 90 leads back along the river to Grenoble. Halfway along the road, a turn to the right leads to Touvet.

★ **Chateau de Touvet** ⊘ - The castle on the slopes of the Chartreuse Massif began as a simple 13C fort surveying the Grésivaudan; two round towers marking the entrance remain from the original defensive wall, but most of the present building dates from the 15C.
The castle was extensively remodelled in the 18C: the courtyard was enclosed, a main staircase was built inside and the **gardens★** were adorned with a remarkable **water stair way★** in the Italian style.
The gallery, adorned with Italian stucco work, houses many archives including letters signed by Henri VIII of England and François I of France, which were preserved for posterity by Guigues Guiffrey, lord of the castle and the ambassador to the English court. The music room contains two harpsichords; one of them, made by Jan Couchet in 1652, is exquisitely decorated.
In the drawing room, there are a few pieces of furniture from the famous Hache work shop in Grenoble, and the walls of the dining room are decorated with Cordoba leather.

Return to St Bernard and continue along the D 30.

★ ② At the foot of the Belledonne Massif

FROM GRENOBLE TO PONTCHARRA 100km/62mi – about 3hr

Leave Grenoble by the D 523 to Domène and Brignoud.

This itinerary explores the slopes of the Belledonne range on the left bank of the River Isère. The D 528 climbs from Brignoud to Laval past the Château du Mas.

Laval - Lovely village with overhanging roofs and a charming manor, the Château de la Martellière. In the **church** ⊘ there is a 15C mural depicting the Virgin Mary pro tecting the congregation.
Between Prabert and the Col des Ayes, there is a fine overall view of the Chartreuse Massif, including the Dent de Crolles and Chamechaude.

Theys – The village, which has retained many old houses, nestles in a green basin.

⚜ **Allevard** – See ALLEVARD.

The spa and town centre of Allevard, not to mention the superb **panorama★★** from the Collet d'Allevard (1 450m/4 757ft) are well worth a short detour.

Between Allevard and Pontcharra, D 9 goes round the heights of Brame Farine *(see ALLEVARD: Excursions)* and gives a fine **view★** of the lower Gelon Valley.

From Pontcharra, follow a small road on the right to Château-Bayard.

Château-Bayard – *The road starts climbing from a tree-shaded square and goes past Pontcharra's schools; at the end of the climb, turn right then immediately left. Leave the car in the car park on the left of the buildings.*

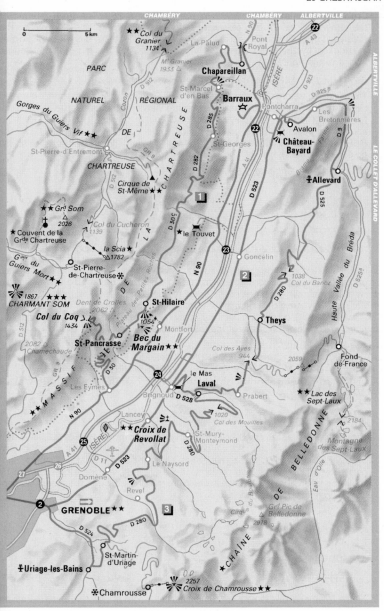

The doorway situated between the farm buildings and the former gatehouse *(now private property)* gives access to the terrace and the **Musée Bayard** ⊘, housed in a 15C square building with mullioned windows which is all that remains of the castle where the "knight without fear and above reproach" was born. The museum contains a few documents and an audio-visual presentation of his life and heroic military career. Impressive **panorama★** of the Grésivaudan and of the Chartreuse, Belledonne and Bauges massifs.

★ ③ Croix de Revollat

79km/49mi – about 2hr 30min. For the itinerary from Grenoble to Laval, see ②.

Laval *– see* ② *above.*

After the Col des Mouilles the D 280 heads down into the St-Mury valley. The Cirque du Boulon, with waterfalls streaming from the glacier, towers above the road and the three peaks of the Belledonne massif (2 913-2 978m/9 557ft-9 770ft) stand out sharply against the sky.

★★Croix de Revollat – *50m/55yd to the right of D 280*. The main interest of the itinerary lies in the **panorama** which unfolds from this viewpoint: the Grésivaudan below and, across the river, the Plateau des Petites Roches overlooked by the Chartreuse; the Vercors Massif to the left and the Bauges Massif to the right.

Drive straight on at the next cross, some 1.5km/0.9mi away.

The road crosses the gorge at La-Combe-de-Lancey. After Le Naysord, the road climbs the terraced slope offering sweeping views of the Chartreuse. 2km/1.2mi further on there are bird's-eye views of Grenoble through the forest. Running above the beautiful Revel Valley, which ends in the forested slopes of the Belledonne, the D 280 heads out of the trees towards **Uriage-les-Bains** *(see Massif de CHAMROUSSE)*.

In Uriage, turn right onto D 524 to Grenoble.

GUILLESTRE★
Population 1 999
Michelin map 334 H5 and 244 fold 43 – Local map see Le QUEYRAS

Guillestre is situated at the centre of a ring of peaks and on the edge of the Queyras, Ecrins and Embrunais regions. The surrounding mountains protect the town from the worst of the weather – it is one of the driest places in the Alps – and make it a natural meeting place, where a thriving market (Monday) has been held since the Middle Ages. The town is also a good starting point for many hiking itineraries which explore the surrounding area. *(Details available at the tourist office.)*

Nearby Sights: ABRIÈS, L'ARGENTIÈRE-LA-BESSÉE, BARCELONNETTE, BRIANÇON, Le BRIANÇONNAIS, CEILLAC, EMBRUN, Vallée de FREISSINIÈRES, Route des GRANDES ALPES, MOLINES-EN-QUEYRAS, MONT-DAUPHIN, MONTGENÈVRE, Le QUEYRAS, ST-VÉRAN, SERRE-CHEVALIER, Lac de SERRE-PONÇON, L'UBAYE, La VALLOUISE, VARS

WALKING ABOUT

Very little remains of the medieval fortifications except for the **Porte du St-Esprit**, which guards the Route de Risoul. Place Albert and its monumental fountain mark the town centre. Built in the 16C, the **church** ⊘ has a similar porch to that of Embrun, supported by four columns; two of them, in pink marble, rest on a base formed by squatting lions carved in Jura limestone from the Briançon area. The doors are decorated with Renaissance panels.

Eating out

MODERATE

L'Epicurien – *R. Frairie* – ☎ *04 92 45 20 02 – closed 1-15 Jun, 1-15 Nov, Mon and Tue except Jul-Aug – 19.82/32.01€*. This small restaurant located in one of the town's narrow streets welcomes diners without any fuss in a vaulted dining room, or on the terrace in summer. Traditional and well prepared dishes.

Where to stay

BUDGET

Camping St-James-les-Pins – *1.5km/1mi W of Guillestre on the Risoul road* – ☎ *04 92 45 08 24 – camping@lesaintjames.com* – ✉ – *reservations recommended – 105 pitches: 11.28€*. This little campsite by a waterfall 1 000m/3 280ft above sea level occupies a pleasant little pine wood. There are numerous sports on offer, including white water sports. Children's play area.

MODERATE

Hôtel Les Barnières – ☎ *04 92 45 04 87 – closed 15 Oct-20 Dec* – 🅿 – *40rms: 64.03/76.22€* – ☲ *7.62€ – restaurant 15.24/30.49€*. This hotel consisting of two chalets is mainly of interest because of the superb panoramic view it offers from the rooms or the terrace, stretching over the valley and the Alps. Relax in the swimming pool, spa bath or sauna. Or try one of the many sports on offer.

HIKES

Rue des Masques – *An easy 2hr walk. Difference in altitude 250m/820ft. Walk from the tourist office to the* gendarmerie *along the rue des Champs-Élysées, then turn right onto the Chemin d'Eygliers. Continue to the top of the hill and follow the signs.* The "road", a deep cleft in the rocks, appears almost man-made but is definitely a natural phenomenon; it penetrates 600m/1 969ft into the mountain and measures 5m/16ft from side to side.

Return to Guillestre along the edge of the plateau and the path skirting the canal.

★ **Mont-Dauphin** – *2hr on foot along an itinerary marked in orange. From Guillestre, follow D 902 towards Briançon until you reach the Chapelles district. Walk across the Plateau de la Chalp and take a footbridge across the Guil.*
The itinerary, leading to the Porte d'Embrun at the entrance of the fort, makes it possible to admire the natural defences of Mont-Dauphin from a different angle *(see MONT-DAUPHIN)*.

EXCURSIONS

Le Cros – *6km by D 37. Drive through Eygliers and continue to Le Cros along a demanding road.* The **views★** of Mont-Dauphin and its surroundings and the Guil gorges make the effort of the drive worthwhile.

★ **Réotier** – Follow the D 902 to the N 94; turn right then left in front of the station. Follow signs for the **"Fontaine Pétrifiante du Réotier"**. The water, high in mineral content, has formed strange concretions including a stalactite looking like a gargoyle.

⁎ **Risoul 1850** – *14km/8.7mi along D 186.*
The winding road offers panoramic views of Mont-Dauphin and its exceptional setting. The resort has a speed-skiing piste and snow-making equipment. The ski area, shared with Vars *(see VARS)* and known as the **Domaine de la Forêt Blanche**, is one of the largest in the southern Alps, with a total of 160km/99.4mi of piste.
An unsurfaced road leads to the Col de Chérine and to the **Belvédère de l'Homme de Pierre** (alt 2 374m/7 789ft). From the viewing table, there is a superb **panorama★★** extending north to the Vanoise Massif, south to Mont Ventoux and southwest to the Lac de Serre-Ponçon.

Les HOUCHES⁎
Population 2 706
Michelin map 328 N5 and 244 fold 21 – Local map see Massif du MONT-BLANC

The view of the massif from this resort at the foot of Mont Blanc is quite simply spectacular. Les Houches has extended across the widest and sunniest part of the Chamonix Valley, while still keeping its village character. Even if the setting is not on a par with that of Chamonix, Les Houches seems content to be a pleasant family resort; well equipped and, at only 1 000m/3 281ft, ideal for skiers who prefer not to take on the steeper, high-altitude slopes.

Nearby Sights: ARGENTIÈRE, CHAMONIX-MONT-BLANC, CLUSES, Les CONTAMINES-MONTJOIE, MÉGÈVE, Massif du MONT-BLANC, ST-GERVAIS-LES-BAINS, Bassin de SALLANCHES

THE RESORT

Ski area – The resort offers skiers a wide range of difficulties in the Lachat, Bellevue and Prarion areas, and 67 snow cannon are on standby to make good any lack of snow. The famous "green run" (black in fact!), brilliantly skied by Émile Allais in 1937, requires a high level of skiing skill. The ski area is linked to that of the main neighbouring resorts.
There are, in addition, some 30km/18.6mi of cross-country skiing trails.

VIEWPOINTS

★★ **Le Prarion** ⊘ – Alt 1 967m/6 453ft. *30min there and back to the viewing table including a 20min cable-car ride.* From the viewing table (alt 1 860m/6 102ft) next to the Hôtel du Prarion, there is an extended **view** of the Mont-Blanc Massif. In order to enjoy the **full panorama★★★**, follow the markings to the summit of Le Prarion *(about 1hr there and back on foot).*

★★ **Bellevue** ⊘ – Alt 1 812m/5 945ft. *1hr there and back including a 15min cable-car ride.*
🚠 It is possible to continue up to the Nid d'Aigle (Glacier de Bionnassay) and go back down via St-Gervais on board the Tramway du Mont-Blanc. *(See ST-GERVAIS and Admission times and charges).*

★★ **Parc du Balcon de Merlet** ⏱ – *6km/3.7mi – 10min there and back on foot. From the Houches station, drive 3km/1.8mi along the mountain road to Coupeau and turn right onto the partly surfaced forest road towards the Parc de Merlet.*
The Balcon de Merlet is a promontory covered with pastures, occupying a prime position opposite Mont Blanc. The park shelters typical mountain fauna (deer, moufflons, chamois, llamas, ibexes, marmots) roaming freely over a steep wooded area covering some 20ha/49 acres. From the terrace of the restaurant or from the chapel (alt 1 534m/5 033ft), there is a superb close-up **view**★★ of the Mont-Blanc Massif.

Where to stay

MODERATE

Auberge Le Montagny – *Le Pont* – ☎ *04 50 54 57 37 – closed 5 Nov-15 Dec –* 🅿 *– 8rms: 62.50€ -* 🍽 *6.40€.* This old farm dating from 1876 has been entirely refurbished by the proprietor himself, a sometime joiner. The peaceful rooms are in typical local style with exposed beams and pale timber roof trusses, blue and white fabrics and pretty tiles in the bathrooms with matching friezes.

Auberge Beau Site – *Near the church* – ☎ *04 50 55 51 16 – closed 21 Apr-19 May and 16 Oct-19 Dec –* 🅿 *– 18rms: 68.60€ -* 🍽 *6.86€ – restaurant 22.87/37.35€.* This chalet is at the heart of the village. Guests sample the proprietor's cooking cosily seated in front of the open fire in the restaurant surrounded by the welcoming wood panelling, or among flowers on the terrace in summer. Traditional-style rooms. Swimming pool in fine weather.

Hôtel du Prarion – *Au Prarion – alt 1 860m/6 100ft – by cable car – 74170 St-Gervais-les-Bains* – ☎ *04 50 54 40 07 – closed mid Apr-22 Jun and 10 Sept-21 Dec – 12rms: 45.73/86.90€ -* 🍽 *7.62€ – restaurant 21.34/33.54€.* This is an invitation to spend the night in the vast peace and quiet of the high mountains, at the summit of Le Prarion. There is a breathtaking panoramic view from the Aravis range to that of Mont Blanc. The rooms and food on offer are simple in the typical style of the mountains.

Route de l'ISERAN★★★
Michelin map 333 L 5/6 and 244 fold 32 and 33

This road, which goes over the Col de l'Iseran, was built in 1936 to link the Tarentaise and Maurienne valleys and climbs to the highest point (2 770m/9 088ft) of the Route des Grandes Alpes. A series of viewpoints along the route reveals the changing landscapes of the high mountains, at once austere and beautiful.

Nearby Sights: AUSSOIS, BESSANS, BONNEVAL-SUR-ARC, BOURG-ST-MAURICE, Route des GRANDES ALPES, La Haute MAURIENNE, La TARENTAISE, TIGNES, VAL D'ISÈRE, Massif de la VANOISE

EXCURSIONS

From the Barrage de Tignes to Bonneval-sur-Arc *32km/20mi – about 1hr 30min*

The Col de l'Iseran is usually blocked by snow from early November to early July. It is recommended to take this road from Val-d'Isère to Bonneval.

The construction of D 902 running from the Barrage de Tignes to Val-d'Isère involved the building of eight tunnels (one of them is 459m/502yd long) and three avalanche barriers. The road therefore offers only intermittent views of the Vanoise Massif to the south and of Mont Pourri downriver.
The Gorges de la Daille open the way into the Val-d'Isère Basin.

★★★**Val-d'Isère** – *See VAL-D'ISÈRE.*

From Val-d'Isère to the Pont St-Charles, the road continues along the Isère Valley, which becomes more and more desolate, and it is closed off upriver by the Pointe de la Galise. Beyond Le Fornet, there are stunning views of the Grande Motte at the heart of the Vanoise Massif and of the Tsanteleina Summit on the Italian border.

The road enters the Parc national de la Vanoise at the Pont St-Charles. *There is a car park for 150 cars just before the bridge.*

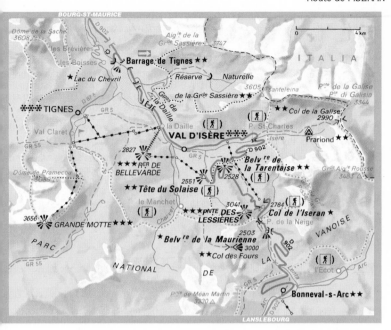

The road then rises along the southern slopes of the valley offering views of the Val-d'Isère Basin with the snow-capped Dôme de la Sache in the background and Mont Pourri just behind it.

★★ Tête du Solaise – Alt 2 551m/8 369ft. *1hr 30min on foot there and back along a path providing a pleasant mountain hike; the summit can also be reached by cable car from Val-d'Isère (see VAL-D'ISÈRE).*

The **panorama** is similar to that which can be admired from the Belvédère de la Tarentaise *(see below)*, but there is a clearer view down the Isère Valley towards Tignes and its dam.

★★ Belvédère de la Tarentaise – Alt 2 528m/8 294. *15min there and back on foot. Park the car as you come out of the bend.*

From the viewing table, the view extends all round from Val-d'Isère, the Lac de Tignes and the Pointe des Lessières in the foreground to the Vanoise Massif, Mont Pourri and the Grande Sassière range in the distance.

★ Col de l'Iseran – Alt 2 770m/9 088ft. The harshness of the landscape is impressive. The snow cover remains throughout the summer on the Tarentaise side of the pass. The Chapelle Notre-Dame-de-l'Iseran was built in a sheltered spot in 1939. The Albaron Summit comes into view on the Maurienne side of the pass.

The view from the Pointe de Lessières

★★★**Pointe des Lessières** – Alt 3 041m/9 977ft. *From the Col de l'Iseran, 2hr 30min there and back on foot along a steep mountain path which can be dangerous for inexperienced hikers (vertiginous handrail-assisted sections towards the top). Climbing boots with non-slip soles are essential. The path starts behind the Chalet-hôtel de l'Iseran.*

🚶 This hike must only be attempted in clear weather; it offers an almost unique opportunity of climbing over 3 000m/9 843ft. The view from the summit is ample reward for one's efforts: the Vanoise Massif, Mont Pourri, the Italian side of Mont Blanc and the border range between the Grande Sassière and the Albaron.

The road continues across the Parc national de la Vanoise, offering views of the barren cirque of the upper Lenta Valley beneath the Grand Pissaillas Glacier.

★ **Belvédère de la Maurienne** – Alt 2 503m/8 212ft. View of the Haute-Maurienne, the Ciamarella and Albaron summits and the Pointe de Charbonnel along the Italian border. Beyond the Pont de la Neige, the "hanging" Lenta Valley offers a landscape of high pastures backed by the snow-capped peak of the Albaron, shaped like an anvil. Lower down, the road overlooks the austere upper Arc Valley which forms the setting of the village of Bonneval.

ISOLA 2000★★

Michelin map 341 D2 and 245 folds 23 and 24

Isola 2000, built in 1972 in a beautiful mountain setting close to the Italian border, is the nearest Alpine ski resort to the Côte d'Azur region. It owes its popularity to its sunny climate and to its good-quality snow cover, which is partly due to the high altitude.

Nearby Sights: AURON, BEUIL, Route de la BONETTE, Gorges du CIANS, ST-ÉTIENNE-DE-TINÉE, Vallée de la TINÉE

THE RESORT

Ski area – It is situated at an altitude ranging from 1 800m/5 906ft to 2 600m/8 539ft and extends towards the Vallon de Chastillon. Snow cover is frequently exceptional considering the southern latitude of Isola 2000, less than 100km/62mi from Nice. The ski runs are varied enough to satisfy the most demanding skiers (Génisserie and Méné black runs) and the less experienced (blue runs starting from Les Marmottes). Adequate snow-making equipment makes up for any lack of snow. Other possibilities: ice-driving and sleigh rides.

HIKES

In summer, Isola 2000 is the ideal **starting point for hikes** through the nearby Parc national du Mercantour and Parc naturel de l'Argentera on the Italian side or among the mountain lakes surrounding the resort. Numerous chamois roam around the area which used to be part of the Italian royal hunting grounds and has retained a network of well-marked paths *(map available from the tourist office)*.

Where to stay and Eating out

EXPENSIVE

Hôtel Chastillon – ☎ 04 93 23 26 00 – closed May-Nov – 🅿 – 51rms: from 154.74€ - ⚏ 10.67€ – restaurant 22.87€. Skiers, strap on your skis, you are at the foot of the ski slopes here! The hotel has 1970s decor and small, peaceful rooms; the dining room predictably has the ambience of a mountain chalet.

On the town

Le Crocodile – Résidence Malinvern – ☎ 04 93 23 18 80 – open daily 6pm-3am – closed mid-Apr-Jun and mid-Sept-Christmas. Contrary to popular belief, it is in the winter that this Crocodile wakes from its torpor to host wild themed evenings (Mexican , Caribbean etc), throbbing to the beat of the music.

Ski in Tarine – Front de Neige – ☎ 06 80 27 70 08/04 93 93 13 55 – open daily 7.30am-midnight, winter: 9.30am-5pm – closed end Oct-Christmas. Friendly and trendy: these two epithets are not necessarily mutually exclusive in the case of this bar where, having shed your hiking boots in summer or your skis in winter, you can really let your hair down. In winter, a main meal eaten here includes admission to and a free drink in the La Tanière disco.

Isola 2000

★**Tête de Pélévos** ◷ – Alt 2 455m/8 054ft. *Take the Pélévos cable-car.*
🚶 From the upper station (alt 2 320m/7 612ft), follow a path on the right, which climbs towards the Marmottes lifts. Bear left at the second lift and go to the summit for a fine **panorama**★ of the ski area, the Lombarde and Malinvern summits.

★★**Lacs de Terre Rouge** – *Difference in altitude: about 650m/2 133ft. Allow 4hr there and back.*
🚶 Start from the restaurant called "La Bergerie" at the end of the resort and climb to the Hôtel Diva. From there, a marked path leads to the lakes lying at the foot of the Cime de Tavels and Mont Malinvern. Continue up to the **Baisse de Druos**★★ (alt 2 628m/8 622ft) which offers a fine view of the Argentera Nature Park on the Italian side and of Mont St-Sauveur and Mont Mounier on the French side.

★★**Mont St-Sauveur** – *Alt 2 711m/8 894ft. Allow 2hr on the way up and 1hr 30min on the way down. Difference in altitude: about 400m/1 312ft.*
🚶 Go up to the Marmottes 2 lift *(see Tête de Pélévos above)* and continue to the Col Valette. From there, take a narrow path *(marked with a wooden signpost)* which runs along the mountainside towards Mont St-Sauveur *(caution is required at the beginning as the path is rather stony).* Turn left at marker 89 and follow the short path running along the crest of the mountain. Extended **panorama**★★ from the summit including the Isola ski area in the foreground as well as a large area of the Parc national du Mercantour and, clockwise, the Gorges de Valabrès, the Valberg ski area, Mont Mounier, Auron, Monte Viso and the snow-capped Pelvoux.

EXCURSIONS

Col de la Lombarde – Alt 2 350m/7 710ft. *5km/3mi north of Isola 2000. Follow the narrow road which is the continuation of D 97 north of Isola 2000 and leads to the Italian border. It is possible to reach the pass on foot (3hr there and back) by following the easy marked path beyond the Belvédère chair lift.*
🚶 The pass is framed on the right by the Lombarde Peak and on the left by the Lausetta Ridge, which provides fine walks or mountain-bike rides. Lovely overall **view** of the Isola 2000 cirque, overlooked by the Tête Mercière, and of the deeper valley on the Italian side.

★★**Santuario di Santa Anna (Italy)** – *12km/7.5mi. 45min drive and 45min walk there and back. Have your identity papers with you.*
🚶 From the Col de la Lombarde, the road runs through a splendid rocky landscape, skirts Lake Orgials and goes down through larch woods. In a bend, turn left towards Santa Anna. As you reach the sanctuary, turn left and continue to the end of the surfaced road. **View**★ of the sanctuary and of the mountains towering over it. Leave the car and walk for 20min to the beautiful **Lago di Santa Anna**★, lying below the Lausfer and Arène Grosse peaks. Walk along the shore to the end of the lake for the best view of it. The lake is the starting point for longer hikes.

★**Vallon de Chastillon** – *17km/10.6mi. D 97 leads from Isola 2000 down to the village of Isola at the confluence of the River Guerche and River Tinée.* The road runs down the steep Vallon de Chastillon, then widens as it leaves the high-pasture area. Many waterfalls cascade down the rock face. Isola's Romanesque bell-tower can be seen from afar.

Isola – *See Vallée de la TINÉE.*

Lacs de LAFFREY ★

Michelin map 333 H7 and 244 fold 39

The Laffrey lakes stretch from north to south along the Route Napoléon *(see ROUTE NAPOLÉON)*. The undoubted highlight of the lakes is the Chemin de Fer de la Mure, a little miracle of 19C railway engineering which offers sublime views from the comfort of a window seat.

Nearby Sights: Le BOURG-D'OISANS, Le CHAMPSAUR, Massif de CHAMROUSSE, Massif de la CHARTREUSE, Le DÉVOLUY, GRENOBLE, Route NAPOLÉON, Le TRIÈVES, Le VALBONNAIS, Le VALGAUDEMAR, VILLARD-DE-LANS, Le VERCORS, VIZILLE

EXCURSIONS

1 Route Napoléon – *see ROUTE NAPOLÉON*

FROM LA MURE TO THE LACS DE LAFFREY – *15km – 45 min.*

★ 2 Route de la Morte

FROM LA MURE TO VIZILLE VIA THE COL DE LA MORTE – *45km – allow 2hr*

La Mure – *See ROUTE NAPOLÉON.*

Between La Mure and the Col de Malissol (alt 1 105m/3 625ft) the D 114 offers views of the Obiou and the eastern escarpments of the Vercors Massif. From the Col de Malissol to the Col de la Morte, it runs along the narrow valley of the Roizonne.

La Morte – Lying at the foot of the Grand Serre and Taillefer summits, La Morte (alt 1 348m/4 423ft) offers beautiful ski runs. In summer, it is the starting point for the ascent of the Taillefer.
The forest road leading to the Lac Poursollet *(6km/3.7mi)* affords fine views of the Romanche Valley, but is only open in summer.

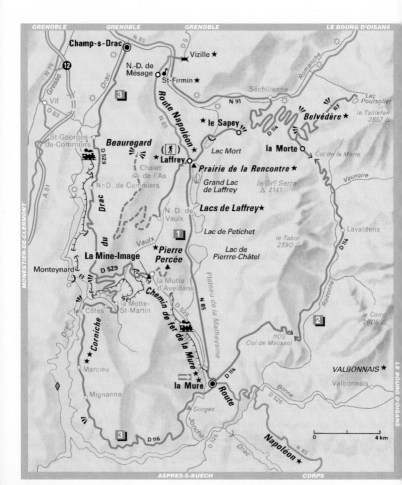

La Mure Mountain Railway

★**Viewpoint over the Vallée de la Romanche** – *By the first hairpin on the way down the Col de la Morte heading north.* There are bird's-eye views of the Romanche Valley 1 000m/3 281ft below.

Road N 91 leads to Vizille.

★**Vizille** – *See VIZILLE.*

To continue to Grenoble, make for Eybens and follow the D 5 through pleasant countryside; this is the final section of the Route Napoléon (see ROUTE NAPOLÉON).

★★ ③ Corniche du Drac

FROM CHAMP-SUR-DRAC TO LA MURE *45km/28mi – about 2hr*

Between Champ-sur-Drac and Monteynard, the road rises gradually and offers views of the deep Drac Valley and of the extensive works carried out to harness the river at Notre-Dame-de-Commiers and Monteynard. On leaving Monteynard, the lake, with Mont Aiguille above, and the dam **(Barrage de Monteynard)** are visible on the right. Stop the car at the intersection of the road leading to La Motte-St-Martin to admire the splendid view.

Continue along D 529 to La Motte-d'Aveillans.

Mine-Image ⊙ – This installation on a former mining site recreates the environment in which the miners worked and shows the evolution of coal-mining technology. The coal seams were worked from the early 19C until 1956 by means of horizontal galleries.
One of the "seven wonders of Dauphiné", known as the **Pierre Percée**, stands just outside La Motte. *Take D 529 towards La Mure, then turn left at the signpost marked "Pierre Percée". A path starting from the car park leads to the ridge (45min).* According to legend, the natural arch, 3m/10ft high, represents the devil turned into stone!

Return to La Motte-d'Aveillans and turn left onto D 116.

Beyond Les Côtes, the cliff road affords striking **views**★★★ of the escarpments plunging into the River Drac, of the power station at Avignonet, of the Monteynard Dam and artificial lake and of the heights of the Vercors Massif.
The panorama unfolding beyond Mignanne includes the Obiou, the highest summit of the Dévoluy mountains (alt 2 790m/9 154ft). The road overlooks the Gorges de la Jonche just before reaching La Mure.

★★ LA MURE MOUNTAIN RAILWAY ⊙

This railway line was built in 1888 over a distance of 30km/18.6mi to transport coal from the mining site of La Mure to St-Georges-de-Commiers, and from there to the national network. At the time, it was a daring technical achievement; the line negotiates a difference in altitude of 560m/1 837ft by means of 12 curved viaducts and 18 tunnels, also curved. At the beginning of the century, the La Mure Railway became the first railway in the world to be

299

powered by high-voltage direct electric current. This modern power source still had its limits, however. Trains could only reach a speed of 40kph/25mph, and even this was only possible on the way down; until 1950 the uphill journey took 2hr 40min.

Variously used to carry coal, to shuttle nuns and pilgrims visiting Notre-Dame-de-la-Salette *(see Le DÉVOLUY,* 2*)* and sometimes to do both at once, the trains are now only operated as a tourist attraction. From St-Georges, the railway rises gradually to the highest point of the line at the Festinière Tunnel (924m/3 032ft). There are some spectacular sections such as those crossing the Gorges du Drac and the Vaulx Viaduct (170m/186yd over nine arches).

Route de la MADELEINE★

Michelin map 333 L5 and 244 fold 30 and 31

Opened in 1969, this road links the Maurienne (N 6) and Tarentaise (N 90) valleys across moderately high mountains, an area of beautiful landscapes and charming hill-side villages.

Nearby Sights: ALBERTVILLE, La Vallée des BELLEVILLE, COURCHEVEL, Route de la CROIX-DE-FER, MÉRIBEL, ST-JEAN-DE-MAURIENNE, La TARENTAISE, Massif de la VANOISE

EXCURSIONS

Betweeen Arc and Isère

FROM LA CHAMBRE TO MOÛTIERS *53km/33mi – about 2hr. The Col de la Madeleine is blocked by snow from November to early June.*

D 213 climbs from La Chambre *(11km/6.8mi northwest of St-Jean-de-Maurienne)* in a series of hairpin bends and offers views of the Allevard and Grandes Rousses massifs through the Glandon Pass.

St-François-Longchamp – This winter sports complex spreads out between St-François (1 450m/4 757ft) and Longchamp (1 610m/5 285ft) on the east side of the Bugeon Valley, beneath the Cheval Noir Summit.

★**Col de la Madeleine** – Alt 2 000m/6 562ft (not to be confused with the pass of the same name on p308). Covered with pastures, this wide gap between the Gros Villan and Cheval Noir (alt 2 832m/9 291ft) summits offers a remarkable view of the Mont-Blanc Massif to the northeast and of the Grandes Rousses and Écrins massifs to the south *(viewing tables)*.

Between Celliers and the Pas de Briançon, the cliff road clings to the western slopes of the Celliers Valley which are dotted with villages, the Beaufortain mountains barring the view downriver.

Drive to La Léchère via Notre-Dame-de-Briançon along D 97.

‡ **La Léchère-les-Bains** – Lying deep down in the lower Tarentaise Valley, La Léchère is the newest Alpine spa resort, specialising in the treatment of vascular diseases, gynecological complaints and rheumatism. The springs were discovered after a land-slide in 1869.

Follow the twisting road on the right, which rises to St-Oyen.

Doucy – The 17C Baroque church is furnished in similar style: note the carved-wood polychrome retable over the **high altar** and the Rosary altar.

Continue along the road to Villaret (D 95⁸).

This road, running along the ridge separating the Morel and Eau Rousse valleys, offers fine views of the Vanoise, Mont Jovet, part of Courchevel and the ski slopes of Méribel-les-Allues.

Drive to Valmorel via Le Meillet.

✱✱ **Valmorel** – 1 400m/4 593ft. At times it seems as if Valmorel, built in 1976, has been part of the landscape for centuries. It is one of the most attractive modern resorts in the Alps, at the upper end of the verdant **Morel Valley** and surrounded by mountains. Trompe-l'œil façades in the Savoyard tradition brighten a traffic-free centre, which has the convivial spirit and architectural style of an old alpine village. Fine old hamlets (Doucy, Les Avanchers) are dotted along the valley, which is renowned for its Beaufort cheese; tourism is expanding rapidly.

Ski area – There is a wide choice of runs for skiers of all levels of proficiency. Experienced skiers prefer the area around St-François-Longchamp via the Madeleine chairlift and around the Massif de la Lauzière. The Morel drag-lift makes it possible to avoid the resort centre and go directly to the Gollet and Mottet ski areas. Snow-cannon more than make up for insufficient snow cover. It is possible to practise night-skiing on the Planchamp runs, and there is a recently opened snowboarding stadium. The Valmorel ski area is linked to that of **St-François-Longchamp** to form the Grand Domaine *(area pass available)*.

In summer, there is a wide choice of outdoor activities and excursions.

Snow to spare in Valmorel

★★ **Crève-Tête** – Alt 2 341m/7 680ft. *Take the Pierrafort gondola.* From the upper station (1 830m/6 004ft) it is easy to reach the **Col du Golet** which offers a fine view. The path to the summit is steeper, but the **panorama** is really superb. *(See also la Vallée des BELLEVILLE.)*

Follow the Morel Valley (D 95) down to Aigueblanche.

Barrage des Échelles d'Annibal – Built across a narrow passage of the Basse Tarentaise Valley, this dam diverts part of the flow of the River Isère to the power station at Randens on the Arc, through an 11.5km/7mi tunnel. The diversion was inaugurated in 1956.

Moûtiers – *See La TARENTAISE, Excursions.*

MANE★
Population 1 169
Michelin map 334 C9 and 245 fold 19 – Local map see FORCALQUIER

Built on an isolated rocky knoll standing in the centre of a plain, this village nestles round its medieval citadel, the last surviving example in Haute-Provence. The local stone, quarried near Porchères, was used in the construction of many buildings, including the Priory of Notre-Dame de Salagon and Sauvan Castle.

Nearby Sights: CÉRESTE, Vallée de la Moyenne DURANCE, FORCALQUIER, Monastère de la GANAGOBIE, GRÉOUX-LES-BAINS, MANOSQUE, Route NAPOLÉON, SISTERON, Plateau de VALENSOLE

WALKING ABOUT

Église St-André – The 16C church has a Florentine doorway decorated with palm leaves. Inside, the Gothic chancel contains a fine marble altar.
Follow the paved street on the left of the church; the old Renaissance houses have carved lintels over the doors.

Citadel *(not open to the public)* – These well-preserved 12C fortifications were built from local stone; note the unusual mullioned windows and the two walls winding round the hillock. From the top there is a fine **view** of the Plateau du Vaucluse, the Luberon, the Observatoire St-Michel and the Durance Valley.

EXCURSIONS

N 100 south of Mane is lined with several monuments which bear witness to the rich historical background of the village.

Medieval bridge across the Laye – *On the right of N 100; follow the sign-posting to the Auberge de la Laye.*
The highest arch of this cutwater bridge is Roma-nesque.

301

Drystone hut

Drystone huts – These circular constructions, half-hidden by the dense vegetation, can be seen to the north and east of Mane. They were built in the 18C and 19C with stones taken from the cultivated fields, both as shelters from the burning sun and as tool sheds. Inside, the roof is in the shape of a corbelled dome, as that of an igloo. There is a narrow window, a fireplace and a cupboard all made of stone. The height of these huts, or *cabanons* in French, varies from 3-7m/10-23ft and their circumference from 10-30m/33-98ft.

Hikers are asked not to pick up stones, even loose ones, not to climb onto walls and not to light fires near or inside them as the heat would split the stones.

★ **Château de Sauvan** ⓥ – This classical building, dating from the early 18C, is shaded by ancient trees. A typical Mediterranean landscape reminiscent of Tuscany unfolds from the terrace. In 1793, the lady of the manor, who bore a striking resemblance to Queen Marie-Antoinette, offered to take her place in the Conciergerie; Marie-Antoinette refused her generous sacrifice and the countess fled the country. However, the lords of the Château de Sauvan were well liked in the area and the château was not destroyed during the Revolution. Neglected for many years, it was eventually restored in 1981.

Particularly noteworthy is the hall separated by pilasters with Ionic capitals from the imposing stone staircase overlooked by the first-floor gallery.

The fine reception rooms contain a rich collection of 17C, 18C and 19C furniture. French-style gardens adorned with fountains surround the château.

Tour de Porchères – *At the end of a path on the right of the road, just beyond the Château de Sauvan*. This massive rectangular keep, in Romanesque style, dates from the 12C; note the long voussoirs forming the arched doorway.

★ **Prieuré de Salagon** ⓥ – The elegant Benedictine **priory**, founded in 1105, rebuilt in the 15C and later used as a farmhouse, was finally restored and turned into an ethnological museum of the Haute-Provence region in 1981. Note the unusual mullioned windows and stair turret. A medieval garden, and two gardens for medicinal and aromatic herbs were planted when the museum was opened. The west front of the **church**★ is decorated with a deeply inset rose-window and a doorway, similar to that of the Ganagobie Monastery *(see Monastère de GANAGOBIE)*. Inside, the capitals and engaged columns denote a definite Provençal influence; the remains of simple 14C frescoes and engraved tableaux add to the charm of this rural church. Gallo-Roman finds have been discovered in the chancel together with evidence of an earlier church dating from the 6C.

Eating out

BUDGET

La Manne Céleste – *N 100* – ☎ *04 92 75 05 70* – *closed 18 Jun-2 Jul, 13 Nov-12 Dec, 24-27 Dec, 31 Dec-2 Jan, Mon evening (except Jul-Aug) and Tue* – *reservations recommended* – *12.96/21.34€*. This old stable houses a small restaurant popular with local people, with a convivial atmosphere guaranteed! Dishes are prepared by the proprietor, with salads and pasta served up on wooden tables without any fancy nonsense. Pizzas are cooked in a charcoal oven as you watch. Round the meal off with one of the delicious homemade sorbets.

MANOSQUE ★

Population 19 603
Michelin map 334 C10 and 245 fold 32
Local map see Vallée de la Moyenne DURANCE

Nestling among foothills at the edge of the Luberon massif, a stone's throw from the River Durance, this peaceful little town has recently expanded owing to its position in the rich agricultural Durance Valley and the proximity of new, high-tech industries; in only twenty years its population has grown from 5 000 to 20 000. This modernisation has altered the rural setting of Manosque, celebrated by the native born novelist, **Jean Giono** (1895-1970), and visitors taking a walk through the town will need sharp eyes to spot the charming little Provençal streets that the writer would have known.

Nearby Sights: CÉRESTE, Vallée de la Moyenne DURANCE, FORCALQUIER, Monastère de la GANAGOBIE, GRÉOUX-LES-BAINS, MANE, Route NAPOLÉON, RIEZ, SISTERON, Plateau de VALENSOLE

★OLD TOWN 1hr

Wide boulevards have replaced the ramparts which once enclosed the old town; the typically Provençal streets are narrow and lined with tall houses concealing secluded gardens, patios, beautiful cellars and galleries. The streets are linked by covered passages and extremely narrow alleyways known as *androns*.

★**Porte Saunerie** – This 12C gate, which formed part of the original town walls, owes its name to the salt warehouses which once stood nearby. Note the twinned openings supported on slender columns and the machicolated side turrets.

Rue Grande – This lively, picturesque high street offers a wealth of old doorways, fine stairwells, courtyards and balconies. **N°14** was the workshop where Giono's father used to mend shoes and where his mother ironed clothes. Note the wrought-iron balconies of the 16C-17C house at n°**23**.

Gates and doorways

In Manosque these are almost a local art form. Some of the finest examples can be seen at: n°5 rue Voland, which runs past St-Sauveur church, n°12 rue Rousseau, n°2 rue des Ormeaux, n°4 rue de la Saunerie and, in the Grande-Rue, n°s31 (the consul's house), 39 and 42.

Église St-Sauveur Ⓥ – The plain façade overlooks a square decorated with a fountain. Look for two blocks of stone set into the north wall of the church; one shows a pilgrim with his staff, the other a cockerel fighting with a snake. By the Gothic doorway are two impressive caryatids. The fine organ case, in carved gilded wood, dates from 1625. The square bell-tower is surmounted by a famous wrought-iron **campanile**, made in 1725 by a blacksmith from Rians.

Hôtel de Ville – The town hall, with its elegant 17C **façade★** and beautiful staircase, is one of the finest buildings in Manosque. A colourful **market** livens up the square three times a week.

Église Notre-Dame-de-Romigier – The church has a Renaissance doorway, but the nave was remodelled in the 17C and the aisles were added. The altar is a splendid 4C or 5C **sarcophagus★** in Carrara marble. According to legend, the **Black Madonna statue★** from which the church takes its name was discovered at the end of the 10C under a bramble bush, where it had been hidden when the Saracens invaded Provence in the 9C; it was later placed inside the church. The Virgin and Child both wear Merovingian crowns, which suggests that the sculpture is one of the oldest of its type in France. Before the statue was restored, its face, neck and hands were darker.

Porte Soubeyran – The 12C gate, remodelled in the 14C like the Porte Saunerie, was later decorated with a lovely stone balustrade and a tower surmounted by a graceful onion-shaped top in wrought iron.

According to a local legend, King François I, on a visit to Manosque, was welcomed at the Porte Saunerie by the beautiful Péronne de Voland, who offered him the town keys on a velvet cushion. The king courted her and, not knowing how to turn him down, the consul's daughter exposed her face to sulphur fumes in order to spoil her looks. Since then, the town has been known as "the bashful Manosque".

303

Eating out

BUDGET

La Source – *1.5km/1mi N of Manosque on Bd M.-Bret and Rte Dauphin* – ☎ *04 92 72 12 79* – *closed during the holidays around 1 Nov and at Christmas, Sa lunchtime and Mon* – *16.77/28.20€*. In summer this restaurant is nice and cool. There are large flagstones on the floor, pale beams overhead, stained wood furniture, and numerous green plants setting off the pastel colours. Provençal cuisine that won't overstretch your wallet.

MODERATE

Le Luberon – *21bis pl. du Terreau* – ☎ *04 92 72 03 09* – *closed 26 Aug-1C Sept, Sun evening and Mon except Jul-Aug* – *18.29/32.01€*. This restaurant in the old town offers food that evokes the sunshine and a good wine list to make you fully aware that you are in Provence. The setting is simple and slightly old fashioned, but the regulars come here for the quality of the food.

Le Petit Laurageais – *6 pl. du Terreau* – ☎ *04 92 72 13 00* – *closed 15-28 Feb, 1-16 Jul, 1-10 Nov, Sat lunchtime and Sun* – *19.06/28.20€*. If you want a change from Provençal cooking, try this restaurant with the understated façade which offers excellently prepared specialities from southwest France; the cooks from this region also know a thing or two… Friendly welcome.

Where to stay

MODERATE

Hôtel Le Pré St-Michel – *1.5km/1mi N of Manosque on Bd M.-Bret and Rte Dauphin* – ☎ *04 92 72 14 27* – ▣ – *24rms: 64.03/74.70€* - ⌁ *6.56€*. This modern hotel with a Provençal appearance offers a pretty panorama overlooking Manosque. The rooms are fairly plain and have a view of either the hills or the swimming pool.

Chambre d'hôte La Maurissime – *Chemin des Oliviers* – *04180 Villeneuve - 12km/7.5mi NE of Manosque on N 96 then D 216 (Rte de Forcalquier)* – ☎ *04 92 78 47 61* – *closed Jan* – ▱ – *4rms: 38.11/45.73€* – *main meal 16.77€*. This guesthouse dispenses its friendly welcome and service with professionalism and good taste. The villa, a recent construction, is a good place for lounging on the terrace or dining. The rooms are decorated in Provençal style and face the garden.

EXPENSIVE

Hostellerie de la Fuste – *04210 Valensole* – *6.5km/4mi SE of Manosque on D 907 then D 4* – ☎ *04 92 72 05 95* – *closed 7 Jan-11 Feb, Sun evening and Mon Oct-Jun except public holidays* – ▣ – *14rms: from 106.71€* - ⌁ *13.72€* – *restaurant 42.69/74.70€*. This pretty inn will delight those who dream of Provence. The rooms are as elegant as the dining room, and the terrace is set in a park with flower beds. The food will also delight those who love to eat, especially in peaceful surroundings.

Shopping

Le Moulin de l'Olivette – *Pl. de l'Olivette* – ☎ *04 92 72 00 99* – *Mon-Sat 8am-noon, 2.30pm-6.30pm Apr-Sept, 8am-noon and 2pm-6pm Oct-Mar*. This olive oil mill received an award in 1999 from the French Ministry of Agriculture and Fisheries. It sells its products retail to the consumer, by the bottle or item. There is a variety of local products and hand-crafted articles for sale, such as vinegars, soaps and different kinds of oil.

Marché (Market) – *Centre of the old town* – *Sat 5am-1pm*. This colourful market, rich with the scent of lavender and olive oil, embodies the essence of Provence. You will find almost everything here that features in Provençal cuisine and everyday life.

Rue Grande – *R. Grande* – The old town's main street, pleasantly shaded and closed to vehicular traffic, has numerous small shops dotted along it (off-the-peg clothes, articles for the home, crafts and more).

Sport and Leisure

Les Vannades – *Office municipal des sports, mairie* – ☎ *04 92 87 41 16 / 41 01 / 20 04* – *Jun-Oct, Mon-Fri 9.30am-6pm, Sat 1pm-6pm, closed Nov-Feb*. At the end of a long and difficult road lies this 11ha/27 acre leisure centre for land and water activities. The arduous journey will be forgotten in the excitement of all it has to offer: swimming (supervised), sailing and rowing courses, rambling, volleyball, boules and miniature golf.

Art

Centre Jean-Giono – *3 bd Élémir-Bourges* – ☎ *04 92 70 54 54* – *Tue-Sat 9am-noon, 2pm-6pm.* Follow in the footsteps of Jean Giono (1895-1970) on informative walks around Manosque and rambles in the local countryside, which had a profound influence on the writer's literary sensibility. This is the principle aim of this centre dedicated to the author of *Que ma joie demeure* (1934). Library and video library can be consulted on site.

M.J.C. (Maison des Jeunes and de la Culture) – *1 allée de Provence* – ☎ *04 92 72 19 70* – *Mon-Sat 8am-noon, 2pm-6pm* – *closed in Aug.* Culture and youth have joined forces in this institution which houses two venues under a single roof. The Jean le Bleu theatre hosts plays, concerts and dance shows. The Café Provisoire – true to its rather poetic name ("temporary café") – attracts crowds of young people to its weekly concert (in term-time only). Music, drama and dance classes.

Turn back, then left onto rue Soubeyran.

Place des Observantins – A former monastery has been turned into the music and dance conservatory. The square is decorated with a lovely old fountain. The library and municipal archives are housed in the **Hôtel d'Herbès**, which has a fine 17C staircase inside.

Return to the Porte Saunerie via rue Jean-Jacques-Rousseau, rue des Ormeaux, past place des Ormeaux and along rue de la Saunerie, admiring some lovely doors on the way.

SIGHTS

Fondation Carzou ⊙ – **Jean Carzou**, a French painter of Armenian descent, born in 1907, departed from Abstract painting and evolved his own intricate style, full of fantasy, against a monochrome background, to depict modern cities, Venice and Provence.

He decorated the former Couvent de la Présentation with murals adapted from a group of paintings on the theme of *The Apocalypse*. The interesting neo-Classical church, built in 1840, has a single nave surmounted by a dome on pendentives, a **coffered vault**, capitals decorated with acanthus leaves and a frieze running round the nave.

★ *The Apocalypse* – It took the artist seven years to complete this amazing fresco. Each decorated panel illustrates one of Carzou's favourite themes. The unity of the work is emphasized by the blue-green backgrounds, shown off to good advantage by the natural light from the dome.

Start with the left-hand side of the nave. In the left wing of the chancel the artist depicts destruction and massacres accomplished by Man; the four columns supporting the dome represent the Evangelists, in the apse he illustrates lust; the right side of the church is devoted to women's accomplishments. Most of the **stained-glass windows★** were also designed by Carzou; the four horsemen of the

MANOSQUE

Apocalypse symbolize the great genocides which have occurred in the history of mankind. The left wing announces the reconstruction of the world through love and work. Note the reference to Millet's **Angelus** in the corner of the left wall. The **Tree-woman** symbolizes the earth's revival; note that, in spite of the disasters brought about by Man, the sky remains blue for there is hope in the future. The lovers clasped in each other's arms represent the universality of Love. Eve appears triumphant whereas Adam, who faces her, is less sure of himself. More information about Carzou's work is available in the adjoining rooms.

Centre Jean-Giono ⊙ – This fine Provençal house, dating from the 18C, houses a museum devoted to the life and works of Jean Giono.

On the ground floor (note the beautiful ceilings), Giono's life, written works and films are presented with the help of documents. The library contains manuscripts of his works and a collection of translations from all over the world.

The Tree-Woman, Fondation Carzou

Fondation Carzou, Manosque

Most of the films to which he contributed, as well as interviews and television programmes, can be seen in the video library on request. The upper floor houses temporary exhibitions.

EXCURSIONS

Chapelle St-Pancrace (also known as Chapelle de Toutes Aures) – *2km/1.2mi southwest. Leave Manosque by ③ on the town plan and follow the signposted road.* Near this chapel, at the top of the hill, there is an extended **view★** (almost 360°) of the Luberon, Manosque and the Préalpes de Digne beyond the Durance Valley and Valensole Plateau.

Mont d'Or – *1.5km/0.9mi northeast. Starting from rue Dauphine, climb up montée des Vraies-Richesses then follow a no-through road on the right to the last house on the right, known as Le Paraïs.*

Le Paraïs ⊙ – *The house is still inhabited by the Giono family and discretion is therefore highly appreciated.* This is the house where Giono wrote most of his works from 1930 onwards. He acquired the property in 1968. The tour goes through his library and the room where he wrote his last works, decorated with a bunch of flowers painted by Giono himself. His study is on the next floor; note the cast of his right hand and other mementoes. The roofs of the old town can be seen from the window, "fitting together" as the author said, "like the plates of a suit of armour".

Mont d'Or Summit – The **view★** gradually extends to embrace the old town and its roofs, the Durance Valley, the Luberon and, in the distance, the Ste-Victoire and Ste-Baume mountains.

Forêt de Pélicier – *10km/6.2mi along D 5; 3hr. Drive out of Manosque along boulevard Martin-Bret; leave the car at the pass.*
The forest was created last century as part of a plan of reafforestation of mountain areas and therefore consists mainly of Austrian pines, which are very hardy trees. From the Col de la Mort d'Imbert, follow the path on the right which skirts a former

tile factory and its clay pits on both sides; turn left 400m/437yd further on and follow another path which goes through gypsum quarries, known as **gipières**, then round Escourteja Hill. Climb up to "Les Deux-Moulins" where an old building houses the **Centre de Découverte de l'Espace Pastoral** (Centre for the Discovery of Rural Environment). The tour continues along a forest road to the Sentier des Roches Aménagées. At the intersection of three tracks, you will find a map of the forest. Return to the Col de la Mort d'Imbert along the signposted track.

> The large tarred slabs which can be seen from the Sentier des Roches mark the area where crude oil and natural gas are being stored beneath the forest. Some 30 wells have been drilled to reach a vast layer of rock salt. Water is pumped in to dissolve the salt, which is then recovered and gradually replaced by oil and gas brought in by pipeline from the Étang de Berre. 10 million m³/353 million cu ft of oil and gas are held on the site.

La Haute MAURIENNE

Michelin map 334 L6 to M6 and 244 folds 30, 31 and 32

The valley of the River Arc, known as La Maurienne, is one of the longest intra-Alpine valleys, deeply enclosed from end to end; in the height of the Middle Ages, traders and clerics, pilgrims and soldiers all passed this way on the road to Italy. There is a striking contrast between the beautiful natural environment and the major industrial complexes lining the valley, although the upper Maurienne between the Col de l'Iseran and the Col du Mont-Cenis has been spared intensive industrialization and still retains its traditional character. Churches and chapels draw art-lovers to the area, and skiers will not be disappointed by the valley's slopes.

Nearby Sights: AUSSOIS, BESSANS, BONNEVAL-SUR-ARC, Route du GALIBIER, Route des GRANDES ALPES, Route de l'ISERAN, MODANE, Route du MONT-CENIS, ST-JEAN-DE-MAURIENNE, TIGNES, VAL D'ISÈRE, Massif de la VANOISE

BACKGROUND

Tourism and industry – The Maurienne lies on an important route between France and Italy across the Col du Mont-Cenis and, since 1980, via the Fréjus Tunnel, so that international traffic can now get through all year round by road and rail.
Between Avrieux, upriver from Modane, and Aiguebelle, near the confluence of the River Arc and River Isère, the course of the middle and lower Maurienne Valley is dotted with some 10 factories (aluminium, steel and chemicals), using the energy produced by about 20 power stations.
Among the most important hydroelectric projects carried out in the area were the building of the generating station at Aussois (1951) and the underground power station at Randens (1954).

Bonneval-sur-Arc and the Arc valley

La Haute MAURIENNE

Busy river – The vast works undertaken to harness the Arc were completed by the building of a dam which led to the creation of a huge reservoir of 320 million m³/259 200acft, at the foot of Mont Cenis, which supplies the power station at Villarodin-Bourget built lower down the valley, near Avrieux.

Three more power stations, situated between Modane and St-Jean-de-Maurienne, regulate the course of the Arc. One of the most daring achievements of the harnessing programme was the building of a 19km/11.8mi-long tunnel going through the Belledonne Massif and intended to divert part of the flow of the Arc to the Isère Valley on the other side of the mountains.

EXCURSIONS

*Haute Maurienne

FROM BONNEVAL-SUR-ARC TO MODANE

56km/34.8mi – about 2hr not including the tour of the chapels decorated with murals in Bessans and Lanslevillard, the detour up the Route du Mont-Cenis and the recommended hikes.

Between December and March the D 902 may be blocked by snow from Bonneval-sur-Arc to Bessans.

*Bonneval-sur-Arc – *See BONNEVAL-SUR-ARC.*

There are many religious monuments left between Bonneval and Lanslebourg: Stations of the Cross, oratories and chapels erected by local people or by pilgrims who had safely travelled over the border passes.

Turn left past Notre-Dame-des-Grâces towards the Refuge d'Avérole.

The **Col de la Madeleine** (not to be confused with the pass of the same name on p 300) between Bessans and Lanslevillard, with its piles of rocks scattered among larches, marks a transition in the landscape: downstream, the slopes appear more rounded, the vegetation is darker and the view extends further towards the **Dent Parrachée** (alt 12 087ft), the most southern peak of the Vanoise Massif, and, behind it, to the jagged Rateau d'Aussois.

Lanslevillard – *Park at the church and continue on foot along the path behind the school.* The church and its high steeple, perched on a promontory, tower over the village. The **Chapelle St-Sébastien** ⊘, which looks very plain from the outside, was built in the 15C by a local man following a vow he made during an epidemic of plague. The **murals★**, painted in tempera on all the walls, have retained their fresh colours and are still extremely vivid, with the martyrdom of St Sebastian on the right and the life of Christ on the other walls. Costumes and backgrounds are 15C, the expressions and gestures are as vivid as ever. The Renaissance coffered ceiling is remarkable.

Lanslebourg-Mont-Cenis – A garrison was stationed in this border town and a monument was erected to Flambeau, the army dog who, between 1928 and 1938, helped to carry the mail from the barracks up to the Sollières Fort (2 780m/9 121ft). The **Espace baroque Maurienne** ⊘ is one of the starting points for the themed tour "**Les Chemins du baroque**" *(see Practical information).*

✳ **Val-Cenis** – In 1967, the *communes* of Lanslevillard and Lanslebourg united under the name of Val-Cenis, a winter resort which occupies a central position in the Haute Maurienne region. It extends over 500ha/1 236 acres, at altitudes

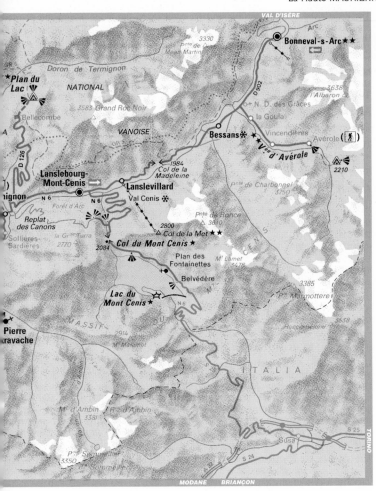

ranging from 1 400m/4 593ft to 2 800m/9 186ft, and a weekly pass giving access to most of the ski resorts in the Maurienne region is available. Europe's longest green run, the **Escargot** or "snail", comes down from the Col du Mont-Cenis *(10km/6.2mi)*; there are also several more difficult runs such as Jacquot, the Lac and the Arcelle. The north-facing aspect and the wind which frequently blows from Italy guarantee adequate snow cover, but the weather is often cold and changeable. A ski pass allows access to most of the slopes in the Maurienne.

Termignon – The name of the town is said to come from the Latin *terminus*, "the end", and in the Middle Ages Termignon was indeed the last community in the Maurienne. The present **church** ⊘ dates from the second half of the 17C; the **pine retable★** over the high altar is the work of Claude and Jean Rey; the other two are by Sébastien Rosaz. From Termignon, a winding road *(D 83)* leads to Bellecombe (alt 2 310m/7 579ft).

★★ **Refuge du Plan du Lac** – *(2hr there and back. Leave Termignon by the D 126 and stop at the car park in Bellecombe).*
🚶 From the viewing table near the refuge, there is a splendid **panorama★★** of the Dent Parrachée, Dôme de Chasseforêt, Vanoise glaciers and the Grande Casse and Grande Motte summits. The path then goes past the Entre-Deux-Eaux refuge through a pastoral landscape dotted with traditional chalets, where ibexes and chamois roam freely, to the Col de la Vanoise affording splendid **views** of the Grande Casse.

Beyond Sollières the route continues to Bramans *(8km/5mi)*. From here, take a detour on the D 100 to **St-Pierre-d'Extravache**. The modest 10C church, which is said to be the oldest in Savoie, has retained a well-preserved chancel and bell-tower.

Return to Sollières and follow D 83.

The road rises among pastures and pine woods to the ledge where the pointed steeple of Sardières can be seen from afar, with the Ambin and Thabor summits in the distance.

Go into Sardières and follow the path leading to the monolith.

★**Monolithe de Sardières** – This 83m/272ft-high pinnacle stands isolated on the southern edge of the Parc national de la Vanoise. It was first climbed in 1957.

⁑**Aussois** – *See AUSSOIS.*

In Aussois, turn left in front of the church.

The cliff road crosses the St-Benoît stream (fine waterfall facing a chapel) and dips into the Avrieux Basin.

Take a small road on the left leading to Avrieux.

Avrieux – The **church** ⊘ is said to have been founded in the 12C by two English families connected with the Archbishop of Canterbury, Thomas Becket, to whom it is dedicated. The façade is decorated with 17C frescoes depicting the seven virtues and the seven capital sins, and the fine interior **decoration**★ is Baroque. On the west wall, there is a diptych dating from 1626 which retraces the life of St Thomas Becket; note also the 16C stone stoup and painted wooden statues of Saints Ours, Anne and Katherine.

The **Souffleries de Modane-Avrieux**, the most important wind-tunnels of their kind in Europe, were designed to try out and experiment on aeroplanes, helicopters, missiles, rockets and space shuttles before test flights are carried out. It all began when the elements of a huge wind tunnel, discovered in Austria by the Allies in 1945, were brought back to this site where the nearby power station supplied the energy necessary to produce wind power.

Just beyond Villarodin, turn left onto D 214 for La Norma.

⁑**La Norma** – This picturesque little resort, founded in 1971, occupies a favourable position on top of a plateau (alt 1 350m/4 429ft) overlooking the upper Maurienne Valley, 6km/3.7mi from Modane. It is possible to combine a **gondola ride**★ to **Le Mélezet** (alt 1 990m/6 529ft, *via the* **Mélezet gondola** ⊘), commanding views of the snow-capped Péclet-Polset, the Aiguille de Doran, the Rateau d'Aussois and Dent Parrachée, with a pleasant **walk**★ down to the resort via **La Repose** and Chapelle Ste-Anne *(in winter beware of skiers)*.

The **ski area**, which extends over 700ha/1 730 acres facing north-northwest, offers good snow cover and 17 ski lifts for 60km/36mi of ski runs of varying levels of difficulty between 1 350 and 2 750m/4 429 and 9 022ft. In addition, there are exceptional **panoramas**★★ of the Thabor and Vanoise massifs.

Via ferrata du Diable – This rock-climbing course located near the Pont du Diable includes five one-way itineraries of varying difficulty and length *(3-6hr)*. Beginners should try the section linking Fort Marie-Thérèse to the Pont du Diable. Information is available from the Bureau des Guides *(see Practical information)*.

Modane – *See MODANE.*

HIGHLIGHT

★**The Esseillon Fortifications** – Between Aussois and Avrieux, the Esseillon is a rocky knoll crowned by impressive fortifications built by the Sards between 1817 and 1834 to repel a possible French invasion. There are five forts situated at different altitudes so that they could defend one another; when fully manned, 1 500 men with 170 artillery pieces would have been stationed here. The highest fortification, **Fort Marie-Christine**, which overlooks Aussois, has been restored and now serves as a gateway into the Parc national de la Vanoise; it is also the starting point of many hikes. Opposite, on the south bank of the Arc, **Fort Marie-Thérèse** is linked to the complex by the impressive Pont du Diable *(see La Norma above)*.

MEGÈVE★★★

Population 4 509

Michelin map 328 M5 and 244 fold 20 – Local map see Massif des ARAVIS

Inaugurated soon after the First World War, Megève remains one of the major French ski resorts thanks to its accommodation potential and fashionable atmosphere. The native town of **Émile Allais**, who was the 1937 downhill, slalom and combination world champion and initiated the "French skiing method", prides itself on its many admirers, who keep on coming back. The nearby pass (1 113m/3 652ft) links the Arly Valley to the Sallanches basin.

Nearby Sights: ALBERTVILLE, Massif des ARAVIS, ARGENTIÈRE, BEAUFORT, CHAMONIX-MONT-BLANC, La CLUSAZ, CLUSES, Les CONTAMINES-MONTJOIE, Les HOUCHES, Massif du MONT-BLANC, ST-GERVAIS-LES-BAINS, Bassin de SALLANCHES

A SUMMER AND WINTER RESORT

Sunny and safe, Megève's slopes are enjoyed more by lovers of "relaxed skiing" than by keen, experienced skiers, although the resort has a reputation for fault-less pistes and equipment and is clearly keen to maintain it. There are many ski lifts and snow cannon are on hand to ensure good snow cover at this relatively low altitude . The ski area, which extends over the slopes of the Mont d'Arbois, Rochebrune and the Aravis, is linked by gondola or shuttle to the other resorts of the Mont Blanc Massif. In addition, Megève has one of the most important ski schools in the world.

Eating out

MODERATE

Auberge du Grenand – *4km/2.5mi S of Megève on the road to Leutaz* – ☎ 04 50 21 30 30 – *closed 22 Apr-9 Jun and 23 Sept-8 Dec* – *15.55/38.11€*. At the foot of Mont Véry stands this farm built entirely in wood with a view of the Megève valley. Guests can sample local specialities surrounded by bunches of dried flowers. There is also an interesting collection of bells from Savoie.

Ferme-auberge des Darbelets – *4km/2.5mi SE of Megève towards Mt d'Arbois* – ☎ 04 50 93 06 12 – *closed 15 Apr-25 Jun, 15 Sept.-20 Dec and Tue in Jan, Mar and Apr* – *reservations compulsory Jul-Aug* – *22.87/28.97€*. This two-hundred year old farm on the slopes of Mont d'Arbois has the per-fect setting. In the winter, the cross-country ski runs are virtually on your doorstep. In summer, the swimming pool and the small "wildlife park" will delight young and old alike.

Les Enfants Terribles – *Pl. de l'Église* – ☎ 04 50 58 76 69 – *closed 7-23 May and Thu (Apr-Jun and 15 Sept-end Nov.)* – *24.39/45.73€*. Jean Cocteau was the happy patron of this restaurant in the resort's pedestrian zone. There is a stained glass window in the ceiling, and displays of books and lithographs by the artist. Colourful cocktails are served from behind a large bar, adding to the fun. There is a piano-bar on some evenings.

La Sauvageonne-Chez Nano – *At Leutaz* – *4km/2.5mi S of Megève on Rte du Bouchet* – ☎ 04 50 91 90 81 – *closed 21 Apr-27 Jun, 17 Sept-14 Dec* – *25.92€*. This restored farm in the middle of unspoiled countryside draws a smart clientele who come to admire its setting. Choose from a fine terrace or cosy dining room, every inch the "mountain chalet" with wood panelling, open fireplace, collection of paintings of chalets in the region and old ski equipment, in which you can dine on typically local cuisine or dishes from fur-ther afield.

Au Vieux Megève – *58 pl. de la Résistance* – ☎ 04 50 21 16 44 – *closed 11 Apr-9 Jul and 11 Sept-14 Dec* – *25.92/47.26€*. This restaurant has been run by the same family for thirty years. Inside, there is a fine open fireplace and a decor typical of "old Megève" with red table cloths and old wood pan-elling. Visitors to the resort can sample local cheese dishes free of fuss and frills.

Idéal – *At the summit of Mont d'Arbois* – *74120 St-Gervais* – *by the Mt d'Arbois or Princesse cable cars* – ☎ 04 50 21 31 26 – *closed 16 Apr-14 Dec and in the evening* – *24.39€*. This is a fine place to stop for a break on the ski slopes. The high altitude chalet combines a pleasant setting with reasonable prices by the standards of the resort. Skiers can enjoy the special dish or "kebab" of the day served in a welcoming dining room or on the vast terrace with its magnificent panoramic view.

Where to stay

BUDGET

Chambre d'hôte Les Oyats – *771 rte de Lady – 1.5km/1mi S of Megève towards Rochebrune then Rte des Perchets* – ☎ *04 50 21 11 56 - jean.claude.tissot@freesbee.fr – closed during holidays around 1 Nov – ⌧ - 2rms: 32.01/39.64€*. This is the ideal place to stay at a reasonable price for this resort. The level of comfort is satisfactory. There is no food served here, but the rooms are fitted with kitchen facilities which can be used if you are desperate to self-cater. There is a country gîte on the first floor. In summer, one or two donkeys come to graze on the grass behind the guesthouse.

MODERATE

Hôtel L'Auguille – *Chemin de l'Auguille* – ☎ *04 50 21 40 00 – closed 26 Apr-31 May and 1 Oct-14 Dec* – ◻ *– 11rms: 53.36/64.03€* - ⌧ *6.10€*. This is a useful little place a short distance out of the village which is simple and well kept. The reception area is well lit, and the plain rooms neat and tidy with functional furniture. It is peaceful and not expensive by the standards of the resort.

Hôtel Chaumine – *36 chemin des Bouleaux, via Chemin du Maz* – ☎ *04 50 21 37 05 – closed 16 Apr-28 Jun and 3 Sept-21 Dec* – ◻ *– 11rms: 76.99/88.42€* - ⌧ *6.40€*. This is just the sort of establishment we like! A pretty chalet with a friendly, homely atmosphere at the end of a quiet track a few minutes away from the centre and well placed for the ski slopes. It has pale golden wood panelling, large patchwork and mountain chalet style furnishings, and a decor reminiscent of Scandinavia.

Hôtel Gai Soleil – *Rte du Crêt-du-Midi* – ☎ *04 50 21 00 70 – closed 16 Apr-14 Jun and 16 Sept-14 Dec* – ◻ *– 21rms: 86.90€* – ⌧ *6.86€* – *restaurant 20.58€*. This comfortable chalet with the welcoming façade is about five minutes from the centre. The rooms vary in size and are plainly decorated with rustic wooden furniture. In summer, guests can enjoy the swimming pool and terrace.

EXPENSIVE

Hôtel Lodge Park – *100 r. d'Arly* – ☎ *04 50 93 05 03 – closed 17 Apr-14 Jun and 16 Sept-14 Dec* – ◻ *– 39rms: from 208.86€* - ⌧ *12.20€* – *restaurant 48.78/68.60€*. Hunting trophies, carvings of animals, logs and comfortable furniture recreate the atmosphere of a Canadian hunter's cabin. But don't be fooled, this is one of the best hotels in Megève, and the "natural" atmosphere in no way compromises the sophisticated luxury and high standard of service.

Les Fermes de Marie – *Chemin de Riante-Colline, via N 212 (rte d'Albertville)* – ☎ *04 50 93 03 10 – closed 16 Apr-30 May and 1 Oct-30 Nov* – ◻ *– 61rms: half-board from 227.15€* - ⌧ *12.20€* – *restaurant 39.64€*. These chalets in the style of summer pasture farms combine the comfort and sophistication of the best hotels and are highly sought after by the high of this society. The accommodation in the chalets on the hillside is warm and the furniture from the Savoie region is made and stained locally. Swimming pool and beauty centre.

On the town

Le Piano à Bretelles – *Chemin Retornes* – ☎ *04 50 58 94 88 – You are advised to reserve*. Lucien and his accordion bring all the old favourites of French popular music back to life here. Every weekend there are dinner-dances which set even the tables spinning.

Les 5 Rues – *Carrefour des 5-Rues – mid-Dec-end Mar Wed-Mon from 5.30pm*. Megève's jazz club. In this rustic bar with an open fireplace patrons sip their aperitif to the accompaniment of piano or guitar music. Night-owls flock to the concerts that start after 10pm.

Palo-Alto – *R. Charles-Feige* – ☎ *04 50 93 01 83 – open daily 6.30pm-5am in winter*. Evenings here begin in the cosseted setting of a luxurious piano-bar and end in the disco where you can strut your stuff to all kinds of music (from retro to techno).

Shopping

Au Crochon – *Rte de Praz-sur-Arly* – ☎ *04 50 21 03 26 – Mon-Sat 7.30am-7.30pm*. Those who love articles hand-crafted from wood will be spoiled for choice here! Whether you are hesitating between a flower pot or a butter mould, a pair of clogs (for Grandma) or a small cask (for Grandpa), a toboggan or snowshoes, it boils down to whether you can fit it into your suitcase…

Flocon de neige – *133 r. Monseigneur-Conseil* – ☎ *04 50 21 20 10 – daily 8.30am-12.30pm, 2.30pm-7.30pm, closed in May, Oct and Nov*. A vital stop for food lovers with chocolates and confectionery, including the famous local speciality, the "Glaçon" (filled chocolate in a delicate "snowy" coating).

In summer the area is popular for its bracing climate, nearby forest, numerous possibilities of mountain hikes and drives and wide choice of sporting activities (tennis, swimming, skating etc). Megève is also a children's health and holiday resort.

SIGHTS

Musée du Haut Val d'Arly ⊘ – *173 rue St-François*. The museum houses collections of traditional objects displayed in reconstructed authentic settings. Several themes are dealt with: domestic life, agricultural tools, milk processing, textiles and winter sports.

Le Calvaire – This is a replica of the Stations of the Cross in Jerusalem, lined with 15 oratories and chapels decorated with paintings and sculptures *(unfortunately in poor condition)* made by local craftsmen between 1844 and 1864. From the lower chapel, there is a pleasant view of the upper Val d'Arly.

HIKES

Viewpoints Accessible by Gondola

★★ **Mont d'Arbois** ⊘ – Alt 1 833m/6 014ft. *Access by gondola from the Plateau du Mont d'Arbois or by the Princesse gondola from the Petit-Bois crossroads.*
Splendid **panoramic view** of the Aravis and Fiz mountains as well as Mont Blanc. It is possible to walk in 20min to the upper station of the cable car which goes back down to St-Gervais.

★★ **Croix des Salles** ⊘ – Alt 1 705m/5 594ft. *About 1hr 30min there and back, including 12min ride in the Jaillet gondola and 45min on foot.*
🚶 Having reached the upper station, continue on foot to the cross through pastures and woodland. **View** of the Fiz range and Mont Blanc Massif.

★ **Rochebrune Super-Megève** ⊘ – Alt 1 754m/5 755ft. *About 1hr there and back, including an 8min cable-car ride.*
🚶 **View** of the Val d'Arly, the Aravis mountains and Mont Blanc.

For Experienced Walkers

A map on sale at the tourist office will enable you to take full advantage of the possibilities the area has to offer.

★★★ **Mont Joly** – Alt 2 525m/8 284ft. *4hr 30min there and back on foot from the Mont d'Arbois via a well-marked path. Climbing boots are recommended, particularly for the last, fairly steep part of the itinerary.*
🚶 The exceptional **panorama★★★** unfolding from the summit *(viewing table)*, includes the Mont-Blanc, Vanoise, Beaufortain, Écrins and Grandes Rousses massifs, the Belledonne range, the Chartreuse and the Aravis.

★★ **Mont de Vorès** – Alt 2 067m/6 781ft. *5hr 30min on foot. Difference in altitude: 800m/2 625ft. This itinerary is not difficult but requires stamina. Board the cable car preferably before 10am. If it is not working, it is possible to make a similar round tour from Leutaz.*
🚶 The path rises to L'Alpette and the Col de Véry on the way to the Mont de Vorès. Splendid **view** of the Mont-Blanc Massif to the east, with the Col du Joly and Lac de la Girotte in the foreground, and the Aravis mountains to the west. The path then follows the mountain ridge to the Crêt du Midi which offers a remarkable **view** of Megève on the right and Le Planay on the left. Walk down to Les Fontanettes then up again to Rochebrune *(hard-going walk for about 1hr)* along a fairly steep path.

MÉRIBEL***

Méribel is an attractive ski resort situated in the Allues Valley, at the heart of the **Trois Vallées**★★★ ski area *(see Massif de la VANOISE)*, the largest in the world.

British skiing enthusiasts were the first to realise the potential of the area for tourism. After the annexation of Austria by Germany in 1938, they stopped going to Austrian resorts and turned to the French Alps in their search for new slopes. Lord Lindsay discovered the Allues Valley with its 13 old hamlets and founded Méribel. After the war, regulations concerning architectural styles were laid down: all residential buildings must be chalets with ridged roofs and wood or stone façades. This concern about blending the resort's architecture with the landscape, combined with the area's potential, has made Méribel one of the finest French ski resorts, welcoming regular international visitors who appreciate the refined atmosphere of this exceptional resort.

More recently, Méribel played its part as an Olympic venue during the 1992 Albertville games, hosting the women's Alpine skiing on the piste du roc de Fer and ice hockey matches on its new rink.

Nearby Sights: La Vallée des BELLEVILLE, CHAMPAGNY-EN-VANOISE, COURCHEVEL, Route de la MADELEINE, La TARENTAISE, Massif de la VANOISE.

THE RESORTS

At the centre of Les Trois Vallées is **Méribel-Mottaret**, situated between 1 700-1 800m/5 577-5 906ft, on the edge of the Parc national de la Vanoise, and offering a successful compromise between modern comfort and traditional architecture. A network of gondolas provides fast and comfortable links with Courchevel, Les Ménuires and Val-Thorens. The recently equipped areas of Mont Vallon, Mont de la Chambre, Roc des Trois Marches and Roc de Fer offer some of the finest ski slopes in Europe, ideal for competent skiers. The fact that they face north-south and west makes it possible for skiers to remain in the sun all day.

The cross-country ski area is not very extensive but delightful; there are 33km/20mi of well-covered trails round the Altiport and Plan du Tuéda, in a fine woodland setting (spruce and arolla pine), at an altitude of 1 700m/5 577ft.

The numerous chalet-apartments of Méribel are dotted around the forest between 1 450-1 600m/4 757-5 249ft; the only drawback is that, apart from La Chaudanne, there is no real resort centre. The road continues to the Altiport (mountain airport), where golf is played in summer. Themed flights are available in all seasons over the Trois Vallées, the Olympic sites and Mont Blanc.

Non-skiers can enjoy the superb landscapes of the Trois Vallées area. Various paths crisscross the forest or skirt the ski runs, and a special **pedestrian pass**, known as a *forfait piéton*, give hikers access to gondolas and chair-lifts in Méribel and Courchevel. In summer, Méribel is a popular **hiking base**, since nearly a quarter of the surrounding area, covering 8 500ha/21 004 acres, is situated inside the Parc national de la Vanoise.

HIGHLIGHT

★★ The Main Summits

★★★**La Saulire** – *Access from Méribel by the Burgin Saulire gondola or from Mottaret by the Pas du Lac gondola.* Splendid **panorama** *(see COURCHEVEL)*.

★★**Mont du Vallon** – Alt 2 952m/9 685ft. *From Mottaret, walk to the Plan des Mains alt 2 150m/7 054ft. Allow 1hr 15min in summer. In winter, the only access is via the Plattières gondola (second section, skiers only). Continue to the summit by the Mont Vallon gondola.* On arrival, go to the panel marked "Réserve de Tuéda": superb close-up **view**★★★ of the Allues Valley's conservation area, including the Aiguille du Borgne and the Gébroulaz Glacier to the south and the surrounding massif. Turn back and take a path leading towards the Lacs du Borgne, giving a fine view of the Vallée des Belleville with the Aiguille d'Arves and Grandes Rousses Massif in the distance.

★★**Roc des Trois Marches** – Alt 2 704m/8 871ft. *In winter, access from Mottaret by the Plattières gondola (three sections).* Beautiful **circular view**, including the Vanoise glaciers and the Meije.

★★**Tougnète** ⊙ – Alt 2 410m/7 907ft. *Access from Méribel by gondola; if possible, sit facing backwards rather than in the direction of travel.* On the way up, there is a view of Méribel and the villages dotted around the valley, with Mont Blanc and the Beaufortain in the background. From the upper station, the view extends over the whole Vallée des Belleville.

Skiers can also enjoy the various panoramas unfolding from the **Roc de Fer**★★, **Pas de Cherferie**★★, **Mont de la Challe**★, **Mont de la Chambre**★★ and **Col de la Loze**★★.

314

Eating out

MODERATE

Le Blanchot – *Rte de l'altiport* – *3.5km/2mi N of Méribel* – ☎ *04 79 00 55 78* – *closed 2 May-14 Jun and 11 Sept-14 Dec* – *24.39/29.73€*. This restaurant is named after the species of hare that turns white as soon as the snow comes. The road that leads to this chalet is an invitation to discover the delights of the outdoors: a pine forest, a summer golf course and cross-country skiing in winter. The food served here is fairly plain at lunchtime and more elaborate in the evening.

La Marée Blanche – *Opposite the ice rink* – ☎ *04 79 08 67 83* – *closed beginning May-beginning Jul and beginning Sept-beginning Dec* – *24.39/48.78€*. In front of the stove, people from Brittany remain faithful to their traditions and even though they are far from their region of origin they continue to cook their traditional, freshly prepared fish and seafood dishes as if they were at home. They will even whip up a few Breton crêpes, by popular demand!

Where to stay

MODERATE

Hôtel Croix Jean-Claude – *Aux Allues* – *7km/4mi N of Méribel on D915°* – ☎ *04 79 08 61 05* – *closed 10 May-25 Jun and 20 Sept-28 Oct* – *18rms: 68.60/83.85€* - ⌧ *7.62€* – *restaurant 19.82/36.59€*. Say hello to the locals quenching their thirst at the bar in this restaurant away from the ski slopes. Nights spent here are peaceful and the cuisine is in the local tradition, served on the terrace or in the rustic-style dining room.

EXPENSIVE

Hôtel Adray Télébar – *On the ski slopes (access on foot only)* – ☎ *04 79 08 60 26* – *closed 21 Apr-19 Dec* – *24rms: from 103.67€* - ⌧ *9.15€* – *restaurant 27.44€*. You can get here on skis, and your luggage will catch up with you in a tracked vehicle. You will be greeted by a friendly family cosily settled in this chalet entirely made from timber, right in the middle of the ski slopes, opposite snow-clad peaks. Large terrace for sunbathing.

Hôtel Yéti – *Rd-pt des Pistes* – ☎ *04 79 00 51 15* – *closed 26 Apr-6 Jul and 1 Sept-14 Dec* – ◲ – *28rms: from 157.02€* - ⌧ *10.67€* – *restaurant 26.68/39.64€*. If you are not the sporty type, you can settle for a deckchair on the panoramic terrace. Inside, the warm tones of pale waxed wood blend with the fabrics and carpets in the vaulted lounge. Spacious rooms with wood panelling. Food-lovers will be well catered for here. Large swimming pool in summer.

Résidence Les Fermes de Méribel – *Rte de la Forêt* – ☎ *04 79 01 32 00* – *closed 28 Apr-30 Jun and 2 Sept-16 Dec* – *67 apartments: 4/10 persons, per week from 1040.46€*. Invitation to chill out in this charming establishment at the gates of the world's largest area of ski slopes. The apartments evoke the style of the Savoie region with wood panelling and colourful fabrics. Once you have shed your skis, it's time for a quick dip in the heated swimming pool.

On the town

Bar la Tueda – *Méribel-Mottaret* – ☎ *04 79 01 07 51* – *open daily* – *access on foot only*. Beauty is worth the effort, so it is on Shanks's pony that you will have to get to this small chalet at the heart of the La Tueda nature reserve. In the winter this haven of peace and quiet is the ideal stopping place for cross-country skiers; in summer, people are mainly drawn here by the lake.

L'Éterlou – *La Chaudanne* – ☎ *04 79 08 89 00* – *lachaudanne@laposte.fr* – *daily from 6pm in season* – *closed May-Jun and Sept-Oct*. This bar located in the hotel of the same name has an atmosphere that is both chic and convivial at once. Numerous themed evenings are run here, and there is a small dance floor.

Le Pub – *Méribel-centre* – ☎ *04 79 08 60 02* – *open daily 11am-1am*. This very popular Irish pub is mainly frequented by an English-speaking clientele. Themed evenings and concerts every evening.

Les Pierres Plates – *La Saulire* – ☎ *04 79 00 46 41* – *www.chaudanne.com* – *Dec-Apr and Jun-Sept, daily 9am-4.45pm* – *in winter accessible only by cable car leaving from Chaudanne*. This bar-restaurant at an altitude of 2 700m/8 860ft on the summit of Saulire commands an incomparable view of the Loze, Grande Casse and Vanoise range.

HIKES

★ **Plan du Tuéda** – *As you reach Mottaret, follow signs for Le Chatelet and park your car at the end of the road.*
The **Réserve naturelle de Tuéda** was created in 1990 for the preservation of one of the last large forests of arolla pines in Savoie. These trees, which sometimes reach 600 years of age, are sought after for making furniture and musical instruments and have therefore been considerably reduced in numbers. The Tuéda Forest surrounds a lovely lake overlooked by the jagged silhouette of the Aiguille du Fruit and by Mont Vallon. A **nature trail**, lined with many flower species, offers hikers the possibility of discovering this exceptional and fragile environment.

★★ **Col de Chanrouge** – *Alt 2 531m/8 304ft. Start from the Plan du Tuéda. On the way up, allow 2hr to the Refuge du Saut then 1hr 15min to the pass. On the way down, allow 2hr.* From the pass, there is a fine **view** of the Courchevel Valley, of the ski area of La Plagne (overlooked by the Sommet de Bellecôte) and of the Mont Blanc Massif.

Tuéda Nature Reserve with the Aiguille du Fruit in the background

MODANE

Population 3 658
Michelin map 333 N6 and 244 fold 32 – Local map see La MAURIENNE

This border town at the beginning of the middle Maurienne Valley, beneath the southern heights of the Vanoise Massif, owes its existence to the Fréjus tunnels linking France and Italy.

Nearby Sights: AUSSOIS, BESSANS, BONNEVAL-SUR-ARC, Route du GALIBIER, Route des GRANDES-ALPES, La Haute MAURIENNE, Route du MONT-CENIS, ST-JEAN-DE-MAURIENNE, Massif de la VANOISE

BACKGROUND

Tunnel Routier du Fréjus – Inaugurated in July 1980 after six years of construction work, the 2 870m/8mi-long road tunnel is shorter than the Arlberg tunnel (Austria) and the St-Gothard tunnel (Switzerland), but longer than the Mont Blanc tunnel. This Franco-Italian project was designed to ease road traffic when the Col du Mont-Cenis is blocked by snow.

The planned construction of a high-speed TGV rail link from Lyon to Turin will involve drilling a 50km/31mi tunnel through the mountains, starting at Modane. The monumental **entrance to the railway tunnel** can be seen from the road. *(Leave Modane and head towards Valfréjus; the road is on the left).*

EXCURSIONS

★**Sentier nature de l'Orgère** – *From N 6 at Le Freney, turn right onto D 106, which rises steeply to the Orgère refuge (parking) over a distance of 13km/8mi.*
This nature trail *(2km/1.2mi)* winds through the Orgère Valley across meadows, woodland and pastures. The first part is lined with information panels about the specific environment. Ask the warden of the Maison du Parc for a leaflet giving details fo the trail.

★★★**Hike to the Col de Chavière** – *Departure from the Orgère refuge: 3hr up (including 2hr to the Lac de Partie); 2hr down. Difference in altitude: about 900m/2 953ft. Climbing boots are recommended, not least because there is still snow on the ground until the end of July. Take a pair of binoculars to observe the fauna.*
🔼 The path, with a view of the Râteau d'Aussois and the Aiguille Doran, climbs to the ruins of the Chalets de l'Estiva: **view★★** of Longe Côte and La Norma. When the path starts going down, after a further hour's walking, the Col de Chavière comes into view flanked by the snow-capped **Péclet-Polset** and high cliffs. Chamois and ibexes roam about the area. Beyond the Lac de Partie, the path climbs steeply to the pass (2 801m/9 190ft), giving a splendid view of the Pralognan Valley and Mont Blanc in the distance.

★ **Valfréjus** – Alt 1 500m/4 921ft. *8km/5mi southwest.* The main attractions of this small ski resort, created in 1983, are its tasteful architecture, which fits in well with the landscape, and the nearby forest planted with spruces, larches and arolla pines. Between 2 000m-2 500m/6 562ft-8 202ft, the north-facing slopes enjoy good snow cover; there are 12 ski lifts and some 20 ski runs. In summer, Valfréjus is the starting point of hikes to the Pointe du Fréjus and Thabor Massif.

★★ **Punta Bagna** ⊘ – Alt 2 750m/9 022ft. *The summit is only accessible by gondola in wintertime; in summer, only the first section operates.*
The **panorama★★** is superb. The Rochebrune and the Italian Alps are visible straight ahead, beyond the Col du Fréjus, to the left is the Pointe de Fréjus. From the terrace of the restaurant, it is possible to see the northern summits of the Écrins Massif (Grande Ruine, Pic Gaspard, Meije and Rateau) to the southwest, and the Valfréjus ski area as well as the Péclet-Posset, Col d'Aussois, the Vanoise glacier, Grande Motte and Dent Parrachée to the north.

MOLINES-EN-QUEYRAS ★

Population 336
Michelin map 334 J4 and 244 fold 44 – Local map see Le QUEYRAS

Not far from St-Véran lie the seven hamlets of Molines. Their picturesque old houses are surmounted by large grain lofts, where crops continue to ripen after the harvest. There are few hotels but accommodation is available in private homes in the old village and surrounding hamlets.
In winter, Molines offers skiing in a lovely woodland setting; the small ski area is linked to that of St-Véran.

Nearby Sights: ABRIÈS, BRIANÇON, Le BRIANÇONNAIS, CEILLAC, Vallée de FREISSINIÈRES, Route des GRANDES ALPES, GUILLESTRE, MONT-DAUPHIN, MONTGENÈVRE, Le QUEYRAS, ST-VERAN, VARS

EXCURSIONS

★★**Route du Col Agnel** (Aigue Agnelle Valley)

15km to the Col Agnel – about 30min. Road closed in winter

Drive to Pierre Grosse, which owes its name to the **erratic blocks** of igneous rock scattered over the surrounding pastures, then on to Fontgillarde, the valley's highest hamlet (1 997m/6 552ft). Beyond Fontgillarde, the road offers a fine **view** of the Pic de Château Renard, towering above the trees. A plaque, fixed to a rock on the right-hand side of the road, reminds passers-by that Hannibal's and Caesar's armies went through here on their way across the Alps.

The road continues to climb through a high-altitude mountain landscape, offering **views** of the snow-covered Pelvoux Massif to the northwest. It finally reaches the Agnel Refuge and, 2km/1.2mi further on, the Agnel Pass on the Italian border. Walk up to the **viewing table** (alt 2 744m/9 003ft) for a splendid **panorama★★** of the Pain de Sucre and Monte Viso to the east, the Grand Queyras and Pointe des Sagnes to the northwest and the Pic de Rochebrune further away and the Meije and Mont Pelvoux in the distance.

Where to stay and Eating out

MODERATE

Hôtel Le Cognarel – *Au Coin – 3km/2mi E of Molines-en-Queyras on D 205 then a minor-road –* ☎ *04 92 45 81 03 – closed 1 Apr-31 May and 16 Sept-21 Dec – 21rms: 61.74/64.49€ -* ⌧ *6.86€ – restaurant 18.29/32.01€.* Nights are peaceful in these two chalets on the slopes above a hamlet. There is nothing to stop you seeking out some fun and company in the local bar which acts as reception. Rooms are furnished in the mountain chalet style. Generous portions of food prepared using good quality produce.

★★ Route de St-Véran (Aigue Blanche Valley) – *See Le QUEYRAS,* ②.

HIKES

★★★**Pain de Sucre** – Alt 3 208m/10 525ft. *Leave the car on the roadside between the refuge and the Col Agnel. 1hr 45min to the top, 1hr 15min down. Difference in altitude: 600m/1 968ft. This itinerary is suitable for experienced hikers equipped with climbing boots; dry weather essential.*

⬛ The **Col Vieux★** (2 806m/9 206ft) is easily reached in 30min; another 15min climb takes you to a ledge; carry straight on to a path which winds up to the Pain de Sucre *(very steep climb, caution is recommended).* The magnificent **panorama★★★**, one of the finest in the Alps, includes Monte Viso and the Italian Alps to the east, the Brec and Aiguille de Chambeyron to the south and the Oisans Massif to the west. To the north, the view extends as far as Mont Blanc in clear weather. Go down along a marked path starting near the cross and leading back to the Col Vieux.

The Caterpillar and the Larch
or
Why evergreens turn brown in summer

Hikers walking through the larch forests in July are sometimes horrified to see acres of blighted trees. What is this strange curse that strikes the "kings of the Queyras" every ten years?

The culprit is a creature called the larch budmoth. Its caterpillars hatch on the tree and gnaw into the buds, eating away at the needles and leaving only a dry husk. These give the tree its dull brown colour, but even a plague which destroys all the needles will not kill off a healthy larch. Pesticides are only used to control the insects in areas well off the beaten track.

Massif du MONT-BLANC★★★

Michelin map 328 O6 and 244 folds 10, 21 and 22

The Mont Blanc Massif surpasses in height all other European mountains, its highest peak reaching 4 807m/15 771ft, yet it owes its fame essentially to the wonderful variety of scenery offered by its domes, needles and glaciers. It was this landscape which inspired pioneering climbers, the first *alpinistes* to take on the challenge of Mont Blanc; thanks to their efforts, countless amateur mountaineers have been able to follow in their footsteps. Motorists can enjoy an excellent overall view by driving up the Chamonix Valley, through which flows the Arve, or delight in the pastoral landscapes of the Val Montjoie (Bon Nant Valley).

The long "Round Tour of Mont Blanc" *(320km/199mi)*, via the Grand and Petit St-Bernard passes, is highly recommended; but there is also the round tour of Mont Blanc on foot, which is a long and fascinating walk suitable for experienced hikers with plenty of stamina. It is also possible to fly over the massif, starting from Megève or Sallanches airfield.

Nearby Sights: ARGENTIÈRE, CHAMONIX-MONT-BLANC, Les CONTAMINES-MONTJOIE, Les HOUCHES, MEGÈVE, ST-GERVAIS-LES-BAINS, Bassin de SALLANCHES

BACKGROUND

The First Ascent of Mont Blanc

In the mid-18C, it became fashionable for wealthy young men on a grand tour of Europe to stop in Chamonix, where they were shown the Mer de Glace by local guides. In 1760, a young scientist from Geneva, **Horace Bénédict de Saussure** offered a reward to the first person to reach the summit of Mont Blanc. A few local people attempted the climb but were all defeated by ignorance, fear, lack of equipment and the conviction that it was impossible to survive a night at such great heights.

In 1776, one **Jacques Balmat**, caught out by nightfall while looking for crystals in the mountains, showed that one could spend a night at very high altitude and survive. **Michel-Gabriel Paccard**, a doctor from Chamonix, found his experience interesting. He had spent many an hour surveying Mont Blanc with his telescope, trying to plot a path to the summit and the two of them took up Saussure's challenge; they left on 7 August 1786 and reached the summit the following evening, completely exhausted.

The following year, it was Saussure's turn to make the ascent accompanied by 18 guides laden with scientific equipment; using barometric instruments, he was able to confirm the height of the peak.

Many more attempts followed, some of them made by women such as **Marie Paradis** in 1809 and **Henriette d'Angeville** in 1838.

Saussure and his team climbing Mont Blanc

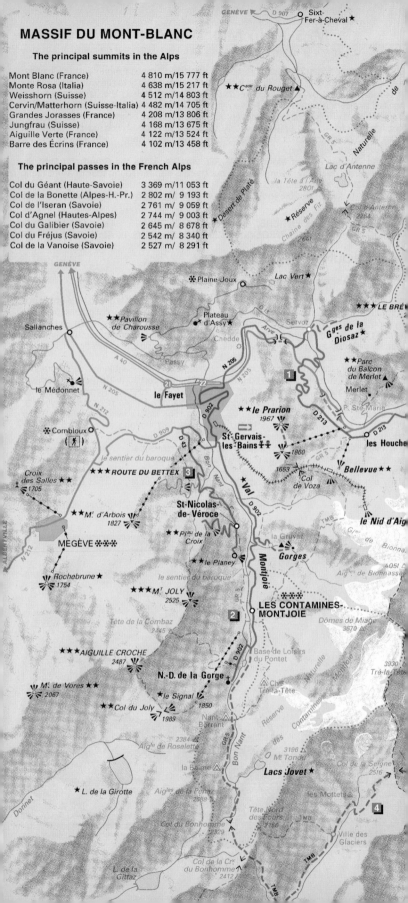

MASSIF DU MONT-BLANC

The principal summits in the Alps

Mont Blanc (France)	4 810 m/15 777 ft	
Monte Rosa (Italia)	4 638 m/15 217 ft	
Weisshorn (Suisse)	4 512 m/14 803 ft	
Cervin/Matterhorn (Suisse-Italia)	4 482 m/14 705 ft	
Grandes Jorasses (France)	4 208 m/13 806 ft	
Jungfrau (Suisse)	4 168 m/13 675 ft	
Aiguille Verte (France)	4 122 m/13 524 ft	
Barre des Écrins (France)	4 102 m/13 458 ft	

The principal passes in the French Alps

Col du Géant (Haute-Savoie)	3 369 m/11 053 ft	
Col de la Bonette (Alpes-H.-Pr.)	2 802 m/ 9 193 ft	
Col de l'Iseran (Savoie)	2 761 m/ 9 059 ft	
Col d'Agnel (Hautes-Alpes)	2 744 m/ 9 003 ft	
Col du Galibier (Savoie)	2 645 m/ 8 678 ft	
Col du Fréjus (Savoie)	2 542 m/ 8 340 ft	
Col de la Vanoise (Savoie)	2 527 m/ 8 291 ft	

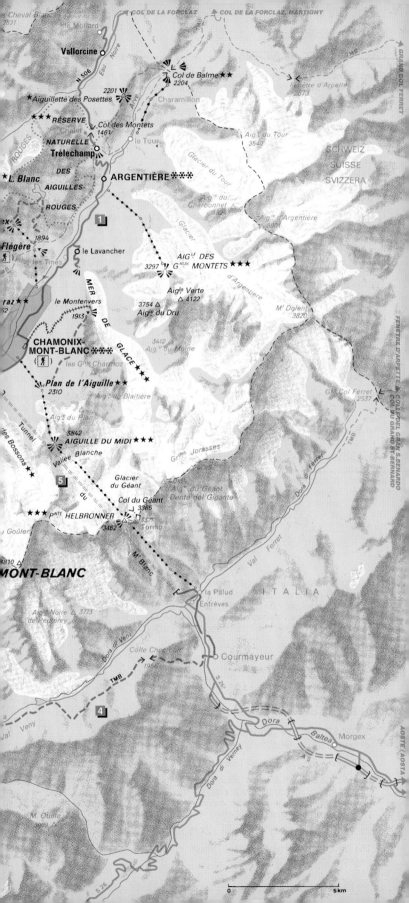

GEOGRAPHICAL NOTES

Mont Blanc... – Like the rest of the Alpine range, Mont Blanc has two different aspects. On the French side, it looks like a "gentle giant", impressively flanked by snow-covered domes underlined by a few rocky escarpments (Aiguille du Goûter and Aiguilles de Bionnassay) whereas the view from the Italian side is of a grim, dark wall bristling with rock pinnacles or needles (Aiguille Noire du Peutérey). The ascent from this side requires a lot of mountaineering skill, but endurance is more important if you want to climb Mont Blanc from Chamonix or St-Gervais.

...and its satellites – The Chamonix Valley owes its fame to the **"needles"**, (aiguilles) carved out of a kind of greenish coarse granite, known as *protogine*. Along the rock face of these splendid pinnacles, mountaineers can find the same hand and footholds year after year, for several decades. The most famous peaks are the Grépon, the Aiguille de Blaitière and the Aiguille du Dru. Three huge **glaciers** are sought after by summer visitors: the **Mer de Glace**, the longest (14km/8.7mi from the head of the Géant Glacier) and most popular, owing to the famous Montenvers scenery; the **Glacier des Bossons** (7km/4.3mi), the most picturesque, thrusting through the forest; the **Glacier d'Argentière** (11km/6.8mi), the most impressive, beneath the imposing north face of the Aiguille Verte. Since the last Ice Age, the size of these glaciers has changed considerably with the fluctuating climate; from the 16C to the mid-18C they stretched so far down that they destroyed houses built below them.

On the other side of the Arve Valley, the Aiguilles Rouges, which are the training ground of rock-climbers, offer some remarkable viewpoints such as the Brévent.

South of Mont Blanc, the snow-covered Dômes de Miage form the typical background of the Val Montjoie.

TUNNEL DU MONT-BLANC

After more than two years of rebuilding work following the disastrous fire of March 1999, the tunnel has been reopened to all vehicles. Improved safety measures are in place and a revised system now only allows heavy goods traffic from one direction at a time. Remember that drivers are required to keep a strictly enforced minimum stopping distance of 150m/492ft.

The Col du Géant (alt 3 365m/11 040ft), which is the lowest pass across the range, could not play an important economic role owing to its high altitude. France and Italy therefore decided to finance the building of the 11.6km/7mi-long Mont Blanc Tunnel, which took place between 1959 and 1965. Chamonix is now only 20km/12.4mi from Courmayeur. The thickness of the layer of rock covering the tunnel is up to 2 480m/8 136ft below the Aiguille du Midi.

The Disaster

Nearly 2 million vehicles of all types went through the tunnel in 1998, but in March 1999 a traffic accident sparked off a fire which claimed the lives of 41 people. The tragedy forced the immediate closure of the tunnel, revealed the inadequacy of the ventilation and safety systems, which have now been entirely rebuilt, and reopened the debate about the problems of transport in the mountains.

EXCURSIONS

★★★① Route de Chamonix

FROM ST-GERVAIS-LES-BAINS TO VALLORCINE
41km/25.5mi – about 2hr – see local map

Le Fayet – *See ST-GERVAIS-LES-BAINS.*

Beyond the modern power station at Passy, the road rises above the Chedde Plain, within sight of the long viaduct, carrying the Autoroute Blanche to Chamonix and of the splendid Chaîne des Fiz to the north, then makes its way through the Défilé du Châtelard and a tunnel to the Servoz Basin.

At Servoz Station, turn left towards D 13.

The road now runs past Montées-Pélissier through the narrow valley carved out by the Arve on its way to Chamonix

Turn right onto D 213.

☀ **Les Houches** – *See Les HOUCHES.*

Continue along D 213 which joins N 205.

The road runs close to the lower end of the Bossons Glacier and the view embraces the superb Aiguilles de Chamonix.

★★**Chamonix and excursions** – *See CHAMONIX-MONT-BLANC.*

Just beyond Chamonix, the slender spire of the Aiguille du Dru standing next to the **Aiguille Verte** forms a striking picture. The Aiguille Verte (alt 4 122m/ 13 523ft) was first climbed by two Swiss guides and an Englishman, Edward Whymper, who is best remembered for his successful ascent of the Cervin in 1865.

Beyond Les Tines, turn right onto the road leading to Le Lavancher.

The road rises rapidly to **Le Lavancher** situated on a spur separating the Argentière and Chamonix basins. *Turn right before the Beausoleil Hotel.*

There are contrasting **views★★** of the Chamonix Valley and its glaciers down-river and of the rocky peaks framing Argentière upriver, with the Glacier d'Argentière in the foreground beneath the Aiguille du Chardonnet.

Take the D 506 to Argentière

★★**Argentière** - *See ARGENTIÈRE.*

As you leave Argentière, turn right towards Le Tour; the landscape becomes more austere and the Glacier du Tour comes into view.
From **Trélechamp**, there is a fine **vista★★** of the high summits of the Mont Blanc Massif.
N 506 *(blocked by snow from December to April)* continues past Trélechamp through scrubland covered with rhododendrons and juniper bushes to the **Col des Montets** (alt 1 461m/4 793ft) overlooked by the Aiguilles Rouges.

★★ **Réserve naturelle des Aiguilles Rouges** – *See ARGENTIÈRE.*

The road follows the wooded valley of the River Eau Noire, offering views of the Swiss Alps.

Vallorcine – *Drive past the station on the right and turn left towards Le Mollard. Turn round at the entrance of the hamlet.*
The Vallorcine Church stands out against the impressive rock face of the Aiguille de Mesure at the northern extremity of the Aiguilles Rouges and Mont-Blanc massifs *(in order to prolong this excursion to Martigny across the Forclaz Pass, see The Green Guide Switzerland).*

★② Val Montjoie

FROM ST-GERVAIS TO NOTRE-DAME-DE-LA-GORGE

16km/10mi – about 45min – See local map.

⚓ **St-Gervais-les-Bains** – *See ST-GERVAIS-LES-BAINS.*

Leave St-Gervais by ② on the town map, D 902 towards Les Contamines.

Beyond Bionnay, a narrow wooded passage opens the way into the Contamines Basin in its picturesque mountain setting.

Gorges de la Gruvaz ⊙ – *On the left, 1.5km/0.9mi from D 902. Caution: the first section includes several footbridges, the second a steep slippery path. Leave the car after La Gruvaz, in front of the entrance to the gorge.*
The path starts by going through the woods, within sight of the stream; once above the tree line, it climbs up the schist slopes of the south side; look back to admire the gorge with St-Nicolas-de-Véroce in the distance. The path leads to a **viewpoint★**; upstream, the gorge forms a perfect V carved out of schist with the raging stream cascading down from the Miage Glacier.

★★**Les Contamines-Montjoie** – *See Les CONTAMINES-MONTJOIE.*

Continue along D 902 to the end of the road.

Notre-Dame-de-la-Gorge – Two pilgrimages to the Virgin Mary *(15 August and 8 September)* take place in this sanctuary, erected at the heart of a wooded valley. The interior decoration of the chapel is one of the finest examples of Baroque art in Haute-Savoie. The high altar (1707) and its **retable** adorned with twisted columns forms the main part of this harmonious ensemble.
Stay on the west bank of the Bon Nant and take a walk through the woods. This place is the starting point for many excursions, and the GR footpath which goes round Mont Blanc passes through here.

★★ ③ VAL MONTJOIE CLIFF-ROAD

FROM ST-GERVAIS-LES-BAINS TO THE PLATEAU DE LA CROIX
(via St-Nicolas-de-Véroce) *15km/9.3mi – about 45min – see local map*

This cliff road overlooking the Bon Nant Valley, known as Val Montjoie, offers clea views of the Mont Blanc Massif.

⚓ **St-Gervais-les-Bains** – *See ST-GERVAIS-LES-BAINS.*

Leave St-Gervais by ③ on the town plan, towards Megève, then turn onto the firs road on the left.

The **Val Montjoie** has retained an interesting group of churches and chapels whose Baroque interior decoration is in striking contrast with the relatively plain façades.

St-Nicolas-de-Véroce – The village occupies a splendid high **position★★** facing the Mont Blanc Massif.
The 18C **church** has retained its original **Baroque altarpiece** situated inside the chance decorated with paintings illustrating scenes from the life of St Nicholas.
The **church treasury** ⊘ is displayed in a room of the presbytery, where monstrances adorned with gems, reliquaries, crucifixes (one of them decorated with the rare moti of the "brass serpent" from the Old Testament) and precious objects are exhibited next to less refined works which are the expression of popular faith (statue of Notre Dame-des-Ermites).

Continue towards Le Planey.

From the last bend before Le Planey, there is a **panoramic view★★** of the whole Va Montjoie and its mountain frame (Mont Tondu, Arête des Fours, Aiguille de la Pena and Aiguille de Roselette).

Return to St-Nicolas and take the road to the Plateau de la Croix.

Plateau de la Croix – *Leave the car near the chalet called "L'Étape" and walk to the base of the cross.* The **view★★** extends to Mont Blanc, the Aiguilles de Bionnassay, the Massif de Miage, the Chaîne des Fiz and the Aiguilles de Chamonix.

HIKES

★★★ ④ A Short Round Tour of Mont Blanc on Foot

Information about this hike is included in the topo-guide of the Tour du Mont Blanc GR path published by the Fédération Française de la Randonnée Pédestre (see Practical information).
Starting from Les Contamines-Montjoie, follow D 902 for 2km/1.2mi, then GR 5 and TMB paths and S 26° (4.5km/2.8mi between Courmayeur and La Palud); a cable-ca ride completes this itinerary. Remember that identification papers are needed to cross the Italian border.

This four-day tour is suitable for determined hikers with stamina and experience o mountain hiking.
Minimum equipment: climbing boots with non-slippery soles, spare warm clothing, rain wear, sunglasses and high factor sun cream.

Suggested programme:
1st day – Les Contamines-Montjoie – Col du Bonhomme – Les Chapieux.
2nd day – Les Chapieux – Ville des Glaciers – Col de la Seigne – Refuge Elisabetta.
3rd day – Refuge Elisabetta – Checrouit cliff path – Courmayeur.
4th day – Courmayeur – La Palud – Cable-car ride across the range to Chamonix.

Start very early in the morning. The full round tour of the Mont-Blanc Massif take. 10 to 12 days including resting periods and excursions. It is only suitable for very experienced hikers with adequate equipment.

⑤ Across the Mont Blanc Massif by Cable Car

It is possible to go on an unforgettable one-day excursion from Chamonix by com bining cable-car rides across the massif with a bus ride through the tunnel. *It i. recommended to inquire about the weather forecast before going. Rapid changes in altitude may affect circulation and can prove unexpectedly tiring; take as much time as possible and take care getting on and off the cable cars.*

The journey from Chamonix is broken up into several sections:

1. Chamonix – Plan de l'Aiguille – Difference in altitude: 1 300m/4 265ft – 9mir cable-car ride.

The Aiguilles d'Argentière, Dru and Aiguille Verte from Planpraz

2. Plan de l'Aiguille – Piton Nord de l'Aiguille du Midi – Difference in altitude: 1 500m/4 921ft – 8min cable-car ride. *See CHAMONIX-MONT-BLANC.*

3. Climb to the Piton Central of the Aiguille du Midi – Difference in altitude: 65m/213ft – 35 seconds by lift. Terrace with panoramic view.

4. Aiguille du Midi - Pointe Helbronner – Difference in altitude: 1 300m/4 265ft – 35min gondola ride above the Glacier du Géant and the Vallée Blanche, offering one of the finest Alpine panoramas.

5. Pointe Helbronner – Refuge Torino – Difference in altitude: 100m/328ft – 3min cable-car ride. Terrace with panoramic view on the Pointe Helbronner.

6. Refuge Torino – La Palud – Difference in altitude: 2 000m/6 562ft – 15min cable-car ride in two sections.

MONTBRUN-LES-BAINS★

Population 467
Michelin map 332 F8 and 245 fold 18

Protected by the Montagne de Lure and Mont Ventoux, this Provençal village is spared the blasts of the mistral and the oppressive heat of summer. Standing at the confluence of the River Anary and River Toulourenc, Montbrun-les-Bains comprises the old village, clinging to the south-facing hillside beneath the castle ruins, and the new district spread in the green valley below, in contrast to the barren countryside around.
In summer, the holiday village and the recently reopened therapeutic baths bring life to the area. Already known to the Romans, the sulphur waters are excellent for the treatment of rheumatism, bronchitis, skin diseases and ear, nose and throat complaints, and in the late 19C, Montbrun was a popular spa town with baths resembling those of Baden-Baden. However, the First World War put an end to this thriving activity which was only resumed much later, in 1987.

Nearby Sights: BUIS-LES-BARONNIES, FORCALQUIER, Route NAPOLÉON, SISTERON

WALKING ABOUT

Place du Beffroi – The square gets its name from the 14C machicolated **Tour de l'Horloge**, which was one of the four fortified town gates. The old village high street begins here. From the terrace there is an extended **view** of the Anary Valley and the hilltop village of Reilhannette standing out against the white silhouette of Mont Ventoux.

Church ⊙ – The plain exterior, which is partly 12C, offers a striking contrast with the rich 17C interior decoration, recently restored. The walls of the nave are covered with wood panelling imitating pink and grey marble. Note in particular the superb **altarpiece★** by a member of the famous Bernus family.

Castle – A few ruins and four round towers overlooking the village are all that remain of the mighty castle, which could accommodate more than 200 men with their horses. Built in the 14C, it was dismantled by Catholic troops during the Wars of

The former spa town basks in the Provençal sun

Religion and partly rebuilt in 1564 by Charles Dupuy-Montbrun, the Protestant fire brand who forcibly converted the Baronnies region; the Renaissance ornamentation of the main doorway dates from this period.

EXCURSION

Haute vallée du Toulourenc *38km/23.6mi round tour – about 1hr 30mi.*

Leave from the top of the village and join D 159.

The road goes through a fertile valley with many orchards.

★**Gorges du Toulourenc** – Squeezing its way between the Montagne de l'Ubac and the Montagne du Buc along a deep gorge overlooked by the cliff road, the impetuous River Toulourenc rushes over rocks.
As the road leaves the gorge, the imposing Château d'Aulan suddenly appears on top of a rocky spur.

Château d'Aulan ⊘ – The original 12C castle was destroyed and the present castle was completely rebuilt in the 19C by the Suarez d'Aulan family who still own it. Inside, there is a fine collection of furniture and mementoes of the owners. Note a fine *Adoration of the Magi* by Leonard Bramer (17C Flemish School).
Next to the castle, the **church** ⊘ has retained its 12C east end in spite of being remodelled in the 17C. It contains a beautiful 18C Baroque altar.
Beyond Aulan, the road runs through arid landscapes dotted with lavender fields.

Turn right onto D 546.

Mévouillon – The village is named after a local family who owned the whole Baronnies region. A fortress, which stood on a ridge on the left-hand side of the road, was at the centre of bitter fighting during the Wars of Religion. Once considered impregnable, it has now completely disappeared.
The **National Hang-gliding Centre** of the Baronnies region is situated in Mévouillon, in a place known as Le Col.

Continue along D 546 then turn right onto D 542.

The road follows the Méouge Valley. (Gorges de la Méouge, *see SISTERON,* **4**).

Séderon – The Montagne de Bergiès (1 367m/4 485ft) towers above this peaceful mountain village.

Turn towards Montbrun-les-Bains at the intersection with D 546.

When you reach the Col de Macuègne (alt 1 968m/3 504ft), turn left towards Ferrassières and stop 50m/55yd further on to admire the fine **views** of the gullied slopes of the Montagne d'Albion and Mont Ventoux.

Return to the pass.

On its way to Montbrun, the road runs down the Anary Valley, dotted with picturesque peaks.

major international road linking France and Italy goes through the vast Mont-Cenis
asin now occupied by a huge artificial lake *(see below)*. Climbing above the Haute
Maurienne Valley, it offers clear views of the Vanoise Massif.

dreaded pass – Before the 19C, travellers had to climb up to the pass on the French
side along a mule track and, from all accounts, it was worse on the way down as
everyone (except, it seems, English travellers) found the sledge ride organised by local
monks positively hair-raising.

Napoleon I ordered the construction of the present road (1803-11) with a carefully
planned gradient averaging 8%.

Nearby Sights: AUSSOIS, BESSANS, BONNEVAL-SUR-ARC, Route des GRANDES ALPES,
la Haute MAURIENNE, MODANE, VAL D'ISÈRE, Massif de la VANOISE

EXCURSIONS

★Route du Lac du Mont-Cenis

FROM LANSLEBOURG TO THE MONT-CENIS LAKE
16km/10mi – about 45min – local map see La MAURIENNE

The Col du Mont-Cenis is usually blocked by snow from December to April.

Lanslebourg – *See la Haute MAURIENNE, Excursions.*

Drive south out of Lanslebourg along N 6 towards Italy.

The road rises through a conifer forest, including fine larches, then continues beyond the tree-line.

Leave the car in a bend to the left (8km/5mi from Lanslebourg, ski lift arrival point).

Beautiful **view**★ of the Vanoise glaciers reclining against the Dent Parrachée and of the Haute Maurienne extending towards Bessans through the narrow opening of the **Col de la Madeleine** *(see La Haute MAURIENNE)*, with ski slopes in the foreground below.

Lac du Mont Cenis

Stop just before the pass near a small monument; walk along the road leading to the **Replat des Canons**; 1km/0.6mi further on, there is a striking **view**★★ of the Dent Parrachée and Bessans village.

★**Col du Mont-Cenis** – Alt 2 084m/6 837ft. The pass used to mark the border between France and Italy, which is now a few kilometres further south. A badly maintained monument, originally erected in Mussolini's honour, is now dedicated to the achievements of the French alpine regiments. The view encompasses the green Mont-Cenis Basin, an ideal place for amateur botanists, framed by Mont Lamet and the Pointe de Clairy, the artificial lake, and to the south, through the opening of the Petit-Mont-Cenis Pass, the high summits of the Aiguille de Scolette (alt 3 508m/11 509ft) and Pointe Sommeiller.

The road skirts the lake past **Plan des Fontainettes**, where there is a busy transport café; the **"Salle historique du Mont-Cenis"** ⊘ can be seen beneath the **chapel** of the priory built above the old hospice, which was flooded by the lake: it shows the Mont-Cenis area before and after the building of the dam. Small Alpine garden nearby.

★**Lac du Mont-Cenis** – From the EDF viewpoint *(parking)*, there is a general **view**★ of the lake and the **dam**. The latter is slightly larger (1 485 000m³/52 442 775cu ft) and much longer at the top (1 400m/1 531yd) but lower (maximum 120m/394ft) and narrower at the base (460m/1 509ft) than the Serre-Ponçon Dam in the southern Alps. It consists of a riprap dyke with clay in the centre to ensure water-tightness.

The lake has a maximum capacity of 315 million m³/255 371acft, mostly at the disposal of the French power station of Villarodin with about one sixth of the capacity being diverted to the Venàus power station in Italy.

MONT-DAUPHIN ★

Population 87
Michelin map 334 H4 and 245 fold 9

Mont-Dauphin (alt 1 030m/3 379ft) is a mighty citadel situated on top of a promontor
commanding a superb **view★★** of the Durance and the Guil. When the duke of Savoie
troops seized the towns of Gap, Embrun and Guillestre in 1692, King Louis XIV of Franc
ordered Vauban, his military engineer, to build fortifications along the border. Mon
Dauphin was one of nine strategic places where Vauban chose to build not just a fortress
but a fortified settlement from which the king's troops could guard the Queyras regior
the Durance Valley and the road leading south across the Col de Vars. Vauban's vision c
a true garrison town took shape, but failed to attract the local people, and when th
army left Mont-Dauphin in 1980, efforts were made to bring in a civilian population, i
particular craftsmen, for whom the **Caserne Campana** ⊘ was turned into workshops.

Nearby Sights: ABRIÈS, L'ARGENTIÈRE-LA-BESSÉE, BARCELONNETTE, BRIANÇON, L
BRIANÇONNAIS, CEILLAC, EMBRUN, Vallée de FREISSINIÈRES, Route des GRANDE
ALPES, GUILLESTRE, MOLINES-EN-QUEYRAS, MONT-GENÈVRE, Le QUEYRAS, S1
VÉRAN, SERRE-CHEVALIER, Lac de SERRE-PONÇON, L'UBAYE, La VALLOUISE, VARS

Where to stay and Eating out

BUDGET

Hôtel Lacour and restaurant de la Gare – *At the station – 05600 Mont
Dauphin-Gare – ☎ 04 92 45 03 08 – closed Sat except Jul-Aug and 1 Sept
20 Dec – ▣ – 46rms: 25.92/48.78€ - ☲ 6.10€ – restaurant 12.65/27.73€*
This hotel-restaurant between the road and the station is a good choice for it
homely atmosphere, simple rooms and generous menus. There are a fev
cheaper rooms without their own bathroom in the annexe which are popula
with young people.

TOUR OF THE TOWN ⊘ 1hr

*Go through the Porte de Briançon which can be reached by turning off N 94 ont
D 37.*

Moat – There is an interesting **view** of the moat from the bridge joining the gate and
the guardhouse; note the scarp and counterscarp, the bastions and the lunette whic
communicates with the outside through an underground passage.

The town – The residential section of the citadel is split into four square blocks. It
buildings, each of which would have had a specific role in time of war, are built o
pink marble from Guillestre, which looks lovely in the sunshine.

★ **Powder magazine** – Only an earth mound and a few air pipes can be seen from the
outside. The building looks fine from the inside; the upper room is covered with
pointed vaulting and the lower room with a solid larch framework. A gallery running
all the way round would have provided ventilation and, of course, light, as a naked
flame could have devastated the town; the locks were even made of bronze to
prevent the tiniest spark from igniting the store. Exhibitions are held here in summer

Mont-Dauphin

Arsenal – Built in the mid-18C, it comprised two wings set at right angles. One of them was destroyed by an Italian bomb dropped in 1940. The other building, with elegant œil-de-boeuf windows, houses an exhibition entitled **Vauban dans les Alpes** ⊙.

Church – The only remaining part of the church designed by Vauban is the chancel, which explains the building's rather strange proportions; the stones of the transept and parts of the nave were used in the construction of munitions bunkers in 1873. In front of the first pew on the right is the fossil of an ammonite. There is a portrait of St Louis (Louis IX), to whom the church is dedicated, but, oddly enough, the figure in wig and regalia bears more than a passing resemblance to Louis XIV!

Plantation – Several tree species were planted as an experiment on this vast area of spare ground.

Caserne Rochambeau – On the outside, these large barracks form a defence wall overlooking the Porte d'Embrun and the ramparts above the gorge of the River Guil. Inside is a remarkable 260m/853ft-long wooden **framework★** which dates from 1820. It is based on a plan by King Henri II's famous architect, Philibert Delorme (1512-70), who designed a framework consisting of a succession of wooden arches held together by wooden dowels, which could easily be dismantled.

A Military Genius

Architect and soldier, builder and destroyer of cities, **Sébastien Le Prestre de Vauban** (1633-1707) was an inspired and utterly untiring man. As Marshal of the army and chief military engineer to Louis XIV, he personally directed 53 sieges, designed countless bridges and public buildings, dug canals, reshaped harbours and built the famous Maintenon aqueduct. He reinforced the defences of over 300 towns and citadels and built 33 of his own, which maintained their daunting reputation as impregnable strongholds for 250 years after his death. An insightful military tactician, adapting his designs to changes in tactics or peculiarities of the terrain, he frequently worked from a star-shaped fortress design with bastions which could protect each other with their arc of fire. In Vauban's hands this basic Italian model was refined, strengthened with demi-lunes and redoubts, encircled by ditches and defended by outer walls. As the Sun King's wars of conquest extended France's borders, Vauban consolidated the new frontiers in Flanders, Alsace, the Ardennes, Franche-Comté, across the Alps and Pyrenees and along the coast. The topography of the Dauphiné and Haute Provence prevented him from planning defences with the aesthetic balance and precision which are his trademarks elsewhere. Nevertheless, twelve fortresses between Antibes and Briançon were built or rebuilt to his plans.

MONTGENÈVRE★★

Population 497

Michelin map 334 I3 and 244 fold 43 – Local map see Le BRIANÇONNAIS

This small border town between France and Italy was the birthplace of French skiing. A young officer garrisoned in Briançon was so convinced of the usefulness of skis for travelling through snow-covered areas that he funded the equipment of seven of his men. In 1901, these *"chasseurs alpins"* (Alpine troops) skied down the slopes of Montgenèvre in front of a panel of military experts. The demonstration was apparently conclusive since, in 1903, the War Ministry founded a school (which later became the École Française de Ski) and ordered all the Alpine troops to be suitably equipped; these measures were even extended to the local population. Technical improvements soon followed: first metal bindings, then the use of two poles instead of one. Today the town is one of the biggest skiing centres in the Briançonnais

Nearby Sights: L'ARGENTIÈRE-LA-BESSÉE, BRIANÇON, Le BRIANÇONNAIS, Vallée de FREISSINIÈRES, GUILLESTRE, MOLINES-EN-QUEYRAS, MONT-DAUPHIN, L'OISANS, LE QUEYRAS, SERRE-CHEVALIER, La VALLOUISE

THE RESORT

Montgenèvre is an important ski resort which forms part of the Franco-Italian **Voie Lactée** together with other resorts such as Clavière, Cesana, Sansicario, Sestrières and Sauze-d'Oulx (representing a total of 400km/249mi of ski runs and 100 ski lifts). The Montgenèvre ski area offers 100km/62mi of pistes with good snow cover and 37 ski lifts, suitable for skiers of all levels. Experienced skiers like the 11 black runs, whereas

---

Talking the talk, boarder style...

The snow park's run is equipped with a quarterpipe, projump and gap, plus a little musical accompaniment. There's also a mogul contest on Thursdays.

---

beginners ski down the lor green run of Le Lac (L Anges area) and intermedia skiers prefer the beautif Souréou run.

The resort is expandir lengthwise along the fl section of the Col c Montgenèvre (alt 1 850n 6 070ft). The pass, which is open all year round, is on a busy commercial and touri route. The obelisk situated near the French customs office is a reminder that the roa was made suitable for wheeled vehicles in 1807.

On the town

La Ca' del Sol – *Rte d'Italie* – ☎ *04 92 21 90 65 – open daily 9am-1am – close May-Jun and Sept-end Nov*. A fine stone fireplace, a copper cauldron hangin there and other items symbolic of life in the mountains mark the decor of th rustic, convivial bar where the regulars engage in an unbroken flow of conve sation. In season, the entertainment culminates in variety concerts and theme evenings at the end of the week.

Sport

Aire de loisirs des lacs – *Zone des lacs* – ☎ *04 92 21 80 50 – daily 9am-7pm closed 15 Sept-15 Jun*. This leisure complex gets the most out of the surround ing lakes and mountains, offering a large range of activities from pedalos t archery, via trout fishing, trampolining and cross-country cycling. Not forgettin also a 9-hole golf course covering 3 000m/2mi.

VIEWPOINTS ACCESSIBLE BY GONDOLA

★★ **Le Chalvet** – *In winter, access by the Chalvet gondola and chair lift (a 2 577m/8 455ft); in summer access on foot: 4hr 15min there and back. Walk up to th viewing table (Check with the ski patrol that there are no avalanche hazards).*
Splendid **panorama**★★ of the Oisans region to the west, including the Bans, the Pointe d Sélé, the Pelvoux, the Barre des Écrins, the Agneaux, the Grande Ruine, the Rateau, th Pic Gaspard and the Meije. The Thabor and Aiguilles d'Arves can be seen to the nort while, to the south, the view encompasses the Montgenèvre ski area overlooked by th Janus and Chenaillet summits, with the Pic de la Font Sancte, Pic de Rochebrune an Monte Viso in the background. The Italian Alps seem very close to the east.

Les Chalmettes gondola – Alt 2 200m/7 218ft. **View** of the Chalvet and Chaberto to the north, of Les Anges and Janus to the south.

★★ **Les Anges and Le Querelay** – Alt 2 400m/7 874ft. *In winter, access to skiers vi Les Anges drag lift or the Observatoire chairlift; in summer, access on foot.* Super **panorama** of the Écrins, the Serre-Chevalier ski area, the Grand Peygu, the Col d'Izoar and the Pic de Rochebrune.

MONTMAUR
Population 423
Michelin map 334 D5 and 245 fold 7

This former medieval "barony" marks the transition between the Bochaine and Dévolu regions. The ruins of the 11C stronghold overlook the village at the foot of the Montagn d'Auroze and the Pic de Bure.
The nearby 18C manor was the birthplace of **Ponson du Terrail** (1829-71), a writer o romantic novels full of extraordinary adventures.

Nearby Sights: Pays du BUËCH, Le CHAMPSAUR, Le DÉVOLUY, GAP, Route NAPOLÉON Lac de SERRE-PONÇON, Le TRIÈVES

CASTLE ⊙

The present castle dates from the 14C. Extended in the 16C and decorated ir Renaissance style, it was more imposing than it is now, its two upper storeys havin been destroyed in a fire. It looks quite austere from the outside, with its two round towers, mullioned windows and lovely 17C rusticated stone gateway, but the inte rior ornamentation is its main attraction. The four reception rooms are decorate with richly carved monumental fireplaces, French-style ceilings with ornamental beams, frescoes and friezes representing scenes on themes of war or morality. Doors carved with symbols, stucco work and *trompe-l'œil* add to the charm of the building. In the 1930s it became a health and beauty retreat which counted Jean Giono, screenwriter and director Henri-Georges Clouzot and the king of Belgium among its clientele. During the Second World War, the castle was occupied by a Resistance network.

HIKE

★Pic de Bure

4hr 30min from Montmaur, drive along D 320 towards the Col de Gaspardon (5km/3mi). Leave the car in the car park near the Maison Forestière des Sauvas (alt 1 320m/4 331ft). A wide stony path rises to the north towards the cliffs of the Pic de Bure, on the west bank of the stream. After an hour's walk, you will reach the Roc des Hirondelles; a path, marked in blue, leads across a small pass to the Plateau de Bure *(3hr 30min altogether).* Continue eastwards for 45min to reach the summit of the Pic de Bure (alt 2 709m/8 888ft) which offers, in clear weather, one of the finest **panoramas★★★** of the Alps, extending from the foothills of Mont Blanc in the north-east to the Cévennes *(to the right of Mont Ventoux)* and the Italian massifs.

Return by the same route.

MORZINE★★

Population 2 948
Michelin map 328 N3 and 244 fold 9 – Local map see CLUSES or
THONON-LES-BAINS

The Morzine-Montriond conurbation lies at an altitude of 980m/3 215ft, in a vast Alpine coomb flanked by the Pointe de Ressachaux and the Pointe de Nyon. Thanks mainly to its prime position at the intersection of six attractive roads, running through densely wooded valleys towards high-pasture areas, Morzine has been the main tourist centre of the Haut Chablais region since the 1930s.

Nearby Sights: ABONDANCE, AVORIAZ, CHÂTEL, CLUSES, ÉVIAN-LES-BAINS, Les GETS, Routes des GRANDES ALPES, Bassin de SALLANCHES, SAMOËNS, SIXT-FER-À-CHEVAL, THONON-LES-BAINS, YVOIRE

THE RESORT

Capital of Haut-Chablais – Three tributaries of the Dranse de Savoie, the Dranse d'Abondance, the Dranse de Morzine and the Brevon, cross this landscape of woodland and meadows. These three long, deep valleys link the Haut Chablais region to the Valais and Faucigny. At the other end of the scale, the Hautforts (alt 2 464m/8 083ft) mark the highest point in the area.

Ski area – Its gentle slopes and beautiful landscapes make it the ideal ski area for those who prefer a more relaxed style of skiing. Itineraries leading from Super-Morzine to Avoriaz are particularly enjoyable. Beginners can also have a go down the "Choucas" green run (from the summit of the Ran Folly). Experienced skiers are mainly drawn to the Creux and Aigle runs or to Avoriaz at the heart of the **Portes du Soleil**★★ ski area. Cross-country skiers can practise along 97km/60mi of fairly easy trails spread over five areas.

HIGHLIGHT

★★Three Viewpoints

★**Pointe de Nyon** ⊙ – *Access by cable car and chairlift.* Impressive view of the rocky barrier of the Dents Blanches and of Mont Blanc on one side, of Lake Geneva and of the Morzine Valley on the other.

★**Le Pléney** ⊙ – *1hr there and back. Access by cable car then on foot.* From the upper cable-car station, walk alongside the Belvédère chairlift to a small mound crowned by a viewing table (alt 1 554m/5 098ft) offering a **panoramic view** of Avoriaz and the Dents Blanches to the east, of the Mont Blanc Massif to the southeast, of the Aravis range to the south and of the Pointe de Marcelly, Mont Chéry and Roc d'Enfer to the west. In clear weather, Lake Geneva is visible through the Dranse Valley.

★★**Chamossière** – Alt 2 000m/6 562ft. *In winter, access is limited to skiers; in summer, access is on foot.* From the viewing table, splendid **panorama★★** of the Dents du Midi, Dents Blanches, Buet, Aiguille du Midi, Mont Blanc and the Aravis range.

Eating out

BUDGET

Le Clin d'Œil – *Opposite the post office* – ☎ *04 50 79 03 10 – closed May, No and Sun in Jun, Sept and Oct – 14.64/47.71€*. This little restaurant in a con verted barn in a quiet street has simple, welcoming decor. The menu features few local specialities and pizzas cooked over charcoal.

Where to stay

MODERATE

L'Hermine Blanche – *Chemin du Mas Metout* – ☎ *04 50 75 76 55 – close 21 Apr-30 Jun and 1 Sept-21 Dec* – 🅿 *– 25rms: 45.73/70.13€ -* 🍽 *5.79€ restaurant 14.48€*. This hotel on the slopes at the side of the resort is favourite of ours! The rooms are fresh and comfortable and some have a ba cony. The restaurant is plain and neat. There is also a pleasant covered swim ming pool and gym. Homely atmosphere for carefree holidays.

Florimontane – *Av. de Joux-Plane* – ☎ *04 50 79 03 87 – florimon@porte. dusoleil.com – closed Nov and 24 Apr-15 May* – 🅿 *– 65rms: 42.23/70.13€ restaurant 17.68€*. These three chalets linked by an underground passag are a great place for holidaymakers, whether in summer or winter. The woo panelled rooms are welcoming and the twenty holiday apartments are ver practical for families. Traditional local cooking. Gym, entertainment an games.

EXCURSIONS

★★ **Lac de Montriond and Col de la Joux Verte** – *20km/12.4mi – about 2hr. Fro Morzine, follow the road to Montriond (east bank of the Dranse). Turn right toward the lake immediately after Montriond Church.*

★ **Lac de Montriond** – Alt 1 049m/3 442ft. Framed by steep escarpments, the area su rounding the lake is well shaded and crisscrossed by footpaths. Continue to th **Cascade d'Ardent** *(stop by the viewpoint on the right-hand side of D 228)*. Th waterfall, which is superb during the spring thaw, drops from a height c 30m/98ft.

The road then climbs up in a series of hairpin bends to a ledge gullied by a succes sion of waterfalls; there is a good view of the Roc d'Enfer downstream. Beyond th village of Les Lindarets, the road rises along the wooded slopes of the Joux Verte within sight of the Mont de Grange to the north.

A road leaves the **Col de la Joux Verte** on the left towards Avoriaz.

★★ **Avoriaz** – *See AVORIAZ.*

★★ **Route du Col de Joux-Plane**

From Morzine to Samoëns via the Col de Joux-Plane – *20km/12.4mi – about 1 hr* The narrow road *(D 354)*, which is passable in summer, rises very quickly above th Morzine Valley, winding across high pastures and some lovely wooded sections. I goes right round the Ran Folly in a 4km/2.5mi loop and over the pass of the sam name (alt 1 650m/5 413ft) before reaching the Plateau de Joux Plane.

★★ **Col de Joux Plane** – Alt 1 698m/5 571ft. The road runs between a small lake and restaurant.

From the restaurant, there is a remarkable **view** of Mont Blanc to the southeast extending south to the Platé Massif and the resort of Flaine.

The road continues beyond the path on the left, which ends at the Col de Joux Plane and runs down towards Samoëns offering bird's-eye **views★** of the Eméru Coomb o the left and the Giffre Valley on the right.

★★ **Samoëns** – *See SAMOËNS.*

★ ② **Route des Gets**

FROM MORZINE TO CLUSES

43km/26.7mi – about 1hr – local map see CLUSES

The Route des Grandes Alpes, D 902-N 202, links the Dranse de Morzine Valley t the Giffre and Arve valleys.

From Morzine, drive west along D 28 then take D 902 south towards Les Gets.

The road affords views of the Roc d'Enfer (alt 2 244m/7 362ft), one of the most rugged Chablais summits.

☀ **Les Gets** – *See Les GETS.*

The road winds its way through the woods along the narrow Arpettaz and Foron valleys.

Turn right at the Pont des Gets onto D 328.

The road climbs above the Foron then veers to the left to reach the vast Praz-de-Lys Basin covered with pastures. From the last bend, there is a wide **panorama★** covering, from left to right, the Dents du Midi, Tour Sallière, Avoudrues, Mont Buet and Chaîne du Reposoir, with Mont Blanc in the distance.

🚶 The peaceful mountain village of **Praz-de-Lys** is overlooked by the Marcelly Peak (alt 2 000m/6 562ft), crowned by a monumental cross and accessible to experienced hikers *(3hr there and back on foot).*

Return to D 902 and drive towards Taninges.

The heights of the Chaîne du Reposoir and Chaîne du Bargy line up on the horizon. Beyond Avonnex, there is an overall **view★** of Taninges and of the Giffre Valley, backed by snow-capped high peaks.

Taninges – This large village is a good starting point for summer walks. The old upper town has partly retained its traditional character.

Beyond Châtillon-sur-Cluses, the mountain setting of the small industrial town of Cluses can be fully appreciated. The road leads on to Cluses.

MOUSTIERS-STE-MARIE★★

Population 630
Michelin map 334 F9 and 245 fold 34
Local map see Grand Canyon du VERDON

Moustiers nestles beneath a large gap in the limestone cliffs towering over the town; 227m/745ft-long chain stretching across this amazing **setting★★** holds a star suspended over Notre-Dame-de-Beauvoir. It was fixed into the rock in fulfillment of a wish made by a knight who returned to Moustiers from the crusades after many years as a prisoner.

Moustiers owes its name to a monastery founded in the 5C by St Maxim, bishop of Riez, but it owes its fame to the manufacture of glazed **ceramics** which reached its peak in the 17C and 18C, disappeared at the end of the 19C and was revived in the 20C.

Built near the downstream exit of the Grand Canyon du Verdon *(see Grand Canyon du VERDON)*, close to the Lac de Ste-Croix *(see Lac de STE-CROIX)*, the town is a very popular centre for excursions.

Nearby Sights: BARGÈME, CASTELLANE, GRÉOUX-LES-BAINS, Route NAPOLÉON, RIEZ, Lac de STE-CROIX, Plateau de VALENSOLE, Grand Canyon du VERDON

BACKGROUND

Parc naturel régional du Verdon – Founded in 1997, the newest of the regional nature parks covers an area of 200 000ha/494 211 acres including the Grand Canyon du Verdon, the Plateau de Valensole, the Pays d'Artuby and the Préalpes de Castellane. The Verdon, which rises at an altitude of 2 500m/8 202ft and flows into the Durance, is the link between Provence and the Alps and the climate of this semi mountainous region (average altitude 700m/2 297ft, highest point: Mourre de Chanier 1 930m/6 332ft) still has a mild, Mediterranean feel. Cicadas chirr in the olive groves and the *garrigue*, wild boar rustle through the undergrowth, chamois climb across rocky ridges and grouse clatter through the larch woods. In the meadows, marmots stand on the qui vive amid the gentian and eagles can be seen circling around the peaks. Less noticeable is one of the smallest creatures in the park, a protected rare species of hairy snail.
Tourist information centres can be found by the five lakes in the park. Walkers, climbers and white-water fans will particularly love the Gorges du Verdon *(see Grand Canyon du VERDON)*.

Eating out

MODERATE

Restaurant La Treille Muscate – *Pl. de l'Église – ☎ 04 92 74 64 31 – close Jan, 15-30 Nov, Mon evening and Tue – 24.39€*. This friendly little Provença bistrot serving regional cooking using only fresh ingredients is a real find.

La Ferme Ste-Cécile – *Rte de Castellane – ☎ 04 92 74 64 18 – closed Fe school holidays, 12 Nov-12 Dec, Sun evening out of season and Mon 28.20/39.64€*. For those seeking a little peace and quiet outside Moustiers. Th restaurant is in an old farmhouse and the natural suroundings can be admire from the terrace. In the small Provençal dining rooms delicious cooking aroma waft their way into your nostrils and set your tastebuds aquiver.

Where to stay

BUDGET

Chambre d'hôte Monastère de Ségriès – *6km/4mi NW of Moustiers on D 952 ☎ 04 92 74 64 32 – c.allegre@free.fr – closed Nov-Mar – ✉ – 5rms 36.59/44.21€ – main meal 13.72€*. Recapture the pleasures of unspoile nature and silence in a forest of holm oaks, chosen as a place to settle by monk in the 19C. The real luxury here is space, both in the lounges and the rooms There is a superb view of the cloister and of the valley.

MODERATE

Hôtel Le Relais – *Pl. du Couvert – ☎ 04 92 74 66 10 – closed 15-22 Oct 31 Dec-24 Feb and Fri except Jul-Aug – 20rms: 42.69/73.18€ - ☕ 8.38€ restaurant 20.58/33.54€*. This pretty hotel between the Lac de Ste-Croix and the Verdon river gorge is in typical Provençal style. The rooms have a balcon or a mezzanine and offer a magnificent view of the village, the valley and th waterfall.

Hôtel Colombier – *Rte de Castellane – ☎ 04 92 74 66 02 – closed 18 Nov 2 Feb – 🅿 – 22rms: 44/58€ - ☕ 7.10€*. The shaded terrace of this hote slightly removed from the village gives a splendid panoramic view. Rooms are functional and well kept.

La Ferme Rose – *4km/2.5mi W of Moustiers on the Ste-Croix road – ☎ 04 9 74 69 47 – closed 15 Nov-28 Feb – 🅿 – 12rms: 59.46/114.34€ - ☕ 7.32€* The style here is characterised by sentimentality and the 1960s. Cicadas abov the doors herald the colour scheme of the bedrooms: blue, pink and pale green Mosquito nets, tiled floors, carefully chosen furniture and a collection of fan complete the decor. Peace and quiet, and a friendly welcome.

EXPENSIVE

Bastide de Moustiers – *S of the village on D 952 then a B-road – ☎ 04 92 7(47 47 – 🅿 – 12rms: from 152.45€ - ☕ 12.96€ – restaurant 35.06/44.97€* Unspoiled nature is here to be enjoyed in this 17C Provençal country house buil on the slopes of the mountains above the Verdon. The estate includes a large park, an enclosure for horses, a wildlife park and a kitchen garden. The room are sophisticated and the bathrooms outstanding. Tasty dishes have a hint of tra ditional local peasant cooking and are served in generous portions.

SIGHTS

★**Church** – Its warm-coloured massive bell-tower, characteristic of the Lombarc Romanesque style, comprises three storeys with twinned openings and blinc arcading resting on pillars or slender columns. The Romanesque chancel wa: replaced in the 14C by a Gothic chancel which forms an angle with the 12C nave The base of the flat east end is decorated with twinned arcading opening ontc rounded arches. Note the beautifully carved 16C and 18C stalls in the chancel and in the nave, a 16C painting depicting Moustiers at that time, without the famous star The room situated beneath the tower houses a collection of holy objects including a votive picture from 1702, 15C copper plates and local ceramics.

★**Musée de la Faïence** ⊙ – The earthenware museum is in the basement of the towr hall. The displays are centred on the ceramic-makers who made Moustiers ceramic: famous: the Clérissy family (1679-1783) who initiated the blue motifs on a white background; the Olérys family who introduced the polychrome motifs in 1738; the Fouque and Pelloquin families (1749-83) who used a yellow background; the Ferrat brothers (1761-94) who were strongly influenced by the technique and decoratior of Strasbourg ceramics.

★ **Chapelle Notre-Dame-de-Beauvoir**
– *2hr there and back on foot*

🚶 This chapel on a ledge overlooking the town has been a place of pilgrimage since early medieval times, when it was known as Notre-Dame d'Entreroches, "Our Lady between the rocks". The wide stepped path leading to it offers glimpses of the village and of the Notre-Dame Gorge; it is lined with 14 Stations of the Cross decorated with ceramic scenes by Simone Garnier. At the end of the path, there is a terrace dating from the Middle Ages, planted with Mediterranean trees and ringed by the remains of the old ramparts; from there, the **view**★ takes in the rooftops of Moustiers, the Maïre Valley and the straight edge of the Valensole Plateau. Protected by an overhanging roof covered with glazed tiles, the Romanesque porch is surmounted by a bell-tower of the same period. The carved wooden door dates from the Renaissance.

The traditional festival known as "la Diane", which takes place every year on 9 September, is the culmination of a week of feasting, dancing and

Moustiers faïence decorated by J Olérys

rejoicing to the sound of pipes and drums. A torch-lit procession to the chapel is followed by mass and celebrations.

EXCURSIONS

★★ **Grand Canyon du Verdon** – *154km/96mi round tour – 1 day – see Grand Canyon du VERDON.*

★★ **Lac de Ste-Croix** – *70km/43.5mi round tour starting from Moustiers – about 3hr – see Lac de STE-CROIX.*

Route NAPOLÉON ★

Michelin maps 341 A/B 5, 334 D/H 3/10, 244 and 245

The Route Napoléon – Napoleon's road – follows the Emperor's route on his return from Elba, from the point where he landed in Golfe Juan to his arrival in Grenoble. The commemorative plaques and monuments bear the flying eagle symbol inspired by Napoleon's remark: 'The eagle will fly from steeple to steeple until he reaches the towers of Notre-Dame'.

The road has always formed an important link between Grenoble and the Verdon and Durance valleys, but only became known as the Route Napoléon in 1913 and was not opened to motor traffic until 1932. The 325km/202mi can be covered in two days, at any time of the year.

Nearby Sights: ANNOT, BARGÈME, Pays du BUËCH, BUIS-LES-BARONNIES, CASTEL-LANE, Le CHAMPSAUR, Massif de CHAMROUSSE, Massif de la CHARTREUSE, CLUES DE HAUTE-PROVENCE, Le DÉVOLUY, DIGNE-LES-BAINS, Préalpes de DIGNE, Vallée de la Moyenne DURANCE, EMBRUN, ENTREVAUX, FORCALQUIER, Monastère de GANAGOBIE, GAP, GRENOBLE, Lacs de LAFFREY, MANE, MANOSQUE, MONTBRUN-LES-BAINS, MONTMAUR, MOUSTIERS-STE-MARIE, ST-JULIEN-DU-VERDON, Lac de STE-CROIX, Lac de SERRE-PONÇON, SISTERON, Le TRIÈVES, Le VALBONNAIS, Plateau de VALENSOLE, Le VALGAUDEMAR, Grand Canyon du VERDON, VIZILLE

"Refuges Napoléon" – As a sign of gratitude for the enthusiastic welcome he received in Gap, Napoleon bequeathed to the Hautes-Alpes *département* a sum of money intended for the construction of refuges at the top of passes particularly exposed in winter. This sum, which was only accepted in 1854, was used to build refuges at the Col de Manse, Col du Lauraret, Col d'Izoard, Col de Vars, Col du Noyer, Col Agnel and Col de la Croix *(the last two are now in ruins and the refuge of the Col du Noyer has been replaced by a hotel).*

The route is described from south to north. The first part of the itinerary from Golfe Juan to the Col de Valferrière is described in the Michelin Green Guide French Riviera.

The Flight of the Eagle

After landing at Golfe Juan on 1 March 1815, Napoleon and his troops, preceded by an advance guard, set up a bivouac and made a brief stop at Cannes. Then, as the moon rose, between one and two o'clock in the morning, they broke camp. Wishing to avoid the Rhône area, which he knew to be hostile, Napoleon planned to get to the valley of the Durance by way of the Alps and made for Grasse. There he expected to find a road which he had ordered to be built when he was Emperor, but discovered that his orders had never been carried out. The little column struggled on, following mule tracks through deep snow. That evening, Napoleon waited impatiently for news from Sisteron, where the fort commanded the narrow passage of the Durance.

Sisteron, however, offered no resistance and, as he left the town, Napoleon realised that support for his cause was already growing; he felt that victory depended on his will power and that France would rally to him if he reached Grenoble. Travelling along a coach road once more, he received an enthusiastic welcome in Gap that night, slept in Corps the next day and on 7 March reached La Mure, only to find troops from the Grenoble garrison facing him at Laffrey. This was the setting for the famous episode which turned events in his favour. It happened on what came to be called the "Prairie de la Rencontre", near the Grand Lac de Laffrey, and is now commemorated by a monument. Seeing the road blocked by a battalion which greatly outnumbered his own escort; the Emperor took a calculated risk, walked forward and, pulling open his grey greatcoat, declared: 'Soldiers, I am your Emperor! If anyone among you wishes to kill his general, here I am'. In spite of being ordered to fire by a young officer, the troops rallied to Napoleon shouting: 'Vive l'Empereur'! and marched with him to Grenoble. That same evening, he entered the town in triumph.

FROM THE COL DE VALFERRIÈRE TO CORPS

210km/130mi – allow 1 day

Beyond the pass, the road goes through the **Clue de Séranon**. Napoleon spent the night (2 to 3 March) in the village of **Séranon** hidden in the midst of a pine forest.
Further on, on the way down from the Col de Luens, the road affords views of Castellane nestling at the foot of its "rock", crowned by Notre-Dame du Roc.

★**Castellane** – *See CASTELLANE.*

On the way up to the **Col des Lèques** (alt 1 148m/3 766ft) there are lovely **views** of Castellane, the Lac de Castillon and the Préalpes de Provence.

★**Clue de Taulanne** – This opening cut through sheer rock leads from the Verdon Valley to the Asse Valley.

6km/3.7mi further on, cross the Asse to enter Senez.

Rock formations in the Clue de Taulanne

Senez – This ancient Gallo-Roman town was one of the oldest and poorest bish-oprics in France, finally dissolved in 1790. It came into the limelight in the 18C, when Bishop **Jean Soanen** refused to condemn Jansenism and was removed from office.

The **former cathedral** ⊙ dates from the early 13C. The east end is decorated with arcading in Lombard style, resting on slender engaged columns. A Gothic doorway gives access to the nave in typical Provençal Romanesque style. Inside, note the 17C stalls, altarpiece and lectern, as well as the 18C antiphonary, a book of antiphonal plainsong.

Return to N 85 and continue towards Digne.

Barrême – The station houses an exhibition concerning one stage of the Cretaceous geological period, particularly well represented in the area.
Napoleon spent the night of 3 March 1815 here *(plaque on a house along N 85).*

The Préalpes de Digne start beyond Chaudon-Norante. Napoleon went to Digne along the route followed by D 20. However, carry on along N 85.

★ **Clue de Chabrières** – The gorge is framed by tall limestone cliffs.

⁺ **Digne-les-Bains** – *See DIGNE-LES-BAINS.*

Leave Digne by ③ *on the town plan.*

The road *(N 85)* continues along the Bléone Valley, between the Plateau de Valensole and the Préalpes de Digne. The imposing Château de Fontenelle stands on the right-hand side of the road, just before Malijai.

Malijai – Napoleon spent the night of 4 to 5 March in the elegant 18C **château** ⊙, famous for its stuccoed interior decoration.

Beyond Malijai, the view embraces the Durance Valley and extends towards the bluish mass of the Montagne de Lure. The road follows the Canal d'Oraison until it reaches L'Escale and the impressive dam across the river.

Leave the bridge to your left and drive north along D 24.

Volonne – This village, clinging to a rocky spur picturesquely crowned by two old towers, is surrounded by lovely orchards. The ruined **Église St-Martin** is a fine specimen of early Romanesque style (11C); the nave flanked by side aisles is open to the sky.

Shortly after the Salignac Dam across the Durance, there is a splendid overall **view★** of Sisteron and its remarkable setting.

★★ **Sisteron** – *See SISTERON.*

The road *(N 85)* follows an EDF (French Electricity Board) feeder canal part of the way to Gap. It is worth stopping at the viewing table situated at the exit of the village of Le Poët *(15min on foot)* to admire the **panorama** of the Gapençais and Embrunais heights and of the Écrins summits. After La Saulce, the road veers northwards.

Tallard – Tallard lies in the middle Durance Valley, surrounded by orchards and vineyards, which produce a popular white wine.

Église St-Grégoire – The church was erected in the 12C and partially rebuilt in the 17C. The main doorway (dated 1549 on the lintel) is the most interesting feature; it is decorated with Renaissance medallions depicting women, children and soldiers. Inside, the 17C pulpit and the 15C christening font supported by lions are particularly noteworthy. An Armenian pilgrimage takes place every year in September.

Castle ⊙ – Its dismantled towers stand on a rock spur overlooking the Durance. Built in the 14C and 16C, it was taken time and again by both sides during the Wars of Religion and seriously damaged by the duke of Savoie's troops in 1692. The castle, which has been extensively repaired, is the venue of a summer festival of music. In the **chapel**, the Flamboyant style is represented by an elegant doorway surmounted by a pinnacle and finial standing between flame-like windows. Inside, note the beautiful keystones, carved capitals and fireplaces. The **main building** dates from the Renaissance. It has a rounded doorway surmounted by the arms of the Clermont-Tonnerre Family (who once owned the castle) and beautiful windows decorated with twisted mullions.

★ **Round tour from Tallard via Urtis** *22km/13.7mi – about 1hr*

From Tallard, drive east across the Durance and turn left almost immediately.
The D 346 rises above the river.

4km/2.5mi further on, turn right towards D 854 leading to Venterol.

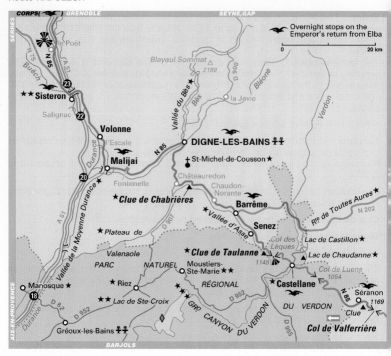

A bend to the left *(cross)* offers a fine **view★** of the Durance. Just beyond Ventero there is an extended **view★** of a large section of the Durance Valley. Soon after Le Marmets, the road runs steeply down to the river and, 2.5km/1.5mi beyond Urtis, small reservoir formed by a dam along the Durance comes into view.

Turn right at the intersection with the road to Curbans to rejoin the Tallard roa within sight of the castle.

★Gap – *See GAP.*

Beyond Gap, N 85 rises sharply to the **Col Bayard** (alt 1 248m/4 094ft, viewing table and comes down again into the open valley of the upper Drac *(see Le CHAMPSAUR,*

Les Baraques – Napoleon stopped here on 6 March 1815 and refused the offer mad by local farmers to join his troops.

The escarpments of the Dévoluy (Montagne de Féraud) lie ahead, the Pic d'Olan i the Écrins Massif can be seen to the northeast, through the **Valgaudemar** Valley *(se Le VALGAUDEMAR)*, and the Obiou to the west of the **Lac du Sautet**.

Corps – *See Le DÉVOLUY.*

① From La Mure to Grenoble

63km/39mi – allow a day – see local map Lacs de LAFFREY or Le TRIÈVES.

The road *(N 85)* winds its way above the Drac Valley, then crosses the Bonne Valle before running straight across the Matheysine Plateau.

La Mure – This lively market town, situated on the southern edge of the Plateau d la Matheysine, owed its prosperity to the nearby coal mines, which produced hun dreds of thousands of tons of coal a year from 1901 until the last mine closed dow in 1996. La Mure is the starting point of the mountain railway line running to St Georges-de-Commiers *(see see Lacs de LAFFREY, La Mure Mountain Railway)*. Nea the covered market, inside a historic building, the **Musée matheysin** ⊘ deals with loca history, including mining, by means of many reconstructions, artefacts and record ings. The road to Laffrey runs along the plateau not far from the former minin complex of Le Villaret, the largest in the area, then along the lakes, sometimes hidde by vegetation, with the heights of the Chartreuse Massif filling the horizon ahead.

The austere Plateau de la Matheysine, with its north-south axis, is windswept an exposed to the full harshness of winter, and fully deserving of its nickname "th Siberia of the Dauphiné"; in spite of its relatively low altitude (belo 1 000m/3 281ft) the lakes often freeze over during the winter months. The **45th par** allel, drawn at an equal distance from the North Pole and the Equator, goes across the southern shore of the Lac de Pierre-Châtel.

★ **Prairie de la Rencontre** – Two monuments bearing the imperial eagle symbol mark the access road. Napoleon's equestrian statue by Frémiet, visible from the road, is a reminder of the famous "meeting" which took place in this pleasant setting of lakes and mountains.

Where to stay and Eating out

MODERATE

Château des Herbeys – *05800 Chauffayer – 2km/1mi N on N 85* – ☎ *04 92 55 26 83 – closed 2 Nov-31 Mar and Tue except school holidays* – 🅿 – *10rms: 68.60/114.34€ -* 🍽 *8.38€ – restaurant 19.06/38.11€.* 13C residence with a beautiful park and a small deer enclosure. Spacious rooms are elegantly furnished, and some have spa baths, not to be missed! The cuisine caters to modern tastes and is served in sumptuously stylish dining rooms, as befits this stately home.

★ **Laffrey** – This holiday resort is particularly popular with by anglers and bathers. A plaque on the wall of the cemetery recalls the speech addressed by Napoleon to the soldiers sent from Grenoble to stop him.

Point de vue de Beauregard – 🚶 An easy walk *(about 2hr)* from Laffrey via the village of Notre-Dame-de-Vaux to the **Montagne de Beauregard**. Park the car near the Chalet de l'As and continue on foot to the top of the ridge which offers a splendid **view** of the plateau, the lakes and the Drac Valley.

★ **Le Sapey** – The narrow road which branches off the N 85 to the right at Laffrey skirts the Lac Mort which supplies a power station in the Romanche Valley. From the end of the road, one can climb to the Chapelle du Sapey *(15min there and back on foot)* which provides a clear view of the Chamrousse-Belledonne and Taillefer massifs.

★ **Vizille** – *See VIZILLE.*

Napoleon went from Vizille to Grenoble along the route now followed by D 5, which offers, on the way down to Eybens, an overall view of Grenoble.

★★ **Grenoble** – *See GRENOBLE.*

L'OISANS★★★

Michelin map 333 J7 or 244 folds 29, 40 and 41

The Oisans region is mostly covered by the high Écrins Massif, bounded by the valleys of the River Romanche, River Durance and River Drac; with a number of summits reaching or exceeding 4 000m/13 000ft, it is the second highest massif in France after Mont Blanc. Since the creation of the **Parc national des Écrins** *(see Le VALGAUDEMAR)*, these imposing mountains with some 10km≤ /4sq mi of glaciers have become better known, but remain wilder, more unspoilt and less visited than their great rivals. The "glorious" **Meije** has a special place in the affections of mountaineers.

The summits of the massif form a huge horseshoe round the Vénéon Valley. The **Barre des Écrins** is the highest point of the massif (alt 4 102m/13 458ft); its icy solitude is so well concealed that the motorist only catches rare and fleeting glimpses of its peak, first reached in 1864 by the British mountaineer **Edward Whymper**. In fact, **Mont Pelvoux** was long regarded as the highest point in the French Alps, Mont Blanc only becoming French after the annexation of Savoie. Mont Pelvoux was first climbed in 1828 by Captain Durand who soon acknowledged that the Barre des Écrins was higher.

Nearby Sights: L'ALPE D'HUEZ, Le BOURG-D'OISANS, BRIANÇON, Le BRIANÇON-NAIS, Les DEUX-ALPES, Le DÉVOLUY, Route du GALIBIER, Route des GRANDES ALPES, La GRAVE, MONTGENÈVRE, SERRE-CHEVALIER, Le VALBONNAIS, Le VALGAUDEMAR

EXCURSIONS

★★★① **Route de la Bérarde et Vallée du Vénéon**

FROM LE BOURG-D'OISANS *31km/19.3mi – about 1hr 30min not including hikes. The last section beyond Champhorent is closed from November to May.*

The road follows the deep, austere Vénéon Valley, giving only occasional glimpses of the high summits; we therefore strongly advise you to go on the hikes suggested below, bearing in mind that some of them are meant for experienced hikers.

Where to stay and Eating out

BUDGET

La Cordée – 38520 St-Christophe-en-Oisans – ☎ 04 76 79 52 37 – 10.52/12.96€. Generations of Alpine guides have recounted anecdotes about their exploits to each other in this hotel founded in 1907. The proprietress, herself an enthusiast, lends books, organises meetings with the authors and serves local dishes. A few rooms are available.

From Le Bourg-d'Oisans, drive eastwards along N 91 towards Briançon.

The road to La Bérarde (D 530), branching off from N 91 at Les Clapiers, enters the wide lower Vénéon Valley, which is in striking contrast with the narrow gorge of the Romanche; this is explained by the fact that, during the Ice Age, the Vénéon Glacier was longer than the Romanche Glacier.

The small depression of the Lac Lauvitel appears straight ahead, overlooked by the Tête de la Muraillette.

★★ **Lac Lauvitel** – *2.5km/1.5mi from D 530 then 3hr there and back on foot. At the bridge in Les Ougiers ,turn right towards La Danchère and leave the car on the roadside. Beyond La Danchère, take the left fork via Les Selles.* This nature trail is lined with markers providing explanations on geology, local fauna and flora, which are detailed in a book on sale in information centres throughout the Parc national des Écrins.

The path follows the natural dam formed by successive landslides, which contains the Lac Lauvitel (60m/197ft deep in parts) set in a wild landscape.

Follow the La Rousse path back to La Danchère.

Venosc – *Turn left off D 530 to a car park.* Walk up to the village which is a thriving centre of local handicrafts. A paved street leads to the church with its onion-shaped spire, which houses a fine altarpiece (17C Italian School). Slate quarrying in the Vénéon Valley was one of the main resources of the Oisans region from the 19C until the Second World War. Nowadays, the mining site has been entirely overgrown by trees.

A cable car, the **Télécabine de Venosc**, links the town with the ski resort at Les Deux-Alpes.

Le Bourg-d'Arud – The village nestles inside a charming verdant basin.

The steepest climb of the route avoids the first glacial obstruction, a jumble of huge boulders. The road then runs through the Plan du Lac Basin, with the Vénéon meandering below, towards St-Christophe-en-Oisans, past the **Cascade de Lanchâtra** on the right and across the Torrent du Diable.

★ **St-Christophe-en-Oisans** – Although it includes 15 hamlets, this vast *commune* (24 000ha/59 304 acres), one of the largest in France, barely has 30 inhabitants in winter, many of whom are professional guides from generation to generation. The **church** shows up against the Barre des Écrins; in the cemetery, young mountaineers who lost their lives in the Écrins Massif are buried next to local guide families like the Turcs and the Gaspards.

★★ **Hike from Champhorent to the Refuge de la Lavey** – Alt 1 797m/5 896ft. *3hr 30min there and back on foot (1hr 45min to reach the refuge); a fairly easy hike. Difference in altitude: 380m/1 247ft. Leave the car just outside Champhorent, in the car park laid out below D 530.*

⚐ The path leads rapidly down to the Vénéon. Markers signal the entrance of the Parc national des Écrins and the view extends towards the **Glacier du Fond** on the left and the **Glaciers des Sellettes** on the right. The path goes through a scree-covered area and the greenery becomes ever more sparse, with only tufts of Alpine sea holly and columbine to brighten up the landscape. A picturesque stone bridge leads over to the left bank of the Muande (*close the cattle gate behind you*); a few lonely patches of grass are the only vegetation to be seen. The glacial hollow of the Lavey and its refuge come into view with the **Glacier d'Entre-Pierroux** and **Glacier du Lac** towering right above and the **Pic d'Olan** filling the horizon to the south. Colonies of marmots live on the northern slopes; you may be able to hear their shrill warning call. *Return to Champhorent along the same route.*

Beyond Champhorent, there is an overall view of the Lavey Valley and the glacial cirque at the end of it before the road goes through a small tunnel into a desolate gorge, followed by the greener Combe des Étages. The Dôme de Neige des Écrins (alt 4 012m/13 163ft) looms ahead in the distance.

La Bérarde – Once a sleepy hamlet, inhabited by the local shepherds, or "bérards" in the old dialect, La Bérarde is now a popular starting point for challenging mountaineering expeditions in the Écrins Massif *(see below)* and a lively place in summer.

★★★ ② Vallée de la Romanche

FROM LE BOURG-D'OISANS TO THE COL DU LAUTARET
57km/35.4mi – about 2hr

This itinerary, combined with those of the Croix de Fer (see Route de la CROIX DE FER) and of the Galibier (see Route du GALIBIER), completes the unforgettable round tour of the Alps' great passes ("Circuit des Grands Cols").

The Col du Lautaret is now open throughout the winter, but can be closed for a few hours in the event of heavy snowfalls or poor visibility; watch out for information panels in Le Bourg-d'Oisans, Le Péage-de-Vizille and Champagnier or listen to the recorded information (see Admission times and charges).

The Briançon road leaves the Bourg-d'Oisans Basin and runs through wild gorges; beyond La Grave, the valley widens, offering lovely views of the summits and glaciers of the Meije.

From Le Bourg-d'Oisans, drive along N 91.

At first, the road runs southeast to the confluence of the River Vénéon and River Romanche, then turns eastwards, leaving the wide Vénéon Valley to the south.

Rampe des Commères – In the days of stagecoaches, tongue-wagging was the favourite pastime of travellers who had to step down and walk up this steep section, hence the name, which translates as "gossips' rise"

★ **Gorges de l'Infernet** – Fine **viewpoint★** over this wild gorge in a tight bend, near a ruined oratory.

The green Freney Basin offers a pleasant contrast.

At the Chambon Dam, take the road to Les Deux-Alpes.

Mont-de-Lans – This hilltop mountain village has retained a few old houses. The **M●sée des Arts et Traditions populaires** ⊙ illustrates daily life in the Oisans region during the 19C to the accompaniment of folksongs and stories; a permanent exhibition is devoted to local pedlars.

Climb up to the church and follow a narrow ridge to a high-voltage pylon for a fine **view★** of Lake Chambon and the Gorges de l'Infernet.

Return to the N 91.

★★ **Barrage du Chambon** – The dam was built across a narrowing of the Romanche Valley in order to regulate the spates of summer and autumn and supply hydroelectric power stations. This gravity dam is 294m/965ft long at the top, 70m/230ft thick at the base, and 90m/295ft high (137m/450ft including the foundations).

The Meije Massif from the Col du Lautaret

The reservoir, which covers an area of 125ha/309 acres, contains 54 million m³/43 778acft. Three hamlets, Le Chambon, Le Dauphin and Le Parizet were flooded when the dam was built.

Turn onto the D 25 at Le Freney.

Beyond Mizoën, the cliff-road climbs up the deep ravine through which flows the Ferrand, affording close-up views of the Grandes Rousses.

Besse – This high **mountain village** (alt 1 550m/5 085ft) is characteristic of the area: the houses lining its narrow twisting lanes have wooden balconies and heavy roof structures, which used to be covered with *lauzes* (thick slabs of schist).

Return to the Chambon Dam and continue along N 91.

★**Combe de Malaval** – The rushing waters of the Romanche are almost level with the road all the way through this long gorge, past two impressive waterfalls on the north bank, the **Cascade de la Pisse★** and **Cascade du Saut de la Pucelle**.

The Mont-de-Lans and the Girose glaciers are visible through gaps in the wall of rock to the right. The Meije and its glaciers come into view as one approaches La Grave.

❊❊**La Grave and excursion** – *See La GRAVE.*

Upstream from Villar-d'Arène, the road leaves the Romanche Valley which veers southeast along the Val d'Arsine; at the end of this glacial valley, the Pic des Agneaux (alt 3 663m/12 018ft) and the Pic de Neige Cordier (alt 3 613m/11 854ft) can be seen towering above the cirque of the Glacier d'Arsine.
Nearer the Col du Lautaret, the jagged peaks of the Combeynot Massif appear in the foreground.

★★**Col du Lautaret** ⊙ – In spite of its relatively high altitude (2 057m/6 749ft), the Col du Lautaret is the busiest pass of the Dauphiné Alps and the road is now kept clear of snow throughout most of the winter. From July until the beginning of August, wild narcissi, anemones, lilies, gentians, rhododendrons and even edelweiss cover vast expanses and brighten up the rather austere landscape.

A path at the highest point of the pass leads off to the **Jardin alpin** ⊙★. This famous garden, created at the beginning of the century contains several rockeries and around 2 000 species of wild and medicinal plants from the Balkans, the Caucasus, the Himalayas and the Rocky Mountains, as well as varieties from closer to home. A research laboratory welcomes scientists and students. From the viewing table situated on top of a knoll, there is a striking **view★★** of the Meije Massif surrounded by glaciers (Glacier de l'Homme).
The **Refuge Napoléon** is an information and exhibition centre devoted to the local fauna, flora and geology.

HIKES

These walks from Bérarde (see ⒈) are suitable for moderately experienced hikers equipped with non-slip shoes.

★★**Tête de la Maye** Alt 2 517m/8 255ft. *North of La Bérarde. 4hr there and back (2hr 30min on the way up); suitable for hikers familiar with steep terrain and not liable to feel dizzy. Difference in altitude: 800m/2 625ft.*
▣ The path starts before the bridge over the Étançons, winds its way across fields hemmed in by stone walls then runs along rows of arolla pines planted as avalanche barriers. *Bear left at the intersection with the path to Le Châtelleret; metal steps and safety cables make the following difficult sections a little easier, but caution is still required.*

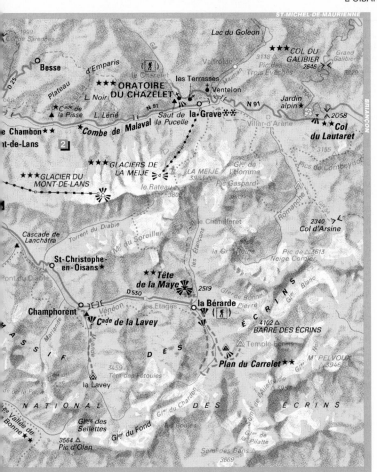

From the viewing table at the summit, there is an overall **view★★** of the Écrins Massif and of the peaks surrounding the Vénéon Valley: note in particular, from left to right, the **Grand Pic de la Meije** (3 983m/13 068ft), the **Glacier des Étançons**, the **Dôme des Écrins** (4 000m/13 123ft) and the **Glacier de la Bonne Pierre**.

It is possible to walk back along the east bank of the stream; at the intersection, bear left towards a bridge, then right to a footbridge and down to La Bérarde. Pleasant view of the Tête de la Maye on the right.

★★ Plan du Carrelet and refuge Alt 2 000m/6 562ft – *South of La Bérarde. 2hr there and back. Difference in altitude: 300m/984ft. For the first half of the year, the névé on the final stretch to the refuge means that this last leg of an otherwise easy walk should only be attempted by experienced and fully equipped hikers.*

🚶 Take the footpath starting beyond the Maison du Parc and following the east bank of the Vénéon. From the park's information panels, there is a fine view of the **Meije** and **Tête de la Maye** overlooking La Bérarde. The Meije has three peaks: the Meije Orientale to the east (3 890m/12 762), the Meije Centrale (3 974m/13 038), known to mountaineers as the Doigt de Dieu, "the finger of God", and the Meije Occidentale or Grand Pic de la Meije in the west. This last, with its steep, dramatic crags, is particularly impressive when seen in silhouette from La Grave. It was first climbed in 1877 – after 17 unsuccessful attempts – by one M. Boileau de Castelnau accompanied by two local guides, a father and son of the Gaspard family.

The U-shaped valley widens at the confluence of the Vénéon and Chardon. From the Plan du Carrelet refuge, the Chardon and Pilatte glaciers appear to fill the horizon to the south.

Retrace your steps, cross the stream and follow the path towards the Chardon Glacier. You then have to go over two footbridges in order to come back along the west bank of the Vénéon. Cross again as you reach the car park in La Bérarde. There is another view of the Meije and Tête de la Maye from here.

La PLAGNE★★

The **Grande Plagne**★★, which covers an area of 10 000ha/24 711 acres, is one of the most extended ski areas in France. Gentle slopes and beautiful views embracing the Mont-Blanc, Beaufortain and Vanoise massifs lend a particular magic to its mountain landscapes, which can be explored on foot in summer and using snowshoes in winter. A superb variety of sports and activities detracts little from the pleasantly unspoilt character of the mountain village.

Nearby Sights: Les ARCS, La Vallée de BELLEVILLE, BOURG-ST-MAURICE, CHAMPAGNY-EN-VANOISE, PRALOGNAN-LA-VANOISE, La TARENTAISE, Massif de la VANOISE

THE RESORTS

Ski area – The 1992 Olympic **bobsleigh** competitions were staged in La Plagne. The 1 500m/0.9mi run, built for the occasion, is the only one of its kind in France. Visitors can try taxi-bob, skeleton and bob-rafting through 19 hair-raising bends, or just watch from a safe distance; there is a good overall view near the intersection with the Plagne-Bellecôte road. Above 2 000m/6 562ft, the quality of the snow is exceptional and ideal for those who like moderately difficult runs (mainly blue runs). Experienced skiers can find a few suitable runs when snow cover is generous. Summer skiing takes place on the Glacier de la Chiaupe and Glacier de Bellecôte.

Created in 1961, La Plagne now includes six high villages and four lower ones. The high villages, situated at altitudes around 2 000m/6 562ft, enjoy good snow cover from December to May; being centrally located, they offer easy access to the whole ski area.
Plagne Bellecôte, **Plagne Centre** and Aime 2000 have a more urban atmosphere than Plagne 1800, Plagne Villages and above all **Belle Plagne** which blend harmoniously with the landscape.
Snow conditions are not so good in the lower villages, situated at altitudes ranging from 1 250m/4 101ft to 1 450m/4 757ft, but they have other advantages.
Champagny-en-Vanoise★★ *(see CHAMPAGNY-EN-VANOISE)* and, to a lesser extent, **Montchavin** have the charm of authentic Savoyard villages and offer superb views of the Vanoise Massif. Hikers can climb up to **Mont Jovet★★**, which offers a beautiful view of the Alps *(a guidebook of the area's hiking itineraries is published by the tourist office)*.

Where to stay

BUDGET

Chambre d'hôte Malezan – *Rte de la Plagne – 73210 Macot-la-Plagne – 16km/10mi N of La Plagne on D 221* – ☎ *04 79 55 69 90* – ⌷ – *4rms: 25.92/54.88€*. You will be guaranteed a warm welcome in this simple, friendly establishment. Whether you are keen on skiing, white-water sports or rambling, you can allow yourself a well-earned meal! It is quiet and peaceful here despite the nearby road. Leave your worries, and your cigarettes, outside the front door. Gîte available.

VIEWPOINTS ACCESSIBLE BY GONDOLA

★★**La Grande Rochette** ⊘ – Alt 2 508m/8 228ft. *Access by gondola from Plagne Centre. From the upper station, climb to the viewing table on the summit.* The splendid **panorama** includes the main summits of the Vanoise Massif (Mont Pourri, Bellecôte, Grande Motte, Grande Casse, Grand Bec) and extends to the Oisans (Meije), the Aiguilles d'Arves, the Étendard, Belledonne, Beaufortain and Mont Blanc massifs.
The high villages of La Plagne can be seen below to the north and Courchevel to the southwest.

★★**Télécabine de Bellecôte** ⊘ – *Access from Plagne Bellecôte*. The exceptionally long gondola ride (6.5km/4mi) leads to Belle Plagne and then to the **Roche de Mio** (2 739m/8 986ft). Climb to the summit *(viewing table)* in 5min to enjoy the splendid **panorama★★**. The Sommet de Bellecôte (3 416m/11 207ft) and its glaciers can be seen in the foreground, with the Grande Motte, the Grande Casse, Péclet-Polset and the Trois Vallées further away to the south. Mont Pourri appears quite close to the northeast with Mont Blanc and the Grandes Jorasses in the distance.
Take the gondola leading to the **Col** and **Glacier de la Chiaupe** (alt 2 994m/9 823ft): beautiful **view** of the Vanoise.

PONT-EN-ROYANS ★

Population 917
Michelin map 333 F7 and 244 fold 38 – Local map see Le VERCORS

Picturesquely situated at the exit of the long gorge of the River Bourne, this village has a definite southern atmosphere.

Nearby Sights: GRENOBLE, Le VERCORS, VILLARD-DE-LANS

Traditional houses line the narrow banks of the Bourne

WALKING ABOUT

★★ Viewpoints

★★ **The site** – *At Pont Picard, take the steps leading to the embankment along the Bourne, from where it is possible to reach the medieval quarter.* In spite of being partly destroyed during the Wars of Religion, the medieval quarter has retained a number of tall old houses clinging to the rock, overlooking the Bourne or dipping their narrow façades into the stream and forming a charming picture which once captured Stendhal's imagination.

★ **Trois Châteaux** – *1hr there and back on foot. Steep paths going across screes; start with a series of steps from place de la Porte-de-France.*
From the belvedere, there is a fine **view** of the Royans region and Isère Valley.

EXCURSIONS

St-Nazaire-en-Royans *9km/5.6mi west along D 531*

As one approaches St-Nazaire-en-Royans along D 531, old houses huddled on the bank of the River Isère appear framed by the arches of an imposing **aqueduct** carrying water from the Bourne into the Valence Plain.
The **Pont St-Hilaire-St-Nazaire** is an elegant single-arched bridge with a 110m/361ft span built across the confluence of the River Isère and River Bourne, now flooded by the more recent building of a dam.
Situated on the shore of the lake, beneath the aqueduct, the **Grotte de Thaïs** ⊘ is a natural cave resulting from the chemical action of the water of an underground river; the deeply carved rock is, in some places, coloured in bright red and grey. Inhabited in prehistoric times, about 13 000 years ago, the cave has yielded a wealth of tools and engraved bones.
There are **paddle-boat trips** ⊘ on the artificial lake (220ha/494 acres), starting from the village of La Sône and going through an important bird sanctuary known as the **Roselière de Creux**.
The **Jardin des Fontaines pétrifiantes** ⊘ is a green open space with 500 different species of plants and flowers, laid out round the petrifying springs at La Sône.

★★ Round tour via Presles *32km/20mi – about 1hr 30min*

From Pont-en-Royans, drive along D 531 towards Villard-de-Lans and turn left onto D 292 immediately after the Pont Rouillard over the Bourne. The road climbs up the sunburnt slopes within sight of the escarpments overlooking the river. From the wide bend known as the "Croix de Toutes Aures", although there's no trace of a cross to be seen, the view extends from the rolling hills of the Royans region to the impressive gorge of the River Bourne overlooked by the Grand Veymont.

345

After a series of hairpin bends, the road finally reaches the Presles Plateau. It continues to rise beyond Presles through the Coulmes Forest to a small hamlet called Le Fas, where the view embraces a long stretch of the lower Isère Valley, including the imposing aqueduct of St-Nazaire-en-Royans.

The road then winds steeply down to St-Pierre-de-Chérennes across green fields, offering more picturesque views.

D 31 reaches N 532. Turn left almost immediately towards Beauvoir-en-Royans.

Château de Beauvoir – The picturesque ruins of the 13C castle, razed by Louis XI, stand on top of an isolated hill overlooking the village. A square tower, a gate, a Gothic window, part of the former chapel and the old, ivy-covered walls are all that remain of the former residence of the "dauphins" *(see also GRENOBLE)*. However the site is pleasant and affords a fine view of the meandering River Isère.

Return to N 532 and, in St-Romans, take D 518 leading back to Pont-en-Royans.

Walnuts from Grenoble

Walnuts from Grenoble have, since 1938, been protected by a label guaranteeing their origin and quality *(appellation d'origine contrôlée)*. Three different kinds are grown in the region:
– the *mayette*, a large walnut with a thin shell and a refined taste;
– the *parisienne*, a round walnut with a brown shell, rich in oil;
– the *franquette*, an oblong walnut with a rough shell, which is the most sought-after by confectioners and the most widely cultivated.
The producing area straddles three *départements*; however, 60% of the annual production (around 10 000 – 15 000t) comes from just four *communes*: Pont-en-Royans, St-Marcellin, Vinay and Tullins.
The September harvest is followed by the washing, drying and conditioning process (there are two sizes: over 30mm/1.2in and between 20mm/0.8in and 30mm/1.2in). This energy-giving fruit can be eaten fresh, within two weeks of the harvest, or dried and used in salads, cakes and confectionery (stuffed walnuts are a Grenoble speciality traditionally eaten during the Christmas period).

PRALOGNAN-LA-VANOISE
Population 756
Michelin map 333 N5 and 244 fold 32 – Local map see Massif de la VANOISE

Set in an imposing glacial valley, this health and ski resort is the best starting point for fine hikes and mountaineering expeditions in the Parc national de la Vanoise, famous as an ibex reserve. The eastern edge of the Pralognan Basin is undoubtedly the most **picturesque area★** with the cirques of the Grand Marchet and Petit Marchet in the foreground, backed by the Glaciers de la Vanoise.
Pralognan, which attracts thousands of hikers and mountaineers, has been one of the liveliest summer resorts in Savoie for over a century. The first climbing attempts date from the late 19C; in 1860, the British mountaineer **William Matthews** and the Frenchman **Michel Croz** hewed their way up one of the peaks of the Grande Casse – now called Pointe Matthews – by carving no fewer than 1 100 steps, 800 of them with an axe.
We strongly advise holidaymakers to attend slide shows organised by the Association des Chasseurs d'Images de Pralognan, which are a useful introduction to the local fauna and flora as well as to hikes and mountain excursions in the surrounding area.
The small but sunny **ski area** offers remarkable possibilities for cross-country skiing.

Nearby Sights: La Vallée de BELLEVILLE, CHAMPAGNY-EN-VANOISE, COURCHEVEL, La PLAGNE, La TARENTAISE, Massif de la VANOISE

HIKES

★ **La Chollière** – *1.5km/0.9mi along a mountain road, then 30min on foot. Start from the Hôtel La Vanoise, cross the Doron and follow the road which winds up to La Chollière. Leave the car above the chalets.* A handsome group of mountains can be seen in the background behind the hamlet: the Pointes de la Glière and the Grande Casse (alt 3 855m/12 648ft, the highest peak of the Vanoise Massif). The surrounding pastures are famous for their wealth of wild flora, including narcissi and edelweiss in June and Alpine sea holly, known as the "Queen of the Alps", in August *(see Introduction: Vegetation).*

★ **Mont Bochor** ⊙ – *About 3hr there and back on foot or 6min by cable car.*

Lac Blanc and Mont Parrachée

From the upper station, walk up to the summit (alt 2 023m/6 637ft, viewing table) for a bird's-eye view of the Pralognan Basin and the Doran de Chavière Valley, closed off upstream by the Péclet-Polset Massif and lined on the left by the huge Vanoise glaciers.

A 1.4km/0.9mi-long **nature trail** enables visitors to become familiar with this typical mountain environment. Information panels detail the geological and ecological wealth of the site.

★★★**Col de la Vanoise** – Alt 2 517m/8 258ft. *Start from Mont Bochor. If the cable car is not operating, start from the Fontanettes car park. 3hr up, 2hr 30min down to Pralognan.*
From the Barmettes refuge, the path rises steeply to the Lac des Vaches before reaching the pass; view of the Grande Casse Glacier and Pointe de la Réchasse. On the way down, there is a fine view of the Lauzière Massif with the Sommet de la Saulire, Dent de la Portetta and Aiguille du Fruit in the foreground. Martagon lily, columbine and houseleek are some of the wildflower species which can be seen along the route. Inexperienced hikers can come down via the Barmettes refuge and Fontanettes car park. Hikers with more experience of the mountains, on the other hand, can, in fine weather conditions only, enjoy a splendid hike via the Arcellin cirque and ravine

★★**Petit Mont Blanc** – Alt 2 677m/8 783ft. *Start from Les Prioux.* 3hr up via the Col du Môme; 2hr down.
For a description of the **panorama**★★, *see COURCHEVEL.*

★★**Lac Blanc** – *Start from the Pont de la Pêche. A long and arduous climb; 3hr 15min up, 2hr 30min down.*
Situated below the Péclet-Polset refuge, the Lac Blanc is one of the loveliest lakes in the Vanoise Massif. Walk along the right side of it and climb towards the Col du Soufre. View of the Aiguille de Polset, the Gébroulaz Glacier, the Col de Chavière, the Pointe de l'Échelle and the Génépy Glacier.

Where to stay

BUDGET

Hôtel Parisien – *R. des Grands-Prés* – ☎ *04 79 08 72 31* – *closed 21 Apr-31 May and 21 Sept-19 Dec* – 🅿 – *24rms: 24.39/54.88€* - 🍽 *5.34€* – *restaurant 12.20/27.44€.* This hotel overlooking the resort has the air of a guesthouse and offers a family welcome. Peace and quiet guaranteed. Plain local fare is served in the dining room or on the terrace overlooking the village, opposite the Vanoise.

MODERATE

Hôtel Les Airelles – *Les Darbelays – 1km/0.6mi N of Pralognan* – ☎ *04 79 08 70 32 – closed 21 Apr-30 May and 23 Sept-19 Dec* – 🅿 – *22rms: 57.93/68.60€* - 🍽 *7.62€* – *restaurant 14.48/21.34€.* Ask the owner to take you to see the ibex. This chalet is just on the edge of the forest. From the balcony of your room, faced with pale wood, you will be able to admire the Vanoise. Good friendly atmosphere, guesthouse style, plain local cooking. Summer swimming pool.

PRA-LOUP*

Michelin map 334 H6 and 245 fold 9 – Local maps see BARCELONNETTE and L'UBAYE

In a dense larch forest, on the edge of a plateau (alt 1 630m/5 347ft) overlooking the Ubaye Valley, the 1960s resort of Pra-Loup is one of the most popular in the Alpes-de-Haute-Provence, owing its fame as much to its facilities, the quality of its environment and to its long hours of sunshine as to an attractive setting.

A natural ice rink marks the centre of an expanding town where fans of new winter sports will feel particularly at home.

Nearby Sights: BARCELONNETTE, Route de la BONETTE, COLMARS, Val d'ENTRAUNES, Lac de SERRE-PONÇON, SEYNE, L'UBAYE, VAL-D'ALLOS

THE RESORT

Ski area – Linked with that of La Foux d'Allos (see VAL-D'ALLOS), it forms a vast area known as the **Espace Lumière**: 54 ski lifts and 230km/143mi of runs. However, the link with La Foux is generally only suitable for experienced skiers. Pra-Loup's own ski area, which rises to a maximum altitude of 2 500m/8 202ft, offers moderately steep snow-fields ideal for intermediate skiers. Cannons ensure adequate snow cover down to the lowest part of the resort. The resort also boasts the most spectacular "big air" run in France and a snow park with its own sound system. Freeriders will want to head for four avalanche-free zones on the edge of the piste for miles of untouched snow.

In summer, Pra-Loup offers a wide choice of activities including swimming, white-water sports and paragliding as well as fine rambles along marked trails.

HIKE

★**Col des Thuiles** – *This itinerary (6hr) is suitable for strong experienced hikers and requires a good sense of direction. The ascent to the pass, alongside the ski lifts, is arduous but the walk down through the Gimette Valley is quite pleasant. Take plenty of drinking water – the only opportunity to replenish supplies is at the Grande Cabane.*
An occasionally vertiginous path running along the mountain slope offers a fine **view★** of the Agneliers area, the Gorges du Bachelard, the Cimet and Chapeau de Gendarme, eventually reaching the Col des Thuiles beneath the Grande Séolane. From here, make for the Rocher Jaumas, cross the Torrent de Langail and follow the yellow markings. A forest path leads steeply downhill for 100m/328ft, then turn right onto a path which crosses the Torrent des Bruns. Beyond the pine woods, a broad path leads to the Pas Lapeine. Carry on through the meadows, the larches and pines of the Gimette forest, across the stream and, after a rest at the Grande Cabane (2 138m/7 014ft), head towards Grande Séolane and the Col de Thuiles (2 376m/7 795ft). The path opposite the Grande Cabane leads back through the Vallon des Agneliers to the Lac de Pra-Loup.

View of the Grande Séolane from the Col des Thuiles

Eating out

BUDGET

La Tisane – *Pra-Loup 1600 – Chenonceau 1 – ☎ 04 92 84 10 55 – closed end Apr-30 Jun and Sept-mid-Dec – 12.96/37.35€.* A mountain restaurant in a shopping centre comes as something of a surprise and is not necessarily appealing, and yet the decor is pleasant and the à la carte and fixed price menus on offer, featuring mainly mountain region dishes, are interesting.

Where to stay

MODERATE

Hôtel Prieuré de Molanès – *At Molanès – ☎ 04 92 84 11 43 – closed 16 Apr-8 Jun and 17 Sept-16 Dec –* 🅿 *– 14rms: 42.69/64.03€ -* 😋 *6.40€ – restaurant 22.20/33.54€.* You are guaranteed an enjoyable stay and relaxed atmosphere in this old 17C priory right in the heart of the Alps. Stone, wood, roughcast and panelling combine to create a warm decor typical of this mountain region. Lounge with open fire for winter evenings, and a swimming pool for the summer.

On the town

Edouard's Pub – *Immeuble Miraval-Miramont – ☎ 04 92 84 07 43 – daily 7am-2am – closed May-Jun and Sept-Nov.* This pub presents a relaxed alternative to the hectic beat of the nightclubs, and offers fair pricing, friendly service and the chance to drink beer by the metre. There is a choice of around thirty cocktails, whiskies, spirits and liqueurs. Piano-bar at weekends during winter.

Shopping

La Cave du Loup – *Immeuble Miraval-Miramont – ☎ 04 92 84 06 29 – daily 9.30am-1pm, 3pm-7.30pm except summer until 8pm – closed May-Jun and Sept-mid-Dec.* This cellar where wine can be bought and tasted enables you to sample spirits and liqueurs from the Ubaye valley, presented in bottles that are often quite original in shape. Do not forget to taste the most famous of these beverages, Génépi, whose manufacture is dictated by the "rule of 40": 40 sprigs of *génépi* (a sort of Alpine wormwood) and 40 sugar lumps soaked in 40° proof spirit for 40 days.

Sport

Mathy-loisirs – 📷 – *Front-des-pistes – ☎ 04 92 84 07 34 – Mon-Fri 9am-12.30pm, 2pm-7pm – closed May-Jun and Sept-Nov.* This is a recreational paradise for 3-15 year olds. Whether toddler or teenager, the budding sportsperson can tackle activities such as tennis, trampolining, downhill racing, pony-riding, and in winter quad and snow-scooter. All activities are run by qualified sports instructors.

PUGET-THÉNIERS ★

Population 1 800
Michelin map 341 C4 and 245 fold 23
Local map see CLUES DE HAUTE-PROVENCE

This small town nestling beneath a rocky spur crowned with the ruins of a castle, at the confluence of the River Var and River Roudoule, is the starting point for excursions to the nearby mountains. Lively and distinctly southern, modern Puget-Théniers also has a historical treasure that is well worth seeking out; cross to the right bank of the Roudole and time seems to stand still in the streets of the old Jewish quarter.

Nearby Sights: ANNOT, BEUIL, Gorges du CIANS, CLUES DE HAUTE-PROVENCE, Val d'ENTRAUNES, ENTREVAUX, ST-JULIEN-DU-VERDON, Vallée de la TINÉE, VILLARS-SUR-VAR

WALKING ABOUT

★ **Old town** – It is mainly concentrated on the west bank of the Roudoule and includes place A.-Conil and its lovely fountain as well as many old houses which have retained beautiful doorways and signs carved in stone.

Church – Built in the 13C by the Knights Templar, this Romanesque church was remodelled and richly decorated in the 17C (chancel vaulting and church furniture). It contains many works of art *(time switch at the entrance on the left)*.

Note the amazing **carved wooden calvary★** consisting of three tiers representing the Crucifixion, the Entombment and the Resurrection. The faces of the different characters are very expressive and the representation of the thieves' bodies, tied to their crosses, and of Christ, carried by his disciples bending beneath the weight, is most realistic.

The high altar **retable of Notre-Dame-de-Secours★**, placed above a polychrome statue of the Virgin Mary carved out of an olive tree trunk, dates from 1525 and is believed to be the work of Antoine Rouzen. Note the beautiful representations of the Virgin Mary and of St James.

★ **"L'Action enchaînée"** – This female nude by Maillol, a powerful figure with her hands bound behind her back, is dedicated to the memory of one of the town's most famous (or infamous) sons. **Louis-Auguste Blanqui** (1805-81), the anticlerical revolutionary who lived by the motto *"Ni Dieu ni maître"* "no God, no master", and helped to fan the flames of revolt in 1830, 1848 and 1870 spent more than 36 years in prison before being elected as member of parliament for Gironde. First unveiled near the church, the statue now stands on a less contentious spot, in a charming square planted with very old plane trees on the edge of N 202.

Eating out

BUDGET

L'Amandier – *11 av. Alexandre-Barety – ☎ 04 93 05 05 13 – closed 22 Dec-13 Jan, Sun evening and Mon – 13.72€/20.58€.* This restaurant near the station for the tourist steam train is a great place to recharge your batteries with some of its generous regional fare. Food is served without any fuss in a neat and tidy dining room or on the terrace.

EXCURSION

Pays de la Roudoule *45km/28mi round tour – about 3hr*

To the north of Puget-Théniers, a succession of unusual landscapes begins; the Roudole has scoured narrow gorges through folds of limestone, red sandstone and black marl, and several picturesque villages, surrounded by larches and olive groves, stand along its path.

From Puget-Théniers, drive along D 16.

The road rises above Puget and offers a lovely view of the old town before entering the Gorges de la Roudoule.

Turn right onto D 116 towards Puget-Rostang.

The road follows the Mairole Valley and goes through a strange landscape darkened by the presence of black marl formations, known as *"robines"*.

Puget-Rostang – This hilltop village is overlooked by the square tower of a restored castle. The **Écomusée du Pays de la Roudoule** ⊘, created to preserve and develop the area's traditional agriculture, rural architecture and cultural heritage, also organises exhibitions here.

From Puget-Rostang, a twisting road leads to **Auvare** *(13km/8mi there and back)* clinging to the rock, which used to be a refuge for all kinds of fugitives.

Return to D 16 and continue along the Gorges de la Roudoule.

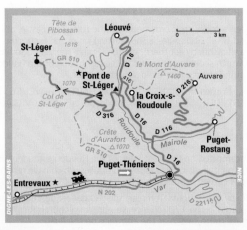

★ **Pont de St-Léger** – This bridge occupies an amazing site. The Roman bridge can be seen below with the paved Roman road at either end.

Continue toward Léouvé and turn right onto D 416 to La Croix sur-Roudoule.

La Croix-sur-Roudoule – Perched high and backing onto the rock in a picturesque **setting★**, this village is still guarded by an old fortified gate. The small Romanesque **church**, which has a wall-belfry with twin openings, houses two panels from an altarpiece by François Bréa representing St John the Baptist on the right of the altar and St Michael on the left. From the top of the village, there is an interesting **view** of the upper Roudoule Valley.

Return to D 16 and turn right.

Léouvé – The Léouvé Cirque is carved out of red sandstone; copper was mined here from 1861 to 1929 and the tall chimneys of the foundry works can still be seen. An exhibition at the **Maison de la Mine** shows the grim reality of everyday life in the mines.

Return to the Pont de St-Léger and cross over.

The road rises to the Col de St-Léger, from where a totally different landscape unfolds. The village of St-Léger lies in verdant surroundings framed by mountains.

Turn back towards Puget-Théniers.

Just before the Pont de St-Léger, there is a fine **view** of the Roman bridge and of the Roman road, as well as of the village of La Croix-sur-Roudoule.

Le QUEYRAS★★★

Michelin map 334 I4 to J5, 244 folds 43 and 44 and 245 folds 9 and 10

Set right on the Italian border, the Queyras region is an isolated bastion, accessible all year round through the Combe du Queyras and in summer via the Col d'Izoard and the Col Agnel (on the Italian border). This geographical, historical and human entity, centred round the Guil Valley, is one of the most authentic areas of the southern Alps, and one of the most culturally independent. Several tributary valleys, including the St-Véran Valley, converge towards the Guil Valley which, as one follows it downstream, is in turn imposing, charming, restful and austere. Even the weather has a distinctive character: the Queyras region has a reputation for blue skies and one of the sunniest climates in France, tempered by a certain coolness in the mountain air. Snow cover is excellent for six months of the year.

Nearby Sights: ABRIÈS, L'ARGENTIÈRE-LA-BESSÉE, BRIANÇON, BRIANÇONNAIS, CEILLAC, EMBRUN, Vallée de FREISSINIÈRES, Route des GRANDES ALPES, GUILLESTRE, MOLINES-EN-QUEYRAS, MONT-DAUPHIN, MONT-GENÈVRE, ST-VÉRAN, SERRE-CHEVALIER, La VALLOUISE, VARS

BACKGROUND

Unusual relief – The Queyras region is divided into two distinct areas. To the east, the Haut Queyras consists of folded sedimentary schist – made from deposits which once formed a **prehistoric seabed** – mixed with layers of volcanic porphyry; these were shaped into jagged summits and shiny mica-schist ridges overlooking rounded glacial valleys. The limestone that predominates in the Bas Queyras to the west produced impressive but austere landscapes such as those of the Casse Déserte near the Col d'Izoard or the Combe du Queyras. The Espace géologique at Château-Queyras *(see below)* offers a detailed view of the region's natural history.

Moufflons

The **moufflon**, a wild sheep which can weigh up to 50kg/110lb, is another example of a successful newcomer; the twelve animals brought over from Corsica in 1973 increased to a colony of over 300 in a little over 20 years. Their splendid horns grow during their first year and, by the third year, curve right round to their neck. In winter, when their short, reddish fleece takes on a black-brown tinge, the search for food brings the moufflons down to the villages, where hay is often provided for them. If taking advantage of this opportunity to observe these surprisingly timid animals, remember to stay at least 50m/55yd away and be careful not to alarm them; binoculars can be used to get a closer look.

A land apart – The natural seclusion of the mountains has always encouraged a sense of independence from the world beyond; the medieval confederation of seven towns in the Aiguilles canton preserved a degree of autonomy until the 18C. Yet even the Queyras region was not spared the ravages of the Wars of Religion; an army of

Huguenots, under the command of Lesdiguières, seized Fort Queyras in 1587. After the revocation of the Edict of Nantes in 1685, many Protestant families emigrated to Switzerland or Germany.

During the 19C, the Queyras remained almost untouched by the Industrial Revolution; the region's first surfaced road, between Guillestre and Château-Queyras, was only built in 1856.

Arts and crafts – The Queyras region is particularly rich in folk art, comprising mainly objects made by peasants during the long winter evenings spent in their traditional houses *(see Introduction: Handicraft)*. Pieces of **furniture** made of larch wood or arolla pine are particularly famous (there are fine collections in the Musée Dauphinois in Grenoble, in the Musée Départemental in Gap and in the Musée des Arts et Traditions Populaires in Paris); they include box beds, wedding chests, spinning-wheels and cots, decorated with geometric motifs carved with a knife.

This tradition has been perpetuated until today with the help of the Traditional Craftsmen's Union. There is a permanent display of their work in the **Maison de l'Artisanat** ⊘, situated on the D 947 towards St-Véran, near the intersection with D 5.

There are many sundials in this exceptionally sunny region (300 days of sunshine a year). They were the work of travelling artists, often natives of Italy, and are decorated with mottos which express popular wisdom *(see Introduction: Traditional architecture, as well as the Practical information section)*.

There are also numerous wooden **fountains**, with a rectangular basin and a circular bowl, which are fine examples of the skill of craftsmen from the Queyras region.

Croix de la Passion – Queyras is famous for these crosses, usually found in front of churches, sometimes inside; fine examples of this devotional art can be seen at St-Véran and Ceillac. Each shows the symbols of Christ's Passion:

– the cock standing at the top is a reminder of Christ's words to Peter: "this night, before the cock crows, thou shalt deny me thrice" (Matthew XXVI, 34);

– the hand suggests Pontius Pilate's gesture at Jesus' trial;

– the coins symbolize the price of Judas' betrayal;

– the weapons, placed on either side of the central upright, represent those used for the Crucifixion;

– in some cases, a crown has been added as a reminder of Jesus' Crown of Thorns.

The Tour du Procureur – Several villages in the Haut Queyras region have a characteristic campanile built of larch logs and crowned with a bell, known as the Tour du Procureur.

Dating from the early Middle Ages, it is all that remains of the original village building. The sound of the bell called the villagers to a meeting where decisions concerning the community were taken: about baking day in the village oven, harvest time, sharing of communal duties and help for widows. The set of rules governing community work was called the "Ruido".

During the 19C, the tower was used for a different purpose in valleys where Protestants had returned; it was used as an ecumenical bell-tower. During the extensive flooding which occurred in 1957, the temporary absence of modern means of communication gave it back its original function.

PARC NATUREL RÉGIONAL DU QUEYRAS

🛈 Tourist information centre
M Museum or exhibit
🏠 Principal mountain refuges or gite for overnight stay

Parc naturel régional du Queyras – By the

mid-20C, isolation and depopulation had considerably slowed down the region's economy so that, in the 1960s, it was decided to modernize traditional agriculture, to develop handicrafts and above all tourism. The **Parc naturel régional du Queyras**, covering some 65 000ha/160 618 acres, was created in 1977 to provide information on the area, mark hiking routes, including the GR 5 and GR 58, and maintain refuges, as well as preserving the landscape and protecting endangered plant and animal species. The **flora** displays a great variety of Mediterranean and Alpine species, around 2 000 in all, and the **fauna** includes the usual mountain-dwellers like the chamois and black grouse as well as rarer animals such as the black salamander. The ibex was successfully reintroduced in 1995; tourist information offices can provide information on where to watch these animals and how to avoid disturbing them.

★★① COMBE DU QUEYRAS

From Guillestre to Château-Queyras

17km/10.6mi – about 1hr, not including the drive to Sommet-Bucher

★ **Guillestre** – *See GUILLESTRE.*

From Guillestre, drive along D 902.

Viewing table at Pied-la-Viste – It is located on top of a mound above the road. The imposing **Pelvoux-Écrins Massif★** can be seen through the gap of the Durance Valley and Vallouise Depression.

Between Pied-la-Viste and Maison du Roy, the valley becomes narrower and the road goes through several tunnels.

Maison du Roy – Tradition has it that King Louis XIII stopped at this inn on his way to Italy in 1629. A painting hanging inside is said to be a gift from the king.

D 60, which goes up the Ceillac Valley (see CEILLAC-EN-QUEYRAS), branches off here. Continue along D 902.

The road enters the **Combe du Queyras★★**, a long steep gorge. The narrowest part lies between La Chapelue and L'Ange Gardien, where there is barely room for the cliff road above the limpid and abundant flow of the river. Beyond the Rocher de l'Ange Gardien, the road offers a fine view of the splendid setting of Château-Queyras with its fort crowning the rocky height.

★ **Château-Queyras** – The village nestles beneath **Fort Queyras** ⊘★, perched on a rugged knoll which almost completely blocks the entrance to the Guil Valley; this is the most characteristic **scenery★** of the Queyras area. *Leave the car on the right, just before climbing to the fort, or on the open space near the river.* This strategic hill at the gateway to the Durance valley has been fortified since medieval times and was occupied by a garrison until 1967. Its defences were improved and extended to the west by Vauban in 1692, before being remodelled three times in the 18C and 19C. Beyond the drawbridge, a marked path leads past casemates and bastions to the machicolated 14C keep where exhibitions are held. Note the picturesque bartizan of the eastern bastion and go to the fortified outwork, or lunette, to get the best overall view of the fort.

★ **Espace géologique** ⊘ – *Turn left at the church and park the car on the open space near the river, then walk back towards the village and go through the porch.* The geological centre, housed in the crypt of the village church, illustrates the formation of the Alps through interactive displays presented in chronological order. One unusual exhibit gives you the chance to smell algae and plankton which were preserved in mud in the Arvieux area for 170 million years.

Where to stay

MODERATE

Chambre d'hôte La Girandole – *At Brunissard – 05350 Arvieux-en-Queyras – ☏ 04 92 46 84 12 – closed 15 Oct-15 Dec – 5rms: 42.69/57.93€.* This cosy guesthouse is full of character, with antique furniture and ornaments, fabrics in warm tones, soft sofas and a piano. In the rooms (which are non-smoking) there are white walls and a prevailing lack of fuss or frills. Two gîtes available.

Résidence Ferme de l'Izoard – *La Chalp – 05350 Arvieux-en-Queyras – ☏ 04 92 46 89 00 – www.laferme.fr – closed 10-30 Apr and 15 Sept-21 Dec – 23rms: 60.62/135.83€ – restaurant 16.01/26.68€.* Do not be misled by appearances, this chalet resembling a traditional farmhouse, with wood panelling and stone slab roof, conceals modern rooms, all with a balcony and some with a kitchenette. Heated swimming pool in view of the mountains.

★**Sommet Bucher** *11km/6.8mi south – about 1hr there and back. The road is in very bad condition – please drive carefully.*

The narrow road, shaded by larches and pines, climbs in a series of hairpin bends, offering fine glimpses of Château-Queyras and the Guil Valley. *From the end of the road, climb to the viewing tables, situated on either side of a military building.* The beautiful **panorama** includes Mont Viso and St-Véran village, framed by the Pic de Châteaurenard, Pointe de Toillies and Sommet de Razis, with the Pic de la Font Sancte to the south, Pelvoux-Écrins Massif to the west and Grand Pic de Rochebrune to the north.

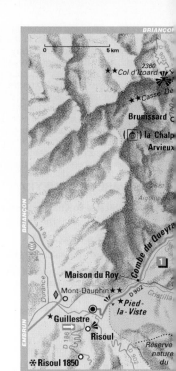

★★ 2 THE ST-VÉRAN ROAD

From Château-Queyras to St-Véran *15km/9.3mi – about 30min*

★**Château-Queyras** – See 1.

From Château-Queyras, drive east along D 947.

Ville-Vieille – This village, administratively linked to Château-Queyras, forms part of **Château-Ville-Vieille**. A nature trail on the left just before the village, the **Sentier écologique des Astragales**, offers a pleasant 1hr 30min walk. ⏁ Views of the valley and of the Bric Bouchet Summit. Rare plant species can be seen along the way, in particular specimens of milk-vetch, pheasant's eye and Ethiopian sage. The path leads to **Pierre Fiche**, probably a prehistoric standing stone, which stood 7m/23ft high before it was broken. *A booklet containing explanations about the trail is on sale in the Maison de l'Artisanat.*

Follow D 5.

Note the **church** doorway, with its arches resting on carved heads, and the lovely sundial decorating the bell-tower.
The road rises along the north-facing slope covered with larches, offering a fine downstream view of the Guil Valley. Beyond a hairpin bend, it enters the Aigue Blanche Valley overlooked by the densely forested slopes of the Sommet Bucher.
At the exit of the Prats Ravine, note the **Demoiselle coiffée** *(see Lac de SERRE-PONÇON, 3)*, a strange rock formation showing above the larches on the opposite slope. The end of the Aigue Blanche Valley is closed off by the Tête de Longet.

A lonely Demoiselle coiffée

La Rua – Go through the village *(narrow street)* and admire the typical architecture of the St-Véran area including a few traditional *mayes* (barns entirely built with beams roughly joined together and covered with laths).

★**Église St-Romain-de-Molines** – Below the village to the right, this isolated church, rebuilt in the 15C, comprises a massive nave and an amazing campanile, next to a tiny enclosed cemetery. Inside, there is a wealth of Baroque decoration; note the imposing altarpiece, framed by twisted columns adorned with vine leaves and surmounted by a broken pediment. The chancel vaulting, restored in the 19C, is decorated with stucco work.

★**Molines-en-Queyras** – See *MOLINES-EN-QUEYRAS.*

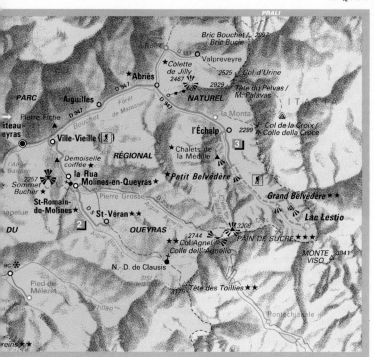

The road continues to climb through a lovely pastoral landscape, and the houses of St-Véran suddenly appear, scattered over the sunny side of the valley.

★★ St-Véran – *See ST-VÉRAN.*

③ HAUT QUEYRAS

From Château-Queyras go the Monte Viso Belvedere
30km/18.6mi – about 1hr

This itinerary takes you through the most open and most pleasant part of the Guil Valley, between Château-Queyras and Abriès, and offers splendid views of Monte Viso.

From Château-Queyras, follow D 947 towards Abriès.

The road runs up the Guil Valley, densely forested with larches and pines on the north-facing side. There is a clear **view** ahead towards the heights lining the Italian border with the Bric Bouchet (alt 3 216m/10 551ft) soaring above.

★ Aiguilles – Lying in pleasant surroundings and enjoying an exceptionally fine climate, Aiguilles is the liveliest resort of the Queyras region. The nearby larch woods are charming and, in winter, the sun shines generously on the ski runs. A large number of local inhabitants emigrated to South America at the beginning of the 19C; most of them came back at the end of the century, having made their fortune across the Atlantic *(see BARCELONNETTE)*. They had sumptuous houses built in a style which was fashionable in large urban areas at the time. The best examples are: the town hall, the Château Margnat (on D 947) and above all the luxurious Villa Challe. Note also the amazing "Maison Eiffel", built entirely of metal for the 1898 Bordeaux Exhibition, but despite the name, not actually the work of Gustave Eiffel.

Beyond Aiguilles, note the contrast between the barren south-facing slope and the densely forested north-facing slope, the forêt de Marassan.

Abriès – *See ABRIÈS.*

Continue along D 947.

The Guil Valley turns southwest and the landscape becomes more austere.

L'Échalp – This is the last village in the valley and the starting point for excursions to the Monte Viso belvederes. The hike to the **Chalets de la Médille★** *(1hr 30min there and back on foot)*, affords a fine view of Monte Viso: take the first bridge over the Guil upstream of L'Échalp and follow the path which rises towards the Plateau de la Médille, a charming meadow surrounded by larches.

Aiguilles is set in pleasant larch woods

The road continues up the Guil Valley, which becomes narrower, passing near a huge rock, known as **"la Roche écroulée"** ⏱, used for rock-climbing practise. The road is closed to traffic at the point where it crosses the Guil.

Leave the car in the car park and continue on foot, in order to get a close-up view of the rocky ridge of Monte Viso. Mountain hiking enthusiasts can make a round tour via the Grand Belvédère, the Lac Lestio and the Refuge du Viso. A shorter and easier itinerary leads to the Petit Belvédère and the Pré Michel Nature trail. For other hiking possibilities, see ABRIÈS.

★ **Petit Belvédère du mont Viso and Sentier écologique du Pré Michel** – *45min on foot and 1hr on the site. The Information Centre near the car park sells a booklet describing the nature trail.*
In addition to the view of Monte Viso, a great variety of plant and flower species are in bloom between late June and early August, including the martagon lily, delphinium and fritillary.

★★ **Hike to the Grand Belvédère, the Lac Lestio and the Refuge du Viso** – *5hr 30min there and back. Difference in altitude: about 700m/2 297ft. This round tour is varied and pleasant but does not offer outstanding panoramas.*
🚶 You will reach the Grand Belvédère after 1hr 45min walk along a landscaped path (explanatory tables) running parallel to the road. From there the **view**★ extends to **Monte Viso** (alt 3 841m/12 602ft) across the Italian border, which seems to close of the upper end of the Guil Valley.
After climbing for a while, take a path on the right which follows the stream. This easy itinerary is recognisable by the yellow markings along the way; after joining the path leading to the refuge and crossing the stream, one reaches the **Lac Lestio** (2 510m/8 235ft).
Retrace your steps and follow the path identified by red and blue markings, which leads to the refuge with a **view**★ of Monte Viso; go back along the road to the Grand Belvédère and the car park.

④ ARVIEUX VALLEY

From Château-Queyras to Brunissard *10km/6.2mi – about 1hr*

This valley is also on the Route de l'Izoard itinerary *(see Le BRIANÇONNAIS, ⑤).*

★ **Château-Queyras** – *See CHÂTEAU-QUEYRAS.*

2km beyond Château-Queyras, turn right onto D 902 towards the Col d'Izoard.

Arvieux – This village and the surrounding hamlets are interesting for their traditional architecture represented by **arcaded houses** covered with larch shingles. Owing to its pleasant climate, Arvieux has become a lively summer resort and winter sports centre.
The 16C **church** has retained an 11C porch and doorway; note the naive-style carvings decorating the capitals.

La Chalp – Situated above Arvieux, this village has been a toy making centre since the 1920s; the wooden toys are decorated by hand *(see Introduction Handicraft).*

Brunissard – An interesting wooden **campanile** rises above the village oven.

RIEZ

Population 1 707

Michelin map 334 E10 and 245 fold 34

This lively ancient town, overlooked by Mont St-Maxime, lies at the confluence of the River Auvestre and River Colostre. Many historical paths also crossed at Riez: first a Celtic settlement, then a Roman colonial town, before the foundation of a bishopric in the 5C, which survived until the Revolution, made Riez an economic as well as a religious force in the region.

From here, every road leads out into the Parc naturel régional du Verdon; the Lac de Ste-Croix and the famous Verdon gorges are almost on the doorstep.

Nearby Sights: CASTELLANE, Vallée de la Moyenne DURANCE, FORCALQUIER, GRÉOUX-LES-BAINS, MANOSQUE, MOUSTIERS-STE-MARIE, Lac de STE-CROIX, Plateau de VALENSOLE, Grand Canyon du VERDON

WALKING ABOUT

★ **Old town** – Start from place Javelly or place du Quinconce, shaded by plane trees, and enter the old town through the 13C **Porte Aiguière**. Grand-Rue, the former main street, is lined with splendidly decorated houses: a corbelled house (n°1), 16C **Hôtel de Mazan** (n°12) with fine stucco work on the staircase, lovely façade decorated with twin windows (n°25), windows surrounded by moulded friezes (n°27).

As you reach the 14C **Porte St-Sols**, turn right towards rue St-Thècle; a tiny square on the left offers an interesting view of what remains of the town walls and of the **Tour de l'Horloge**. The **town hall** is housed in the former bishop's palace.

Go back to the church past the Porte St-Sols.

Church – Rebuilt during the 19C, it has retained the bell-tower and apsidal chapels of the 15C cathedral.

SIGHTS

★ **Baptistère** ⊙ – This is one of the few Merovingian buildings still standing in France. It probably dates from the 5C, but its cupola was rebuilt in the 12C. The square edifice comprises an octagonal room with four radiating chapels. Eight granite columns with marble Corinthian capitals form a circle round the christening font which has almost entirely disappeared.

A museum displays finds excavated on the site: altars, Roman inscriptions, sarcophagi, mosaics etc. Part of the Gallo-Roman town and the foundations of a cathedral dating from the 5C have been excavated opposite the baptistery.

Roman columns – Four beautiful granite columns, surmounted by white-marble Corinthian capitals and supporting an architrave, stand 6m/20ft high in a meadow. It is all that remains of a late 1C temple, believed to have been dedicated to Apollo.

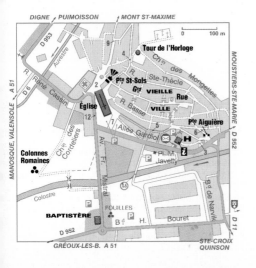

RIEZ

[Hôtel de Ville .... **H**]

Where to stay

MODERATE

Hôtel Carina – ☎ *04 92 77 85 43 – closed Nov-Mar –* 🅿 *– 30rms. 45.73/57.93€ -* ⌐ *6.10€.* Hardly have you left the medieval village when you are off on your journey back in time once again. This modern 1980s hotel has a main lounge and a breakfast room in which the Louis XV and Louis XVI styles mix with modern fireplaces and balustrades.

Chambre d'hôte Le Château d'Allemagne-en-Provence – *04500 Allemagne-en-Provence –* ☎ *04 92 77 46 78 – http://perso.wanadoo.fr/himmel – closed Oct-Mar -* ✉ *– 3rms: 76.22/137.20€.* Charm and history meet in this restored castle. You will be delighted by its large guest rooms furnished with character. A vast apartment is available on request. Swimming pool secluded from the gaze of onlookers in the park.

NEARBY SIGHTS

Allemagne-en-Provence – *12km/7.5mi northeast along D 952.* A fine Renaissance **castle** ⊘, restored in the 19C, stands beside the River Colostre. The crenellated 12C keep was remodelled in the 16C and mullioned windows, surmounted by carved gables, were opened. The great hall, in Renaissance style, has a monumental **fireplace★** decorated with gypsum carvings and framed by two mythological characters: Hercules and Minerva. Note the fine **spiral staircase** linking the medieval and Renaissance wings. Part of the park is laid out as a medieval herb garden.

Maison de l'Abeille et du Miel ⊘ – 📷 *2km/1.2mi northeast on the Puimoisson road.* A bee-keeper and lavender-grower presents an exhibition about bee-keeping: the life of a bee (5 weeks in summer), what goes on inside a beehive (which houses as many as 50 000 working bees), the honey harvest (about 12kg/26lb per beehive) and the conditioning of honey to be sold. *Tasting and sale on the premises.*

EXCURSION

Mont St-Maxime – *2km/1.2mi northeast along rue du Faubourg-St-Sébastien.* This 636m/2 087ft-high hill is a familiar landmark in the Riez area. The **Chapelle St-Maxime** has retained its Romanesque apse: the ambulatory is lined with six beautiful Corinthian columns clearly taken from a much older building. From the shaded terrace in front of the chapel, the **panorama★** extends over part of Riez, the Valensole Plateau, the Préalpes de Castellane, the Plans de Canjuers, the hills of the Haut Var area, the Luberon and the Montagne de Lure.

The "black gold" of Haute-Provence

There are two kinds of truffle, known as **rabasse** in Provençal dialect.
The white truffle, picked in the spring, has little culinary value; it is used to train truffle hounds.
The rarer and tastier black truffle is gathered in December; it is used to enhance the taste of dishes and sauces.
Truffles, which are buried beneath oak and hazelnut trees, are the signs of a disease in these trees. Nowadays, the harvest takes place in fields containing trees which favour the growth of these sought-after mushrooms.
Montagnac, near Riez, is a famous centre of production in the Haute-Provence region.

La ROCHE-SUR-FORON★

Population 7 116
Michelin map 328 K4 and 244 fold 8

This town of Reblochon, Beaufort and Tomme cheeses has a thousand year-old city at its centre. An important crossroads above the lower Arve Valley, La Roche-sur-Foron belonged to the Genevan nobility in the 11C and came to be as important as Geneva or Annecy in the 14C, becoming a Savoyard posession one hundred years later.
In 1885, La Roche-sur-Foron was the first European town to enjoy electric lighting; a plaque in the castle park commemorates the event.

Nearby Sights: ANNECY, Lac d'ANNECY, Massif des ARAVIS, La CLUSAZ, CLUSES, Les GETS, MORZINE, ST-GERVAIS-LES-BAINS, Bassin de SALLANCHES, SAMOËNS, THONON-LES-BAINS, THORENS-GLIÈRES, YVOIRE

★★ OLD TOWN *1hr 30min*

This round tour of the medieval town leads past many houses with ogee-arched mullioned windows. This charming district is being carefully restored; several houses and public buildings have been repainted with bright colours, in typical Piedmontese style.

The Plain-Château district is accessible from place St-Jean.

Follow rue des Fours on the left of the church to reach the tower.

Go through the Porte Falquet into the school yard. The entrance to the tower is at the end, on the right.

Tower ⊘ – It is all that remains of the counts of Geneva's castle, built on the rocky spur which gave the town its name.

On the way down, take **rue du Plain-Château** (on the right) and admire the carved façades of the 17C houses; note in particular the **Maison des Chevaliers** (1565), once home to an order of knights founded by Amedée VI of Savoy.

Turn right at the end of the street towards the Château de l'Échelle.
Retrace your steps and walk down rue du Cretet beyond the Porte St-Martin (remains of the 13C wall).

There are a couple of interesting houses in rue du Silence, in particular n°30. Walk round the church and onto rue des Halles; a **stone bench** dating from 1558 has three **grain measures**, for 20, 40 and 80l/4.4, 8.8 and 17.6gal.

Église St-Jean-Baptiste – The arms of the counts of Geneva can be seen above the doorway of this early 12C church, surmounted by an onion-shaped steeple dating from the 19C which replaced the one destroyed in 1793. The chancel and the apse are Romanesque.

In rue Perrine, note the **Maison Boniface** (n°79) in Renaissance style and the emblazoned lintels inside the courtyard. The picturesque *halle aux grains* (corn exchange), known as **"La Grenette"**, is near the town hall.

Walk onto the Pont-Neuf in order to admire the fine view of the Foron overlooked by terraced gardens.

EXCURSION

★ **Le Salève** – The tiered cliffs of Mont Salève, towering above Geneva on the French side of the border, are one of the favourite haunts of Swiss tourists, especially rock-climbers.

A road following the ridge leads past the main peaks: the Petit Salève, the Grand Salève and the Grand Piton, the highest of the three at 1 380m/4 528ft. All along the way, the route offers splendid views of the Arve Valley and the Faucigny heights to the east with the Mont Blanc Massif in the distance, and of Geneva and its lake to the west with the Jura mountains in the background.

★★ **Les Treize Arbres viewpoint** - *Follow the road from the hotel car park. 15min there and back on foot along the D 41* Splendid *view* of the peaks between the Dents du Midi and Mont Blanc. The edge of the rock is a favourite spot for hangliders.

★ ③ Route de Mont-Saxonnex

From La Roche-sur-Foron to Cluses

36km/22.4mi – about 1hr 30min – local map see CLUSES.

Drive east along N 203.

Bonneville – The former capital of the Faucigny region is today an administrative centre, situated at a tourist-road junction and at the confluence of the River Borne and River Arve. A column, standing at the entrance of the bridge across the Arve, commemorates the regulation of this mighty stream in the early 19C, following the initiative of Charles-Félix de Sardaigne.

From Bonneville, drive east along N 205; after crossing the motorway, turn right towards Mont-Saxonnex then right again to Brizon. Leave the car near a sharp bend to the right.

★ **Point de vue de Brizon** – From the viewpoint at the side of the road, there is a bird's-eye view of the Gorges du Bronze with the Môle summits and Pointe de Marcelly in the distance across the Arve Valley.

Return to the Mont-Saxonnex road.

Gorges du Bronze – Leave the car 100m/109yd beyond the first of four hairpin bends and climb onto a rock overlooking the deep wooded ravine.

★ **Mont-Saxonnex** – This summer resort, popular for its high position overlooking the Arve Valley *(more than 500m/1 640ft above the river bed)*, includes two main villages: **Le Bourgeal** nestling below the church and **Pincru** at the beginning of the Gorges du Bronze. Leave the car in front of the church and walk round the east end for a bird's-eye **view★★** of the confluence of the Arve and Giffre.

After a dizzying view down to the Arve plain, the road runs through a wooded area and joins D 4 before passing a number of small metalworking workshops and finally reaching Cluses.

ST-ÉTIENNE-DE-TINÉE ★
Population 1 668
Michelin map 341 C2 and 245 folds 23 and 24

This charming Alpine town, rebuilt after the devastating fire which occurred in 1929, lies on the banks of a fast-flowing river, in a pleasant **setting★** of pastures and terrace cultivation against a beautiful mountain background.

In summer, St-Étienne-de-Tinée is the ideal starting point of very interesting hikes, in particular from the Route de la Bonette. In winter, it offers a small **ski area** – highest point: **Cime de la Berchia**, alt 2 274m/7 461ft – linked to that of Auron by cable car and chairlift.

Nearby Sights: AURON, BARCELONNETTE, BEUIL, Route de la BONETTE, Gorges du CIANS, ISOLA 2000, Vallée de la TINÉE, L'UBAYE, VAL-D'ALLOS

SIGHTS

Church – The most striking feature is the 4-tiered **steeple★** in Lombard Romanesque style, surmounted by a tall octagonal stone spire surrounded by four gargoyled pinnacles; the date inscribed on the base of the steeple is 1492. Inside, the high altar in gilded wood bears the mark of Spanish influence; note, on the left, some carved wood panels depicting scenes of Christ's life surrounding a statue of the Virgin Mary with Child.

The Chapels – Well-preserved frescoes by Baleison and Canavesio in the **Chapelle St-Sébastien** ⊙ include the creation of Adam and Eve on the vaulting, Jesus between the two thieves on the back wall and scenes from the life of St Sebastian on the right. The **Chapelle St-Michel** ⊙ contains a small museum devoted to the penitent orders. The **Chapelle des Trinitaires** ⊙, which belonged to the former monastery (now a school), is decorated with fine carved wood panels 17C frescoes, including one showing the battle of Lepanto and two paintings depicting the life of the monks who used to buy back Christians enslaved on the Barbary Coast. The **Chapelle St-Maur** ⊙ *(2km along the road to Auron)* was decorated in the 15C with picturesque frescoes depicting the legends of St Maur and St Sebastian.

Two small museums illustrate aspects of traditional life: the **Musée des Traditions** ⊙, housed in the former village bakery, explains the process of making rye bread and the **Musée du Lait** ⊙ displays the equipment used in cheese-making.

HIKES

There are numerous possibilities starting from St-Étienne-de-Tinée or Auron. A wide choice of itineraries is available from the tourist office in both resorts.

Starting from Le Pra

★★ **The Lacs de Vens** – *Leave the car in Le Pra, on the road to La Bonette (10km/6.2mi north of St-Étienne-de-Tinée). 6hr on foot via the Col de Fer. Difference in altitude: about 940m/3 084ft. Easy but long and taxing itinerary.*

▨ The path goes through a larch forest to reach the Plateau de Morgon *(after 1hr)* then past waymark no 33 to the Tortisse forest lodges. From there it is possible to go straight to the Refuge de Vens, but the detour via the **Col de Fer** (alt 2 584m/8 478ft) is recommended for the **view★** it offers, even if the additional distance demands extra strength.

Y. Bontoux

Lacs de Vens

Well-equipped hikers, who do not suffer from vertigo, can climb up to the Cime de Fer (alt 2 700m/8 858ft; *add 35min there and back on foot*), where a splendid **panorama★★** includes Mont Vallonnet and the Lacs de Vens in the foreground, the road to the Col de Larche and the Tête de Moïse Summit further north.

From the Col de Fer, the path leads to the refuge and **Lacs de Vens★★**. The reflection of the mountains and of the sky in the clear waters of the lakes enhances the beauty of the landscape. Skirt the first lake and part of the second then turn right beyond a pile of huge rocks. The path divides several times; keep left every time in order to reach the top of the ridge. On the other side there is a splendid **view★** of the Cime de la Bonette and Crête de la Blanche.

Go up the path, running just below, to waymark 23 and turn towards Le Pra. The path runs along the mountain slope in a splendid **setting**, then down to the Tortisse forest lodges. From there, retrace your steps to Le Pra.

★★ **Hike to the Refuge de Rabuons** – *This extension of the previous hike includes a night in the Refuge des Lacs de Vens. About 5hr on foot. Marked itinerary.*

🔲 The main purpose in combining these hikes is to link the two highest mountain refuges in the Parc national du Mercantour along a route which overlooks the Tinée Valley and offers a succession of superb panoramic views. Walk along the right side of the middle and lower lakes, cross a footbridge then climb up to the Crête des Babarottes. On the way down, follow part of the *"Chemin de l'énergie"* to the Lac de Rabuons and the refuge of the same name.

The **"Chemin de l'énergie"** was built in the 1930s at high altitude, through very uneven terrain with retaining walls and tunnels, in order to supply a power station in St-Étienne-de-Tinée which was never completed.

Starting from the Camp des Fourches

★★ **The Pas de la Cavale** – Alt 2 671m/8 763ft. *Leave the car at the Camp des Fourches, on the road to La Bonette (see Route de la BONETTE) and walk to the Col des Fourches (5min). Climbing boots recommended. 3hr 30min there and back on foot. Difference in altitude: about 750m/2 461ft.*

🔲 Walk down a narrow path, marked in white and red, to an old shack just below the Salso Moreno Cirque. The austere yet splendid landscape is very interesting from a geological point of view: sink-holes have resulted from the action of water and snow erosion. Colonies of marmots inhabit the area.

From waymark 37 onwards, the stony, slippery path climbs steadily to the Pas de la Cavale framed by the Rocher des Trois Évêques and the Tête Carrée. The **view★★** embraces the Lacs d'Agnel, the heights lining the Italian border and the Auron ski area to the south, the Vallon du Lauzanier and the Brec de Chambeyron to the north. The Lac de Derrière la Croix lies just below.

361

ST-GERVAIS-LES-BAINS‡‡

Population 5 276

Michelin map 328 N5 and 244 fold 20 – Local map see Massif du MONT-BLANC

St-Gervais-les-Bains occupies one of the most open sites in the Alps, at the meeting point of the Autoroute Blanche and where the Val Montjoie widens out into the Sallanches Basin. Known for more than a century for its hot springs, the spa town is now regarded as the main health resort in the Mont-Blanc Massif and is sometimes called St-Gervais-Mont-Blanc. This important holiday resort welcomes many children and is the starting point of many drives and cable-car rides offering outstanding views of the Mont-Blanc Massif.

Mountaineers traditionally start the ascent of Mont Blanc from St-Gervais, via the Tramway du Mont Blanc, Tête Rousse and the Aiguille du Goûter.

Finally, owing to its position at the centre of the network of cable cars and mountain railways linking Megève to the Chamonix Valley via the Mont d'Arbois, the Col de Voza and Bellevue, the town, together with its high-altitude satellites of Le Bettex, Voza-Prarion and St-Nicolas-de-Véroce, has become an important ski resort.

Nearby Sights: Massif des ARAVIS, ARGENTIÈRE, CHAMONIX-MONT-BLANC, CLUSES, Les CONTAMINES-MONTJOIE, Les HOUCHES, MEGÈVE, Massif du MONT-BLANC, LA-ROCHE-SUR-FORON, Bassin de SALLANCHES

ST-GERVAIS

The town nestles round its church, on the last gentle slopes of the Val Montjoie above the wooded gorge through which flows the River Bon Nant, spanned here by the **Pont du Diable**. This bridge spans the wooded gorge of the Bon Nant. Looking up the valley from the bridge, there is a clear view of Mont Joly, Mont Tondu and the Dômes de Miage framing the Val Montjoie; downriver, the view extends to the escarpments of the Chaîne des Fiz (Pointe and Désert de Platé).

Le Fayet – This is the spa district. The **Établissement thermal** (hydrotherapy centre) is situated at the exit of the Bon Nant Gorge, inside a park with a lovely waterfall. The waters are used for the treatment of skin diseases and respiratory complaints. The local church, the **Église Notre-Dame-des-Alpes**, was designed in 1938 by Novarina; it is a good example of religious art at that time.

EXCURSIONS

★★★**Le Bettex** – *8km/5mi along D 909 to Megève, then left along D 43 to Le Bettex. It is also possible to reach Le Bettex from St-Gervais by the* **Mont d'Arbois cable car** ⊘.

ST-GERVAIS-LES-BAINS
LE FAYET

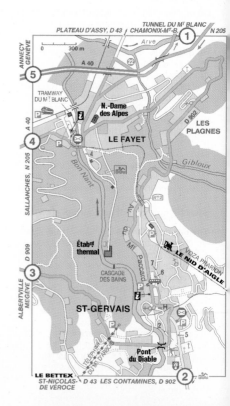

Eating out

MODERATE

Lou Grangni – *50 r. de la Vignette – ☎ 04 50 47 76 39 – closed 15 May-15 Jun, 15 Nov-15 Dec and Mon out of season – 21.04€*. Behind the timber façade of this restaurant in the centre of town the chef plies his trade as you watch. Take a seat in one of the alcoves in the back room and discover the joys of regional dishes or a more classic meal, but don't count the calories! Those who do not like the smell of cheese should stay on the terrace.

Ferme-auberge de Bionnassay – *3084 rte de Bionnassay – 3.5km/2mi S of St-Gervais towards Les Contamines then Bionnay – ☎ 04 50 93 45 23 – closed 1 Nov-Christmas and Tue out of season – 22.87/37.35€*. This farm-inn dating from 1810 stands at a crossroads and is an ideal stopping place for ramblers. The welcoming interior, which also has a small stable, reflects the charm of life in the mountains in years gone by. Don't be put off by the fact that it is hard to get to in winter!

Where to stay

MODERATE

Hôtel Carlina – *R. Rosay – ☎ 04 50 93 41 10 – closed 16 Apr-14 Jun and 1 Oct-19 Dec – ▣ – 34rms: 66.32/94.52€ - ⌇ 7.62€ – restaurant 20.58/27.44€*. This is a large building on the slopes, near the Bettex cable car. The pleasant dining room opens onto the garden and resort. During your stay, a fine indoor heated swimming pool will help you keep fit.

Hôtel Chez la Tante – *On Mont-d'Arbois via cable-car at the upper station (access on foot) – 74190 Le Fayet – ☎ 04 50 21 31 30 – closed May-14 Jul and 16 Sept-14 Dec – 45.73/53.36€*. This isolated chalet, perched at 1 850m/6 070ft above sea level, offers a unique panorama of the Mont-Blanc range. You are guaranteed a breath of really fresh air in this magnificent site. Access via cable car and tracker vehicle, on skis or on foot. Accommodation is simple, as is the food.

On the town

Il Était Une Fois – *85 av. du Mont-Paccard – ☎ 04 50 93 66 01 – daily 9am-3am in season – closed end Oct-Dec*. Cosy atmosphere and original decoration in this tea room which transforms itself into a piano-bar in the evenings. Literature also has its place here, and numerous authors come for readings, discussions and book-signings. Home-made pastries and exclusively leaf tea.

Extremely varied views of the Mont Blanc, Fiz and Aravis massifs.
It is possible to continue by cable car up to the **Mont d'Arbois★★★** (alt 1 827m/5 994ft, viewing table) for an even finer **panoramic view**.

Col de Voza – Alt 1 653m/5 423ft. *Journey from Le Fayet or St-Gervais-Ville aboard the* **Tramway du Mont-Blanc** ⊙.
The electric tram on its way to the Nid d'Aigle *(see below)* stops at the Col de Voza; halfway up the mountainside, above the Bionnassay Valley, there are splendid **views★★** of the Mont Blanc Massif.

★★ **The Nid d'Aigle (Glacier de Bionnassay)** – Alt 2 286m/7 828ft. *Allow 3hr there and back by the Tramway du Mont-Blanc (see above).*
This journey provides a good introduction to high-altitude mountain landscapes by opening up the wild setting of the Bionnassay Glacier *(from the upper station, 1hr there and back on foot to the moraine)* stretched out at the foot of the Aiguilles de Bionnassay *(spectacular avalanches)* and of the Aiguille du Goûter. **View** of the massifs surrounding the Bassin de Sallanches.

★ **Gorges de la Diosaz** ⊙ – On its way to join the River Arve, the Diosaz flows through a famous gorge with a **succession of waterfalls★★**, particularly abundant in July and August, when the dam upstream opens its floodgates
The entrance of the gorge can be reached by car (1km/0.6mi) from Servoz.
The itinerary follows a path and overhanging galleries to several waterfalls including the Cascade des Danses, the Cascade de Barme-Rousse and the triple Cascade de l'Aigle, the most impressive of them all. The galleries continue as far as the natural bridge formed by a rock which fell in the 16C and stuck inside a fissure from which springs the **Cascade du Soufflet**.

St-Nicolas-de-Véroce and excursions – *12km/7.5mi along D 909 to Megève, then left along D 43. See Massif du MONT-BLANC.*

ST-JEAN-DE-MAURIENNE

Population 8 902
Michelin map 334 L6 or 244 fold 30

Did you know that three of St. John the Baptist's fingers are still proudly preserved in St-Jean-de Maurienne? The historic capital of the Maurienne region, situated at the confluence of the River Arc and River Arvan, owes its development to its role as diocesan town until 1966.

Nearby Sights: AUSSOIS, Route de la CROIX-DE-FER, Route du GALIBIER, Route de la MADELEINE, La Haute MAURIENNE, MODANE

SIGHTS

A long-term project to restore the town's historic centre has been a visible success; typical alpine houses boast colourful façades and pretty doorways.

Cathédrale St-Jean-Baptiste ⊙ – An isolated square tower (11C-12C), which was the bell-tower of the Église Notre-Dame and was partly dismantled during the Revolution, stands in front of the cathedral.

The cathedral, dedicated to the city's patron saint and dating from the 11C and 15C, was built over a **crypt** excavated in 1958; it is preceded by a peristyle built in 1771, beneath which stands a mausoleum dedicated to Humbert "White Hands", the founder of the House of Savoie. The interior, partly restored, contains some splendid 15C church furniture and two frescoes: one of them, on the north side, shows the Annunciation, the other, on the south side, depicts the Entombment. On the left-hand side of the apse is the **Ciborium★**, a delicate Flamboyant masterpiece carved in alabaster. Three of St John the Baptist's fingers used to be kept in the central recess (they are now in the vestry). The choir **stalls★★** were carved between 1483 and 1498 by Pierre Mochet from Geneva; this superb piece of woodwork was restored in 1969. There are 43 high stalls and 39 low ones. The high backs are decorated with low-relief carvings depicting various saints whereas the backrests and misericords show a freer inspiration. There are two stalls under a baldaquin, near the high altar; the one on the right is the bishop's seat and the other is intended for the president of France, who is an honorary canon of the cathedral. On the north side of the church, the well-preserved 15C **cloister** has retained its original alabaster arches. A flight of steps in the south gallery leads to the crypt.

Musée Opinel ⊙ – The museum illustrates the history of the famous knives from Savoie produced by the Opinel dynasty of cutlers, who were natives of St-Jean-de-Maurienne.

EXCURSION

Route de la Toussuire *36km/22.4mi – allow 2hr*

From St-Jean, drive along D 926 then turn right towards La Toussuire.

During the drive, the **Aiguilles d'Arves★★** stand out from a broad horizon of mountains. The road rises above the St-Jean-de-Maurienne Basin offering bird's-eye views of the valley below.

The misericords in the Cathédrale St-Jean-Baptiste are worth a closer look

Opinel

Opinel – The famous knife from Savoie

At the end of the 19C, Joseph Opinel, a toolmaker from a nearby village, began to make folding pocket knives for his friends during the long winters. Opinel met with such success that he launched into the manufacture of knives in a big way and put the finishing touch to his prototype in 1890. Available in twelve different sizes, the knives sold well in local markets and fairs and soon became popular across the border in Italy and Switzerland. The Opinel trademark was added in 1905: the hand of St. John beneath a crown, symbolising loyalty to the house of Savoie, is also the insignia of the Canon of the cathedral. Chosen by the Museum of Modern Art in New York as a functional design classic, the knives are now produced at Cognin, near Chambéry.

The ancient hilltop village of **Fontcouverte★** commands a panoramic view of the surrounding area. The ski area of **Le Corbier**, at the heart of the massif, is linked to that of the neighbouring resorts of **La Toussuire**, in a setting of barren slopes, and St-Sorlin-d'Arves (Les Sybelles in the massif de l'Avan-Villards 1 100-2 600m/3 609-8 530ft: ☎ 04 79 59 88 00, www.les-sybelles.com)

On the way down to St-Jean-de-Maurienne, the road goes through **La Rochette**; note the isolated rock which gave its name to the hamlet.

ST-JULIEN-DU-VERDON ★
Population 110
Michelin map 334 H9 and 245 fold 22

A village which once clung to a hilltop now stands at the water's edge; a miracle worthy of St Julien himself, but one worked as part of the hydro-engineering project which saw the building of five dams in the space of 30 years and the creation of the Lac de Castillon. The hamlet at the foot of the white cliffs of Pinadoux is the perfect starting point for a tour of this remarkable man-made landscape.

Nearby Sights: ANNOT, BARGÈME, CASTELLANE, CLUES DE HAUT-PROVNCE, COLMARS, ENTREVAUX, Route NAPOLÉON, PUGET-THÉNIERS, Plateau de VALENSOLE, Grand Canyon du VERDON

EXCURSION

★Lac de Castillon and Lac de Chaudanne

TOUR OF THE LAKES *47km/29.2mi – allow 3hr*

The road runs across the dam, then follows the right shore of the lake; a road to the left leads to the Col de Toutes Aures.

Barrage de Castillon – Stop by the belvedere to get a good view of the site; there are explanatory panels about the dam and the harnessing of the Verdon. This elegant arch dam is only 26m/85ft thick at the base. It is 200m/218yd long across the top and 100m/328ft high. The hydroelectric power station has a capacity of 77 million kWh.

★ **Panorama from Blaron** – *Leave the car at the entrance to Blaron village and continue along the footpath (15min there and back).* From the promontory there is a magnificent **view** of the Lac de Castillon, its tiny island and St-Julien-du-Verdon.

Return to D 955 and continue along the edge of the lake.

★ **Castellane** – *see CASTELLANE*

St-Julien, now home to a water sports centre, is the only village on the slopes not to have been submerged by the flooding of the valley.

Go back along the same road and turn left onto D 102 towards Demandolx.

The road rises in a series of hairpin bends. At the Croix de la Mission, there is a fine **view★★** of the Lac de Castillon. On the way down towards the Lac de Chaudanne, there are bird's-eye **views★★** of this dark green mountain lake.

Barrage de Chaudanne – This arch dam (total height 70m/230ft, length across the top 95m/104yd) is built across a gorge of the Verdon downstream from the Barrage de Castillon. The power station can produce 67 million kWh.

Return to St-Julien-du-Verdon by D 955.

Route de Toutes Aures

FROM ST-JULIEN-DU-VERDON TO ENTREVAUX *30km/18.6mi – allow 1hr*

This road is a section of the "winter Alpine route" *(N°202)* linking the upper valleys of the River Verdon and the River Var.

From St-Julien, drive along N 202.

Mountain streams, which are subject to fearsome spates, have cut across the barren plateaux at an angle to the mountain crests, carving deep valleys which often narrow to form wild gorges known as *"clues" (see CLUES DE HAUTE-PROVENCE).*

★**Clue de Vergons** – The road rises as it goes through the gorge, offering fine views of the lake and the lovely setting of St-Julien-du-Verdon.
The Romanesque **Chapelle Notre-Dame-de-Valvert** stands on the roadside just beyond Vergons.

Col de Toutes Aures – Alt 1 124m/3 688ft. Tilted rock strata – sometimes almost vertical – form a striking contrast with the forested slopes.

★**Clue de Rouaine** – The road runs between impressive cliffs.

Beyond Les Scaffarels, where one can see the famous Grès d'Annot *(see ANNOT),* the Coulomp Valley is deep and narrow, except where the river joins the Var (Pont de Gueydan). The road then follows the Var Valley, and the typically southern character of the arid landscape is enhanced by the Mediterranean sun.

★**Entrevaux** – *See ENTREVAUX.*

Where to stay

BUDGET

Camping Le Lac – *Rte de St-André-les-Alpes* – ☎ *04 92 89 07 93 – open 15 Jun-15 Sept – reservations recommended – 70 pitches: 9.15€.* A simple camp site at the exit to the village. Many people come here regularly, won over by the shaded pitches and friendly atmosphere.

ST-PIERRE-DE-CHARTREUSE✻
Population 770
Michelin map 333 H5 and 244 fold 28 – Local map see Massif de la CHARTREUSE

This medium-altitude health resort is sought after in summer and winter by those who enjoy the peaceful setting. 270km/168mi of marked paths lead out into the beautiful forested landscapes of the Chartreuse Massif.

Nearby Sights: ALLEVARD, CHAMBÉRY, Massif de CHAMROUSSE, Massif de la CHARTREUSE, GRENOBLE, Le GRÉSIVAUDAN, VIZILLE

THE TOWN

The slopes of the Scia, at altitudes ranging between 900m/2 953ft and 1 800m/5 906ft, offer 35km/21.7mi of ski runs at all levels of difficulty, plus 50km/31.1mi in St-Hugues.
In summer, St-Pierre-de-Chartreuse is a popular touring and hiking base for excursions across the Chartreuse massif The ascent of the **Dent de Crolles** or of **Mont Granier** is ideal for experienced hikers who do not suffer from vertigo.
There is a splendid **view** of the elegant silhouette of Chamechaude (alt 2 082m/6 831ft) and of the rocky summit of the Pinea across the Col de Porte from the **Terrasse de la Mairie**.

EXCURSION

Église St-Hugues-de-Chartreuse – *4km south.* The 19C **church** ⊘ looks quite ordinary from the outside, but, inside, the contemporary **sacred art★** with decoration in reds and golds is amazing; paintings, sculptures, stained glass and holy objects are all the work of a single artist, Jean-Marie Pirot Arcabas, who worked from 1953 to 1986.

Where to stay and Eating out

MODERATE

Hôtel Beau Site – *Pl. de l'Église* – ☎ *04 76 88 61 34 – closed 23 Mar-14 Apr and 15 Oct-21 Dec – 27rms: 48.78/54.88€ -* ⌂ *6.10€ – restaurant 14.48/30.49€.* The Sestier family has been running this hotel opposite the church for four generations. There is a comfortable lounge-bar and a dining room with a view of the valley and forest. Ask for a room in the more recently built part. Summer swimming pool.

HIKES

★★**Grand Som** – *Alt 2 026m/6 647ft. Difference in altitude: 1 175m/3 855ft. Taxing hike: 4hr ascent. The main interest of this itinerary lies in the panoramic view from the summit.*
From St-Pierre, drive west along D 520^B for 3km/2mi; leave the car in the car park reserved for hikers of La Correrie .
🚶 Walk 300m/328yd back along the road and take the road on the right leading to the monastery, la Grande Chartreuse. Walk alongside it and turn right past a house on the left. The path leads to a calvary; climb to the top of the meadow on the edge of the forest. There is a fine **view** of the monastery.
Return to the road and continue in the direction of the Grand Som via the Col de la Ruchère. After walking for 30min and reaching two chapels, take the steep path *(marked in orange)* on the right; 15min later, turn right again onto a signposted path and shortly after that turn left onto a steep path leading to the Habert de Bovinan refuge *(45min)*. Continue until you reach the foot of the Grand Som. then take the path on the right marked with arrows painted on the rock. At the next intersection, take the stony path used by sheep. From the cross at the summit, there is a magnificent **panorama★★★** of the whole Chartreuse Massif and a bird's-eye view of the monastery. Mont Blanc and the Belledonne range can just be seen on the eastern horizon.

★★**Belvédère des Sangles** – *2km/1.2mi then 2hr 30min there and back on foot. Drive to La Diat and follow the road to St-Laurent-du-Pont. Leave the car beyond the bridge on the Guiers Mort, then cross back and take the Valombré Forest road.*
It leads to the lovely **Prairie de Valombré** which offers the best **view★** of the Grande Chartreuse Monastery, framed by the escarpments of the Grand Som on the right and the forested ridges of the Aliénard on the left.
The road ends at a roundabout. From there, a path climbs up to the **belvedere** overlooking the wooded gorge of the Guiers Mort.

★**Perquelin** – *3km/2mi east.* The path ends in the upper valley of the River Guiers Mort, beneath the escarpments of the Dent de Crolles.

★**The Scia** – *1hr 30min there and back, including a 45min ride on the* **Essarts gondola and Scia chairlift** ⊘.
🚶 It is easy to climb from the upper station of the second section of the gondola to the summit of the Scia (alt 1 782m/5 846ft), which offers a fine **panorama** of the Chartreuse, with the Taillefer, the Obiou and the Vercors to the south, the Dent du Chat and the Grand Colombier to the north.

ST-VÉRAN★★

Population 280
Michelin map 334 J4 and 244 fold 43
Local map see Le QUEYRAS

St-Véran, lying at altitudes ranging from 1 990m/6 529ft to 2 040m/6 693ft, is the highest village in Europe. It owes its name to a 6C archbishop who is the hero of a local legend. **St Véran** is said to have fought and wounded a dragon which was terrorising the area. While the beast was flying off to Provence, 12 drops of blood dripped from its wounds. These later symbolised each of the places where shepherds used to stop when moving livestock from the Luberon to summer grazing in the Queyras.
The houses are built in the midst of pastures on a gentle slope, which rises to 2 990m/9 810ft at its highest point, the **Pic de Châteaurenard**. In summer, the main attractions of St-Véran are the quality of its environment and the interesting hikes it offers. In winter, the resort's fairly easy and very sunny ski area is linked to that of Molines-en-Queyras.

Nearby Sights: ABRIÈS, BRIANÇON, Le BRIANÇONNAIS, CEILLAC, Route des GRANDES ALPES, GUILLESTRE, MOLINES-EN-QUEYRAS, MONT-DAUPHIN, Le QUEYRAS, VARS

St-Véran

WALKING ABOUT

Traffic is banned in summer, except for temporary residents' vehicles, for which a disc must be obtained from the tourist office. There are several car parks at the entrance to the village.

From June to the end of August, the road to the Chapelle Notre-Dame-de-Clausis is only open to the shuttle service vehicles *(charge)* and to ramblers.

The Italian border being quite close, hikers may wish to cross it and should therefore make sure they carry their identity papers at all times.

La Chalp and Le Raux – The two neighbouring hamlets are known locally for their handcrafted wooden furniture.

★★ **Old village** – Built entirely of wood and stone, the village has a characteristic archi-tectural style. Alpine farmhouses, facing south and built in a line stretching for 1km/0.6mi have long galleries in front of their storage lofts, where cereals go on ripening after the harvest. Each of St-Véran's six districts has its own wooden foun-tain, *croix de la Passion* and communal oven. Many houses are decorated with elaborate sundials.

At the bottom of the village, on the left as you go in, note the workshop of one of the most famous woodcarvers in the Queyras region. The road climbs up to the village square surrounded by the church, the town hall and the tourist office. The **church** at the centre of the cemetery dates from the 17C. The porch is supported by two columns resting on lions, which belonged to an earlier building. Inside, note the stone stoup, the 18C pulpit and the 17C **altarpiece★** carved by Italian artists. The east-end wall is decorated with a sundial; its inscription, in the old dialect, celebrates "the highest village in which God's bread is eaten".

SIGHTS

★ **Musée du Soum** ⊘ – *On the right as you go in through the western car park.* The name means "the end" (of one of the districts); built in 1641, it is the oldest house in the village. The museum illustrates traditional life in St-Véran through a succession of rooms furnished in local style. It is representative of Haut Queyras houses, in spite of its typically local features: an outside pen for the household's pig; an inner courtyard floored with tree trunks and intended for cattle, and on the ground floor; a "shepher-d's room" intended for seasonal workers, usually itinerant farmhands from Piedmont. In the living room, note the box bed (1842) used by several members of the family, the fireplace – an unusual feature as the kitchen would normally be the only room to have a chimney – and the hay rack which is a reminder that humans and cattle cohabited in winter. Upstairs, the joiner's and the lapidary's workshops have been reconstructed.

Ancienne Maison traditionelle – Until 1976, the residents shared this house with their animals, in the traditional way. The members of the family who lived here guide visitors around their old home.

Musée de l'Habitat ancien ⊘ – The interior of a house has been preserved exactly as it was at the beginning of the century. It illustrates the daily life of the villagers at that time.

HIKES

★★Drive to the Col Agnel and hike to the Pain de Sucre – *Allow a minimum of 4hr.*
Follow the 4km/2.5mi-long **Route des Amoureux★** starting in St-Véran and offering views of the northern side of the Guil Valley overlooked by the Pic de Rochebrune. The road leads to Pierre Grosse. Turn right twice towards the Col Agnel *(for the rest of the itinerary, see MOLINES-EN-QUEYRAS).*

Chapelle Notre-Dame-de-Clausis – Alt 2 390m/7 841ft. *Road closed to motor vehicles. Access by shuttle (charge; journey: 20min then 15min on foot as the last section of the road is not suitable for wheeled vehicles) or on foot (3hr there and back).*
As the road runs past disused marble quarries and copper mines, spare a thought for the miners who worked here at high altitude, on meagre rations and who would get so covered in verdigris during their shift that they were known as "diables verts" (green devils). Colonies of marmots live in the area. The chapel, where a Franco-Italian pilgrimage takes place on 16 July, stands in the centre of a vast cirque within sight of the surrounding summits soaring to 3 000m/9 843ft.

★★Tête des Toillies round tour – *A splendid but taxing hike offering varied scenery: allow 5hr 30min for the walk and at least 1hr 30min for the breaks. Difference in altitude: 1 050m/3 445ft. Leave early in the morning, catching the shuttle to Notre-Dame-de-Clausis no later than 10am.*
Leave the road on the last bend before the chapel and follow a path straight ahead, which leads to the Lac du Blanchet and to the refuge of the same name. Turn right before the refuge *(yellow markings)* towards the **Col de la Noire** (alt 2 955m/9 695ft) affording **views★** of the impressive rocky summit of the Tête des Toillies and of nearby peaks.

The ibex in the Queyras

The ibex gradually disappeared from the Alps during the 17C. At the beginning of the 19C, there were fewer than 100 head in the Grand Paradisio Massif on the Italian side. The reintroduction of the ibex within the Parc naturel régional du Queyras took place in 1995 when 12 ibexes were transferred from the Parc national de la Vanoise. The animals are given electronic chips make it possible to locate them.

The path drops steeply down to the **Lac de la Noire**; walk past the lake for another 10min and turn left then immediately head for the bottom of the valley. Shortly afterwards, there is a tricky passage through the rocks then the path runs along the mountainside to the Lac du Longet and disappears. Join another path leading to the **Col du Longet**, set in a wild landscape of screes dotted with lakes; **view** of Monte Viso. Walk down for 10min and turn left towards the **Col Blanchet**. Allow 45min to climb up to the pass through pastures: striking **panorama★★** of the Tête des Toillies soaring up to the sky, of the Pelvoux, Pic de Rochebrune, Monte Viso and the Italian Alps. *Allow 1hr 15min to return to the shuttle.*

★★Col St-Véran and Pic de Caramantran – *Take the shuttle to the Chapelle Notre-Dame-de-Clausis. Continue on foot for 5min then, just before a bridge, take GR 58. Difference in altitude: about 700m/2 297ft.*
It takes 1hr 30min to get to the pass: **view★** of Monte Viso and Lake Castello on the Italian side. Follow the ridge line on the left, which leads in 30min to the Pic de Caramantran (alt 3 021m/9 911ft): superb **panorama★★** of the surrounding peaks on both sides of the border.
Follow a path running between the two peaks of the Caramantran to the **Col de Chamoussière★** offering a fine view of the Pain de Sucre, and return to the shuttle in 1hr 15min along the path marked in white and red.

Lac de STE-CROIX★★

Michelin map 334 E10 and 245 fold 34

The turquoise-coloured lake, into which flows the green River Verdon as it comes out of the famous canyon, is framed by the desolate heights of the Plateau de Valensole and Plan de Canjuers. As large as the Lac d'Annecy, it stretches from the Grand Canyon du Verdon to the Gorges of the lower Verdon; its shores are now lined with pleasant beaches and popular summer resorts and its vast expanse is ideal for water sports.

Nearby Sights: BARGÈME, CASTELLANE, GRÉOUX-LES-BAINS, MOUTIERS-STE-MARIE, Route NAPOLÉON, RIEZ, Plateau de VALENSOLE, Grand Canyon du VERDON

EXCURSION

Tour of the Lake *70km/44mi – about 3hr*

★★ Moustiers-Ste-Marie – *See MOUSTIERS-STE-MARIE.*

From Moustiers, drive towards Riez then turn left towards Ste-Croix.

The road rises in a series of hairpin bends, offering interesting views of Moustiers and its remarkable setting, then runs along the top of the plateau as the lake comes into view.

Ste-Croix-de-Verdon – This old hilltop village, which gave its name to the lake, is today almost level with the water. There is a beach along the shore.
The road goes down to the lake.

Lac de Ste-Croix

Barrage de Ste-Croix – The reservoir created by the dam contains 767 million m³/621 807acft of water supplying a power station which produces 150 million kWh per year.

Beyond the dam, turn right onto D 71.

The road runs through the Gorges de Baudinard.

🚶 Beyond Baudinard, turn left onto the path leading to the chapel, which is best reached on foot (allow 1hr there and back).

★ View from Notre-Dame-de-Baudinard – A small viewing platform has been set up on the roof of the chapel; the **view** extends over the Lac de Ste-Croix, the Plateau de Valensole, Plan de Canjuers and, beyond, towards the Alpine summits.

Return to the lake and continue eastwards.

Bauduen – This Provençal village, formerly situated on high ground, is now on the edge of the lake. The **setting★** is nevertheless remarkable. Old houses, their lovely rounded doorways flanked with hollyhocks, line the picturesque streets climbing towards the church, which stands out against the rocks overlooking the village. The lake shores are equipped for water sports.

The scenic road planned between Bauduen and Les Salles will avoid the detour via St-Andrieux, along D 49 and D 957.

Les Salles-sur-Verdon – The old village of Les Salles is now lying 40m/131ft below the surface of the lake. A few architectural features (doors, tiles), as well as the church steeple and the village fountain were saved and used again when the new village was built on the shores of the lake.

The entire valley was flooded after the dam was built in 1975; orchards and fields disappeared beneath the lake surface (2 200ha/5 436 acres)

Continue along D 957 to Moustiers past the leisure park.

It is easy to see why Victor Hugo compared Sallanches to a colossal stage: the tiered escarpments form a vast amphitheatre to the north, with Mont Blanc, towering some 4 000m/13 000ft above the town, providing the most spectacular of backdrops. The scene is just as remakable on either side: to the west stands the Pointe Percée (alt 2 752m/9 029ft), the highest summit of the Aravis range. The **Chaîne des Fiz** extends its strange rocky heights to the east; the most striking of these is the **Désert de Platé**, a desolate and deeply fissured limestone plateau covering an area of 15km²/6sq mi.
The area has one more surprise in store on the nearby Lacs de la Cavettaz: enjoy swimming and summer sports at Mont-Blanc-Plage in sight of the "Giant of the Alps".

Nearby Sights: ARGENTIÈRE, CHAMONIX-MONT-BLANC, Les CONTAMINES-MONTJOIE, Les GETS, Les HOUCHES, Massif du MONT-BLANC, MEGÈVE, MORZINE, La ROCHE-SUR-FORON, SAINT-GERVAIS-LES-BAINS, SAMOËNS, SIXT-FER-A-CHEVAL

SIGHTS

Church – This imposing edifice is decorated in Italian style. The christening chapel on the left as you go in houses a small Flamboyant ciborium and, inside a glass case, a collection of silver religious objects, including a 15C monstrance. A viewing table in place Charles-Albert gives a detailed overview of the Mont Blanc massif.

Château des Rubins – Introduction to nature in mountainous areas ⊘ – This 17C castle displays, on two levels, an instructive presentation of ecosystems in mountainous areas.

Mont Blanc from the air – *Cross the Arve and turn left after the bridge to reach the airfield.*
The AMS Company organizes **plane trips** over the Mont Blanc Massif all year round (☎ 04 50 58 05 99)

Near Sallanches

★**Cascade d'Arpenaz** – *From Sallanches take the D 205 towards Cluses as far as Luzier.* This impressive 200m/656ft-high waterfall gushes from a curiously stratified channel in the rock.

EXCURSIONS

★ The Old Servoz Road

13km from Sallanches – allow 30min

This itinerary follows the old Sallanches to Chamonix road, described by generations of travellers – particularly during the Romantic period – thrilled to be getting close to Mont Blanc.

From Sallanches, D 13 crosses the motorway and then the River Arve, 150m/164yd upstream of the old humpback bridge of **St-Martin**, painted and photographed many times over the past 100 years.
The road then climbs up the last slopes of the Plateau d'Assy and, between Passy and Servoz, it overlooks the narrow industrial Chedde Plain and the gorge through which the railway enters the Servoz Basin. Ahead is the narrow wooded valley of the Diosaz. Just beyond the hamlet of Joux, the imposing **Viaduc des Egratz** comes into view: this masterpiece of modern engineering, carrying the Chamonix motorway, is 2 277m/2 490yd long and some of its pillars are 68m/223ft high.
The road then goes through a wood, crosses a stream, offers glimpses of the Arve Valley towards the glaciers of the Dôme du Goûter and enters the verdant Servoz Basin.

Servoz – The village lies at the heart of a wooded basin beneath the cliffs of the Fiz mountains and the scree-covered slopes of the Pas du Dérochoir.

★★ Route du Plateau d'Assy

FROM PASSY TO PLAINE-JOUX *12km/7.5mi – allow 1hr 30min*

The D 43, branching off the Servoz road in Passy, rises onto wooded south-facing ledges, well sheltered from the wind and dotted with health establishments and family holiday homes. During the climb, the view gets gradually broader, embracing the Mont-Blanc Massif and the Chaîne des Fiz.

★★**Pavillon de Charousse** – *500m/547yd southwest of Bay. Leave the car in front of the Relais de Charousse and take the path on the left of the chapel leading to the wooded mound on which the house stands.* Remarkable **panorama**. It is possible to walk along the edge of the escarpment, on the right of the house, to admire the view of Sallanches and the Aravis Massif.

Eating out

MODERATE

La Chaumière – *73 ancienne rte de Combloux* – ☎ *04 50 58 00 59* – *closed 28 Aug-4 Sept, 25 Sept-3 Oct, holidays around 1 Nov, Sun evening and Mon* – *21.04/33.54€*. A small establishment for food-lovers not far from the town hall. In the rustic-style dining room of this typical local house there is a varied menu of essentially traditional dishes.

Where to stay

MODERATE

Les Gorges de la Diosaz – *Near the post office* – *74310 Servoz* – ☎ *04 50 47 20 97* – *closed 8-25 May and 25 Oct-15 Nov* – *9rms: 44.21/59.46€* – *restaurant 16.01/20.58€*. This homely chalet in a small peaceful village is simple and charming. Enter through the bar to get to the typical dining room, the setting for traditional cooking. There is a terrace with flowers in summer. The rooms have mountain chalet-style decor.

Hôtel Cordonant – *Les Darbaillets* – *74700 Cordon* – *4km/2.5mi from Sallanches on D 113* – ☎ *04 50 58 34 56* – *closed 16 Apr-19 May and 21 Sept-19 Dec* – ▣ – *16rms: 54.88/64.03€* - ⌑ *5.79€* – *restaurant 19.51/27.44€*. This chalet with wood-panelled walls has a floral decor and windows with a view of the Mont Blanc range. In summer, dinner can be taken on the pleasant terrace with its abundance of plants. In winter, the hotel has a warm and cosy atmosphere. Good value for money.

As the road reaches Plateau d'Assy, the Aiguille Verte can be seen sticking up behind the Brévent.

★**Plateau d'Assy** -This well-known health resort is spread over several terraces backing on to the Fiz range, at altitudes ranging from 1 000m/3 281ft to 1 500m/4 921ft; from this prime position, there is a magnificent **panorama**★★ of the Mont Blanc Massif.
The highlight of the town is the **Église Notre-Dame-de-Toute-Grâce★**, a good example of the contemporary revival of religious art. It was built between 1937 and 1945 by Novarina who took his inspiration from the region's traditional domestic architecture; the result is a solid, stocky church, adapted to Alpine climatic conditions and in harmony with traditional architecture, which is surmounted by a 29m/95ft-high campanile.
Famous contemporary artists contributed to the exterior and interior **decoration**★★: **Fernand Léger** made the mosaic which brightens up the façade, **Lurçat** decorated the chancel with a huge tapestry on the theme of the Woman triumphing over the Dragon of the Apocalypse. **Bazaine** designed the stained-glass windows lighting up the gallery, **Rouault** designed those situated at the back of the façade, notably in the side chapel on the north side. **Germaine Richier's** bronze crucifix, which caused a critical stir when first displayed, stands in front of the high altar, while **Bonnard, Matisse, Braque, Chagall** and **Lipchitz** are also represented. Walk round the building and go through the east-end doorway down to the crypt decorated with stained glass by Marguerite Huré and a representation of the Last Supper by Kijno.

The road then goes through a forested area, after which the Chamonix glacier comes into view.

✳**Plaine-Joux** – A chalet at the centre of this small ski resort houses the Information Centre of the **Réserve naturelle de Passy** covering 2 000ha/4 942 acres.

Beyond Plaine-Joux, the road reaches an open area of high pastures giving glimpses of Mont-Blanc through the pines and close-up **views** of the cliffs of the Fiz range and the scree-covered Pas du Dérochoir.

★**Lac Vert** – The lake, surrounded by firs and overlooked by the escarpments of the Fiz mountains, is of a dark green colour *(you can walk round in about 15min)*.

★★★**Route de Combloux**

FROM SALLANCHES TO ST-GERVAIS *18km/11.2mi – allow 45min*

The roads running along the mountainside offer splendid and varied overall views of the massifs.

From Sallanches, drive south along N 212 towards Albertville.

The approach to Combloux affords a **panorama**★★★ of the Aravis range, the Fiz mountains and the southern part of the Mont Blanc Massif.

✳**Combloux** ⊙ – This summer and winter resort, famous for its mild climate, has retained its traditional farms and old-world charm. The Baroque spire of the **church** is of typical 18C Alpine design; set against the backdrop of Mont Blanc, it has become one of the most popular images of Savoy. The elaborate retable decorating the high-altar also dates from the 18C. The **ski resort** (1 200-1 853m/3 937-6 079ft) specialises in family entertainment and skiing without risk. The ski area is linked to that of Jaillet (Megève) by numerous ski lifts. There are three separate cross-country loops totalling 15km/9.3mi. Experienced skiers looking for more of a challenge should head to Évasion Mont Blanc (1 100-2 353m/3 609-7 720ft) which offers 420km/261mi of piste, kept in good condition by 260 snow cannon.

3km/1.9mi away in La Cry *(turn right onto Route du Haut-Combloux)* is a **viewing table★**.

3km/1.9mi north of Megève, turn left towards Chamonix.

Between Gemoëns and Le Freney there are views of the *cluse* (transverse valley) of the Arve, downstream of Sallanches, framed by the Aravis and Fiz mountains. The Dôme du Goûter, Mont Blanc and the Aiguille de Bionnassay and its glacier are visible on the other side.

D 909 reaches St-Gervais.

St-Gervais-les-Bains – *See ST-GERVAIS-LES-BAINS.*

★ Round tour via Cordon *11km/6.8mi – allow 1hr*

From Sallanches, drive west along D 113 towards Cordon.

The road winds its way along the ridge separating the gorges of the River Sallanche and River Frasse, as Mont Blanc comes into sight.

★ Cordon – This charming village, backed by the Aravis mountains, occupies an attractive **position★** facing the prestigious Mont Blanc Massif, amid orchards of cherry and walnut trees. In winter, the resort offers possibilities of Alpine and cross-country skiing, as well as sledge rides. The 18C **church** is a fine example of Savoyard Baroque style, including interesting paintings and a rich central **altarpiece** with twisted columns.

As you leave Cordon, follow the road to Combloux then turn left towards Nant Cruy. Drive through the village.

The gilded onion spire of Cordon's church can be seen above the orchards.

The road runs down to an intersection (2km/1.2mi); turn right to the Chapelle du Médonnet (600m/656yd).

Chapelle du Médonnet – The east end of this unassuming little chapel faces a magnificent **panorama★★** which includes, from left to right, the Pointe d'Areu, the Chaîne des Fiz, the Aiguilles Rouges and the Mont-Blanc Massif from the Aiguille Verte to the Aiguille de la Bérangère.

Turn round to go back to Sallanches then right towards N 212.

C. Sénéchal/PHOTONONSTOP

Désert de Platé

SAMOËNS**

Population 2 148
Michelin map 328 N4 and 244 folds 9 and 10 – Local map see Le FAUCIGNY

Samoëns lies at the bottom of a wide glacial valley through which flows the River Giff
Each of its nine satellite hamlets, scattered over the forested slopes, has a chapel st
mounted by a graceful onion-shaped spire. In spite of its considerable expansic
Samoëns has retained a wealth for traditional stone houses built by its famous stor
masons.

This tourist centre of the Haut Faucigny is the ideal starting point of untaxi
hikes and splendid mountain excursions. Summer activities include mou
taineering, canoeing and rafting on the Giffre, swimming, tennis as well
paragliding and hang-gliding which have become a local speciality. In wint
60km/37mi of pistes and 90km/56mi of cross-country loops tempt skiers fro
miles around.

Nearby Sights: AVORIAZ, CLUSES, Les GETS, MORZINE, La ROCHE-SUR-FORON, Bass
de SALLANCHES, SIXT FER-À-CHEVAL

Where to stay and Eating out

MODERATE

Le Moulin de Bathieu – *2km/1mi SW of Samoëns towards Vercland (follc
Samoëns 1600)* – ☎ *04 50 34 48 07* – *moulin-du-bathieu@wanadoo.fr
closed May and 5 Nov-22 Dec* – 🅿 – *7rms: 48.78/91.47€ -* ☕ *6.10€ – resta
rant 16.77/27.44€.* This old walnut oil mill now houses seven rooms, four
which have a mezzanine. There is a splendid view of the Dents Blanches mou
tains. Take a look at the hundred-year-old "mazot" (local word for barn), in pe
fect condition.

BACKGROUND

The Stonemasons of Samoëns – Stone-cutting has been a local speciali
since 1659, when the village's stonemasons and builders founded a brothe
hood taking as their patron saints four Hungarian stonemasons who we
martyred by the emperor Diocletian for refusing to sculpt a pagan ide
Members of this guild were called to work all over France, taking part
Vauban's military projects or building canals, and even went abroad, as f
afield as Poland and Louisiana. The brotherhood also undertook benevole
work, looking after the sick and training the young; it had its own drawir
school and a large library. It was revived in 1979 when an association w
created to preserve the architectural heritage of Samoëns and organise guidc
tours.

A local speciality

What could be better at end of a tiring hike than a fortifying bowl of the
local "soupe châtrée"? This nourishing soup is made with slices of bread
soaked in onion sauce, covered with Tomme de Savoie, the local cheese,
and browned under the grill. Wooden spoons are best to deal with the
melted cheese.

WALKING ABOUT

★ **Place du Gros-Tilleul** – Located at the centre of the village, the square owes its nam
to the lime tree planted here in 1438.

The **Grenette**, a 16C covered market, restored in the 18C, stands on the south sid
note the strange bulges on the central pillars: the arms of Samoëns were to be carve
on these pillars, but the mason did not complete his work following a disagreeme
with the municipality over his contract. A lovely fountain stands in the centre of th
square. The **church**, next to the Château de la Tour on the north side of the squar
was rebuilt in the 16C and 17C; at the foot of the 12C bell-tower, a graceful canop
covered with copper tiles shelters a 16C doorway with older features, including tv
lions supporting twisted columns.

The stained-glass windows on the left, dating from 1982, depict the four patrc
saints of the stonemasons' brotherhood. The baptistery chapel is in Flamboya
Gothic style. The 19C stoup was carved out of a single block of marble.

Chapelle de la Jasinia, Samoëns

A sundial on the front of the **presbytery** indicates the time in 12 large cities of the world.

★ **Jardin botanique alpin Jasinia** ⊘ – These botanical gardens, complete with pools and waterfalls and covering an area of 3ha/7.5 acres, were created in 1906 on sloping ground overlooking the village; they contain more than 5 000 species of mountain plants from the main temperate areas of the world. Walking past the **Chapelle de la Jasinia**, one reaches the terrace and its ruined castle offering an extended view of Samoëns and the surrounding mountains. The garden was one of many gifts to the town from local girl Louise Cognacq-Ja, a local girl from a humble background who made her fortune as owner of the famous "La Samaritaine" department store in Paris. The **Maison de la Jasinia** at the garden entrance contains documents relating to the village's benefactress.

EXCURSIONS

Les Vallons – *2km/1.2mi along D 907 towards Sixt, then a road on the left.* This hamlet is interesting for its lovely stone fountains and its chapel.

★★ **La Rosière (view)** – *6km/3.7mi. Leave Samoëns along D 907 towards Sixt; turn left almost immediately towards Les Allamands, left again 750m/0.5mi further on and sharp right 1km/0.6mi after that.* From la Rosière, there is a particularly fine view of Mont Blanc framed by the forested Rochers du Criou and the rock face of the Pointe de Sales.

★ Drive to the Cirque du Fer à Cheval

13km/8mi from Samoëns – allow 45min

Leave Samoëns by the D 907 heading southeast

The Cascade de Nant d'Ant rushes down the rock on the opposite bank of the Giffre; the valley narrows as the road approaches the Gorges de Tines.

Gorges de Tines – This narrow gorge, through which the Giffre splashes, is best explored on foot. *Park the car in the car park just before the quarry and head right towards the footbridge over the river.*

Sixt-Fer-à-Cheval and Cirque du Fer à Cheval★★ – *13km/8mi east. See SIXT-FER-À-CHEVAL.*

★★ **Col de Joux Plane** – *10km/6.2mi via Chantemerle and D 354. See MORZINE, Excursions*

SERRE-CHEVALIER✳✳✳

Michelin map 334 H3 and 244 fold 42
Local map see Le BRIANÇONNAIS

Situated in the Guisane Valley, between the Col du Lautaret and Briançon, Serre
Chevalier is the largest winter sports complex in the southern Alps. The resort, shelter
by the surrounding mountains, enjoys a microclimate characterised by 300 days of sui
shine a year.
Facilities and accommodation are spread over four main sites (Le Monêtier, Villeneuve
Chantemerle and Briançon), but there are in fact 13 villages and hamlets on either si
of the road leading to the Col du Lautaret.

Nearby Sights: L'ARGENTIÈRE-LA-BESSÉE, BRIANÇON, Le BRIANÇONNAIS, Vallée c
FREISSINIÈRES, Route du GALIBIER, La GRAVE, GUILLESTRE, MONT-DAUPHII
MONTGENÈVRE, L'OISANS, Le QUEYRAS, La VALLOUISE

Eating out

BUDGET

La Goustarine – *Allée des Boutiques RN 91 – 05330 Chantemerle – ☎ 04 9
24 17 13 – la.goustarine@wanadoo.fr – closed 15 Apr-20 Jun, 20 Sept-20 De
and Sun evening in winter – reservations recommended in winter –
14.94/19.82€.* The restaurant serves dishes from the local mountain region ar
Piedmont just across the nearby Italian border. There is a shop selling cure
hams, naturally, and less predictably sausages with bilberries or hazelnut
among other things.

MODERATE

La Boîte à Fromages – *R. St-Eldrade – 05220 Monêtier-les-Bains – ☎ 04 9
24 50 08 – closed May, Oct and Nov – 30.49/45.73€.* A few steps lead dow
into this old house hidden in a narrow alley. Cheese reigns supreme here! This
an address to note if you enjoy raclette and other local cheese specialities.

Where to stay

BUDGET

Camping Caravaneige-Serre-Chevalier – *05330 Chantemerle – ☎ 04 92 24 0
14 – open 9 Jun-9 Sept and 1 Dec-29 Apr – reservations recommended – 17
pitches: 18.29€ – catering available on site.* In winter you can camp in the snov
and in summer amid an oasis of greenery; this is what makes this campsite s
original. It is entirely devoted to sports and is very well kept. There is a heate
swimming pool with a children's pool.

MODERATE

Hôtel Boule de Neige – *05330 Chantemerle – ☎ 04 92 24 00 16 – closed 2
Apr-15 Jun and 3 Sept-14 Dec – 10rms: 65/120€ - ☲ 7.60€ – restaurar
22/34€.* This 17C chalet has the appearance of a stately home. The rooms hav
vaulted ceilings and are decorated in pastel colours and with pale wood furn
ture. Sculptures are artfully placed here and there. There is also an apartmer
which is particularly smart and commands a good view of the ski slopes.

EXPENSIVE

Auberge du Choucas – *05220 Monêtier-les-Bains – ☎ 04 92 24 42 73 – close
2-23 May and 1 Oct-8 Dec – 8rms: from 117.33€ - ☲ 10.67€ – restaurar
21.34/57.93€.* At the foot of the 15C church in the famous mountain villag
stands this inn redolent of local tradition. The rooms are warm and well lit, an
the four suites on two floors are very practical. The dining room has a vaulte
ceiling and stone walls and features an open fireplace decorated with a fine co
lection of coppers.

On the town

Cocoon café – *C.C. "Le Prélong" – 05240 La Salle-les-Alpes – ☎ 04 92 24 9
25 – open daily 8am-1am, closed mid Apr-mid Jun and Sept-Nov.* In tune wit
the seasons, this café offers a menu with the emphasis on coffees, teas and beer
in the winter, whereas in summer cocktails are to the fore and there is also a ter
race open to the sunshine. The interior combines warmth and good taste.

L'Escapade – *Allée des Boutiques – 05330 Chantemerle – ☎ 04 92 24 15 90 – ope
daily 9.30pm-4am, in spring: Sat-Sun 9.30pm-4am – closed May-Jun and Sept-en
Dec.* This is a temple to karaoke: buzzing with the latest hit tunes and the adrenali
of would-be pop stars, the atmosphere can get quite wild, especially in season.

a **Baïta** – *1 chemin de l'Enfer – 05240 La Salle-les-Alpes – ☎ 04 92 24 74 41 – daily 6pm-5am in season – closed mid Apr-end Jun and Sept-end Dec.* Even ough this nightclub occupies an old stable, it is no less charming for all at, with its fine vaulted ceiling in the main room and a fireplace to combat e chill of winter. The music programme is joyfully eclectic, spanning blues · techno, via rock, jazz and disco. Themed nights include an annual Hallowe'en rty.

Shopping

a **Soupière** – *30 r. de la Guisane – 05240 La Salle-les-Alpes – ☎ 04 92 24 88 2 – daily 8.30am-12.30pm, 2.30pm-7.30pm in winter, 8.30am-7.30pm in mmer – closed in May, Oct, Nov.* Having crossed the threshold of this food op, let yourself by guided by your taste buds and you will not regret it. Nettle ıup, charcuterie, cheeses, honey and preserves, and last but not least, a pear eritif. There is nothing here that it is not a joy to eat, or drink.

a **Vitrine** – *3 pl. du Marché – 05220 Monêtier-les-Bains – ☎ 04 92 24 51 11 – Tue-Sun 10am-noon, 3pm-7pm – closed 1 May-15 Jun and 15 Sept-15 Dec.* t the heart of this cooperative, artists, craftspeople and local producers have ecided to join forces and set up a joint permanent exhibition where their cre- ions and produce can be sold retail. Besides honey and preserves, there are rned wood pieces, pottery, original jewellery, unusual oil lamps etc. What is on splay changes constantly, as the local producers regularly bring along their lat- st creations.

Sports

venture Parc – 🖻 – *BP 26 – 05240 La Salle-les-Alpes – ☎ 04 92 24 90 57 – ww.aventure-parc.com – opening times vary depending on the season – closed ɔv-Apr.* About twenty varied activities (wooden bridge, rope bridge, bungy mping etc) in this park, each a miniature adventure, mean that visitors will not e bored.

THE RESORT

The valley's 13 villages are grouped into three municipalities: Saint-Chaffrey, La Salle- les-Alpes and Monêtier-les-Bains. Traditional stone houses, nestling round 13C and 15C churches, stand next to modern shops, hotels and apartments. Yet each resort retains its own character and activities within the vast ski area known as the "**Grand Serre-Che**".

Monêtier-les-Bains, also called **Serre-Chevalier 1500**, owes its name to a monastery and its hot springs, already famous in Roman times. Today, Monêtier is a spa and ski resort with reasonable access to the "Grand Serre-Che" ski runs and adequate snow- making equipment. Its appeal lies in its traditional architecture and its peaceful atmosphere; the **Musée d'Art et Traditions populaires d'Antan** presents tools and everyday objects from the past.

Le Lauzet – 2 800m/9 186ft. *Leave Monetier by the D 300 to Col du Lautaret.* This is the highest point in the valley, giving a superb view of the Aiguillette du Lauzet (Massif des Cerces). It is easy to imagine the hardships of life as a miner in the old graphite mines which were worked here at the beginning of the 20C.

Villeneuve (Serre-Chevalier 1400) and **Chantemerle (Serre-Chevalier 1350)** – These modern functional resorts lack charm but offer direct access to the ski runs and a choice of après-ski activities (swimming, skating, fitness club, riding, ice-driving). **St- Chaffrey**, which was the starting point of the skiing complex, has an interesting bridge which can be raised in case of flooding. The 11C **Chapelle St-Arnoult** ☉, situated on high ground behind the church, contains fine frescoes.

Briançon *(see BRIANÇON)*, now linked to the ski area by the **Téléphérique du Prorel**, is known as **Serre-Chevalier 1200** and has an impressive number of snow-cannon. Night- skiing by floodlights is offered on certain pistes.

Ski area – Created in 1941, the resort is now equipped with more than 70 lifts giving access to 250km/155mi of north-facing ski runs suitable for skiers of all levels. Of the 109 pistes, 21 are green, 20 are blue, 55 are red and 13 are black. The first- section runs go through a larch forest and are equipped with snow-cannon. The second section is more exposed, and snow cover is adequate until mid-April. The Serre-Chevalier Summit, rapidly accessible from Chantemerle and Villeneuve, is at the heart of the ski area. Le Monêtier offers the wildest and most appealing section, suit- able for experienced skiers. A bus shuttles tourists to and from their resort.

Serre Chevalier and the valley

In addition, there are 45km/28mi of cross-country skiing tracks at the bottom of the valley, from Le Lauzet to Villeneuve and from Chantemerle to Briançon.

In summer, the valley offers a wide range of activities: mountain biking, canoeing on the Guisane, riding tours, paragliding and hang-gliding. It is also a good place to start medium-altitude hikes in the Parc national des Écrins.

HIKES

★★Sommet de Serre-Chevalier – Alt 2 483m/8 146ft. *Access from Chantemerle by two-section* **cable car** ⊙.

🔼 From the upper station, climb to the viewing table: splendid **panorama★★** of the Oisans Massif to the west, the Aiguilles d'Arves and Pic du Galibier to the northwest, the Vanoise to the north and the Queyras to the east.

★★Hike round the Eychauda Summit – *5hr on foot on fairly level ground. A 1:25 000 map is strongly recommended. The hike starts in Chantemerle and ends in Le Monêtier; return to Chantemerle by coach (information from the tourist office).*

🔼 Take the cable car to the top of Serre-Chevalier. From the viewing table, go down towards the Col de Serre-Chevalier and follow tracks leading to the path going round the Eychauda and walk up to the **Col de la Pisse** (alt 2 501m/8 205ft).

The path runs across the mountainside, offering lovely **views★★** of Lake Eychauda and the Pelvoux Massif *(a few tricky sections)*, and finally reaches the **Col de l'Eychauda** overlooking the Col du Lautaret road. A wide path leads down to a mountain restaurant. Go to the left, leave the path and take another one to the right *(GR 54, marked in white and red, sometimes in yellow)*. It follows the stream, crosses it and enters a pleasant larch forest.

Towards the end of the hike, continue straight on past a chapel and follow a small road going down to the left. When you reach a square with a playground, turn right, cross a small bridge and walk up rue de la Grande-Turière. As you join the Route Nationale, the coach stop is on your right, in front of the post office.

From Le Bez (Villeneuve) to Le Monêtier – *Start from the rock-climbing school. 4hr there and back on foot; untaxing hike.*

🔼 Walk towards Fréjus then take the path rising to the Clos de la Salette above the rock-climbing site; at the intersection, turn right to Le Monêtier. The viewpoint offers a panorama of the Guisane Valley. The path runs down to a stream, the Chanteloube, and continues into the Monêtier Valley.

★★Lac du Combeynot – *5hr there and back along a path marked in blue. Please abide by the rules of the Parc national des Écrins: do not pick flowers, disturb the animals or bring dogs within the central zone of the park.*

🔼 Start from Les Boussardes, 200m/219yd south of Le Lauzet. On the way up to the lake, hikers are likely to meet chamois *(keep to the path)*. The Tête de Vallon rises above the splendid glacial lake (alt 2 555m/8 383ft and 16m/52ft deep).

★Via ferrata de l'Aiguillette du Lauzet – These high limestone cliffs are the favourite haunt of rock-climbers from the Briançon area. *Via ferrata* climbing has become very popular in the last few years and the car park near the starting point of the different courses is very congested *(see Practical information)*.

★ **Réserve naturelle du Combeynot** – *This hike takes at least 7hr and should not be attempted by anyone without a good level of stamina, a good head for heights and experience of long walks. Start from the Refuge Napoléon at the Col du Lautaret. Not recommended in rainy weather or after a snowfall. Walkers must arrange to be picked up by car from Le Casset.*

🚶 Walk across N 91, then due west along the marked Sentier des Crevasses. The path goes through the nature reserve and round the west side of the Pic du Combeynot before joining GR 54 at the Col d'Arsine. On the way up to the Refuge de l'Alpe du Villard *(food available)*, there are fine views of the Romanche Valley and numerous opportunities to observe high-altitude flora and birdlife. Continue to the Col d'Arsine and enjoy the splendid panorama of the glacial valleys, the Pic de Neige Cordier (3 613m/11 854ft) and the Arsine Glacier. The path then runs down to the lovely Lac de la Douche and back to the Guisane along the Petit Tabuc Valley.

Barrage et lac de SERRE-PONÇON ★★
Michelin map 334 F6 and 245 folds 8 and 9

rget any ideas you may have about artificial landscapes; no-one could fail to be armed by the largest man-made lake in Europe, set against a line of mountain peaks aching towards the sun. The picturesque road winds around the lake in a series of rves, turning away into the hills, only to reappear around the next bend for another ew of the deep blue water, dotted with white sails.

earby Sights: BARCELONNETTE, CEILLAC, Le CHAMPSAUR, Le DÉVOLUY, Préalpes de GNE, EMBRUN, GAP, Route des GRANDES ALPES, GUILLESTRE, MONT-DAUPHIN, ONTMAUR, Route NAPOLÉON, PRA-LOUP, SEYNE, L'UBAYE, VAL-D'ALLOS, VARS

HIGHLIGHTS

★ **Barrage de Serre-Ponçon** – Work on a project to control the Durance, this most unpredictable of rivers, began in 1955, but nothing could check the torrential floods which devastated the region two years later. The project at Serre-Ponçon was the first time an earth dam with a waterproof core of clay was built on such a scale in France, by applying a technique widely used in the USA. The dyke, made up of alluvial material from the river bed, is 600m/1 969ft long at the top, 650m/2 133ft wide at the base and 123m/404ft high. The clay core has a volume of 2 million m³/1 621acft against a total volume of 14 million m³/11 350acft. A mixture of clay and concrete is used to prevent seepage. The lake, created in 1960 and covering an area of 3 000ha/7 413 acres, is one of the largest reservoirs in Europe *(20km/12.5mi long, 3km/1.9mi at its widest point; capacity: 1 270 million m³/1 029 589cu ft)*.

Power station ⊙ – As well as safeguarding the lower valley and improving irrigation, the dam is also an important energy provider. Imbedded in the rock of the south bank, its power station can produce 720 million kWh per year. In order to regulate the flow of the Durance downstream of the dam, a reservoir covering 100ha/247 acres was created on the site where the alluvial soil was removed.

★ **The lake** – The curved shape of the lake, its indented shores and the promontory marking the confluence of the Durance and the Ubaye have made it easier for this vast expanse of water to blend with the natural scenery and to offer at the same time a variety of water sports.

EXCURSIONS

1️⃣ **From the lower dam to Embrun** *39km/24mi – allow 1hr 30min*

D 3 to Chorges follows the downstream reservoir before rising sharply within sight of the riprap embankment of the dam.

★ **Belvédère Ivan-Wilhem** – This viewpoint (alt 847m/2 779ft), built along the axis of the ridge line of the dam and named after the engineer who designed it, offers a fine overall view. Films and models at the **Muséoscope du Lac** ⊙ immediately above offer reminders of the villages which were submerged under the lake.
Beyond the tunnel, the road veers away from the lake.

Col Lebraut – Alt 1 110m/3 642ft. From the pass, there is a view of the Gap Basin to the west and of the lake to the east. Further on *(1.2km/0.7mi)*, the **panorama**★ extends to the whole northeast arm of the lake.

Chorges – From its prosperous past, the village has retained a few old houses, a lovely 16C fountain and a hilltop church with a rounded 12C porch; to the right stands an imposing pink-marble stela, known as "Nero's stone", which might be the pedestal of a Roman statue. Also noteworthy is the 14C bell-tower with its two tiers of windows and its narrow-stone bond.

Where to stay

BUDGET

Camping La Viste – *Rousset – 05190 Espinasses – 2km/1mi W of the Iva*
Wilhem lookout point on D 103 – ☎ 04 92 54 43 39 – campingla
iste@minitel.net – open 15 May-15 Sept – reservations recommended
160 pitches: 14.18€ – catering available on site. Come and get a breath
fresh air on this campsite in which every detail has been anticipated. The
is a snack bar with a terrace and a veranda with a superb view of the lak
Swimming pool.

MODERATE

Chambre d'hôte Les Carlines – *Les Vignes – 05230 Prunières – 4km/2.5mi*
of Chorges on D 9 then D 109 – ☎ 04 92 50 63 27 – chambredhotelesca
lines@hotmail.com – closed Nov-20 Dec – ✉ – 5rms: 39.64/47.26€. Th
chalet situated on the south slope of the Écrins range offers an idyl
panorama of the Lac de Serre-Ponçon and the Morgon peak. This view w
transform your breakfast on the terrace into a dream. Rooms are fairly plain
decorated. Garden.

From Chorges, the Savines road runs east towards the lake; note, on th
right, a chapel standing on a tiny island in the **Baie St-Michel**. Further o
N 94 runs across the lake over the **Pont de Savines**, almost level with th
water.

Savines-le-Lac – The village, which disappeared beneath the surface of the lake, w
rebuilt here. **Boat trips** ⊘ are organised.

Crots – Lying on the edge of the lake, this ancient village and its 14C church are ove
looked by the 13C **Château de Picomtal**, extended in the 16C.
Just before Embrun, the road crosses the Durance near the expanse of wat
reserved for sailing and water sports.

★ **Embrun** – *See EMBRUN.*

② **Vallée de Réallon** *18km/11mi – allow 1hr*

Two alternative access roads: D 41 north from the Pont de Savines or D 9 fro
Chorges; choose the second one in preference.
From Chorges, D 9 offers lovely views on its way to **St-Apollinaire**, a picturesque villa
overlooking the Lac de Serre-Ponçon; this section of the route sometimes forms pa
of the Monte-Carlo Rally. The pastoral Lac de St-Apollinaire can be reached along
road on the left.

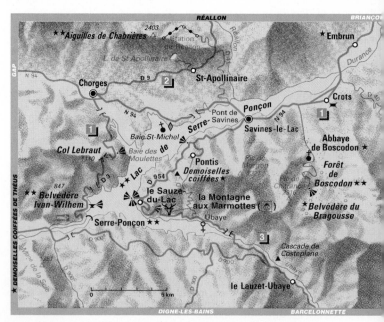

Réallon – The church spire soars above the village which has retained its Alpine atmosphere and is now a pleasant family ski resort. It has also been a famous archaeological site since the discovery last century of Bronze-Age precious objects, including a set of jewellery exhibited in the Gap Museum. A chairllift to the viewing table (2 135m/7 005m) runs all year round.

★**Aiguilles de Chabrières** – *5hr hike to be attempted in clear weather only. From Réallon, follow the path with yellow markings known as the "Tour des Aiguilles-Serre-du-Mouton"; detailed topo-guides are available at the tourist office.* The itinerary goes across a deeply gullied limestone plateau to the ridge of the Aiguilles de Chabrières.

③ From Savines-le-Lac to Le Lauzet-Ubaye *25km/15.5mi – allow 1hr*

Savines-le-Lac – *See drive ①.*

From Savines, D 954 winds along the indented shore of the lake; the **view**★ becomes gradually broader, embracing the wild southern part of the lake *(parking spaces on a bend to the left)*.

A small road branching off to the left leads to Pontis.

Pontis – The old school houses the **Musée de la Vallée** ⊘, a museum illustrating the life of schoolchildren and teachers in the 19C.

Turn back towards D 954.

The waters of the Durance, tamed at last by a man-made lake

★**Demoiselles coiffées de Pontis** – *For more details about these strange rock formations, see Demoiselles coiffées de Théus below.* It is possible to get quite close to these 12 strange stone columns by following the stony path *(30min there and back on foot; please do not touch the stones)*.

Le Sauze-du-Lac – A picturesque **site**★★, on top of a promontory overlooking the lake, at the confluence of the River Durance and River Ubaye. There is a fine **view**★ back towards Le Sauze from the road beyond.
The road winds steeply down the slope, offering a clear **view** of the Ubaye arm of the lake. On the opposite shore, the scenery is wild and the shoreline deeply indented.

Montagne aux Marmottes ⊘ ⊡ – The "Marmot Mountain" is an educational centre, studying and protecting animals from nature reserves and private collections. Every two hours, children can pet the marmots after a short introduction to these retiring creatures. Also on show are a prehistoric cave, a selection of minerals and fossils and a mountain fauna museum. Take a picnic if the weather is fine.

Ubaye – The church and the cemetery are all that remain of the flooded village.

The road runs through two tunnels *(single lane)* then across a bridge at the extremity of the lake. The **Cascade de Costeplane** flows through a deep gorge near the intersection of D 954 and D 900.

Continue along D 900 towards Barcelonnette.

Le Lauzet-Ubaye – The village lies next to a small lake (*lauzet* in local dialect). Roman bridge spans the river near the modern one *(15min there and back on foo*

For a description of the lower-Ubaye itinerary from Le Lauzet-Ubaye Barcelonnette, see L'UBAYE **1**.

SIGHTS NEARBY

★ **Demoiselles coiffées** – *From the dam along the D 900 towards Tallard, then rig towards Théus.* Among the most remarkable geological wonders of the southe Alps, the **"demoiselles coiffées"** (capped maidens), sometimes called *"cheminées fées"* (fairies' chimneys), are columns of soft material – in this case morainic deb – preserved from erosion by their harder rocky caps. These help to compress the s material underneath making it last longer. However, the column quickly disappea once its cap has toppled over.

Leave the car at the **Salle de Bal**★, or ballroom, where there is a great concentrati of these rock formations. It is possible to continue *(4.5km/2.8mi)* to the **Mont Colom** transmitter (alt 1 733m/5 686ft) for a panoramic **view** of the Lac de Serre-Ponço

★ **Abbaye de Boscodon** – *Turn right onto the D 568 between Savines and Embrun.* local preservation society acquired the buildings in 1972 and teams of young peo have worked hard to restore it ever since. The abbey is also home to a small commun of Dominican nuns. The recently restored east end of the **abbey church** is remarkab inside, one is overwhelmed by the architectural simplicity of this single-nave edifice a the amount of light pouring through its semicircular-arched windows. The chapter h **(Aile des Moines)**, has been completely restored and is used as a reception and exhibiti area. Excavations are still in progress in the lay community wing, **Aile des Convers**.

★★ **Forêt de Boscdon** – *From the abbey, take the forest road (surfaced) leading* Fontaine de l'Ours. The forest, which formed part of the estate of the abbey a extends over 850ha/2 100 acres, is famous for its beautiful specimens of larch and trees. 600m/656yd further on, a **nature trail** guides walkers past 24 different types tree and conifer. A **map** of the wood, showing the various walks, is on display in a h

★ **Belvédère de Bragousse** – The gullied cirque forms a striking landscape enhanc by the beautiful colour of the soil; chamois can be seen (with the aid of binocula roaming around in the upper part of the cirque. The mountain stream, subject sudden summer flooding when the snow melts, has been tamed by a series of dam the first of these can be seen from the belvedere.

Drive another 500m/0.3mi to reach Fontaine de l'Ours; park the car at the end of t road. A 2hr 30min walk along the Chantier de la Charance leads to the Cirque Morgon (difference in altitude: 530m/1 739ft).

SEYNE★

Population 1 440
Michelin map 334 G6 and 245 fold 8

1 200m/3 937ft up in the verdant Blanche valley, Seyne is a sunny summer and wint resort (with an annexe at Grand-Puy), which keeps up its traditions, including its rep tation for horse and mule breeding.

Nearby Sights: BARCELONNETTE, DIGNE-LES-BAINS, Préalpes de DIGNE, EMBRU PRA-LOUP, Lac de SERRE-PONÇON, L'UBAYE, VAL-D'ALLOS

BACKGROUND

Mules from Seyne – The mule show (second Saturday in August) and the mule a horse fair (St Matthew's day, 21 September) testify to a strong tradition whi brought fame and prosperity to the town. The mule is a remarkable beast of burde used in the past in mountain areas for farming and for carrying munitions and foo to isolated mountain troops *(chasseurs alpins)*. Young mules, which are the steri offspring of a male donkey and a female horse, were cared for and trained by sp cialists until the age of two. This activity remained vital until the 1950s, but th introduction of tractors and the progress made by artificial-insemination techniqu caused it to decline rapidly. However, the development of tourism and pony-trekkin in rural areas has recently given it a new lease of life.

WALKING ABOUT

Vieille ville – Traces of Seyne's past as a defensive stronghold can still be seen in the cent of the old town. Closely set ranks of tall houses follow the line of the old town wall, which only the machicolated southern gate, the **Porte Basse**, remains; Vauban's glacis now a grassy park. Across the rue Basse stands the Chapelle des Dominicans ☉, whi contains an interesting **picture** of a penitential procession: the townspeople are depicte by class, with every citizen knowing his place in the social order. The Maison de Pays houses an **Exposition mulassière** explaining everything there is to know about the history of mule-breeding.

Église Notre-Dame de Nazareth ⊘ – This 13C church in attractive pink and blue stone is a fine example of Alpine Romanesque architecture. The nave, surmounted by a broken barrel vault, contains a beautiful 17C set of stalls, pulpit and retable as well as a large single-block christening font. Note the strange monsters which stalk the sculpted capitals of the nave.

Citadel ⊘ – Commissioned by Vauban in 1693, but rendered obsolete by the Treaty of Utrecht which handed nearby Ubaye to France, the citadel still has its 12C watch-tower. It now plays host to summer exhibitions about the history of the fortress and mule-breeding in Seyne.

EXCURSION

Vallée de la Blanche – Near the Col des Maures, where the larches give way to open meadow, the little winter sports resort of Chabanon (1 600m/2 549ft) looks down into the Blanche valley. Rising at the Cabane des Mulets, not far from the Col des Maures, the Blanche cuts straight across the area around Seyne. To the north, down-stream from Selonnet, it has cut deep gorges on its way to the Durance. The broad valley still bears traces of the glacier which once stretched as far as Col St-Jean.

St-Jean-Montclar – *12km/7.5mi north along D 900.*
This family ski resort, backed by the Dormillouse Massif, is situated on a plateau which is the starting point of the ski runs. The **ski area** is linked to that of **Le Lauzet**, situated on the north side of the Dormillouse Massif, via the Brèche runs. The village of **Montclar** has retained a 17C castle framed by two round towers *(not open to the public)* and the 13C Chapelle St-Léger.

★ **A hike to the Dormillouse** – (alt 2 505m/8 218ft) *The summit is accessible by chairlift to the Plateau de la Chau and then by a forest road (45min on foot).* From the 17C fort, there is a fine **view**★ of the Ubaye Valley. The cliff below the fort is used for paragliding, and has even hosted a paragliding world championship.

SISTERON★★

Population 6 964
Michelin map 334 D7 and 245 fold 20
Local maps see Vallée de la Moyenne DURANCE

Sisteron is situated along a transverse section *(cluse)* of the Durance Valley which marks the transition between Dauphiné and Provence. Arriving from the south along D 4, one enjoys a remarkable view of the highly impressive **setting**★★: the town climbing up the steep side of a hillock crowned by a citadel facing the impressive Rocher de la Baume, whose almost vertical strata seem to rise from the river bed. Tall narrow houses, covered with tiles, nestle between the ruined 14C walls.

Nearby Sights: Pays du BUËCH, BUIS-LES-BARONNIES, DIGNE-LES-BAINS, Préalpes de DIGNE, Vallée de la Moyenne DURANCE, FORCALQUIER, Monastère de GANAGOBIE, GAP, MANE, MANOSQUE, MONTBRUN-LES-BAINS, Route NAPOLÉON, Plateau de VALENSOLE

BACKGROUND

From Roman legions to GIs – During the Roman occupation, Sisteron, known as Segustero, was a major stopover along the **Domitian Way** linking Italy and the Rhône Delta. It became a bishopric in the 6C and was fortified by the lords of Forcalquier when it came into their possession some five hundred years later. After unification with Provence, the stronghold guarded the territory's northern border, until Provence itself was ceded to the king of France in 1483. The citadel was built during

the Wars of Religion (late 16C). Napoleon, returning from the island of Elba in 181
found luck was on his side when he entered Sisteron to discover that its royalist re
iment had withdrawn the day before; the emperor was able to stop for lunch in th
town before marching on to Grenoble. Towards the end of the Second World Wa
the town was partly destroyed by an Allied bombing raid on 15 August 1944 at
cost of 300 lives, but was then liberated by American troops a week later.

The programme for harnessing the Durance, completed in 1977, includes the unde
ground power station at Sisteron, supplied by a pressure pipeline, and the Saligna
Dam with its 118ha/292-acre reservoir. The town's economic activities are centre
round the production of lamb meat and the food-processing industry.

A theatre and dance festival, **Les Nuits de la Citadelle**, takes place in the open-air theatre belo
the citadel. Chamber music concerts are given in the Église St-Dominique and the cathedra

Eating out

BUDGET

L'Iris de Suse – *04200 Mison-Village – 12km/7.5mi NW of Sisteron on N 75 the
D 124 –* ☎ *04 92 62 21 69 – closed during holidays around 1 Nov –
14.48/15.40€.* Treat yourself to a moment of privacy in the small dining room com
posed of three platforms, or in fine weather on this restaurant's small terrace-ga
den. For the post-prandial constitutional, why not take a stroll around the village

MODERATE

Les Becs Fins – *16 r. Saunerie –* ☎ *04 92 61 12 04 – closed 16-23 Jun, 2
Oct-4 Nov, Sun evening, Tue evening and Wed except 15 Jul-15 Aug –
19.06/53.36€.* In a town where there are restaurants aplenty, this one certain
lives up to its name ("the gourmets"). The food served here is simple but tast
attractively presented and reasonably priced. Large terrace on the partia
pedestrianised street.

Where to stay

BUDGET

Hôtel Touring Napoléon – *22 av. de la Libération via Rte de Digne –* ☎ *04 9
61 00 06 –* 🅿 *– 28rms: 38.11/45.73€ -* ☕ *6.10€ – restaurant 15.24/20.58€*
This hotel on the road out of town has simple, functional rooms which are hand
as a stopover while travelling to or from your holiday destination. The foo
served here is also perfectly palatable. Children's menus available.

MODERATE

Grand Hôtel du Cours – *Pl. de l'Église –* ☎ *04 92 61 04 51 – closed 16 Nov-2
Feb –* 🅿 *– 51rms: 42.69/71.65€ -* ☕ *7.17€ – restaurant 18.29/23.63€.* Th
hotel with 1960s decor stands at the heart of the historic old town. Ask for room
at the back of the hotel, as these have more room and are more comfortable.

On the town

La Citadelle – *126 r. Saunerie –* ☎ *04 92 61 13 52 – daily 7am-11pm.* Whe
approaching Sisteron from the north, you cannot miss this establishment with the te
race overlooking the Durance valley. The chink of ice cubes in glasses is accompanie
by the clicking of cameras capturing this idyllic scene, subject of many a postcard...

Shopping

Pâtisserie-confiserie Canteperdrix – *131 r. de Provence –* ☎ *04 92 61 02 49
Tue-Sat 7.45am-12.30pm, 2.30pm-7.30pm – closed 1st week in Oct.* This confec
tioner's displays a choice selection of some of the finest flavours of Haute-Provenc
nougats, *calissons* (small iced almond cakes), *brioche sisteronnaise* and variou
other local specialities, as well as for good measure a range of *génépi* liqueurs.

Rue Droite and Rue Saunerie – The streets of Sisteron's old town and especiall
the Rues Droite and Saunerie are good places for a stroll. Rue Droite is a sho
per's paradise, while Rue Saunerie is lined with little bars tucked beneath ston
vaults, shops selling local produce and craft workshops.

Leisure

Base de loisirs des Marres – *Les Marres –* ☎ *04 92 61 00 37 / 04 92 61 34 44
daily 11am-7pm in Jul-Aug – closed beginning Sept-Jun.* This leisure park is sprea
out at the foot of the old town and includes a lake with supervised swimming, volle
ball pitches, a miniature golf course, several fitness circuits and children's play areas

SISTERON

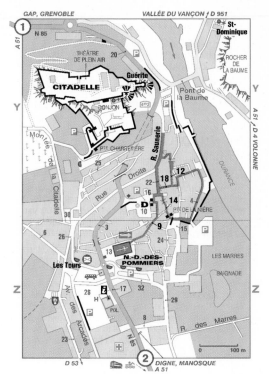

WALKING ABOUT

★ **Cathédrale Notre-Dame-des-Pommiers** ⊙ – This church, built between 1160 and 1220, is a fine example of Provençal Romanesque architecture. As so often in Provence, the influence of Lombard style is immediately apparent: an elegant doorway has alternate black and white voussoirs extended by half-rounded arches leaning against strong buttresses. The main pediment is also flanked by two half pediments; jambs and slender columns are decorated with carvings and capitals forming a continuous frieze representing a bestiary.

With its three naves, Notre-Dame is one of the largest churches in Provence. The square bell-tower is surmounted by a spire in the shape of a pyramid.

A slightly pointed barrel vault, supported by massive square pillars, rests over the dark nave flanked by narrow aisles. Paintings include works by Van Loo, Mignard and Coypel. As for the unusual name of the church, it refers not to *pommiers* (apple trees) but rather to the *pomœrii*, the Latin word for the town walls.

Towers – Sisteron has retained five towers dating from 1370, which formed part of the town's fortifications; four of them stand just south of Notre-Dame, the fifth guards the foot of the citadel. Each bears an evocative name: during the Wars of Religion, the Protestants fled the town through the Porte Sauve, the "escaping gate"; women used to gather for a gossip at the Porte de la Médisance, or "scandalmongers' gate".

★ **Old Sisteron** – *Follow the arrows, starting on the left of Notre-Dame; guided tours of the old town are organised in summer by the Tourist Information Centre.* The old town lies between rue Droite and the Durance; narrow streets running down to the river are lined with tall houses sometimes linked by vaulted passages known as **andrônes**. Note the elegant carved doorways (16C, 17C and 18C) along the way. Walk along **rue Deleuze** to the **Tour de l'Horloge**★ surmounted by a magnificent wrought-iron campanile bearing Sisteron's motto: *"Tuta montibus et fluviis"* (Safe between its mountains and its rivers). The **Longue Andrône**, a narrow arcaded passageway, branches off rue Mercerie. Continue along **rue du Glissoir** *(often icy in winter, as the name "slippery street" suggests),* which has retained a 13C Romanesque façade (no 5). Beyond the square, rue Basse-des-Remparts leads to **rue Font-Chaude** then through a covered passageway up to **rue Saunerie**; Napoleon had lunch at no 64, the old **Hostellerie du Bras d'Or**. Note the attractive 16C door at no 2, rue Mercerie; the **porte d'Ornano** takes its name from the noble family who once lived here, and whose arms it bears.

> **"Waste not, want not..."**
>
> The people of Sisteron believe in making the most of their local lamb. *Pieds et paquets* are a traditional speciality consisting of stuffed mutton tripe cooked with lardons, seasoned with herbs and pepper and served with grilled sheep's feet.

Église St-Dominique
Situated on the opposit bank of the Durance, belo the Rocher de la Baum this former monaster church has retained Lombard bell-towe Concerts and literar evenings take place i summer.

★ THE CITADEL ⊘ 1hr

The Porte Charretière leading into the citadel is accessible by car and on foot. In summe a small tourist train provides a shuttle service between the town hall and the citadel.

There is nothing left of the 11C castle. The keep and the watch-path are late 12 and the mighty walls set around the rock are the work of **Jean Errard**, Henri IV's chie military engineer. New defences, designed by Vauban in 1692, were added to th powerful 16C fortifications. Part of the citadel, including the chapel, was damage by bombing in 1944 but later tastefully restored.

A marked tour leads up a succession of steps and terraces, offering views of the town an the Durance Valley, and on to the watch-path. Walk on below the keep, where Ja Kazimierz, prince of Poland, was imprisoned in 1639, to reach the terrace *(viewing tabl* and enjoy the bird's-eye **view★** of the lower part of town, the reservoir and the mountain dominating the horizon to the north. The 15C **chapel**, partly rebuilt, is an exhibition centr Walk to the north side of the citadel, to the **"Guérite du Diable"** offering an impressive **view★** the Rocher de la Baume. The steps leading downwards were once part of an undergroun staircase, built to link the citadel to the Porte de Dauphiné, which was destroyed in 1944 The citadel museum includes a room devoted to Napoleon's "Return from Elba" an an exhibition featuring horse-drawn vehicles.

EXCURSIONS

① Prieuré de Vilhosc ⊘ 10km/6mi east along D 4 towards Volonne

Drive 5km/3mi then turn left onto D 217; 4km/2.5mi further on, cross the Riou d Jabron and follow the signposted road on the right.

The 3-naved **crypt** of an ancient monastery, located near the river beneath farm build ings, is a rare example of 11C early Romanesque art.
Continue along D 217 for 5km/3mi to reach the single-arched **Pont de la Reine-Jeann** spanning the Vançon in a picturesque wooded setting.

★ ② Haute vallée du Vançon 92km/57mi round tour – allow 3hr

Cross the bridge over the Durance and drive northeast along D 951 then D 3.

The road rises, offering interesting **views★** of Sisteron and of the Buëch Valley in the foregroun with the Montagne de Lure to the southwest. Beyond the pass, there are bird's-eye views the Riou de Jabron as it comes out of the Défilé de Pierre Écrite and flows towards the Duranc

Sisteron – the citadel and the banks of the Durance

Défilé de Pierre Écrite – The rock face of this deep gorge, on the left of the road near a small bridge, bears a Roman inscription celebrating Dardanus, a prefect of Gaul who converted to Christianity and who ordered the building of the first road through the gorge in the 5C AD. He founded Théopolis, a "city of God", the remains of which were discovered between Chardavon and St-Geniez.

Beyond St-Geniez on the right, Notre-Dame-de-Dromon can be seen at the foot of the Rocher de Dromon.

Notre-Dame-de-Dromon ○ – *Leave the car near a farm and continue on foot (15min there and back). This plain 11C chapel was a place of pilgrimage until the 19C. The vaulting dates from the 17C. The tiny crypt beneath the building, which has alabaster columns and capitals, is a fine example of early Romanesque art.*

Continue along D 3.

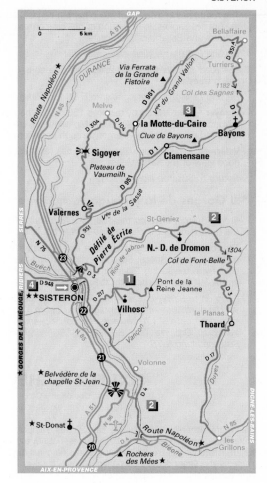

The road overlooks the wooded upper Vançon Valley, and the view extends through the Durance Valley to the Luberon and the Montagne Ste-Victoire. The road, which narrows considerably beyond Authon, goes over the **Col de Fontbelle** (alt 1 304m/4 278ft) and through the Mélan Forest.

At Le Planas, follow the small road to Thoard.

Thoard – This picturesque old village has retained part of its medieval walls and a Romanesque keep which is now the bell-tower.

From Thoard, continue along D 17 to reach N 85 and follow the Route Napoléon (see ROUTE NAPOLÉON) back to Sisteron.

③ Pays de la Motte-Turriers *85km/53mi round tour – allow 3hr*

From Sisteron, drive north along D 951.

The Sasse Valley, lying northeast of Sisteron, is an area modelled by erosion into a succession of ravines and gorges.

Turn right onto D 1.

Clamensane – This village is perched on a rocky spur. The landscape becomes gradually wilder and more austere. Beyond the **Clue de Bayons**, the road enters an open basin.

Bayons – A large and beautiful abbey **church** overlooks the village square. Built in the 12C and 13C, it is a harmonious mixture of Romanesque and Gothic art: the nave is surmounted by a broken barrel vault and the chancel has a ribbed vault with an Agnus Dei on the fine keystone. The archivolt of the 14C porch is framed by lancet arcades.

Beyond Bayons, D 1 veers due north towards Turriers.

The road rises in a series of steep hairpin bends, known locally as "tourniquets", t
the Col des Sagnes, in its setting of gullied mountain slopes, before running down t
Turriers and Bellaffaire (18C castle).

Beyond Bellaffaire, turn left onto D 951.

The road follows the **Grand Vallon** Valley, famous for its orchards (apple, pear an
peach trees).

Beyond La Motte, turn right onto D 104 to Melve then left onto D 304.

Sigoyer – From the partly restored 15C castle, the **view**★ extends to the Durance and
beyond, to the Baronnies and the Montagne de Lure.
The road runs down to Valernes through lavender fields.

Valernes – This hilltop village, which has retained part of its fortifications, offers
good view of the Sasse Valley.

Return to Sisteron along D 951.

★ 4 **Gorges de la Méouge** *90km/56km round tour – allow 4hr*

*From Sisteron, drive northeast on D 948 towards Ribiers; continue to Le Plan alon
the right bank of the Buëch then turn left onto D 942.*

The road winds through the gorge along the north bank of the rushing Méouge,
tributary of the Buëch. Several sections of the river are suitable for canoeing, par
ticularly in the spring. There are excellent views of the water and the jagged rock
on the left bank, particularly at **Pomet**.

*Carry on to Barret-le-Bas at the end of the gorge. It is possible to return to Sisteron
via the north side of the Montagne de Chabre. Otherwise, continue to La Calandre
turn right onto D 170 towards the Col St-Jean and Laborel then follow the Céan
Valley to Orpierre (see BUIS-LES-BARONNIES, 2) and Eyguiers, returning t
Sisteron along N 75.*

SIXT-FER-À-CHEVAL ★
Population 706
Michelin map 328 N4 and 244 fold 10

Like many other communities in Savoie, this traditional village at the top of the Giffr
valley has managed to move with the times, but not too far, successfully reinventing itsel
as an attractive centre for walking and skiing holidays. Its main attraction, howeve
remains the **Cirque du Fer-a-Cheval** from which it takes its name. Hollowed out by an Ic
Age glacier, this horseshoe-shaped ridge is characterised by the waterfalls which splas
down its steep, rocky face and wooded slopes. What better invitation could a walker c
a climber need?

Nearby Sights: AVORIAZ, CLUSES, Les GETS, MORZINE, Bassin de SALLANCHES
SAMOËNS

SIGHTS

Église – The village church still has its 13C nave. Beside it, handsome old houses fac
onto the square, where an ancient lime tree lends welcome shade in summer. A com
memorative plaque on the wall of the church is dedicated to Jacques Balmat, th
conqueror of Mont Blanc, who died in the mountains around Sixt while searching fo
gold.

Maison de la Réserve naturelle ⊘ – Three-quarters of the Sixt are
(9 200ha/22 734 acres) has been designated as a nature reserve. This visitors
centre in the middle of th
village presents a shor
history of the area and a
introduction to its flora
fauna and geology.

Eating out

MODERATE

La Feuille d'Érable – *Au Chef-lieu* – ☎ *04
50 34 44 47 – closed 15 May-15 Jun, 1-26
Oct and Mon lunchtime – 21.34/30.49€.*
Leaving the village in the direction of the
Rouget waterfall, you will come across this
massive house typical of the Savoie region
built in the early 20C. The delightful little
rustic dining room, decorated with mirrors
featuring advertisements, is the setting for
you to enjoy some well-cooked local cuisine.

HIKES

The Limestone Alps of Faucigny

The limestone peaks in th
French Alpine range reac
their highest point i
Faucigny *(see also CLUSES
Excursions)*. Twisted an

The Fond de la Combe, the source of the Giffre

crumpled rocks have been shaped into a magnificent landscape of outcrops and steep cliff walls which climbers and hikers love to explore; ever-present on the skyline is the snow-capped peak of the **Buet** (3 099m/10 167ft), but the superb **Fer à Cheval**★★ is the undisputed highlight.

Dedicated walkers can follow part of the GR 5 route over the **col d'Anterne** (2 264m/7 428ft), linking the Sixt valley with the bassin de Sallanches or the Chamonix valley across the Chaîne des Fiz.

★ Réserve naturel de Sixt

★★ **Cirque du Fer-à-Cheval** – *6.5km/4mi from Sixt on D 907.* On leaving Sixt, there is a fine view of the pyramid-shaped peak of the Tenneverge (2 985m/9 793ft), and its Corne du Chamois, the "chamois horn", at the end of the basin. The limestone walls (500-700m/1 640-2 297ft) run with waterfalls; in June, as many as thirty stream down the cliffs and add to the magical attraction of the place. The cirque forms a near-perfect ring, broken only at its north end, where the Giffre has cut a path through the rock. The **Maison de la Réserve naturelle** presents exhibitions on mountain flora and fauna during the season.

★ **Fond de la Combe** – *1hr 30min on foot there and back*

A marked path branches off at the end of the road, 50m/55yd beyond the kiosk, and leads to the Bout du Monde, "the End of the World", where the Giffre rises at the foot of the Ruan and Prazon glaciers.

★★ **Cascade du Rouget** – *5km/3mi from Sixt. Cross the Giffre in Sixt and follow the small road to Salvagny.* Beyond Salvagny, the road runs down to the foot of this double waterfall, the largest in a whole chain of cascades which continues downstream.

La TARENTAISE★★

Michelin map 333 L4 to N5 and 244 fold 21 and 31
Local map see Massif de la VANOISE

The sinuous course of the upper Isère Valley is the main geographical feature of the Tarentaise region. The long and narrow defiles of the Haute and Basse Tarentaise provide a contrast with the more open Moyenne Tarentaise stretching from Moûtiers to Bourg-St-Maurice. This pastoral and wooded middle Tarentaise is the natural habitat of the fawn-coloured **Tarine cows**, one of the most carefully preserved mountain breeds in France which, owing to their high milk yield, have spread to areas outside the Alps, particularly in the southern part of the country. The Moûtiers area is the only industrialised part of the region, although hydroelectric power is produced in other areas such as Tignes *(see TIGNES)*. The Tarentaise is also known as the home of the *"frontière"*, which has become one of the symbols of traditional life in Savoie. This black-velvet headdress decorated with gold braid has probably been worn by women since the 16C. There's something of an art to wearing the bonnet, which may need up to an hour of careful adjustment before it sits perfectly.

La TARENTAISE

Nearby Sights: ALBERTVILLE, Les ARCS, BEAUFORT, La Vallée des BELLEVILLE
BOURG-ST-MAURICE, CHAMPAGNY-EN-VANOISE, COURCHEVEL, Route des GRANDES
ALPES, Route de l'ISERAN, Route de la MADELEINE, MÉRIBEL, La PLAGNE
PRALOGNAN-LA-VANOISE, TIGNES, VAL-D'ISÈRE, Massif de la VANOISE

EXCURSIONS

★Moyenne Tarentaise

FROM MOÛTIERS TO BOURG-ST-MAURICE *41km/25.5mi – allow 2hr*

Beyond Aime, the itinerary leaves N 90 and follows secondary roads through
orchards and fields on the south side of the valley, within sight of the wooded slope
across the river, backed by the tall silhouette of Mont Pourri (alt 3 779m/12 398ft)

Moûtiers – Moûtiers, which lies deep inside a basin, at the confluence of the River
Dorons and River Isère, used to be the capital of the Tarentaise region and a major religious centre whose feudal lords boasted the title of "princes of the Holy Roman Empire".
Inside the **Cathédrale St-Pierre** note the wooden bishop's throne, dating from the 15C, and
on the left of the nave, a Romanesque Virgin Mary, reminiscent of a 13C Burgundian
statue. It is worth walking up to the north transept to admire a large and expressive representation of the Entombment (16C). On the first floor of the archbishop's palace is the
Musée de l'Académie de la Val d'Isère ⓥ, a small museum displaying historical finds from the
Tarentaise region (Bronze-Age jewellery, Roman pottery, medieval books and documents). The 17C archbishop's drawing room, decorated with paintings of the Good
Samaritan on wood panelling, and the 18C chapel are nearby. **The Musée des Traditions pop
ulaires de Tarentaise** ⓥ presents forgotten rural professions and ways of life.
Two spas in the lower Doron de Bozel Valley are within easy reach of Moutiers: **Brides-
les-Bains**‡ (for obesity and circulatory complaints) and **Salins-les-Bains**‡, which offers
stimulating salty waters, recommended in the treatment of gynaecological problems
and complaints affecting the lymph glands. Salins-les-Bains was once a major salt-
producing centre, processing 1 000 tons per year until the 18C.

The **Chapelle St-Jacques** stands on a rocky spur at the entrance of the Étroit du Siaix
Gorge, in front of the village of St-Marcel.

Étroit du Siaix – It is recommended to stop 50m/55yd before the tunnel *(beware
of falling rocks)* in order to appreciate the depth of this gorge, which is the narrowest
passage of the whole Isère Valley.
On the way to Aime, the valley is blocked by two glacial obstructions which bar its way.
Beyond the first of these, within sight of the Mont Pourri Summit and glaciers lies the
small **Centron Basin** which takes its name from the Celtic tribe who settled in the area.

Aime – Aime is the site of the **Ancienne basilique St-Martin**. This 11C church with its
massive bell-tower is the best example of early Romanesque architecture in Savoie.
The chancel and the apse are decorated with 12C and 14C frescoes – partly restored
in the 19C – which illustrate scenes of the Old and New Testament (Adam and Eve,
the massacre of the Innocents). Excavations have revealed traces of two previous edifices: the older of these, which may have been Roman, was used by the first
Christians, the "newer" building dates from the Merovingian period. The 11C crypt,
with its plain square capitals, supports the chancel.
Housed in a former 14C chapel, the small **Musée Pierre-Borrione** ⓥ displays
Gallo-Roman and Merovingian finds including coins, skeletons and sarcophagi plus a
collection of minerals and fossils found in the area and other parts of France.

Turn left onto D 218 towards Tessens and Granier, then take D 86.

On leaving Valezan, the view extends over the other bank of the Isère, along the
Ponturin Valley to the Bellecôte Massif (highest point: 3 416m/11 207ft). Beyond
Montgirod, Bourg-St-Maurice gradually comes into view, backed by the Col du Petit-
St-Bernard flanked on the left by the jagged silhouette of the Roc de Belleface.

Bourg-St-Maurice – See *BOURG-ST-MAURICE*.

★Haute Tarentaise

FROM BOURG-ST-MAURICE TO TIGNES
32km/20mi – allow 1hr, not including the hikes from Ste-Foy.

From Bourg-St-Maurice there is a view of the Malgovert power station, which is fed
by the Tignes dam. Beyond the town, D 902 leaves the broad valley and leads up in
a series of tight bends to Ste-Foy.

Ste-Foy-Tarentaise – Built on high ground overlooking the east bank of the River
Isère, between Bourg-St-Maurice and Val-d'Isère, and surrounded by traditional villages and hamlets, Ste-Foy-Tarentaise is the ideal starting point for pleasant
excursions in the area.

*La Sassière – *10km/6.2mi then 2hr there and back on foot. Leave Ste-Foy-Tarentaise towards the Col de l'Iseran and turn onto the first road on the left.*
After driving for 2km/1.2mi, you will come within sight of **Le Miroir**, a large hamlet whose chalets, climbing up the south-facing slope, have wooden balconies.
The road continues to rise, eventually reaching the high-pasture area where houses are built of stone with small openings and flat roofs covered with *lauzes* (heavy slabs of schist) in order to withstand bitter winter conditions.

Flocks on the high pastures

Leave the car at the end of the road and continue on foot.

🔼 The path rises among clusters of rhododendrons. As you approach the Chapelle de la Sassière, the Rutor Glacier, situated across the Italian border and overlooking a pastoral landscape, suddenly comes into **view****.

*Le Monal – *8km/5mi then 1hr there and back on foot. Drive south along D 902 then turn left to Chenal. Leave the car there and continue on foot.*

🔼 From the hamlet, there is a remarkable **view**** of the Mont Pourri and its glaciers, in particular the waterfalls coming down from the Glaciers de la Gurra and the village of La Gurraz below.

Upstream of Ste-Foy, the wild wooded valley widens slightly between La Raie and the Pont de la Balme. Water can be seen cascading down the opposite slope from the Mont Pourri glaciers (the view is particularly interesting from Le Monal). Towards the end of the drive, the huge fresco of a giant decorating the Barrage de Tignes seems to bar the end of the valley.

Tignes – *See TIGNES.*

THONON-LES-BAINS♨♨
Conurbation 53 078
Michelin map 328 L2 and 244 fold 8 and 9

Thonon is the historic capital of the Chablais region as well as a health and spa resort specialising in the treatment of kidney and bladder diseases; the season lasts from 15 May to 15 September. In addition to the resort and the handsome lakeside villas, set back behind lush gardens, visitors should make time for the **Rives** district, near the harbour on Lake Geneva, which has retained a few picturesque fishermen's cottages.

Nearby Sights: ABONDANCE, AVORIAZ, CHÂTEL, CLUSES, ÉVIAN-LES-BAINS, Les GETS, Route des GRANDES ALPES, MORZINE, La ROCHE-SUR-FORON, YVOIRE

AROUND THE SPA TOWN

The lake shore – On the way to Ripaille, there is a neatly appointed beach. The cruise ships which cross the lake have their moorings in the well-preserved port of Rives; from here Thonon can be reached by car, by a picturesque **funicular** ⊙ or even by walking up several inclines, preferably through the gardens laid out beneath the Château de Sonnaz.

Eating out

BUDGET

Le Bétandi – *2 r. des Italiens –* ☎ *04 50 71 37 71 – closed Sun lunchtime -
10.67/28.20€.* This small restaurant not far from the centre of town has
decor reminiscent of a traditional farm of the Savoie region. The materials
and old objects on display are all authentic. The cooking is also regional and
good.

MODERATE

Château de Ripaille – ☎ *04 50 26 64 44 – open Jul-Aug and at lunchtime only
– 23.63€.* This château typical of the Savoie has towered above Lake Geneva
since the 15C. A special package on offer during July and August enables visitors to sample the wine made on the estate, visit part of the château and have
a meal in one of the pleasure gardens.

Auberge d'Anthy – *74200 Anthy-sur-Léman – 6km/4mi SW of Thonon on N 5
and D 33 –* ☎ *04 50 70 35 00 – closed 1-13 Mar, 29 Oct-6 Nov, Mon evening
and Tue – 24.39/35.06€.* This is a happy discovery. Go through the bar-tobac-
conist's to get to a dining room in which well-cooked local fare is served. There
is a very attractively priced lunchtime menu. The setting is simple and friendly.
There are a few rooms available if you are in need.

Where to stay

MODERATE

À l'Ombre des Marronniers – *17 pl. de Crête –* ☎ *04 50 71 26 18 – closed 24
Dec-8 Jan –* 🅿 *– 17rms: 44.21/48.78€ –* ☕ *5.34€ – restaurant 11.43/27.44€*
Ask for one of the rooms in typical local style, which are real little bijou apart-
ments, in the picturesque chalet nestling amid the greenery of a flower garden.
The rest of the hotel is more run-of-the-mill, but clean and plain, like the restau-
rant. A good family place.

La Villa des Fleurs – *4 av. des Jardins –* ☎ *04 50 71 11 38 – closed 16 Oct-
31 Mar – 11rms: 44.21/53.36€ –* ☕ *5.34€.* Annexe to the Ombre des
Marronniers, where its reception now is, but the rooms here are peaceful and
have a little more charm, as well as being bigger; some have a balcony.

On the town

Le France – *2 av. de la Gare –* ☎ *04 50 70 10 51 – daily 5pm-3am – closed for
a fortnight at the end of Aug-beginning Sept.* This small piano-bar is smart and
comfortable. It offers a warm welcome and elegant service. Every day from 9pm
there is live musical entertainment. This is an ideal place to come and relax over
a cocktail.

Art

Maison des Arts – *4 bis av. d'Évian –* ☎ *04 50 71 39 47 – www.mal
thonon.org – opening hours depend on the programme of events.* This is the
hub of cultural life in Thonon and Evian, and puts on a pleasantly eclectic programme of exhibitions, plays, operas, variety shows etc.

★★ VIEWPOINTS

Several viewpoints line the way from boulevard de la Corniche to the Jardin
Anglais.

Place du Château – This was the site of the dukes of Savoie's castle destroyed by
the French in 1589. In the centre of the square stands the statue of **Général Dessaix**
(1764-1834), a native of Thonon, who fought courageously for the reunion of
France and Savoie and was made a general by Napoleon.
From the terraces, there is an open **view★** of the Swiss side of Lake Geneva from Nyon
to Lausanne. Below, the Rives district clusters round the brownish roofs of Rives.
Montjoux Castle and Ripaille Castle can be seen to the right. The Vaudois Alps and
Jura mountains form the panoramic background.

Jardin du château de Sonnaz and Jardin Paul-Jacquier – A pleasant place to relax;
situated at the end of the vast open space of the Jardin Paul-Jacquier, the ancient
Chapelle St-Bon, adjacent to a 13C tower (part of the town's fortifications), attracts
water-colourists.
The Maison des Arts et Loisirs, designed by Novarina, was completed in 1966.

SIGHTS

Musée du Chablais ⊙ – Housed in the 17C Château de Sonnaz, this regional folk museum illustrates local history; a room is devoted to the lakeside village period and to local Gallo-Roman finds.

Église St-Hippolyte ⊙ – St François de Sales preached in this church and the local population renounced Protestantism within its walls. The building illustrates different styles; the interior decoration, dating from the 17C, includes stucco work as well as painted cartouches and medallions over the nave **vaulting★**.
Note, on the right-hand side of the first nave, a 13C stoup bearing the arms of Savoie.
The pulpit dates from the 16C and the organ loft from 1672.
The three-naved Romanesque **crypt** (12C) was partly rebuilt in the 17C.

Basilique St-François-de-Sales – The neo-Gothic basilica is adjacent to Église St-Hippolyte. It contains the last work painted by Maurice Denis, one of the founders of the Nabis movement: two large frescoes entitled **Chemin de Croix** (1943), depicting Christ dying on the cross and his apparition to the holy women after his resurrection. The christening font dates from the 13C, the Virgin and Child from the 14C.

Monastère de la Visitation – It was erected in the 17C and recently restored. The chapel is surmounted by Gothic ribbed vaulting.

Hôtel-Dieu ⊙ – Occupying the site of the former Minimes Convent, founded in 1636, the edifice is centred round a cloister whose upper part is decorated in Baroque style.

Foyer Don-Bosco – The small modern chapel of this institution is decorated with ceramics.

EXCURSIONS

★ **Domaine de Ripaille** – *7km/4.3mi round tour. Go down to Rives and follow quai de Ripaille to the end then turn left into the avenue leading to the Château de Ripaille.*

This monastery and castle comprises a group of imposing buildings in typical Savoyard style, set in the midst of fine vineyards.

Fondation Ripaille ⊙ – The castle has, since 1976, been the headquarters of the Fondation Ripaille whose aim is to promote a research centre concerned with ecology, geology and the development of natural resources. A doorway in French classical style leads to the main courtyard. The castle is on the right – four out of the seven towers are still standing – while the monastery buildings are on the left; between 1619 and the Revolution, they were occupied by Carthusian monks, hence the name of *chartreuse* by which they are known today.

Castle – The interior was restored at the end of the 19C and decorated in neo-Gothic and modern styles. There are exhibitions about the castle's history.

Chartreuse – The winepress and 17C kitchens are open to visitors.

Forest and arboretum ⊙ – *Leave the grounds and take the first road on the left.* The Ripaille Forest, which was the hunting ground of the dukes of Savoie, covers an area of 53ha/131 acres. Marked paths lead to the arboretum whose trees, including firs, thujas, red oaks from America and black walnuts, were planted between 1930 and 1934. In a clearing nearby, the **monument national des Justes** commemorates the bravery of those who risked their lives to save French Jews from deportation during the Second World War.

VONGY

Église Notre-Dame-du-Léman is a graceful modern church decorated in tones of blue in honour of Our Lady. A large roof is supported by transverse gables and surmounted by a slender spire. The apse is adorned with a large mosaic depicting the Virgin Mary surrounded by local saints.

CHÂTEAU DES ALLINGES

7km/4.3mi south, leave Thonon by ③ on the town plan and following D 12. Take the first road on the right as you enter Macheron.

The hilltop was originally crowned by two castles belonging to rival feudal lords until 1355 when they both came into the possession of the count of Savoie. In 1594, St François de Sales made it his headquarters when he preached in the area.

Walk through the two fortified gates to the east platform offering an open **view** of the Bas Chablais region and the Dent d'Oche; the west platform affords an extended **view★** of Lake Geneva, Thonon and the Jura mountains. The restored **chapel** ⊙ has retained its oven-vaulted apse *(Light switch to the left of the door)* decorated with a late 10C Romanesque fresco, its rich colours and hieratic figures showing a clear Byzantine influence. Christ is represented in Glory, surrounded by the Evangelists, the Virgin Mary on the left, St John the Baptist on the right and personifications of the virtues below. Note the round stones embedded in the castle's east walls by a Carolingian catapult.

CHABLAIS

★★ The Chablais, extending between Lake Geneva and the Giffre Valley, is the largest massif in the Préalpes with some imposing summits such as the Dent d'Oche and its twin peak the Château d'Oche. The complex geological structure comprises three distinct areas. The **Bas-Chablais** is a relatively low, hilly area bordering the southern shore of Lake Geneva (Lac Léman in French), where woods of chestnut trees alternate with vineyards along the Savoyard Riviera. The **Pays Gavot** is the name given to the area inland from Évian. The **Haut-Chablais** (highest point: the Hautforts, at 2 464m/8 083ft), centred round Morzine, is an area of pastures and forests. Three rivers have cut their way through it: the Dranse d'Abondance, Dranse de Morzine and Brevon, all of which are tributaries of the Dranse de Savoie flowing into Lake Geneva.

★ ① **ROUTE DES TROIS COLS** *55km/34.2mi round tour – about 3hr 30min*

Leave Thonon-les-Bains by the road to Bellevaux

The D 26 runs above the Gorges de la Dranse; here and there the route gives a glimpse of the picturesque valley of Bellevaux and the Dent d'Oche in the distance.

Cow bells

Bellevaux – The village lies on the west bank of the Brevon, in the charming green **valley★** of the same name. The church, surmounted by a copper onion-shaped spire, contains some elegant woodwork and has retained a 14C chapel.

Turn right past the cemetery, cross the Brevon and take the forest road on the left.

The road rises very steeply above the Bellevaux Valley.

Chalets de Buchille – Fine view of the Mont d'Hermone to the northwest.

★ **Vallon de la Chèvrerie** – The upper Brevon Valley, guarded by the narrow pass of La Clusaz, was the secluded site chosen for the **Chartreuse de Vallon** dedicated to St Bruno in the 12C and abandoned in 1619 when the order moved to Ripaille. The road ends at La Chèvrerie, beneath a cirque over which the Roc d'Enfer towers at 2 244m/7 362ft.

Go back to the Col de Jambaz, turn left and almost immediately right onto D 32.

Between the Col de Jambaz and the Col de Terramont, the road leaves the Risse Valley, briefly enters the Lullin Valley then the Vallon de Terramont. Further on, towards the Col du Cou, the road reveals the peaceful landscapes of the Vallée Verte framed by forested heights, including the Voirons, Mont d'Hirmentaz and Mont Forchat (the latter bearing a white statue of St François de Sales).

★ **Col de Cou** – Alt 1 116m/3 661ft. Beyond the forested pass, there is a **view★** of Lake Geneva with the Jura mountain range in the distance.
During the drive down from the pass (16km/10mi), the road offers glimpses through the trees of the lake, of the Yvoire promontory, of the Voirons and of the Jura mountains. Further down, there are lovely **views★** of the pleasant Bas Chablais countryside overlooked by the ruins of the Château des Allinges.

In Mâcheron, turn left towards the Château des Allinges.

Château des Allinges – *See above.*

Road D 12 leads to Thonon.

② GORGES DE LA DRANSE

From Thonon to Morzine

33km/20.5mi – allow 1hr 45min. Leave Thonon by ② on the town plan, D 902 towards Cluses.

The route follows the Dranse de Savoie Valley through a succession of narrow sections and small basins. From Thonon to Bioge, the road follows the wooded Gorges of the Dranse where impressive red and ochre cliffs tower over the rushing mountain stream.

★★ **Gorges du Pont du Diable** ⊙ – *200 steps.* Enormous rocks, coloured in ochre, grey, green and blue by various deposits and eroded into all kinds of shapes, luxuriant vegetation and smooth vertical cliffs up to 60m/197ft high all contribute to make this visit a fascinating one; landslides have occurred in places, forming huge piles of boulders and a spectacular natural bridge known as the Pont du Diable.

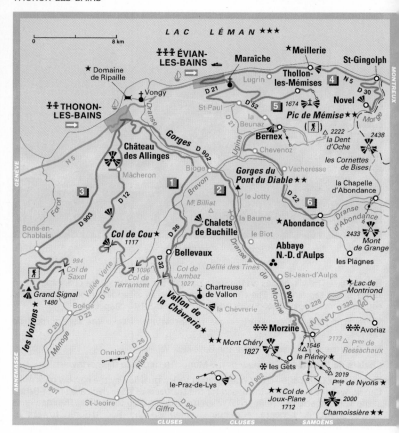

Stop further on by the Le Jotty Dam and the Église de la Baume, perched on a ledge. Beyond the Défilé de Tines (tunnel) are the ruins of Notre-Dame d'Aulps.

Abbaye Notre-Dame d'Aulps – The ruins of the 12C-13C church are the only remaining part of this Cistercian abbey. The pilgrimage dedicated to St Guérin, a former abbot, now takes place in the neo-Gothic church of St-Jean-d'Aulps. Note the attractive rose window.

The road now leads into the broad, more densely populated Morzine valley with the Pointe de Ressachaux and Pointe de Nyon rising above it. Return by the same route or via Taninges and St-Jeoire.

HIKE

③ Grand Signal des Voirons

Take the D 903 to Annemasse as far as Bons-en-Chablais. From Bons, drive south-east along D 20 towards Boëge.

The road rises gently through the woods, offering lovely glimpses of the Bas Chablais and Lake Geneva. From the Col de Saxel, D 50 follows the line of the ridge to the right through a small wood; the view gradually extends to the east beyond the Chaîne du Reposoir to the Dents du Midi, Mont Buet and the snow-capped peaks of the Mont Blanc Massif.

▶ Leave the car at the end of the road, in the car park near the monastery. 1hr there and back. From the car park, take the path marked "voie sans issue" and head uphill through the wood. At the edge of the wood, follow a path 50m/55yd ahead on the left marked "Les Crêtes". After 200m/219yd this path joins the Chemin des Crêtes; turn right here. The path divides in front of the monastery building; take the left fork to the ridge and follow it to the right to the cross which marks the summit of the Grand Signal (1 480m/4 856ft).

The **view** of Lake Geneva is partly blocked, but takes in the Mont Blanc Massif and the high chalk cliffs of Faucigny on the eastern and southern sides.

THORENS-GLIÈRES ★
Population 2 560
Michelin map 328 K5 and 244 fold 19

This small town lies on the banks of the River Fillière, a tributary of the Fier, at the point where the narrow valley opens out. It is the birthplace of St François de Sales who was christened and later ordained as a bishop in the parish church; its chancel, built in 1450, is the one that de Sales would have known. Nothing remains of the castle where François de Sales was born, but the Chapelle de Sales standing on the site, along the Usillon road, has become a place of annual pilgrimage; a procession in traditional costume takes place in Thorens on the same day *(Sunday following 15 August)*.

Thorens-Glières is also proud of its role as a focal point of resistance during the Second World War; the plateau around the town was the scene of bitter fighting against the Wehrmacht and the Vichy militia.

Nearby Sights: L'ALBANAIS, ANNECY, Lac d'ANNECY, Massif des ARAVIS, La CLUSAZ, CLUSES, La ROCHE-SUR-FORON

★ CHÂTEAU DE THORENS ⊘

The castle stands in an attractive setting, within sight of the Vallon de la Fillière and the Parmelan Mountain. The foundations date from the 11C, the round keep – unusual in Savoie – from the 13C, and the whole edifice was remodelled in the 19C.

The vaulted basement was originally given over to a guardroom and prison cells. The ground-floor rooms contain mementoes of St François de Sales, 16C tapestries from Brussels, a wealth of furniture and a collection of paintings; note in particular **St Stephen** by Marco d'Oggiono, 16C Lombard School, *Portrait of the Infanta Isabella* by Van Dyck and *Portrait of the Marquise de Grollier* by Madame Vigée-Lebrun. Two rooms are devoted to the architect of Italian unification, Count Cavour, who was related to the Sales family; portraits and letters are housed here, as well as the desk on which the treaty uniting France and Savoie was signed.

PLATEAU DES GLIÈRES
14km/8.7mi east along a forest road.

During the Second World War, the high-pasture area of the Plateau des Glières was chosen by Resistance leaders as the site of one of their fortified camps. It was unsuccessfully attacked in February 1944 by Vichy security forces. A second attempt in March also failed. The Germans then sent 12 000 soldiers, and the 465 besieged men were forced to retreat in spite of putting up a fierce resistance. There were heavy losses on both sides and the surrounding towns and villages suffered fierce reprisals. However, the local Resistance group became gradually stronger, regained possession of the plateau and eventually liberated the *département* with the help of other Resistance groups in the area; Haute-Savoie became the first French territory to be liberated without the help of the Allied forces.

The surfaced road ends at the **Col des Glières** (alt 1 440m/4 724ft), where a panel explains the sequence of the military operations which took place in 1944. The **memorial**, standing slightly below on the right, symbolises the V for Victory together with renewed hope and life. There is a chapel inside.

The Resistance fighters killed in 1944 are buried in the "Nécropole nationale des Glières".

A trail called "Nature et Paysages des Glières" (nature and landscapes of the Glières region) offers a marked itinerary which includes the main historic sites *(1hr 30min)*.

TIGNES ✳✳✳
Population 2 220
Michelin map 333 O5 and 244 fold 32 – Local map see Massif de la VANOISE

Almost every skier knows the name and its reputation as a modern winter resort; but few realise that Tignes was not always a sporting paradise. The old village, flooded in 1952 as a result of the building of the dam *(see Excursions: Barrage de Tignes)*, was replaced five years later by a ski resort which developed 6km/3.7mi higher up. The **setting★★** could hardly be more delightful, near a lake surrounded by meadows, with the **Grande Motte** to the south and the **Grande Sassière** to the east. To the east of the lake, a cable car runs up to the peak of the Tovière. To the west, the Parc national de la Vanoise lies over the Col du Palet and the Col de Tourne. Golf and lake fishing are among the sports to be enjoyed in summer.

Nearby Sights: Les ARCS, BESSANS, BONNEVAL-SUR-ARC, BOURG-ST-MAURICE, Route des GRANDES ALPES, Route de l'ISERAN, La Haute MAURIENNE, La TARENTAISE, VAL-D'ISÈRE, Massif de la VANOISE

Lac de Tignes – This small natural lake lies at the centre of a treeless high-pasture basin backed by the snowfields of the **Grande Motte** sloping down to the Rochers de la Grande Balme. The setting of the **Grande Sassière** across the river is very similar. The Tovière Summit to the east, facing Val-d'Isère, is accessible by gondola. The Col du Palet and Col de la Tourne to the west give access to the Parc national de la Vanoise. In summer, the lake offers a variety of water sports and there is an 18-hole golf course nearby.

THE RESORT

Situated at an altitude of 2 100m/6 890ft, Tignes has gradually expanded into several districts spread around the lake: Tignes-le-Lac, Le Lavachet and Val Claret further south. The world championships of artistic and acrobatic skiing take place every year in Tignes. The events include mogul skiing as well as ballet and jumping in the Lognan Olympic stadium.

Ski area – It is linked to that of Val-d'Isère to form the famous **Espace Killy**✳✳✳ *(see Massif de la VANOISE)*, one of the largest and most beautiful ski areas in the world, in a totally treeless high-mountain setting. Snow cover is excellent and available all year round (with summer skiing on the Grande Motte Glacier). Some 100 snow-cannons make it possible for skiers to ski down to the resort from October to May. Slopes are generally less steep than in Val-d'Isère, but some ski runs are however suitable for advanced skiers (Le Vallon de la Sache, Les Pâquerettes and La Ves). In addition, it is possible to practise mogul skiing and experience non-pisted powder runs.

HIGHLIGHTS

✳✳**Barrage de Tignes** – The reservoir, known as the **Lac du Chevril**✳, holds 230 million m³/186 461acft, held back by a wall which is 180m/591ft high including its foundations. The massive downstream side of this arch dam, inaugurated in 1953, is decorated with a huge fresco covering 12 000m≤ /129 120sq ft depicting **Le Géant** (the giant) (fine view from D 902 and the village of Les Brévières). The water falls a total height of 1 000m/3 281ft, first supplying the **Brévières** power station (yearly production: 154 million kWh), before travelling along a 15km/9mi-long tunnel to the **Malgovert** power station (yearly production: 750 million kWh).

In addition, the Chevril power station is partly supplied by the Réservoir de la Sassière (2 460m/8 071ft).

A **viewpoint** on the roof of the Chevril power station, just off D 902, offers an overall **view**✳ of the dam, its reservoir and the mountains.

Tignes

Where to stay

MODERATE

Le Paquis – *Au Lac* – ☎ *04 79 06 37 33 – closed 3 May-13 Jul and 31 Aug-30 Oct – 36rms: 60.98/91.47€ -* ☂ *8.08€ – restaurant 20.58/57.93€.* This hotel on the slopes above the resort has been entirely refurbished and is run by friendly local people. The rooms are decorated in traditional local style and have painted wood panelling.

EXPENSIVE

Résidence Village Montana – *Les Almes* – ☎ *04 79 40 01 44 – www.vmontana.com – closed 5 May-30 Jun and Sept-Nov – 99 apartments 4/10 persons: per week from 1344.60€.* This establishment is part of the Hôtel Village Montana, but is some distance away from it. It consists of fine timber apartments, some of which have an open fireplace and others a mezzanine. They all have a kitchen, but there is nothing to stop you from dining in one of the hotel restaurants!

On the town

Grizzly's Bar – *Val-Claret* – ☎ *04 79 06 34 17 – Nov-Apr 8.30am-7.30pm, Jul-Aug: daily 10.30am-12.30pm, 3.30pm-7.30pm – closed May-Jun, Sept-Oct.* Beneath the benevolent gaze of one or two bears carved from wood, skiers and ramblers can take a break here and warm themselves by the fireside. There is also a fashion boutique and gift shop.

L'Étoile des Neiges – *Les Brévières* – ☎ *04 79 06 41 16 – daily 8.30am-9pm – closed May-Dec.* The immense terrace in this bar at the foot of the ski slopes opposite the La Sache cable car overlooks the whole of this busy area.

La Grande Chute – *Les Brévières* – ☎ *04 79 06 47 63 – open daily 11am-1.30am – closed May-Nov.* This little mountain bar occupies a house built in 1789. The setting is slightly old-fashioned and rustic (old photographs and skis) in keeping with its relaxed and happy atmosphere.

Le Panoramic – ☎ *04 79 06 47 21 – daily 9am-4.45pm – accessible in winter via the Grande Motte funicular.* The terrace of this bar-restaurant is perched at an altitude of 3 032m/9 945ft. In very cold weather, there is only one remedy: rikiki, hot chocolate with a shot of kirsch! Every Thursday there is a torch-lit procession downhill.

Shopping

Boucherie du Lac – J. Grégoire – *Au Lac* – ☎ *04 79 06 30 13 – open daily 6am-8pm – closed beginning Sept-beginning Dec and May-Jun.* This specialist in the art of curing meat has won many an international prize for his charcuteries (jambon sec, noix de jambon, saucissons secs in a huge variety of flavours) and especially for his Bœuf séché de Tignes (dried beef).

★★★ **The Grande Motte** – This glacier is famous for its scenery and for its summer skiing. An underground **rack railway** ⊘, starting from Val Claret, runs over a distance of 3 400m/2.2mi to a viewing platform offering an overall view of the glacier. From there, a huge cable car *(capacity: 125)* takes skiers up to 3 450m/11 319ft, near the Grande Motte Summit (3 656m/11 995ft). The **panorama★★** of the surrounding peaks is breathtaking.

★★ **The Tovière** – Alt 2 696m/8 845ft. *Access from Tignes-le-Lac by the Aéro-Ski gondola in winter.* **Panorama** including the Espace Killy, the Grande Motte, Dôme de la Sache, Mont Blanc and the Grande Sassière.

HIKES

★★★ **Col du Palet and Col de la Tourne** – *Allow 1 day. Difference in altitude: 750m/2 461ft minimum. Experienced hikers can extend the itinerary if they wish: Col de la Grassaz or Lac de la Plagne are two splendid detours which can be included in the following tour.* Start from Tignes-le-Lac; 1hr 30min to the Col du Palet (alt 2 653m/8 704ft) with interesting flora; from the pass, a further 30min to the **Pointe du Chardonnet★★★** (2 870m/9 416ft) *(for hikers not suffering from vertigo; mountain boots essential)*: exceptional panoramic view of the Tarentaise region. Less adventurous hikers can aim for the **Col de la Croix des Frêtes★★**, 10min further on from the Col du Palet. Walk down to the Lac du Grataleu then up again to the **Col de la Tourne★★** (2 656m/8 714ft), offering splendid views of the Espace Killy. On the way down, note the superb **Aiguille Percée** on the left.

★★ **Refuge de la Martin** – Alt 2 154m/7 067ft. *5hr there and back from Tignes-le-Lac or Les Boisses.*
🚶 This undemanding hike offers lovely views of the Lac du Chevril, the surrounding summits and Mont Blanc in the distance. Walkers can continue as far as the edge of the glacier and admire the view *(Remember that it is highly dangerous for inexperienced walkers to venture onto a glacier).*

EXCURSIONS

★★ **Réserve naturelle de la Grande Sassière** – *From the Tignes Dam, follow the road to Val-d'Isère. Immediately beyond the Giettaz tunnel, turn left up a steep, narrow road towards the Barrage du Saut (6km/3.7mi), at an altitude of 2 300m/7 546ft (car park).*
The nature reserve covering 2 230ha/5 511 acres was created in 1973, and the beauty of the environment has been totally preserved in spite of important investments in hydroelectric projects. Overlooked by the **Grande Sassière** (3 747m/12 293ft) and **Tsanteleina** (3 605m/11 827ft) summits, it extends to the Glacier de Rhêmes-Golette on the Italian border.

★★ **Lac de la Sassière** – Alt 2 460m/8 071ft. *1hr 45min there and back on foot from Le Saut; go up along a path following the stream and return by the EDF road on the opposite bank.*
🚶 This undemanding hike leads to a pleasant lake with the Aiguille de Dôme towering above it.

★★ **Glacier de Rhême-Golette** – Alt about 3 000m/9 843ft. *1hr 30min steep climb from the Lac de la Sassière; it is dangerous to go onto the glacier.*
🚶 Beautiful scenery with the Grande Casse and Grande Motte in the distance.

Vallée de la TINÉE★★

Michelin map 341 C2 to E4 and 245 folds 23 and 24

The River Tinée flows southwards from the Col de la Bonette to its confluence with the Var. Gorges and open basins alternate along this green valley covered with forests of chestnuts, firs and larches. Hilltop villages line the way on both sides of the river, their simple little churches often brightened with **frescoes★** on the inside.

Nearby Sights: AURON, BARCELONNETTE, BEUIL, Gorges du CIANS, CLUES DE HAUTE-PROVENCE, Route de la BONETTE, Val d'ENTRAUNES, ENTREVAUX, Route des GRANDES ALPES, ISOLA 2000, PUGET-THÉNIERS, ST-ÉTIENNE-DE-TINÉE, L'UBAYE, VILLARS-SUR-VAR

EXCURSION

A Drive through the Gorges *143km/89mi – allow 1 day*

This itinerary, which begins at the confluence of the Tinée and the Var, requires a full day as the detours to hilltop villages involve taking narrow, winding roads.

From the Pont de la Mescla, drive along D 2205.

★ **Gorges de la Mescla** – The road runs along the bottom of the gorge, beneath overhanging rocks; the name Mescla, a Provençal word meaning "mix", refers to the joining of the two rivers.

At the Pont de la Lune, turn right onto D 32.

La Tour – This isolated village, perched on a rocky spur above the Tinée Valley, has retained its medieval character and boasts a charming square, lined with arcades, a shaded fountain and *trompe-l'œil* façades.
The Romanesque-Gothic **church** ⊘ is decorated with three beautiful Renaissance retables and two 15C stoups.
Several 16C water-powered oil-mills are still in working order.
The **Chapelle des Pénitents-Blancs** ⊘ stands along D 32 at the northeast end of the village. The side walls are covered with **frescoes★** by Brevesi and Nadale, dating from 1491, depicting 20 scenes from the Passion. Older frescoes, painted on the east-end wall, illustrate the Last Judgement.

Return to D 2205 and drive north to Pons-de-Clans then turn left onto D 56.

The road winds its way to Bairols in a series of spectacular hairpin bends, amid olive, oak and chestnut trees.

Bairols – This hilltop village (alt 830m/2 723ft) has been tastefully restored. It offers bird's-eye **views★** of the valley below. The old flour-mill has been turned into a restaurant and the oil-mill into a bar.

Rejoin D 2205 and turn immediately right onto D 55 to Clans.

Clans – This pleasant village, overlooking the steep Clans Valley on one side and the Tinée on the other, is surrounded by a large forest of spruces, larches and firs and framed by mountains. Note its many fountains, which date back to medieval times.
The Romanesque **church** was rebuilt in Baroque style, so the beautiful doorway, dating from 1702, is preceded by a portico. The interior decoration is rather elaborate: the chancel contains two panels of a retable from the Nice School; in the side chapel on the left of the chancel and there is a Baroque altarpiece in 17 parts.

Life of St Anthony – a fresco from the Chapelle St. Antoine

11C **frescoes** representing hunting scenes have been discovered behind the high altar, together with a 15C Christ in Glory. The organ case was made in 1792 by **Honoré Grinda** from Nice. *Walk along the left-hand side of the church to the end of the surfaced road.* **Chapelle St-Michel** stands at the top of the village. The flat east end is adorned with 16C **frescoes**; the Archangel Michael can be seen in the centre, weighing souls. From the terrace, the **view** embraces Clans, the Tinée Valley with Bairols and the Pointe des Quatre Cantons across the river.
On the left of the Pont-de-Clans road stands **Chapelle St-Antoine** *(500m/547yd from the village)*. The small rustic chapel has a wall-belfry and a large porch. The interior is extensively decorated with 15C **frescoes★** depicting virtues and vices and scenes from the life of St Anthony, with texts in the old local dialect.

Return to D 2205 once more and, a little further on, turn left to Ilonse.

Ilonse – Ilonse lies in a beautiful mountain setting, at an altitude of 1 210m/3 970ft. From the viewing table at the top of the village several hilltop villages can be seen standing out against dark forest patches.

Back to D 2205; continue towards St-Sauveur-sur-Tinée.

The Valdeblore road on the right links the Tinée and Vésubie valleys. Red schists add colour to the landscape.

St-Sauveur-sur-Tinée – Situated at the confluence of the River Tinée and River Vionène, this village is a maze of twisting lanes lined with tall buildings with projecting roofs. It houses an information centre of the **Parc national du Mercantour**.
The 15C **church** has a Romanesque bell-tower decorated with gargoyles. Inside, the rich ornaments include the **Retable Notre-Dame** (1483) by Guillaume Planeta. A painting of the betrothal of St Catherine, showing Tinée as it was in the 17C, can be seen behind the wrought-iron grille of the chapelle St-Joseph
Beyond St-Sauveur, D 30 winds its way westwards along the Vionène and across the Col de la Couillole *(see BEUIL, Excursions)*, linking the Tinée and Cians valleys. D 2205 follows the Tinée through the dark and barren corridor of the **Gorges de Valabres★**, between Mont Gravières on one side and the Cime des Lauses and Mont St-Sauveur on the other.

Isola – The lovely Romanesque bell-tower of the church, destroyed by a flood of the Guerche, stands at the entrance of the village. The rounded twinned windows with carved capitals are typical of the Lombard influence.
The road on the left leads to the **Cascade de Louch★**; the water falls from a hanging valley, 100m/328ft above the Tinée.

To reach **Isola 2000**★★ *(see ISOLA 2000), turn right onto D 97 and follow the Vallon de Chastillon.*

The road runs close to the Italian border, which is lined with snow-capped peaks. Mountain streams come rushing down the slopes on both sides of the River Tinée and the valley widens within sight of St-Étienne-de-Tinée.

※ **Auron** - *See AURON.*

Via Ferrata d'Auron – The climb is made up of seven separate sections, which can be completed in three to four hours, combining the thrill of close contact with the rock and the security of a safety line. France's longest via ferrata bridge (46m/151ft) is guaranteed to impress.

★ **St-Étienne-de-Tinée** – *See ST-ÉTIENNE-DE-TINÉE.*

Beyond St-Étienne-de-Tinée, the road rises above the Tinée Valley, towards the Col de la Bonette *(see Route de la BONETTE, Excursions).*

Le TRIÈVES ★

Michelin map 333 H9 and 244 folds 39 and 40

The River Drac and River Ébron have carved deep trenches through the green Trièves Depression. To the west, the landscape almost takes on the look of the Savoyard High Alps; guarding the approaches of the Vercors Massif like a bastion is **Mont Aiguille** (alt 2 086m/6 844ft), one of the "Seven Wonders of the Dauphiné". This isolated table mountain inspired one of the first recorded mountaineering expeditions in France. It was climbed in 1492 at the request of King Charles VIII who came to Notre-Dame d'Embrun on a pilgrimage and, hearing tales of supernatural manifestations on the top of the mountain, ordered Antoine de Ville to lead an expedition of ten men. These early *alpinistes* reached the top, only to find not the dancing angels of local legend but a charming meadow dotted with flowers and a flock of chamois.

Nearby Sights: Pays du BUËCH, Massif de CHAMROUSSE, Le DÉVOLUY, GRENOBLE, Lacs de LAFFREY, MONTMAUR, Route NAPOLÉON, Le VALGAUDEMAR, Le VERCORS, VIZILLE

EXCURSIONS

★ 1 Route du Col de la Croix Haute

FROM MONESTIER TO THE COL DE LA CROIX HAUTE

36km/22.4mi – about 1hr 30min

Monestier-de-Clermont – The surrounding woods offer numerous possibilities for shaded walks and the nearby village of Avignonet to the northeast has an excellent belvedere overlooking the Drac, the Monteynard Dam and its reservoir *(water sports)*.
The road leading to the Col de la Croix Haute affords a vast panorama of mountains, with the splendid escarpments of **Mont Aiguille** in the foreground on the right.

Col de la Croix Haute (1 179m/3 858ft)– Its landscape of pastures and dark fir forests is characteristic of northern Alpine scenery.

2 Upper Gresse Valley

ROUND TOUR STARTING FROM MONESTIER *61km/38mi – about 2hr*

From Monestier-de-Clermont, drive northwest along D 8.

The road goes through St-Guillaume, a typical village of the Trièves region, with its stocky houses covered with steep, tiled roofs. It then rises above the Gresse Valley to Miribel-Lanchâtre *(lovely views)* and runs down again to St-Barthélemy.

Turn left onto D 8e.

Prélenfrey – This small summer resort lies at the heart of a **vale**★ beneath the escarpments of the Vercors Massif (Arêtes du Gerbier). The Échaillon flows through a narrow gorge, through which there is a pleasant view of the Drac valley.

Continue along D 8e to the Col de l'Arzelier.

The road rises to the **Col de l'Arzelier** (ski area), then runs down to Château-Bernard, offering more fine views of the Vercors.

Follow D 242 towards St-Andéol.

The pastoral landscapes of the Trièves are backed by the impressive cliffs of the Vercors, including the Grand Veymont (alt 2 341m/7 680ft), the massif's highest peak.

D 242 goes over the Col des Deux to join the road leading to Gresse-en-Vercors.

Gresse-en-Vercors – Note the strange local means of transport known as *trinqueballes*, which look vaguely like sledges and are designed to cope with uneven ground. The Maison du Parc naturel régional du Vercors is in the village centre.

★ **Col de l'Allimas** – From the pass there is a striking view of Mont Aiguille, followed by fine views of the Trièves on the way down to St-Michel-les-Portes.

Return to Monestier along N 75 towards Grenoble.

★ ③ **Across the Trièves**

FROM MONESTIER-DE-CLERMONT TO CORPS

46km/28.6mi – about 1hr 30min

From Monestier, drive south along N 75 then turn left onto D 34.

★ **Pont de Brion** – This suspension bridge, looking surprisingly light, spans the sombre gorge of the Ébron. It used to be 126m/413ft above the river bed, but since the building of the Monteynard Dam on the Drac downstream, the level of the Ébron has been raised by 60m/197ft.

Near the Col de Cornillon, there is a clear **view** on the left of the Corniche du Drac and the reservoir of the Monteynard Dam.

Where to stay

BUDGET

Hôtel Au Sans Souci – *38650 St-Paul-lès-Monestier – 2km/1mi NW of Monestier-de-Clermont on N 75 and D 8 – ☎ 04 76 34 03 60 – closed 20 Dec-end Jan, Sun evening and Mon except Jul-Aug – 🅿 – 13rms: 27/49€ – 5.80€ – restaurant 13.50/35€.* For a short break in the countryside, stay at this peaceful vine-clad hotel. The warm decor is typical of the local mountain region, with frills and beams, solid wooden tables and floral wallpaper in the bedrooms. There are tennis courts and a swimming pool. Good value for money.

Accueil paysan Ferme de Préfaucon – *Préfaucon – 38710 Mens – 2km/1mi S of Mens on D 66 towards St-Baudille-et-Pipet – ☎ 04 76 34 62 50 – sc.jlg@wanadoo.fr – ✉ – 5rms. half-board: 30.49/38.11€.* This old farm has been tastefully refurbished and boasts a large vaulted hall supported on a single column, typical of the Trièves. It offers nature lovers and rambling enthusiasts a friendly welcome at the foot of Mont Obiou. Food served uses organic products grown in the kitchen garden. It is possible to take part in some farm activities.

Hôtel Au Gai Soleil du Mont Aiguille – *At La Richardière – 38930 Chichilianne – 4km/2.5mi NW of Chichilianne on B-road – ☎ 04 76 34 41 71 – closed beginning Nov-20 Dec – 🅿 – 20rms: 31.25/44.21€ - 🛏 6.10€ – restaurant 12.20/30.49€.* This family hotel occupies an outstanding site at the foot of Mont Aiguille, ready for departure on one of many possible rambles. It treats its guests as one of the family. In winter, you can take off your cross-country skis on the threshold.

MODERATE

Chambre d'hôte Le Château de Pâquier – *38650 St-Michel-les-Portes – 12km/7.5mi N of Monestier-de-Clermont on N 75 and B-road – ☎ 04 76 72 77 33 – hrossi@club-internet.fr – closed 1 Nov-1 Mar – 5rms: 44.21/48.78€ – main meal 13.72€.* This small Renaissance castle at the end of a track is surrounded by a pretty garden. Downstairs, there is a fine French-style ceiling, mullioned windows and a spiral staircase, which leads you up to the tastefully furnished rooms. One of the bedrooms is in the old chapel.

Château de Passières – *38930 Chichilianne – ☎ 04 76 34 45 48 – closed Dec, Jan, Sun evening and Mon out of season – 🅿 – 23rms: 48.78/64.03€ - 🛏 6.86€ – restaurant 21.34/30.49€.* This castle was built in the 14C at the foot of Mont Aiguille, and retains numerous mementoes of its past, including objets d'art and dark wood panelling in three of the bedrooms, which are accessed via an old spiral stone staircase. Tennis court and swimming pool.

Auberge du Goutarou – *Les Granges Thoranne – 38650 St-Michel-les-Portes – ☎ 04 76 34 08 28 – auberge-du-goutarou@magros.com – closed 15-30 Nov and Tue lunchtime except Jul-Aug – 6rms: 49.55/70.13€ – main meal 14.48€.* You can take your meals in an old stall with a vaulted ceiling in this 18C farm and sleep in rooms with bunk beds and bare beams. The owner uses the old bread oven to prepare traditional dishes for his guests.

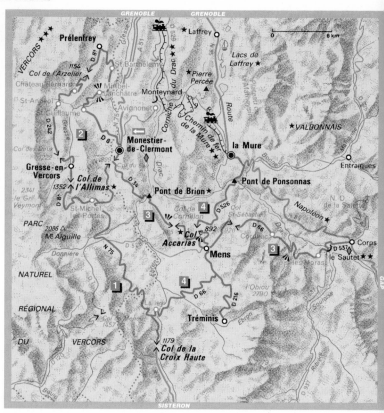

Mens – The capital of the Trièves region was a stopping point on the Roman road; the old covered **market** and the 17C townhouses in the rue du Bourg hint at the prosperity and importance which Mens once enjoyed. The **Café des Arts**, mentioned in Jean Giono's *Triomphe de la Vie*, features a mural (1896) by Gustave Riquet depicting local landscapes and farming scenes

Musée du Trièves ⊘ – Rural life in the region is remembered in this collection of artefacts, housed in a historic building.

Pony trekking near Tréminis

Beyond Mens, drive northeastwards along D 66.

Between the Col de St-Sébastien and Cordéac, the road skirts the Obiou Massif before passing the terraced fields above the left bank of the Drac.

★★ **Barrage et lac du Sautet and Corps** – *See Le DÉVOLUY* 2.

4 From La Mure to the Col de la Croix Haute

65km/40mi – allow 2hr

La Mure – *See Route NAPOLÉON* 1

Between La Mure and the Pont de Ponsonnas, the snow-capped southern peaks of the Écrins Massif can be seen through the Valbonnais Corridor.

Pont de Ponsonnas – This bridge spans the gorge of the Drac 100m/328ft above the river bed.

★ **Col Accarias** – Alt 892m/2 927ft. Extended **view**★ of the Trièves enclosed by the Obiou, the Grand Ferrand and the Tête du Lauzon.

From Mens, drive south along D 66, then turn left onto D 216.

Tréminis – Tréminis lies in the upper Ébron Valley, which is covered with fir forests and overlooked by the limestone escarpments of the Dévoluy. This **setting**★ is one of most attractive of the whole area and the resort is a pleasant place to spend a summer holiday.

Return to D 66 and continue towards Lalley.

Col de la Croix Haute – *See* 1.

L'UBAYE★★

Michelin map 334 6 to 17 and 245 folds 9 and 10

The valley of the River Ubaye, a tributary of the Durance, forms the most northern region of the Provençal Alps. It is an area of deeply gullied marly slopes, of huge alluvial fans covered with scrub, but also of fine conifer forests and rocky peaks, conveying an impression of spaciousness to travellers used to the deep valleys of the northern Alps.

The Ubaye region remained cut off during the long winter months until 1883, when the road linking Barcelonnette to the Durance Valley *(D 900)* was completed. This isolation also had a political side: the region was within the Duchy of Savoy's sphere of influence from the 14C to the 18C and maintained strong links with Piedmont.

The Barcelonnette Basin, lying at the intersection of the international Gap-Cuneo Route *(D 900-S 21)* and the Route des Grandes Alpes *(D 902)* from the Col de Vars to the Col de la Cayolle, forms the central part of the region.

Nearby Sights: BARCELONNETTE, Route de la BONETTE, EMBRUN, Val d'ENTRAUNES, Route des GRANDES ALPES, GUILLESTRE, MONT-DAUPHIN, PRA-LOUP, ST-ÉTIENNE-DE-TINÉE, Lac de SERRE-PONÇON, SEYNE, Vallée de la TINÉE, VAL D'ALLOS, VARS

EXCURSIONS

1 The Lower Ubaye Valley

FROM LE LAUZET-UBAYE TO BARCELONNETTE

21km/13mi along D 900 – about 30min

Le Lauzet-Ubaye – *See Barrage et Lac de SERRE-PONÇON,* 2.

Beyond Serre-Ponçon the gorges become narrower and the landscape takes on a very different aspect. Before the construction of the road in 1883, travellers had no choice but to brave a dangerous, 23km/14mi path through the gorges of the Durance and negotiate some infamous, life-threatening stretches. The road skirts the south bank of the Ubaye flowing between wooded slopes, within sight of the snow-capped summits of the Petite and Grande Séolane. Between Le Lauzet and Le Martinet, several viewpoints offer the possibility of observing the numerous rafters and canoeists. Just before Le Martinet is the rock known as Tête de Louis XVI; but don't worry, this "head" is unlikely to roll!

Le Martinet – As you drive through the village, look right up the Grand Riou Valley sloping down from the Montagne de la Blanche. Before the bridge, a road runs down to an important water sports park.

The landscape becomes more open beyond Les Thuiles and the view embraces the Barcelonnette Basin at the heart of the valley. To the right, the ski resort of **Pra-Loup**⁎ *(see PRA-LOUP)* can be seen clinging to the steep slopes of the Péguieu. On its way to Barcelonnette, the road runs between the tributary valleys of the Riou Bourdoux *(see BARCELONNETTE)* and of the Bachelard.

★ **Barcelonnette** – *See BARCELONNETTE.*

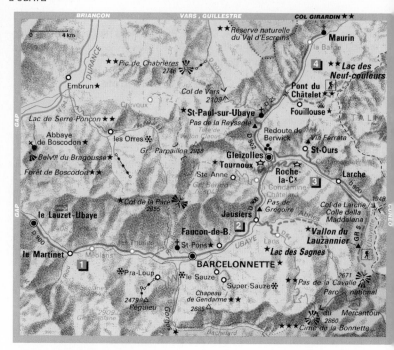

② Barcelonnette Basin

FROM BARCELONNETTE TO LES GLEIZOLLES 15km/9.3mi – about 1hr

★ **Barcelonnette** – *See BARCELONNETTE.*

The road *(D 900)* runs across the Barcelonnette Basin where crops alternate with scree.

Faucon-de-Barcelonnette – This ancient village going back to Roman times is said to owe its name to the numerous birds of prey (falcons) inhabiting the area.
An elegant 12C **campanile** overlooks the village. Note the carved cover of a Gallo-Roman sarcophagus on the right of the church doorway.

The characteristic silhouettes of the Pain de Sucre and Chapeau de Gendarme summits can be seen on the horizon to the south.

Jausiers – The Arnaud brothers, who pioneered the mass emigration of the local population to Mexico in 1805 *(see BARCELONNETTE)*, were natives of this village which has been twinned with Arnaudville in Louisiana since 1995.
Several buildings testify to the success of the emigrants in the New World (Villa Morélia, Villa Manon).

Beyond Jausiers, wooded basins alternate with deep gorges. The strategic importance of the narrow **Pas de Grégoire** and **Pas de la Reyssole** *(see* ④*, Upper Ubaye Valley)* was at the origin of the construction of the Fort de Tournoux.
A road branching off D 900 at La Condamine leads to the small ski resort of **Sainte-Anne**.

★ **Fort de Tournoux** ⊘ – *Turn left before the bridge over the Ubaye, 1km/0.6mi beyond La Condamine-Châtelard, leave the car on the open space. Follow the twisting track which goes up to the middle fort. This is only possible on days when there are guided tours. Hiking boots recommended.*
These extensive fortifications, straddling a ridge line at the confluence of the Ubaye and Ubayette valleys, are a real feat of engineering: there is a difference in height of 700m/2 297ft between the barracks on the river and the upper fort. The main part was built from 1843 to 1865 and the different batteries are linked by underground passages and steps (including a flight of 808 steps). Other batteries were added later on the heights surrounding the fort. The tour includes the middle fort with its monumental machicolated gate, several other buildings and the ramps giving access to the upper fort; from the upper batteries, there is a splendid **view**★ of the two valleys.

Fort de Roche-la-Croix ⊘ – *7km/4.3mi along a forest road branching off D 900 to the right, just before the intersection with D 902.*

This fort, built between 1931 and 1940, formed part of the Maginot line of defence in the Alps; it was designed to be able to survive as independently as a submarine at sea. The tour illustrates the fighting which took place here in 1940 and 1945. Other fortifications along the Ubayette Valley may be open to the public during the season *(inquire at the tourist office in Barcelonnette).*

Fort de Tournoux

★ ③ **Ubayette**

FROM LES GLEIZOLLES TO THE COL DE LARCHE (on the Italian border) *11km6.8mi – about 30min*

The road *(D 900)* follows the Ubayette Valley lined with villages destroyed in 1944 and rebuilt after the war.

St-Ours – A narrow twisting road, branching off D 900, leads to this isolated hamlet, famous for its fortifications which withstood attacks by the Italians in 1940. On the north side of the Rochers de St-Ours, a path gives access to the base of the **Via ferrata de St-Ours** offering rock-climbers two different courses, *l'Ourson* and *l'Aiguille de Luce (see Practical information).*

Tour of the fortifications – *3km/1.9mi round tour starting from the village.* The fort of **St-Ours-Haut** ⊘, an infantry and artillery station, forms the central part of the fortifications. It was used together with the Roche-la-Croix Fort to block the Col de Larche.

A path up the north side of the Rocher de St-Ours leads to the **Via Ferrata de St-Ours** (car park at the end of the village) offering two different routes, "L'Ourson" and "L'Aiguille de Luce".

Larche – This is the last French village on the way to the Italian border, beyond the Col de Larche (1 948m/6 391ft), on the Italian side, lies the lovely Lago della Magdalena.

★★ ④ **Upper Ubaye Valley**

FROM LES GLEIZOLLES TO MAURIN *28km/17.4mi – about 3hr.*

The Briançon road *(D 902),* follows the upper Ubaye Valley. The **Redoute de Berwick** on the right formed part of fortifications built at the beginning of the 18C in anticipation of the union of the Ubaye region with France. The road and the river then go through the corridor formed by the **Pas de la Reyssole.**

St-Paul-sur-Ubaye – This pleasant village is the starting point of numerous excursions. The **church★** dates from the early Middle Ages but the chancel was rebuilt in the 15C and the vault in the 16C, at the end of the Wars of Religion. The doorway is surmounted by a three-lobed rose-window. Note the partly Romanesque octagonal bell-tower with twinned openings, surmounted by a pyramid. Inside, there is a 17C rood beam, interesting 16C paintings and some fine woodwork including a larch ceiling.

The former barn of the Maison Arnaud houses the **Musée Albert-Manuel** ⊘, an annexe of the Musée de la Vallée de Barcelonnette devoted to agriculture and forestry. It displays tools and machinery from the Ubaye region and illustrates traditional techniques, some of which are also demonstrated at a picturesque fair of local produce takes place every year on the third Sunday in August.

From St-Paul, continue along D 25 and the River Ubaye.

The road goes through a succession of small hamlets overlooked by the slender steeples of their remarkably well-restored churches, in particular the façades, often decorated with frescoes.

★★ **Pont du Châtelet** – This site is famous throughout the region; the single-arched bridge, built in 1880, spans the gorge 100m/328ft above the stream.

Turn right towards Fouillouse for an excellent view of the valley around St-Paul.

★ **Fouillouse** – This high-mountain hamlet (alt 1 907m/6 257ft) lies on the edge of a desolate glacial cirque overlooked by the Brec de Chambeyron (alt 3 389m/11 119ft). The houses occupy the south-facing slope; note the charming 16C Église St-Jean-Baptiste. *Food is available at the inn-café in a former shepherd's hut.*

Return to the valley and turn right towards Maurin.

The road rises towards Maurin through a lonely mountain landscape, enhanced by the Mediterranean light, until suddenly the view opens onto the valley, framed by rocky slopes. Farmsteads with tall chimneys and grey schist roofs on larch timbers stand by the roadside. A 3hr hike from the hamlets of La Barge and Maljasset leads to the **Col Girardin**★★.

Église de Maurin – The church stands on an isolated site, surrounded by the old cemetery. An inscription in Provençal tells how an avalanche destroyed the previous 12C church in 1531. This explains why the present edifice, although built in the 16C, has a Romanesque appearance.

Pines of Haute-Provence

Five varieties of pine may be found in the region. You might spot:

An Austrian or **black pine**, regularly used for reforestation and easily identified by its sticky buds and its hard, sharp, dark green needles, which can grow up to 15cm/6in long.

A **Swiss mountain pine**, with its short, shiny needles and rounded hooks on its cones.

An **Aleppo pine**, which has reddish-brown bark, a twisted trunk and grows well in dry soil, but only below 500m/1 640ft. Its soft, comparatively pale green needles grow in pairs.

A **Scots pine**, which prefers higher altitudes. It also bears needles in pairs, although they are darker and more curved than on an Aleppo pine. Its bark peels off in thin strips.

A **larch**, with its distinctive bunches of light green needles and its furrowed, reddish brown trunk. The larch is the only pine which loses its needles in winter

---

HIKES

★ **Vallon du Chambreyon and the Lac des Neuf Couleurs** – *6hr there and back starting from Fouillouse. Leave the car at the entrance of the village. It is possible to make it a two-day trip by booking a night in the Refuge du Chambeyron. It may be necessary to go across névés and it is therefore essential to wear climbing boots.*
🔾 Go through the village and take the path on the left winding its way through a pine wood to a ledge. After climbing for 2hr, hikers will reach the **Refuge du Chambeyron** and **Refuge Jean-Coste** overlooking Lac Premier. The superb mountain landscape is framed by the Aiguille de Chambeyron (3 412m/11 194ft) to the north and the Brec de Chambeyron (3 389m/11 119ft) to the east. The Brec de Chambeyron was always regarded as impossible to climb until two climbers from Fouillouse reached the top in 1878, to be followed the next year by the English mountaineer **Coolidge**.
The path runs northeast to Lac Long. From the top of a mound on the left there is a fine view of Lac Noir. Continue along the path which goes past the Lac de l'Étoile before reaching the magnificent **Lac des Neuf Couleurs**★★ (2 834m/9 298ft). It is possible to continue climbing for another hour to the **Col de la Gypière** (2 927m/9 603ft), in clear weather only; hikers must be used to walking across steep screes.

Return to Fouillouse by the same route.

★ **Hike to the Lac du Lauzanier** – *In Larche, turn right after the border post and leave the car in the Pont Rouge car park (alt 1 907m/6 257ft), 6km/3.7mi further on. 2hr walk to the Lac de Lauzanier along GR 5-56.*
🔾 A great number of sheep spend the summer in this area of the Parc national du Mercantour; the grass is dense and the path is lined with typical high-pasture huts. Continue along the green valley, past a series of waterfalls. The lake (alt 2 284m/7 493ft) fills one of the finest glacial depressions in this part of the Alps. The small chapel used to be a place of pilgrimage.
Experienced hikers can continue to the **Pas de la Cavalle**★★ *(see ST-ÉTIENNE-DE-TINÉE, Hikes). Allow at least 2hr there and back.*

MOUNTAIN BIKE TOUR

★ **Parpaillon round tour** – There is a difference in altitude of almost 1 000m/3 281ft over a distance of 30km/18.6mi. Start from Ste-Anne towards the Chapelle Ste-Anne and the Pont Bérard. This cycle tour is interesting on two counts: it satisfies sports enthusiasts and offers them the opportunity of discovering the Parpaillon military road, build by the *chasseurs alpins* (mountain troops) at the end of the 19C to link the upper Ubaye Valley and the Embrun region from La Condamine to Crévoux.

Keeping the lakes crystal-clear

The high Alpine lakes, without plant life or sediment to cloud the waters, reflect the sky with all the clarity of a mirror, sometimes even taking on a hint of turquiose. But this remarkable purity has its disadvantages. The low oxygen content means that any waste which is thrown into the water, even biodegradeable material, may take years to be broken down, during which time it may damage the delicate biological balance of the lake.

Le VALBONNAIS ★

Michelin map 333 I8 and 244 folds 39, 40 and 41

The lower valley of the River Bonne, a tributary of the Drac, is known as the **Valbonnais**, whereas its upper valley, upstream of Entraigues, is called **Valjouffrey**. This is a region of deep valleys and wild landscapes characteristic of the Dauphiné mountains. At the turn of the 19C, farming supported a population around ten times the size it is today in near self-sufficiency, before the development of forestry brought with it a need for roads to the outside world. The natural environment has survived the changes well, still offering space to roam for hikers as well as for the reintroduced ibexes which returned to the valley in 1989 and 1990.

A beautiful road passes through the valley of the Malsanne, a tributary of the Bonne to the Bourg-d'Oisans *(see BOURG D'OISANS)* region via the Col d'Ornon.

Nearby Sights: L'ALPE d'HUEZ, Le BOURG-D'OISANS, Le CHAMPSAUR, Massif de CHAMROUSSE, Les DEUX-ALPES, Le DÉVOLUY, Route NAPOLÉON, Lacs de LAFFREY, L'OISANS, Le VALGAUDEMAR, VIZILLE

EXCURSION

From La Mure to Valsenestre *55km/34mi – about 1hr 30min*

La Mure – *See Route NAPOLÉON,* **1**.

Between La Mure and Le Pont-Haut, N 85 offers panoramic views, south towards the imposing Obiou and east towards the snow-capped peaks of the Écrins Massif (Roche de la Muzelle, Pic d'Olan).

Pont-Haut – Capped columns (the *demoiselles coiffées*, literally "capped maidens"), more common to the south, are forming in the nearby ravines *(see Lac de SERRE-PONÇON,* **3** *)*.

At Pont-Haut, turn onto D 526.

Valbonnais – Together with Entraigues, Valbonnais is the region's trading centre. As you leave, note the small lake below on the right where the Bonne has been dammed.

Entraigues – This unassuming village is pleasantly situated on a sunny ledge overlooking the confluence of the River Bonne and River Malsanne.

From Entraigues, follow D 117 towards Valjouffrey. At the Pont de la Chapelle, turn left onto D 117ᴬ and follow the Valsenestre road.

★ **Route de Valsenestre** – The road rises above the **Gorges du Béranger★**, then runs along the wooded slopes (larches and firs). Many waterfalls can be seen on the way. Valsenestre, situated at the entrance of a vast glacial cirque, is the starting point of numerous mountain excursions.

Return to D 117.

HIKE

★★ **Haute vallée de la Bonne** – *3hr there and back on foot. Parking compulsory at the entrance of Le Désert-en-Valjouffrey.*

⊠ This pleasant, untaxing itinerary follows the bottom of the glacial valley carved through the crystalline massif.

Le Désert-en-Valjouffrey (1 267m/4 157ft) is the last village along the upper Bonne Valley; barns still line the main street, testifying to the strong rural traditions. Some still bear the year in which they were built and the farmer's initials.

Beyond the hamlet, the U-shaped valley can be seen clearly; it is blocked by an impressive rock wall reaching over 3 000m/9 843ft. On the left, the alluvial cone of a side valley is cultivated thanks to the patient stone-extracting done by the farmers. The dark-grey Aiguille des Marmes (3 046m/9 993ft) soars above the area. On the right, the Bonne flows at the centre of a vast stony river bed. Beyond the park's gate, the landscape becomes wilder *(please read the park regulations carefully)*; at such high altitudes, the stunted, twisted trees become more and more scarce. Heather and juniper grow on the south-facing slope whereas the shadier north-facing slope is dotted with rhododendrons. The path goes across a scree before reaching the **Cascade de la Pisse** on the left.

Walk over the footbridge then through a small pine wood: the trees owe their twisted trunks to the fact that they had to adapt to severe conditions. The meagre pastures give way to bare rock within sight of the imposing Pic d'Olan (3 564m/11 693ft) overlooking the **Cirque de Font-Turbat** glacial cirque.

Return to Le Désert along the same path.

Plateau de VALENSOLE★

Michelin map 334 D9 and 245 folds 21, 33 and 34

This region extends from the central Durance Valley to the first escarpments of the Préalpes de Digne and Préalpes de Castellane, and from the River Bléone to the lower Verdon. It is a vast plateau sloping from east to west and towering 200-300m/656-984ft above the River Durance. The Asse Valley splits it into two: the north includes arid wooded areas and a few inhabited valleys; the south is flatter and more open with vast fields of cereals and *lavandin* (cultivated lavender), laid out like a blue and gold chessboard and dotted with traditional almond trees. The best time to drive across the plateau is at almond blossom time in March, or in July when the scent of the *lavandin* flowers fills the air.

Nearby Sights: CASTELLANE, CÉRESTE, DIGNE-LES-BAINS, Préalpes de DIGNE, Vallée de la Moyenne DURANCE, FORCALQUIER, Monastère de GANAGOBIE, GRÉOUX-LES-BAINS, MANE, MANOSQUE, MOUSTIERS-STE-MARIE, Route NAPOLÉON, RIEZ, ST-JULIEN-DU-VERDON, Lac de STE-CROIX, SISTERON, Grand Canyon du VERDON

EXCURSIONS

Through the lavender fields *89km/55mi – allow 5hr*

Valensole – This large village, spread over a gently sloping hill, is the birthplace of Nelson's great rival during the Napoleonic War, Admiral de Villeneuve (1763-1806), who was defeated and captured at the battle of Trafalgar. St. Mayeul, the founder of the abbey of Cluny (965), was also a native of the town. The townhouses, some with 17C or 18C doors, stand in the shadow of the church and its massive tower; the flat Gothic apse is lit by six lancet windows. The stalls in the chancel date from the 16C. Visit on All Saints' Day (1 November) for the **Rencontres mondiales du conte**, an international storyteller's convention, and spin a yarn or simply listen.

Where to stay

BUDGET

Camping Le Soleil – *Rte de Quinson – 04800 Esparron-de-Verdon – ☎ 04 92 77 13 78 – open Easter-Sept – reservations recommended – 100 pitches: 14.18€ – catering available on site.* This campsite has an exceptional position on the shores of the lake. The pitches are either marked out or on terraces and are well shaded by pines and oak trees. There are facilities for water sports and children's games, a snack bar and a pleasant raised terrace.

EXPENSIVE

Chambre d'hôte Château d'Esparron – *04800 Esparron-de-Verdon – ☎ 04 92 77 12 05 – bernard.de.castellane@wanadoo.fr – closed 1 Nov-Easter – 5rms: from 106.71€.* This castle has belonged to the Castellane family since the 15C and still boasts its keep and main courtyard. A monumental spiral staircase leads to the bedrooms which are vast, with four-poster beds, a fireplace and an antechamber. They are decorated with furniture which in some cases is still in its original position.

Lavender fields on the Plateau de Valensole

From Valensole, drive northeast along D 8.

The road skirts the edge of the Valensole Plateau and runs through fields of cereals and *lavandin*, offering interesting **views** of the Asse Valley.

Turn right onto D 953 towards Puimoisson then left to St-Jurs.

St-Jurs – From the church overlooking this ancient hilltop village, the **view★** extends over the Valensole Plateau and the southern Alps.

Return to D 953.

Puimoisson – In the 12C, Puimoisson belonged to the Knights of the Hospital of St John at Jerusalem. The 15C church stands on a vast square planted with nettle trees, but it was not always as peaceful as it seems today. In the 16C, building work uncovered the buried relics of two saints. Pilgrims flocked to the tiny village until the local people lost patience with the unending streams of visitors and secretly reinterred the relics somewhere else, where they remain hidden to this day.

Continue along D 953.

Riez – *See RIEZ.*

Drive southeast along D 952.

The road follows the Colostre Valley which abounds in lavender distilleries.

Allemagne-en-Provence – *See RIEZ.*

Continue along D 952 through fields of *lavandin* and tulips alternating with vineyards.

★ St-Martin-de-Brômes – Note the date and various inscriptions over the doors of the village's old Romanesque or classical houses. The Romanesque **church** ⊙, dating from the 11C, has a lovely rustic east end and a steeple surmounted by a stone pyramid. Inside, note the carved corbels and, behind the altar, an interesting polychrome tabernacle. The 14C **Tour templière** ⊙, once part of the castle, houses a Roman grave found in 1972, dating from the early 4C AD.

Drive southeast along D 82 to Esparron.

Esparron-de-Verdon – The old village built on either side of a ravine is overlooked by the **Château des Castellane**. Today, Esparron is a small resort for sailing and fishing enthusiasts on the shore of the Gréoux artificial lake.

Go back along the same road and turn left towards Gréoux after 6km/3.7mi.

Barrage de Gréoux – It is 260m/853ft thick at the base, 67m/220ft high and 220m/722ft long. The reservoir holds water from the River Verdon, which supplies the power station at Vinon (producing 130 million kWh) and the Canal de Provence. There is a fine **view★** of Esparron-de-Verdon and the Chateau
The road reaches the lower Verdon Valley and leads to Gréoux.

♯♯ **Gréoux-les-Bains** – *See GRÉOUX-LES-BAINS.*

Return to Valensole along D 8 which follows the Ravin de Laval.

The bees move to summer pastures too

Between early June and mid-July, a feverish activity invades the Plateau de Valensole as beehives are set up everywhere, in time for the flowering of aromatic plants. The honey "season" starts in spring with the flowering of rosemary and reaches its height at the end of June when the lavender fields are in bloom.
At that time, some 250 000 beehives are set up on the plateau; they belong to 500 beekeepers from the nearby *départements* and even from abroad, who rent the land from the farmers. The transport of beehives is strictly regulated; lorries can only operate at night for obvious security reasons but also because the bees do not return to the beehive until after dusk.

Le VALGAUDEMAR★★

Michelin map 334 E/F4 and 244 folds 40 and 41

The Séveraisse, a clear mountain stream, penetrates deeper than any other tributary of the upper Drac into the Écrins Massif; this is the reason why the Valgaudemar Valley is such a popular mountaineering area.
The scenery changes dramatically at Villar-Loubière. Downstream, the deep smiling valley is covered with pastures separated by rows of poplars and dotted with picturesque villages lost amid clusters of trees, whereas upstream, the valley becomes almost oppressively narrow as the river runs between screes collected at the foot of south-facing slopes and densely forested north-facing slopes.

Nearby Sights: Le CHAMPSAUR, Le DÉVOLUY, GAP, Lacs de LAFFREY, Route NAPOLÉON, L'OISANS, Le TRIÈVES, Le VALBONNAIS

BACKGROUND

Parc national des Écrins – Created in 1973, it is France's largest national park, covering an area of 92 000ha/227 332 acres, a third of which are in the Isère *département* and two thirds in the Hautes-Alpes *département.* This high mountain region includes

numerous peaks above 3 000m/9 843ft including the Meije, Pelvoux, Bans, Olan and Agneaux peaks and the highest of them all, the Barre des Écrins which reaches 4 102m/13 458ft. Within the park, which was formerly known as the Parc domanial du Pelvoux, there are glaciers covering an area of 12 000ha/29 653 acres, such as the Glacier Blanc on the north side of the Barre des Écrins, and lakes such as Lac Lauvitel, Lac de Vallon and Lac de l'Eychauda.
The Massif du Pelvoux, situated at the heart of the park, offers marvellous possibilities for mountain climbing, whereas the diverging Vénéon, Valgaudemar and Vallouise valleys are ideal starting points for hiking. More than 1 000km/621mi of footpaths are available inside the park, including the GR 54 "Tour de l'Oisans", the GR 50 "Tour du Dauphiné" offering a wider round trip and the "Tour du Vieux Chaillol" which leads through Champsaur.
A combination of Alpine and Mediterranean climates encourages an extremely varied flora; hardy, resistant species and plants vulnerable to the cold can often be found on the shady and the sunny slopes of the same valley. 1 800 different species of flowering plants grow here, including the lady's slipper, the orange lily, the wormwood, the Alpine columbine and the Alpine sea holly.
This rich habitat also supports 7 000 chamois as well as golden eagles. More than 50 000 sheep spend the summer in the area; in October, their trek down from the high summer pastures is marked by picturesque fairs in the villages of La Chapelle-en-Valgaudemar and St-Bonnet.

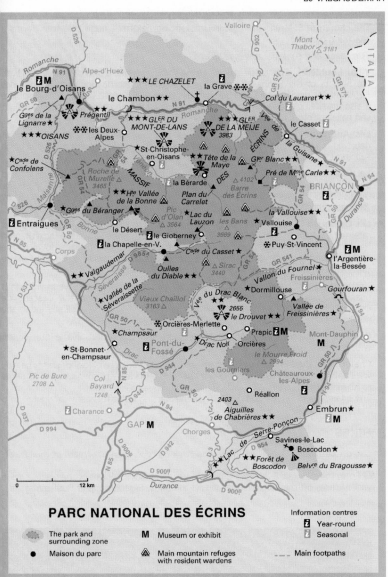

PARC NATIONAL DES ÉCRINS

The park and surrounding zone	M Museum or exhibit	Information centres
● Maison du parc	⚠ Main mountain refuges with resident wardens	🛈 Year-round 🛈 Seasonal
		___ Main footpaths

The peripheral zone, which covers an area of 178 000ha/439 838 acres, comprises the upper valleys of the Drac, Romanche, Malsanne, Guisane and Durance rivers where several winter resorts have developed in recent years.

Information and exhibition centres have been set up at the entrances to the park and the Maison du parc national des Écrins is situated near the village of Vallouise. In summer, guided tours are organised by the Guides de l'Oisans.

EXCURSION

The Upper Séveraisse

FROM THE ROUTE NAPOLÉON TO LE GIOBERNEY ★★

27km/16.8mi – allow 1hr 30min

Leave N 85 3km/1.9mi north of Chauffayer (between Gap and Corps), turning right onto D 16.

This narrow twisting road, which follows the left bank of the Séveraisse and goes through several villages, is nicely shaded. The elegant pyramid of the Pic d'Olan (alt 3 564m/11 693ft) looms ahead.

Le VALGAUDEMAR

Cross the Séveraisse at L'Ubac and turn left towards St-Firmin.

The church of **St-Maurice-en-Valgaudemar**, standing next to a huge lime tree, forms a charming picture.

Turn back and continue towards Villar-Loubière.

Villar-Loubière – The village clinging to the rockside forms a picturesque setting with the heights of the Écrins Massif in the background: Pic de Bonvoisin, Glacier des Aupillous, Pic des Aupillous and Sommet des Bans (3 669m/12 037ft). Villar-Loubière is also the site of Valgaudemar's **last working mill**, used to grind corn but also as a walnut and hazelnut press for oil. Restored in 1979, the thatched mill dates back to 1838.

Les Andrieux – The Aiguille du Midi des Andrieux towering above this hamlet deprives it of any sun for **100 days every year**, as the locals say, from November to February.

La Chapelle-en-Valgaudemar – This mountaineering centre is ideally located beneath the Pic d'Olan. The local Maison du Parc des Écrins can be contacted on ☏ 04 92 55 25 19. Note how many of the house and stable doorways are sheltered by "tounes", the large, arched porches which are typical of the village.

★★ **Les Oulles du Diable** – From La Chapelle it is easy to walk to **Les Portes**, which has retained a few lovely old houses *(1hr there and back)*; fine view of the Pic d'Olan on the left and of the Cime du Vallon. Beyond the hamlet, a path leads down to the bridge spanning the **"Oulles du Diable"**★, a series of potholes carved by erosion, where the River Navette whirls round with a thundering noise.

Upstream of La Chapelle-en-Valgaudemar, D 480 offers views of several waterfalls gushing down from the slopes or from the glaciers; beyond the Cascade de Combefroide, the road enters the wildest part of the valley and climbs along the northern slope.

★ **Cascade du Casset** – This fine waterfall can be seen on the left, at the intersection with the road leading to Le Bourg.

Chalet-hôtel du Gioberney – It lies inside a wild and austere glacial **cirque**★★, nearby waterfalls include the famous **"Voile de la Mariée"**★, ("Bride's Veil") which owes its name to its long, frothy train.
The *chalet-hôtel* (alt 1 700m/5 577ft) is the starting point for many excursions into the Écrins Massif.

HIKES

★ **Lac du Lauzon** – *2hr 30min there and back on foot; start upstream of the Chalet-hôtel du Gioberney, on the left.*
🔲 From the lake (alt 2 200m/7 218ft) there is a splendid **view**★★ of the glacial cirque which closes off the Valgaudemar Valley: the Bans, Pigeonnier and Rouies massifs.

The Valgaudemar in autumn – Pic d'Olan in the background on the right

Where to stay

BUDGET

Hôtel du Mont-Olan – *05800 La Chapelle-en-Valgaudemar* – ☎ *04 92 55 23 03 - closed 16 Sept-30 Mar – ▣ – 28rms: 30.49/41.16€ - ☐ 5.34€ – restaurant 10.67/21.34€.* Join the numerous ramblers who make a stopover in this mountain village and share with them the friendly, lively atmosphere of these two chalets nestling in the bottom of the valley. Modest but comfortable rooms, laundry, traditional dishes and snack menu.

Ferme-auberge Les Clarines – *At Entrepierres – 05800 St-Jacques-en-Valgaudemar – 1km/0.6mi S of St-Jacques-en-Valgaudemar – ☎ 04 92 55 20 31 -☐ – reservations compulsory – 4rms: 35.06/41.92€ – main meal 14.48€.* This farm-inn offers accommodation and meals. Individual tables for passing guests are set up on one side of the dining room. On the other, there is a farm table for all the guests staying here. A choice of holiday appartments and guest rooms.

★**Refuge de Vallonpierre** – 2 280m/7 480ft. *3hr on foot to the refuge by the direct path. Hikers wishing to continue beyond the refuge will need experience of crossing névés and scree slopes.*

🏔 The relatively easy walk up to the refuge offers a good view of the **Glacier de Sirac**, one of the most impressive glaciers in the Écrins massif. The "Sentier du Ministre" joins the winding GR 54, which in turn leads to the Lac de Vallonpierre; the pleasant refuge on the shore is a relaxing place to stop in summer.

The high-pasture lookout

Marmots, who live in colonies above 1 000m/3 281ft, have evolved an unusually exact warning system: one single strident cry announces the presence of a golden eagle or other bird of prey, whereas a series of cries warns of the arrival of a four-legged predator such as a fox or a dog.

Marmots lead a strictly regulated family life. The colony, which forms the social unit, includes several families living in communicating burrows up to 10m/11yd long. During their six-month hibernation period, their body temperature falls to 4°C/39.2°F and they lose around half their weight. At the end of the mating season, which lasts from mid-April to the mid-May, three to four baby marmots are born to every couple.

The species is protected throughout the Alpine nature parks and reserves. The southern part of the Parc national des Écrins, in particular the Valgaudemar region, is known to shelter large colonies.

La VALLOUISE★★
Michelin map 334 G3 and 244 fold 42

The valley of an important tributary of the Durance, which penetrates deep into the Écrins Massif, was named Vallouise in the 15C after Louis XI, who was king of France at the time. The verdant landscapes are reminiscent of Savoie but the luminous sky is characteristic of the southern Alps. Large villages and spacious stone-built houses, typical of the Briançonnais region *(see Introduction)*, add to the charm of the area. The ski resort of Puy-St-Vincent *(see PUY-ST-VINCENT)* has contributed to the development of tourism.

Nearby Sights: L'ARGENTIÈRE-LA-BESSÉE, BRIANÇON, Le BRIANÇONNAIS, Vallée de FREISSINIÈRES, GUILLESTRE, MONT-DAUPHIN, MONTGENÈVRE, Le QUEYRAS, SERRE-CHEVALIER, VARS

BACKGROUND

The Vaudois – Not to be confused with the Swiss from the Vaud canton, these Vaudois or Waldenses were members of a sect founded in the 12C by a rich merchant from Lyon, **Pierre Valdo** (or de Vaux) who believed that salvation depended on the renunciation of all worldly possessions and put his beliefs into practice. Vaudois worship centred on praying, reading the Scriptures and lay preaching, and it was this last that brought Valdo's followers into conflict with the church authorities. As this new sect, which was a forerunner of the Reformation, spread throughout the Lyon region, the Church became worried and the Pope denounced the schismatics, excommunicating Pierre Valdo in 1184.

The Vaudois scattered and took refuge in nearby regions, settling in remote valleys where they were forgotten for two centuries. Ultimately, however, the persecution began again in earnest; the campaign led by the Catholics of Grenoble in 1488 inspired merciless crusades against the "heretics", who were rooted out and slaughtered. The valley of the Gyronde, where many of the new sect had settled, was devastated and came to be known as *Val pute*, or "the bad valley". Louis XI brought the grim persecution to an end, and the area was renamed in his honour.

The final blow came in the 17C, after the Revocation of the Edict of Nantes: 8 000 soldiers were sent to "cleanse" the Vallouise, Valgaudemar and Champsaur valleys and the Vaudois took refuge over the border in the valleys of Piedmont.

Farmhouses – The three-storey houses still common in Vallouise are a reminder of the region's strong farming traditions. The vaulted ground floor would have served as accommodation for the animals, the first floor, often with a larch balcony painted with flowers, provided living quarters for the family and the top floor, or "*baouti*" in local dialect, was designed to be used as a grain store.

EXCURSION

From l'Argentière-la-Bessée to the Pré de Madame Carle

38km – allow 3hr

From L'Argentière, drive along D 994ᴱ which follows the Vallouise Valley.

The road crosses the Durance and the Gyronde near their confluence. Note on the right the ruins of some 14C fortifications improperly called **Mur des Vaudois**, which might equally have been built to keep out marauding mercenaries, or in a vain attempt to halt the spread of the plague.

As you drive through La Bâtie, the twin peaks of Mont Pelvoux come into view with, further south, the Sommet des Bans and the Pic des Aupillous.

Turn right towards Les Vigneaux.

Les Vigneaux – The outside wall of the 15C **church**, to the right of the traditional *réa* (porch), is decorated with **murals** on the theme of vices and their punishments.

At Pont des Vigneaux, follow the road leading to Puy-St-Vincent.

The cliff road rises through a larch forest, opposite the beautifully coloured escarpments of the Tête d'Aval and Tête d'Amont.

The view becomes more open and the Glacier Blanc can be seen overlooked by the Pic de Neige Cordier.

٭ **Puy-St-Vincent** – The fast-expanding ski resort and the summer hiking routes in the nearby Parc national des Écrins have greatly contributed to the development of this village. The Combe de Narreyoux, a lovely pastoral conservation area, also offers fine walks through the beautiful countryside of a high valley. The traditional and peaceful village, **Puy-St-Vincent 1400**, comprises the main resort's hotels. It is linked by chairlift to Puy-St-Vincent 1600. Go round the Église des Prés for a lovely **panorama★** of the

Mountain landscape near the Pré de Madame Carle

Vallouise, framed by mountains: the Pelvoux, Glacier Blanc and Pic de Clouzis to the northwest, the Sommet des Bans to the west, the Pic de Peyre-Eyraute to the east. Then park the car near L'Aiglière and walk up through the meadow to the 16C **Chapelle St-Romain**, which is used for exhibitions. There is a splendid **panorama★** of Vallouise, overlooked by the Pelvoux, Condamine and Montbrison summits. *(Follow the road to Puy-St-Vincent 1600 and park the car on the right, at the intersection of the Narreyoux Valley road)*. Finally, admire the remarkable 15C **frescoes★** in the **Chapelle St-Vincent** ⊘. The modern resort of **Puy-St-Vincent 1600**, situated above the old village and sheltered from the wind by Mont Pelvoux, faces the ski runs on two levels; in winter and summer, a gondola gives access to the upper part of the ski area, just below the Pendine (2 749m/9 019ft). The forested **ski area** is well known for the quality of its snow cover, due to its northern aspect and its location near the Écrins Massif. It comprises 28 runs suitable for all levels of skiing; international competitions, such as the ladies' downhill of the world championship, have been held on the steepest runs. There are 30km/18.6mi of cross-country trails, in particular on the Tournoux Plateau at an altitude of 1 800m/5 906ft.

From Puy-St-Vincent, drive down to Vallouise.

The **Maison du Parc national des Écrins** ⊘ stands on the left, near the intersection with D 994ᴱ. It houses exhibitions relating the flora, fauna and geology of the area and also to the traditional architecture inside the park. Various shows and activities are designed to make children aware of the environment. A nature trail *(30min walk)* offers an introduction to the natural environment.

★ **Vallouise** – This picturesque village has retained a wealth of architectural interest, including large houses with arcades and sundials.
The 15C-16C **church★** with an elegant porch is a fine example of Lombard style in the Alps. Note the splendid wrought-iron chimera's head **lock★** on the carved door.
The chapel on the right of the entrance, dedicated to souls in Purgatory, is covered with frescoes and houses a 15C polychrome Pietà carved in wood. Note the old grain measures and the lengths marked out at the foot of the bell-tower.

Continue along D 994ᵀ running close to the Gyr. Beyond Le Poët-en-Pelvoux, turn right towards Les Choulières.

The road climbs in a series of hairpin bends and offers **close-up views★★** of the Grande Sagne, the twin peaks of the Pelvoux, the Pic Sans Nom and the Ailefroide.

Turn back at Les Choulières and rejoin D 994ᵀ.

Pelvoux – Pelvoux is a family resort with twelve pistes, covering a difference in altitude of 1 050m/3 445ft; some slopes are floodlit at night. A 5km/3.1mi off-piste route is reserved for accomplished skiers and snowboarders.

★★ **Ailefroide** – This hamlet, which seems crushed by the Pelvoux foothills, makes an ideal mountaineering base.

D 204ᵀ follows the bottom of the valley which becomes wilder as it gains altitude; larches become rarer. The jagged Pic de Clouzis soars quite near on the right.

★★ **Pré de Madame Carle** – This hollow, once filled by a lake and since planted with larches is today nothing more than a stony **landscape★★**, characteristic of the Dauphiné mountains. Legend has it that the field is named after a local woman whose husband, a rich nobleman, was consumed with anger on returning from his campaigns and learning of her infidelity. He revenged himself by depriving his wife's horse of water before she went on one of her favourite rides through the fields of Ailefroide. Dying of thirst, the horse plunged into the fast-flowing river and drowned its rider.

HIKES

While the following hikes do not require an understanding of mountaineering techniques, as long as the glaciers are avoided, the correct equipment is absolutely essential. Walkers should not attempt the following itineraries without good hiking boots, rainproof clothing and sunglasses.

The Vallouise offers numerous possibilities for hikes along 50 paths totalling 250km/155mi and it is also a superb mountaineering area. It is one of the rare valleys of the southern Alps to afford views of snow-capped high mountains and many glaciers all year round. It is also fascinating from a geological point of view, and its varied flora and fauna (chamois) are an added attraction.

★★ **Glacier Blanc** – *Fine hike, very popular in summer; 4hr there and back on foot. Difference in altitude: 676m/2 218ft to the refuge. Start from the Pré de Madame Carle, waymarked path. Average difficulty.*
🚶 The path crosses the mountain stream and climbs up the lateral moraine of the glacier, then, leaving the path leading to the Glacier Noir on the left, it winds its way to the Glacier Blanc, once linked to the Glacier Noir but now receding. Continue to

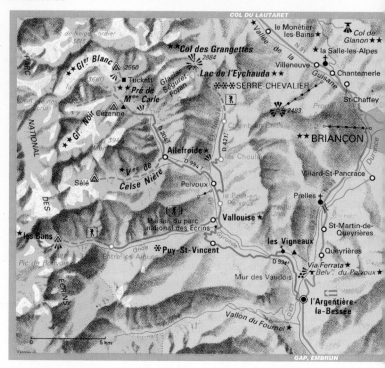

the refuge; difficult sections are fitted with metal ladders. Standing on a ledge on th
right, the former **Refuge Tuckett** (alt 2 438m/7 999ft) has been turned into a moun
taineering museum. In July 1862, the British mountaineer Francis Tuckett and h
French guides set up camp here before attempting the ascent of the Barre des Écrins
From the refuge, there is a fine **view★★** of the glacier and the north side of Mor
Pelvoux.

★★ **Glacier Noir** – *Start from the Pré de Madame Carle (parking area); 1hr 45min up
steep path; 1hr 15min on the way down. Narrow path not suitable for people pron
to vertigo.*
Follow the same itinerary as for the Glacier Blanc but turn left towards the Glacie
Noir and walk alongside it. It takes its name, "the black glacier", from the thick laye
of stones which covers it. The Pic Coolidge stands straight ahead with the Ailefroid
and **Mont Pelvoux** on the left.
There is a fine view of the southern Écrins peaks on the way up.

★ **Refuge des Bans** – *Alt 2 076m/6 811. From Vallouise, drive west along D 504 an
park the car at the end of the road (Entre-les-Aigues, alt 1 615m/5 299ft). This hik
requires a certain amount of stamina: 2hr on the way up and 1hr 30min on the wa
down. Difference in altitude: 540m/1 772ft.*
The Sommet des Bans is already visible from the car park. There is a great variety o
wild flowers along the path which runs close to the mountain stream then climbs .
rocky escarpment to reach the refuge; view★ of the Glacier des Bruyères, the Pic an
Glacier de Bonvoisin.

★ **Lac de l'Eychauda** – *Alt 2 514m/8 248ft. From Vallouise, drive along D 994
along the Gyr Valley towards Ailefroide, then turn right to Les Choulières. Par
the car at the Chalets de Chambran car park (1 720m/5 643ft). Continue on foo
2hr 30min to the lake; 1hr 45min on the way down. Try to start this walk as earl
as possible, as the path is exposed to the full glare of the sun and can be gruellin
in the midday heat.* The ascent is very tiring and monotonous, but the beaut
of the lake makes up for it. Walk along the right side of the lake towards the Co
des Grangettes to get a good view of the **Glacier de Séguret Foran**, which feeds th
lake.

★★ **Col des Grangettes** – *Alt 2 884m/9 462ft. 45min climb from the Lac d
l'Eychauda. Steep, stony path suitable for experienced hikers equipped with non
slip boots.*
Splendid **panorama★★**: the Guisanne Valley in the foreground, backed by Mont Thabo
the Col du Lautaret and Col du Galibier. On a clear day, Mont Blanc can just be see
in the far distance.

VAL-D'ALLOS**

Population 709
Michelin map 334 H7 and 245 fold 22

Situated in the upper Verdon Valley, on the edge of the Parc national du Mercantour, the Val d'Allos includes Allos village and two nearby ski resorts, Le Seignus and La Foux-d'Allos. Owing to its sunny climate, its beautiful landscape, overlooked by the Trois Évêchés, the Grande Séolane and Mont Pelat, and its important facilities the Val d'Allos has become one of the most favoured resorts in the southern Alps.

Nearby Sights: BARCELONNETTE, Route de la BONETTE, COLMARS, EMBRUN, Val d'ENTRAUNES, Route des GRANDES ALPES, PRA-LOUP, ST-ÉTIENNE-DE-TINÉE, Lac de SERRE-PONÇON, SEYNE, UBAYE

THE RESORTS

Allos – Alt 1 400m/4 593ft. This old village is the starting point for many excursions including the popular hike to the Lac d'Allos.
In summer, the outdoor leisure park, set in green surroundings round a large expanse of water, offers swimming plus water chutes, canoeing and also tennis.

The 13C **Église Notre-Dame-de-Valvert** ⊘ is an interesting example of Provençal Romanesque art.

Ski area – cross-country skiers have 25km/15.5mi of marked trails at their disposal near the village, which is linked by gondola to Le Seignus and the ski runs.

Le Seignus – Alt 1 500m/4 921ft. This long-established family resort inaugurated the first ski lift of the upper Verdon region in 1936.

Ski area – Situated just above Allos village, Le Seignus offers a limited but varied ski area; 12 ski lifts and some 20 runs (including the Valcibière red run) between 1 500m/4 921 and 2 400m/7 874ft. The first section is equipped with snow cannon.

** **La Foux-d'Allos** – Alt 1 708m/5 604ft. La Foux is an important modern resort, situated between Allos and the Col d'Allos, whose wooden houses decorated with small balconies blend well with the surroundings.

Parc national du Mercantour

The newest of the national parks, founded in 1979, covers 68 500ha of the Alpes-Maritimes and Alpes-de-Haute-Provence *départements*. The park, which was part of the Italian royal hunting estates until 1861, renewed the transalpine connection in 1987 by agreeing to work in partnership with the Parco naturale delle Alpe Marittime, with which it shares 33km/20.5mi of common boundary.

The altitude of this high mountain region ranges from 500m/1 640ft to 3 143m/10 308ft and the park offers beautiful views of cirques, glacial valleys and deep gorges. It is home to around 6 300 chamois, 300 ibexes and 1 250 mouflons, all well adapted to the Mediterranean climate. Lower wooded areas are inhabited by red deer and roe deer, as well as smaller mammals such as the blue hare, the stoat and the marmot. Among the more common birds are the black grouse and the snow-partridge, and visitors may also spot the short-toed eagle and the golden eagle; the bearded eagle was successfully reintroduced during the summer of 1993. Wolves are also returning, crossing the border from Italy where this protected species is growing in number. Of the 2 000 species of plants in the area, ranging from olive trees  to rhododendrons, the rare *saxifraga florulenta* was chosen as the park's emblem. Walkers can choose from 600km/373mi of paths, not to mention several nature trails, like those at Lac d'Allos and the Col de la Bonette. Two long-distance hiking routes, GR 5 and GR 52 ("Sentier panoramique du Mercantour") also cross park territory.

Information: Information centre in Entraunes: open every day from 3pm to 7pm ☎04 93 05 53 07; Col de la Cayolle refuge: 15 June-15 Sept., ☎04 92 81 24 25.

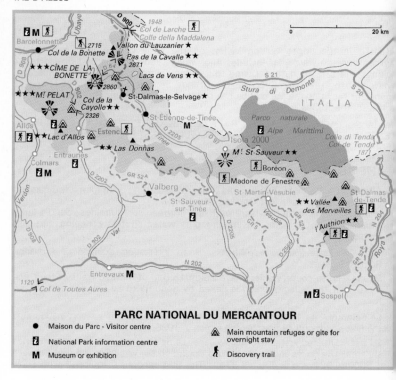

PARC NATIONAL DU MERCANTOUR

●   Maison du Parc - Visitor centre

🛈   National Park information centre

M   Museum or exhibition

⛰   Main mountain refuges or gîte for overnight stay

🚶   Discovery trail

Ski area – Situated inside a glacial cirque, overlooked by the Trois Évêchés Massif, the ski area is spread over five slopes, which catch the sun in turn. It is linked to that of Pra-Loup *(see PRA-LOUP)* to form the **Espace Lumière**, one of the largest ski areas in France with a total of 167km/104mi of runs. The snowfields around La Foux are ideal for advanced skiers, particularly the runs starting from the upper station of the Observatoire gondola and the Pouret chairlift. Snowmaking guarantees resort-level snow until late in the season.

★ **Observatoire gondola** – Alt 2 600m/8 530ft. **View** of the Tête de l'Estrop, the Préalpes de Digne, the Grande Séolane and Mont Pelat from the top station.

Nature trail – *Park the car near the tennis courts and the Pont de Labrau chair-lift as you go into the resort (on the Allos side)*. This hike enables visitors to get to know the area surrounding La Foux-d'Allos and its history.

Lac d'Allos

HIKES

Through the Parc du Mercantour

★★ Lac d'Allos – *This excursion attracts many tourists from mid-July to mid-August. Leave very early. Drive east along D 226 for 13km/8mi; twisting road, narrow and steep from Allos onwards. From the end of the road (parking) allow 1hr there and back on foot and 30min to read the panels and admire the landscape.*

Situated at the heart of the Parc national du Mercantour, the 60ha/148 acre **lake**, which has a maximum depth of 50m/164ft, is the largest natural lake in Europe at that altitude (2 230m/7 316ft). The lake and the surrounding jagged peaks form a splendid barren landscape. The azure-coloured expanse of water is supplied by melting snow and numerous springs. Another glacial lake situated below has been replaced by a bog. This and other phenomena concerning Alpine geology and flora are explained on panels dotted along the **nature trail** linking the car park and the lake. Experienced hikers can combine this excursion to the Lac d'Allos with the one described below.

★★ Mont Pelat – Alt 3 050m/10 007ft. *5hr there and back Difference in altitude: 925m/3 035ft. Leave the car in the same car park as for the previous excursion. The yellow and green-marked path is not too taxing but it is steep and stony towards the end and climbing boots are strongly recommended.*

From the summit, the magnificent **panoramic view★★★** of the roads leading to the Col d'Allos, Col de la Cayolle and Col de la Bonette and of the surrounding summits extends in clear weather to Mont Blanc, Monte Viso and Mont Ventoux. A recently discovered underground glacier runs beneath the surface of Mont Pelat. Twenty-two ibexes, fitted with transmitters, were reintroduced into the Mont Pelat Massif in 1994. This is just one of several projects designed to encourage the survival of this species in the Mercantour (upper Var, upper Verdon and upper Ubaye valleys).

EXCURSION

★★ Route du Col d'Allos

FROM BARCELONNETTE TO COLMARS 44km/27mi – about 2hr

*Please exercise **extreme caution** at crossroads. The Col d'Allos is blocked by snow from November to May.*

Through the rugged landscape between Barcelonnette and the upper Verdon Valley the twisting, narrow track clings to a near-vertical rock face. Extra care is needed, but exhilarating views are guaranteed.

★ Barcelonnette – *See BARCELONNETTE.*

Leaving Barcelonnette and the Ubaye Valley, D 908 climbs above the wild, forested **Gorges du Bachelard★** *(see Route des GRANDES ALPES).*
After the bridge across the Fau, road D 908 makes a detour via the Vallon des Agneliers, overlooked by the ridge of the Grande Séolane (alt 2 909m/9 544ft), before affording more breathtaking bird's-eye views of the deep Gorges du Bachelard.

★★ Col d'Allos - Alt 2 247m/7 372ft. From the platform of the refuge situated just below the pass *(viewing table)*, there is a fine **panorama★** of Barcelonnette to the north, of the Pain de Sucre and Chapeau de Gendarme to the northeast and of the Grand Cheval de Bois to the east. The Grande Séolane and the ski area of La Foux d'Allos can be seen from the pass itself.
The road continues down to the pastures where the Verdon takes its source.

As one approaches Colmars, the road affords a lovely view of the fortified town.

★ Colmars – *See COLMARS.*

VAL-D'ISÈRE ✳✳✳

Population 1 632
Michelin map 333 O5 and 244 fold 32
Local maps see Route de l'ISERAN and Massif de la VANOISE

Val-d'Isère is one of the most prestigious Alpine ski resorts, located in the deep valley o
the upper River Isère at an altitude of 1 850m/6 070ft beneath the imposing Rocher d
Bellevarde, Tête du Solaise and Grande Sassière summits. Beside the resort centre, Va
d'Isère includes the old hamlet of Le Fornet to the east and the modern La Daille to th
north.

Nearby sights: Les ARCS, AUSSOIS, BESSANS, BONNEVAL-SUR-ARC
BOURG-ST-MAURICE, Route des GRANDES ALPES, Route de l'ISERAN, L
Haute MAURIENNE, Route du MONT-CENIS, La TARENTAISE, TIGNES
Massif de la VANOISE

THE RESORT

Ski area – Val d'Isère owes its success and its reputation among experienced skiers t
its abundant snow cover and to its extensive snowfields, linke
with the Tignes area to form the **Espace Killy**✳✳✳; the Face de Bellevarde, "S" de Solais
and Tunnel runs are all well known as impressive tests of skil
Some 30 passes and summits soaring to 3 000m/9 843ft, in a 10km/6mi radius o
the resort, ensure that cross-country enthusiasts are also well catered for.

The **Critérium de la Première Neige**, held on the Oreiller Killy run, has marked th
beginning of the international Alpine skiing season since 1955, and the men
Alpine events of the 1992 Olympic Games were held along the spectacula
Bellevarde slopes.

In summer, Val-d'Isère is also a lively holiday resort with summer skiing on th
Grand Pissaillas Glacier and an International Four-wheel-drive Vehicles Show. I
addition, Val d'Isère is also part of the beautiful **Route de l'Iseran**✳✳✳ *(see Route d
l'ISERAN)*.

HIGHLIGHT

Viewpoints accessible by cable car

✳✳✳**Rocher de Bellevarde** ⊙ – Alt 2 826m/9 272ft. *1hr there and back, including
7min cable-car ride or 4.5min by* **Funival** ⊙ *mountain railway starting from La Daille
From the upper station, steep flights of steps lead to the viewing table in 5min. Th
splendid **panoramic view**✳✳✳ includes Val-d'Isère 1 000m/3 281ft below, and th
summits all around.

✳✳**Tête du Solaise** ⊙ – Alt 2 551m/8 369ft. *45min there and back, including
6min cable-car ride.* During the journey and from the platform of the café situate
on the summit, the magnificent view embraces the Isère Valley, Val-d'Isère an

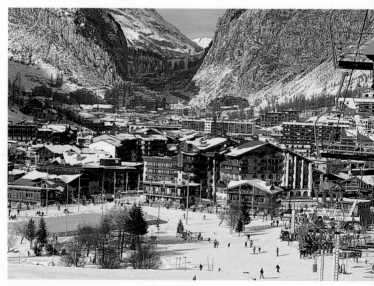

Val-d'Isère

the Lac du Chevril, the Bellevarde Olympic run immediately opposite and a **panorama** of the Grande Sassière, Mont Pourri, the Grande Motte and the Pointe de la Sana.

★ **Col de l'Iseran** – *Access by the Fornet cable car and the Vallon de l'Iseran gondola in winter. In summer it is preferable to drive up to the pass along the impressive Route de l'Iseran (see Route de l'ISERAN).*
From the pass, skiers can go up to the Grand Pissaillas Glacier (3 300m/10 827ft) where they can enjoy superb **views**★★ of the Haute Maurienne and Haute Tarentaise.

HIKES

There is little to inspire walkers in the ski area itself, but some excellent itineraries begin in the Parc national de la Vanoise, a few kilometres from Val-d'Isère.

★★ **Refuge de Prariond and Col de la Galise** – *Park the car by the Pont St-Charles on the way to the Col de l'Iseran. 1hr on foot up to the refuge then 2hr to the pass. Difference in altitude: 900m/2 953ft. 2hr on the way down.*
🔼 The steep path goes through the Gorges du Malpasset, where ibexes roam freely, to the foot of the Glacier des Sources de l'Isère. Beyond the refuge it becomes steeper until it reaches the Col de la Galise (alt 2 990m/9 810ft).

★★ **Col des Fours** – *Taxing hike requiring a lot of stamina. From the centre of Val-d'Isère, drive south to Le Manchet (3km/1.9mi, parking area). 1hr 30min on foot up to the Fonds des Fours refuge then 1hr to the pass. Difference in altitude: 1 100m/3 609ft. 2hr on the way down. It is recommended to wear a waterproof windcheater and warm clothing, as the wind at the top of the pass can be bitterly cold.*
🔼 At the refuge, pause to take in the **view**★ of the Grande Sassière, the Mont-Blanc Massif, the Dôme de la Sache and Bellevarde. The path then veers to the left and climbs to the pass (3 000m/9 843ft): splendid **view**★★ of a lake surrounded by the Glacier de la Jave and of the Maurienne and Tarentaise mountains. Chamois are frequently seen in the area.

Massif de la VANOISE★★★

Michelin map 333 M4 to 06 and 244 folds 20, 21 and 31-33

The magnificent landscapes of the massif have fascinated mountaineers since the 19C; it seemed therefore quite natural to create the first French national park in the Vanoise. As one of its goals was the preservation of the last ibexes in the Alps, this animal was chosen as the first emblem of the park, but it is only one of a thousand species of flora and fauna in the park's 53 000ha/130 966 acres. The park is the ideal setting for romantic walks and breathtaking rock-climbing, not to mention some exhilarating ski runs on the 1 000km/621mi of pistes to be found in the area.

Nearby Sights: Les ARCS, AUSSOIS, Vallée des BELLEVILLE, BESSANS, BONNEVAL-SUR-ARC, BOURG-ST-MAURICE, CHAMPAGNY-EN-VANOISE, COURCHEVEL, Route des GRANDES ALPES, Route de l'ISERAN, Route de la MADELEINE, La Haute MAURIENNE, MÉRIBEL, MODANE, Route du MONT-CENIS, PRALOGNAN, La TARENTAISE, TIGNES, VAL-D'ISÈRE

SKI AREA

The peripheral zone of the Vanoise Massif includes an exceptionally fine skiing area with three major assets: its size, the quality of its equipment and of its snow cover. The Maurienne Valley specialises in charming family resorts, whereas the Tarentaise has, since the 1930s, acquired an impressive number of winter sports resorts. The high quality of these resorts was officially acknowledged when the 1992 Winter Olympics were held there. The Espace Olympique Pass gives access to the following areas: the Trois Vallées, the Espace Killy, the Espace La Plagne-les-Arcs, Pralognan, Ste-Foy-Tarentaise, La Rosière, Valmorel and Les Saisies.

Tourist offices will be able to supply a copy of the "Guide du skieur Trois-Vallées" to help you plan your route through the ski area. The well-marked pistes are generally open from December to May; if possible, always ask one of the "pisteurs" on patrol about snow conditions and any avalanche warnings. Once on the slopes, be aware of the time and the weather so that you may be sure to return to your base in good time.

★★★**Espace Killy** – This skiing area, linking that of **Tignes**★★★ and **Val-d'Isère**★★★, has gained international fame because of its size (100km²/39sq mi), its high-quality snow cover (all year skiing on the Grande Motte Glacier) and its superb high-mountain scenery. There are some 100 ski lifts and 300km/186mi of runs.
Val-d'Isère is particularly suitable for advanced skiers whereas Tignes has easier runs and skiers are able to ski right down to the resort.

★★★**Trois Vallées** – This ski area, covering 400km≤ /154sq mi and extending over the **St-Bon Valley** (**Courchevel**★★★, **La Tania**), the **Allues Valley** (**Méribel**★★★) and the **Belleville Valley**★★★ (**St-Martin-de-Belleville**★, **Les Ménuires**★★ and **Val-Thorens**★★★), is the largest in the Alps: 210 ski lifts including 37 gondolas and cable cars, 300 runs and itineraries totalling 700km/435mi. These are extremely varied: there are large pisted runs for all levels of proficiency, technical pistes – among the most difficult in the Alps – and numerous possibilities of off-piste skiing in conservation areas, as well as 110km/68mi of cross-country skiing trails. The Trois-Vallées owe their success to the efficient links between resorts, to their excellent snow conditions and a superb diversity of mountain landscapes and life.
In addition to the two main ski areas of the Trois-Vallées and the Espace Killy, the Tarentaise offers a choice of first-class resorts such as **La Plagne**★★ and **Les Arcs** ★★★/**Peisey-Nancroix**★.
There are also smaller resorts which are interesting from a sightseeing point of view and enjoy very good snow cover conditions, such as **La Rosière**★ and **Valmorel**★.

THE NATIONAL PARK

The **peripheral zone (1 450km²/560sq mi)** offers an impressive range of first-class accommodation and sports facilities. The Tarentaise region alone includes some of France's largest and most prestigious winter sports resorts, whereas picturesque hamlets and villages like Bonneval-sur-Arc and Le Monal take life at a more restful pace. Churches and chapels including St-Martin-de-Belleville, Champagny, Peisey-Nancroix, Bessans and Lanslevillard are proof of a remarkable architectural and artistic heritage. Five information centres known as *"portes du Parc"*, are located at Orgère (near Modane), at Fort Marie-Christine (Aussois), at Plan du Lac (above Termignon), at Rosuel (Peisey-Nancroix) and at Le Bois (Champagny-le-Haut).

The **central zone (530km²/205sq mi)** is essentially a high-mountain area, with 107 summits above 3 000m/9 843ft and glaciers covering an area of 88km²/34sq mi.
The name Vanoise refers to the huge ice cap extending from the Col de la Vanoise to the Col d'Aussois. The most famous summits are: Mont Pourri (3 779m/12 398ft) and the Sommet de Bellecôte (3 416m/11 207ft) in the north; the Aiguille de la Grande Sassière (3 747m/12 293ft) in the northeast; the Grande Casse

Y. Bontoux

Lac Blanc and the Col de Soufre *(see PRALOGNAN-LA-VANOISE)*

(3 855m/12 648ft) and the Grande Motte (3 656m/11 995ft) in the centre; the Pointe de la Sana (3 456m/11 339ft) and the Pointe de Méan Martin (3 330m/10 925ft) in the east, and finally the Massif de Péclet-Polset (3 562m/11 686ft) and the Dent Parrachée (3 684m/12 087ft) in the south.
Below 2 000m/6 562ft, there are some beautiful forests with a variety of species including spruce, larch and arolla pine. An exceptionally rich flora includes some very rare arctic species such as the buttercup and the catchfly, as well as the familiar gentians, rhododendron and anemones, sprouting freely by the side of the road and, here and there, the famous edelweiss.
The fauna has considerably expanded since the creation of the park, in which time the population of 40 ibexes has grown to 1 000. Hikers are likely to meet marmots along their way, but spotting rarer species, such as the ptarmigan, rock partridge, black grouse and golden eagle, requires a great deal of patience and a fair knowledge of animal life in mountain areas.

EXCURSIONS

Roads running through the picturesque Isère and Arc valleys are ideal for a drive around the park, but the heart of the massif cannot be explored by car; the best scenery is only available to skiers in winter and hikers in summer. The following sections may be useful:

★★ **La Tarentaise** *(see La TARENTAISE)*

★ **La Haute Maurienne** *(see La MAURIENNE)*

★★ **Route du Petit-Saint-Bernard** *(see BOURG-ST-MAURICE: Excursions)*

★ **Route du Mont-Cenis** *(see Route du MONT-CENIS)*

★★ **Route de l'Iseran** *(see Route de l'ISERAN)*

★★★ **Vallée des Belleville** *(see La Vallée des BELLEVILLE)*

★★ HIKES

The Vanoise massif offers an almost limitless variety of paths to explore. It can be hard to know where to start, but first-time visitors should consider basing themselves in Pralognan, Champagny, Peisey-Nancroix or Bonneville-sur-Arc, although Tignes, Les Ménuires at St-Martin-de-Belleville, Méribel and Courchevel, better known as ski resorts, also make good starting points for walking expeditions. Paths in the central zone are the most frequented, so consider setting out on one of the quieter routes on the periphery, where the landscape is every bit as beautiful.
The best time for a walking holiday is between 4 July and 15 August, when the flowers are in bloom. Bear in mind that there may still be snow on the ground until the beginning of July, which can add to the difficulty of walks above 2 000m/6 562ft, but a holiday in early summer or early autumn does at least have the advantage of avoiding the crowds at the height of the season. The best hikes described in this guide are listed below and graded according to their length and level of difficulty.

MASSIF DE LA VANOISE

CHAMONIX, AOSTE

2928 ebranlette

2188 Col du P^it St-Bernard ★

★★ ROUTE DU P^it ST-BERNARD ★★

N 90

la Rosière 1850 ✳

le Châtelard

D 902

le Miroir

la Sassière ★★

Becca du Lac 3402

△ 3456
TESTA
DEL RUTOR

ITALIA

Ghiacciaio del Rutor
Glacier du Rutor

△ 3300
Mt Paramont

Grisanche

Ste-Foy-Tarentaise

HAUTE TARENTAISE ★

Arc 2000

le Monal ★★

Chenal

▲ 3226
le Rouge ★★★

Mt POURRI △ 3779

Dôme de la Sache 3608

ISÈRE

D 902

Barrage de Tignes ★★

les Boisses

Aig^le Percée △ 2778

le Saut

★★ Col de Tourne 2656

hardonnet 2870

2653 du Palet

Val Claret

ESPACE

Gr^de Rousse 3607 △

Pointe du Nantcruet 3610

Réserve de la Gr^de Sassière ★★

AIGUILLE DE LA GR^de SASSIÈRE 3747

Lac de la Sassière ★★

Aig^le du Dôme △ 3026

Gl. de Rhême-Golette

Tsanteleina 2605

L. du Chevril

TIGNES ★★★

Pont St-Charles

VAL D'ISÈRE ★★★

Col de la Galise ★★ 2990

Prariond ★★

ITALIA

VAL DI RHÊMES

PARCO NAZIONALE DEL GRAN PARADISO

2826 R^er de Bellevarde ★★★

KILLY ★★★

le Manchet

D 902

Col de l'Iseran ★ 2764

Gr^de Aig^le Rousse

le Carro ★★

Glacier de la Gr^de Motte

LA GR^de MOTTE ★★★ 3656

GR 55

★★★ Pointe des Lessières 3041

▲ 3000

Col des Fours ★★

GR 5

Chalets de la Duis ★★

l'Ecot

les Evettes ★★

ASSE

léise

P^nte DE LA SANA 3456

P^nte DE MEAN MARTIN 3330 △

Bonneval-s-Arc ★★

L. des Pareis

Gl^er des Evettes

Entre-deux-Eaux

Rocheure

ARC

3638 △ Albaron

Plan du Lac ★★

Gr^e Roc Noir △ 3583

Bessans ✳

Vallée d'Avérole ★★

Bessanese 3592

D 83

GR 5

D 902

Lanslebourg-Mont-Cenis

Lanslevillard

HAUTE MAURIENNE ★

Avérole

△ 2210

N 6

Val-Cenis ✳

P^nte de Charbonnel 3750 △

mignon

ères

2770 △ la Gr^de Turra

2084

Col du Mont Cenis ★

2800 Col de la Met ★★

P^nte de Ronce 3612 △

Ribon

N 6

ROUTE DU Mt CENIS ★

Lac du Mont Cenis ★

△ 3478 Mt Lamet

CENIS

MASSIF

DU

nay

MONT

ITALIA

S 25

0   5km

Family rambles

These short and easy itineraries are suitable for families with children, but it is advisable to be properly equipped all the same.

★★ **Lac de la Sassière** *(see TIGNES)*

★★ **Le Monal** *(see LA TARENTAISE)*

★★ **Refuge de Prariond** *(see VAL-D'ISÈRE)*

★★ **Plan du Lac** *(see la Haute MAURIENNE)*

★★ **Refuge d'Avérole** *(see BESSANS)*

★★ **Fond d'Aussois** *(see AUSSOIS)*

★ **Chalets de la Duis** *(see BONNEVAL-SUR-ARC)*

★ **Plan de Tuéda** *(see MÉRIBEL)*

Hikes

These itineraries require stamina and physical fitness but are not technically difficult

★★★ **Col de la Vanoise** *(see PRALOGNAN-LA-VANOISE)*

★★★ **Col du Palet and Col de la Tourne** *(see TIGNES)*

★★★ **Col de Chavière** *(see MODANE)*

★★★ **Crève-Tête** *(see Route de la MADELEINE or La vallée des BELLEVILLE)*

★★ **Lac de la Plagne** *(see Les ARCS)*

★★ **Refuge du Carro** *(see BONNEVAL-SUR-ARC)*

★★ **Refuge des Évettes** *(see BONNEVAL-SUR-ARC)*

★★ **Lacs Merlet** *(see COURCHEVEL)*

★★ **Col des Fours** *(see VAL-D'ISÈRE)*

Itineraries for experienced hikers

These itineraries require stamina and include difficult sections (extremely steep o vertiginous paths). They do not, however, require any knowledge of rock-climbin or mountaineering techniques *(non-slip climbing boots essential)*.

★★★ **Pointe du Chardonnet** *(see TIGNES)*

★★★ **Pointe de l'Observatoire** *(see AUSSOIS)*

★★★ **Pointe des Lessières** *(see Route de l'ISERAN)*

Three-day round tour of the Vanoise glaciers

This itinerary is suitable for experienced hikers in good physical condition. Befor leaving, it is essential to book overnight stays in refuges (ask at the Pralognan touris office) and to inquire about the weather forecast over several days. Leave very ear in the morning in order to reach the refuge before 7pm (reservations are cancelle after that time). See the advice on hiking given in the Practical information sectior.

First day: Pralognan – **Mont Bochor★** (by cable car) – **Col de la Vanoise★★★** – **Refuge d l'Arpont**.

Second day: Refuge de l'Arpont – La Loza – La Turra – **Refuge du Fond d'Aussois★★★**.

Third day: Refuge du Fond d'Aussois – Col d'Aussois – **Pointe de l'Observatoire★★★** – Le Prioux – Pralognan.

Main viewpoints accessible by lift

★★★ **Cime de Caron** – *See La vallée des BELLEVILLE: Val-Thorens*

★★★ **Bellevarde** – *See VAL-D'ISÈRE*

★★★ **Aiguille Rouge** – *See Les ARCS*

★★★ **La Grande Motte** – *See TIGNES*

★★★ **La Saulire** – *See COURCHEVEL*

★★ **Mont du Vallon** – *See MÉRIBEL*

★★ **Sommet de Bellecôte Gondola** – *See La PLAGNE*

VARS★★

Population 941
Michelin map 334 I5 and 245 fold 10

Situated between Guillestre and Barcelonnette, near the pass (2 109m/6 919ft) that links l'Ubaye and the Haut-Embrunnais, Vars is one of the main winter and summer resorts of the southern Alps, highly regarded for its sunny climate, the quality of its facilities and the beauty of its natural environment.

Nearby sights: ABRIÈS, L'ARGENTIÈRE-LA-BESSÉE, BARCELONNETTE, BRIANÇON, Le BRIANÇONNAIS, CEILLAC, EMBRUN, Vallée de FREISSINIÈRES, Route des GRANDES ALPES, GUILLESTRE, MOLINES-EN-QUEYRAS, MONT-DAUPHIN, Le QUEYRAS, ST-VÉRAN, Lac de SERRE-PONÇON, L'UBAYE, La VALLOUISE

THE RESORT

Accommodation is spread over three traditional hamlets (Ste-Marie, St-Marcellin and Ste-Catherine) and a modern resort (Les Claux) at altitudes ranging from 1 600m/5 249ft to 1 800m/5 906ft. **Ste-Marie-de-Vars** and **Les Claux** alone offer direct access to the ski runs.

Ski area – Linked to the slopes of Risoul under the name of **Domaine de la Forêt Blanche**, the resort is constantly expanding; at present, it includes 56 ski lifts and 170km of runs with adequate snow cover. Its mostly quite gentle slopes are ideal for intermediate skiers who love beautiful scenery. Several fine runs start from the Pic de Chabrières, and advanced skiers can enjoy the "Olympic" run above Ste-Marie and the "Mur du Grand Ubac" near Les Claux. Vars also boasts a number of high-speed runs on which the **Speed-skiing** World Championships are held. Off-piste skiing can be practised in the Risoul area and there are 25km/16mi of marked cross-country skiing trails.

In summer, Vars is an excellent hiking base. In addition to skiing and rambling, the resort offers a wide choice of summer and winter activities including skating, snowmobiling, swimming, riding, paragliding and squash. Mountain bikers can test their stamina on the longest course in Europe (32km/20mi).

EXCURSIONS

The Col de Vars may be blocked by snow from December to April.

From Guillestre, drive south along D 902.

Between Guillestre and Peyre-Haute, there are views of the fortified city of Mont-Dauphin *(see MONT-DAUPHIN)* perched on its promontory, of the Durance Valley upstream of Embrun and of the Guil Valley. The road rises up to a rocky ridge separating the Rif-Bel (Val d'Escreins) and Chagne valleys.

Peyre-Haute viewing table – *15min there and back on foot; 100m/109yd upstream of Peyre-Haute (panel), climb onto the mound on the left.* The **view★** includes, from left to right, the Ailefroide, the Pic sans Nom, Mont Pelvoux, and the Pic de Neige Cordier with the Glacier Blanc coming down from it.
The next few bends offer views of the snow-capped summits of the Écrins Massif. The **Route du Val d'Escreins★★** *(see below)* branches off on the left.

The road goes through the hamlets which make up the resort of Vars.

★★ **Vars** – From Vars to the pass, the road runs along the foot of the slopes, equipped with ski lifts between Ste-Marie and the Refuge Napoléon.

Musée du KL (Refuge Napoléon) – This museum just off N 902, before the pass, is devoted to speed skiing, from its origins in the 1930s to the latest refinements of the **Kilomètre Lancé** or "flying Kilometre". Open to amateurs as well as speed specialists, the Pic de Chabrières is the site of the world's fastest piste, but be warned: the 1.4km/0.87mi slope has an average gradient of 52%, reaching a dizzying 98% at its steepest point. No wonder, then, that racers need a full 850m braking zone to slow down. *(For more on the refuges Napoléon, see Le BRIANÇONNAIS, ⑤).*

Col de Vars – Alt 2 109m/6 926ft. In the middle of meagre pastures dotted with blocks of sandstone stands a monument commemorating the renovation of the road by Alpine troops. On the way down to l'Ubaye, the pastoral landscape remains austere. The truncated summit of the Brec de Chambeyron (alt 3 390m/11 122ft), preceded by a long ridge, can be seen to the east.
Between Melezen and St-Paul, there is an interesting group of *"demoiselles coiffées"* (capped maidens) on the roadside. It is possible to park the car before the small bridge and walk close to them *(see SERRE-PONÇON, ③ and Sights Nearby)*.

Eating out

MODERATE

Chez Plumot – *Aux Claux* – ☎ *04 92 46 52 12* – *closed 28 Apr-9 Jun and 3 7 Dec* – *21.34/30.49€*. The dining room here is cosy and private with a mez zanine level, and the food served is simple, generous and tasty. If it is avail able, we recommend the *tarte tatin*.... Special fast service menu option a lunchtime.

Where to stay

MODERATE

Hôtel L'Écureuil – *Aux Claux* – ☎ *04 92 46 50 72* – *closed 25 Apr-9 Jun and 10 Sept-7 Dec* – 🅿 – *19rms: 68.60/80.80€* – 🍴 *6.10€*. This small chalet off the beaten track, is no exception to the rule; wood dominates the deco and gives the premises a warm and friendly atmosphere. There is a pleasan lounge-bar with a modern fireplace. Rooms are partially panelled with colour ful fabrics.

On the town

La Gruate – *Cours Rohner* – ☎ *04 92 46 67 00* – *www.hotel-les-escondus.com* – *daily 7am-1.30am* – *closed end Apr-Jun and Sept-Christmas*. The piano-bar a the Hôtel des Escondus is named after the winch that was once used to hois bundles of hay into the haylofts. Nowadays, with a terrace that is heated in win ter and a well-kept garden, La Gruate is a popular place, especially on concer nights and when the big game is being shown on the giant screen. One furthe point in its favour: the owner is a master without peer when it comes to con cocting delicious little cocktails.

Le Shuss – *Cours Brayer* – ☎ *04 92 46 53 28* – *daily 9am-11pm* – *closed mi Apr-Jun and Sept-mid-Dec*. This is a shining example of a classic and unpreten tious little bar in which it is pleasant to stop for a quick drink or for a pancake Nice terrace with a view of the ski slopes.

Shopping

Le Point Show – *Cours Rohner* – *depending on the shops, closed mid Apr Jun and Sept-mid Dec*. This shopping arcade is without a doubt the livelies of those in the resort. In fact, it not only offers shops of every kind, but also bars and small restaurants, as well as a cinema, games arcade and swimming pool.

Sports

Indiana Forest – 🎬 – *La Charpenterie* – ☎ *04 92 46 52 10 / 06 09 52 35 62* – *Jun-Sept: daily 10am-7pm* – *closed Sept-Jun*. Inspired by archaeologica adventurer Indiana Jones, well known to fans of Steven Spielberg's films, this adventure circuit is riddled with pitfalls and obstacles such as rope ladders anc footbridges made from lianas. Children will have a whale of a time while the grown-ups can also put their skills to the test.

** Réserve naturelle du Val d'Escreins

From Vars, drive down towards Guillestre along D 902; turn right onto a small roac following the Val d'Escreins.

The Rif-Bel Valley, which is inaccessible for eight months of the year, became the **Réserve naturelle du Val d'Escreins** ⊘ (2 500ha/3 707 acres) in 1964 and was later com bined with the Parc naturel régional du Queyras.

At the end of the valley, the forested slopes give way to barren summits, including the **Pic de la Font Sancte** (alt 3 387m/11 112ft). The name, meaning "holy fountain", comes, according to tradition, from a spring discovered by a young shepherdess which became a place of pilgrimage in times of drought. The climb to the summit is only suitable for experienced hikers, who are rewarded with one of the finest panoramas in the Alps.

The reserve, open to visitors in summer, offers 37km/23mi of marked footpaths linking this valley to that of Ceillac in the north and Maurin in the east. Accommodation is available during the season at the Basse Rua refuge, allowing sea soned walkers to climb to the Col des Houerts *(map available from tourist information centres)*.

St-Marcellin-de-Vars – This ancient hamlet has retained its mountain-village atmosphere.

A pleasant **walk to the castle ruins★** starts in St. Marcellin. *Leave the car in one of St-Marcellin's car parks. Allow 1hr 30min there and back on foot (steep path).*
Walk along the right side of the church. The path is marked in yellow. After the first bend to the left, carry straight on *(ignore the house up on the right)*. The path crosses a small road. Continue to the summit where you will find explanations about the ruined castle and enjoy an extended **view★** of the various hamlets around Vars, of Guillestre and of Mont-Dauphin.

HIKES

★★ Pic de Chabrières – *In winter: access via the* **Chabrières gondola** ⊙, *the Crévoux and Chabrières chairlifts. In summer: access via the Chabrières gondola, then on foot (3hr 30min there and back). Climbing boots recommended.*
🚶 The upper station of the **Télecabine de Chabrières** stands at the foot of the **Kilometre lancé** speed-record trial run; view of Ste-Marie, Ste-Catherine, the Col de Vars and the Crêtes de l'Eyssina.
The **Pic de Chabrières** (alt 2 727m/8 947ft) offers a magnificent **panorama★★** of the "Forêt Blanche" backed by the Pic de la Font Sancte, the Queyras Massif, the snow-capped Pelvoux and the peaks surrounding the Lac de Serre-Ponçon, which is visible from the **Col de Crévoux★**.

★★ Hike to the Tête de Paneyron – Alt 2 787m/9 144ft. *Leave the car at the Col de Vars. 3hr 30min there and back on foot. Difference in height: 677m/2 221ft. It is advisable to wear mountain boots.*
🚶 Walk down towards Barcelonnette for a few minutes and turn left onto a wide path which, after around 20min, leads to a shepherd's house; above and to the right are some cairns which mark the way. After a 10min walk across pastures, you will find a clearer path which climbs very steeply as it nears the summit. Beautiful **panorama★★** of the ski area from the Pointe de l'Eyssina to the Val d'Escreins and of the road to the Col de Vars, from Guillestre to the River Ubaye.

Return by the same route.

Le VERCORS★★★

Michelin map 332 F2 to E3 and 244 folds 27,28 and 37-39

Rising above Grenoble like a fortress, the massive limestone plateau of the Vercors forms the largest natural park in the northern Alps. Daring cliff roads follow the deep gorges carved by tributaries of the lower Isère and run deep into thick beech and conifer forests. Its southern uplands, arid and deserted, feel like the plains of the Midi; the forested northern heights have the open, untouched look of the Canadian wilderness. The Vercors attracts alpine and cross-country skiers who brave the bitter winters in search of peace and quiet and natural beauty.

Nearby Sights: Massif de CHAMROUSSE, Massif de la CHARTREUSE, DIE, GRENOBLE, Lacs de LAFFREY, PONT-EN-ROYANS, Le TRIÈVES, VILLARD-DE-LANS, VIZILLE

A POTHOLER'S PARADISE

The "crust" of the Vercors Plateau consists of a gently undulating layer of limestone from the Cretaceous period, up to 300m/984ft thick in places, which forms impressive cliffs in the gorges and along the edge of the massif. Water flows freely through these calcareous rocks, streams disappear into sink-holes known as *scialets* similar to the *chourums* of the Dévoluy region, and reappear as resurgent springs. The most striking example of this phenomenon is the underground **Vernaison**; identified in the depths of the Luire Cave, it reappears in the Bournillon Cave, 20km/12mi further on, which makes it one of the major underground rivers in France.

The exploration of the **Gouffre Berger**, which opens on the Sornin Plateau (west of Sassenage), led the Spéléo-club de la Seine to a depth of 1 141m/3 743ft.

STRONGHOLD OF THE RESISTANCE

The strategic advantage of the Vercors Massif, thinly populated and easy to defend, became apparent to the local resistance movements, or *maquis*, as early as 1942 and several defensive camps were established from 1943 onwards.

Two keen amateur mountaineers, the writer Jean Prévost and the architect Pierre Dalloz, and the head of the Secret Army, General Delestraint, hatched a scheme, known as the **"plan Montagnards"**, to establish an allied bridgehead in the Vercors.

By March 1944 there were two Resistance groups in the Vercors, totalling 400 men. After D-day, there were 4 000 volunteers receiving military training from professional soldiers. A first German assault on St-Nizier was beaten back on the 15 June; and on 3 July the "République du Vercors" was proclaimed and supplied with Allied airdrops of light armament and material. The area was soon surrounded by two German Alpine divisions numbering 15 000 men and, on 21 July, German gliders used the airfield intended for allied planes to drop special commandos and SS troops. After three days of fierce fighting, the outnumbered Resistance fighters retreated towards the Forêt de Lente while the St-Martin Hospital was evacuated south to the Grotte de la Luire. The hospital was stormed by a commando unit on 27 July: one Resistance fighter managed to survive by hiding in a fissure in the rock, but the remaining patients, two doctors and a priest were killed and the nurses deported to Ravensbrück concentration camp. Reprisals continued until 19 August. A number of memorials in the Vercors Massif commemorate these events.

HIGHLIGHT

Parc naturel régional du Vercors ⊘

Created in 1970, the park covers an area of 175 000ha/432 425 acres and includes 62 municipalities situated in the limestone Massif du Vercors and also in the Royans, Trièves and Diois regions.

A number of local museums document the area, five nature trails have been set up and the high plateaux, overlooked by Mont Aiguille, are now designated as a nature reserve. The Vercors has also gained a reputation for cross-country skiing, thanks mainly to the resorts of Autrans and Villard-de-Lans; the area is crisscrossed with marked trails and cross-country ski clubs. Several hiking footpaths go through the area, including the GR 91 which crosses the high plateaux.

A remarkable ecosystem – Forests cover more than half the total area of the Vercors Massif and offer great variety: beeches and firs are gradually replaced by pines in the south of the region. There are more than 1 800 different plant varieties including some very rare protected species: the lady's slipper, martagon lily and forest tulip.

The Vercors is one of the rare areas where the six species of wild hoofed animals living in France can be found: chamois, deer, roe-deer, wild boars, moufflons and ibexes. Birds of prey are also well represented: golden eagles, peregrines, eagle owls, Bonelli's eagles (in the south) and a few bearded vultures. Since 1994, griffon vultures have also been gradually reintroduced to the park's skies.

Eating out

Le Pertuzon – *Av. du Vercors* – *38112 Méaudre* – ☎ *04 76 95 21 17* – *closed 20 Nov-20 Dec, Sun evening, Tue evening and Wed out of season* – *14.94/38.87€.* This hotel-restaurant in a little village on the edge of the river gorge with its rich plant life offers its guests a warm welcome. It serves good food, and ensures peace and quiet in its well sound-proofed rooms, on the terrace or in the garden beneath a parasol.

Where to stay

Hôtel des Grands Goulets – *26420 Les Barraques-en-Vercors* – ☎ *04 75 48 22 45* – *closed 1 Oct-30 Apr* – ▯ – *29rms: 26.68/48.78€* - ☒ *5.79€* – *restaurant 14.94/28.20€.* This long imposing building by the roadside clings to the mountain. If the weather is good enough, leave your room to dine on the terrace. The garden is the perfect place for a siesta.

Hôtel Montbrand – *38880 Autrans* – ☎ *04 76 95 34 58* – *closed end Mar-May and Oct-Christmas* – ▯ – *8rms: 48.02/51.83€* - ☒ *6.40€.* Cross-country skiing enthusiasts, keen ramblers and nature lovers will be delighted with this hotel. The proprietress is a good handywoman and sees to the maintenance of the rooms herself, which are decorated in the style of the mountain region.

★★① GRANDS GOULETS

From Villard-de-Lans to Pont-en-Royans *36km/22.4mi – allow 2hr – see local map*

From Villard de Lans (see VILLARD-DE-LANS), drive along D 531 towards Pont-en-Royans.

Beyond Les Jarrands, the road runs beside the Méaudre through a deep gorge, which narrows until there is only just room for the road and the stream.

At the Pont de la Goule Noire, bear left along D 103.

La Goule Noire – This significant spring is visible downstream of the Pont de la Goule Noire, level with the river bed.

The cliff road rises above the south bank of the Bourne, offering lovely views of cliffs known as the Rochers du Rang. Before St-Martin-en-Vercors, note the impressive rock, standing like a statue; it is known as the Vierge de Vercors, "the Virgin Mary of the Vercors".

St-Martin-en-Vercors – This was the French headquarters during the 1944 fighting. The last bear was seen here in 1937.

Caverne de l'ours ⊘ – This exhibition uses reconstructions and the display of stuffed animals to illustrate the often difficult relationship between men and bears sharing the same habitat.

Beyond Les Barraques, D 518 enters the Grands Goulets.
Parking facilities at the entrance of Les Barraques.

★★**Grands Goulets** – *Extreme care is required as you drive through the Grands Goulets. Stopping points for one or two cars are on the right-hand side of the road driving towards Les Barraques. The tunnels are not designed for large vehicles.*
This deep narrow gorge is the most impressive natural sight of the Vercors region. Before driving through, walk as far as the second bridge over the Vernaison *(15min there and back)*. Daylight barely reaches the road through the thick vegetation and when you suddenly enter the gorge on a blazing summer's day, the effect is striking. Near the last tunnels, the cliff

The Grands Goulets

S. Sauvignier/MICHELIN

road clings to the rock face above the river bed (numerous waterfalls). Downstream, the ravine opens out; look back after the last tunnel to appreciate the depth of the gorge. The road continues high above the valley, whose arid slopes, overlooked by rocky escarpments high in colour, contribute to the southern atmosphere which pervades the scenery.

★ **Petits Goulets** – The sharp-edged rocky slabs plunging almost vertically into the river are remarkable.
Beyond Ste-Eulalie, the smiling Royans countryside offers a strong contrast with the last *cluse* (gorge) of the Bourne, looking like a natural gateway.

★ **Pont-en-Royans** – *See PONT-EN-ROYANS.*

The following itinerary describes the return journey to Villard-de-Lans.

★★★② GORGES DE LA BOURNE

From Pont-en-Royans to Villars-de-Lans
24km/15mi – allow 1hr 30min – see local map.

This gorge, lined with thick layers of coloured limestone, gets deeper and deeper as one heads upstream along the Bourne, which is reduced to a trickle in summer.

After Pont-en-Royans, the D 531 enters the gorge immediately and follows the river. The valley widens slightly before Choranche, then becomes narrow again and the road leaves the river bed to climb along the steep north bank, where many waterfalls cascade down the cliffside in rainy weather.

Grotte du Bournillon – *1km/0.6mi south of D 531, then 1hr there and back on foot. Turn onto the private road leading to the power station, cross its yard and turn right; the path giving access to the cave starts on the left, on the other side of a bridge over the Bournillon (parking allowed, but beware of falling rocks).* Continue left along a steep, difficult path at the base of the escarpments to reach the huge **entrance★** (100m/328ft high) of the cave. Walk as far as the footbridge to appreciate the size of this enormous arch. The Bournillon spring, now piped, was the continuation of the underground river Vernaison which has its source in the Grotte de la Luire. Opposite the semicircular walls around the spring are the red rocks of the cirque de Choranche.

★★ **Grottes de Choranche** - *2.5km/1.5mi from D 531 across the Bourne (car park); continue on foot.*
There are seven caves in all at the foot of tall cliffs overlooking the village of Choranche. Two of them are open to the public.
The **Grotte de Coufin** ⏱★★ is the most spectacular cave in the Vercors Massif. Discovered in 1875, it includes a vast chamber where thousands of snow-white **stalactites★★**, 1-3m/3-10ft long, are reflected in the water of a lake. The tour continues along a winding gallery where light effects create a supernatural atmosphere. The visit ends with an **audio-visual show★**. An aquarium contains an olm, a blind cave-dwelling salamander with external gills. Outside, there is an exhibition about prehistoric men who lived in the area; a very pleasant and interesting walk along the scientific **nature trail** *(allow 1hr)* provides an introduction to the flora, fauna and geology of the area.

Grottes de Choranche

The **Grotte du Gournier** contains a beautiful lake, 50m/164ft long and 8m/26ft deep, fed by an underwater spring. This underground network, known to stretch over 18km/11mi, consists of a succession of waterfalls with a considerable difference in altitude, but you will need the right equipment and an experienced guide to explore the caves properly.

The road then runs through the basin of La Balme at the confluence of the Rencurel and Bourne valleys *(see Route des Écouges below)*, then enters the Goule Noire Gorge. Note the large Calvaire de Valchevrière standing on the opposite bank. After the Pont de la Goule Noire and the Grotte de la Goule Blanche, its water now used to generate electricity, the road continues to Villard-de-Lans *(see Villard-de-Lans)*.

★★ ③ ROUTE DES ÉCOUGES ET DU NAN

Round trip from La Balme-de-Rencurel to N 532

21km/13mi – allow 1hr – see local map

This itinerary includes one of the most vertiginous sections in the Vercors region, but promises superb views of the Bas-Dauphiné.

From La Balme, drive north along D 35.

The road runs up the Rencurel Valley along to the Col de Romeyère (alt 1 074m/3 524ft), where a forest road leads to the vast Coulmes Forest. The valley itself is densely forested and uninhabited. At Pont Chabert-d'Hières, the Drevenne leaves this wide coomb and veers left through a spectacular **gorge★** towards the Isère Valley, running along the side of the cliff. There are bird's-eye **views★★** of the Isère Valley and the hills of the Bas Dauphiné.

Bridge over the Drevenne – It is worth stopping for a moment to admire the **waterfall** dropping from a height of 50m/164ft.

Just beyond St-Gervais, the road joins N 532 along the east bank of the Isère to Cognin-les-Gorges. Continue on the D 55 to Malleval.

★**Gorges de Nan** – The Nan, a mountain stream flowing down from the western foothills of the Vercors, is followed from a great height by a small picturesque cliff road. The stretch along the left bank of the River Isère is still more spectacular. D 22 rises in a series of hairpin bends along the escarpment overlooking the Nan Valley. Stop between the second and third tunnels on the most impressive section of the route, on the edge of a precipice with a drop of 200m/656ft. A second, less vertiginous narrow defile leads to the cool and verdant upper valley. The road continues upwards through meadows to Malleval, from where a relatively new road, built in 1983, gives access to the Coulmes Forest and the D 31 leads up to the Vercors Plateau (in summer only).

The route along the D 292 via Presles is described in reverse order under PONT-DE-ROYANS.

At the crossroads with the D 531, turn left towards La Balme-de-Rencurel and **Gorges de la Bourne★★★** (see ② above).

★★ ④ ROUTE DU COL DE ROUSSET

From Chapelle-en-Vercors to the Col de Rousset

24km/15mi – allow 1hr 30min – see local map

From Les Barraques-en-Vercors, drive south along D 518.

La Chapelle-en-Vercors – This tourist centre located near the Forêt de Lente was bombed and burnt down in July 1944. Two plaques in a farmyard (Ferme Albert), one of the rare places which was not destroyed, honour the memory of 16 inhabitants of the village who were shot.

Follow D 518 towards Grotte de la Luire and Col du Rousset.

Grotte de la Luire ◷ – *0.5km/0.3mi off D 518 on the left and 15min there and back on foot; allow 30min more to see the Decombaz Chamber.* The cave is interesting from a geological and a historical point of view. In July 1944, the Nazis killed or deported the wounded and the staff of the Resistance movement hospital set up inside the cave *(see above: Stronghold of the Resistance)*.
The **Decombaz Chamber** is 60m/197ft high under a natural vault; deep inside it, there is a chasm which led potholers 470m/1 542ft down to what is thought to be the underground Vernaison. During periods of exceptional spates, the water of the river rises up the chasm and overflows into the cave.

Continue south along D 518 to the Col de Rousset station and go through the tunnel.

★★**Col de Rousset** – Alt 1 254m/4 114ft. *Leave the car at the tunnel exit and walk to a viewpoint (1 367m/4 485ft).* The Col de Rousset marks the climatic limit between the northern and southern Alps: the green landscapes of the Vercors on the northside, the arid **Bassin de Die★★** on the southside.

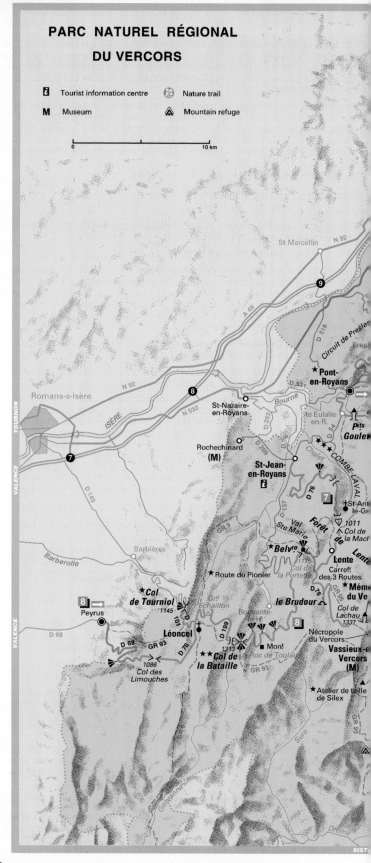

PARC NATUREL RÉGIONAL
DU VERCORS

i Tourist information centre   🌐 Nature trail

M Museum   ⛰ Mountain refuge

0   10 km

St-Marcellin   N 92

9

Circuit de Presles

★ **Pont-en-Royans**

D 531

Pits Goule

Romans-s-Isère

ISÈRE   N 532

8

St-Nazaire-en-Royans

Bourne

Ste Eulalie-en-R.

Chôlet   COMBE LAVAL

7

D 149

Rochechinard **(M)**

D 253

D 209

St-Jean-en-Royans **i**

D 76

★St-Ant le-Gr

D 137

7

▽ 1011
⚓ Col de la Mach

Barbières

GR 9

Val Ste Marie

Forêt de

Lente

★ **Belv'e**

Lente

Carref des 3 Routes

Col de la Portette

D 76

GR 9 ★ **Mém du Ve**

★ Route du Pionier

8
Peyrus

★ **Col de Tourniol**
1145

D 101

Gr Échaillon

le Brudour ⌂

Col de Lachau 1337

8

Nécropole du Vercors

Vassieux-en-Vercors (M)

Barberolle

D 68

Léoncel

D 68   GR 93

D 199

Bouvante

★ Mon!

D 70

1313

★★ **Col de la Bataille**

GR 93

Roc de Toulau

▲ 1086
Col des Limouches

Sure

★ Atelier de taille de Silex

GR 95

Gervanne

⛰

Drôme

SIST

436

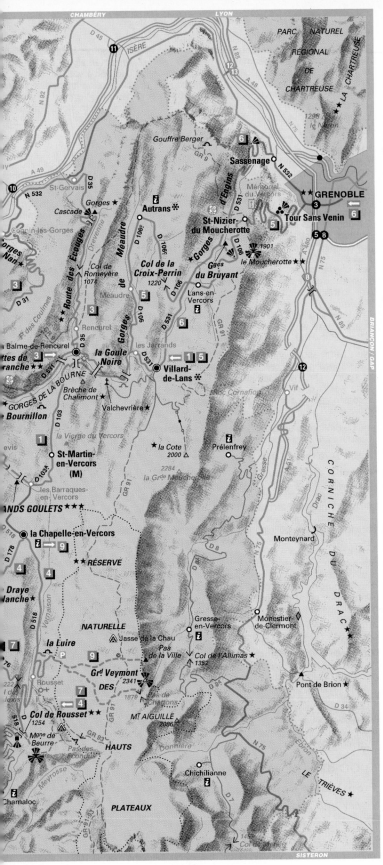

The ski runs of the recent **Col de Rousset** ski resort are on the slopes of the **Montagne de Beurre**, near the pass. In summer, a new fun vehicle takes advantage of the available slopes: the **"trottinherbe"**, a cross between a mountain bike and a scooter.

From the viewing table, situated on the edge of the plateau, an impressive **panorama★★** unfolds: the Grande Moucherolle to the north, the Grand Veymont to the east (in the foreground) and the heights of the Diois to the south with Mont Ventoux on the horizon.

Head north and turn left onto D 76 to Vassieux-en-Vercors.

The road leads gradually uphill through the woods above the Vernaison, crosses the Col de St-Alexis and heads down through stony fields into the valley of Vassieux 500m/550yd from the town, on the left side of the road, lie the remains of German gliders from the Second World War.

Vassieux-en-Vercors – In 1944, while fierce fighting was going on in the region, the Resistance built an airfield for the Allies near Vassieux, but early on the morning of 21 July it was used by German gliders filled with commandos. The resistance fighters, at first believing them to be their liberators, realised their mistake too late. the German troops killed the population and burnt the village to the ground. Vassieux was entirely rebuilt and a monument, surmounted by a recumbent figure by Gilioli, was erected to the "Martyrs of the Vercors, 1944"; a commemorative plaque on the town hall square bears the names of the 74 civilian victims.

The **church**, built after the war, is decorated with a fresco by Jean Aujame *(The Assumption)* and bears a touching commemorative plaque.

The **Musée de la Résistance du Vercors** ⊘ was founded by a former member of the Secret Army. It deals with the events which took place in the region in 1944, as well as the horror of the Nazi camps and the joy of the Liberation.

3km/1.9mi south of Vassieux by D 615 is the Musée du Site préhistorique ⊘. Excavations in 1969 revealed numerous flints shards and blades spread over an area of 100m². The specialised knife and dagger blades cut in this 4 000-year-old workshop were exported all over Europe. Displays, films, practical demonstrations and reconstructions of pre-historic dwellings reveal the working methods of these early craftsmen.

1km/0.6mi north along D 76, the **Cimetière national du Vercors** contains the graves of 193 Resistance fighters and civilian victims who died during the operations of July 1944.

Follow D 76 to the Col de Lachau.

★**Mémorial du Vercors (Col de la Chau)** ⊘ – *3km/1.9mi from Vassieux; from the cemetery, take D 76 on the left. Car park at the pass.*

The memorial stands out like the prow of a ship against the dense Forêt de Lente. Built by a group of architects from Grenoble at an altitude of 1 305m/4 282ft, it is covered with junipers and pines which grow naturally in the Vercors Massif. The intentionally plain building is devoted to the Vercors Resistance Movement and to national events which took place at the time. Themed reconstructions and dioramas cover collaboration with the Germans, interrogations by the Milice (French paramilitary organisation created by the Vichy Government) and the role of women in the Resistance movements; recorded individual accounts and contemporary films recall the "République du Vercors" which lasted until 23 July 1944.

On the way out, the names of 840 civilian victims are inscribed in recesses along a large wall. From the terrace, the view embraces the Vassieux Valley.

Turn right after the cemetery and take the D 178 towards La Chapelle-en-Vercors and follow the signs to la Draye Blanche.

★**Grotte de la Draye Blanche** ⊘ – One of the most ancient caves in the Vercors region, la Grotte de la Draye Blanche was discovered in 1918 by one Fabien Rey, who had the foresight to block off the entrance. The cave remained perfectly preserved until it was finally opened to the public in 1970 and is now directly accessible from the car park via a tunnel. This most recent work led to the discovery of another pothole containing animal remains from many thousands of years ago, a find which sheds new light on the prehistory of the Vercors. The tour includes the **Grande Salle★**, a vast chamber, 100m/110yd long, in which calcite comes in different colours, white, ochre or blue-grey. A stalagmite, 12m/40ft high and 2m/6.5ft thick, looks like a petrified waterfall.

⑤ GORGES DE MÉAUDRE

From Villard-de-Lans to Grenoble *46km/29mi – allow 5hr – see local map.*

From Villard, drive west along D 531.

The road follows the River Bourne. At Les Jarrands, where the valley suddenly narrows, turn right onto D 106 which goes up the **Gorges de Méaudre** through pastoral scenery. Beyond Méaudre, bear left onto D 106C and continue through **Autrans**✳, a popular cross-country skiing resort, before rejoining the main D 106.

Col de la Croix Perrin – Alt 1 220m/4 003ft. The pass is a vast clearing between slopes clad with splendid forests of firs. In Jaume, D 106 veers to the right, goes through **Lans-en-Vercors** then rises above the Furon Valley, offering bird's-eye views of the picturesque Gorges d'Engins and Gorges du Bruyant.

St-Nizier-du-Moucherotte – *see GRENOBLE, Nearby Sights.*

On the way down to Grenoble, there are views of the Grenoble Basin where the River Isère and River Drac meet. In the foreground on the right are three peaks known as the Trois Pucelles or "Three Maidens", the site of a climbing school.

Tour Sans Venin – *15min there and back on foot.* One of the Seven Wonders of Dauphiné. According to legend, a crusader brought back some soil from the Holy Land and, by spreading it round his castle, rid the area of all venomous snakes, hence the name which translates as "the tower without venom". From the foot of the ruined tower, the **view★** extends south to the Dévoluy.

6 GORGES D'ENGINS

From Grenoble to Villard-de-Lans *32km/20mi – allow 2hr*

From Grenoble, drive northwest to Sassenage along D 532, which runs parallel to the Casque de Néron along the Isère valley.

Sassenage – *see GRENOBLE, Nearby Sights*

★**Gorges d'Engins** – The smooth rock walls of this deep trench frame the verdant valley of the Furon.

Gorges du Bruyant – A convenient footpath, linking D 531 and D 106, leads to the bottom of the gorge *(1hr there and back).*

From Jaume to Villard-de-Lans, the road follows the Lans Valley, whose gentle slopes are clad with dense forests of fir, within sight of the peaks marking the eastern edge of the Vercors. Note the stepped gables of traditional houses.

★★★7 ROUTE DU COMBE LAVAL

From the Col de Rousset to St-Jean en Royans *41km/25.5mi – allow 3hr – see local map*

Drive north and bear left onto D 76 to Vassieux, passing the memorial.

Grotte du Brudour – *From the bridge across the Brudour, 30min there and back on foot along a very pleasant path.* It leads to a cave where water from nearby Urle bubbles up as a resurgent spring. It is possible to follow the left-hand gallery to a chamber containing a small lake *(30min there and back).* The Brudour itself soon disappears into various sink-holes to reappear as the Cholet below the cirque of the Combe Laval.

Combe Laval

From the Carrefour des Trois Routes to St-Jean-en-Royans

After heavy rain, look out for the waterfall just before **Lente**, a small forestry village the cascade disappears straight into a funnel-shaped sinkhole known as a *doline*.

★★ **Forêt de Lente** – The forest consists essentially of firs and beeches; the timber was used in the 19C by the navy and the coal industry.

★★★ **Combe Laval** – The spine-chilling journey starts from the **Col de la Machine**. The road hewn out of the rock face, literally hangs above the gorge of the upper Cholet from a height of 600m/1 968ft. Note the Cascalde du Cholet, a resurgent spring of the Brudour. After going through several tunnels, the road suddenly overlooks the whole Royans region, offering bird's-eye **views**★★ of this deeply burrowed area and of the Bas Dauphiné plateaux (Chambaran Forest). To the north are the deep furrows dug through the mountain by the River Bourne and River Vernaison.

St-Jean-en-Royans – Lying below the cliffs of the Vercors Plateau, this small town is the starting point of magnificent excursions on foot or by car and also the home of Royans ravioli, a local treat. The chancel of the church is decorated with fine 18C woodwork from a former Carthusian monastery. There is an interesting **viewpoint** on top of the **Toura** Hill accessible via the cemetery lane.
Situated 5km/3mi west along D 209, **Rochechinard** is overlooked by the ruins of an 11C-12C **castle**; its small country church and its presbytery form a lovely picture with the cliffs of the Combe Laval in the background; the **Musée de la Mémoire** ⊘ contains a collection of tools and regional costumes as well as reconstructions of traditional interiors.
There is a fine excursion to be made south of St-Jean *(17km/10.6mi on D 131 and D 331)* along a cliff road known as the **Route du Pionnier**★, which overlooks the Lyonne Valley. *It is possible to make it a round tour by returning via the Combe Laval (see above) or via the Col de la Bataille (see drive* 🎱 *).*

Monastère St-Antoine-le-Grand ⊘ – *Take the D 54 to Combe de Laval and follow signs for the Gorges de Laval along the D 2 and D 239.* This short diversion leads to an Orthodox monastery with unusual Russian murals.

★ 🎱 COL DE LA BATAILLE

From Peyrus to the Carrefour des Trois Routes
45km/28mi – allow 2hr – see local map

From Peyrus, drive along D 68.

The road rises in a series of wide hairpin bends above a wooded vale. About half a mile before it reaches the plateau, there is an extended view of the Valence Plain with the Cevennes in the background. The Col des Limouches gives access to the Léoncel Valley, whose meagre pastures, dotted with box and juniper bushes, look distinctly Mediterranean.

Léoncel – From its Cistercian abbey founded in 1137, the village has retained a vast Romanesque **abbey church** ⊘★ dating from the late 12C, surmounted by a stocky square bell-tower topped by a pyramid. Built in stages from 1150 to 1210, the interior demonstrates the changing taste in architecture: the oven-vaulted apse and apsidal chapels are typical of Provençal Romanesque style, whereas the quadripartite vaulting of the nave already bears the mark of Gothic art. Note the arms of the abbey chiselled into the wall near the door, on the right, plus a 16C lectern and a fine modern icon in the northern transept.

From Léoncel, follow D 101 to the Col de Tourniol.

★ **Col de Tourniol** – The **view** extends beyond the Vercors foothills across the Valence Basin.

Return to Léoncel.

The road climbs up the eastern slope of the valley and reaches the densely forested plateau.

★★ **Col de la Bataille** – *The road is closed from 15 November to 15 May.* A tunnel gives access to the pass (alt 1 313m/4 308ft) overlooked by the Roc de Toulau. The **panorama** is impressive.
From the pass to Malatra *(2km/1.2mi)*, the **cliff road**★★ winds it way above the Bouvante Cirque and its small lake; there are three viewpoints along this section, before the road veers north towards the Col de la Portette.

★ **Belvédère de la Portette** – *15min on foot there and back from the Col de la Portette. Leave the car in the last bend and follow the stony path which starts behind a forest marker; bear right 200m/219yd further on.* From the belvedere, the **view** looks down over the Val Ste-Marie, with the Royans region and Isère Valley beyond; note the huge modern bridge of St-Hilaire-St-Nazaire.

From the pass, it is only a short distance to the Carrefour des Trois Routes.

HIKES

★★ ⑨ RÉSERVE NATURELLE DES HAUTS-PLATEAUX

This desolate area, covering 16 600ha/41 020 acres and situated at altitudes ranging from 1 200m/3 846ft to 2 300m/7 546ft, was declared a nature reserve in 1985 in order to safeguard the balance which existed between traditional activities (foresters and shepherds) and natural ecosystems. No road goes through it and there are no permanent dwellings.

The area consists of karst-like limestone plateaux, dotted with fissures and sinkholes into which surface water disappears, and includes the two highest summits of the Vercors Massif, the Grand Veymont (2 341m/7 680ft) and Mont Aiguille (2 086m/6 844ft); it is bounded by impressive cliffs on the east and west sides.

Wildlife is less diverse here than in the rest of the Vercors. The main species of fauna are the black grouse, the blue hare and the chamois, as well as around 100 ibexes and the recently reintroduced wild vultures. Cave-dwellers, on the other hand, are plentiful, in particular the many species of bat.

Many marked footpaths such as GR 91 and 93 crisscross the high plateaux, but in the absence of access roads, hikes are inevitably lengthened and often involve camping overnight. Specialised topo-guides are available at tourist offices.

From Rousset to the Col des Escondus – *The excursion described below is relatively easy and should only take half a day; start from Rousset, where you can leave the car. Difference in altitude: 400m/1 312ft.*

Aim for the Chapelle St-Alexis, cross a stream then walk south along its east bank to the end of the Combe Male and then to the Col des Escondus at the intersection of GR 93. Impressive views of the hamlet of La Grange and the Montagne de Beurre. Follow the path going north through the woods to the Chalet des Ours *(it is also possible to go west to the Col de Rousset across high pastures)*. Take the path running behind the chalet towards the Combe Male and follow it back to your starting point.

★★ Grand Veymont – *Allow 1 day – Difference in altitude: 1 000m/3 281ft – Altitude at the starting point: 1 350m/4 429ft.*

From La Chapelle-en-Vercors, drive along D 518 towards the Col de Rousset; 1km/0.6mi before Rousset, turn left onto a narrow forest road signposted "Route forestière de la Coche". Follow it to the vast car park of the Maison Forestière de la Coche (9km/5.6mi). Leave the car there.

Continue on foot to the Maison Forestière de Pré Grandu. Walk east along the marked path running across the plateau, past rocks and pine woods; the stern wall of the Grand Veymont bars the horizon straight ahead. On the way down through the central depression, make for the **Nouvelle Jasse de la Chau**, where you can get a fresh supply of water.

Behind the information panel, a path climbs towards the **Pas de la Ville**, the last stage before the summit, exposed to high winds *(make sure you have warm clothing with you)*. A path on the right of the iron cross leads up to the summit but it is worth walking a few extra metres east beyond the pass for some wonderful bird's-eye views of the Trièves Valley.

The climb to the summit along the scree-covered slope requires particular care. Several cairns mark the summit (2 341m/7 680ft); the impressive **panorama★★★** includes the major part of the Alps from Mont Blanc in the northeast to Mont Pelvoux and the Meije facing the Grand Veymont, with the solitary Mont Ventoux in Provence. But the most striking silhouette is undoubtedly that of Mont Aiguille (2 086m/6 844ft) in the foreground.

The way down to the south is very steep. At the foot of the ridge, take the path on the right which runs west to the Pas de Chattons and joins GR 91 just before La Grande Cabane. Continue westwards and turn right at the intersection. The path runs north for 5km/3mi to meet the large path leading to the Maison Forestière du Pré Grandu.

BEFORE GOING

– Water is rare on the Vercors plateaux: an extra supply is never superfluous.
– Do not go off marked paths, even when going across open spaces.
– Sheepfolds which look deserted always belong to shepherds; if you want to stop for a break or to take cover, make sure you do not leave anything behind.
– When a flock or herd approaches, make a wide detour round it without sudden movements or noises.
– Paragliding, camping and fires are forbidden and dogs are not allowed inside the reserve's perimeter. Mountain bikes are only permitted on the "Grande Traversée du Vercors" (GTV)

The River Verdon, a tributary of the Durance, has carved magnificent gorges throug the limestone plateaux of the Haute-Provence region, the most spectacular bein the Grand Canyon which extends for 21km/13mi from Rougon to Aiguines. Th sight of this vast furrow lined with sheer walls in wild unspoilt surroundings is uniqu in Europe; as Jean Giono would say: "Here, it is more than remote, it is elsewhere..."

Nearby Sights: BARGÈME, CASTELLANE, CLUES DE HAUTE-PROVENCE GRÉOUX-LES-BAINS, MOUSTIERS-STE-MARIE, Route NAPOLÉON, RIEZ ST-JULIEN-DU-VERDON, Lac de STE-CROIX, Plateau de VALENSOLE

BACKGROUND

How can so deep a gorge have been carved out by so small a river? The reason that when the Alpine area folded during the Tertiary tectonic upheaval, the hug layers of limestone deposits rose slowly and the existing river bed sank deeper an deeper. The Verdon subsequently widened and modelled the sinuous corrido through which it now flows. Intense erosion carved huge caves in the cliffside, an water penetrating through the karst of the plateau created a vast network of under ground caves and galleries.

The width of the gorge varies from 6/20ft to 100m/328ft at water level and from 200m/656ft to 1 500m/4 921ft at the top of the cliffs. Its depth varies from 250m/820ft to 700m/2 297ft.

Edouard Martel (1859-1938), the inventor of potholing, was the first to explor the 21km/13mi-long gorge. In 1928, part of the canyon was equipped t receive visitors, but still only on foot; the main viewpoints were signposted. In 1947 the cliff road *(D 71)*, known as the Corniche Sublime, was hewn out of the rock, thu opening the way to motorists. The north bank road, on the other hand, was onl completed in 1973. In 1997 the Parc naturel régional du Verdon was inaugurated t safeguard the outstanding natural site of the Grand-Canyon du Verdon.

Motorists arriving from Draguignan may occasionally find D 955 closed as it run through the Canjuers Firing Range.

Eating out

MODERATE

Auberge du Point Sublime – *04120 Point-Sublime* – ☎ *04 92 83 60 35 closed 16 Oct-31 Mar, Wed except Jul-Aug* – *17.53/32.01€*. This small tradi tional restaurant on the road that follows the Gorges du Verdon has a delightfu lounge with a panoramic view and a shaded terrace. The rooms are simple an in keeping with the establishment's friendly atmosphere.

Where to stay

BUDGET

Hôtel Les Gorges du Verdon – *04120 La Palud-sur-Verdon* – *1km/0.6mi S* La Palud – ☎ *04 92 77 38 26* – *closed 1 Nov-31 Mar* – 🅿 – *28rms: half-boar 70.13/82.32€* – *restaurant 18.29/25.92€*. Before embarking on one of th numerous adventurous activities open to you in the Gorges de Verdon, enjoy th peace and quiet of this hotel on the hillside above the river gorge. The rooms ar well lit and decorated in Provençal colours, and they overlook the village Traditional cuisine. Swimming pool.

MODERATE

Auberge des Crêtes – *04120 La Palud-sur-Verdon* – *1km/0.6mi E on D 952* ☎ *04 92 77 38 47* – *closed 2 Oct-6 Apr* – 🅿 – *12rms: 41.77/48 78€* - 🖵 *5.95€* – *restaurant 13.57/20.58€*. This is an unpretentious and prac tical inn on the Gorges du Verdon road. The rooms are simple and have simp fitted bathrooms. There is a large terrace at the front and a shaded patio at th back of the house. Good cooking and friendly atmosphere.

Chambre d'hôte Mme Colombéro – *Campagne l'Enchastre* – *04120 La Palud sur-Verdon* – *12km/7.5mi N of La Palud on D 123 (towards Châteauneuf) the D 17* – ☎ *04 92 83 76 12* – *closed Nov-Mar* – *5rms: 42.69€* – *main me 13.72€*. Those who love unspoiled nature and peace and quiet will be delighte with this guesthouse in the middle of nowhere at the end of a very narrow roac The modern house stands on a farm estate 1 100m/3 608ft above sea level. Th rooms are fairly plain, but comfortable and decorated in colourful tones.

EXCURSIONS

★★Route de la Corniche Sublime *81km/50.3mi – half a day*

This itinerary is almost perfect from a tourist's point of view, the road twisting and turning to reach the most impressive viewpoints. The bird's-eye views of the canyon are amazing, but drivers are unlikely to have this idyllic route all to themselves: the Gorges du Verdon attract over one million visitors every year.

FROM CASTELLANE TO THE BALCONS DE LA MESCLA

★**Castellane** – *See CASTELLANE.*

Leave Castellane by ② on the town plan and drive along D 952.

The road follows the north bank of the Verdon meandering beneath impressive escarpments. The rocky ridge of the Cadières de Brandis can be seen on the right.

★**Porte de St-Jean** – Beyond this narrow passage cut through limestone heights, the river takes a wide turn to the left and flows southwards.

Falaise des Cavaliers, Gorges du Verdon

★**Clue de Chasteuil** – This long transverse gorge is lined with vertical rock strata.

In Pont-de-Soleils, turn left into D 955.

The road leaves the Verdon to follow the green Jabron Valley. On the right, the hilltop village of **Trigance** is overlooked by an imposing medieval castle remodelled in the 16C, now turned into a hotel.

Comps-sur-Artuby – This ancient village, which once belonged to the Knights Templar and later to the Knights Hospitaller, nestles at the foot of a rock crowned by the 13C **Église St-André**; the nave, surmounted by a pointed vault, ends with an oven-vaulted apse. Note the christening font.
From the church, there are fine views of the Artuby Gorge and the entrances of several caves.

From Comps, drive west along D 71.

A bend in the road affords a wide **view**★ of the arid Préalpes de Castellane and Préalpes de Digne.

★★★**Balcons de la Mescla** – *On the right side of the road and on either side of the Café-Relais des Balcons.* From these rock terraces, there are bird's-eye views of the *Mescla* 250m/820ft below, the name taken from the Provençal word for "mix" and given to the confluence of the Verdon and its tributary the Artuby. The Verdon takes a sharp bend round a narrow promontory and the view embraces the upstream part of the gorge, 400-500m/1 312-1 640ft deep. The upper viewing terrace offers the most impressive view.
The road then runs towards the Artuby.

FROM THE BALCONS DE LA MESCLA TO MOUSTIERS-STE-MARIE

The road may be blocked by snow from December to March.

★**Pont de l'Artuby** – *Car park at the end of the bridge.* This remarkable piece of engineering in reinforced concrete comprises a single arch with a 110m/361ft span thrown across the Artuby Canyon lined with vertical cliffs. Anyone keen to get a closer look at the gorge may like to know that this is a popular bungee jumping spot. The road goes round the Pilon du Fayet to reach the Verdon Canyon.

Tunnels de Fayet – Between the two tunnels and immediately beyond there is a breathtaking **view**★★★ of the curve of the canyon near the Étroit des Cavaliers.

★**Falaise des Cavaliers** – The road follows the edge of the cliff where there are two viewpoints. Turn right towards the Restaurant des Cavaliers. From the terrace, there is a striking **view** of the 300m/984ft-high cliff.
Over the next 3km/1.9mi, the road runs 250-400m/820-1 312ft above the gorge: it is one of the most impressive sections of the whole itinerary.

★**Falaise de Baucher** – Lovely view of the Pré Baucher Basin upstream.

The acrobats of the River Verdon

For a long time, the bottom of the gorge and the river bed provided the local population with their main means of support: boxwood and wild honey.
It required a great deal of skill and courage to reach the virtually inaccessible sites where box and honey could be found. Honey gatherers moved about on a plank held by a hemp rope, whereas box cutters climbed up and down a succession of long poles fitted with bars. The most daring among them worked their way along the cliffs by driving spikes into the rock; they were the forerunners of today's rock-climbers whose demonstrations up and down the Falaise de l'Escalès win the admiration of onlookers.

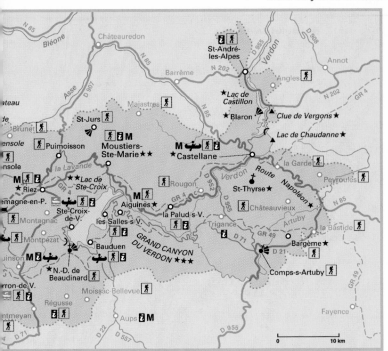

Pas de l'Imbut – Bird's-eye view of the Verdon overlooked by huge sheer cliffs; the river disappears 400m/1 312ft below under a pile of fallen rocks.

Further on, the road leaves the edge of the cliffs and one loses sight of the gorge for a while.

★★ Cirque de Vaumale – The road enters the cirque after a sharp bend to the left and the view then embraces the downstream section of the gorge. The road reaches its highest point at an altitude of 1 204m/3 950ft. The gorge backed by the heights of the opposite bank forms a superb landscape.

As it comes out of the cirque, the road leaves the gorge once more and winds its way westwards, offering **views★** of the Lac de Ste-Croix and, further away, of the Luberon, the Montagne de Lure and Mont Ventoux beyond the Durance Valley.

★★ Col d'Illoire – The road comes out of the gorge for good. Stop and admire the Grand Canyon once more.

The **view★** now embraces the flat expanse of the Plateau de Valensole, with a line of bluish heights on the horizon.

Aiguines – This village, in a superb sitea overlooking the vast expanse of the Lac de Ste-Croix, has retained its old-world charm, twisting lanes, old houses and a 17C castle with four corner towers covered in colourful tiles. Aiguines was famous for the work of its wood-turners who used boxwood from the nearby forests. The Musée des Tourneurs K presents the various species of wood used by turners and illustrates their work. It contains lathes and a collection of objects made this way, from bottle cases and powder boxes to tool handles and potato-mashers. Animated models show the process of collecting and turning the wood.A video show is devoted to the speciality of Aiguines: **nail-studded boules** for playing *pétanque*

Beyond Aiguines, the road winds down to the Lac de Ste-Croix.

Turn right onto D 957.

★★ Lac de Ste-Croix – See Lac de STE-CROIX.

There is a fine **view★** of the entrance of the canyon from the bridge across the Verdon; the road then follows the Maïre Valley and skirts the outdoor leisure park of Moustiers-Ste-Marie.

★★ Moustiers-Ste-Marie – See MOUSTIERS-STE-MARIE.

★★ North Bank 73km/45mi – allow half a day

The direct road *(D 952)* from Moustiers to Castellane only runs close to the Grand Canyon at each end. However, the "Route des Crêtes" *(D 23)* offers an unforgettable round tour from La Palud-sur-Verdon via a number of viewpoints.

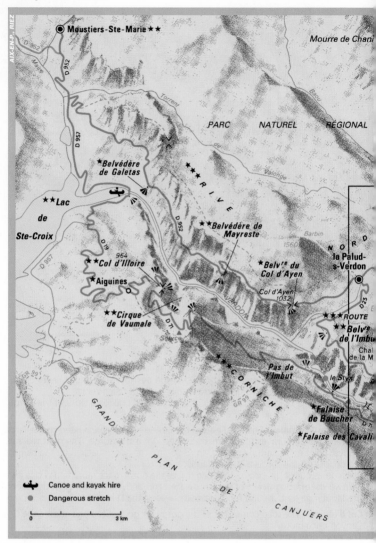

FROM MOUSTIERS-STE-MARIE TO LA PALUD-SUR-VERDON

★★ Moustiers-Ste-Marie – *See MOUSTIERS-STE-MARIE.*

On the way down the Maïre Valley, the scenery is unmistakably Provençal with its lavender fields and twisted olive trees. The view embraces the edge of the Plateau de Valensole, overlooking the vast turquoise expanse of the Lac de Ste-Croix, and takes in Aiguines and its castle as well.

★ Belvédère de Galetas – This viewpoint marks the entrance of the gorge. View of the gateway of the Grand Canyon and of the Lac de Ste-Croix in a picturesque landscape of ochre-coloured cliffs.

The road enters the Cirque de Mayreste and climbs steeply.

★★ Belvédère de Mayreste – *15min on foot there and back along a marked stony path.* First overall upstream view of the deep furrow.

★ Belvédère du col d'Ayen – *15min on foot there and back.* Interesting upstream view of the twisted course of the canyon; however, the bottom remains out of sight.

The road veers away from the Verdon towards the cultivated area surrounding La Palud-sur-Verdon.

La Palud-sur-Verdon – This family resort is the ideal starting point of hikes through the canyon and a good base for rock-climbers.

A 12C Romanesque bell-tower is all that remains of the original church. The 18C castle and its four corner towers overlook the village.

★★ROUTE DES CRÊTES (Round tour starting from La Palud-sur-Verdon)

A succession of belvederes or viewing points line this itinerary; they are sometimes situated so high above the gorge that it feels as if one were looking at an aerial view. The main belvederes are listed below.

From La Palud, continue along D 952 towards Castellane then turn right into D 23.

The road rises through lavender fields and woodland areas.

★★ **Belvédère de Trescaïre** – Looking upstream, the Verdon is seen to flow through a jumble of fallen rocks and disappear under the vault of the Baulme aux Pigeons Cave, in the Samson Corridor. In summer, take a moment to watch the rock climbers inching their way up the rock face.

★★ **Belvédère de Carelle** – Bird's-eye view of the river meandering deep down in the gorge. To the left is the Auberge du Point Sublime and, above it, the hilltop village of Rougon. It is one of the main free-climbing sites in the Grand Canyon.

★★ **Belvédère de l'Escalès** – It is situated on top of the sheer cliffs below which runs the Sentier Martel. In summer, numerous rock-climbers add to the interest of the site.

★★ **Belvédère de la Dent d'Aire** – Alt 1 300m/4 265ft. The golden cliffs of the Dent d'Aire and of the Barre de l'Escalès can be seen towering on the left; straight ahead is the narrow corridor of the Baumes-Frères.

447

★★ Belvédère du Tilleul – The confluence of the Verdon and Artuby, known as the "Mescla", lies ahead and the single-arched Pont de l'Artuby behind. The Verdon changes course to the northwest.

★★ Belvédère des Glacières – Impressive view of the Mescla and its enormous promontory, of the Verdon and Plan de Canjuers. When the weather is clear, it is possible to see the Mediterranean Sea.

The road runs past the Chalet de la Maline, which is the starting point of the hike through the Grand Canyon *(see Sentier Martel)*.

★★ Belvédère de l'Imbut – The Verdon disappears under a pile of fallen rocks and the Sentier Vidal and Sentier de l'Imbut can be seen running along the opposite bank. The **view** embraces the mighty cliffs of the Baou Béni. Upstream, the narrowing of the **"Passage du Styx"** affords glimpses of the Pré Baucher.

The road veers away from the Verdon to return to La Palud-sur-Verdon.

FROM LA PALUD-SUR-VERDON TO CASTELLANE

Don't miss the fine **view** on the next bend: the picturesque hilltop village of Rougon suddenly appears ahead, slightly to the left, and the road runs within sight of the gorge once more.

USEFUL TIPS FOR A SUCCESSFUL TRIP

Duration – Allow 2hr extra as a safety precaution, to make sure you will return before nightfall. Stick to the times indicated for each section of the itinerary so as not to be caught by surprise. Follow the itinerary in the direction that is recommended (usually the easiest) to avoid encountering awkward crossings and having to make too great an effort climbing out of the gorge.

Equipment – Take some food and 2litres (4 pints) pints of water (the river water is not suitable for drinking), one or two torches, additional clothing (the tunnels and a few places are quite cool) and climbing boots.

Strictly prohibited – Camping on unauthorised sites, lighting a fire, digging up fossils. Hikers are also asked to refrain from taking shortcuts (it tends to increase the gullying of slopes), crossing the river except via bridges and picking flowers (they fade rapidly anyway) as many species are protected.

Domestic animals – Dogs should not be taken along the Sentier Vidal as they would find the 240 steps along the Sentier Martel difficult to tackle.

Children – Going into the gorge with children under 10 is not recommended; the Sentier Vidal is too difficult for them.

Variation of the water level – Water released by the Chaudanne or Castillon plants can cause a sudden rise in the level of the Verdon; the flow of the river is liable to increase from 10-100m³/353-3 531cu ft per second. The EDF recorded information only lists forecast rates of flow, so it is essential, when stopping for any length of time, to choose a few rocks at water level as markers and watch them carefully. Releases from the dams are usually preceded by warning releases intended for informed hikers.
The Sentier de l'Imbut, which is only suitable for experienced hikers, is accessible under special conditions *(see hike* 4 *)*.

Recorded information – Weather forecast in St-Auban: ☎ 04 92 64 90 60. Rate of flow of the Verdon: ☎ 04 92 83 62 68.

Taxis – A taxi service operates between the Auberge du Point Sublime, La Palud-sur-Verdon and the Chalet de la Maline. It enables hikers to return to where they left their car.

Maps and topo-guides – In addition to the local maps included in this chapter, it would be useful to buy the Moustiers-Ste-Marie local map (1:50 000) and the Grand Canyon du Verdon map by A Monier. "Le Guide du Verdon" by JF Bettus, is on sale in La Palud-sur-Verdon; another useful guide is "Randonnées pédestres dans le pays du Verdon", published by Édisud.

Exploration of the bottom of the gorge – It can be done mostly on foot, but swimming is necessary in places, so in general it is closer to canyoning *(see Practical information)*. Whatever the conditions and the length of the exploration planned, it is a sporting feat which entails danger and requires a thorough knowledge of the techniques of white-water sports.

Rock-climbing sites – The main one is the Belvédère de Carelle, where it is easy to film rock-climbers at work; there is also the Belvédère de Trescaïre and the Falaise de l'Escalès.

The Canyon du Verdon from the Sentier Martel

★**Point Sublime** – *15min there and back on foot. Leave the car in the car park near the Auberge du Point Sublime.* Follow the signposted path on the right across the deeply fissured Plateau des Lauves to the belvedere towering 180m/590ft above the confluence of the Verdon and its tributary the Baou. Splendid **view**★★★ of the entrance of the Grand Canyon and of the Samson Corridor.

Return to the car and follow D 17 to Rougon.

Rougon – Alt 960m/3 150ft. This "eyrie", overlooked by medieval ruins, affords a fine **view**★ of the entrance of the Grand Canyon from the slope above the car park. *Access to the ruins can be tricky as there is no path, so extra care is required.*

Return to D 952 and follow it towards Castellane.

★**Couloir Samson** – *Just before the Tunnel du Tusset, a dead-end road branching off to the right leads to the confluence of the Verdon and the Baou (car park); it meets the path running along the river from the Chalet de la Maline.*
From this spot, the narrowing of the Grand Canyon downstream looks wild and impressive as huge rocks lie across the river bed.

Beyond the tunnel, the cliff road runs down towards the river.

★**Clue de Carejuan** – The limestone strata are strangely coloured. The water cascades over fallen rocks and its clear, green surface is temporarily disturbed.
After the heavy spates of Autumn 1994, the banks of the stream had to be reinforced.

For the section of the itinerary from Pont-de-Soleils to Castellane, see the drive entitled Corniche Sublime.

HIKES THROUGH THE GRAND CANYON

★ 1 Sentier Martel

Between the Chalet de la Maline and the Point Sublime, GR 4, known as the Sentier Martel, offers tourists who do not mind a tiring day's hike an unforgettable close contact with the Grand Canyon.

FROM THE CHALET DE LA MALINE TO THE POINT SUBLIME

5hr hike, not counting resting time, along a difficult itinerary ; see local map – torch essential. GR 4 is marked in white and red.

FOOTPATHS ALONG THE GRAND CANYON

🛈 Tourist information centre	🚶 Start of long-distance footpath	🧗 Rock climbing
● Resting place	✳ Dangerous stretch	0 ——— 1500 m

🛤 From the steps going down to the river, there are fine views of the Pas de l'Estellié.

Ignore the path branching off to the right towards the Estellié Footbridge; it leads to the Restaurant des Cavaliers and the Corniche Sublime.

At the Pré d'Issane, the path runs close to the river and follows it through the Étroit des Cavaliers with sheer cliffs towering 300m/984ft above. The gorge widens and the path reaches the Talus de Guègues, a scree framed by steep slopes.

Continue upstream past the vast Baumes-aux-Bœufs Cave and take the second path to the right leading to the **Mescla★★★**, where the flow of the Verdon mixes with that of the Artuby. There is a splendid view upstream of the Défilé des Baumes-Frères.

Retrace your steps to the intersection and turn right.

The path winds its way up to the Brèche Imbert *(steps)*: superb view of the Baumes-Frères and the Barre de l'Escalès. The canyon, overlooked by very high cliffs (400-500m/1 312-1 640ft), becomes wider then suddenly narrower. The Chaos de

Trescaïre, on the right, is an extraordinary jumble of fallen rocks. The hilltop village of Rougon can be seen in the distance. Next come two tunnels; inside the second, metal steps lead to the **Baume-aux-Pigeons★**, a vast cave, 30m/98ft high, situated at the foot of a 350m/1 148ft-high cliff. From the bottom of the stairs, it is possible to see, on the opposite bank, the huge blocks which fell when the roof caved in. This cave and the collapsed roof indicate that in the past the Verdon partly flowed underground. From the last opening, there is a view of the **Couloir Samson★★**, a very narrow corridor with smooth vertical sides. Beyond the tunnel, the path goes over the footbridge across the Baou and climbs to the parking area. The hike ends at the **Belvédère du Point Sublime★★★**.

Walk to the inn where you can call a taxi. You can join D 952 from the Auberge du Point Sublime by taking shortcuts.

If you wish to go to La Palud-sur-Verdon without going past the Point Sublime, take the path on the left just before the footbridge over the Baou; it goes up along the south bank of the stream and joins D 952 4km/2.5mi from La Palud-sur-Verdon. This shortens the hike by 3km/1.9mi.

② Sentier de Découverte des Lézards

★ 🔲 ⊙ **From the Point Sublime** – This well-marked nature trail starts from the Plateau des Lauves. A small explanatory booklet is available at the Auberge du Point Sublime or at the tourist office in La Palud-sur-Verdon.
Another itinerary leads to the Pont de Tusset along GR 49.
These round tours usually last between 1hr and 3hr 30min.

③ Belvédère de Rancoumas

★★ **East bank starting from the Point Sublime** – *3hr 30min there and back. It is possible to start from the Point Sublime car park and to walk south, following GR 49 markings, or to drive towards the Couloir Samson (D 23ᴱ) and park the car on the last bend before the straight stretch ending in the car park.*
🔲 2km/1.2mi before reaching the car park, take GR 49 on the left, marked in white and red; it leads through an oak forest down to the **Pont de Tusset★**, dating from the early 17C.
The path starts rising through a forest of pines, maples and beeches, then joins a wide track. Leave the marked path and follow the track on the right; it crosses a stream before reaching the ruins of Encastel. Go up to the edge of the cliff. The natural Belvédère de Rancoumas offers a striking **panorama★★** of the whole Falaise de l'Escalès with the Sentier Martel running below. The **Mourre de Chanier** (alt 1 930m/6 332ft), the highest summit of the Verdon region, soars in the distance to the northwest.

Return along the same route.

★★④ Sentier de l'Imbut *3km/1.9mi.*

Do not take on this difficult itinerary without first having spent a day along the Sentier Martel to prepare for this sort of terrain.
– The path must be followed in one direction only, i.e. exit via the Vidal steps.
– Do not take domestic animals or children under 10 on this hike.
– Do not undertake this hike if the forecast flow rate reaches 40m³/1 413cu ft per second.
– Qualified guides are available (☎ 04 9274 63 95)
– It is possible to cross the Verdon over the Estellié footbridge and follow the Sentier Martel to the Chalet de la Maline.
Start from the Auberge des Cavaliers, 2.5km/1.5mi to the Estellié footbridge including 340m/372yd downwards. The itinerary runs entirely on the south bank, along a cliff path equipped with handrails in several places.
This is the most secluded and impressive part of the canyon where one can see huge beech trees, caves, groves of hazelnut trees and potholes. The itinerary follows the long Styx Corridor and reaches the Imbut Beach, where the path ends. This is the point where the water disappears down a sump. Great caution is required if you wish to go over the jumble of rocks forming the "Chaos de l'Imbut".
The return journey up the steep Vidal steps requires a considerable effort to negotiate the difference in altitude of 400m/1 312ft; the steps are often 50cm/20in high and the only help comes from a steel handrail.
Walkers can also cross the Estellié footbridge and continue along the Sentier Martel to the Chalet de la Maline.

VILLARD-DE-LANS

Population 3 798
Michelin map 333 G7 and 244 fold 39

The tourist capital of the Vercors region has the best facilities of all the resorts in the Dauphiné Préalpes. Its dry, sunny climate, clean air and sheltered position at the foot of the Cornafion, Gerbier and Moucherotte make it an ideal resort for children and adults; outdoor activities include skiing, paragliding, potholing, canyoning and ballooning. In the 1980s, Villars-de-Lans and Corrençon-en-Vercors joined forces to form a single holiday resort with a greater variety of ski slopes, hikes and climbing routes.

Nearby Sights: Massif de CHAMROUSSE, Massif de la CHARTREUSE, GRENOBLE, Lacs de LAFFREY, PONT-EN-ROYANS, Le VERCORS, VIZILLE

EXCURSIONS

★ Cote 2000 *4.5km/2.8mi southeast*

From Villard-de-Lans, take the avenue des Bains to the end of the valley. Turn left onto D 215 to Corrençon and left again to the gondola station. Take the **Cote 2000 gondola** ⊘ to the mountain station and continue on foot *(1hr there and back for the ride and the walk)*.

The **view** embraces the undulating plateaux of the Montagnes de Lans and Vercors to the north and west and stretches as far as the distant brown line of the Cevennes

★ Route de Valchevrière

Leave Villard-de-Lans by the avenue des Bains. At the junction at the end of the valley, follow the D 215C towards Le Bois-Barbu.

A small scenic road is lined with the Stations of the Cross dedicated to the victims of the fighting which took place in 1944. Views of the Gorges de la Bourne and the Méaudre valley.

★ **Calvaire de Valchevrière** – *(8km/5mi west along D 215C)* The twelfth cross was erected on the last position held on 23 and 24 July 1944 by members of the Resistance.

Eating out

BUDGET

Le Bacha – *42 pl. de la Libération* – ☎ *04 76 95 15 24* – *closed 10-30 Apr, 10-30 Nov, Mon evening and Tue* – *14.48/24.39€*. This family restaurant on a small and lively square in the village centre has rustic decor and a vaulted basement dining room. Take a seat on the terrace in season.

MODERATE

La Ferme du Bois Barbu – *Au Bois-Barbu – 3km/2mi W of Villard-de-Lans on D 215E* – ☎ *04 76 95 13 09* – *closed 18-23 Jun, 12 Nov-7 Dec, Sun evening and Wed except school holidays* – *18.29/45.73€*. This farmhouse stands in an unspoiled natural setting almost at the end of the road, just before the start of the cross-country ski trails. It has a painted façade and peaceful mountain chalet style decor. Ramblers can rest here and be lulled by the piano in the evenings.

Where to stay

BUDGET

Villa Primerose – *147 av. des Bains* – ☎ *04 76 95 13 17 – closed 1 Oct-20 De* – 🅿 – *18rms: 33.54/38.11€* – ⌣ *3.81€*. Take a seat in the garden or on the terrace here to be spellbound by the view of the mountains in a setting of greenery. Keen sportspeople can play tennis opposite the hotel and go either cross country or downhill skiing in winter. The kitchen is made available to residents which is practical!

Chambre d'hôte Le Val Ste-Marie – *Au Bois-Barbu – near the start of the cross country ski trails – 4km/2.5mi W of Villard-de-Lans on D 215ᴱ towards Bois Barbu then La Glisse mountain refuge, track to the left after the signpost t Caisse* – ☎ *04 76 95 92 80* – ⊠ – *3rms: 35.06/43.30€ – main meal 13.72€* This two hundred year-old farm has been well restored and is a comfortabl place to stay. Nature lovers can make the most of the surrounding countrysid in summer and the cross-country ski trails in winter. In the evening, guests din with their hosts.

View of the Gorges de la Bourne and of Valchevrière. The chapel, now the fourteenth station of the cross, was the only building to survive the fire that destroyed the old village.

★**Brèche de Chalimont** – Continue to the Chalets de Chalimont. Turn right along a forest road *(1hr there and back on foot – the road is also suitable for cars in dry weather)*. A narrow ridge offers extended views of the whole area.

★★Gorges de la Bourne

From Villard-de-Lans to Pont-en-Royans – *Itinerary described in reverse under VERCORS,* 2

The likely return of the bear

Since it was last seen near St-Martin-en-Vercors in 1938, the European brown bear has completely disappeared from the French Alps. This animal, which lives in forests, is particularly shy and can sense human presence several hundred yards away. Occasionally carnivorous, it lives mainly on plants and looks for them in remote and steep wooded areas. The Haut-Vercors region, which is totally desolate in winter and has no permanent settlements, offers the ideal conditions for the return of the bear, which is represented by statues in many villages. However, the Parc naturel régional du Vercors authorities, who have drawn up plans for its possible return, are first looking for the support and active involvement of the local population, particularly farmers

---

VILLARS-SUR-VAR

Population 507
Michelin map 341 D4 and 245 fold 24

Set in the midst of rocks, vines and olive groves, Villars-sur-Var was once a stronghold of the mighty Grimaldi family. The remains of the old walls and the Porte St-Antoine guard a peaceful village, perched on a sunny mountain terrace above the Var, only 40 minutes' drive from Nice

Nearby Sights:

ANNOT, BEUIL, Gorges du CIANS, CLUES DE HAUTE-PROVENCE, ENTREVAUX, PUGET-THÉNIERS, Vallée de la TINÉE

THE OLD TOWN

Within the walls, a walk along the cobbled streets, closed to traffic, leads past a number of doorways with carved 18C and 19C porches.

Church – The highlight of the rich interior decoration is a large **high-altar retable★** made up of 10 panels in Franciscan style, painted by an unknown artist; the central panel represents a splendid **Entombment★★**, below are St. Claire and St. Francis to the left and St. Lucy and St. Honoratus to the right. The polychrome woodwork bears the arms of the Grimaldi, a powerful family bitterly opposed to the dukes of Savoie from the 14C to the 17C. The **Annunciation altarpiece★** (Nice School c 1520), located on the left of the chancel, is also remarkable, as are the three paintings above it; a Nativity, a Pietà and a depiction of the Flight into Egypt. The church contains some fine statues, including one of St. Petronilla and another of John the Baptist by Mathieu Danvers (1524), plus a painting from the school of Veronese entitled *Martyrdom of St Bartholomew*. The Madonna with rosary (late 16C) on the right of the chancel, was a favourite subject of the Nice Gothic school.

St Lucy (detail) from the high-altar retable, Villars-sur-Var

P. et G. Leclerc

453

EXCURSIONS

* **Thiéry** – *14km/8.7mi northwest along D 226*. A place of narrow streets and covered alleyways, this isolated village overlooking the Gorges du Cians **(viewpoint)** has stood on the hilltop since the 11C.

★ Route de Tournefort

This picturesque road (D 25) linking the River Var and River Tinée across the foothills of the Pointe des Quatre-Cantons, some 10km/6mi upstream from their confluence, presents some of the best of the local landscape. 11km/6.8mi west of the Pont de la Mescla, the road branches off ,5from N 202 and climbs the slopes towards Villars.

Villars-sur-Var – *see above*

D 26 winds its way along the forested slopes of Mont Falourde, offering glimpses of the Chapelle de la Madone d'Utelle across the River Tinée.

Massoins – From this mountain village, there is a fine **view** of the Var Valley. The ruins of a 14C castle stand above the centre.

2km/1.2mi further on, turn right onto a small road.

Tournefort – The village clings to a steep rock spur. Near the chapel, the **view★** embraces the Var and Tinée valleys framed by mountains, the Madone d'Utelle and the hilltop village of La Tour *(see Vallée de la TINÉE)*.

Return to D 26 and follow it down to the Tinée Valley.

VIZILLE★

Population 7 495
Michelin map 333 H7 and 244 fold 39 – Local map see Lacs de LAFFREY

This small industrial town has retained one of the major historic buildings of the Dauphiné region, the château of François de Bonne de **Lesdiguières** (1543-1627). Until 1972, it was one of the national estates at the disposal of the French President.

Nearby Sights: Le BOURG D'OISANS, Massif de CHAMROUSSE, Massif de la CHARTREUSE, GRENOBLE, Le GRÉSIVAUDAN, Lacs de LAFFREY, Route NAPOLÉON, ST-PIERRE-DE-CHARTREUSE, Le TRIÈVES, Le VALBONNAIS, Le VERCORS, VILLARD-DE-LANS

BACKGROUND

The Duc de Lesdiguières rose from the minor aristocracy to become one of the most colourful characters of his time. A staunch supporter of the Reformation, who had made his name at 22 as a Huguenot leader, he was made governor of Dauphiné by King Henri IV and for the next thirty years exercised his authority with vigour and such cunning that he was nicknamed "the Fox". Lesdiguières was created duke, peer of the realm and marshal of France, but his ambition was not yet satisfied. In 1622 he finally became the last constable of France, but only after renouncing the Protestant faith.
In 1602 he supervised the building of the Château de Vizille, exacting forced labour from the local villagers to get the job done. His son-in-law Marshal Créqui added the monumental staircase leading down to the park. In 1780, the château was bought by Claude Périer, a wealthy financier from Grenoble who lent it to the États du Dauphiné for their historic meeting in 1788.
The major event in the history of this little town took place on 21 July 1788, one year before the French Revolution began. The meeting of the regional assembly, which was banned in Grenoble, took place instead in the Château de Vizille. Discussions between 165 members of the nobility, 50 clergymen and 325 representatives of the middle and lower classes went on from 8am to 3am the next morning. The resolution finally voted by the **Assemblée de Vizille** protested against the suppression of Parliament by Louis XVI, called for a meeting of all the regional assemblies and demanded individual freedom for all French citizens. For having expressed wishes that the whole nation adopted a year later, Vizille can rightly be called the "cradle" of the French Revolution.

★CHÂTEAU ⊙ *1hr*

The asymmetric silhouette of the château, deprived of its east wing by a fire in 1865 and flanked by a round and a square tower, looks quite original. One of the entrances is decorated with a bronze low relief by Jacob Richier, depicting Lesdiguières on horseback. The austere main façade faces the Romanche whereas a more elegant Renaissance façade overlooks the park.

Interior – It is divided into two parts: the **Musée de la Révolution française** and the old château. The museum is arranged on three floors. French and English earthenware is on display in the orangery; also on the ground floor, in the "salle des Colonnes" carved

Château de Vizille

out of the rock, are some large canvases, stored for the Musée du Louvre and the Château de Versailles. The first floor is devoted to themed temporary exhibitions and the second floor houses a collection of portraits and furniture.

The historic part of the old château comprises several reception rooms including the Grand Salon des Tapisseries (17C tapestries, portraits of Lesdiguières) and the Salon Lesdiguières (Louis XIII furniture), the terrace (lovely view of the park with the Mont Thabor in the distance) and the library (Louis XIV panelling).

Park – In the vast park (100ha/247 acres), extending south of the château, deer, moufflons and herons roam freely and huge trout can be seen swimming in the lake.

Jardin du Roi – *Access during the summer*. Medieval ruins of the old feudal fortress crown the "King's Garden", a rocky promontory overlooking the old town, north of the present building.

EXCURSION

Notre-Dame-de-Mésage – *2.6km/1.6mi south along N 85*. The church stands on the right of the main road; note its fine Romanesque stone bell-tower.
Slightly further on, the **Chapelle St-Firmin★**, a 13C chapel of the Knights Templar, has an elegant east end.

YVOIRE★★
Population 650
Michelin map 328 K2 and 244 fold 8

Yvoire occupies a splendid position on the shores of Lake Geneva, at the tip of the promontory which separates the "Petit Lac" and the "Grand Lac".
Flowers abound in this picturesque village which has retained its medieval character. Its restaurants are renowned for their fish specialities, and in summer the marina is kept busy by keen yachtsmen from Switzerland and Savoie.

Nearby Sights: ABONDANCE, AVORIAZ, CHÂTEL, ÉVIAN-LES-BAINS, MORZINE, La ROCHE-SUR-FORON, THONON-LES-BAINS

★★THE MEDIEVAL VILLAGE

Yvoire has retained part of its 14C fortifications, including two gateways, the **castle** *(not open to the public)* with its massive square keep flanked by turrets, and a few old houses.

Leave the car outside the fortifications, in the paying car park, on the right coming from Thonon.

Take a stroll through the lively streets lined with workshops; now and then a lovely square decorated with flowers offers views of the lake.

The **Église St-Pancrace** adds the finishing touch to this attractive picture; the chancel dates from the 14C but the building was only completed at the end of the 17C.

The château at Yvoire

From the end of the pier, where boats offering trips round the lake have their moorings *(see ÉVIAN: Practical information)*, there are views of the Swiss shore backed by the Jura mountains. Day excursions are organised along the opposite shore.

★ **Jardin des Cinq Sens** ⊘ – *Rue du Lac.* The former kitchen garden of the castle has been turned into a reconstruction of a medieval enclosed garden where monks used to grow vegetables and herbs. Gentian and rhododendrons grow in the Alpine garden, from where there is a fine view of the castle. Next comes the **Labyrinthe végétal**, a maze on the theme of the five senses: the Jardin du goût (taste) with its strawberries, raspberries and apple trees, the Jardin des textures (touch) with its subtle variety of foliage, the Jardin des couleurs (sight) with its harmonious range of colours changing with the seasons (geraniums, roses, bluebells) and the Jardin des senteurs (smell) with its lilies, honeysuckle and daphnes; at the centre of the garden, an aviary, full of pheasants and turtledoves, symbolises the sense of hearing.

Vivarium ⊘ – *Rue de l'Église.* This observation centre, housed in a medieval building, contains more than 50 different species of reptiles and amphibians from the five continents: green mambas, rare snakes, lizards, batrachians and crocodiles.

Eating out

BUDGET

Le Denieu – *74140 Bonnatrait – 6km/4mi SE of Yvoire on D 25 and N 5 -* ☎ *04 50 72 35 06 – 13.72/29.73€.* Dare to cross the threshold of this large harmonious-looking house by the side of the main road. The dining room is very fine with aged wood decor and a display of old farming implements in deference to its agricultural past. Specialities from the Savoie region.

MODERATE

La Vieille Porte – ☎ *04 50 72 80 14 – closed 26 Nov-28 Feb, and Mon except Jul-Aug and public holidays – 26.68/42.69€.* This house is located in the walls of the old town and has belonged to the same family since 1587. Its terrace between the village and the lake becomes popular as soon as the sun comes out. In winter, there is a peaceful dining room with an open fire.

Where to stay

BUDGET

Camping Municipal la Pinède – *74140 Excenevex – 4km/2.5mi SE of Yvoire on D 25 –* ☎ *04 50 72 85 05 – open Mar-Oct – reservations recommended - 619 pitches: 10.98€.* Set up camp among the pine trees and sand dunes, on the shores of Lake Geneva. You can indulge in your favourite sport: tennis, sailing, wind-surfing, table-tennis, boules… There is a fine sandy beach for lying on, if nothing else appeals. Children's play area.

MODERATE

Hôtel Le Vieux Logis – *R. Principale –* ☎ *04 50 72 80 24 – closed Dec-Feb -* 🅿 *– 11rms: 53.36/56.41€ -* ⌑ *6.40€ – restaurant 21.65€/36.59€.* This 14C house is totally in keeping with the style of the old town. The hotel inside it does not quite match up to the charm of the beautiful façade, but it is unfussy and well kept. The dining room is set up inside the fortified curtain walls.

Hôtel Le Pré de la Cure – ☎ *04 50 72 83 58 – closed 12 Nov-1 Mar –* 🅿 *- 25rms: 56.41/64.03€ -* ⌑ *7.93€ – restaurant 16.77/42.69€.* This modern house opposite one of the fortified gateways of the old town is set in a pleasant garden. There is a fine view of the lake from its terrace and balconies. The rooms are quite spacious and functional. Friendly welcome and well-prepared food.

EXCURSION

★ **Excenevex** – *3km/1.9mi southeast along D 25.*
This charming lakeside resort, sheltering in the Golfe de Coudrée, is famous for having the most extensive beach on the French side of Lake Geneva. The coast is lined with luxury holiday villas.

France's last manufacturers of gold leaf, which is used for bookbinding, picture-framing and decorative wrought-iron, have been working here since 1939 *(not open to the public)*. Some of the gold leaf produced in Excenevex was used for the restoration of Versailles.

Admission times and charges

As admission times and charges are liable to alteration, the information printed below is for guidance only. In cases where it has not been possible to obtain up-to-date information, the admission times and charges from the previous edition of the guide have been given in italics.

Every sight for which times and charges are listed below is indicated by the symbol ⊘ after the title in the Sights Section of the guide.

Order: The information is listed in the same order as in the Sights Section of the guide.

Dates: Dates given are inclusive.

Last admission: Ticket offices usually shut 30min before closing time. Some places issue timed tickets owing to limited space and facilities.

Lecture tours: These are regularly organised during the tourist season in towns of specaill interest. The information is given under the appropriate heading. In towns labelled "Villes d'Art et d'Histoire" and "Villes d'Art" , tours are conducted by lecturers/guides approved by the "Caisse des Monuments Historiques et des Sites".

Charge: The charge given is for an individual adult. Concessionary rates may be available for families, children, old-age pensioners and the unemployed. Many places offer special rates for group bookings and some have special days for group visits. Large parties should apply in advance.

Churches: Churches cannot be visited during services and are usually closed between noon and 2pm. They are included in the following list if the interior is of particular interest.

Facilities for the disabled: All venues offering facilities for the disabled are followed by the symbol ♿. As the range of possible facilities is great (for impaired mobility, sight and hearing) readers are advised to telephone in advance to check what is available.

A

ABONDANCE
🄱 74360 Abondance, ☎ 04 50 73 02 90. www.valdabondance.com

Abbey – Possibility of guided tours. Ask at the cloisters. ☎ 04 50 81 60 54.

Cloister – ♿ Mar-Oct: 10am-noon, 2-5pm; from Christmas school holidays to end Feb: daily except Sat 10am-noon, 2-5pm. Guided tours 10am and 3pm. Closed from All Saints to Christmas. 1,75€ unaccompanied visits, 3.20€ guided tours. ☎ 04 50 81 60 54.

Museum of Religious Art – Ask at the cloisters. ☎ 04 50 81 60 54.

ABRIÈS
🄱 Le Bourg, 05460 Abriès, ☎ 04 92 46 72 26.

Jilly chairlift – Jul and Aug: daily except Sat 9.15am-12.15pm, 1.30-4.30pm. 5€. ☎ 04 92 46 78 08.

AIX-LES-BAINS
🄱 Pl. Maurice-Mollard, 73100 Aix-Les-Bains, ☎ 04 79 88 68 00. www.aixlesbains.com

Aquarium – Jul and Aug: 10-11am, 2-6pm; May, Jun and Sep: 2-6pm; Feb-Apr, Oct and Nov: Wed, Sat-Sun 2-5pm. Closed Dec and Jan. 4,5€. ☎ 04 79 61 08 22. www.lacdubourget.com

Musée Faure – ♿ Mar-Oct: daily except Tue 10am-noon, 1.30-6pm; Nov-Feb: daily except Tue and Wed 10am-noon, 1.30-6pm. Closed mid-Dec to mid-Jan and public holidays. 3,5€. ☎ 04 79 61 06 57.

Thermes nationaux – Apr-Oct: daily except Sun and Mon 3-4.30pm; Nov-Mar: Wed 3-4.30pm. 4€. ☎ 04 79 35 38 50.

Musée d'Archéologie et de Préhistoire – Jun-Aug: 9am-6.30pm; Apr, May and Sep: 9am-12.15pm, 2-6pm; Oct-Mar: daily except Sun 9am-noon, 2-6pm; Dec-Feb: daily except Sun 9am-noon, 2-5.30pm. No charge. ☎ 04 79 88 68 00.

L'ALBANAIS

Rumilly   🖪 4, pl. de l'Hotel de Ville, 74152 Rumilly, ☎ 04 50 64 58 32. www.ot-albanais74.fr

Guided tours of the town – Contact the tourist office.

Musée régional de l'Albanais – ♿ Jul and Aug: daily except Tue 10am-noon, 3-7pm; Jun and Sep: daily except Tue 9-11am, 2-6pm. No charge. ☎ 04 50 01 19 53.

Chapelle N.-D.-de-l'Aumône – 2-6pm.

Vaulx: Jardins Secrets – ♿ Early Jul to mid-Sep: guided tours (1hr15min, last tour leaves 1hr before closing time) 1.30-7pm; mid-Apr to end Jun: Sat-Sun and public holidays 1.30-7pm; mid-Sep to mid-Oct: Sun and public holidays 1.30-6pm. 6€ (under 16s: 2,5€). ☎ 04 50 60 53 18.

Alby-sur-Chéran

Guided tour of the old town – Contact the Maison du Pays d'Alby.

Musée de la Cordonnerie – Early Jul to mid-Sep: 10am-noon, 2-6pm; mid-Sep to end Jun: daily except Sun and Mon 10am-noon, 1.30-5.30pm. Closed public holidays. No charge. ☎ 04 50 68 39 44.

Gruffy: Musée de la Nature – ♿ Jul and Aug: 2-6pm (last admission 30min before closing); mid-Mar to end of Jun and early Sep to mid-Nov: daily except Mon and Tue. 2-6pm. 3,8€. ☎ 04 50 77 58 60.

Marcellaz-Albanais: Musée l'Art de l'enfance – Apr-Oct: Mon, Wed, Thu, Sun 2-8pm. 4,5€ (children: 2,25€). ☎ 04 50 69 73 74.

Château de Clermont – May-Oct: 10.30am-6.30pm. 3€. ☎ 04 50 63 69 15.

ALBERTVILLE
🖪 Pl. de l'Europe, 73204 Albertville, ☎ 04 79 32 04 22. www.albertville.com

Guided tours of the town 🔳 – Jul and Aug: daily except Sat-Sun.

Maison des 16es Jeux Olympiques d'hiver – ♿ Jul and Aug: 9am-7pm, Sun and public holidays 2-7pm; Sep-Jun: daily except Sun and Public holidays 9am-noon, 2-6pm. 3€. ☎ 04 79 37 75 71.

Conflans

Guided tours of the town – Jul and Aug: 10.30am, 2.30pm and 4.30pm. 5€. Contact the Albertville-Conflans guide-lecturers. ☎ 04 79 32 29 93.

Château Manuel de Locatel – Jul and Aug: guided tours (45min) by appointment 3pm and 4.30pm. 2,5€. ☎ 04 79 32 04 22.

Maison Rouge – Mid-Jun to mid-Sep: 10am-7pm; early Nov to mid-Jun: daily except Tue 2-6pm; school holidays: daily except Tue 2-6pm. Closed Oct, 1 Jan, 1 May and 25 Dec. 2,5€. ☎ 04 79 37 86 86.

ALLEVARD
🖪 Pl. de la Résistance, 38580 Allevard, ☎ 04 76 45 10 11. www.allevard-les-bains.com

Chartreuse de St-Hugon/Buddhist temple – Jul and Aug: guided tours (1hr) daily except Wed 4pm; Sep-Jun: Sun and public holidays 4pm Closed Jan. 4,6€. ☎ 04 79 25 78 00.

L'ALPE-D'HUEZ
🖪 Pl. Paganon, 38750 Alpe-D'huez, ☎ 04 76 11 44 44. www.alpedhuez.com

Musée d'Huez et de l'Oisans – Jul, Aug and Nov-Apr: daily except Sat 10am-noon, 3-7pm. Closed May, Jun, Sep, Oct and public holidays (except in Jul and Aug). 2€. ☎ 04 76 11 21 74. www.musee.alpedhuez.com

Pic du Lac Blanc gondola and cable car– Summer: 8.15am-5.10pm (30min). 12,5€. ☎ 04 76 80 30 30.

la Grande Sure chairlift – Dec-Apr: 9am-3.45pm (10min). 1,52€. ☎ 04 76 80 30 30.

ANNECY
🖪 Centre Bonlieu, 1 r. J.-Jaurès, 74000 Annecy, ☎ 04 50 45 00 33. www.lac-annecy.com

Guided Tours 🔳

Palais de l'Isle – As for château-museum. 4,6€ (children: no charge). ☎ 04 50 33 87 31.

Musée de l'Histoire d'Annecy – Jun-Sep: 10am-6.30pm; Oct-May: daily except Tue 10am-noon, 2-5pm. Closed 1 Jan, Easter Sunday and Monday, 1 May, 1 and 11 Nov, 24, 25 and 31Dec. 4.60€ (children: no charge). ☎ 04 50 33 87 31.

Observatoire régional des lacs alpins – As for château-museum. Combined ticket.

Conservatoire d'Art et d'Histoire de la Haute-Savoie – Daily except Sat-Sun and public holidays 9am-noon. No charge.

Basilique de la Visitation – Guided tours possible by appointment. ☎ 04 50 45 22 76.

Basilique St-Joseph-des-Fins – Ask at the presbytery. ☎ 04 50 57 03 12.

Circuits

Gorges du Fier – Mid-Jun to mid-Sep: 9am-7pm; mid-Mar to mid-Jun and mid-Sep to mid-Oct: 9am-noon, 2-6pm. 4,2€. ☎ 04 50 46 23 07.

Château du Montrottier – Jun-Aug: guided tours (1hr15min, last tour 1hr before closing time) daily except Tue 10am-1pm, 2-7pm; mid-Mar to end May and Sep: daily except Tue 10am-1pm, 2-6pm; early Oct to mid-Oct: daily except Tue 2-5pm. 5,34€. ☎ 04 50 46 23 02.

Boat trips on the lake – Apr to end Oct: several types of boat trips with commentaries (1hr). 9,8€. May to mid-Sep: Boats stopping at various places (2hr). 12,1€. Lunch trip and dinner-dance on board the MS Libellule. Times and reservations: Compagnie des Bateaux du lac d'Annecy, ☎ 04 50 51 08 40. www.annecy-croisieres.com.

Lac d'ANNECY

Écomusée du Costume savoyard – Jun-Sep: daily except Sun morning and Mon 10am-noon, 2.30-6.30pm; May: daily except Mon 2-6pm. 3,4€. ☎ 04 50 52 41 05.

Musée de la Cloche – ♿ Jun-Aug: daily except Mon 10am-noon, 2.30-6.30pm, Sun 2.30-6.30pm (last admission 1hr before closing); Sep-May: daily except Mon 10am-noon, 2.30-5.30pm, Sun 2.30-5.30pm. Closed early to mid-Dec, 1st week in Jan and 25 Dec. 4.27€. ☎ 04 50 52 47 11.

Seythenex

Grotte and Cascade de Seythenex – Jul and Aug: guided tours (30min) 9.30am-6pm; mid-May to end Jun and early to mid-Sep: 10am-5.30pm. 6,1€ (children: 4,45€). ☎ 04 50 44 55 97. www.cascade.fr

Montagne de la Sambuy (Seythenex chairlift) – Mid-Jun to end Aug: 10am-5pm (20min, continuous). 6€ return. ☎ 04 50 44 44 45.

Viuz: Musée archéologique - Jul and Aug: 2.30-6.30pm; Sep-Jun: daily except Sat-Sun 2.30-6.30pm. Closed public holidays (except 14 Jul and 15 Aug). 2,35€. ☎ 04 50 32 45 99.

Menthon-Saint-Bernard　　　　　🛈 74290 Menthon-St-Bernard, ☎ 04 50 60 14 30.

Château – Jul and Aug: guided tours (1hr) noon-6pm; May, Jun and Sep: Fri 2-6pm. 5,5€ (costumed visit Sat-Sun and public holidays: 6€). ☎ 04 50 60 12 05.

ANNOT　　　　　🛈 Bd St Pierre, 04240 Annot, ☎ 04 92 83 23 03. www.annot.com

Massif des ARAVIS　　　　　🛈 74220 La Clusaz, ☎ 04 50 32 65 00. www.laclusaz.com

Cimetière des Glières: Musée de la Résistance – Jun to mid-Sep: 10am-noon, 2-7pm (last admission 15min before closing). No charge. ☎ 04 50 51 87 00.

Thônes　　　　　🛈 Pl. Avet, 74230 Thônes, ☎ 04 50 02 00 26. www.thones-tourisme.com

Musée du Pays de Thônes – Jul and Aug: daily except Sun 10am-noon, 3-7pm; Sep-Jun: daily except Sun 9am-noon, 1.30-5.30pm, Mon and Wed 1.30-5.30pm. Closed public holidays (except 14 Jul and 15 Aug). 2,5€. ☎ 04 50 02 97 76.

Écomusée du Bois et de la Forêt – ♿ Jul and Aug: guided tours (1hr) daily except Wed 9.30am-noon; Apr-Jun, Sep and Oct: Tue and Thu 4-5pm, Sun 2.30-6.30pm. 3,35€. ☎ 04 50 32 18 10.

Entremont: Church – Jun-Aug: guided tours (1hr30min) Wed 2-5pm by request. ☎ 04 50 03 56 87.

Les ARCS　　　　　🛈 73706 Les Arcs, ☎ 04 79 07 12 57. www.lesarcs.com

Arc-en-Ciel funicular – Jul and Aug: 8.30am-7.30pm (7min, departure every 30min). 9,5€ return, 5,5€ single. ☎ 04 79 04 24 40.

l'Aiguille Rouge – Jul and Aug: Varet gondola 9.45am-4.30pm, Aiguille Rouge cable-car 10am-4.30pm (continuous). 12,5€ return (both stages).

Télécabine le Transarc – Jul and Aug: 9.15am-4.30pm (15min, continuous). 9,5€ return, 5,5€ single.

Télésiège de la Cachette – Jul and Aug: 9.15am-5.30pm (continuous). 9,5€ return, 5,5€ single. ☎ 04 79 04 24 40.

Peisey-Nancroix　　　　　🛈 Pl. de Roscanvel, 73210 Peisey-Nancroix, ☎ 04 79 07 94 28.
www.peisey-vallandry.com

ARGENTIÈRE　　　　　🛈 Pl. du Triangle de l'Amitié, BP 25, 74400 Chamonix-Mont-Blanc,
☎ 04 50 53 00 24. www.chamonix.com

Lognan and Grands-Montets cable cars – Jul and Aug: 7.15am-5.15pm; Sep-Jun: 8.30am-12.30pm, 1.30-4.30pm. 23€ return, 17€ single. ☎ 04 50 54 00 71.

Col de Balme gondola – de mid-Jul to mid-Sep: 8.30am-5.15pm (16min, continuous); mid-Jun to mid-Jul: 9am-4.45pm. 12€ return, 9€ single. ☎ 04 50 54 00 58.

Réserve naturelle des Aiguilles-Rouges, Information Centre – Reception and information chalet early Jun to mid-Sep: 9am-12.30pm, 1.30-6.30pm. No charge. ☎ 04 50 54 08 06.

L'ARGENTIÈRE-LA-BESSÉE
🖪 Pl. de la Poste, 05120 L'Argentière-La-Bessée, ☎ 04 92 23 03 11.

Chapelle St-Jean – Contact the tourist office.

Church – Contact the tourist office.

Musée des Mines d'Argent – ⅃ Mid-Jun to mid-Sep and Easter school holidays: 9am-noon, 2-6pm; other school holidays: Wed 2-6pm, other days by request. 1,5€. ☎ 04 92 23 02 94.

Anciennes Mines d'Argent – Mid-Jun to mid-Sep: guided tours 9.30am, 11am, 2pm and 4.30pm; school holidays: 9.30am and 2pm (unless blocked by snow). Visitors must reserve. 6,85€ (children: 5,85€). Minimum age: 6 years. ☎ 04 92 23 02 94.

Réserve biologique des Deslioures – Mid-Jul to mid-Aug: guided tours: early Apr to mid-Jul and mid-Aug to end Oct: unaccompanied tours. 8,35€ guided tours (children: 6€). ☎ 04 92 23 02 94.

AURON
🖪 Le Riou, Grange Cossa, 06660 Auron, ☎ 04 93 23 02 66. www.auron.fr.st

Chapelle St-Érige – The key is available at the tourist office (identity document retained as guarantee). ☎ 04 93 23 02 66.

Las Donnas cable car – Contact the tourist office for information. ☎ 04 93 23 02 66.

AUSSOIS
🖪 Rte des Barrages, 73500 Aussois, ☎ 04 79 20 30 80. www.aussois.com

AVORIAZ
🖪 Pl. Centrale, 74110 Avoriaz, ☎ 04 50 74 02 11. www.avoriaz.com

BARCELONNETTE
🖪 Pl. Frédéric-Mistral, 04400 Barcelonnette, ☎ 04 92 81 04 71. www.barcelonnette.net
Maison de la vallée, 4 av. des Trois-Frères-Arnaud, 04400 Barcelonnette, ☎ 04 92 81 03 68.

Villa la Sapinière, Musée de la Vallée – Jul and Aug: 10am-noon, 2.30-7pm (last admission 1hr before closing); school holidays: 2.30-6pm; Jun, Sep: daily except Sun and Mon 3-7pm; outside school holidays: Wed, Thu, Sat 2.30-6pm. Closed 1 Jan and 25 Dec. 3,2€. ☎ 04 92 81 27 15.

Maison du Parc du Mercantour – Jul and Aug: 10am-noon, 3-7pm; mid to end Jun and early to mid-Sep: 3-6pm. No charge. ☎ 04 92 81 21 31. www.parc-mercantour.fr

Le Sauze 🖪 Immeuble le Perce-Neige, 04400 Le Sauze, ☎ 04 92 81 05 61. www.sauze.com
Super-Sauze cable car – Jul and Aug: 9am-4.45pm. 5€ return. ☎ 04 92 81 05 35.

BARGÈME
🖪 Mairie, 83840 Bargème, ☎ 04 94 76 81 25.

Église Saint Nicolas – Jul and Aug: guided tours 2.30pm, 3.30pm, 4.30pm and 5.30pm.

Les BAUGES

Le Châtelard 🖪 Pl. de la Grenette, 73630 Le Châtelard, ☎ 04 79 54 84 28. www.lesbauges.com
Parc naturel régional du massif des Bauges, Le Châtelard, ☎ 04 79 54 86 40.

Château de Miolans – Jul and Aug: 10am-7pm; May, Jun and Sep: 10am-noon, 1.30-7pm; Apr: Sat-Sun and public holidays 1.30-7pm; Nov school holidays: 1.30-7pm. Closed rest of the year. 5,5€ (children: 2,5€). ☎ 04 79 28 57 04.

BEAUFORT
🖪 Grande Rue, 73270 Beaufort, ☎ 04 79 38 37 57.

Les Saisies 🖪 Av. des Jeux Olympiques, 73620 Les Saisies, ☎ 04 79 38 90 30. www.lessaisies.com

Hauteluce: Écomusée – Jul and Aug: daily except Mon 10am-noon, 3-7pm; Sep-Jun: ask for information at the town hall. No charge. ☎ 04 79 38 80 31.

Ugine: Musée des arts et traditions populaires du val d'Arly – Mid-Jun to mid-Sep: guided tours (1hr15min) daily except Tue 2-6pm. 4€. ☎ 04 79 37 56 33. www.ugine.com

Vallée des BELLEVILLE

🛈 Imm. l'Epervière, 73440 St-Martin-De-Belleville.
☎ 04 79 08 93 09. www.qt-martin-belleville.com

Val-Thorens

Caron cable car – Once a week (call for information). 8€. ☎ 04 79 00 07 08.

Funitel du Péclet – A few days per week (call for information). 8€. ☎ 04 79 00 08 08.

BESSANS

🛈 73480 Bessans, ☎ 04 79 05 96 52. www.bessans.com

Church – For guided tours, make an appointment at the tourist office. ☎ 04 79 05 96 52.

BEUIL

🛈 Quartier du Passaire, 06470 Beuil, ☎ 04 93 02 32 58.

Chapelle des Pénitents Blancs – Guided tours. Contact M. Noble, pl. de l'église.

Valberg

🛈 Pl. Centrale, 06470 Péone, ☎ 04 93 23 24 25. www.valberg.com

Roubion

🛈 06420 Roubion, ☎ 04 93 02 00 70. C

Chapelle St-Sébastien – For guided tours, ask at the tourist office. ☎ 04 93 02 10 30.

Roure

🛈 Mairie, 06420 Roure, ☎ 04 93 02 00 70. C

Chapelle St-Bernard-et-St-Sébastien – The key is available at the "Le Robur" inn. ☎ 04 93 02 03 57 or at the town hall. ☎ 04 93 02 00 70.

Route de la BONETTE

St-Dalmas-le-Selvage: Church – Contact the administration office at the town hall. ☎ 04 93 02 41 01 or the tourist office. ☎ 04 93 02 46 40.

BONNEVAL-SUR-ARC

🛈 73480 Bonneval-Sur-Arc, ☎ 04 79 05 95 95.
www.bonneval-sur-arc.com

Cheese dairy – 8am-noon. ☎ 04 79 05 93 10.

Le BOURG-D'OISANS

🛈 Quai Girard, 38520 Le Bourg-D'oisans, ☎ 04 76 80 03 25.

Musée des Minéraux et de la Faune des Alpes – Jul and Aug: 11am-7pm; Sep-Jun: 2-6pm. Closed from mid-Nov to mid-Dec and 1 Jan. 4€ (children: 1,5€). ☎ 04 76 80 27 54. www.oisans.com/musee

Lac du BOURGET

Le Bourget du Lac 🛈 73371 Le Bourget-Du-Lac, ☎ 04 79 25 01 99. www.bourgetdulac.com

Church – By request at the tourist office. ☎ 04 79 25 01 99.

Château-Prieuré – Jul and Aug: guided tours (1hr30min) Tue and Fri 10.30am by request at the tourist office. 5€. ☎ 04 79 25 01 99.

Château Thomas II – Jul and Aug: guided tours (1hr) 9-11am, 2-5pm, Tue and Fri 4pm, Sun 2-5pm. Price information not provided. ☎ 04 79 25 01 99.

Abbaye royale de Hautecombe: Church – Guided audio tours (30min) daily except Tue 10-11.30am, 2-5pm. ☎ 04 79 54 58 80.

BOURG-ST-MAURICE

🛈 Pl. de la Gare, BP 49, 73700 Bourg-St-Maurice,
☎ 04 79 07 04 92.

Musée des Minéraux et Faune de l'Alpe – Jul and Aug: 10am-noon, 3-7pm, Sun and Mon 3-7pm; Sep-Jun: by appointment. 4€. ☎ 04 79 07 12 74.

Alentours

Vulmix: Chapelle St-Gras – For guided tours, ask at the tourist office. ☎ 04 79 07 04 92.

Hauteville-Gondon

Musée du Costume – ♿ Daily except Tue 2-6pm (last admission 1hr before closing). Closed 1 Jan, 1 May and 25 Dec. Contact the tourist office during school holidays. 1.6€. ☎ 04 79 07 04 92 or 04 79 07 09 01.

Eglise Saint-Martin – Possibility of guided tours. Contact the tourist office. ☎ 04 79 07 04 92.

Circuits

La Rosière 1850 🛈 La Rosière Bourg, 73700 La Rosière-1850, ☎ 04 79 06 80 51. www.larosiere.net

BRIANÇON

🛈 1 pl. du Temple, 05100 Briançon, ☎ 04 92 21 08 50. www.ot-briancon.fr

Guided tours of the town 🄰 – Jul and Aug: 3pm; Sep: Wed, Fri and Sat a 3pm; Oct-May: Fri and Sat at 2pm. 4,27€.

Porte Pignerol – Jul and Aug: tours (2hr) daily except Sun 9.30am-noon, 2-6pm; Sep-Jun: daily except Sat-Sun 9.30am-noon, 2-5.30pm. 4,5€. ☎ 04 92 20 29 49.

Fort du Château (Citadelle) – Jul and Aug: 10am-6pm. 4€. ☎ 04 92 20 29 49

Musée de la mesure du temps – ♿ Jul and Aug: 10am-7pm; May, Jun and early Sep to mid-Nov: 10am-12.30pm, 3-6.30pm. 4€. 04 92 21 07 93.

Church – Jul and Aug: guided tours (1hr30min) by appointment Tue-Fri 4.30pm. ☎ 04 92 20 29 49.

Maison du Parc national des Écrins – ♿ Jul and Aug: 10am-7pm; Sep-Jun: daily except Sun and Mon 10am-noon, 1.30-5.30pm; school holidays: 10am-noon, 1.30-5.30 Closed public holidays. No charge. ☎ 04 92 21 42 15.

Alentours

Puy-Chalvin: Chapelle Ste-Lucie – Daily except Sat-Sun 5-6.30. ☎ 04 92 20 24 26.

Puy-St-Pierre: Musée de plein air sur les canaux d'irrigation – Free admission to the "Les Prenailles" locality, near the "Serre Che soleil" path.

Fort des Salettes – Jul and Aug: 10am-noon, 2-6pm. 4€. ☎ 04 92 20 29 49. www.briancon.com/vah

Prorel cable car – Jul, Aug and early Sep to mid-Dec: 10am-5pm (20min, continuous). 8,5€ (return ticket for pedestrians). ☎ 04 92 25 55 00.

BRIANÇONNAIS

La Salle-les-Alpes:

Eglise St-Marcellin – Possibility of guided tours Wed 2-3pm.

Chapelle St-Barthélemy – Guided tours by appointment with Mme Barbara. ☎ 04 92 24 76 17.

Plampinet: Église St-Sébastien – Contact the service du Patrimoine (Heritage Dept.) at the tourist office. ☎ 04 92 22 30 18.

Chapelle N.-D.-des-Grâces – Guided tours possible daily except Sat-Sun. No charge (guided tours: 3€). Contact the service du Patrimoine (Heritage Dept.) or the tourist office. ☎ 04 92 22 38 19 or 04 92 21 30 18.

Névache ☐ Ville Haute, 05100 Névache, ☎ 04 92 21 38 19. www.hautes-alpes.com/laclarée

Église St-Marcellin – Jul and Aug: 10.30am-6pm; Sep-Jun: Sat-Sun and Wed 10.30am-6pm. Possibility of guided tours: contact the service du Patrimoine (Heritage Dept.) or the tourist office. 3€. ☎ 04 92 21 30 18 or 04 92 21 38 19.

Cervières: maison Faure Vincent-Dubois – Jul and Aug: 3-6pm; Sep-Jun: by appointment. 4€. ☎ 04 92 21 07 59.

Col d'Izoard: museum – Jul and Aug: daily except Sun 10am-noon, 2.30-6.15pm. ☎ 04 92 45 06 23.

Villard-St-Pancras: Chapelle St-Pancrace – Contact the town hall. ☎ 04 92 21 05 27.

Prelles: Chapelle St-Jacques – Tours by appointment with Mr Bortino, next to the chapel. ☎ 04 92 21 05 03.

Le pays du BUËCH ☐ Rte de Grenoble, 05140 Aspres-Sur-Buëch, ☎ 04 92 58 68 88.

Veynes: Écomusée du Cheminot veynois – ♿ Jun-Sep: Wed-Sat 3-7pm; other school holidays: Wed-Sat 2-6pm. 3,10€. ☎ 04 92 58 00 49.

Serres ☐ Pl. du Lac, 05700 Serres, ☎ 04 92 67 00 67. www.buech-serrois.com

BUIS-LES-BARONNIES ☐ Pl. du Quinconce, 26170 Buis-Les-Baronnies, ☎ 04 75 28 04 59. www.buislesbaronnies.com

Church – Closed for renovation work.

Lagrand: Church – Jul and Aug: daily; Sep-Jun: daily except Sat-Sun. ☎ 04 92 66 25 35 (town hall).

CASTELLANE ☐ R. Nationale, 04120 Castellane, ☎ 04 92 83 61 14. www.castellane.org

Ethnological museum – ♿ Jul-Sep: daily except Mon 9am-noon, 2-6pm; Jun: daily except Sun and Mon 9am-noon, 2-6pm. Closed public holidays. 2€. ☎ 04 92 83 71 80.

Église St-Victor – Key available at the tourist office.

Réserve géologique de Haute Provence (Maison des Sirènes) – ♿ May-Sep: 10am-1pm, 2-6pm; Oct and Apr: daily except Sat-Sun and public holidays 9am-noon, 2-6pm. 3,81€. ☎ 04 92 83 19 23.

CEILLAC

🏠 Le village, 05600 Ceillac, ☎ 04 92 45 05 74.

Église St-Sébastien: Chapelle des Pénitents – Jul and Aug: daily except Sat-Sun 5-7pm.

CÉRESTE

🏠 Pl. de la République, 04280 Céreste, ☎ 04 92 79 09 84. www.cereste.fr

Prieuré de Carluc – Jul: 3-7.30pm; rest of the year: by appointment. 1,5€. ☎ 04 42 54 22 70.

CHAMBÉRY

🏠 24 bd de la Colonne, 73000 Chambéry, ☎ 04 79 33 42 47. www.chambery-tourisme.com

Guided tours of the town 🅰

Train – May-Sep: guided tours (45min, every hour) 10am-noon, 2-6pm. 5€ (children: 3€). ☎ 04 79 33 42 47.

Cathédrale métropolitaine St-François-de-Sales: Treasury – Jun-Aug: Sat 3-6pm. No charge. ☎ 04 79 33 23 91.

Château – Jul and Aug: guided tours (1hr) at 10.30am, 2.30pm, 3.30pm, 4.30pm, Sun and 15 Aug at 2.30pm, 3.30pm, 4.30pm; May, Jun and Sep: 2.30pm. Closed 1 Jan and 25 Dec. 4€. ☎ 04 79 33 42 47. www.chateau-tourisme.com

Sainte Chapelle – Guided tours only (see Practical Information).

Grand Carillon – Sat 3pm (departure from pl. du Château). 2,5€. ☎ 04 79 33 42 47.

Musée Savoisien – Daily except Tue and Public holidays 10am-noon, 2-6pm. 3,1€, no charge 1st Sunday in the month. ☎ 04 79 33 44 48.

Musée des Beaux-Arts – Daily except Tue and Public holidays 10am-noon, 2-6pm. 3,1€, no charge 1st Sunday in the month. ☎ 04 79 33 75 03.

Église St-Pierre-de-Lémenc – Sat 5-6pm, Sun 9.30-10.30am. ☎ 04 79 33 35 53.

Alentours

Les Charmettes – Apr-Sep: guided tours (30min) daily except Tue 10am-noon, 2-6pm; Oct-Mar: daily except Tue 10am-noon, 2-4.30pm. Closed public holidays. 3,1€, no charge 1st Sunday in the month. ☎ 04 79 33 75 03.

Montmélian 🏠 BP 1, 73800 Montmélian, ☎ 04 79 84 07 31. www.montmelian.com

Musée d'Histoire – Apr to Nov: Wed 5-6.30pm; Dec-Mar: Wed 3.30-4.30pm. No Charge. Town hall. ☎ 04 79 84 07 31. www.montmelian.com

Aoste: Musée archéologique – ♿ Daily except Tue 10am-noon, 2-6pm. Closed Dec, 1 Jan and 1 May. 3,6€. ☎ 04 76 32 58 27.

CHAMONIX-MONT-BLANC

🏠 Pl. du Triangle de l'Amitié, BP 25, 74400 Chamonix-Mont-Blanc, ☎ 04 50 53 00 24 www.chamonix.com

Musée alpin – School holidays: 10am-noon, 3-7pm; outside school holidays: 3-7pm. Closed May, Sep, Oct and 25 Dec. 4€. ☎ 04 50 53 25 93.

l'Aiguille du Midi cable car – Jul and Aug: 6am-4.45pm; Sep-Jun: 8am-3.45pm. Journey in two stages: Chamonix-Plan de l'aiguille and Plan de l'aiguille-Aiguille du Midi. (departures every 30min). 33€ return (children: 23,10€). ☎ 04 50 53 30 80 (Jul and Aug: places can be booked: ☎ 08 36 68 00 67).

Piton Central lift – Jul and Aug: 7am-5pm; Sep-Jun: 8am-3.45pm. Closed mid-Nov to mid-Dec. No charge (summer: 3€). ☎ 04 50 53 30 80. www.aiguilledumidi.com

Brévent gondola and cable car – Mid-Jun to mid-Sep: 8am-6pm; Mid-Dec to end Apr: 9am-5pm. Chamonix-Planpraz by gondola (20min), Planpraz-Brévent by cable-car (10min). Closed early May to mid-Jun and early Oct to mid-Dec. 14.3€ return (children under 11: 10€; under 15s: 12,2€). ☎ 04 50 53 30 80.

Les Praz-La Flégère cable car – Jun-Sep: 7.30am-5.30pm; mid-Dec to end Apr: 8.30am-4.50pm. 14,3€ return. ☎ 04 50 53 18 58.

La Flégère-Index – Mid-Jun to end Aug: 8.40am-4.50pm (7min, continuous); early Sep to mid-Jun: 7.40am-5.50pm. Closed May, Oct and Nov. 15€ return (ticket combined with the Praz cable-car), 10.5€ single. ☎ 04 50 53 18 58.

Montenvers mountain railway – Early Jun to mid-Nov: 7am-6pm (departure every 30min); mid-Nov to end May: 9am-4pm. 3€ (gondola only), 19.60€ return (combined ticket for train and gondola). ☎ 04 50 53 12 54.

Montenvers-ice cave gondola – Jul and Aug: 8am-6pm (20min); May, Jun and Sep: 8.30am-5.30pm; Oct-Apr: 10am-4pm (every hour). Closed mid-Nov to mid-Dec. 13€ (Montenvers and Mer de Glace). ☎ 04 50 53 12 54.

Ice cave – Jul and Aug: 8am-6pm; May, Jun and Sep: 8.30am-3.30pm; Oct-Apr: 10am-4pm. Closed mid-Nov to mid-Dec. Cost of admission included in the Montenvers railway ticket price. ☏ 04 50 53 12 54.

Musée Alpin - Early Jun to mid-Oct: 2-7pm; mid-Oct to end May: 3-7pm; school holidays: 10am-noon, 3-7pm. Closed 1 Jan and 25 Dec. 4€. ☏ 04 50 53 25 93.

CHAMPAGNY-EN-VANOISE

🛈 Le Centre, 73830 Champagny-En-Vanoise, ☏ 04 79 55 06 55. www.champagny.com

Church – Mid-Jun to end Aug: daily except Tue 3-6pm. Jul and Aug: 1 guided tour per week (enquire at the tourist office). ☏ 04 79 55 06 55.

Télécabine de Champagny (gondola) – Jul and Aug: daily except Sat-Sun 9.15am-1pm, 2.15-5.30pm. 6€. ☏ 04 79 09 67 00.

CHAMPSAUR

🛈 Haut-Champsaur, 05260 Pont-Du-Fossé, ☏ 04 92 55 95 71. 0

Pont du Fossé: Musée des arts et traditions du Champsaur – School holidays: daily except Sat-Sun and public holidays 3-5pm. Guided tours possible by appointment. 2,25€. ☏ 04 92 51 91 19.

Orcières-Merlette
🛈 05170 Orcières-Merlette, ☏ 04 92 55 89 89. www.orcieres.com

Drouvet gondola – Jul and Aug: 8.50am-12.30pm, 1.50-4.45pm (15min, continuous). 8€ (children: 6,10€). ☏ 04 92 55 89 89.

Prapic: Museum – Jun to Oct: 9am-noon, 2-7pm. 2,29€. ☏ 04 92 55 62 58.

Massif de CHAMROUSSE

Chamrousse
🛈 24 pl. de Belledonne, 38410 Chamrousse, ☏ 04 76 89 92 65. www.chamrousse.com

Réserve naturelle du Luitel – Jul and Aug: 10.30am-noon, 1.30-6pm. 4€ (children: 2€). ☏ 04 38 92 12 36.

Croix de Chamrousse cable car – Mid-Jun to mid-Sep: 8am-12.30pm, 1.30-5.30pm (7min, every 30min). 7,01€ return, 5,49€ single. ☏ 04 76 59 09 09.

Massif de la CHARTREUSE

🛈 Pl. de la Mairie, 38380 St-Pierre-De-Chartreuse, ☏ 04 76 88 62 08. www.st-pierre-chartreuse.com

Couvent de la Grande-Chartreuse: Museum – Jul and Aug: 9am-6.30pm; May, Jun and Sep: 9.30am-noon, 2-6.30pm; Apr and Oct: 10am-noon, 2-6pm. 3€. ☏ 04 76 88 60 45.

Voiron: Chartreuse cellars – Apr-Oct: guided tours (1hr) 9-11.30am, 2-6.30pm; Nov-Mar: 9-11.30am, 2-5.30pm. No charge. ☏ 04 76 05 81 77. www.chartreuse.fr

Les Échelles Entre-Deux-Guiers
🛈 R. Stendhal, 73360 Les Échelles, ☏ 04 79 36 56 24. www.parc-chartreuse.net

Tour of the caves – Mid-Jun to end Oct: guided tours (1hr) 10am-6.30pm; mid-Apr to mid-Jun: Sat-Sun and public holidays 10am-6.30pm. 5€ (children: 3,5€). ☏ 04 79 36 65 95.

CHÂTEL

🛈 74390 Châtel, ☏ 04 50 73 22 44.

Morclan chairlift – Jul and Aug: 9am-4.30pm (2 stages: Super-Châtel gondola and Morclan chair-lift). 6€ return (day ticket for hikers and paragliding enthusiasts). ☏ 04 50 73 22 44.

Gorges du CIANS

🛈 Quartier du Passaire, 06470 Beuil, ☏ 04 93 02 32 58.

CLUES DE HAUTE-PROVENCE

🛈 R. Alziary, 06910 Roquesteron, ☏ 04 93 05 92 92.

Sigale: Chapelle Notre-Dame d'Entrevignes – To visit, contact the town hall in Sigale. ☏ 04 93 05 83 52.

La CLUSAZ

🛈 74220 La Clusaz, ☏ 04 50 32 65 00. www.laclusaz.com

CLUSES

🛈 Espace Carpano et Pons, 100 pl. du 11 novembre, 74300 Cluses, ☏ 04 50 98 31 79.

Musée de l'Horlogerie et du Décolletage (Espace Carpano et Pons) – ♿ Jul and Aug: audio tours (1hr30min) 10am-noon, 2-5.30pm, Sun 2-5.30pm; Sep-Jun: daily except Sun 10am-noon, 2-5.30pm. Closed 1 Jan, 1 and 8 May, 25 Dec. 5.5€. ☏ 04 50 89 13 02.

Flaine
🛈 Galerie des Marchands, 74300 Flaine, ☏ 04 50 90 80 01. www.flaine.com

CLUSES

Téléphérique des Grandes Platières – Jul and Aug: 10am-5pm (10min, departure every 30min). 10€ return, 8,5€ single (under 15s: 7,5€ return, 6,5€ single). ☎ 04 50 90 40 00.

COLMARS
🛈 Pl. Joseph-Girieud, 04370 Colmars, ☎ 04 92 83 41 92.

Église St-Martin – Possibility of guided tours in summer: contact the tourist office. ☎ 04 92 83 41 92.

Fort de Savoie – Jul and Aug: guided tours (1hr) by request 10am-noon, unaccompanied visits 2.30-7pm. 4€. ☎ 04 92 83 41 92.

Les CONTAMINES-MONTJOIE
🛈 Pl. de la mairie, 74170 Les Contamines-Montjoie, ☎ 04 50 47 01 58. www.lescontamines.com

Gorge and Signal gondolas – Jul and Aug: La Gorge gondola 8.45am-5.30pm (20min, continuous), Signal gondola 9am-12.15pm, 1.30-5pm. 9,22€ return. ☎ 04 50 47 02 05.

COURCHEVEL
🛈 La Croisette, BP 37, 73122 Courchevel, ☎ 04 79 08 00 29. www.courchevel.com

Verdons gondola and Saulire cable car – Jul and Aug: alternate morning and afternoon service. 5,13€. ☎ 04 79 08 04 09.

Chenus gondola – Jul and Aug: alternate morning and afternoon service. 5,13€.

Mont Bel Air (Arondiaz gondola) – Jul and Aug: alternate morning and afternoon service. 5,13€. ☎ 04 79 08 04 09.

Route de la CROIX-DE-FER

Hydrelec – ♿ Mid-Jun to mid-Sep: 10am-6pm; mid-Sep to mid-Jun: Sat-Sun, public and school holidays, 2-6pm. Closed 1 Jan, 1 May and 25 Dec. No charge. ☎ 04 76 80 78 00.

Les DEUX-ALPES
🛈 4 pl. des Deux Alpes, 38860 Les Deux-Alpes, ☎ 04 76 79 22 00. www.les2alpes.com

Glacier du Mont-de-Lans – Jul and Aug: 7.30am-4pm. 17,5€ return (combined ticket includes a visit to the grotte de glace (ice cave). 18.29€). ☎ 04 76 79 75 01.

Croisière Blanche – 23,5€ (ascent by cable-car from Les Deux-Alpes, tour of the grotte de glace (ice cave), excursion by minibus). Visitors must reserve. ☎ 04 76 79 75 01.

Le DÉVOLUY
🛈 Le Pré, 05250 St-Étienne-En-Dévoluy, ☎ 04 92 58 91 91. www.ledevoluy.com

Corps: Chapelle St-Roch – 16 Aug and St Roch's day.

Notre-Dame de la Salette: Chapelle – Closed Nov ☎ 04 76 30 00 11.

DIE
🛈 Pl. St-Pierre, 26150 Die, ☎ 04 75 22 03 03. www.vallee-drome.com/die

Chapelle St-Nicolas – Guided tours Tue and Fri 2pm. 2€. ☎ 04 75 22 03 03.

Museum – Jul and Aug: daily except Sun 3.30-6.30pm; May, Jun and Sep: Tue and Sat 3-6pm; Apr and May: Sat 3-6pm. Closed 15 Aug. 3,5€. ☎ 04 75 22 03 03.

Environs

Abbaye de Valcroissant – Jul and Aug: guided tours by appointment Mon, Wed and Fri 5pm; Jun and Sep: Wed 5pm; May: Fri 5pm. ☎ 04 75 22 12 70.

DIGNE-LES-BAINS
🛈 Rond Point du 11 Novembre, 04000 Digne-Les-Bains, ☎ 04 92 36 62 62. www.ot-dignelesbains.fr

Guided tours of the town – You will discover all there is to discover in the old town. Mar-Oct: Wed afternoon. No charge. Contact the tourist office.

Église St-Jérôme – Daily except Mon and Fri 3-6pm.

Musée départemental de Digne – Closed for renovation work. Reopening planned for 2003.

Musée d'Art religieux – Jul-Sep: 10am-6pm. No charge. ☎ 04 92 36 75 00.

Musée de la Seconde Guerre mondiale – ♿ Jul and Aug: daily except Sat-Sun 2pm-6pm; Sep-Jun: Wed 2-5pm. Closed public holidays. No charge. ☎ 04 92 31 28 95.

Jardin botanique des Cordeliers – ♿ Jul and Aug: 9am-noon, 3-7pm; Apr-Jun, Sep and Oct: daily except Sun and Mon 9am-noon, 2-6pm. No charge. ☎ 04 92 31 59 59.

Cathédrale N.-D. du Bourg – Jun to Oct: 3-6pm; make an appointment at the vicarage. No charge. ☎ 04 92 32 06 48.

Musée Alexandra David-Néel – Jul-Sep: guided tours (1hr30min) at 10am, 2pm, 3.30pm and 5pm; Oct-Jun: 10am, 2pm and 4pm. No charge. ☎ 04 92 31 32 38. www.alexandra-david-neel.org

Musée-promenade St-Benoît/geological museum – Apr-Oct: 9am-noon, 2-5.30pm; Nov-Mar: daily except Sat-Sun 9am-noon, 2-5.30pm. 4,6€. ☎ 04 92 36 70 70.

Vallée de la Moyenne DURANCE

🖪 Ferme Font-Robert, 04160 Château-Arnoux-St-Auban, ☎ 04 92 64 02 64. 0

EMBRUN

🖪 Pl. du Gén.-Dosse, 05202 Embrun, ☎ 04 92 43 72 72. www.embrun.net

Guided tours of the town – They take place every Thursday at 10am in Jul and Aug. Visitors must book. The meeting point is in front of the tourist office. 5,2€.

Tour Brune – Mid-Jun to mid-Sep: 10.30am-12.30pm, 2.30-7pm; early May to mid-Jun and mid to end Sep: Sat-Sun and public holidays 10.30am-12.30pm, 2.30-7pm; school holidays: daily except Sun 2-6pm. 3,05€. ☎ 04 92 43 49 48.

Cathédrale Notre-Dame-du-Réal – Possibility of guided tours: contact the tourist office. ☎ 04 92 43 72 72.

Treasury – Jul and Aug: 10am-noon. Contact the tourist office. 2,8€. ☎ 04 92 43 72 72.

Chapelle des Cordeliers – Jul and Aug: 9am-7pm, Sun and public holidays 10am-noon, 4-7pm; Sep-Jun: daily except Sun 9am-noon, 2-6.30pm. No charge. ☎ 04 92 43 72 72.

Alentours

Les Orres: Prelongis et Fontaine chairlifts – Jul and Aug: 10am-5pm. 6,86€. ☎ 04 92 44 00 39 or 04 92 44 00 39.

Val d'ENTRAUNES

Entraunes 🖪 Pl. Napoléon-III, 06470 Guillaumes, ☎ 04 93 05 57 76.

Parc National du Mercantour – To obtain information on the park's activities in Jul and Aug: 3-7pm at the Entraunes information area, noon to 6pm at the col de la Cayolle refuge. ☎ 04 93 05 53 07.

St-Martin-d'Entraunes: Church – To visit, contact Mrs. Liautaud who lives opposite the church.

ENTREVAUX

🖪 Pl. Charles-Panier, 04320 Entrevaux, ☎ 04 93 05 46 73.

Guided tours of the town – Contact the tourist office.

Cathedral – Possibility of guided tours: contact the tourist office. ☎ 04 93 05 46 73.

Citadel – 3€. ☎ 04 93 05 46 73.

Musée de la Moto – Jul-Sep: 10am-noon, 2-6pm; May-Jun: Sat-Sun 10am-noon, 2-6pm. No charge. ☎ 04 93 79 12 70.

Moulins à huile et à farine – Jul and Aug: 9am-noon, 2-5.30pm. Possibility of guided tours, make an appointment at the reception office. 2,3€. ☎ 04 93 05 46 73.

ÉVIAN-LES-BAINS

🖪 Pl. d'Allinges, 74500 Évian-Les-Bains, ☎ 04 50 75 04 26. www.eviantourism.com

Exhibition and Information Centre about Évian water ⊙ – Mid-Jun to mid-Sep: 10.30am-12.30pm, 3-7pm; early May to mid-Jun and mid to end Sep: 2.30-6.30pm. No charge. ☎ 04 50 26 80 80.

Villa Lumière (town hall) – Daily except Sat-Sun 9-11.30am, 1.30-5pm. ☎ 04 50 83 10 00.

Musée Pré-Lude – Closed temporarily. Information at the tourist office. ☎ 04 50 75 04 26.

Bottling factory – ♿ Early Jan to mid-Dec: guided tours (1hr30min) 9-10.30am, 2-3.30pm. Reservations to be made with the Service des Visites (Dept. which deals with visits to the plant), Eaux Minérales d'Évian, 22 avenue des Sources, 74 503 Évian les Bains. ☎ 04 50 26 80 51 or 04 50 26 93 23.

FORCALQUIER

🖪 Pl. du Bourguet, 04301 Forcalquier, ☎ 04 92 75 10 02. www.forcalquier.com

Guided tours – The tourist office organises 2-hour visits of the old town, the town hall, the cathedral, the citadel and mansion houses. Mid-Jun to mid-Sep: Thu at 10am (Jul and Aug: Wed evening at 8.30pm); mid-Sep to mid-Jun: Sat at 10am. 3,05€

FORCALQUIER

Couvent des Cordeliers – Mid-Jun to mid-Sep: guided tours (1hr) 11am, 2.30 and 4.30pm. At other times of the year, contact the tourist office. Closed Dec and Jan (except school holidays). 3.8€ ☎ 04 92 75 10 02. www.forcalquier.com

Museum – Apr-Sep: daily except Tue, Wed and public holidays 3-6pm. 2€. ☎ 04 92 70 91 19.

Alentours

St-Michel-l'Observatoire

Observatoire de Haute-Provence – Apr-Sep: guided tours (1hr) Wed 2-4pm; Oct-Mar: Wed at 3pm. Closed public holidays. 2,3€. ☎ 04 92 70 64 00. www.obs-hp.fr

Centre d'Astronomie de St-Michel – Jul: evening observation sessions 9.30pm, observation of the sun 4.30, entertainment based on the visit of the Observatoire de Haute-Provence Wed; Aug: evening observation sessions 9pm, observation of the sun 4pm; Sep-Jun: evening observation sessions one Sat per month. 8€ evening observation sessions, 5€ observation of the sun. Book by calling ☎ 04 92 76 69 69.

Montfuron: windmill – Guided tours (15min) by appointment at the town hall (2 weeks in advance). 1,52€. ☎ 04 92 76 41 65.

Vachères: museum – &. May-Sep: 10am-noon, 3-6pm; Oct-Apr: 2-5pm. Closed in Jan and during Christmas school holidays. 2.3€. ☎ 04 92 75 62 15.

Simiane-la-Rotonde: La Rotonde – Mid-Jun to end Aug: 10am-12.30pm, 3-7pm, Sun 3-7pm; early Apr to mid-Jun and Sep: daily except Tue 3-5.30pm. 1,53€. ☎ 04 92 75 90 14.

Lurs 🛈 Allée Arthur-Gouin, 04700 Lurs, ☎ 04 92 79 10 20.

Notre-Dame de Lure – Visits by appointment at the town hall, ☎ 04 92 73 02 00 or the tourist office. ☎ 04 92 73 02 57. Key available in exchange for an identity document.

Vallée de Freissinières 🛈 Le Moulin Les Ribes, 05310 Vallée De Freissinières, ☎ 04 92 20 95 49. 0

Route du GALIBIER

Valloire 🛈 73450 Valloire, ☎ 04 79 59 03 96. www.valloire.net
Church – Jul and Aug: possibility of guided tours 10am-noon, 3-6pm; Sep-Jun: by request at the tourist office. ☎ 04 79 59 03 96.

GAP 🛈 12 r. Faure-du-Serre, 05002 Gap, ☎ 04 92 52 56 56. www.tourisme.fr/gap

Guided tour – The tourist office organises complete discovery tours (1hr15min) covering the old town centre, the town hall and the cathedral. Jul and Aug: Tue and Thu 5pm, Fri 10am. 3,20€.

Musée départemental – &. Jul and Aug: 10am-noon, 2-6pm; Sep-Jun: daily except Tue 2-5.30pm, Sat-Sun 2-6pm. Closed public holidays. 3€. ☎ 04 92 51 01 58 or 04 92 52 05 44.

Les GETS 🛈 BP 27, 74260 Les Gets, ☎ 04 50 75 80 80. www.lesgets.com

Musée de la Musique mécanique – &. Jul and Aug: guided tours (1hr15min, last departure at 6pm) 10.30am-noon, 2.30-7.30pm (2pm in rainy weather); Sep-Jun: 2.30-7.30pm. Closed early Nov to mid-Dec. 6.5 €. ☎ 04 50 79 85 75. www.museedesgets.free.fr

Mont Chéry gondola and chairlift – Jul and Aug: 9.30am-5.30pm. 4,1€ single. ☎ 04 50 75 80 99.

La GRAVE 🛈 RN 91, 05320 La Grave, ☎ 04 76 79 90 05.

Chapelle des Pénitents – Apply to the presbytery to visit. ☎ 04 76 79 91 29.

Glaciers de la Meije cable car – Mid-Jun to end Aug and Jan-May (journey in 2 stages). 17€ return. ☎ 04 76 79 91 09.

Grotte de Glace de la Meije – Times are the same as for the Meije glacier cable-cars. 3,5€. ☎ 04 76 79 90 05. www.grottedeglace.com

GRENOBLE 🛈 14 r. de la République, 38000 Grenoble, ☎ 04 76 42 41 41. www.grenoble-isere-tourisme.com

Guided tours of the town 🅰 – Jul and Aug: Sat at 10am. 6,8€.

Fort de la Bastille cable car – Jun-Sep: 9.15am-11.45pm, Mon 11am-11.45pm, Sun 9.15am-7.25pm (Jul and Aug: 12.15am); Mar-May and Oct: 9.15am-11.45pm, Mon 11am-7.25pm, Sun 9.15am-7.25pm; Nov-Mar: 10.45am-6.30pm, Mon 11am-6.30pm. Closed 2nd week in Jan. 5,5€ return, 3,8€ single. ☎ 04 76 44 33 65.

Maison Stendhal – Mid-Jul to mid-Sep: daily except Mon 10am-noon, 2-6pm; mid-Sep to mid-Jul: daily except Mon 9am-noon. Closed public holidays. No charge. ☎ 04 76 42 02 62.

Musée Stendhal – Mid-Jul to mid-Sep: daily except Mon 10am-noon, 2-6pm; mid-Sep to mid-Jul: daily except Mon 2-6pm. Closed public holidays. No charge. ☎ 04 76 54 44 14.

Palais de Justice – 1st Sat in the month at 10am. 5,5€. ☎ 04 76 85 16 15.

Musée de Grenoble – ♿ Jul-Sep: daily except Tue 10am-6pm, Wed 10am-9pm; Oct-Jun: daily except Tue 11am-7pm, Wed 11am-10pm. Closed 1 Jan, 1 May, 25 Dec. 4€, no charge 1st Sunday in the month. ☎ 04 76 63 44 44.

Musée de l'Ancien Évêché/Patrimoines de l'Isère – ♿ Daily except Tue 9am-6pm, Sun 10am-7pm. Closed 1 Jan, 1 May, 25 Dec. 3.20, no charge 1st Sunday in the month. ☎ 04 76 03 15 25.

Musée Dauphinois – ♿ Jun-Sep: 10am-7pm; Oct-May: daily except Tue 10am-6pm. Closed 1 Jan and 1 May. 3.2€. ☎ 04 76 85 19 01. www.musee.dauphinois.fr

Musée-église St-Laurent – ♿ Daily except Tue 9am-6pm. Closed 1 Jan, 1 May, 25 Dec. 3,2€, no charge 1st Sunday in the month. ☎ 04 76 44 78 68.

Musée de la Résistance et de la Déportation – ♿ Jul and Aug: 10am-7pm; Sep-Jun: daily except Tue 9am-6pm, Sat-Sun and public holidays 10am-6pm. Closed 1 Jan, 1 May, 25 Dec. 3,20€. ☎ 04 76 42 38 53. www.resistance-en-isere.com

Musée des Troupes de montagne – Daily except Sat-Sun and public holidays 10am-noon, 2pm-5.30pm. No charge. ☎ 04 76 76 22 12.

Musée des Rêves mécaniques – ♿ Guided tours (1hr, last admission 45min before closing) 2-6.30pm. 5€. ☎ 04 76 43 33 33.

Musée d'Histoire naturelle – ♿ 9.30am-noon, 1.30-5.30pm, Sat-Sun and public holidays 2-6pm. Closed 1 Jan, 1 May, 25 Dec. 2,2€, no charge Wed afternoon (Oct-May). ☎ 04 76 44 05 35. www.ville-grenoble.fr/museum

Centre national d'Art contemporain (Le Magasin) – ♿ According to the exhibition programme, daily except Mon noon-7pm. 3,5€. ☎ 04 76 21 95 84. www.magasin-cnac.org

Alentours

La Tronche: Musée départemental E.-Hébert – Closed for renovation work. Reopening planned for Sep 2003.

Lancey: Musée de la Houille Blanche – Closed for reorganisation. Reopening planned for 2004. ☎ 04 76 45 66 81.

Sassenage

Les Cuves – Jul and Aug: guided tours 10am-6pm; May, Jun and Sep: daily except Mon at 11am, 1.30pm, 3pm, 4.30pm, 6pm; Apr and Oct: Sat-Sun and school holidays 11am, 1.30pm, 3pm, 4.30pm and 6pm; from the weekend before Christmas to Christmas: 11am, 1pm, 2.30pm, 4pm. Closed rest of the year. 4,64€ ☎ 04 76 27 48 63.

Château – Early Jul to mid-Sep: guided tours (1hr) daily except Mon at 11am, 2pm, 3pm, 4pm and 5pm. 6€. ☎ 04 76 27 54 44. www.domaine-de-sassenage.com

GRÉOUX-LES-BAINS 🛈 5 av. des Marroniers, 04800 Gréoux-Les-Bains, ☎ 04 92 78 01 08. www.greoux-les-bains.com

Guided tours of the town – Lasting 1hr30min, the tour gives you the opportunity to discover the town's old streets, the Templars' castle and the church. Thu 2.30pm (4pm Jul and Aug). Meet at the tourist office. 3,80€.

Crèche de Haute Provence – ♿ Jul and Aug: guided tours (30min) daily except Mon 10am-noon, 2.30-7pm; Apr-Jun, Sep and Oct: daily except Sun and Mon 10am-noon, 2.30-5.30pm. 4€ (children: no charge). ☎ 04 92 77 61 08.

Alentours

St-Julien-le-Montagnier: Church – Jul and Aug: 10am-7pm; Sep-Jun: Sat-Sun 10am-5pm. By appointment with Mme Pascal. ☎ 04 94 80 03 07.

Le GRÉSIVAUDAN

St-Hilaire-du-Touvet: Rack Railway – Jun-Aug: 10am-7pm (20min, departure every hour); Sep-May: 10am-noon, 2-6pm, Sun and public holidays 10am-noon, 1.30-7pm 10€ return, 6,50€ single (children: 6€ return, 4,30€ single). ☎ 04 76 08 00 02.

Château du Touvet – ♿ Jul and Aug: guided tours (45min) daily except Sat 2-6pm; Mid-Apr to end Jun, Sep and Oct: Sun and public holidays 2-6pm; All Saints to Easter: by appointment. 5,8€. ☎ 04 76 08 42 27. www.touvet.com

Laval: Church – Contact M. Chalaye, ☎ 04 76 71 48 60.

Château-Bayard – Jul and Aug: daily except Tue 2-6pm; May, Jun and Sep: Sat-Sun and public holidays 2-6pm. 2,5€. ☎ 04 76 97 11 65.

GUILLESTRE
🄸 Pl. Joseph-Salva, 05600 Guillestre, ☎ 04 92 45 04 37.

Les HOUCHES
🄸 Pl. de l'Église, BP 09, 74310 Les Houches, ☎ 04 50 55 50 62.
www.leshouches.com

Prarion cable car – Jul and Aug: 9am-5.30pm; early to mid-Sep: 9am-noon, 1.30-4.45pm. 11,4€ return. ☎ 04 50 54 42 65.

Bellevue cable car – Mid-Jun to mid-Sep: 8am-6pm. 11,4€ return. ☎ 04 50 54 40 32.

Parc du Balcon de Merlet – Jul and Aug: 9.30am-7.30pm (last admission 45min before closing); May, Jun and Sep: 10am-6pm. 4,2€ (children: 2,9€). ☎ 04 50 53 47 89.

ISOLA 2000
🄸 Immeuble Le Pélevos, 06420 Isola 2000, ☎ 04 93 23 15 15.
www.isola-2000.com

Pélévos cable car – Dec-Apr 5min. 3€ return. ☎ 04 93 23 25 25.

Lacs de LAFFREY
🄸 43 r. de Breuil, 38350 La Mure, ☎ 04 76 81 05 71.

La Motte-d'Aveillans: Mine-Image – Early Jun to mid-Sep: guided tours (1hr) 10am, 11.15am, 1.30pm, 2.30pm, 3.30pm, 4.30pm and 5.30pm, Sun and public holidays 2.30pm, 3.30pm and 4.30pm. 5,5€. ☎ 04 76 30 68 74.

La Mure Mountain Railway – Jul and Aug: departure from La Mure and St-Georges de Commiers 9.45am, noon, 2.30pm (round trip 4hr); May, Jun and Sep: departure from St-Georges 9.45am, 2.30pm; Apr and Oct: departure from St-Georges 2.30pm. 17€ return (children: 12€ return). ☎ 0892 39 14 26.

Route de la MADELEINE
🄸 73260 Valmorel, ☎ 04 79 09 85 55. www.valmorel.com

MANE
🄸 Mairie, 04300 Mane, ☎ 04 92 75 05 64. 0

Alentours

Château de Sauvan: – Jul and Aug: guided tours (1hr30min) daily except Sat 3.30pm; Sep-Jun: Thu, Sun and public holidays 3.30pm. 5,6€. ☎ 04 92 75 05 64.

Prieuré de Salagon – May-Sep: 10am-noon, 2-7pm, Sat 2-7pm; Oct-Apr: Sat-Sun and school holidays 2-6pm. Closed Jan. 4,6€. ☎ 04 92 75 70 50.

MANOSQUE
🄸 Pl. du Dr-Joubert, 04100 Manosque, ☎ 04 92 72 16 00. ville-manosque.fr

Guided tour – Tours are organised by the tourist office (tours last 1hr30min to 2hr) from Jun to end Sep Thu and Fri 3.30pm; rest of the year Thu 2.30pm every fortnight. 3€. ☎ 04 92 72 16 00.

Église St-Sauveur – Daily except Sat-Sun 8.30am-6.30pm.

Fondation Carzou – Jul and Aug: daily except Mon 10am-noon, 2.30-6.30pm; Sep and Jun: daily except Sun and Mon 2.30-6.30pm; Oct-May: Wed, Thu, Fri and Sat 2.30-6.30pm. 4€. ☎ 04 92 87 40 49.

Centre Jean-Giono – Apr-Sep: daily except Sun and Mon 9.30am-12.30pm, 2-6pm, Sat 10am-noon, 2-6pm; Oct-Mar: 2-6pm. Closed public holidays. 4€. ☎ 04 92 70 54 54.

Alentours

Giono's House "Le Paraïs" – Guided tours (1hr30min) Fri 3-5pm by appointment (at least 3 days in advance). No charge. ☎ 04 92 87 73 03.

La haute MAURIENNE
🄸 Grande Rue, 73480 Val-Cenis, ☎ 04 79 05 23 66.
www.Valcenis.com

Lanslevillard: Chapelle St-Sébastien – Possibility of visits during summer and winter school holidays by request at the town hall. ☎ 04 79 05 93 78.

Lanslebourg-Mont-Cenis: Espace baroque Maurienne – Early Jul to mid-Sep: Mon, Tue and Wed 9.30am-12.30pm, Thu, Fri and Sun 3.30-7.30pm; mid-Sep to end Jun: call for information. 2,5€. ☎ 04 79 05 90 78.

Termignon: Church – Daily except Mon 3-6pm. ☎ 04 79 05 51 49 (town hall).

Avrieux: Church – Ask for information at the town hall in Avrieux, 154 r. de l'Église, ☎ 04 79 20 33 16.

La Norma   🄸 Maison de la Norma, 73500 La Norma, ☎ 04 79 20 31 46.

Mélézet gondola – Jun-Aug: daily except Sat 9.30am-12.30pm, 2-4.45pm; Apr: daily except Sat 9.45am-5.30pm; Jan-Mar: daily except Sat 9.15am-5pm. 5€. ☎ 04 79 20 31 46.

MEGÈVE   🄸 R. Monseigneur Conseil, BP 24, 74120 Megève, ☎ 04 50 21 27 28.

Musée du Haut-Val d'Arly – Jul-Sep and Jan-Apr: guided tours (1hr) daily except Sun 2.30-6.30pm. Closed rest of the year. 3€. ☎ 04 50 91 81 00.

Princesse gondola – Mid-Dec to end Mar. ☎ 04 50 93 00 83.

Mont d'Arbois gondola – Jul and Aug: 9am-1pm, 2-6pm. ☎ 04 50 21 22 07.

Jaillet gondola– Jul and Aug: 9am-1pm, 2-6pm; Mid-Dec to end Mar: 9am-5pm. Closed rest of the year. 8€ return. ☎ 04 50 21 01 50.

Rochebrune cable car – Early Jul to mid-Sep: 9am-1pm, 2-6pm (7min, continuous). 5,5€ single, 9.5€ return. ☎ 04 50 21 38 39.

MÉRIBEL   🄸 BP 1, 73551 Méribel, ☎ 04 79 08 60 01. www.meribel.net

Saulire gondolas -Jul and Aug: Burgin gondola Mon, Tue and Wed; Pas du Lac gondola Mon, Tue, Thu and Sun (2 stages: 20min). 8,2€ return. ☎ 04 79 08 65 32.

Tougnète gondolas – Jul and Aug: daily except Fri and Sat-Sun 9am-5pm (2 stages, 20min, continuous). 8.2 return. ☎ 04 79 08 63 32.

MODANE   🄸 Les Mélèzets, 73500 Modane, ☎ 04 79 05 33 83.

Valfréjus   🄸 73500 Valfréjus, ☎ 04 79 05 33 83.

Punta Bagna gondola – Early May to mid-Dec (departure every 30min). 5,5€. ☎ 04 79 05 33 33.

MOLINES-EN-QUEYRAS   🄸 Clot la Chalp, 05350 Molines-En-Queyras, ☎ 04 92 45 83 22. 0

Massif du MONT-BLANC

Gorges de la Gruvaz – Mid-Jun to mid-Sep: 9am-7pm. ☎ 04 50 47 50 71.

St-Nicolas-de-Véroce: church treasury – Jul and Aug: daily except Mon and Wed 4-6pm. No charge. ☎ 04 50 93 20 63.

Panoramic Mont-Blanc – Jul and Aug: 8am-3.30pm (round trip with stop for panoramic view: 3hr); May, Jun and Sep: 9am-2.30pm. 33€ return (under 15s: 23€). ☎ 04 50 53 30 80.

MONTBRUN-LES-BAINS   🄸 L'Autin, 26570 Montbrun-Les-Bains, ☎ 04 75 28 82 49.

Church – Visit by appointment with Mme Arnoux ("Le Beffroi" shop). ☎ 04 75 28 82 24.

Circuit

Aulan: Château – Possibility of guided tours by request to the comte d'Aulan. Closed early Jan to mid-Mar. 4€. ☎ 04 75 28 80 00.

Route du MONT-CENIS

Salle historique du Mont-Cenis -Mid-Jun to end Aug: 10am-12.30pm, 2-6pm; early to mid-Sep: Sat-Sun 10am-12.30pm, 2-6pm. 2,5€. ☎ 04 79 05 92 95.

MONT-DAUPHIN   🄸 Quartier des Artisans d'Art, 05600 Mont-Dauphin, ☎ 04 92 45 17 80.

Caserne Campana – 10am-noon, 2.30-6pm.

Guided tour of the citadel – The guided tour (2hr) gives access to the Rochambeau barracks and the powder magazine; not to be missed. Contact the Centre des Monuments Nationaux (National Monuments Centre). ☎ 01 44 61 21 50. Apr-Sep: 9am-noon, 2-6pm; Oct-Mar: 10am-noon, 2-5pm. 4€.

MONT-DAUPHIN

Vauban exhibition – Apr-Sep: 9am-noon, 2-6pm; Oct-Mar: 2-5pm. Arsenal: Jun-Sep Sat-Sun and public holidays 2-6pm. 4€. ☎ 04 92 45 42 40.

MONTMAUR

🖪 Av. du Cdt-Dumont, 05400 Veynes, ☎ 04 92 57 27 43.

Château – Jul and Aug: guided tours (1hr) at 3pm, 4pm and 5pm. 4,5€ (children: 2,3€). ☎ 04 92 58 11 42.

MORZINE

🖪 Pl. de la Crusaz, 74110 Morzine, ☎ 04 50 74 72 72. www.morzine-avoriaz.com

Pointe de Nyon: chairlift and cable car – Contact the tourist office, ☎ 04 50 74 72 72.

Le Pléney cable car– Mid-Jun to mid-Sep: 9am-5.45pm (10min, continuous). Toboggan run: May-Sep 10am-12.30pm, 2.30-6.30pm. 4€ single. ☎ 04 50 79 00 38.

MOUSTIERS-STE-MARIE

🖪 04360 Moustiers-Ste-Marie, ☎ 04 92 74 67 84.
www.ville-moustiers-sainte-marie.fr

Musée de la Faïence – Jul and Aug: 9am-noon, 2-7pm; Apr-Jun, Sep and Oct: daily except Tue 9am-noon, 2-6pm; Nov-Mar: Sat-Sun and school holidays (daily except Tue) 2-5pm. Closed 1 Nov and 25 Dec. 2€. ☎ 04 92 74 61 64.

Route NAPOLÉON

Senez Cathedral – Guided tours possible by appointment with Mme Mestre. ☎ 04 92 34 23 87.

Château de Malijai – ♿ Daily except Sat-Sun and public holidays 9am-noon, 3-6pm. No charge. ☎ 04 92 34 01 12.

Tallard: Château – Jul and Aug: daily except Tue 2-5pm, guide tours 5-6pm. 2,5€ (children under 10: no charge; guided tours: 3,5€). ☎ 04 92 54 10 14.

La Mure: Musée Matheysin – May-Oct: daily except Tue 1-6.30pm. 2,3€. ☎ 04 76 30 98 15.

L'OISANS

🖪 Quai Girard, 38520 Le Bourg-D'oisans, ☎ 04 76 80 03 25.

Vanosc cable car – Jul and Aug: 8am-7pm (5min, continuous). 6,5€ return. ☎ 04 76 79 75 01.

Mont-de-Lans: Musée des arts et traditions populaires – Jul and Aug: 8-10am, 3-7pm; Dec-Apr: 2-6pm. Closed May, Jun, Oct and Nov. 2€. ☎ 04 76 80 23 97.

Col du Lautaret: answering machine– An answering machine gives information on access conditions to the pass: ☎ 04 92 24 44 44.

Jardin alpin – Mid-Jun to mid-Sep: 9.30am-7pm. 4,2€ (children: no charge). ☎ 04 92 24 41 62.

La PLAGNE

🖪 Le Chalet, 73210 La Plagne, ☎ 04 79 09 79 79. www.la-plagne.com

la Grande Rochette gondola – Summer: Mon-Thu (6min, continuous). 6€. Enquire for information on opening times. ☎ 04 79 09 67 00.

Bellecôte gondola – Summer: 8-1am (45min, continuous). 16€. ☎ 04 79 09 67 00.

PONT-EN-ROYANS

🖪 Grande Rue, 38680 Pont-En-Royans, ☎ 04 76 36 09 10.

Alentours

St-Nazaire-en-Royans: Grotte de Thaïs – Jul and Aug: guided tours (45min) 10am-noon, 2-5pm; Jun: 2-5pm, Sun and public holidays 10am-noon, 2-5pm; Apr, May and Oct: Sun and public holidays 10am-noon, 2-5pm. 5,5€ (children: 3,25€). ☎ 04 75 48 45 76.

Jardin des Fontaines Pétrifiantes – Jun-Aug: 10am-6.30pm; May and early Sep to mid-Oct: daily except Mon 10am-6pm. Dogs prohibited. 5,5€. ☎ 04 76 64 43 42.

PRALOGNON-LA-VANOISE

🖪 73710 Pralognan-La-Vanoise, ☎ 04 79 08 79 08.
www.pralognan.com

Mont-Bochor cable car – Jul and Aug: 8.10am-12.25pm, 1.50-5.50pm (every 10min); Jun: 8.10-11.50am, 1.35-5.20pm (every 20min). 4,6€ return. ☎ 04 79 08 79 09.

PRA-LOUP

🖪 Maison de Pra-Loup, 04400 Pra-Loup, ☎ 04 92 84 10 04. www.praloup.com

PUGET-THÉNIERS

🚶 2 av. Alexandre-Barety, 06260 Puget-Théniers,☎ 04 93 05 05 05.
www.provence-valdazur.com

Puget-Rostang: Écomusée du Pays de la Roudoule – ♿ Apr-Oct: 8am-noon, 2-6pm; Nov-Mar: daily except Sat-Sun 8am-noon, 2-6pm. Closed during Christmas school holidays. 4,57€. ☎ 04 93 05 07 38.

Léouvé: Maison de la mine – ♿ May-Sep: daily except Mon 10am-noon, 2.30-5.30pm; Mar, Apr, Oct and Nov: daily except Mon 2.30-5.30pm. 2,50€. ☎ 04 93 05 14 64.

QUEYRAS

🚶 Château-Ville-Vieille, 05350 Château-Queyras, ☎ 04 92 46 70 70. 0

Maison de l'artisanat – Jul and Aug: 10am-7pm; school holidays: 10am-noon, 3-7pm; rest of the year: 3-7pm. Closed 1 Jan and 25 Dec. No charge. ☎ 04 92 46 80 29 or 04 92 46 75 06.

Château-Queyras: Fort Queyras – May-Sep: 9am-7pm, Sun and public holidays 9am-6pm. 5€ (children: 2€). 06 15 95 69 83.

Espace géologique – Jul and Aug: 10am-noon, 2.45-6.15pm by request. 3,5€ (children: 2,5€). ☎ 04 92 45 06 23.

RIEZ

🚶 Allée Louis-Gardiol, 04500 Riez, ☎ 04 92 77 99 33.

Baptistère – Jun-Sep: Tue and Fri 3-7pm. Contact the tourist office. 2,29€. ☎ 04 92 77 99 09.

Château d'Allemagne-en-Provence – Early Jul to mid-Sep: guided tours (1hr) daily except Mon and Tue 4-5pm; Apr-Jun and mid-Sep to end Oct: Sat-Sun and public holidays 4pm and 5pm. 5€. ☎ 04 92 77 46 78.

Maison de l'Abeille et du Miel – ♿ 10am-12.30pm, 2.30-7pm. No charge. ☎ 04 92 77 84 15.

ROCHE-SUR-FORON

🚶 Pl. Andrevetan, 74800 La Roche-Sur-Foron, ☎ 04 50 03 36 68.
www.larochesurforon.com

Guided tours of the town – Contact the tourist office.

Tour des Comtes de Genève: tower – Mid-Jul to end Aug: 10am-noon, 2-6.30pm; mid-Jun to mid-Jul and early to mid-Sep: 2-6.30pm. 2€. ☎ 04 50 03 36 68. www.larochesurforon.com

ST-ÉTIENNE-DE-TINÉE

Chapelles St-Sébastien, St-Michel, des Trinitaires Guided tours (1hr30min) by appointment at the tourist office. 3,1€. ☎ 04 93 02 41 96.

Musée des Traditions – Guided tours (15min) by request. No charge. ☎ 04 93 02 41 96.

Musée du Lait – Contact the tourist office. ☎ 04 93 02 41 96.

ST-GERVAIS-LES-BAINS

🚶 115 av. du Mont-Paccard, 74170 St-Gervais-Les-Bains,
☎ 04 50 47 76 08. www.st-gervais.net

Le Bettex-Mont-Arbois cable car - Mid-Jun to end Aug: 9am-noon, 2-6pm (10min, every 30min). 12,5€ return. ☎ 04 50 93 11 87.

Tramway du Mont-Blanc – Mid-Jun to end Sep and mid-Dec to mid-Apr: from St-Gervais to Voza pass (5905ft) Mid-Jun to mid-Sep: from St-Gervais to the Nid d'Aigle (7874ft). ☎ 04 50 47 51 83.

Gorges de la Diosaz – Mid-Jun to end Aug: 8am-7.30pm (last admission 1hr before closing); early to mid-Jun: 8.30am-5.30pm; Sep: 8.30am-4.30pm. 4,2€. ☎ 04 50 47 21 13.

ST-JEAN-EN-MAURIENNE

🚶 Ancien Évêché, pl. de la Cathédrale,
73300 St-Jean-De-Maurienne, ☎ 04 79 83 51 51.
www.ville-saint-jean-de-maurienne.fr

Cathédrale St-Jean-Baptiste – Daily except Sun morning. Possibility of guided tours by request at the tourist office or by contacting the cathedral priest, 60 pl. de la cathédrale, 73300 St-Jean-de-Maurienne.

Musée Opinel – ♿ Daily except Sun and Public holidays 9am-noon, 2-7pm. No charge. ☎ 04 79 64 04 78. www.opinel-musee.com

ST-JULIEN DU VERDON

Barrage de Chaudanne – Visits cancelled due to the government "Vigipirate" security plan. Call for information: ☎ 04 92 70 68 00.

ST-PIERRE-DE-CHARTREUSE

Pl. de la Mairie, 38380 St-Pierre-De-Chartreuse. ☎ 04 76 88 62 08. www.st-pierre-chartreuse.com

Alentours

Église St-Hugues-de-Chartreuse – Possibility of guided tours daily except Tue 9am-noon, 2-7pm, Thu 10am-noon, 2-7pm. Closed Jan and 1 May. 3,8€. ☎ 04 76 88 65 01.

La Scia, Essarts gondola/Scia chairlift – Jul and Aug: certain days 11am-6pm. Price information not provided. Call for information: ☎ 04 76 88 62 08.

ST-VÉRAN

05350 St-Véran, ☎ 04 92 45 82 21.

Musée Le Soum – Jul and Aug: 10am-1pm, 2-6.30pm; Sep-Jun: daily except Mon 2-6pm. 3,5€. ☎ 04 92 45 86 42.

Musée de l'habitat ancien/Ancienne maison traditionnelle – Jul and Aug: guided tours 10am-noon, 2-6pm; Sep-Jun: by appointment. 2,29€. ☎ 04 92 45 84 77.

Lac de SAINTE-CROIX

04500 Ste-Croix-De-Verdon, ☎ 04 92 77 85 29. 0

Bassin de SALLANCHES

Sallanches ☐ 31 quai de l'Hôtel-de-Ville, 74700 Sallanches, ☎ 04 50 58 04 25. www.sallanches.com
Château des Rubins – Jul and Aug: 9am-6.30pm, Sun and public holidays 2-6pm; Sep-Jun: 9am-noon, 2-6pm, Sun and public holidays 2-6pm. Closed 1 Jan and 25 Dec. 4,3€. ☎ 04 50 58 32 13.

Combloux ☐ 49 ch. des Passerands, 74920 Combloux, ☎ 04 50 58 60 49. www.combloux.com

SAMOËNS

BP 42, 74340 Samoëns, ☎ 04 50 34 40 28. www.samoens.com

Guided tours of the town – Contact the tourist office.

Jardin botanique alpin Jaüsinia – Mid-Jun to mid-Aug: 10am-noon, 3-6pm. No charge. ☎ 04 50 34 11 93.

SERRE-CHEVALIER

05240 Serre-Chevalier, ☎ 04 92 24 98 98. www.serre-chevalier.com

Musée d'Arts et Traditions populaires d'Antan – Closed temporarily. ☎ 04 92 24 57 46.

St-Chaffrey: Chapelle St-Arnoult – Visits by appointment with M. Peythieu. ☎ 04 92 24 17 54.

Chantemerle cable car – Jul and Aug: 9am-1pm, 2-5pm (15min, departure every 20min). Closed May, Jun and Sep to Nov. 6,71€ (foot passengers, both stages). ☎ 04 92 24 29 29.

Barrage et Lac de SERRE-PONÇON

Embrun ☐ Pl. du Gén.-Dosse, 05202 Embrun, ☎ 04 92 43 72 72. www.embrun.net
Chorges ☐ Grande Rue, 05230 Chorges, ☎ 04 92 50 64 25.
Savines-le-Lac ☐ Av. de la Combe-d'Or, 05160 Savines-Le-Lac, ☎ 04 92 44 31 00.
Power station – Jul and Aug: guided tours (1hr30min) daily except Sun 9.30-11am, 2-4pm; Jun and Sep: 2-4pm, morning by request; Oct-May: morning by request. Closed public holidays. No charge. ☎ 04 92 54 41 18. www.serre-poncon.com

Muséoscope du lac – ♿ Jul and Aug: 10am,11am, noon and 1.30-6pm; Jun and Sep: daily except Tue 2pm, 3pm, 4pm and 5pm; May: daily except Tue 2pm, 3pm and 4pm; Apr and Oct: daily except Tue and Thu 2pm, 3pm and 4pm; Feb and Mar: daily except Thu 2pm, 3pm and 4pm. 7€ (children: 5€). ☎ 04 92 54 50 00. www.museoscope-du-lac.com

Pontis: Musée de la Vallée – Jul and Aug: 3-7pm. 1,52€ (children: 0,76€). ☎ 04 92 44 26 94.

La Montagne aux Marmottes – Mid-May to end Aug: 9.30am-7pm; mid-Apr to mid-May and early Sep to mid-Nov: 9.30am-6pm. 10€ (children: 7€). ☎ 04 92 44 32 00.

Abbaye de Boscodon – Abbey church: 8am-7pm. Cloister and exhibitions; Apr-Oct: 10am-noon, 2-5pm; Jan-Mar: daily except Thu 2-5pm. Jul and Aug: possibility of guided tours (2hr) at fixed times (call for information); Sep-Jun: by request. Closed Nov and Dec 3€ (under 16s: no charge). ☎ 04 92 43 14 45.

SEYNE

Pl. d'Armes, 04140 Seyne, ☎ 04 92 35 11 00.

Chapelle des Dominicains – Tours by appointment. ☎ 04 92 35 00 51 or 06 88 71 05 49.

Exposition mulassière – ♿ Jul and Aug: Wed, Thu and Sun 9-10am; Sep-Jun: by request 2,7€. ☎ 04 92 35 00 51 ("Fort et Patrimoine" association).

Église N.-D.-de-Nazareth – Contact the presbytery. ☎ 04 92 35 01 89.

Citadel – Jul and Aug: 10am-noon, 3-6pm; Nov school holidays: 2-5pm; early Jan to mid-Feb and Christmas school holidays: 2-4pm. Closed rest of the year. 2,7€. ☎ 06 88 71 05 49.

SISTERON
🅸 Hôtel de Ville, 04202 Sisteron, ☎ 04 92 61 36 50. www.sisteron.com

Cathédrale Notre-Dame-des-Pommiers – Daily except Sat-Sun 3-6pm. ☎ 04 92 61 12 03.

Citadel – Jul and Aug: 9am-8pm (last admission 1hr before closing); Jun and Sep: 9am-7.30pm; May and Oct: 9am-6.30pm; Apr and Nov: 9am-5.30pm. 4,60€. ☎ 04 92 61 27 57.

Alentours

Prieuré de Vilhosc – Guided tours by appointment with proprietor. ☎ 04 92 61 26 70.

N.-D.-de-Dromon – Jul and Aug: Tue, Thu and Sat-Sun 3-6pm; Jun and Sep: Sun 3-6pm. ☎ 04 92 61 27 54.

La Motte-du-Caire: Via ferrata de la Grande Fistoire – 5,5€ (toll), 8€ (equipment rental). ☎ 04 92 68 40 39.

Sixt-Fer-à-Cheval
🅸 Pl. de la gare, 74740 Sixt-Fer-À-Cheval, ☎ 04 50 34 49 36. www.sixtferacheval.com

Maison de la réserve naturelle – Jul and Aug: 9am-1pm, 2-7pm. No charge. ☎ 04 50 34 91 90.

La TARENTAISE
🅸 Station, 73640 Ste-Foy-Tarentaise, ☎ 04 79 06 95 19.

Moûtiers 🅸 Pl. St-Pierre, 73600 Moûtiers, ☎ 04 79 24 04 23. www.ot-moutiers.com
Cathédrale St-Pierre – Possibility of guided tours. Contact the tourist office. ☎ 04 79 24 04 23.

Musée de l'Académie de la Val d'Isère – Daily except Sun and Public holidays 9am-noon, 2-6pm (last admission 30min before closing) by request at the tourist office. 2€. ☎ 04 79 24 04 23.

Musée des Traditions populaires de Tarentaise – Daily except Sun and Public holidays 9am-noon, 2-6pm. 2,3€. ☎ 04 79 24 04 23. www.ot-moutiers.com

Aime: Musée Pierre-Borrione – Jul and Aug: possibility of guided tours 10am-noon, 2-6pm. 1,5€ (under 16s: no charge). ☎ 04 79 55 67 00.

THONON-LES-BAINS
🅸 1 pl. du Marché, BP 82, 74023 Thonon-Les-Bains, ☎ 04 50 71 55 55. www.thononlesbains.com

Funicular – Mid-May to mid-Sep: 8am-11pm (2min30sec, every 15min); Mid-Sep to mid-May: 8am-12.30pm, 1.30-6.30pm, Sun 2-6pm. 1,8€ return. ☎ 04 50 71 21 54.

Musée du Chablais – Jul and Aug: 10am-noon, 2.30-6.30pm (last admission 30min before closing); Sep-Jun: daily except Mon and Tue. 2.30-6.30pm. Closed public holidays (except 15 Aug). 2€. ☎ 04 50 71 56 34.

Église St-Hippolyte – Closed for renovation work.

La fondation Ripaille – Jul and Aug: guided tours (1hr) at 11am, 2.30pm, 3pm, 3.30pm, 4pm, 4.30pm, 5pm; Apr-Jun and Sep: 11am, 2.30pm, 4pm; Feb, Mar, Oct and Nov: 3pm. 5€ (children: 2,5€). ☎ 04 50 26 64 44.

Arboretum – May-Sep: daily except Mon 10am-7pm; Oct-Apr: daily except Mon 10am-4.30pm. Closed Dec. No charge. ☎ 04 50 70 69 59.

Gorges de la Dranse: Gorges du Pont du Diable – May-Sep: guided tours (45min) 9am-6pm. 4,2€ (6-15 years: 2,1€). ☎ 04 50 72 10 39.

THORENS-GLIÈRES
🅸 Pl. du Commerce, 74570 Thorens-Glières, ☎ 04 50 22 40 31.

Château – Jul and Aug: guided tours (1hr, last visit 1hr before closing time) 2-6pm; Jun and Sep: Sat-Sun and public holidays 2-6pm. 5,5€ (children: 2,5€). ☎ 04 50 22 42 02.

TIGNES
🅸 BP 51, 73320 Tignes, ☎ 04 79 40 04 40. www.tignes.net

Grande Motte rack railway – 7.15am-4.45pm (6min, every 30 min). Closed Sep and mid-May to mid-Jun. From 16,5€ to 21€ return depending on the time of year (children under 5: no charge). ☎ 04 79 06 60 12.

Vallée de la TINÉE

🛈 06660 St-Étienne-De-Tinée, ☎ 04 93 23 07 39.
St-Étienne-De-Tinée, ☎ 04 93 02 41 96.
St-Étienne-De-Tinée, ☎ 04 93 23 02 66.

La Tour: Church – Guided tours 10am-noon, 2-4pm. Town hall. ☎ 04 93 02 05 27.
Chapelle des Pénitents Blancs – As for the church.

Le TRIÈVES

Mens   🛈 R. du Breuil, 38710 Mens, ☎ 04 76 34 84 25. www.alpes-trieves.com
Musée du Trièves – ♿ May-Sep: daily except Mon 3-7pm; Oct-Apr: Sat-Sun 2-5pm; school holidays: daily except Mon 2-5pm. Closed 1 Jan, 1 and 11 Nov, Easter Monday and 25 Dec. 2.3€. ☎ 04 76 34 88 28.

L'UBAYE

🛈 Pl. Frédéric-Mistral, 04400 Barcelonnette, ☎ 04 92 81 04 71. www.barcelonnette.net –
Maison de la vallée, 4 av. des Trois-Frères-Arnaud, 04400 Barcelonnette, ☎ 04 92 81 03 68.

Fort de Tournoux – Early Jul to early Sep: guided tours (1hr30min) (middle fort) Tue 10-11.30am, 2.30-6pm, Thu, Sat 10-11.30am and Sun 2.30-6pm. (Upper fort) Tue, Thu 2.30-6pm, Sat 2.30-6pm. Go directly to the site. 5,5€ (children under 12: 3,5€). ☎ 04 92 81 03 68. www.ubaye.com

Fort de Roche-la-Croix – Jul and Aug: guided tours (1hr30min) Mon 10-11.30am, Fri 10-11.30am, 2.30-6pm. Go directly to the site. 5,5€ (children under 12: 3,5€). ☎ 04 92 81 03 68. www.ubaye.com

Fort de St-Ours-Haut – Jul and Aug: guided tours (1hr30min) Mon 2.30-4pm, Wed 10-11.30am, 2.30-6pm. Go directly to the site. 5,5€ (children under 12: 3,5€. ☎ 04 92 81 03 68. www.ubaye.com

St-Paul-sur-Ubaye: Musée Albert-Manuel – Mid-Jul to end Aug: 3-7pm. 2,75€. ☎ 04 92 84 32 36.

VAL-D'ALLOS

🛈 04260 Allos, ☎ 04 92 83 02 81.

Notre-Dame-de-Valvert – Jul and Aug: To visit, make an appointment at the tourist office. ☎ 04 92 83 02 81.

VAL-D'ISÈRE

🛈 BP 228, 73150 Val-D'isère, ☎ 04 79 06 06 60. www.valdisere.com

Rocher de Bellevarde cable car – Reopening planned for Dec 2003.

Funival mountain railway – Mid-Aug, during the 4x4 motor show (4min). Price included in the entrance fee to the motor show. ☎ 04 79 06 00 35.

Tête du Solaise cable car – Jul and Aug: 9am-4.50pm (departure every hour) 8€ return. ☎ 04 79 06 00 35.

Le VALBONNAIS

🛈 38740 Valbonnais, ☎ 04 76 30 25 26. www.tignes.net

Plateau de VALENSOLE

St-Martin-de-Brômes: Church – Early May to mid-Sep: guided tours (45min) daily except Mon and public holidays 3-7pm. 1,55€. ☎ 04 92 78 02 02.
Tour templière – Early May to mid-Sep: guided tours (45min) daily except Mon and public holidays 3-7pm. 1,55€. ☎ 04 92 78 02 02.

Le VALGAUDEMAR

🛈 05800 La Chapelle-En-Valgaudémar, ☎ 04 92 55 23 21.

La VALLOUISE

🛈 Pl. de l'Église, 05290 Vallouise, ☎ 04 92 23 36 12.

Maison du Parc national des Écrins – ♿ Mid-Jun to mid-Sep: 10am-noon, 2-6pm; mid-Sep to mid-Jun: daily except Wed and Sat-Sun. 1.30-5.30pm. Closed public holidays (except in Jul and Aug). No charge. ☎ 04 92 23 58 08.

VARS

🛈 Cours Fontanarosa, 05560 Vars, ☎ 04 92 46 51 31. www.alpes-net.fr/vars

Musée du KL – Closed temporarily. ☎ 04 92 46 51 31.

Reserve naturelle du Val d'Escreins – From Whitsun for as long as weather permits. 1,83€. ☎ 04 92 46 51 31. www.vars-ski.com

Chabrières gondola – Jul and Aug: 10am-5.30pm (10min, continuous). 4,1€ single. ☎ 04 92 46 51 04.

Le VERCORS

Parc Naturel Régional du Vercors – 255 chemin des Fusillés, 38250 Lans-en-Vercors, ☎ 04 76 94 38 26. www.parc-du-vercors.fr

Grottes de Choranche/Grotte du Coufin – ᚶ Jul and Aug: guided tours (1hr, departure every 30min) 9.30am-6.30pm; May, Jun and Sep: 9.30am-noon, 1.30-6.30pm; Apr and Oct: 10am-noon, 1.30-6pm; Nov-Mar: 10.30am, 11.30am, 12.30pm (during school holidays) and 1.30pm, 2.30pm, 3.30pm, 4.30pm. 6,86€ (under 14s: 4,57€). ☎ 04 76 36 09 88.

La Chapelle-en-Vercors   🄴 Pl. Pietri, BP 5, 26420 La Chapelle-En-Vercors, ☎ 04 75 48 22 54. www.vercors-net.com

Grotte de la Luire – Jul and Aug: guided tours (30min) 9.30am-6.30pm; May-Jun: 9.30am-noon, 1.30-6pm; Apr and Sep: 10am-noon, 1.30-5.30 4,7€. ☎ 04 75 48 25 83.

Vassieux-en-Vercors: Musée de la Résistance du Vercors – Apr-Oct: 10am-noon, 2-6pm; Feb: daily except Mon and Sat 10am-noon, 2-5pm. Closed rest of the year. No charge. ☎ 04 75 48 28 46.

Musée du Site préhistorique – Jul and Aug: 10am-6pm; Apr-Jun and Sep: 10am-12.30pm, 2-6pm; Oct-Mar: Sat-Sun and public holidays 10am-12.30pm, 2pm-5pm; school holidays: 10am-12.30pm, 2-5pm. Closed Nov, Dec and 1 Jan. 3.85€. ☎ 04 75 48 27 81. www.prehistoire-vercors.fr

Mémorial de la Résistance (Col de Lachau) – ᚶ Apr-Sep: 10am-6pm; Oct-Dec: 10am-5pm; Jan-Mar: daily except Mon and Tue (apart from school holidays) 10am-5pm. Closed mid-Nov to beginning of Christmas school holidays, 1 Jan and 25 Dec. 3.85€ (children: 1,55€). ☎ 04 75 48 26 00. www.memorial-vercors.fr

Grotte de la Draye Blanche – Jul and Aug: guided tours (45min) 9.30am-7pm; Feb, Mar, Sep and Oct: 9.30am-noon, 2-6pm; Dec to Jan: 10am-noon, 2-5pm; Apr-Jun and Nov: Sat 10am-noon, 2-5pm. 5,1€. ☎ 04 75 48 24 96.

Saint-Jean-en-Royans   🄴 Pl. de l'Église, 26190 St-Jean-En-Royans, ☎ 04 75 48 61 39. www.royans.com

Rochechinard: Musée de la Mémoire – Jul and Aug: guided tours (1hr) daily except Mon 3-7pm. 3,5€. ☎ 04 75 48 62 53 or 04 75 47 74 23.

Monastère St-Antoine-le-Grand – ᚶ Guided tours 11.30am-12.30pm, 2-5.30pm. 3€ (children under 12: no charge). ☎ 04 75 47 72 02.

Grand Canyon du VERDON   🄴 04360 Moustiers-Ste-Marie, ☎ 04 92 74 67 84. www.ville-moustiers-sainte-marie.fr

Aiguines   🄴 Les Buis, 86360 Aiguines, ☎ 04 94 70 21 64. 0

Musée des Tourneurs – Mid-Jun to mid-Sep: daily except Mon 9am-noon, 2-6pm; Apr and May: daily except Mon 2-6pm; rest of the year: by request 2€. ☎ 04 94 70 20 89.

VILLARD-DE-LANS   🄴 Pl. Mure-Ravaud, 38250 Villard-De-Lans, ☎ 04 76 95 10 38. www.ot-villard-de-lans.fr

Télécabine Cote 2000 – Jul and Aug: 9.30am-1pm, 2-5.30pm (10min, continuous). 5,5€. ☎ 04 76 94 50 50.

VILLARS-SUR-VAR   🄴 Mairie, 04710 Villars-Sur-Var, ☎ 04 93 05 32 32.

Church – If closed, ask at the presbytery. Possibility of guided tours by appointment (2 weeks in advance). ☎ 04 93 84 44 32.

VIZILLE   🄴 Pl. du Château, 38220 Vizille, ☎ 04 76 68 15 16.

Château – ᚶ Apr-Oct: daily except Tue 10am-6pm; Nov-Mar: daily except Tue 10am-5pm. Closed 25 Dec to 1 Jan and 1 May. 3€, no charge 1st Sunday in the month. ☎ 04 76 68 07 35.

Notre-Dame-de-Mésage: Church – ☎ 04 76 68 07 33.

YVOIRE   🄴 Pl. de la Mairie, 74140 Yvoire, ☎ 04 50 72 80 21. www.presquile-leman.com

Jardin des Cinq Sens – ᚶ Mid-May to mid-Sep: 10am-7pm; Mid-Apr to mid-May: 11am-6pm; mid-Sep to mid-Oct: 1-5pm. 8€ (under 16s: 4,5€). ☎ 04 50 72 88 80.

Vivarium – Mid-Apr to end Sep: 10am-12.30pm, 2-8pm; early Oct to mid-Apr: daily except Mon 2-5.30pm. Closed Nov, 1 Jan and 25 Dec. 6.5€. ☎ 04 50 72 82 28.

Index

478